THE EU AND AFRICA

ADEKEYE ADEBAJO AND KAYE WHITEMAN
(*editors*)

The EU and Africa

From Eurafrique to Afro-Europa

HURST & COMPANY, LONDON

First published in the United Kingdom in 2012 by
C. Hurst & Co. (Publishers) Ltd.,
41 Great Russell Street, London, WC1B 3PL
© Centre for Conflict Resolution, Cape Town, South Africa, 2012
All rights reserved.
Printed in India

The right of Adekeye Adebajo, Kaye Whiteman and the Contributors to be
identified as the authors of this publication is asserted by them in accordance
with the Copyright, Designs and Patents Act, 1988.

A Cataloguing-in-Publication data record for this book is available from the
British Library.

ISBN: 978-1-84904-171-3 (paperback original)

This book is printed using paper from registered sustainable
and managed sources.

www.hurstpub.co.uk

CONTENTS

Acknowledgements   vii
About the Contributors   ix

1. Introduction   *Kaye Whiteman*   1

PART 1
AFRICA AND EUROPE IN HISTORICAL PERSPECTIVE

2. The Rise and Fall of *Eurafrique:* From the Berlin Conference of
   1884–1885 to the Tripoli EU-Africa Summit of 2010
                                             Kaye Whiteman   23
3. Paradise Lost and Found: The African Union and the
   European Union   *Adekeye Adebajo*   45

PART 2
POLITICAL, ECONOMIC AND STRATEGIC DIMENSIONS

4. The Travails of Regional Integration in Africa
                                            Adebayo Adedeji   83
5. Europe, Africa and Aid: Towards a Genuine Partnership
                                               Rob de Vos   105
6. South Africa and the EU: Where Lies the Strategic Partnership?
                                   Talitha Bertelsmann-Scott   121
7. The EU, the Maghreb and the Mediterranean   *George Joffé*   137
8. The EU and Asia: Lessons for Africa?   *Shada Islam*   153

v

CONTENTS

PART 3
TRADE, INVESTMENT, AND DEVELOPMENT

9. Global Africa: The Last Investment Frontier?   *Liam Halligan*   171
10. An Anatomy of the Economic Partnership Agreements
                                        Mareike Meyn   197
11. Africa and Europe: Ending a Dialogue of the Deaf?
                                        Gilbert M. Khadiagala   217
12. A Critique of the EU's Common Agricultural Policy
                                        Charles Mutasa   237

PART 4
SECURITY AND GOVERNANCE

13. AU-EU Security and Governance Cooperation   *Garth le Pere*   257
14. The EU Security Role in the Great Lakes Region   *Aldo Ajello*   277
15. The EU Security Role in Chad and the Central African
    Republic   *Winrich Kühne*   295

PART 5
THE EU-AFRICA POLICIES OF FRANCE, BRITAIN, PORTUGAL, AND THE NORDICS

16. France, the EU, and Africa   *Douglas A. Yates*   317
17. Britain, the EU, and Africa   *Paul D. Williams*   343
18. Portugal, the EU, and Africa   *Alex Vines*   365
19. The Nordics, the EU, and Africa   *Anne Hammerstad*   385

PART 6
MIGRATION AND IDENTITY

20. Migration and 'Fortress Europe'   *Andrew Geddes*   405
21. The Black Atlantic from Othello to Obama: In Search of a
    Post-Racial Society   *Ali A. Mazrui*   419
22. Europe's Postcolonial Role and Identity   *Hartmut Mayer*   441
Annex   459

Notes   463
Index   521

ACKNOWLEDGEMENTS

Even though the European Union (EU) has been Africa's largest trading partner over the last five decades, this is an area in which few African institutions have produced academically rigorous and policy-relevant knowledge. This volume seeks to correct this anomaly and to contribute to a better understanding of the historically difficult relationship between Africa and the EU in the areas of history, politics, economics, security, migration, and identity. The Centre for Conflict Resolution (CCR) in Cape Town, South Africa, organised two research and policy seminars on relations between Africa and the EU in October/November 2007 and September 2008. Both meetings sought to foster greater understanding of the political, economic, and security aspects of this important relationship. We thank the 21 authors on three continents involved in this volume who demonstrated great professionalism, perseverance, and punctiliousness during what must sometimes have seemed a tortuous editing process. The editors also wish to thank all the participants at the two meetings in 2007 and 2008 who shared their rich insights with us and provided substantive and candid feedback to the authors in this volume which greatly strengthened their chapters. These have all been revised and updated to take into account the tremendous changes that have occurred in the world over the last few years.

The two policy briefs and policy reports produced from the seminars in 2007 and 2008 have been widely employed by African and European policymakers, academics, and civil society actors in their work. This unique 22-chapter book will be similarly disseminated, and contains rich insights from African and European scholars and practitioners, as well as an Asian and an American scholar. We hope that it will be useful for African, European, and other scholars and policymakers with an interest in relations

ACKNOWLEDGEMENTS

between both continents. It is important that academic institutions on both continents engage constructively on these issues for the mutual benefit of both Africa and the EU. In conducting research for this book, the editors also visited Brussels twice between 2008 and 2010 and interviewed key officials in both the Secretariat and government of the African, Caribbean, and Pacific (ACP) Group, as well as EU Commission, Council, and Parliament officials. We wish to thank all the officials—too numerous to mention—who patiently and generously shared their practical insights and vast experience with us. We aim to disseminate the main findings of this project directly to these policymakers as well as to key regional organisations in Africa. There are many others in the academic world and in the private sector, as well as in diverse parts of the media, whose perceptions and insights have played a part that would often surprise them in moulding our own appreciation of such complex and multi-dimensional subject matter.

We would like to thank Jason Cook for copyediting the manuscript so meticulously. Jonathan Derrick also deserves credit for his copyediting efforts. We thank Michael Dwyer, Daisy Leitch, and the team at Hurst Publishers who drove this process; Meredith Howard at Columbia University; and Veronica Klipp and Roshan Cader at Wits University Press.

Finally, we would like to thank the staff and board of the Centre for Conflict Resolution for the support that allowed us to complete this project. We must especially acknowledge the tremendous assistance of CCR researchers Dawn Nagar and Elizabeth Otitodun, and the centre's librarian Margaret Struthers, as well as other colleagues in the training, communications, finance, and human resources departments. We also wish to thank the main funders of CCR's Africa programme, who supported the production of this book: the Netherlands, Denmark, and Sweden. All three are appropriately the governments of EU states that have traditionally strongly supported both African development efforts and the European project.

Adekeye Adebajo and Kaye Whiteman

ABOUT THE CONTRIBUTORS

Adekeye Adebajo has been Executive Director of the Centre for Conflict Resolution (CCR) in Cape Town, South Africa, since 2003. He served on United Nations (UN) missions in South Africa, Western Sahara, and Iraq. Dr Adebajo is the author of four books: *Building Peace in West Africa*; *Liberia's Civil War*; *The Curse of Berlin: Africa After the Cold War*; and *UN Peacekeeping in Africa: From the Suez Crisis to the Sudan Conflicts*. He has edited or co-edited six books on: managing global conflicts; the United Nations; the European Union; West African security; and South Africa and Nigeria's foreign policies in Africa. He obtained his doctorate from Oxford University, where he studied as a Rhodes Scholar.

Adebayo Adedeji has been a proponent and architect of regional integration in Africa since the early 1970s, beginning with the establishment of the Economic Community of West African States (ECOWAS). Between 1971 and 1975, he was Minister of Economic Reconstruction and Development in Nigeria. During his tenure as Executive Secretary of the UN Economic Commission for Africa from 1975 to 1991, Adedeji led the development of the Preferential Trade Agreement, which later became the Common Market for Eastern and Southern Africa. He is the editor of *Africa Within the World: Beyond Dispossession and Dependence; Towards a Dynamic African Economy: Selected Speeches and Lectures; South Africa and Africa: Within or Apart?; South Africa: The Post Apartheid Era* and many publications on African political economy, development and security. He is the Executive Director of the African Centre for Development and Strategic Studies in Ijebu Ode, Nigeria, and the former Chair of the African Peer Review Mechanism Panel of Eminent Persons.

ABOUT THE CONTRIBUTORS

Aldo Ajello was the European Union's Special representative for the Great Lakes Region between 1997 and 2007. He previously served as the Special Representative of the United Nations Secretary-General in Mozambique between 1992 and 1995, worked with the UN Development Programme (UNDP) and was an Italian legislator. He is the author of *Brasiers d'Afrique: Mémoires d'un émissaire pour la paix.*

Talitha Bertelsmann-Scott is an independent analyst. She is also Research Associate at the South African Institute of International Affairs (SAIIA), Johannesburg, South Africa. She has worked extensively in the areas of EU-South and Southern African trade relations, as well as Southern African integration. Her co-edited publications include: *Regional Integration and Economic Partnership Agreements: Southern Africa at the Crossroads,* and *The EU-SA Agreement: South Africa, Southern Africa and the European Union.*

Andrew Geddes is a Professor in the Department of Politics at the University of Sheffield, United Kingdom. He specialises in the comparative analysis of politics and policymaking with a particular interest in international migration. He has published a large number of books and articles on European and international migration, as well as work on British elections and British relations with the EU.

Liam Halligan is Chief Economist at Prosperity Capital Management in London. He holds an MPhil in Economics from the University of Oxford. Previously he held positions at the International Monetary Fund (IMF), the International Food Policy Research Institute (IFPRI), the Social Market Foundation, and the London School of Economics (LSE).

Anne Hammerstad is a Lecturer in International Relations at the University of Kent in England, an Economic and Social Research Council (ESRC) Fellow, and a South African Institute of International Affairs research associate. Before joining the University of Kent, she was a Research and Teaching Fellow at the Royal Holloway College, University of London. She has published articles, chapters, reports and monographs, as well as an edited volume on topics relating to the Southern African Development Community (SADC) and regional security in Southern Africa, South Africa's role in Africa, the African Union, and the relationship between displacement, conflict, and development.

ABOUT THE CONTRIBUTORS

Shada Islam is Head of Policy at the Friends of Europe, a think-tank, in Brussels, Belgium. She was previously Senior Programme Executive at the Brussels-based European Policy Centre (EPC). She is an experienced journalist, columnist, policy analyst and communication specialist with a strong background in geo-political, foreign, economic and trade policy issues involving Europe, Asia, the Middle East, Africa, and the United States. She is also a regular contributor to Asian, African and Middle Eastern publications on issues relating to the EU, including foreign policy, security issues, economic and monetary union, immigration, and institutional reform and enlargement.

George Joffé is Deputy Director and Professorial Research Fellow at the Global Policy Institute, London Metropolitan University, England. He was Deputy Director and Director of Studies at the Royal Institute of International Affairs (Chatham House) between 1997 and 2000. Professor Joffé is also a Research Fellow at the Centre of International Studies, Cambridge University; and Director of the Royal United Services Institute (RUSI), Qatar.

Gilbert M. Khadiagala is the Jan Smuts Professor of International Relations at the University of the Witwatersrand in Johannesburg. He has taught African politics in Kenya, Canada and the United States, most recently at the Johns Hopkins School of Advanced International Studies in Washington, DC. He is the editor of *Security Dynamics in Africa's Great Lakes Region*; co-author of *Sudan: The Elusive Quest for Peace* and co-editor of *Getting In: The Entry of African Mediators in the Settlement of African Conflicts*. He has consulted for various governments, NGOs and international organisations.

Winrich Kühne is the Steven Muller Professor in German Studies at the Paul H. Nitze School of International Studies at John Hopkins University, Bologna, Italy. He is the founding Director of the German Centre for International Peace Operations (ZiF), Berlin; former Deputy Director of the German Research Institute for International and Security Affairs (SWP); consultant to the Association of European Parliamentarians (AWEPA); member of the international advisory group to the UN Peacekeeping Lessons Learned Unit; senior adviser to the former EU Crisis Prevention Network; member of the United Nations and Civilian Crisis Prevention advisory groups of the German Foreign Office; and a member of the editorial boards of the *Journal of International Peacekeeping* and *Global Governance.*

Hartmut Mayer is a Fellow and Lecturer in Politics and International Relations at St. Peter's College, University of Oxford, England. Prior to becoming a Fellow of St. Peter's, he held College Lectureships at Worcester, St. John's and St. Peter's Colleges, University of Oxford. He received his doctorate from Oxford University. His publications include two co-edited volumes: *A Responsible Europe? Ethical Foundations of EU External Affairs,* and *German-British Relations and the Spirit of Cadenabbia.*

Ali A. Mazrui is Director of the Institute of Global Cultural Studies at the State University of New York. Previously, he was Head of the Political Science department and Dean of the Faculty of Social Sciences at Makerere University in Uganda; and Director of the University of Michigan's Centre for Afro-American and African studies. In 1986, Professor Mazrui wrote and narrated the influential nine-part documentary, 'The Africans: A Triple Heritage', which established his global reputation. The author of more than thirty books and hundreds of essays, he holds a doctorate from Oxford University, and has served in an advisory capacity to numerous organisations, including the United Nations.

Mareike Meyn is a Consultant with GFA Consulting Group in Hamburg, Germany, focusing on EU/ACP Relations. She was previously a Research Fellow in the International Economic Development Group (IEDG) at the Overseas Development Institute (ODI) in London.

Charles Mutasa is an independent development policy consultant and development studies doctoral student at the University of Zimbabwe. He served as Deputy Presiding Officer of the first African Union–Civil Society Organisations (CSO) Bureau and as a member of the Organisation for Economic Cooperation and Development (OECD) 2008 Aid Effectiveness CSO working group. He is the former Head of Programme Policy at Christian Aid and the former Executive Director of the African Forum and Network on Debt and Development (AFRODAD). He has written extensively on Africa's development challenges and state-civil society relations.

Garth le Pere is the former Executive Director of the Institute for Global Dialogue (IGD) in Midrand, South Africa, a position he held for fifteen years until joining DAJO Associates as a senior partner in January 2010. He is also Extraordinary Professor of Political Science at the University of Pretoria. His academic research and publishing record includes work on China's increasing role in Africa, a focus on state-society dynamics in Africa, EU-Africa relations, theories of international relations, South African foreign policy, multilateral trade, global conflict, regional integration and South-South cooperation.

Alex Vines is Research Director, Regional and Security Studies and Head of the Africa Programme at Chatham House in London. Between 2005 and 2007, he was a member and later Chair of the UN Panel of Experts on Côte d'Ivoire and a member of the UN Panel of Experts on Liberia between 2001 and 2003. He is the author of *RENAMO: Terrorism in Mozambique*.

Rob de Vos is Consul-General of the Netherlands in New York, United States. He previously served as Ambassador of the Netherlands to South Africa. He studied economics at the University of Amsterdam and entered the Dutch Foreign Service in 1978. He served at the Dutch Ministry of Foreign Affairs as Deputy Director-General for International Cooperation and acting Director-General for International Cooperation. He is a member of the Executive Committee of the African Economic Research Consortium (AERC).

Kaye Whiteman is a journalist and writer on African affairs. He is currently a London-based editorial adviser to *Business Day* (Nigeria), and writes for other publications such as *Africa Today*, *The Annual Register*, and *Geopolitique Africaine*. He was based at *Business Day* in Lagos, served as Director of Information and Public Affairs at the Commonwealth Secretariat in London, and was Editor-in-Chief, General Manager and Managing Editor of the London-based weekly magazine *West Africa*. He was also a senior Information Official at the European Commission in Brussels, working on development issues between 1973 and 1982. He is the author of *Lagos: A Cultural and Historical Companion*, and has an MA in history from Oxford University. He has written extensively on West African affairs, Europe-Africa relations, and the Commonwealth.

Paul D. Williams is Associate Professor of International Affairs and Associate Director of the Security Policy Studies Programme at the Elliot School of International Affairs, George Washington University in Washington, DC. He previously taught at the Universities of Aberystwyth, Birmingham, and Warwick in the United Kingdom. He has also served as a Visiting Professor at the Institute for Peace and Security Studies at Addis Ababa University in Ethiopia. He currently serves on the editorial boards of two journals, *African Affairs* and *Global Responsibility to Protect*. His latest book, *War and Conflict in Africa*, was published in 2011.

Douglas A. Yates teaches political science at the American Graduate School of International Relations and Diplomacy in Paris, international relations at the American University of Paris, and Anglo-American jurisprudence at the French state law school of the University of Cergy-Pontoise. He is the author of the *Rentier state in Africa: Oil-Rent Dependency and Neo-colonialism in the Republic of Gabon*; and *The Scramble for African Oil*; co-author of *Oil Policy in the Gulf of Guinea*; and co-editor of the third edition of the *Historical Dictionary of Gabon*.

1

INTRODUCTION

Kaye Whiteman

This book offers a holistic and comprehensive assessment of the relations of the European Union with Africa, focusing on their historical, political, socio-economic and cultural dimensions. In the high imperial period in the early twentieth century, some in Europe advocated the idea of *Eurafrique*—a formula for putting Africa's resources at the disposal of Europe's industries. After tracing Europe's historical attempts to remodel relations following African independence beginning in the 1960s, and Europe's own quest for unity, the book examines the current strategic dimensions of the relationship, especially the place of Africa in Europe's own need for global partnerships. Key issues are then analysed, from trade and investment to the growing priorities of security and governance, through case histories of the role of key European players in Africa—France, Britain, Portugal, and the Nordics—within the context of the EU. The volume concludes by examining the important issues of migration and identity, especially in view of Europe's controversial immigration policies and complex relations with the Maghreb and the Mediterranean, as well as perceptions of past and current European identity.

For some time, there has clearly been a need for an overarching study of the relations of the European Union with Africa. This is a pioneering volume focusing on this important relationship, written mostly by African and Euro-

1

pean scholars and practitioners, but also involving a Pakistani and an American citizen. The book is sponsored by the Centre for Conflict Resolution (CCR) in Cape Town, South Africa—which organised two policy seminars on Africa-Europe relations, in November 2007 and September 2008—and represents a groundbreaking effort by an African think-tank to enter a field hitherto largely dominated by institutions in Europe. The aim of this study is to encourage a constructive dialogue between scholars, policymakers, civil society groups, and the general public interested in Africa and Europe.

The EU-Africa Strategy put forward at the summit in the Portuguese capital of Lisbon in December 2007, and reviewed at the Tripoli summit in Libya in November 2010, has refocused on a subject that had seemed to drift down the Brussels agenda, even as the question is repeatedly asked: what kind of relationship should there be between the two continents? At present, Africa and Europe seem still not to have fully escaped from the burden of history. Also, their relations are beset by the ambiguities that surround this particular 'partnership' in the context of a wider European development policy. Does the 'African priority' in European policy—once an important theme—mean very much anymore? As Europe faces the buffeting of the global financial crisis, affecting the very future of the euro currency zone, does the relationship with Africa assume more significance, or is a new subtle process of marginalisation at work?

This is why the subtitle of this book, 'From Eurafrique to Afro-Europa', has a particular relevance. The expression *Eurafrique* is very much a hangover from the colonial past, from the less attractive areas of European history. It was a theory of empire devised by a Frenchman in the 1920s, which later became attractive in Nazi Germany and Fascist Italy, as they saw advantages in a pan-European strategy for exploiting Africa's resources and markets (which individual European colonial powers had for long been doing). While for the French and Italians this concept was part of an extended Mediterranean strategy that extended Europe to the south in a zone of continuous domination, for Adolf Hitler's Germany in the 1930s it represented a way of recovering lost colonies, while fuelling Germany's industrial powerhouse. This was also taken up by the Nazi-allied Vichy regime in France in the Second World War (1939–1945), but was revived, very much with French inspiration, as a postcolonial strategy.

By the 1960s, France found that its former sub-Saharan African territories were the only part of its former empire where it could maintain a powerful influence (unlike North Africa and Indo-China). The system of intensified cooperation that had been developed by France's President Charles de Gaulle at that time was seen as having a European extension, using the 'association' policy that had been included in the Rome Treaty of 1957 at France's insistence. This was often referred to as the 'Eurafrican Association', and posited a special symbiotic relationship between the two continents, involving prioritised markets and privileged aid, modelled on France's own special relationship with its former territories.

The relationship was incarnated in the ten years of the Yaoundé Conventions of 1963 and 1968, which were criticised heavily by radical African leaders such as Guinea's Sékou Touré and Ghana's Kwame Nkrumah.[1] While the successor to Yaoundé, the Lomé Convention of 1975, eliminated the by now discredited language of 'association', and indeed of *Eurafrique*, the idea of an African priority for Europe (this time including all of independent sub-Saharan Africa) remained dominant in the twenty-five years of the Lomé Convention, which even Sekou Touré's Guinea was persuaded to join. It also remained implicit in the Cotonou Partnership Agreement of 2000, although the geopolitical priorities within the EU Commission in Brussels had changed substantially.

There was a bizarre resuscitation of the *Eurafrique* concept by France's President Nicolas Sarkozy on his first African tour in 2007,[2] encouraged by one of his advisers, Henri Guaino, who also revived the idea of a Europe-Mediterranean-Africa bloc, with the new Mediterranean Union as a central building brick. (See chapter 7 in this volume.) If this produced a negative reaction in Africa where *Eurafrique* is still equated with the neocolonial notion of *Françafrique*, the idea can sometimes be detected (without having its name spoken) in some of the new security-conscious thinking about Europe and Africa increasingly prevalent in Brussels. The purpose of this book is thus in part to examine how far attitudes have changed in this relationship, and whether a new, more balanced concept, which we choose to baptise 'Afro-Europa'—that is, an equal partnership of mutual interests without suggestion of a special relationship of more significance than others—can now become predominant.

One of the problems of writing about the relations that the European Union has with the developing world, and more particularly with Africa, is that this large and complex subject covers several disciplines. This means that the book has to deal not just with politics and economics but also with security, governance, migration, and identity. Most academic studies of the EU and its predecessor organisations, however, have focused disproportionately on economic aspects to the disadvantage of other critical subjects in this relationship.[3] Even the substantial and serious body of work carried out by research institutes and think-tanks in Europe has steered around grappling with the more overtly sensitive political subject matter that is an essential part of the EU's external relations. In short, there is a shortage of all-embracing treatments of the subject, extending to the history of European institutions and activities as a critical part of the history of the continent, including the history of ideas.

It is to be regretted, for example, that most of the major players in this relationship have never written memoirs of their experiences, from commissioners such as Claude Cheysson and Edgard Pisani, to some of the architects of Cotonou, and to more recent commissioners such as Louis Michel. The same can be said of the main Africa, Caribbean, and Pacific (ACP) participants in this drama, with the exception of Nigeria's former ambassador to Brussels, Olu Sanu, whose 1998 account offered an illuminating appraisal of Nigeria's relations with Europe.[4] Pius Okigbo, another former Nigerian ambassador to the European Economic Community (EEC), also wrote an early study on Brussels's relations with Africa in 1967.[5] There were a few helpful academic studies of Lomé in its early days, notably John Ravenhill's *Collective Clientelism*,[6] one of the first analyses of why the convention was not functioning well. More recently, the work of Kunibert Raffer[7] has contained a series of telling arguments as to why Cotonou marked a definite step backwards from the positive aspects of Lomé, from the point of view of all developing countries.[8]

This absence of personal accounts may be one of the reasons why the relationship is, to put it mildly, underpublicised, and in many cases unsung. This has sometimes meant that while it has been convenient and advantageous to operate without the glare of publicity, the relationship has often not received the sort of scrutiny that would have been useful to a deeper understanding of EU-Africa relations. Moreover, there are major changes going on in Brussels, arising notably from the enlargement of the EU from its initial six members in 1957 to twenty-seven countries and the consolidation of EU institutions in the Lisbon Treaty of 2007, that now inevitably demand much more attention.

On top of which, the dramatic troubles of the euro in the context of the EU's poorer member states—such as Greece, Portugal, and Ireland—mean that a coherent global trade and development policy, targeted on a series of equal partnerships, especially in the 'emerging markets', seems to have assumed greater urgency. As several of our chapters explain, in the context of a newly coalescing multipolar world the African partnership has its own place, especially in view of the mounting crisis between Europe and Africa over migration, one of the topics prioritised in this book (see chapter 20), but it is still hard to push it to the top of the EU agenda.

The growth of development policy

In November 1974, Claude Cheysson, then French commissioner for development in the European Commission, released a document called 'Development Aid: Fresco of Community Action Tomorrow'.[9] This was probably the first serious attempt by the Commission, which was then still at the core of the European project's dynamic, to produce a coherent policy on relations with the developing world. It was way ahead of its time, because the early years of the concept had confined Europe's relations with the developing world to the limited and partial device of the Yaoundé Conventions: a trade and aid treaty between the EEC and eighteen African countries, mainly former French territories, as well as a few limited trade agreements.

It was the enlargement of the EEC from six to nine countries in 1973, including Britain, that offered the opportunity for wider perspectives in the developing world. The context of the severe oil crisis of that year, which tripled global oil prices, ushered in a number of new ideas, such as that of a 'New International Economic Order' (NIEO). In the two-year negotiations that eventually produced the EEC-ACP Lomé Convention in 1975, there were those who would have liked it to extend to all developing countries. These aspirations came not just from the British, but also from those who had been keenest for British entry into the EEC, the Germans and the Dutch, with less enthusiasm from the French.

In fact, just as the North Africans had not wanted an intensive Yaoundé-style relationship with Brussels, neither did the Asians and the Latin Americans, who preferred a more relaxed development of relations with more emphasis on trade. Thus the fresco at that time was perforce incomplete, with many areas still to be painted in, while the traditional priority interest in sub-Saharan Africa remained for some time. Sights had been raised, however, and the cosy French-dominated Yaoundé idea, backed up, as we have seen, by the neocolonial geopolitical notion of *Eurafrique*, was buried, with the idea of 'partnership' replacing that of the 'association' policy that had been built into the philosophy of the Rome Treaty of 1957. The desire to reflect new thinking was seen in the opening paragraphs of the Fresco, which contained this statement redolent with aspiration, not to mention wishful thinking: 'there are no longer donors and recipients: equality between partners is established'.[10]

Now, about forty years on, the European Union can claim to have put in place many of the ambitions expressed in the fresco. The concept of a development policy found its place in European treaties for the first time in Maastricht (1992), but has continued to acquire more substance. There is now a network of different instruments, not just extending to a variety of treaties, but also offering one of the world's largest sources of total overseas development assistance. The financial prioritisation of Africa (and the Caribbean and Pacific companions) has faded as more and more financial provisions find their way to Asia (see chapter 8 in this volume) and Latin America, even if the European Development Fund (EDF) even now derives its budget separate from the Commission's budget, an arrangement that goes back to the 1957 Treaty of Rome. The network of relations that began with the EDF delegates in each of the 'associated' states still reflects, to some extent, the piecemeal way it has grown. However, the Lisbon Treaty of 2007 has completed the establishment of a full European diplomatic service in which the idea of a delegation even in a place like Vanuatu is now subsumed into that of a European embassy, which accounts in part for the excessively high (and much-criticised) cost of the exercise.

Historically, the high point in Europe's relations with Africa was the Lomé Convention of 1975.[11] It was also, notably, seen as one of Britain's main contributions to the new enlarging Europe, with a variety of progressive instruments, most notably the abandonment of trade reciprocity, or mutual access to markets, which was seen as unfair to developing countries. This concession persuaded a number of countries that Lomé would be worth joining, as did the fact that it was open to all forty-eight countries in sub-Saharan Africa. It was also, as is made clear by Adebayo Adedeji in chapter 4 of this volume, a great facilitator of Africa's budding regional groupings, notably the Economic Community of West African States (ECOWAS), whose treaty was signed in 1975—led by Adedeji's own vision and energy—three months after the Lomé Convention itself.[12]

Over the years, Lomé proved a disappointment, as its substantial aid programmes were mired in bureaucracy, and the principles of equality and partnership it proclaimed were occluded by continuing dependence, which worsened after Africa's economic crisis of the 1980s. The convention had also become too bulky and unmanageable, growing in size but not in effectiveness, with each new accord. In 1990, Lomé's life was extended from five to ten years, to relieve some of the pressure of negotiation.

After twenty-five years, revision was needed, but the opportunity was used by some, in what was by now the EU, to ditch the non-reciprocity that had been Lomé's 'jewel in the crown'. This was justified by the increasing pressures from the strong free-traders in the newly strengthened World Trade Organisation (WTO)—created in 1995 as a successor to the General Agreement on Tariffs and Trade (GATT)—but it was still too easily abandoned. The apologists for the Cotonou Agreement of 2000 proclaimed somewhat speciously that Lomé itself was outdated and even 'neocolonial', saying they were seeking 'normalisation'.

From the 'bonfire of the vanities' of development nostra of an earlier era, for example the scrapping of subsidising mechanisms such as Stabex (for commodities) and Sysmin (for minerals), as well as chapters on industrial and cultural cooperation, a simplified text was produced. This had a more pronounced political dimension concerning human rights and governance. Increasing importance was also accorded to the private sector's role in development. But the main motivation for the ACP states to sign Cotonou in 2000 was, as with Lomé in 1975, the substantial funds available in the European Development Fund with which Cotonou entered its ninth incarnation.

In Cotonou, however, the EU, from guile or unimaginative thinking, imposed on the ACP group a new trade regime that, as well as incorporating revived reciprocity, divided the ACP into six regions—four in Africa (West, East, Central, and Southern), plus the Caribbean and the Pacific—that would be open to economic partnership agreements (EPAs). These would include free trade areas alongside other development instruments. Thus, at a stroke, in seeking, however admirably, to promote regional cooperation, Brussels managed to create new divisions both in the ACP group and within Africa, because regional groupings are still fledgling in the developing world.[13] (See chapters 10 and 11 in this volume.)

This may have been well-intentioned, but it was bound to be seen as part of 'divide and rule' tactics, especially in 2007, when the EPA provisions of Cotonou were due to come into force. Thus the EU, and especially the Commission, which had anticipated some of these more divisive changes in its Green Paper on EU-ACP relations,[14] were wrong-footed in a manner that damaged relations between both organisations, and caused the ACP to feel that Europe was trying to break up the grouping. It was true that the ACP countries, through having established a secretariat in Brussels in 1976, were not necessarily a very homogeneous alliance, but since the negotiations of the first Lomé Convention, of 1975, they have established a useful South-South solidarity that could still have its place with the right leadership. The EPAs, only partially completed by 2011, are still a source of distress and confusion.

Since 2006, visitors to Brussels have become more and more painfully aware that the EU is now pursuing two parallel strategies in Africa, which gives an impression of dysfunctionality. Since 2000, Brussels has sought to develop a partnership with Africa, largely through the African Union—then about to replace the Organization of African Unity (OAU)—although the absence of Morocco from the AU has meant that the 'partnership' is not officially with the AU. At the same time, strategic partnerships were developed separately with the Caribbean and Pacific countries.

This may well be seen as a logical evolution, but it springs from the view (now quite prevalent in European circles) that, for present-day Europe, the harnessing of three groups together as the ACP is an anachronistic absurdity. Some in Brussels have persuaded themselves that even Cotonou is 'a relic'. This is ironic, since in the 1990s this was something that used to be said about Lomé. If anything, Cotonou was in fact a regressive step back from Lomé, a proposition few want to admit. Some have also argued that it belonged to the Cold War era, which is historically inaccurate, for the ethos of Lomé was above all politically neutral, providing large amounts of money to countries like 'Marxist' Ethiopia as well as 'capitalist' Côte d'Ivoire. The current increased attention to Africa, pushed by the Portuguese and encouraged by the French, has also been useful in masking any covert 'Eurafricanism' (see chapters 16 and 18 in this volume) by playing to wider security preoccupations in the post–11 September 2001 era.

This idea was articulated in the Africa Strategy of 2007, devised in Europe but filled out into a joint partnership strategy by the third EU-Africa summit in Lisbon.[15] In many respects, this document duplicated areas of partnership in Cotonou, with the added dimension of security, as the EU itself has been falteringly developing its own security identity. (See chapters 13–15 in this volume.) In practical terms, this has involved close cooperation with the AU in assisting both capacity-building and peacekeeping operations, such as in Darfur, with funds taken from the European Development Fund, very definitely a Cotonou institution. The disconnect between the Africa Strategy/Action Plan and Cotonou was visible at the EU-Africa Lisbon summit of December 2007, although the sour atmosphere there, expressed by the presidents of Senegal, Abdoulaye Wade,[16] and South Africa, Thabo Mbeki, was more focused on the EPA muddle.

Reports from the fourth EU-Africa summit, in Tripoli in November 2010, suggest that the problems surrounding this relationship have not fully dissipated. Although officially all went well, a story in *Le Monde*[17] after the summit suggested that there were still serious areas of disagreement between Africa and Europe. Beyond the obvious continuing aggravation of the EPAs, the report mentioned immigration, human rights, and climate change, where the EU and Africa signally failed to find a common position prior to the most recent round of UN-sponsored talks in Cancún in December 2010, but a revised version of the 2007 joint strategy was agreed.

The report in *Le Monde* also noted that while there were eighty heads of state and government present, the leaders of Britain, France, and Germany were absent. And under a special deal, the host, Libya's leader Muammar Qaddafi (subsequently toppled and killed by rebels backed by an Anglo-French-led North Atlantic Treaty Organisation [NATO] operation in 2011) agreed not to invite Sudan's leader, Omar al-Bashir, for whom an international arrest warrant had been issued in 2009 by the Hague-based International Criminal Court (ICC) for alleged war crimes committed in Darfur. In return, African leaders appealed for the ICC process to be postponed. Even the predictable presence of the Zimbabwean leader, Robert Mugabe, produced little controversy, and there was little of the 'sacred drama' of Lisbon of three years earlier. The departure from power and later death of Qaddafi in October 2011 pushed the summit back further in political consciousness, even as there have been increasing admissions from European officials that implementation of the Europe-Africa Strategy continues to experience difficulties.

More positive takes on the partnership (and the Tripoli summit of 2010) have come not just from the usual official Brussels sources. A month prior to the summit itself, there was an optimistic take on EU-Africa relations from Ambassador John Shinkaiye, the Nigerian chief of staff of the chairperson of the AU, Jean Ping, at a conference at Chatham House in London on peace and security in Africa. Among the positive assessments of the AU-EU relationship, Shinkaiye's speech contained two profoundly significant statements: first, that in endeavouring to build international partnerships, the AU has borne in mind that they should be 'fully based on Africa's leadership, because without such leadership there will be no ownership and sustainability, because we understand those problems far better than those who come from far away, because we know which solutions will work, and how we can get there, and because, fundamentally, these problems are ours and we will live with their consequences'.[18]

Second, Shinkaiye delivered a clear warning:

Our continent is keenly following the European integration project and the efforts being made to meet the challenges arising from this project. In particular, Africa is interested in how an integrated Europe, at peace with itself, would project power as a cohesive whole. We are watching how Europe is balancing the re-nationalisation of political life, which one could detect from recent developments, and the pursuit of a collective ideal. If the former tips the balance, Africa will once again have to revert to the old *modus operandi* of interacting individually with European governments in peace and development matters, which will be a serious setback to the EU-AU partnership.[19]

The increasing stress on security

Just as the 2007 Lisbon Treaty somewhat shifts power from the EU Commission to the Council, so the development of the 2007 Lisbon partnership represents a certain move in emphasis away from the ACP in the direction of the AU, even if, as one is still told in Brussels, 'Cotonou is money'.[20] The preference now in some Brussels circles is definitely for the Africa Strategic Partnership of 2007, with more emphasis on security considerations, which may eventually lead to the burying of the ACP in 2020 when Cotonou expires. There are those who apparently intend to work for that objective, pointing out that the functioning of the ACP group is entirely based on European money, and what Brussels proposes, Brussels can dispose of. But for the most part, such views are not found within the ACP group. Those on the European side concerned with implementing the strategy in 2010 seemed sublimely unconcerned about funding, saying 'we are now beyond aid'. But we are also a long way from having an EU-Africa partnership that is a substantive power relationship. There are still too many ghosts of the past to overcome.

Meanwhile, it is Cotonou that still has the resources of the EDF, and remains the guardian of what is left of the emotional engagement with the ACP that was there from the 1970s. This spirit, surprisingly to some, has been revived by the signing in June 2010 of the renewal of Cotonou for another five years, at an EU-ACP Council of Ministers in the Burkinabè capital of Ouagadougou. Significantly, for the first time, there is reference to the AU in a Cotonou document, which is encouraging, as there was absolutely no reference to Cotonou in the joint strategy of 2007, and the security aspects of the relationship bypass the ACP secretariat in Brussels, which has no military function.

Although this latest Cotonou renewal is no longer tied to that of the EDF (the tenth fund, totalling 22.6 million euros, lasts from 2007 to 2013), it has been accompanied by a new ray of hope for a flagging relationship. This has coincided with the arrival at the ACP House in March 2010 of a new secretary-general, Mohamed Ibn Chambas, fresh from running ECOWAS for ten years between 2000 and 2010, and is very familiar with the key trade issues. The Ghanaian diplomat has been facing up to the challenge by trying to infuse a new spirit of dynamism and direction into ACP House. All those familiar with the disconnected ways of the EU institutions (painfully on display in 2010 in the confusion over foreign policy and the laborious and costly setting up of a European diplomatic service) will be painfully aware of the mammoth dimensions of this challenge. There are those who doubt that the ACP as a group can last beyond the legal expiry of Cotonou in 2020, but as we have seen, there are others who would deeply regret its disappearance.

The holistic approach of the volume

The need to examine the EU-Africa relationship in a holistic way has dictated the priorities of this diverse collection of essays. There are many subjects of importance in EU-Africa relations that this volume is able to touch on only tangentially. For example, the tale of the European Commission's particular and groundbreaking involvement in Africa from the Treaty of Rome in 1957 onwards is a mammoth study in its own right.[21]

With this in mind, the editors have divided the book into six parts, each with several chapters, to illustrate the multidimensional nature of the subject matter and facilitate the emergence of common themes, just as the parts interact with each other and the chapters speak to each other. Part 1 assesses the historical relationship of Europe with Africa. The first question it asks is how historical and institutional relations are analysed, given the compartmentalisation of disciplines. The second question, the one that lies behind the ethos of the whole book, is why the idea of *Eurafrique* has had such survival power beyond the colonial period, during which it flourished in certain circles. A third question posed is how the Lomé-Cotonou trade-aid continuum has come to relate so dysfunctionally with the ambitious plans for a Europe-Africa strategy. And last, part 1 asks whether the African Union has been wise to have placed so much emphasis on the EU as an institutional model.

In examining some of the EU's strategic partnerships, part 2 poses the question of why Brussels has so far been unable to develop satisfactory partnerships with South Africa and the countries of North Africa, even before the latter faced the turbulence of 2011. It also poses the question of how such seriously diverse groups of countries can achieve an equal partnership. Part 2 further speculates on whether the struggles over regional integration in Europe (seen dramatically in the Eurozone crisis that raged in 2011) have lessons for Africa. Another question is whether Europe is not increasingly turning to consolidation of other partnerships. Finally there is a powerful question to be posed especially in view of 'the rise of the rest', most dramatically seen in Asia, about how Europe can maintain its strong ties with Africa, whose strongest trading partner is still Europe, in the face of rising challenges in the global balance of economic power from countries like China and India. From this naturally flows the crucial question of why Africa should in any way prioritise relations with Europe over partnerships with other possibly more sympathetic areas in the world.

Part 3, focusing on trade, aid, and investment, asks how sustainable Africa's current investment boom is, and also how far the considerable economic potential of African states can last. This leads to the doubts cast on one of Europe's major policy innovations of recent years: the economic partnership agreements in the Cotonou Agreement. Again, how far are these EPAs really promoting Africa's regional integration as against Europe's mercantilist inclinations? Part 3 also highlights the EU's Common Agricultural Policy, asking with passion, how damaging this is for Africa's legitimate trading ambitions, especially on a planet growing increasingly aware of the need for food security. These discordant policies pose a basic question about whether the EU is really able to cope with the demands of international relations in a globalising world.

Likewise, part 4 examines the increasing role of the conditionality of 'good governance' in EU-Africa relations, asking about Europe's uncertain ventures into the field of security, and assessing the effectiveness of these initiatives in the Great Lakes region and in Chad and the Central African Republic. It also asks the question of how far the EU, as an entity, should really venture into the field of security in Africa, and whether the continent's own need for security sometimes concedes too much in an area that in the past had been a proud and essential yardstick of independence. Another sensitive and related question is how far development budgets, above all the European Development Fund, should be reallocated for security purposes, however pressing may be the need of security as a prerequisite for development.

Part 5 examines the Africa policies within the EU context of France, Britain, Portugal, and the Nordic countries in order to assess how far their bilateral and multilateral relations in Africa have influenced their EU positions. It further asks how far it is possible to harmonise these relations in Brussels. It also asks how many similarities and differences there are between the countries selected, along with the question of how much those with strong historical connections with Africa have influenced the EU's own policies towards Africa in the five and a half decades since the signing of the Treaty of Rome in 1957. How far do the historically progressive-minded Nordic countries have policies that resemble former colonial powers with strong historical African connections? Moreover, how can the interests of these strong relations coexist with those of the majority of the twenty-seven countries of the EU for which Africa relations are more marginal?

The concluding section, part 6, has to be seen very much in the context of changes already burgeoning in the twenty-first century. Not surprisingly, this part focuses first on the migration phenomenon from Africa to Europe. The pressing question is asked: how can Europe manage coordinated policies in an increasingly difficult economic situation? The deadly follow-up is to ask: how can Europe contain evident reversions to strident nationalism, bearing as it does the dangers of racism and xenophobia? A related question is: what further transformations could take place in the established mind-set of Europe's view of Africa as the world potentially moves increasingly towards the development of 'postracial societies', as evidenced by the historic election of Barack Obama in the US in 2008. This leads to a final question: how do we solve the ultimate riddle of Europe's true postcolonial identity and role? Indeed, how far can that role be relieved of the delusions of the past, and sanitised and modernised?

Part 1 begins with a chapter by Kaye Whiteman, a former *fonctionnaire* at the European Commission in Brussels between 1973 and 1982 and a British historian and journalist, who provides detailed historical background. He examines the rise and fall of the idea of *Eurafrique* from the

Berlin Conference of 1884–1885 to the EU-Africa summit in Tripoli in 2010. He then looks at aspects of the historical relationship, especially the evolution from the colonial nexus to the different ways in which more equal relations were often painfully sought in the postcolonial relationship, as recounted in the first part of this introduction.

Whiteman's chapter also details the central role that France has played in European policy on Africa from the beginning. Indeed it is probably the France-Africa relationship that has moulded how Europe-Africa relations have been structured and perceived more than any other. Next, Nigerian scholar Adekeye Adebajo undertakes a comparative study of the evolution, development, and achievements of the African Union and the European Union, focusing on the key political, economic, and legal institutions of both bodies, before seeking to draw some lessons for regional integration in Africa from the European experience.

In part 2, five chapters assess the political, economic, and strategic dimensions of the Africa-Europe relationship. Two chapters—from opposite ends of the development spectrum—analyse the continued difficulties in the dialogue between the Europe and Africa. Nigerian scholar-administrator Adebayo Adedeji draws from his varied experiences as academic, politician, and international civil servant, which has permitted him to cover magisterially the widest range of material and dwell frankly on some of the underlying political issues that have all too often been ducked in some of the blander literature on Europe-Africa relations. He provides a history of integration efforts in Africa and what he regards as Europe's often pernicious role in stalling such efforts, before suggesting constructive ways in which the EU can support contemporary African efforts at pursuing regional integration.

Rob de Vos, a distinguished Dutch diplomat with long experience of Africa, calls for an end to Western economic aid to Africa, urging greater investment instead. He also recommends better institutional organisation in Africa and more honesty in Europe, but above all advises that 'the sooner this dependence on aid funding vanishes, the better the EU-Africa relationship will become'. Three more chapters focus on strategic engagement with the EU. South African scholar Talitha Bertelsmann-Scott examines the important strategic relationship between South Africa and the EU, noting that this is only one of ten such bilateral relations (along with the US, Canada, Mexico, China, Japan, South Korea, Russia, Brazil, and India). She examines both the political relationship and the free trade agreement that

Tshwane (Pretoria) concluded with Brussels in 2000, as well as the impact of the damaging spat over the EPAs. Longtime Maghreb and Middle East observer and British scholar George Joffé, in his chapter on the EU and North Africa, argues that the Maghreb countries in particular are on the front line of migration problems. Their imperatives are different from those of the wider Middle East, and whereas the succession of European plans for a political settlement in the Middle East have tended to become blocked, the Mahgreb and Egypt will be on the front line of any quest for genuine partnership in the Mediterranean. The cataclysmic events of the 'Arab Spring' of 2011 and their implications for Brussels's plans with the Mediterranean are also briefly discussed.

Pakistani analyst Shada Islam shows in the final chapter of this section how much the rise of the economic power of Asia, and Europe's need to take this into account, underline the continuing tendency to marginalise of Africa, in spite of recent signs of a turnaround in Africa's economies, due in part to the growing influence of Asian power.[22] She argues that Africa can learn lessons about how Asia is engaging the EU.

In part 3, four chapters focus on issues of trade, investment, and development. These chapters bring an important global perspective to the Europe-Africa framework, indicating how much the growth of relations between the EU and all developing countries (many of which now also come into the definition of 'emerging markets') have altered perspectives in Brussels. Irish economist Liam Halligan brings a refreshingly frank economic perspective, especially in the context of the global financial crisis of 2008–2009, arguing for a strong private sector role in Africa's socio-economic development and viewing Africa as the world's 'last investment frontier', in stark contrast to widespread stereotypical views of the 'Dark Continent' of European lore.

German economist Mareike Meyn revealingly dissects the vexed and complex question of the economic partnership agreements, which hang like a pall over the relationships in Africa of both the EU's member states and its own institutions. There is also room for one of the great unstudied areas: the political dimensions of the operation of the European Development Fund. This is now in its tenth incarnation, and has spawned a great deal of developmental literature, some of it adulatory and respectful, some of it doubting or, in a few cases, deeply damning. Despite this coverage there has been prevarication around the political story—for example, the extent to which there have been disasters, wastefulness, and the funding of 'white elephants' is a subject that has only occasionally been excavated, and this volume is unable to dwell on it.

Kenyan scholar Gilbert Khadiagala, in his forthright analysis, provides an African perspective on the EPA debate, tracing the pernicious impact of what he regards as Europe's mercantilist approach on each subregion in sub-Saharan Africa. He further argues that Europe is disengaging from its former African ties through the multilateralisation of its relations with Africa using institutions such as the Group of Eight (G8) industrialised countries. More work has been done on the EU's 50 million euro (in 2010) annual Common Agricultural Policy (CAP), but not so much as far as its interrelationship with the development policy, with which it is often in contradiction. This is one of the main themes of Zimbabwean scholar Charles Mutasa's chapter on the CAP which calls on EU governments to provide more generous development assistance to African governments, especially in the area of agriculture and human development, and advocates a phasing out of agricultural subsidies.

The way in which the development policies of European member states impact on the EU's own policies is a major and intricate subject in its own right, one on which it has not been possible to dwell in detail, although it cannot help intruding on this volume. In part 4, three chapters examine the security and governance aspects of the EU-Africa relationship. South African scholar Garth le Pere provides a critical overarching frame of the governance and security aspects of the relationship, arguing that the EU has continued some of the colonial practices of the past even as it seems to be striving to become an 'ethical power'.

Aldo Ajello, the veteran Italian diplomat who was EU Special Representative to the Great Lakes region between 1996 and 2007, provides a firsthand account of the EU and the turbulent politics of the Democratic Republic of the Congo (DRC), while German analyst Winrich Kühne provides a fascinating treatment of the involvement of the EU in deploying troops to Chad and the Central African Republic in 2008–2009. Both of these rich case histories assess the interplay of national politics—particularly the controversial French role, Brussels's evolving security role, and the difficulties in the peacekeeping partnership between the EU and the United Nations—on the EU's geostrategic chessboard, which forms an essential part of these narratives. The limited success of pan-European attempts at intervention,[23] despite some positive contributions to stability in both regions, highlights the continuing struggle the EU has been experiencing in building its unity, even though it is felt in Brussels that there has been slow but gradual progress in that direction.

The security dimension of the EU's relations with Africa has to be considered in its broadest sense, a sense that is now taken on board in Brussels. While Europe is aware of the limits to its possibilities of intervening in Africa in the way that France, for example, was able to do in the first forty years of the post-independence era, since 1960, there has still been a concerted effort to pursue a European security policy in Africa. This has been helped by Africa being forced to take more responsibility for its own security as a result of Western military disengagement from the continent after the UN debacle in Somalia in 1993.

The EU's willingness to find ways of being militarily involved in Africa has been encouraged by France (seeking ways to justify its own continued military presence in Africa). This has been seen in the way that, from 2005 onwards, 250 million euros over three-year periods have been diverted from the European Development Fund into a security project, called the African Peace Facility, most notably in support of the AU's operations in Darfur, but also backing the proposed African Standby Force, consisting of five subregional peacekeeping brigades. This is a development that would have been hard to imagine in the early days of the EDF. Even though there was always a certain amount of what the French call *dosage*—or political payoffs—there had never been a security element to the fund.

We have, in part 5, examined the positions of some of the leading European players. Our four chapters—on France, Britain, Portugal, and the Nordic countries—have been chosen in part because of the heavy legacy of the colonial policies of Paris, London, and Lisbon in Africa, but also because of the proactive role that, on various occasions, these countries and the Nordics have played in EU policy formulation. In a rich case study, Paris-based American scholar Douglas Yates shows how the French administration of Nicolas Sarkozy has sought, since 2007, to use the EU to multilateralise its military interventions in Africa, as a result of the discrediting of the French military role on the continent after the Rwandan genocide in 1994. Yates's chapter trenchantly examines some of the more dangerous moves by France's unpredictable president, Nicolas Sarkozy. Disillusionment on the part of francophone Africans with Paris's attitude and policies could become a determining factor in changing views on Europe in Africa, as the whole continent reacts to some of the more intolerant and racist positions that 'the old continent' has been taking. The inconvenient truth is that the presence of millions of African migrants in Europe, and the desire of many more to be there, is a direct consequence of the colonial past. Since the turn of the twenty-first century, migration has moved up everyone's agenda because of the impact of the terrorist attacks on the US on 11 September 2001. Concern at perceived 'terrorist' issues has not only enhanced preoccupation with security, but also exacerbated both xenophobia and Islamophobia.

British scholar Paul Williams dissects the various points at which Britain's role has been significant, noting that between 1997 and 2011 London did not treat the EU as a major theatre for conducting its foreign policy towards Africa, with the exception of Zimbabwe. Britain played a more active economic role in Africa than a military one, with the exception of a brief intervention in Sierra Leone in 2000. Likewise, British analyst and longtime Lusophone Africa expert Alex Vines shows how Portugal has increasingly sought to act as a bridge between Europe and Africa on the basis of historical ties with its former African colonies: Angola, Mozambique, Guinea-Bissau, Cape Verde, and São Tomé and Príncipe.

Norwegian scholar Anne Hammerstad skilfully explains the evolving Africa policies of the Nordic states (Sweden, Denmark, Norway, Iceland, and Finland), arguing that while still among the most generous and progressive aid donors in the world, these countries are increasingly pursuing their national interests in their Africa policies. Highlighting these countries is in no way to deny the importance in the complex kaleidoscopic picture of the Germans, the Belgians, the Spanish, and the Dutch, all of whom figure prominently in Europe's history in Africa, and crop up again and again in different chapters in this book—for example in the views of Dutch diplomat and experienced development expert Rob de Vos in part 2.

The three chapters of the final part of this book focus on migration and identity issues that have been an important part of Africa-Europe relations. Migration has a direct link to the increasingly pressing question of security, which also features prominently in several chapters in this book. The impact on Europe's own politics has been seen alarmingly in well-known liberal countries such as Sweden, Denmark, and the Netherlands, where immigration issues caused swings to the xenophobic right, a trend seen in several other EU member countries. British scholar Andrew Geddes is concerned in his chapter with migration issues and with attempts to regulate them at a European level, and argues that growing tensions on migration in EU member states have now acquired an important EU resonance. From now on, he concludes, any analysis of migration and asylum issues in Europe must factor developing countries into the framework. Two chapters focusing on different aspects of 'identity', broadly defined, then round off the volume. Kenyan scholar Ali Mazrui has put forward, over fifty years, views that have often challenged the received wisdom of Western academia on issues such as cultural colonialism and neocolonialism, peace and security, the vagaries of development aid, and the significance of regional integration. His prophetic contribution here focuses on the impact of the rise of the Kenyan-Kansan president of the US, Barack Obama, on international perceptions of Africa and its place in the international community in the era of what Mazrui calls 'post-racialism'. He uses powerful examples from the European literary canon—William Shakespeare and Aleksander Pushkin—to make diasporic links between Africa, Europe, and the US, a geographical area that has been described as the 'Black Atlantic'.

The concluding chapter by German scholar Hartmut Mayer considers the issue of Europe's own evolving identity in the twenty-first-century world and its attempts to become an 'ethical power' defined by promoting what American scholar Joseph Nye described as 'soft power': getting others to desire what one wants, and using nonmilitary tools of persuasion to attract allies rather than using military tools of 'hard power'.

We have followed the language of the 2007 joint strategy agreed at Lisbon in referring to the EU partnering with 'Africa' rather than as such with the AU, as strictly speaking, for complex political reasons, the partnership, while existing *de facto*, is not between two organisations. This has historical roots in the Western Sahara issue, which nearly broke up the former OAU in the early 1980s, and has still been frozen ever since Morocco quit the organisation in November 1984 after diplomatic recognition of the Algerian-backed Saharawi Arab Democratic Republic by a majority of the organisation's membership.

Finally, this study hopes to contribute to the promotion of dialogue between Africa and Europe based on genuine equality and mutual respect. We argue that Africa and Europe still appear not to have fully escaped the burdens of history, and examine the feasibility of elaborating and practising, in future, an 'Afro-Europa'. At the heart of the book is the desire to make the Afro-European relationship equal. By highlighting the negative impact of some European policies, and drawing attention to the lack of commitment in some quarters in Africa truly to stand up to these policies, the book challenges our current understanding of benign policies in Europe towards

Africa. The year 2011 showed how rapidly assumptions can change, and how swiftly the balance of global economic power can unleash unexpected forces. Europe should be grateful that it still has some advantages in Africa, and must ensure that it is not too late to work out a new relationship of genuine equality, partnership, and mutual self-interest between both continents that sheds the baggage of the *Eurafrique* past.

PART 1

AFRICA AND EUROPE
IN HISTORICAL PERSPECTIVE

2

THE RISE AND FALL OF *EURAFRIQUE*

FROM THE BERLIN CONFERENCE OF 1884–1885 TO THE TRIPOLI EU-AFRICA SUMMIT OF 2010

Kaye Whiteman

Cessons de ressasser le passé et tournons-nous ensemble vers l'avenir. Cet avenir a un nom: l'Eurafrique, et l'Union pour la Méditerranée est le premier étape. [Let us stop going over the past and turn to face the future. This future has a name: *Eurafrique*, of which the Mediterranean Union is the first stage.]

Author's translation of an article by Henri Guaino, special adviser to French president Nicolas Sarkozy, published in *Le Monde*, 27–28 July 2008

Introduction

Since the Centre for Conflict Resolution (CCR) in Cape Town, South Africa, has now held two conferences, in November 2007 and September 2008, with the word *Eurafrique* in the title,[1] I feel obliged to enlarge on the meaning of this vexatious expression lurking under the surface of the relationship between Europe and Africa. Note first of all that its usage is most often in French. To my knowledge, informed by my own research, there has never been any currency in any political or geopolitical context in the English language for the expression 'Eurafrica', although it exists with limited use in German, Italian, Spanish, and Portuguese. One researcher, after

23

painstaking effort, did find the expression in English used by an American anthropologist[2] in the 1890s, but the usage was only for purposes of geographical definition and had no geopolitical overtones. Any time *Eurafrique* has subsequently been used in English, it has most often been a translation from the French, although we are talking of a French political/cultural notion that found credence in other countries of continental Europe, notably Germany and Italy. The continued psychological power emanating from the concept was demonstrated at the seminar held by the CCR in November 2007, when there was an embittered Franco-African clash on the subject.

When I first went to Brussels to work as a *fonctionnaire* under the European Commission in 1973, *Eurafrique* had been a popular concept, particularly associated with the Yaoundé Conventions of 1963 and 1969, as some of the French and Francophone African leaders adopted it to describe the relationship that had existed between them and the European Economic Community (EEC) since its inception in 1957. But the idea did have more antecedents. Although first coined, it seems, by Eugène Guernier, a French writer,[3] in 1923, it was taken up by both Italian and German politicians who dwelt on the concept of Africa as a source of raw materials for industrialised Europe and sought a concerted European policy on the subject. The expression was in no way current at the time of the historic and infamous Conference on Africa organised in Berlin from 15 November 1884 to 26 February 1885,[4] the starting point for this chapter.

The Conference of Berlin, 1884–1885

If Berlin was a defining moment in Europe-Africa relations, it was because it was clearly a central event in the geopolitical process that came to be known as the 'Scramble for Africa'. This was the great competition by European powers to grab as much land as they could on the African continent, so that between the 1870s and the beginning of the First World War in 1914, what had been a collection of enclaves and trading posts scattered all around the coast of the continent, from west to south to east, became—through conquest—a patchwork of territories, some of enormous size, covering the whole continent and almost all under the sovereignty of one or another European power.[5]

The words 'through conquest' should be stressed as a historical description of how this process happened, because it is sometimes glossed over or even forgotten that the European connection to Africa as we know it today had violent roots. Treaties, protectorates, and concessions were negotiated but were all too often fronts: ruses covering the superior military power of the colonisers.

The immediate context of the gathering of fourteen largely European powers (Germany, France, Britain, Portugal, Belgium, Spain, Italy, Russia, Austria-Hungary, the United States, Denmark, Sweden/Norway, the Netherlands, and Turkey) in Berlin was the convergence of interest between two dominant figures in Europe at the time: the German chancellor, Prince Otto von Bismarck, head of the government of the most significant power of continental Europe, and King Leopold II of Belgium, who was not personally in Berlin but sent his representatives to the conference to promote his interests. Adding to this was intensification of the rivalry between the British and the French, especially in West Africa, then coming to a head with French ambitions to move into the 'Oil Rivers' in the Niger Delta, which was already regarded by the British as part of their sphere of influence. The Third Republic in France had been encouraged by Bismarck to seek colonies in Africa to distract the country from seeking revenge after the humiliating defeat in the Franco-Prussian war of 1870–1871, after which Bismarck himself had consolidated the unification of Germany and the creation of the Reich, before promoting the Prussian king to German kaiser (emperor).

Even in 1880 Africans largely ruled the continent, and most of it was unknown to Europeans, but in this new situation it was wide open, and the British takeover of Egypt in 1882 (again to the annoyance of the French, who had been the main promoters of the Suez Canal) ushered in an era of more intense competition. Bismarck had been against the idea of German colonies, but in the early 1880s began to change his mind, partly under pressure from public opinion but also because European competition in Africa was growing, and it was felt that Germany should be part of it, especially with a share of trade in mind. In May 1884 he cabled secret orders to the German agent Nachtigal to raise the German flag at posts in Cameroon, Togo, and South West Africa (now Namibia). The move was the immediate trigger for a grand meeting to regulate the situation, as what Bismarck called the *Kolonialtummel* ('colonial whirl')—the competition to grab territory by different European powers—was getting out of hand. Thus it was Germany's 'Iron Chancellor', by now the most important statesman in Europe, who called the meeting for 15 November 1884, in snow-filled Berlin, although it was actually at the request of Portugal, a power in decline that nonetheless still saw the mouth of the Congo as part of its sphere of influence.

The Irish historian Thomas Pakenham, in his *magnum opus* of 1991, *The Scramble for Africa*,[6] noted that the Berlin Conference was a meeting of middle-level delegations, in no way a summit, unlike the Congress of Berlin six years before, which had tried to regulate the problems of the Near and Middle East. In many respects, the Berlin Conference, in its three months, drew much less attention to itself than the dramatic and unsuccessful battle to save the hapless British general, Charles Gordon, in Khartoum, which went on at almost exactly the same period.[7]

At the same time, Belgium's King Leopold[8] sought by all means to realise the ambition he had developed in the late 1870s to be among the imperial European powers, with a huge colony of his own in the still wide-open territory of the Congo basin. Although he himself was absent from Berlin, as was his recently formed International Association of the Congo, it was his subtle and ruthless diplomacy, often in alliance with Bismarck, that played Britain and France against each other, as well as Britain's ally Portugal. Leopold ended up obtaining the huge prize of the Congo, even if the Portuguese still kept Cabinda on one shore of the river's mouth. Even today, Leopold's hubris in posing as a great disinterested humanitarian, aided by his publicist, the adventurer Henry Morton Stanley, when his agenda was really one of land-grab, remains the most astonishing aspect of the Berlin Conference. Pakenham observed that 'the self-styled philanthropic king had been chosen to act in Africa as the trustee for the whole of Europe'.[9]

The French lost both the mouth of the Congo (while retaining the north bank) and the mouth of the Niger. Securing the latter had been the main objective of the British in Berlin. Bismarck, in the end, while happy to tease the British, did not want to give the French such a prize as the huge wealth of the Congo,[10] which they had also coveted. This spurred the French, in the next fifteen years, to try to secure as much territory as they could both in Central and West Africa, even if much of what they took was uninhabited desert.[11]

The aftermath of Berlin

If this chapter dwells on Berlin and its significance, it is because of the way in which the historic conference formed a kind of dress rehearsal for *Eurafrique* and the great set-pieces between Europe and Africa, such as the opening of the negotiations for what became the Lomé Convention, at one of the historic palaces of Brussels, the Egmont, in 1973. It is true that the peace conference of Versailles in 1919 (after the First World War of 1914–1918) and the later agreements regarding defeated Fascist Italy (after the Second World War of 1939–1945) also disposed of and reorganised African frontiers, much as had been done at Berlin. They were thus events that played a role in perpetrating the idea of *Eurafrique:* at none of them were Africans in any way represented. But Berlin set the scene and triggered the process. This was also an early exercise in pan-European cooperation on African issues, even if its purpose was to regulate conquest. The poisonous memory that lingers today of those three months of intricate negotiations that had such far-reaching consequences for a continent is precisely that, in deciding the boundaries of what became independent countries in the twentieth century, there was not one single African representative present at the horseshoe negotiating table in Berlin.[12]

This is not the place to go into the detail of the 'Scramble for Africa'. But it is enough to say that the process was accompanied by a surge of dangerous ideas of European racial superiority, and also of the *mission civilisatrice* (civilising mission), a concept that infuses the language of the document from Berlin. At the signature of the third Lomé Convention, in November 1984, which I personally witnessed as a reporter, it was impossible not to be struck that it coincided exactly with the centenary of the Berlin Conference. Although the historical context was vastly different, there was a comparable odour of sanctity and hypocrisy around the language of the text that had been negotiated. If in 1884 there were high-minded concerns for the abolition of slavery, in 1984 there was high-minded language on socioeconomic development in Africa, even if human rights concerns only seriously entered the Europe-Africa relationship with the Cotonou Agreement in 2000. The difference in the late twentieth century was that a united Europe was sitting down with delegations from independent countries in Africa (along with representatives from the Caribbean and Pacific).

Also, while the nitty-gritty of negotiations had been about questions of demarcation of borders a century earlier (not mainly at the Berlin Conference, for the actual demarcation was made after 1885 in several agreements), now they were about real interests concerning commodities and raw materials. For Lomé was about trade as well as aid. If commerce had also been a preoccupation of the powers at Berlin, it was the other 'Cs'— Christianity and civilisation—that Bismarck, drawing from an aphorism of the sainted British explorer David Livingstone, advised including among the main preoccupations of the conference. The Lomé and Cotonou agreements had no such presumption. Most of the earlier theories of imperialism that prevailed at the end of the nineteenth century had an economic basis, although there were always two schools of thought in most European capitals as to whether the possession of colonies—especially African colonies—was in fact an economically viable proposition. But there was a remarkable persistence of the theory of the *pacte coloniale*, in which Africa under European control offered a source of commodities and raw materials, especially minerals, for Europe's industries, and at the same time provided a captive market.

If Leopold had promoted the idea of the Congo as a free trade zone as a tactical move to help fulfil his ambition, the great ideas of free trade put forward by Britain in the mid-nineteenth century, which had been so much a part of conventional wisdom, faded under the new theories of protectionism in the guise of imperial preference (later Commonwealth Preference) as promoted by Joseph Chamberlain as British colonial secretary. The French had always been among the most protectionist of powers (indeed in certain respects they still are), but with the new empires, the rest followed. Leopold ran the Congo Free State as his own private estate in a regime of appalling brutality (resulting in an estimated 10 million deaths), until a European campaign against his rule evicted him and transferred the huge colony to the Belgian state.

The tales of wealth that fired the so-called explorers found greater substance with the gold and diamond boom in South Africa beginning in the 1870s, and the legend of the British-born imperialist Cecil John Rhodes. The mineral wealth in the South was not unrelated to the final Great Power struggle of the Scramble, the Anglo-Boer War of 1899–1902, whose brutal and inconclusive nature put a damper on imperial adventurism, and helped to return the focus of the power struggle to Europe. Most of the carve-up of African territory had by then been sorted out, although rebellions continued in places like Tanganyika (now Tanzania) and Chad (even if the true and persistent nature of African resistance, as well as the brutal way in which it was suppressed, has tended to be underplayed in most European histories of the period).

The increasing struggle for domination in Europe from the 1890s onwards was enhanced by the arrival in office in 1890 of Kaiser Wilhelm II. Bismarck was out of power five years after Berlin, and the new era saw an eclipse of what, in retrospect, was seen as the moderating influence of Bismarck's *Realpolitik*. Most important of all, the rise of German military and naval power caused Britain and France to seek to settle their differences, and engage in the complex diplomatic process that led to the signing of the Entente Cordiale of 1904, much of which dealt with a series of agreements regarding Africa.[13] This was not quite *Eurafrique*, as there was still competition and compartmentalisation, but it was certainly a precursor of the Franco-British cooperation in Africa drawn up at the summit between the French president Jacques Chirac and the British prime minister Tony Blair at Saint-Malo in 1998, and seen more recently in the Anglo-French collaboration in the North Atlantic Treaty Organisation's (NATO) toppling of Libyan autocrat Muammar Qaddafi's regime in October 2011. The paradox of the Entente, which is still summoned up whenever the need for cooperation between Paris and London in Africa is invoked, was that it came only six years after one of the lowest points in the whole story of Anglo-French relations. This was the incident in 1898, when a confrontation at Fashoda[14] on the Upper Nile nearly brought the two nations to war. It left the British in control of the vast area of Sudan, but drove the French on the rebound to take over the whole tract of land, much of it in the Sahara, that was to become the territory of Chad.[15]

The birth of Eurafrique

In her 1973 doctoral thesis for the University of Virginia in the US, Judith Trunzo's "Eurafrica Counterpart? Counterpoint?"[16] noted that if the First World War had brought a heightened awareness of the use of colonies to European powers (in raw materials and manpower), the period between the wars was particularly conducive to the development of ideas of *Eurafrique*, if only because of the weakened state of Europe's Great Powers after the depradations of the war. While the French writer Eugène Guernier had laid claim to having coined the expression in 1923, Trunzo emphasised that 'the concept itself seems to have been given its widest circulation by Italian thinkers', including its high priest, Paolo Agostino Orsini di Camerota, who wrote a book titled *Eurafrica* in 1934.[17] Italy, noted Trunzo, was a major defender of European rights of access to, and distribution of, raw materials 'guaranteed by regional organisations'. Both the French and the Italians in their more strategic moments saw an extension of Europe southwards across the Mediterranean. For example, the French general André Meynier started a magazine called *Eurafrique* in Algiers in the 1930s, and continued advocating the idea into the 1950s.[18]

The concept was also fervently subscribed to by the German führer Adolf Hitler's economy minister, Hjalmar Schacht, who used the argument of *Eurafrika* to support the claim for restitution of Germany's colonies lost by 1919: in Africa, Cameroon, Tanganyika, Togo, Rwanda, Burundi, and South West Africa. Hjalmar Schacht argued, in 1937,[19] that the sealing off of markets, the decline in world trade, the brake on immigration (especially to the US), and the break in international credit procedures had been harmful to Germany, and that colonies had assumed much greater importance for European powers. He felt that Europe should pool its colonies in Africa the better to exploit them, an idea also advocated by the Vichy regime in France, perhaps by virtue of necessity. Vichy's paternalist and racist views of Africa also tied in with the known views of the Third Reich.[20]

After the Second World War ended in 1945 there were two parallel trends of profound importance. One was the movement for decolonisation of Europe's empires, all of which had become unsustainable for a continent that had been all but destroyed. The triumph of American power and the rise of the Soviet Union to superpower status gave a boost to nationalist movements, in theoretical support of the self-determination of peoples as articulated in the Charter of the United Nations, which, it was hoped in 1945, would be more effective than the ill-fated League of Nations had been between the two world wars.[21] The second trend was the strong impulse to build European unity as a means of never again having to experience the horror of two world wars. The role of colonies in such a union was the subject of a number of studies in amorphous new bodies like the Council of Europe, but not all pro-Europeans were necessarily enthused by the idea of *Eurafrique*, which had all too recently had such unattractive supporters.

France's president between 1959 and 1969, General Charles de Gaulle, as far as one can establish, never gave currency to the expression (perhaps from his dislike of vague notions—he had a similar aversion to *la Francophonie*). However, de Gaulle was well known to favour a new alternative relationship with Africa that sought to chart a middle way between what he used to call 'the two hegemons': the US and Russia. The Franco-African Community project, which was submitted to referendum in France's African territories in September 1958 only to be sabotaged by its rejection by Sékou Touré's Guinea, was essentially Euro-African in spirit. Moreover, some of de Gaulle's supporters in the various Gaullist parties that succeeded each other were among the most enthusiastic about the concept, since the idea fitted in with the Gaullist focus on the existence of a tight sphere of influence in France's sub-Saharan back yard, which later came to be generally known as *Françafrique*.[22] Having lost both Indo-China (by 1954) and Algeria (by 1962) in long and disastrous colonial wars, France was the more determined to hold on to what was left of its empire in Africa, as a ticket to maintaining its role as a middle-ranking power. *Lâchons l'Asie, gardons l'Afrique* (leave Asia, hold on to Africa) was a popular slogan of the 1950s.[23] (See chapter 16 in this volume.)

There were a number of France's African clients who favoured the idea of the Euro-African project. Senegal's president from 1960 to 1980, Léopold Senghor, sensitive to history, supported the concept devoutly, as part of his universalist worldview, while deploring the *Eurafrique* of Hitler and Vichy. Senghor genuinely believed in a symbiotic relationship between the two continents, whereas others, perhaps because of the sinister weight of history, felt that Africa's relations should be equal with all continents, despite the strength of economic and traditional ties.[24]

From Yaoundé to Lomé

The high point of postwar Euro-Africanism came after the Treaty of Rome established the European Economic Community in 1957. The French had more or less wished on its five partners in the Rome Treaty a provision for an 'association' of all those overseas territories, mainly in Africa, connected to member states (France, Belgium, the Netherlands, and Italy). It was the need to look after the interests of the African territories that was the motivating factor. After independence in the 1960s, this arrangement took the form of the Yaoundé Conventions (1963 and 1968), signed by eighteen African countries (fourteen ex-French, three ex-Belgian, and one ex-Italian).[25] This arrangement was frequently referred to as *l'Association Eurafricaine*, even if it was largely a French interest. However, there had always been a tendency in France to believe that what was good for France was also good for Europe.

Even for some of the original six countries of the EEC, the Yaoundé Conventions were too limited and distorted an approach to survive for long, but the process of widening the relationship only came with the enlargement of the Community to nine states by 1973, including notably Britain (Denmark and Ireland also joined in 1973). London's entry had been a painful process, as the British had always felt a certain separateness from Europe, but reduced circumstances, economic difficulties, and the advanced process of disengaging from empire, begun with the Indian sub-continent in 1947 and advancing steadily in Africa in the 1950s (starting with Sudan and Ghana), made the move towards the European experiment seem both attractive and apparently inevitable.

For Africa, British membership in the EEC was a political breakthrough, as the British Accession Treaty included a protocol for those in Africa, the Caribbean, and the Pacific (ACP) group who enjoyed Commonwealth Preference and the Commonwealth Sugar Agreement. Asia was too big a fish to swallow, while Canada and the Antipodes were left on their own, but the development money offered to the African, Caribbean, and Pacific countries in the first Lomé Convention by the EEC, of 3 billion ECU over a five-year period (at that time the second largest European expenditure item after the Common Agricultural Policy; see chapter 12 in this volume), was a tempting addition. However, the main concern of the African Commonwealth countries that decided, after some agonising, to join the negotiations, was with trade.

This was also an opportunity to try to put into practice some of the new ideas circulating in the early 1970s in the global South for a 'New International Economic Order' (NIEO). These hit international politics in a big way after the 1973 Arab-Israeli War and the arrival of the 'oil weapon' deployed by the Arabs. For a while there was a heady feeling of international revolution, until the West, on the receiving end of the 'oil shock', discovered that the best counteraction lay in neutralising the demand for producer power, about which the developing countries had begun to fantasise, for other commodities than oil. But context was all, and 1973 was coincidentally the year in which the Lomé Convention negotiations began. While there were those in Brussels who had been keen to compartmentalise the negotiations into 'associates' and 'associables', this was soon overcome by political imperatives dictated by the so-called Associables of the Commonwealth themselves.[26]

Researching the role of the former Commonwealth Secretary-General, Shridath 'Sonny' Ramphal, in the creation of Lomé and the ACP group when he was Guyana's foreign minister,[27] it became clearer that from the beginning, the Caribbean countries, just formed into a regional grouping called Caricom, sought African support for a joint negotiation. The vital endorsement came from a now almost forgotten document from the tenth-anniversary session of the Organisation of African Unity (OAU) in May 1973, the Declaration on Cooperation, Development, and Economic Independence,[28] which reads curiously like a precursor of the New Partnership for Africa's Development (NEPAD), produced by African leaders by 2001.[29] This process took Europe-Africa relations decisively away from the close and claustrophobic proximity of *Eurafrique* (which too closely resembled *Françafrique*) into something that promised to be a bigger, more open, and more innovative concept of relations. Where the Yaoundé Association had been the target of critics such as Sékou Touré, who felt it was fundamentally neocolonial, here was the same Guinean president signing up to Lomé along with the Marxist regime of Ethiopia and the newly independent Marxist regimes of Angola and Mozambique. Lomé, it was said, was politically neutral, and all-African, even if, by common consent, the North Africans chose to have their own agreements with Europe, leaving sub-Saharan Africa for Lomé. (See chapter 7 in this volume.)

There had thus been a strongly political decision to secure support from the OAU for a joint negotiation under a big tent that eventually became the Africa, Caribbean, and Pacific group. While the Yaoundé formula of a legally based 'trade and aid' treaty between equal partners was kept, there were a number of progressive innovations in the Lomé platform, including industrial cooperation and a scheme for the stabilisation of export earnings, which met the persistent complaints of developing countries about uncertain fluctuations in income. Nothing was more important in Lomé than the abandonment of the reciprocity built into a free trade area that had been a governing feature of Yaoundé. Without this change, an agreement would have been much harder to reach, and in retrospect it appears to have been Lomé's 'jewel in the crown'. The accord endured until 1975, right up to the Cotonou Partnership Agreement of 2000,[30] and even now is at the root of the crisis caused by its abandonment, coming from its replacement by the reciprocity clauses in the controversial and heavy-handed economic partnership agreements (EPAs). (See chapters 10 and 11 in this volume.)

A fundamental question thus has to be posed when looking at the more than thirty years between the signing of the first Lomé Convention in 1975 and the launch of the Europe-Africa Strategy in Lisbon in 2007: Was the new deal of Lomé a real future model for relations, or was it only a myth to cover and justify increasingly anachronistic postcolonial relations?

From Lomé to Cotonou

With the signing of Lomé, the expression *Eurafrique* dropped out of fashion and usage, much as did the expression 'association', although some in Southern Africa also had doubts about the new vogue for the word 'partnership', recalling the Rhodesian settler politician Godfrey Huggins (later Lord Malvern) in the 1950s, who had notoriously spoken of the 'partnership of the rider and the horse' in the subsequently defunct Federation of Rhodesia and Nyasaland (comprising what are now Zimbabwe, Zambia, and Malawi). However, these memories had (and still have) no weight in Brussels, just as the political support found in 1973 from the Organisation of African Unity was also later forgotten. But was the fall into disuse of the expression *Eurafrique* really a decline of the reality?

Some left-wing analysts such as the Malian scholar Guy Martin, writing in 1982,[31] considered that Lomé was nothing more than a more effective reworking of the neocolonial principles of Yaoundé. Indeed, from another perspective, it could be argued that since Lomé included all of sub-Saharan Africa, it was *de facto* a more effective articulation of the better aspects of *Eurafrique* than Yaoundé had been. One of the main believers in the benefits of *Eurafrique*, Léopold Senghor, certainly thought so. This was why he had urged his friend the French president Georges Pompidou (1969–1974) to welcome Britain into the new Europe, where de Gaulle had been hostile. The main movers in the European Commission, Claude Cheysson, the French commissioner for Development from 1974 to 1981, and former British minister Maurice Foley, the deputy director-general for development from 1973 to 1988,[32] recognised that there was an element in Lomé of making up for the crimes of the 'Scramble for Africa' by helping to reunite Africa in accordance with the aspirations of its countries and citizens. Although it was not a word normally used in diplomacy, there was an element of 'atonement' here for historical sins dating back to the era of the Berlin Conference.

Senghor, with some of the other Francophone African leaders, also feared a loss of interest in Africa, by both France and Europe, since they felt that Africa still needed European aid. The same fear later focused on the 'marginalisation' of the continent. Although this dependency syndrome was not felt by other African states such as Nigeria,[33] they all signed up to Lomé in the interests of unity, and in order to move at the pace of the slowest members. Moreover, signing up to Lomé proved to be the green light for the great project of the Economic Community of West African States (ECO-

WAS), whose treaty was signed in 1975, some three months after the signing of the first Lomé Convention (see chapter 4 in this volume). The greater African input into Lomé also ensured that priority was given in the Treaty to regional cooperation, with a provision of 10 per cent of the 3 billion ECU European Development Fund for regional projects.

The major change in Lomé, a significant move away from what some had lauded as the special *Eurafrique* aspects of Yaoundé—which curiously vaunted its attachment to reciprocity—was in trade. A speech made by the leader of Nigeria at the time, General Yakubu Gowon, as chair of the OAU, to the economic debate at the Commonwealth Heads of Government Meeting in Ottawa, Canada, in August 1973, is worth quoting in relation to the OAU's May 1973 Declaration:

That Declaration was not a protest. Both in its conception and thrust, it was an offer of partnership between Africa and the rest of the world in terms of sovereign equality and mutual non-exploitation. For we must, of necessity, trade with Europe and the rest of the world. But we also want the world to know that it is a fiction to speak of a free trade area between developed and developing countries.[34]

My concern here, however, is to concentrate on the *politics* of this relationship, which is often ignored by students, many of whom believe that the relationship is essentially economic. Although Lomé had its critics from both left and right, the support from heavyweight leaders of the ACP such as Guyana's Forbes Burnham and Jamaica's Michael Manley, and Zambia's Kenneth Kaunda and Tanzania's Julius Nyerere (the latter of whom once described the group as the 'trade union of the poor'), gave enough legitimacy to the group. The 'radical' development commissioner in Brussels, French diplomat Claude Cheysson, had a persuasive discourse that preached equality, even if in practice this could not have been an equal relationship. Cheysson also argued that because Lomé was a treaty, the money in the European Development Fund belonged to the ACP, which idea, although a pleasing legal fiction, was contradicted by his successors as patently untrue. In the Cotonou Partnership Agreement, with the introduction of flexible amounts, this became even less true. The Cheysson discourse also emphasised the concept of political neutrality cited earlier. This was fine in the atmosphere of the Cold War, because it committed huge sums of European aid money to the Marxist dictatorship of Haile Mariam Mengistu, but with the end of the Cold War by 1990 the rise of preoccupations on human rights and governance transformed Western views of aid and made the spirit of Lomé—despite the insertion of provisions on human rights and democratic governance—appear increasingly obsolete. (See chapter 5 in this volume.)

Although the 1979 negotiations for Lomé II showed some fight on the part of the ACP, it was less than the genuinely tough negotiations of Lomé I.[35] By the 'lost decade'[36] of the 1980s, Africa's economic decline meant that most of the continent's negotiators were grateful for 'any port in a storm', which further debilitated the whole partnership operation of the convention, so that by the time the 1990s arrived, the accord was in desperate need of renewal.[37] The convention itself, by Lomé IV, had grown and grown in size to incorporate more and more chapters, including cultural cooperation, but had not grown in effectiveness.

Lomé's much extolled chapter on regional cooperation (the amount devoted to regional cooperation was increased from 10 to 15 per cent of funds—to 1,116 billion ECU of the total sixth European Development Fund of 7,440 billion ECU in 1984 in Lomé III) had increasing difficulty in finding projects to fund, especially as some of those funded proved to have their own problems, such as the Senegal River Scheme and the West African Cement Works (CIMAO) in Togo. Brussels's support for regional groups often seemed opaque, confused by the different interests of Europe's member states and caught between different groupings, such as between ECOWAS and the Francophone grouping that became the West African Economic and Monetary Union (UEMOA), or between the Community of Eastern and Southern Africa (COMESA) and the Southern African Development Community (SADC, formerly the Southern African Development Coordination Conference, SADCC), which Brussels had encouraged.

The ACP states themselves were occasionally divided by damaging disputes between Anglophones and Francophones over jobs. Moreover, the European Commission's Green Paper of 1997[38] suggested that the three regions—Africa, the Caribbean, and the Pacific—might be treated separately, thus breaking up the Lomé alliance. An appeal from Ramphal, still watching over relations on behalf of the Caribbean, helped to reinforce some solidarity, so that the Cotonou Partnership Agreement of June 2000 was still in the end an EU-ACP agreement. Some aspects were an improvement: Cotonou was simplified in its form, with many of its instruments dropped, like industrial and cultural cooperation as well as Stabex and Sysmin (a parallel system for mineral prices introduced against some opposition under Lomé II in 1979). 'Cooperation' thus became more dependent on bilateral priorities, at the same time as being, up to a point, decentralised away from Brussels to delegates and their counterparts in each country.

But Cotonou's farthest-reaching change was the dropping of nonreciprocity, which had been the keystone in the Lomé arch. The ACP states had bitterly opposed this decision, but were powerless to stop it. Reciprocity had been dressed up in the notorious system of economic partnership agreements and given a time delay of seven years before application. The idea was to encourage regional groupings, but also on the table was the concept that the EPAs should be free trade areas. But the ending of nonreciprocity, it was calculated, could mean a loss to ACP countries of as much as one year's development money.[39] Although much delayed, the granting of a five-year World Trade Organisation (WTO) waiver in 2002, permitting nonreciprocity to continue, eased the pain enough for some interim EPA agreements to be signed, but there was a lot of disappointment and bad feeling. (See chapters 10 and 11 in this volume.)

The introduction in 2001 of a proposal for free access to the European market for 'Everything but Arms' from the least-developed countries covered over half of the ACP states, and so only a group of middle-income countries that were serious potential exporters to Europe, such as Ghana, Kenya, Mauritius, Namibia, Botswana, and many of the Caribbean states, would be seriously affected by this proposal, unless they were to sign up to the EPAs. This distress was further eased by the prolongation once again of the European Development Fund in its eighth (1995–2000) and ninth (2000–2007) incarnations, allocating 12.9 billion euros and 13.2 billion euros respectively, to which was added 9.9 billion euros in unspent balances, and 2007 was a long way away. Politically, however, the spirit had been taken out of the Europe-Africa relationship, and the EU itself no longer seemed to be engaged towards the ACP.[40] It was an extreme irony that, when faced with the challenges of the EU-Africa summit in Lisbon in 2007, the ghost of the apparent failure of the ACP connection should have returned to haunt EU-Africa relations, to the point that the summit was perceived as being only partially successful, and received a lukewarm international press.

Cotonou, however, was also a more profoundly political agreement than Lomé, reflecting the changes in international perceptions of development, as well as Africa's own appreciation of what was already coming to be called its 'renaissance': a term particularly associated with Thabo Mbeki, South Africa's president between 1999 and 2008. More important were Cotonou's provisions on human rights and governance, providing for the suspension of aid for those whose democratic governance performance fell short. This had already been present in Lomé IV (indeed aid had been suspended to Uganda as long ago as 1977 in the era of Idi Amin, mainly because of eventual British pressure, though no such suspension was applied to the equally repugnant Jean-Bédel Bokassa's French-backed regime in the Central African Republic). In the 1990s the EU was encouraged by signs that Africa was finally beginning to put its own governance house in order, even as conflicts multiplied in parts of the continent.

From Cairo to Tripoli

This is where context again becomes important. The plans for reform of the OAU were already well under way when the Portuguese presidency of the EU invited all African states to the first EU-Africa summit, in Cairo in 2000. It was held on the African side 'under the aegis of the OAU', a formula designed to permit Morocco, with which the EU had a bilateral aid and trade agreement, to attend the meeting, although it was not an OAU member. A similar formula was eventually applied with the AU in Lisbon in 2007 and Tripoli in 2010—hence the name 'EU-Africa summit'. There were a lot of important-sounding declarations on subjects like security and governance, but there was no follow-up, and an attempt to hold a second summit, in Lisbon in 2003, failed mainly because of British objections to the presence of Zimbabwe's Robert Mugabe. In fact, the rebirth of the OAU as the African Union in 2002 made the idea of a strategic partnership more attractive to the EU, which already was becoming increasingly keen on the idea of security involvement in Africa (as indeed security cooperation developed within the EU).

The idea of EU security forces deployed in Africa, unthinkable thirty years earlier, was now entirely accepted, even if pioneered by a few countries with more developed interests. (See chapters 13–16 in this volume.) Drawing on the European Development Fund to finance such forces would have been even more unthinkable thirty years earlier, but this had again become part of the new paradigm. As the US involved itself militarily more and more in Africa in the post–11 September 2001 environment, so we even saw NATO in Libya in 2011 attempting anew to develop an African interest of a kind that was absolutely ruled out at the time of the Franco-Belgian intervention in Zaire's (now the Democratic Republic of the Congo) Shaba region in 1978. The question still remains: How far are these actions actually in Africa's interest?

One development that encouraged the belief that a greater political involvement by the EU in Africa was possible was an improvement in relations between the French and the British. French involvement in the Rwandan genocide in 1994 and the fall of the dictatorship of Mobutu Sese Seko in 1997 had exacerbated relations between France and the so-called Anglo-Saxons. One French diplomat in Kinshasa had even perceived the British as playing the role of 'useful idiot' given the US support for the rebellion against Mobutu. But rather than risk further confrontation, by 1998 the British and the French were again on speaking terms and talking at a Blair-Chirac summit in Saint-Malo that year not just about reinforcing European defence but also about embarking on a range of areas of cooperation in Africa, followed by further discussions at successive summits.

The extent of this understanding was made clearer after the unexpected British intervention in Sierra Leone in April 2000 to assist a crumbling UN mission: the most concrete evidence yet of a major change in British policy towards Africa (see chapter 17 in this volume). Until Tony Blair came to power in 1997, as the British analyst Tom Porteous noted,[41] relations 'had been characterised by disengagement, withdrawal and damage limitation', dominated by coping with the negative effects of the crises first in Rhodesia and then in South Africa. Porteous further observed that, for Blair, initially 'Africa was simply not on the radar. But he gradually came to realise the possibilities. Determining factors were the push for a new and better-funded development policy from those who oversaw the creation of the Department for International Development (DFID); and the need for New Labour to conduct an ethical foreign policy'.[42]

Although this was a fairly early casualty of political realities, it was one of the main factors behind the Sierra Leone intervention, initially to shore up a faltering UN operation, but eventually growing into a mission to save a country. This was the kind of military intervention in Africa to which the French were more accustomed, and they took comfort from the initiative. These developments led to greater mutual comprehension, so that when the French intervened in Côte d'Ivoire in September 2002, they had immediate British support. Indeed, the 4,600-strong Operation Licorne marked a new Gallic approach to intervention, with important UN cover and EU endorsement of a kind that back in the 1960s and 1970s would never have been sought.

Moreover, from 2001 onwards, Britain turned Africa into a major foreign policy priority, from Blair's October 2001 speech on Africa as a 'scar on the conscience of the world' to the setting up of the Commission for Africa of 2005 to the Group of Eight (G8) industrialised countries' summit at Gleneagles in Scotland in 2005, best remembered for major commitments to increase aid, which had by 2011 been mostly unrealised. Complete with dubious accompanying celebrity culture involving the likes of Bono and Bob Geldof, Blair's Africa policy (continued between 2007 and 2010 under Gordon Brown, who in fact had been one of its most important architects) might be called '*Eurafrique* Lite'. This approach made Africa, for the first time since its independence, a highlight of British foreign policy, but without any real commitment to some deeper engagement in a 'special relationship' for which others in Europe seemed to want to push.

The second EU-Africa summit, in Lisbon, was seven years in the making. It was the prospect of the Portuguese (always the main champions of the idea of the summit, with discreet support from the French) holding the EU presidency in the second part of 2007 that caused it to happen. Lisbon intended to hold the summit regardless, in spite of the continued 'Zimbabwe problem'. Cover was provided by the fact that the AU was determined in its insistence that President Mugabe, as an AU head of state, attend the summit. Most EU members accepted the Portuguese position, and only Gordon Brown, among major EU leaders, refused to attend, although he did send a delegation. The summit—though in many respects a great and well-attended show, which approved all the strategy papers and declarations about a strategic partnership that had been intended for some time—had a mixed impact. This was due in part to the fact that, although the development of a partnership with the AU might have seemed a straightforward and desirable development, the ghosts of the past could not be escaped. The spectre of *Eurafrique* still cast a long shadow over this relationship.

Students of the documents drawn up for Lisbon[43] could not ignore the fact that there was virtually no reference to the existing Cotonou agreement, despite the fact that the latter contained negotiated provisions on a range of subjects put up for consideration in Lisbon, such as governance, human rights, and security. This could only have been because of the unfortunate coincidence that the summit fell at the worst point in the knotty discussions in the EPAs, on which there was much disgruntlement in Africa. If the Portuguese had hoped that they could insulate the summit from the issue, they were disappointed, as there were fiery speeches from a number of African leaders, notably the Senegalese president, Abdoulaye Wade, who condemned both the concept of EPAs and the way they were being handled.

Most significant, Africans were upset at the effect, probably unintended, that the EPAs had on the regional groupings that the continent had for some years been trying to put together; whereas the policy was supposed to be furthering regional unity, it was actually causing more divisions. Although the return to reciprocity had been negotiated away in 2000 and been accepted as unavoidable, if damaging, the strong-arm tactics of EU commissioners—Peter Mandelson of Britain and Louis Michel of Belgium—caused great offence, which is likely to have lasting consequences, as the issue, although quiescent, was still not resolved by early 2012. Mandelson's remarks in November 2007 that Nigeria and South Africa were obstructing the EPA talks were particularly impolitic. The comment of ACP ministers, ten days after Lisbon, regretting that 'the EU's mercantilist interests have taken precedence over the ACP's developmental and regional interests',[44] contained the bitter truth, even if many of them were obliged to go on and sign up to interim EPAs owing to their own short-term national interest of not being denied access to the lucrative European market. These were the real issues, as opposed to the high-sounding good intentions about 'strategic partnership' of the Lisbon Declaration and the strategy papers. Concern about the top-heavy structures of the EU-Africa strategy continued in the series of implementation discussions, and the agenda of the subsequent EU-Africa summit in Tripoli in November 2010 included a measure of simplification.

Reports on the fourth EU-Africa summit, in Tripoli in 2010, suggested that the problems surrounding this relationship have not fully dissipated, and several areas of disagreement remain between Africa and Europe.[45] Beyond the obvious continuing aggravation of the EPAs, the reports mentioned immigration, human rights, and climate change, on which the EU and Africa signally failed to find a common position prior to the most recent round of United Nations-sponsored talks in Cancún in December 2010, though a revised version of the 2007 joint strategy was agreed in Tripoli. However, the predictable presence of Zimbabwean leader Robert Mugabe produced little controversy this time, and there was little of the drama of Lisbon three years earlier.

Concluding reflections: the demise of Eurafrique

Since this chapter has essentially been an attempt to trace a political itinerary of the concept of *Eurafrique*, I must include a last word about the views of French president Nicolas Sarkozy, on which there has been much commentary. Although before coming to power in 2007 Sarkozy said that he would introduce change, even 'rupture', in France's Africa policy, and his views on immigration seemed to bear this out, his attacks on the cronyism of his predecessor, Jacques Chirac, were apparently forgotten as soon as he came to power, given the thrust to cultivate Gabon's late autocratic leader, Omar Bongo, the crony to end all cronies. More serious, in the context of this chapter, in his speeches in both Senegal and Gabon, Sarkozy openly used the discredited term *Eurafrique*, the first politician in years to do so, although one suspects that EU commissioner Louis Michel did not disagree, since the Belgian largely spoke of 'Europe-Africa' in the context of an 'indispensable partnership' in November 2007.[46]

There was some suggestion that Sarkozy was somewhat concerned at the hostile reaction to the speech he made in Dakar, where disparaging remarks about Africa's history and culture brought a barrage of hostile reactions in Africa. Thus the French president's speech in Cape Town in February 2008[47] was couched in more palatable language, and even promised a renegotiation of France's defence agreements in Africa, without any commitment to abandon them. This was followed, however, by the removal from the post of minister of cooperation of Jean-Marie Bockel, who had the temerity to announce prematurely that *Françafrique* was dead, perhaps taking some of Sarkozy's words about 'rupture' too seriously, to the point that Bockel had been criticised by some of France's old friends in Africa, from Gabon to Cameroon to Congo-Brazzaville.

Then, in July 2008, as if to demonstrate the point more emphatically, Henri Guaino, Sarkozy's special adviser on African and Mediterranean affairs, penned an article in *Le Monde* defending the controversial speech in Dakar (which he was said to have drafted), and, more pointedly, called for a revival of *Eurafrique*, a call he made again in Gabon, where it was likely to be received more sympathetically. As if to rub salt in the wound, Guaino reaffirmed everything that he had said in the speech, noting that Africa was not succeeding because it could not 'liberate itself from its myths'. The bluntspeaking adviser then went on to use the statement quoted at the beginning of this chapter: '"Let us stop going over the past and turn to face the future. This future has a name: *Eurafrique*, of which the Mediterranean Union is the first stage." That is what the President of the Republic said in Dakar'.[48]

Sarkozy's project of a Mediterranean Union, launched amid many misgivings both in Europe and in North Africa in July 2008, was ambiguous and devoid of content (see chapter 7 in this volume). But the idea at least had the virtue of historical consistency: it goes back to the old dream of a French sphere of influence stretching southwards from France across the Mediterranean to take in all of Africa or as much of it as could be swallowed. One had the distinct impression that Sarkozy was trying on different policies for size, and would continue to wear those that suited him, and discard those that were ill-fitting, as the situation demanded.

Sarkozy and some others in Europe, including some in Brussels, were mindful of the international configuration and feared losing out on Europe's once privileged position in Africa to the new Asian superpowers: China and India. But effectively the idea of *Eurafrique*, with its colonial and neocolonial overtones, is historically dead, and any attempt to revive it will cause apprehension in many quarters. The expression's present survival has a certain ghostly aspect, and the word was dropped from the mercurial Sarkozy's discourse after 2008, perhaps in deference to expressions of sensitivity on the subject. Whatever the advantages the African Union may see in having a strategic partnership with Europe, much as it seeks to do with China, India, Japan, and the US, a symbiotic connection with Europe privileged over all others is surely, above all now, not what Africa should be seeking (see chapter 8 in this volume). Some may see this questioning as tilting at windmills, and argue that it is now best to let sleeping dogs lie. But one can safely say that any idea that an already unsettling, if nebulous, 'Mediterranean Union' might be extended in some form of 'Eurafrican Union' has surely got to be a nonstarter given the present mind-set and lingering historical suspicions of *Eurafrique* prevailing in Africa.

3

PARADISE LOST AND FOUND

THE AFRICAN UNION AND THE EUROPEAN UNION[1]

Adekeye Adebajo

Introduction

The English poet John Milton's classic *Paradise Lost* of 1667 portrayed a vain God—wanting to be forever worshipped, for hymns to be sung to him, and demanding absolute obedience—being plunged into a celestial civil war by a 'radical' Satan who instigated a third of the angels in rebellion against 'Heav'n's awful Monarch'. Lucifer reasoned that it was 'Better to reign in Hell than serve in Heav'n'. Though Milton sees God as just and loving and acknowledges his ultimate triumph over Satan, some critics have noted that his portrayal can be read as support for a revolt against tyrannical rule, particularly since God had banished Adam and Eve from the paradisiacal Garden of Eden for eating an apple—and thus introduced Death to the world—and then, according to those critics, taken satisfaction at his own son's crucifixion.[2] Whatever the merits of this debate, for our own purposes this chapter deals with Africa's continuing quest for regional integration following the decay of its own 'Garden of Eden'[3] as a result of the pernicious actions of avaricious European imperialists.

We will assess the African Union and the European Union in comparative perspective. Africa was the birthplace of humankind, with the biblical

Garden of Eden believed to have been located on the continent. Africa also remains the site of some of the world's most breathtaking scenery: rolling hills, dense rainforests, cloud-covered mountains, bountiful wildlife, barren deserts, and majestic rivers. Four centuries of slavery and another century of colonialism by Western states distorted Africa's politics, economics, societies and culture. After the continent's independence from the late 1950s, the Cold War also had a destabilising effect on Africa's security—with France, the United States, and the Soviet Union being the main interventionist culprits[4]—even as many autocratic African leaders failed to reverse the 'Curse of Berlin'.[5] This 'Curse' had been invoked during the infamous Berlin Conference of 1884–1885, where Germany's 'Iron Chancellor', Otto von Bismarck, hosted the meeting at which the rules were effectively set for the partition of Africa during the European 'Scramble' for the continent's riches (see chapter 2 in this volume). As many African states celebrated their fiftieth year of nationhood in 2010, their continuing socioeconomic and political problems and lack of regional integration meant that less than 10 per cent of trade on the continent was conducted with other African countries. The African Union remained more aspiration than reality, and the continent represented a Miltonian case of 'Paradise Lost'.

Europe had been the epicentre of two world wars between 1914 and 1945, after which Britain, France, Portugal, Belgium, and Spain were eventually forced to give up their African colonies. That continent was thus itself partitioned and forced to cede global preeminence to two superpowers, the US and Russia. The 'curse' of Africa's ancestors had wrought revenge for Europe's 'original sin' against Africa, as Berlin itself—the site of the conference where the rules for Africa's partition were set—was partitioned, becoming the symbol of the division of Germany and Europe. However, the incredible economic integration of Europe after 1945, which ensured an end to large-scale conflicts on the continent, suggested that, in contrast to Africa, Europe now represented a case of 'Paradise Regained'.

In a sense, Africa and Europe have been seeking to create their own paradise on Earth through regional integration. I argue in this chapter that the African Union—and before it the Organisation of African Unity (OAU)—as well as the European Economic Community (EEC) and the European Union, can be seen as efforts to create 'perfect unions', modern Towers of Babel, by bringing together scattered African and European diasporas. This is, of course, not a perfect comparison: the fifty-three-member AU, with some of the poorest countries in the world, was born in 2002, while the twenty-seven-member EU, with some of the world's wealthiest states, celebrated its fiftieth birthday in 2007.[6] But the African Union is the successor organisation of the thirty-nine-year-old OAU and has consciously modelled itself on the European Union's institutions, creating similar political, economic, and legal institutions. This comparison is thus worth making to see if the AU can draw useful lessons from the five-decade integration experiences of the EU.

The African Union has identified as a sixth subregion (in addition to North, West, Eastern, Central, and Southern Africa)—the diaspora of Africans in the Americas, for example in the US, Brazil, and the West Indies, together with expatriate Africans living largely in the West.[7] The organisation is currently attempting to unite a continent of 800 million inhabitants in fifty-four countries from the Cape to Cairo; some of its leaders, like Libya's late autocrat Muammar Qaddafi, have talked of creating a 'United States of Africa'; and the AU seeks to establish an African Economic Community (AEC) by 2028. The European Union is striving towards unity by bringing together 500 million people in twenty-seven countries, from Sofia to Stockholm, creating in the process the world's largest market and its only international organisation with some supranational powers. The Union has now become the world's largest trading power. The EU accounted, in 2010, for about 30 per cent of the world's nominal gross domestic product, at about $16.2 trillion. Africa in contrast accounted for less than 2 per cent of world trade in 2010.

This chapter is divided into three main sections that comparatively assess experiences and actors in Africa and Europe. First it analyses the quest for economic and political integration in Africa, adopting a historical approach that examines pan-African efforts to attain political freedom, from the first Pan-African Conference in 1900 up until the fifth Pan-African Congress at Manchester in 1945. This section also assesses the struggle for African unity after decolonisation, which in the 1950s culminated in the creation of the OAU by 1963 and the birth of the AU in 2002. The second section of the chapter examines European efforts at integration after two bloody civil wars—more popularly known as the First and Second World Wars—and the expansion of the six-member EEC of 1957 into the twenty-seven-member EU by 2007. The third section examines comparatively, and in more detail, the structures, challenges, and achievements of the key institutions of the AU and the EU. The chapter concludes with a few reflections on why regional integration has been more successful in Europe than in Africa.

Africa's integrationists

From London to Addis Ababa: the Organisation of African Unity.[8] Fifteen years after the 1884–1885 Conference of Berlin effectively set the rules for Africa's partition, the pan-African movement was born in 1900. A Trinidadian lawyer, Henry Sylvester Williams, organised the first Pan-African Conference in London. This was the same year that eminent African American scholar-activist William E.B. DuBois, the 'Father of Pan-Africanism', uttered the remarkably prescient prophecy: 'The problem of the twentieth century is the problem of the colour line'.[9] Between 1919 and 1945, five Pan-African Congresses took place, in Paris (1919), London (1921 and 1923), New York (1927), and Manchester (1945).[10] These meetings were at first dominated by African Americans like DuBois. But in time, black Caribbeans in Europe, and Africans from countries like Sierra Leone, Ghana, Ethiopia, Liberia, and Nigeria, increasingly participated in them.[11]

Initially, the demands of these early pan-Africanists were limited to education for Africans, economic development, and racial equality. Eventually, however, the doctrine of pan-Africanism not only emphasised the existence, worth, and strength of African cultures, but also called for African unity so that these cultures might flourish in freedom, unhampered by the denigrating influences of Western 'civilisation', which in Africa signified slavery and colonialism.[12] Pan-Africanism, therefore, represented the reaction by the black African diaspora to the indignities that blacks had suffered from Caucasian Euro-Americans. Some sought refuge in an idealised African past, free of slavery and xenophobia. In the Francophone world, writers like Martinique's Aimé Césaire and Senegal's Léopold Senghor also contributed to the movement, developing the idea of *négritude*, which glorified black culture, looked back nostalgically at a rich African past, and affirmed the worth and dignity of black people across the globe.[13] As Césaire noted: 'My Négritude is no tower and no cathedral / It delves into the deeper red flesh of the soil'.[14]

The Nigerian Nobel Literature laureate Wole Soyinka famously ridiculed the romanticisation of this apolitical, moderate approach to pan-Africanism in wryly noting: 'The tiger does not profess its tigritude, it pounces'.[15] It was ironically one of the apostles of *négritude*, Césaire, who in 1969 turned a Western classic into a parable of the Western exploitation of Africa and its diaspora. Set in the Caribbean, Césaire's play, *Une Tempête*, adapted William Shakespeare's 1610 play *The Tempest* to portray a European Prospero enslaving a black Caliban. Shakespeare's Caliban is a primitive half-beast, half-man creature, reported to be fathered by a devil and a witch who had been banished from Algiers to a deserted island. Prospero treats Caliban harshly, enslaving and tormenting him. Césaire's Caliban—unlike Shakespeare's—eventually rebels against Prospero.[16]

By the time of the fifth Pan-African Congress, held in the English city of Manchester in 1945, not only had the Second World War of 1939–1945 shifted the global balance of power away from the imperial European powers, but the pan-African movement had also shifted its centre of influence to Africa itself. This conference was dominated by indigenous Africans like Ghana's Kwame Nkrumah, Nigeria's Obafemi Awolowo, Kenya's Jomo Kenyatta, and Malawi's Hastings Banda, men who later led their countries to independence. William DuBois, in fact, was the only African American at the 1945 congress. He passed the torch of pan-Africanism to Nkrumah and later moved to Ghana, where he spent the last years of his life. Both DuBois and Trinidad's George Padmore (who worked in Ghana under Nkrumah's government as an adviser on African affairs) lie buried in Accra.

It is not within the scope of this chapter to explain the swift decolonisation of Africa after the Second World War. Suffice it to say that there were many reasons—including the economic exhaustion of Europe after the war; the emergence of two professedly anticolonial superpowers, the United States and the Soviet Union; the growth of anticolonial sentiments in the metropolis; and the growing strength of African nationalists—that led to the near-complete decolonisation of Africa by the mid-1960s. In a classic 1967 study, the American scholar Immanuel Wallerstein discusses mass social movements into which many people are drawn without sharing or even understanding the aims of those movements. These movements feature a core and a periphery, with the former believing firmly in the movement's end-goal and the latter hoping only to use the mass support to achieve more parochial ends.[17] The pan-African movement conformed to this paradigm. Many nationalist politicians subscribed to the movement merely as an expedient for the consolidation of their domestic power.

A historic battle was waged for the soul of pan-Africanism, between a 'radical' Casablanca minority bloc led by Kwame Nkrumah, and the majority of African leaders, grouped under the Brazzaville and Monrovia blocs, who favoured a more gradualist approach to continental unity.[18] Nkrumah's rejected vision of a 'Union Government of African States' would have involved common economic planning (including a common currency and monetary zone), an African military command, and a common foreign policy. The Ghanaian leader was widely distrusted by his fellow African leaders for backing armed dissidents, and even his union with Guinea in 1958 and later including Mali in 1961 proved to be short-lived, dying by 1962.

Despite Nkrumah's attempts to fulfil pan-African dreams of a 'United States of Africa', African politics had become extremely divisive by 1963. The Monrovia and Brazzaville groups favoured a gradualist, functionalist approach to African union, and stressed the importance of noninterference in the affairs of other African states. The 'moderate' periphery of the pan-African movement consisted of the majority of Africa's independent leaders, who jealously guarded their newly won independence and opposed surrendering sovereignty to any supranational body. The core of the movement, on the other hand, called for close military, political, and economic cooperation towards the creation of a supranational African state. The 'radical' states—Ghana, Egypt, Morocco, Algeria, Guinea, and Mali—appeared to be more prepared to sanction intervention in other African states in order to cleanse the vestiges of colonialism from the continent. Thus Nkrumah harboured and supported critics of pro-Western 'moderate' regimes.

It is doubtful, though, that all members of the Casablanca group were prepared to cede sovereignty to a supranational African body. Indeed, one of the presidents of these states, Mali's Modibo Keita, supported the status quo on colonial boundaries in 1963, and the conservative kingdom of Morocco under King Hassan II and the United Arab Republic (UAR) under Egypt's Gamal Abdel Nasser—which involved a union with Syria— would scarcely have been ready to surrender power to an African body run from, and influenced by, Accra. The protracted Congo crisis of 1960–1964 further illustrated the divisions among African states, as the 'moderates' mostly backed President Joseph Kasavubu against Prime Minister Patrice Lumumba, who was supported by the 'radicals'.[19] The threat of further foreign intervention in the heart of Africa, this time as an extension of the Cold War, brought home anew the need for what Kenyan scholar Ali Mazrui, in a seminal 1967 study, described as a Pax Africana[20]—a peace secured, kept, and consolidated by Africans themselves—which would allow African states to resolve their disputes independently. This would be a stark contrast to the militarily expansionist and culturally destructive Pax Europa of the previous century. Where Pax Africana sought to stabilise and unite a continent, Pax Europa had sought to divide and conquer a continent.

In May 1963, thirty African states met in the Ethiopian capital of Addis Ababa and signed the Charter of the Organisation of African Unity, effecting the disintegration of the rival African blocs of Casablanca, Brazzaville, and Monrovia. The OAU Charter clearly reflected the triumph of the gradualist, evolutionary path over the speedy, revolutionary course of the 'radicals'. Four of its seven principles were concerned with sovereign rights, an emphasis of the Monrovia group. The two concessions to the Casablanca group—nonalignment and support for Africa's emancipation—had already been adopted by almost all African states as part of their foreign policy objectives. There is no reference in the charter to pan-Africanism or political union. There were two noteworthy institutional flaws in the charter that plagued the organisation during its three decades of existence. First, the charter rendered the OAU's executive and administrative branches ineffective by according them only limited powers. Resolutions of the OAU Assembly (consisting of all member states) were not legally binding, and this rendered the Assembly little more than a deliberative forum at best, or a 'talk shop' with no implementation mechanisms at worst. Second, the OAU's Commission of Mediation, Conciliation, and Arbitration, set up as the organisation's diplomatic machinery for conflict resolution, was not a judicial organ and did not have any powers of sanction. Along with the Economic and Social Commission, the Educational, Cultural, Scientific, and Health Commission, and the Defence Commission, the conflict resolution machinery of the OAU remained largely moribund after its creation in 1963.[21]

OAU aspirations for a Pax Africana were further weakened by the increasing 'proxy wars' waged by the superpowers in Africa, and the ongoing adventures of the French gendarme in Africa.[22] (See chapter 16 in this volume.) While the OAU's legitimisation of Cuba's 1975 intervention in Angola was consistent with its anti-South African stance, from the point of view of the Pax Africana it was an acknowledgement of its own military impotence. The Francophone states sanctioned French intervention in Zaire, while the OAU gave the nod to Cuban interference in Angola, which encouraged the Cubans, and their Soviet backers, to intervene in Ethiopia in 1977. At the end of the decade, the OAU did not bother to react collectively when Tanzania invaded Uganda in 1979 to depose the 'butcher of Kampala': Idi Amin had been elected as OAU chair in 1975–1976 despite killing an estimated 300,000 of his citizens in a bloody reign of terror. As heinous a dictator as Amin certainly was, Tanzania had violated one of the OAU's cardinal principles: respect for the sovereignty and territorial integrity of member states. Nyerere's impeccable pan-African credentials—in hosting the OAU Liberation Committee—combined with Ugandan military provocation, however, inoculated the *Mwalimu* (Teacher) from much criticism.

Africa's 'Thirty Years War' involved the OAU's Cold War struggle between 1963 and 1993 to achieve a Pax Africana in which Africans themselves would resolve their own conflicts. Ironically, the seat of the OAU secretariat, Ethiopia, itself experienced a thirty-year civil war, with the federal government fighting Eritrean and Tigrayan rebel groups.[23] The backdrop of the OAU's debates and attempts to maintain peace throughout Africa was thus a bloody civil war in its host country. It would be difficult to imagine diplomats at the United Nations trying to resolve global disputes while civil war raged in the United States. This, though, was the very situation confronting African multilateral diplomacy.[24] But despite its shortcomings, the OAU deserves credit for its firm commitment to decolonisation and the anti-apartheid struggle in South Africa. The continental body displayed pragmatism and flexibility in pursuing its dogged struggles on an issue over which most of its members were not prepared to compromise. The organisation furnished ideological and diplomatic support to African liberation movements through multilateral forums in which it was well represented, such as the UN, the Group of 77 (G77) developing countries, and the Non-Aligned Movement (NAM). With admirable tenacity and diplomatic skills, African governments sponsored resolutions in the UN condemning Rhodesian and South African excesses,[25] leading to the imposition of economic sanctions against the two pariah states—the first in UN history.[26]

Tanzania's Salim Ahmed Salim served as Secretary-General of the OAU from 1989 to 2001: the longest tenure in the institution's history. His main contribution to African unity was in the area of peace. As the Cold War came to an end in Africa, the Tanzanian diplomat bluntly noted in 1992: 'The image of a continent in which conflicts seem to be endemic and in which human suffering seems to be callously taken for granted, must be altered … without further delay'.[27] He warned African leaders of the need to observe human rights and stop regarding the notion of state sovereignty as absolute: 'We should talk about the need for accountability of governments and of their national and international responsibilities. In the process, we shall be redefining sovereignty'.[28] Salim regarded Africa's regional organisations as the 'first line of defence' and called on them to promote democracy, human rights, and economic development.[29] He further argued that 'every African is his brother's keeper', and called for the use of African culture and social relations to manage conflicts.[30] He finally succeeded in his efforts to convince African leaders to establish an OAU conflict resolution mechanism in 1993.[31]

From Durban to Accra: the African Union and the new interventionists. In creating the African Union in the South African port city of Durban in 2002, it seemed at first that African leaders had finally realised that the grandiose plans, ad hoc committees, and numerous high-sounding resolutions of the OAU era could not bring about the continent's economic and political integration. African governments were thus forced to recognise that economic development and integration could not simply be legislated into existence. The glue that had held the OAU together for three decades—the liberation of Southern Africa and the elimination of apartheid—had come unstuck by 1994 with the election of the saintly Nelson Mandela as South Africa's first post-apartheid president. With growing poverty and continued insecurity replacing apartheid and colonialism as the common enemy, the OAU was forced to commit suicide in 2002 in the hope that another body, the African Union, could rise from its ashes like the Egyptian Phoenix, to invigorate the four-decade efforts to integrate the continent. Unlike the OAU Charter, the AU's Constitutive Act of 2000 allowed for interference in the internal affairs of its members in cases of unconstitutional changes of governments, egregious human rights abuses and genocide, and conflicts that threaten regional stability. This is potentially revolutionary in light of the OAU's rigid, noninterventionist posture in the first three decades of its existence. Learning from the difficulties of the OAU, the AU also sought to establish an African Standby Force, consisting of five subregional brigades, by 2010.

We now turn to the 'Grand Debate' on a 'United States of Africa' that took place at the African Union summit in Accra in July 2007. In the early nineteenth century, Mali's Timbuktu was a fabled city of gold in the grasping imagination of European explorers; the AU summit in Accra in 2007 evoked images of a similar elusive quest for an African El Dorado. A 'Grand Debate' was staged between Africa's leaders that revived some of the early battles of African diplomacy in the 1960s. In Africa's contemporary battle, the gladiators had changed but the issues had not. Libya, under its mercurial leader Muammar Qaddafi, launched the vision of an African Union that would be loosely modelled after the European Union. Tripoli called for a

'United States of Africa' with an appointed president and ministers, as well as a central bank. Senegal's Abdoulaye Wade came closest to backing this vision, continuing to advocate a limited continental government, with the AU serving as an embryonic federation with a common currency and appointing its own ministers of foreign affairs, infrastructure, health, and education. Uganda's Yoweri Museveni pushed for a subfederalism that would eventually culminate in a political federation with Kenya, Tanzania, Burundi, and Rwanda under a revived East African Community (EAC).

This contemporary debate, however, seems ahistorical, quixotic, and impractical. The lessons of the divisions of the 1960s must be learned before progress can be made today. African leaders in Accra in 2007 were presented with three options: first, to strengthen the AU and existing regional groupings; second, to create a 'Union Government' by 2015 with executive powers in specific areas as a transitory phase towards a 'United States of Africa'; and third, to proceed immediately towards a 'United States of Africa'. Nigeria, South Africa, and the majority of African states appeared to favour the second option. As in the days of Nkrumah, the more federalist vision of Africa (in particular, the third option) was rejected by African leaders. This is an idea whose time has not yet come. There appears to be a lack of priority, sequencing, or reality in these federalist schemes. Putting old wine in new bottles will clearly not integrate Africa. African leaders must revert to the first option and focus on the hard work of strengthening and funding fledgling institutions that they have created, and establishing one effective economic pillar in each African subregion. They must get their domestic houses in order and build strong economies and stable democracies. After all, there has to be something to integrate for integration to succeed. Otherwise, this 'Grand Debate' could turn out to have been another 'Grand Distraction'. A 'Big Bang' approach to African unity by Africa's alchemists will clearly not turn lead into gold.[32]

Europe's integrationists

From Paris to Maastricht: the European Economic Community. Charlemagne, the king of the Franks (a Germanic group), was one of the earliest visionaries of European integration. After thirty years of military campaigns, he united parts of modern-day Germany, Austria, France, Italy, Spain, Switzerland, Belgium, Luxembourg, and the Netherlands into an empire. By C.E. 800, Charlemagne had established central government over much of Western Europe.[33] This paved the way for the subsequent creation of the Holy Roman Empire. The modern roots of European integration, however, are often traced back to the Treaty of Westphalia in 1648, which ended thirty years of bloody religious conflicts and the delusions of the hegemony of the Holy Roman Empire, thus starting the long process of creating recognised sovereign states. 'Emperor' Napoleon Bonaparte sought to unite Europe through force of arms in the nineteenth century, while Germany's Adolf Hitler unsuccessfully attempted a similar forced integration of the continent in the twentieth century.

The real impetus for contemporary European integration came about as a result of the slaughter of the Second World War of 1939–1945, which left the continent in ruins. Jean Monnet is generally regarded as the 'Father of European integration'. This Frenchman became the architect of European integration, authoring the Schuman Plan of May 1950 (named after the French foreign minister Robert Schuman), becoming president of the High Authority of the Luxembourg-based European Coal and Steel Community (ECSC) from 1952 to 1955—with institutions such as the High Authority, the Common Assembly, the Special Council of Ministers, and the Court of Justice, which were all forerunners of current European Union institutions; and he was the moving force of the Action Committee for a United States of Europe, a platform he used to push for the 1957 Treaty of Rome in creating the European Economic Community. Monnet worked closely with Walter Hallstein, a former German professor at Frankfurt and strong advocate of European federalism, who went on to become the first president of the European Commission. The Frenchman regarded the Schuman Plan as chiefly a political means of dealing with economic problems.[34] Thus even though coal and steel were not the best industries to integrate economically—coal would soon decline as a source of energy in much of Europe—they had a potent symbolism, as steel was viewed as a symbol of arms merchants and German military power in France. Cooperation in this area would thus send a powerful symbol of pacific intent.

The European Coal and Steel Community was thus created in Paris in 1951 to integrate the coal and steel markets of its six founding members: France, Germany, Italy, Belgium, the Netherlands, and Luxembourg. The ECSC, however, did not succeed in integrating European coal and steel by preventing and promoting competition. National interests of members often prevailed over those of the Community. But this was an effort at supranationalism that laid the foundations for closer cooperation among 'the Six'. The basic strategy at the heart of this largely French initiative was to bring an end to the perpetual conflict between France and Germany by integrating their markets closer together. America's need for strong allies and viable markets and its provision of a $100 billion (in today's currency) Marshall Plan of economic aid to Europe, as well as a nuclear umbrella to counter the threat of Soviet expansionism, were also key factors in the integration of Western Europe.[35]

In June 1955 the founding members of the ECSC met in the Italian city of Messina and agreed to establish a common market. The Treaty of Rome of 1957 established the European Economic Community and the European Atomic Energy Community (Euratom). Rome's preamble noted that the EEC sought to 'lay the foundations of an ever closer union among the peoples of Europe'. The basic bargain of the EEC was essentially a deal between French agriculture and German industry as a way of bringing peace to Europe. Where pan-Africanism was an ideology of liberation, pan-Europeanism was an ideology of peacemaking (though within the framework of the North Atlantic Treaty Organisation [NATO] and the Cold War).[36] The EEC saw immediate results: trade in industrial products doubled in four years and average growth within the Community in the 1960s was 5 to 6 per cent. The customs union was completed in July 1968, eighteen months ahead of schedule. The Common Agricultural Policy (CAP) was launched in 1962, which at $50 billion a year has now become a profligate monstrosity of food mountains and corpulent farmers. (See chapter 12 in this volume.)

While the EEC made economic strides, the organisation experienced one of its most difficult political periods during the quasi-monarchical 'reign' of French president Charles de Gaulle from 1959 and 1969. This was ironic, since France had done more than any other country to create the EEC. De Gaulle practised a *politique de grandeur* that seemed to stress style over substance by pretending that France was still a Great Power that could rival the United States and the Soviet Union. He thus sidelined the collective reliance on American nuclear military power in favour of an independent French nuclear *force de frappe*. De Gaulle's view of the EEC was of an intergovernmental body in which governments largely made decisions, the parliament debated, and the bureaucrats prepared technical reports. He famously noted in May 1962 that the only option for the continent was 'a Europe of countries ... for Dante, Goethe, Chateaubriand would not have served Europe well if they had been stateless, men thinking and writing some form of integrated Esperanto or Volapuk'.[37] After the European Commission—supported by the European Court of Justice (ECJ)—sought its own resources to be paid by states from agricultural levies as well as oversight by the European Parliament, and after a French-backed plan for major decisions on foreign and defence plans to be taken unanimously by heads of state at summit meetings failed, de Gaulle instituted the 'Empty Chair policy' for the last six months of 1965, during which he withdrew his representatives from the Council of Ministers. The 'Luxembourg Compromise' of January 1966, which ensured France's return to the Council, effectively handed member states a veto over issues of vital national interests. De Gaulle then vindictively vetoed Britain's application to join the EEC twice, in 1963 and 1967.[38]

In 1965 the ECSC, the EEC, and Euratom were merged into the European Community (EC). The *Trente Glorieuses* (Thirty Glorious Years) of sustained economic growth after 1945 delivered peace and prosperity to Europe. The 1970s, however, ended as a dismal decade for European integration, with oil shocks in 1973 and 1979 and a global economic crisis that led to 'Eurosclerosis' in an era of stagflation. Even as Britain, Denmark, and Ireland joined the Community in 1973, member states seemed paralysed by indecision, and restricted supranational decisionmaking. Three of the few positive developments of the epoch were the first direct elections of the European Parliament, in 1979, establishment of the European Monetary System in the same year, and the evolution of the European Court of Justice as a source of European law. But high inflation and low growth afflicted most European economies during the 1970s.[39] The gloomy mood of the EEC was captured in a cover of the London-based magazine *The Economist*. After the first president of the European Commission, Walter Hallstein, died in March 1982, the influential but opinionated magazine—not renowned for its restraint and sense of proportion—depicted a front cover with a gravestone that read: 'EEC. Born March 25, 1957. Moribund March 25, 1982'.

The mid-1980s, however, saw a *relance* (relaunch) of European integration. The appointment of the Frenchman Jacques Delors as Commission president in January 1985 started a period of dynamism for the European Community that saw the creation of a single market by 1992. Delors was undoubtedly the heir of Jean Monnet. With strong working-class roots, the former Socialist French finance minister was president of the European Commission from 1985 to 1994, overseeing a period of unparalleled success not witnessed since the halcyon integration days of the 1960s. The dynamism of the new Commission was evidenced by the fact that in the first six months of 1988 alone, the EC took more decisions than it had done between 1974 and 1984.[40] During Delors's tenure, the European Commission achieved a single market in 1992, moved towards a single currency, promoted a common defence and foreign policy, and oversaw the birth of the European Union in November 1993. The Single European Act of 1986 also gave the Community 'competences' in the areas of social policies (including employment), development, the environment, and technological research.

The Single Market sought to promote freedom of goods, services, capital, and labour through the reduction of nontariff barriers and other measures. The ramparts of 'Fortress Europe' were finally being lifted. Qualified majority voting (instead of a requirement for unanimity) was increasingly used, and 297 pieces of Community legislation were identified to facilitate the creation of the Single Market. One of the big drivers of European integration during this period was European big business. Spain and Portugal joined the EC in 1986 (Greece had joined in 1981) and democracy-building was clearly shown to be an additional goal of the Community.[41] The road to Maastricht appeared to be paved with gold.

From Maastricht to Lisbon: the European Union. The Maastricht Treaty was signed in December 1991. It soon suffered a setback, however, when it was rejected in a Danish referendum in 1992, with both Denmark and Britain winning opt-outs from the European Monetary Union (Sweden would also win an opt-out after a failed referendum in 2003, having joined the EC with Austria and Finland in 1995). The Maastricht Treaty also enhanced the powers of the European Parliament. Two new 'pillars'—foreign and security policy, and freedom of movement and internal security—were established alongside the European Community, with the whole structure being renamed the European Union. But a French referendum on Maastricht in 1992 only managed a wafer-thin 51 per cent majority in favour. Despite the epoch-making achievements of the treaty, there were signs that Europe's leaders were not taking their populations with them on this integrationist journey without maps. The Yugoslav wars of succession between 1992 and 1995 further exposed the EU as an economic giant and military dwarf. The late US diplomat Richard Holbrooke openly questioned Europe's inability to take care of security issues within its own neighbourhood. The conflict in Kosovo in 1999 would also require American military might to reach a conclusion.

The Amsterdam Treaty of 1997 added new chapters on employment to the Community's treaty. The powers of the European Parliament were enhanced with co-decisions with the European Council on most legislative decisions, and the power to approve not just the Commission but its president, who was also given the right to accept or reject other members of the Commission. Amsterdam also created 'enhanced cooperation' in which groups of states could proceed with projects in which a minority did not want to participate, raising the prospect of a 'two-speed Europe'.

The launch of a European currency—the euro—in 1999 (the bills and coins appeared in 2002) was the main achievement of European integration between 1999 and 2009. The prospect of German reunification accelerated the pace of monetary union, as France looked to tie the German Gulliver into a web of interdependence: a common thread in the whole project of European integration. The euro has proved to be a volatile currency. Its value fell 15 per cent in relation to the dollar in its first year. But by 2003 it had recovered ground. By 2008 the euro had yet to prove its worth in terms of creating economies of scale and lowering prices.[42] Though it was widely viewed as a source of stability in the wake of the global financial crisis of 2008–2009, by 2010 questions were being widely raised about the long-term future of the euro after two eurozone members, Greece in May 2010 and Ireland in November 2010, had to be bailed out with loans from the EU of 80 billion and 67.5 billion euros respectively, as the banking and debt crisis threatened the viability of the eurozone; Portugal, another eurozone member, had to seek similar help in 2011.

By 2007 the EU had brought in twelve states largely from Central and Eastern Europe,[43] but the gloomy mood of the 1970s seemed to be returning. The divisions triggered by the US-led invasion of Iraq in 2003 led to divisions between 'Old Europe'—led by France, Germany, and Belgium—and a 'New Europe' led by Britain, Spain, Denmark, and several Eastern European countries like Poland and the Czech Republic. These events also embarrassingly exposed the failings of the EU's efforts to develop its Common Foreign and Security Policy. By 2008 the Union seemed to be suffering from indigestion, and was clearly having problems integrating the less wealthy countries as well as those, like Poland, having large agricultural sectors.

In February 2002 the former French president Valéry Giscard d'Estaing was asked to chair a convention to draft a European constitution to build more effective and democratic institutions for the EU. But the constitution was rejected by large majorities in referendums in two founding and usually reliable supporters: France and the Netherlands.[44] Attempts to salvage the constitution by making amendments were agreed in October 2007, but ran into more trouble when Irish voters (whose economy had benefitted more than most from the EU) rejected the new Lisbon Treaty of 2007 in a June 2008 referendum. A second Irish referendum produced a different result and the treaty came into force, but Europe's elites seemed once again to be far ahead of their electorates, and the 'democratic deficit' at the heart of the European project was once again embarrassingly laid bare. There was, however, a paradox: needing to seek the support of citizens to approve technically dense and incomprehensible documents rendered leaders vulnerable to protest votes about parochial domestic issues that had nothing to do with the draft treaties. The political horse-trading that resulted in the election of a Belgian, Herman Van Rompuy, and a Briton, Catherine Ashton, as president of the EU Council and the EU's foreign policy chief respectively, in November 2009, was also widely criticised.[45]

The key institutions of the AU and the EU

The key organs of the African Union and the European Union include the AU and EU Commissions; the AU Assembly of Heads of State and the European Council (of heads of state); the AU Executive Council and the European Council of Ministers; the Pan-African Parliament (PAP) and the European Parliament (EP); and the African Commission on Human and Peoples' Rights (ACHPR), the African Court on Human and Peoples' Rights (AfCHPR), and the European Court of Justice. It is important to reiterate here that many of the organs of the AU were inherited from the OAU, while many EU organs derived from the ECSC and the EEC. Both the AU and the EU have been accused of being elite-driven bodies that suffer from a 'democratic deficit' in which their citizens have not been properly consulted or informed sufficiently about decisions taken in their name. But while the EU represents a carefully calibrated balance between supranationalism and sovereignty, decisionmaking within the AU remains dominated by its heads of state. Many of the institutions of the AU appear to be modelled specifically on the EU, and some—the Commission and the Council—even borrow their names directly from the EU. But can the EU really serve as a useful model for the AU?

The AU Commission and the EU Commission. The Addis Ababa-based AU Commission is the secretariat of the body and is headed by a chair (former Gabonese foreign minister Jean Ping since 2008), a deputy, and eight commissioners. Its six main tasks include: to represent the AU and to defend its interests as mandated and directed by the Assembly of Heads of State and the Executive Council; to initiate proposals for other AU organs to consider; to implement the decisions of these organs; to coordinate and monitor implementation of AU decisions in conjunction with the Permanent Representatives Committee (PRC) of African ambassadors in Ethiopia and with regular reporting to the Executive Council; to draft common positions and coordinate the actions of member states in international negotiations; and to prepare the AU's programme of activities and budget for approval.

In practice, however, the AU Commission struggled in the first decade of its existence to establish its independence and ability to take initiatives on behalf of the fifty-three members. The chair of the Commission is the chief executive officer, legal representative, and accounting officer of the African Union. However, under the leadership of the AU's first chair, former Malian president Alpha Oumar Konaré, between 2003 and 2008, the deputy chairperson appeared to have been given sole responsibility for administration and finance. The eight other commissioners also often acted as if they were not accountable to the chair, with some arguing that since they had been elected by the AU Assembly of Heads of State, they did not have to answer to the chair. The situation was further exacerbated by the fact that most of the commissioners had never before worked in an international organisation.[46]

The AU audit report of December 2007 was scathing about the administrative and management failings of the AU Commission under Konaré's leadership. The relationship between the chair, his deputy, and eight commissioners was described as 'dysfunctional', with infrequent meetings, a misunderstanding of mandates and authority levels, and a lack of coordination of overlapping mandates. After assuming office in September 2003, the commissioners—effectively Konaré's cabinet—did not have their first joint meeting for two years. Weekly meetings were thereafter agreed, but only thirty-seven meetings took place between September 2005 and October 2007, a total of 138 working weeks! No agenda items were submitted for these meetings, and strategic and substantive discussions rarely took place. The chair of the Commission and his deputy often tendered their apologies, and on average five to six commissioners failed to attend meetings owing to travel problems, while only four times did at least seven commissioners attend. Minutes of the meetings also had not been circulated in a year, while current meetings did not review decisions of previous meetings.

Inadequate leadership, weak management systems, and poor supervision were also identified between and within AU departments, as well as a lack of understanding and acceptance of a proper chain of command. Also criticised by the 2007 audit report were the lack of clarity on delegation and exercise of power; the frequent absence of commissioners; the lack of internal communications strategies; ineffective accountability mechanisms; the 'unhealthy organisational culture'; and the lack of reports from field missions. In 2007 the Commission was operating with only 617 out of 912 approved staff (60 per cent), relying heavily on short-term consultants.[47] Another source of tension was between Konaré and the plenipotentiaries on the AU's Permanent Representatives Committee, with the ambassadors accusing the Malian of continuing to act like a head of state and going over their heads to deal directly with his former colleagues.

In 2007 the AU's annual budget stood at $132 million. In the same year, donors were expected to contribute $142 million to the AU Peace Fund (more than its entire annual budget), while member states were assessed at $2.9 million. The AU audit report of 2007 assessed the first five years of the organisation. Its panel, chaired by the former executive secretary of the UN Economic Commission for Africa (ECA) between 1975 and 1991, Nigeria's Adebayo Adedeji, found that the Commission's secretariat had weak financial accountability, with no centralised controls of funds raised by AU organs and departments. This sometimes resulted in unapproved activities being undertaken, funded by external donors. There was also a lack of implementation of programmes, with only 50 per cent of approved tasks implemented in 2006, and with most directorates underspending by 70–90 per cent. Procurement processes were also slow, and it could take up to five months to purchase essential equipment.[48]

The Brussels-based EU Commission, in stark contrast to its AU counterpart, is the 'guardian of the treaties' and the main executive body of the Union, initiating most of its legislation. The body derives its powers and substantial autonomy from the *acquis communautaire:* the rights and obligations flowing from the EU's treaties, laws, and regulations. The Commission issues about 5,000 directives, regulations, and decisions annually on issues such as health and safety, environmental standards, and product guidelines. It is also the only international body of its kind with supranational powers delegated by European leaders. The Commission's powers to initiate legislation, however, are somewhat constrained, in practice, by the European Council's role of setting the strategic direction for the organisation.[49] The European Council and the EU Council of Ministers thus still largely determine, in effect, the political direction of the Union.[50] Power still flows directly from national capitals like Berlin, Paris, London, and Rome, and not just from Brussels.

The European Commission has seven key roles: to propose legislation; to ensure implementation of EU treaties and provisions; to make recommendations and formulate opinions; to manage the budget; to conduct external relations; to help prepare activities of the European Council and the European Parliament; and to implement rules agreed by the Council.[51] The body is headed by a president (Portugal's José Manuel Barroso since November 2004), assisted by a College of Commissioners, composed of twenty-six other officials, who make decisions mostly by consensus and sometimes by majority vote. The College of Commissioners usually meets once a week and each commissioner has a cabinet, reflecting the influence of the French administrative system. The Commission has the sole right to initiate EU legislation, proposing texts of laws to the European Council and the European Parliament.

As earlier noted, the Commission's 'golden age' occurred under its most dynamic president, the French politician Jacques Delors, who pushed through legislation to create the Single Market during his tenure between 1985 and 1994. The body is also referred to as a 'watchdog' in its role of ensuring that the EU's treaty and laws are implemented by its twenty-seven member states. If governments refuse to abide by a 'reasoned opinion' of the Commission, it can take them to the European Court of Justice to seek a judgement. In some cases, fines are imposed on EU governments for refusing to comply with Commission requests. However, the Commission is usually astute enough to work with members and often seeks to accommodate rather than confront governments. The EU Commission has performed well in areas such as competition policy, but has been weaker at administering expenditure programmes.[52]

Like the EU Commission, the AU Commission has a mandate to initiate proposals and to negotiate in international forums on behalf of the organisation. However, in practice, the AU Commission lacks both the capacity and the power to do either very effectively. Unlike the EU Commission, which has some supranational powers explicitly delegated to it by its member states, the AU Commission has no such powers. The European Commission, unlike its African counterpart, can also take initiatives, make laws, and enforce rules. Brussels has also been engaged in negotiating trade deals in forums like the World Trade Organisation (WTO), and has acquired a reputation for being able to match the strength of countries such as the US, China, and Japan in such institutions. The AU Commission, on the other hand, has not been able to act in a similar manner, both because its leaders have yet to give it such a mandate and because of its own limited capacity. The EU Commission can also refer to the Court of Justice and fine states to push them to implement its decisions: a far cry from the powers of the AU.

The European Commission has a staff of 24,000, compared to the AU Commission's paltry 617 personnel, despite the African body having twice as many member states (fifty-three) as the EU (twenty-seven). While the AU budget was $260 million in 2011 and was irregularly paid by its member states, the EU budget in the same year was 141.9 billion euros and is always paid by all its members, with the sum representing only 1 per cent of the EU's total gross national product. The president of the EU Commission—unlike the chair of the AU Commission—now takes part in picking his commissioners, can reshuffle their portfolios, and can fire them with the collective support of the Commission. Unlike the AU Commission staff, the EU Commission staff are paid at the level of top international organisations like the United Nations, are multilingual, and often believe in the ideals of the organisation. Entry into the EU also requires competitive written and language exams, and some of the 'best and brightest' of Europe's technocrats work in the organisation. While the AU does have some impressive staff, it also has a good deal of incompetent 'dead wood' and clearly lacks the depth and breath of staff that the EU has. There have also been numerous complaints of an anti-intellectual culture within the AU Commission.

Unlike the AU Commission staff (with a few exceptions), senior EU Commission staff typically work fifty- to fifty-five-hour weeks. Both the AU and the EU have their own national and linguistic mafias. Neither organisation bases promotions strictly on a meritocratic system; they are often based on the power of influential networks and godfathers. Both have suffered from mismanagement and corruption. Both AU and EU commissioners spend much time travelling. The EU may be even more nepotistically nationalistic than the AU, as the cabinets of EU commissioners are chosen along largely national lines. EU commissioners also tend to show less independence of their national governments than do AU commissioners, while the EU traditionally reserves certain positions for specific nationalities. In 1993, for example, the European Court of Justice had to annul the appointment of several Spaniards and Italians in the EU Commission's fisheries department, noting that nationality had largely determined the appointments. While the EU Commission has delegations in over 120 countries and set up a European External Action Service (EEAS) as an international foreign service in January 2011, the AU has offices only in New York, Washington, and Brussels. The AU Commission is, however, more progressive in the area of gender than the EU's College of Commissioners, with half of the ten AU commissioners always mandated to be female, in contrast to the EU's nine women out of twenty-seven commissioners in 2011—representing only a third of the most senior officials.

The AU Assembly and the European Council. The AU Assembly of Heads of State is the 'supreme organ' and highest decisionmaking body of the organisation. Its tasks include forging common positions of the AU; determining when interventions and sanctions are to be imposed on erring members; monitoring implementation of its decisions; issuing directives and regulations to the Executive Council; ensuring oversight of the Union; establishing new organs; and appointing certain levels of staff. Since January 2005 the Assembly has met twice a year, in January and July, instead of once a year as previously.

Many African leaders tend, however, to arrive at the two-day summits on the day that they begin, and most heads of state have left by the second day. Since the first day is largely consumed by procedural issues, consultations, and ceremonial duties, this leaves little time for substantive discussions, which, because most leaders have already departed, are then left for ministers and the Permanent Representatives Committee of ambassadors in Addis Ababa to deal with. The Assembly's agenda is thus able to address only one or two policy issues. By June 2007, OAU/AU leaders had adopted thirty-three treaties since 1963, but only eighteen—about half of them— had been ratified by member states and come into force. Of forty-two decisions that were adopted by the AU Assembly at its two summits in 2006, only twenty-one had been fully implemented by December 2007. Another major deficiency is that the Assembly appoints a chair among its heads of state to direct the body's affairs for a year. But there is no national or AU Commission structure to direct this chairing, and AU leaders thus develop their own style of coordination with the Commission,[53] resulting in various levels of effectiveness.

In December 2007, only nine AU members had paid all their outstanding financial arrears,[54] and twenty-one countries were over a year in arrears, raising serious questions about the commitment of African leaders to their continental organisation. Five countries—Algeria, Egypt, Libya, Nigeria, and South Africa—contribute 75 per cent (15 per cent each) of the African contributions to the AU's annual budget, which was $260 million in 2010. That three North African countries—Algeria, Egypt, and Libya—which also traditionally play an important role in the Arab world, account for nearly half of the AU's budget, raises serious issues about exposing the continental body to changing political vicissitudes. For example, the late Libyan leader Muammar Qaddafi's interest in pan-Arabism and pan-Africanism often fluctuated with the prevailing international political winds during his four decades in power between 1969 and 2011. Only 40 per cent of the AU's budget is actually paid by its members, with China, the EU, and the US mostly paying the rest. Even the AU Commission chair, Jean Ping, conceded in January 2011 that the parsimony of African leaders 'does not do honour to the African cause'.[55] As the French scholar Daniel Bach also insightfully noted: 'Institution-building requires the growth of a sense of ownership that should not be confined to rhetorical pledges. The AU, unlike the EU, cannot rely on a stock of commonly shared values and criteria to ensure its sustainability'.[56]

One positive development within the AU was the clause in its Constitutive Act of 2000 excluding members who had engaged in unconstitutional changes of power: usually military coups d'état. Military regimes in Togo, Mauritania, Madagascar, and Niger have thus been sanctioned by the AU. The criticism of this approach, however, is that African leaders who have engaged in 'civilian coups d'état' (rigged elections, human rights abuses, clampdowns on the media) often escape sanction, and the focus on punishing military coups is sometimes seen by critics as a way for autocratic leaders to ensure regime survival.

The European Council was created at a summit in Paris in 1974. Like the European Union itself, the body of heads of state was the brainchild of a French citizen, in this case Valéry Giscard d'Estaing. This French president managed to convince his colleagues that European countries needed a regular and high-profile forum to offer strategic direction and to shape the direction and pace of European integration in an informal setting.[57] The

Council is sometimes referred to as the 'summit' and discusses topics relating to the economic situation in Europe, the Single Market, monetary union, enlargement, and foreign and security issues. It also makes decisions on treaty amendments, new policies, and institutional reforms, which the EU Commission is then asked to implement. The Council reaches decisions by unanimity and consists of heads of state and government of the twenty-seven EU members as well as the president of the EU Commission. It is assisted in its work by a Council secretariat in Brussels, as well as by both the EU Commission and its Council of Ministers.

The European Council meets three or four times a year for two days, and discusses political issues of strategic importance to the EU such as new treaties, financial packages, or issues that European ministers have been unable to resolve. The body is mandated to 'define general political guidelines'. It has worked on the basis of a six-month rotating presidency, with each country taking a turn at setting and driving its agenda. Most of the Council's work is legislative, while some of it is executive. Under the Maastricht Treaty of 1993 (signed in 1992), the Council is responsible for implementing the Common Foreign and Security Policy (the second pillar) and Justice and Home Affairs (the third pillar). Since 1974 the body has imposed trade sanctions on apartheid South Africa and Slobodan Milosevic's Yugoslavia, as well as an arms embargo on China.[58]

Unlike the EU, where power is shared between the European Council, the Commission, the European Parliament, and the European Court of Justice in a carefully balanced relationship of interdependence in which cooperation is needed to get things done, the AU is a top-down heads of state-driven body where even decisions that could be dealt with by the Executive Council or ambassadors are often placed on its agenda. AU leaders thus do not adhere to the principle of subsidiarity (decisions being taken at the lowest practical level) in their own decisionmaking. AU and EU leaders, however, share the perception that their deliberations are far removed from their citizens, with populations often left uninformed about the details of their leaders' integration efforts. The EU Council, unlike the AU Assembly, also has a permanent secretariat that coordinates its work with the EU Commission, thus ensuring that implementation of decisions is followed up. While the EU has gradually developed a complicated system of qualified majority voting for 80 per cent of its legislation (excluding treaty amendments, employment-related social policy, tax harmonisation, health and safety issues, foreign and security policy, and criminal-related police and judicial issues), the AU still conducts most of its business through unanimity (though the AU's fifteen-member Peace and Security Council takes decisions on substantive issues by a two-thirds majority).

The AU Executive Council and the Council of European Ministers. The AU's Executive Council consists, in practice, of its member states' foreign ministers, even though other ministers are authorised to discuss sectoral specialisations. Issues addressed by the Council range across international relations, foreign trade, energy, industry, agriculture, environmental protection, education, health, technology, and immigration. No matter how talented, AU foreign ministers can surely not be expected to have the requisite expertise and time to deal with these substantive matters fully. Decisions of the Council are thus sometimes superficial, reinforcing a triumph of style over substance. Foreign ministers have sometimes sought to modify the recommendations of sectoral ministers before sending them to the Assembly of Heads of State, without consultation with their sectoral counterparts.[59]

The powers of the AU Executive Council include supporting the Assembly in monitoring and implementing decisions, and making recommendations to the heads of state on issues such as budgets, appointing commissioners, and electing judges to the African Commission on Human and Peoples' Rights and the proposed African Court of Justice (ACJ). Although the AU Council and Assembly appear to have co-decisionmaking powers, in practice the Assembly makes all the major decisions in the AU, since all Council decisions require Assembly endorsement.[60]

Below the AU Executive Council is the powerful Permanent Representatives Committee, composed of ambassadors who are tasked with supporting the Council in its functions; liaising between member states and the Commission; exercising oversight over the Commission; and helping to prepare the AU's programme of activities. The PRC is mandated to meet at least once a month to discuss the Executive Council's recommendations, but its meetings have been less frequent. The body has created subcommittees on such issues as administration, budget, refugees, drought, and famine. But these subcommittees focused largely, in the first five years of the AU's work (2002–2007), on oversight rather than substantive issues; this led to charges of micro-management from, and tensions with, the AU Commission. These subcommittees often struggled to achieve a quorum, with some permanent representatives failing to attend PRC meetings regularly, instead delegating this work to their subordinates. Some of these problems were also due to African embassies of insufficient capacity in Addis Ababa, and the quality of the personnel in these permanent missions remains uneven.[61] Other problems relating to the PRC have involved tensions with the Commission, particularly under the leadership of Alpha Konaré between 2003 and 2008. The PRC criticised the administration and management of the Konaré Commission, while the Commission accused the ambassadors of going beyond their advisory role and attempting to micro-manage the Commission. PRC members were, however, also accused of seeking to recruit their relatives and nationals to the Commission, and AU staff sometimes used their embassies in Addis Ababa to intervene in internal management disputes.[62]

The European Council of Ministers sets the medium-term policy goals of the EU and approves the budget and legislation proposed by the European Commission, along with the European Parliament. This body has some executive powers in foreign and security issues as well as justice and immigration issues.[63] It meets in up to nine different sectors spanning general affairs and external affairs; economic and financial affairs; agriculture and fisheries; transport, telecommunications, and energy; competitiveness; justice and home affairs; environment; education, youth, and culture; and employment, social policy, health, and consumer affairs. The General Affairs Council of EU foreign ministers coordinates the work of the Council of Ministers. The relevant EU commissioners also attend these meetings. The EU Council of Ministers has many committees that help to supervise implementation of the Commission's work. These bodies are overseen by the Committee of Permanent Representatives (Coreper), composed of the EU ambassadors in Brussels and equivalent to the AU's PRC. Coreper was established in 1958 and meets once a week to prepare Council meetings, supported by about 200 well-staffed working groups.

The European Council of Ministers clearly has more decisionmaking powers (both executive and legislative) and influence than the AU Executive Council. EU heads of state also seem to have more trust in the ability of their ministers to make decisions than African leaders have in their foreign ministers. Furthermore, the EU's institutions are structurally more genuinely decentralised than the equivalent AU bodies, to allow its foreign ministers to take decisions.

The Pan-African Parliament and the European Parliament. The AU's Pan-African Parliament was established in Midrand, South Africa, in March

2004 as an organ of the African Union reporting to the AU Assembly of Heads of State. Led by a bureau composed of a president and four vice presidents, the PAP set up committees to investigate such broad-ranging issues as agriculture, monetary and financial issues, trade, immigration, conflict resolution, transport, communications, health, labour, education, culture, gender, justice, and human rights. The parliament has advisory and consultative functions and each member state appoints five representatives from national parliaments or other deliberative bodies (with at least one required to be a woman). By 2007 the PAP had 265 members. The president of the parliament (Tanzania's Gertrude Mongella between 2004 and 2009, until replaced by Chad's Idriss Moussa) also attends annual AU summits.

The PAP's early years involved adopting its procedural rules, establishing its permanent commissions, sending an observer mission to Sudan's wartorn Darfur region in 2004, and deploying other observers to the Democratic Republic of the Congo for elections in 2006–2007 and to Mauritania after a coup in August 2008.[64] But as the AU audit report of 2007 noted: 'The PAP has had little impact on substantive issues of significance to the continent'.[65] The parliament attracted much controversy in its short life when the PRC—through the Executive Council—noted that the PAP Fund had been established without following proper AU procedures and processes, and should thus be frozen until such systems were in place. The Executive Council (at the recommendation of AU ambassadors) also requested that the $375,000 in the fund should be returned to the PAP's general coffers. Questions about the PAP's financial management and allowances were also raised, which contributed to the resignation of its president, Gertrude Mongella, in May 2009. Again the lack of clarity of authority lines among AU bodies was evident, as some of the parliamentarians argued that, since the institution reports directly to the Assembly, it could not adhere to Executive Council directives. The Assembly had, however, delegated some powers to the Executive Council.[66]

The PAP has effectively been a toothless talk-shop, and represents one of Africa's most notorious examples of political alchemy. With national parliaments barely functioning effectively enough to hold dominant executives accountable in many African countries in which legislatures are essentially presidential rubber-stamps, the creation of a costly continental parliament did not really appear to be a sensible and practical idea. It would surely have made more sense to strengthen and make more effective such AU organs as the Commission, the Assembly, the Executive Council, and the PRC before embarking on such an ambitious project.

In contrast to the PAP, the European Parliament has a long history, with the European Assembly having been set up for the ECSC in 1952. The European Parliament's members were directly elected for the first time in 1979, and the parliament remains the only EU body that enjoys this democratic distinction. Paradoxically, however, this quasi-legislative body has no powers to propose legislation, which is the task of the EU Commission and its Council. The European Parliament's 785 members are elected every five years. They range from 99 members from Germany, and 78 each from France, Britain, and Italy, to 5 from Malta. Unlike meetings of the EU Council, sessions of the European Parliament are open to the public. The centre-right European People's Party, the centre-left Party of European Socialists, and the European Liberals, Democrats, and Reformists are the three main groups and voting blocs in the parliament.

The European Parliament is headed by a bureau composed of a president and vice presidents, and a college of quaestors, with the president (German politician Martin Schulz since January 2012) representing the parliament to the outside world. Committee meetings are held in Brussels for two weeks each month, which EU Council and Commission officials are able to attend. The parliament also meets as a full body at its main headquarters in the French city of Strasbourg for a week each month to vote on legislation. Its secretariat resides in Luxembourg. This three-headed monstrosity of cities has, however, resulted in much criticism of the parliament's expenses (estimated at 200 million euros a year),[67] and the large travel expenses of its members have also come under much negative media scrutiny.

By 2007 the European Parliament accounted for over half of EU legislation. It could accept, reject, or amend legislation proposed by the EU Council, and suggest laws to the European Commission on issues as broad as social policy, transport, the environment, health, culture, consumer protection, and the Single Market.[68] The European Parliament works through committees, and has increasingly acquired co-decision powers (with the Council) over approving the EU budget: its most important powers. Since 2004 the parliament has had powers over the appointment of the president of the Commission (proposed by the Council), and dismissal of the College of Commissioners. The parliament forced the whole Commission of Jacques Santer to resign in 1999 after a devastating report on mismanagement and corruption within that body.[69]

The European Parliament also approves agreements with third countries, appoints the European Ombudsman, and is consulted on appointments to the European Court of Justice. But the parliament has no oversight in areas of justice and home affairs. Though it has only a consultative role in foreign and security policy, the European Parliament has sought to flex its muscles by increasing aid massively to Central and Eastern Europe. It has also spoken out over issues such as human rights abuses in Turkey, Palestinian rights, and the rights of the people of Western Sahara. The parliament has also met with the Pan-African Parliament and sought to increase European aid to Africa, to assist the continent's agricultural sector, to reduce tensions in European immigration policies towards Africa, and to support peace efforts on the continent.[70] However, foreign policy still remains largely the domain of the European Council, though the European Parliament's agreement is needed to bring in new EU member states, and the parliament ratifies deals with external bodies. Within Europe itself, the parliament has successfully insisted that airlines compensate European passengers for cancelled flights.[71] The European Parliament, however, has many critics among citizens in EU member states. The low turnout at elections to the parliament clearly demonstrates the low priority that EU citizens accord their parliament: after a high of 63 per cent in 1979, only 46 per cent of eligible Europeans voted in the 2004 election, and turnout fell further, to 43 per cent, in 2009. Such polls are often used to punish ruling or mainstream parties on domestic issues that are totally unrelated to European affairs.[72]

The Pan-African Parliament was modelled on the European Parliament's bureau, but was not yet directly elected in 2011 and did not have the supranational legislative, supervisory, or budgetary powers of its European counterpart. Unlike the PAP, the European Parliament has funding, researchers, and a well-staffed secretariat. Although the European Parliament is better endowed than its African counterpart, one should not exaggerate its financial resources and research capacity, particularly when compared with the impressive financial and intellectual support of the US Congress.[73] Whereas the EU Commission and its Council can take part in the discussions of the European Parliament's working committees in Brussels, the Pan-African Parliament's location in South Africa means that the AU Commission and other bodies in Addis Ababa do not have direct access to its deliberations, which weakens cooperation between key organs of the organisation. The PAP can perhaps take comfort in the fact that it took the European Parliament nearly three decades to institute direct elections of its members. But financial resources are not as scarce within the EU as they are within the AU, and it seems that Africa has more pressing priorities for use of its resources than a powerless, unelected legislative body. The fact that Egypt and Libya—with hardly accountably elected parliaments—felt bold enough to apply to host the PAP in 2004 further reinforces the air of surreal fantasy that surrounds this institution.

The African Commission on Human and Peoples' Rights, the African courts, and the European Court of Justice. The African Commission on Human and Peoples' Rights, based in Banjul, Gambia, was set up as a result of the African Charter of Human and Peoples' Rights of 1981, which entered into force five years later. The commission is incorporated into the AU system as a *de facto* organ reporting to the Executive Council, and its budget is provided by the African Union. The commission's two main goals are to promote and protect human rights, and to interpret the provisions of the charter and any other tasks given to the commission by the AU Assembly of Heads of State. The commission's eleven members are appointed by the Assembly and serve six-year terms. The body also appoints special rapporteurs on issues such as prisons, human rights, and extrajudicial executions in order to carry out its work. By 2011 the commission had held about fifty ordinary sessions, to which national and international human rights bodies and nongovernmental organisation (NGOs) were invited to participate in public sessions. The ACHPR also sent missions to member states such as Sudan's Darfur region in 2004. Topics tackled by the commission have included violation of women's rights, rights of refugees and internally displaced persons, and prison conditions.

The ACHPR receives about fifty complaints a year, and since 2006 has been obliged to submit such complaints to states against which they are lodged before passing them on to the Assembly. As the AU audit report of 2007 noted about this development: 'This, in effect, undermines the substance and spirit of Article 46 of its Charter which requires the ACHPR to conduct its work with impartiality and without interference'.[74] This again reinforces the fact that the AU often appears to be totally dominated by the whims and caprices of its leaders, many of whom are accustomed to acting in an autocratic manner at home, where the idea of checks and balances is sometimes alien.

The greatest weakness of the African Commission on Human and Peoples' Rights has been its lack of 'teeth', since it has no powers to enforce its nonbinding decisions on AU member states.[75] There are other challenges to the work of the commission. For example, some AU members do not grant the body permission to undertake missions to their countries, in violation of the charter they had earlier ratified; only fourteen out of fifty-three African states had submitted and presented all their reports to the commission by May 2007; several states do not comply with the recommendations of the commission; and African national human rights institutions do not participate actively in the body's work. The ACHPR has also suffered from staffing problems (with only seventeen staff posts in December 2007, though thirty-three more were promised by the AU between 2010 and 2014), while most of its budget has been spent on operating costs, with very little devoted to its core mandate (for example, in 2006, out of a budget of $1.1 million, only $47,000 was spent on the latter). There have been criticisms that the body is too dependent on donor funding ($530,000 in 2006), though the same could of course be said about the AU Commission itself. While the ACHPR's judges are mandated to be independent, the fact that some of them have held official posts simultaneously in their countries has raised further questions about their impartiality.[76] The location of the commission in Banjul also continues to raise eyebrows: Gambia has been led, since 1994, by Yahya Jammeh, a military coup leader turned civilian head of state, who has conducted elections of dubious legitimacy and has himself been accused of countless human rights abuses against political opponents and journalists.

More positively, the African Commission on Human and Peoples' Rights has contributed significantly to the interpretation of human rights protection in cases such as the one that sought to hold the government of Malawi responsible for the human rights abuses of its predecessor (1995); it has condemned the expulsion of Burundian nationals from Rwanda (1996), of West Africans from Zambia (1996) and Angola (1997); and it has criticised attempts by the Zambian government to exclude a presidential candidate (Kenneth Kaunda, who had previously ruled the country for twenty-seven years) whose parents were said to have been born in Malawi (2001). It has also raised concerns about unfair and inhumane detention in Cameroon (1997) as well as in Sierra Leone, Nigeria, and Kenya (2000); found, in 2006, that Rwanda, Uganda, and Burundi had violated the rights of the Congolese people by their military invasion of the DRC in 1998; and openly condemned human rights abuses in Zimbabwe in 2006, as well as the suppression of a peaceful demonstration in Guinea in 2007.[77]

Related to the ACHPR is the African Court on Human and Peoples' Rights, which was established in January 2006 with the election of eleven judges. Unlike the commission, the court was able to request African states to provide remedies after finding against them, including paying compensation or reparations. It was, however, hard to imagine how these sanctions would be enforced, since they still relied on the AU Assembly of Heads of State for implementation. The court is located in the Tanzanian town of Arusha, and had fifty-seven staff members in December 2007.

The AU Assembly, under the direction of the Nigerian president at the time, Olusegun Obasanjo, decided in July 2004 that the AfCHPR and the proposed AU Court of Justice should be merged into one body in order to save costs, noting that both courts had similar competences. This decision again confirmed the head of state-driven nature of the AU. It reversed an earlier Executive Council decision not to merge both courts,[78] and in an uncharacteristic display of independence the AU Commission cautioned the heads of state against merging both courts, as they had distinct roles to play. The AfCHPR identified three key challenges for itself: human resources, financial autonomy, and a need to clarify its role within the AU.[79] By July 2008, African leaders had drafted a protocol for a merged court to be known as the African Court of Justice and Human Rights, which would serve as the AU's main judicial organ. The court would have two sections: one to deal with disputes over the powers of the AU and breaches of treaty obligations, and another to hear human rights cases. The main advantage of the new court would be that it could impose political and economic sanctions on states that failed to comply with its judgements, though the uncertain support of the AU heads of state would still be needed to enforce this role.[80] At a very late stage in negotiations, Egypt and Tunisia led other African states in denying automatic access to the new court by individuals and NGOs wanting to lodge human rights complaints, unless the state in question had previously accepted the competence of the court.[81]

The African Charter on Human and Peoples' Rights of 1981 appears to have been honoured more in its breach than in its observance. Between 1960 and 1990, only four civilian heads of state in Africa voluntarily handed over power, mostly after decades in office (Senegal's Léopold Senghor, Sierra Leone's Siaka Stevens, Tanzania's Julius Nyerere, and Cameroon's Ahmadou Ahidjo). During the same period, no ruling party in Africa lost power.[82] This was scarcely an auspicious environment in which to promote human rights. While the situation has improved somewhat in the post-Cold War era, and ruling parties in Ghana, Senegal, Kenya, and Zambia have since been voted out of power, many African autocrats are still able to rig polls or manipulate the media and national institutions to their advantage. The fact that African leaders set up courts whose decisions they often have no intention of adhering to also demonstrates the same sort of recklessness that led so many African leaders to sign up to the Hague-based International Criminal Court (ICC), but only to complain later that the ICC was selectively targeting African governments. This leads one to question whether African leaders are signing agreements to make themselves feel part of international society without interrogating or researching the consequences of signing legally binding documents.

The European Court of Justice is based in the Grand Duchy of Luxembourg and was set up in 1958 to ensure that the treaties and legislation of European bodies are observed. As the continent's 'apex' court, its decisions are final and cannot be appealed. The ECJ has one judge from each of its twenty-seven member states, selected for six-year terms and assisted by eight advocates-general. The Court judges the legality of both Community acts and Commission actions against member states. The ECJ can also remove individual commissioners from office for serious offences or for not meeting their conditions of office. Most of the Court's cases, however, are brought by European citizens or companies, though domestic remedies must first be exhausted, and these cases must relate to Community issues. Some of the Court's landmark rulings have had a great impact on how the EU itself has developed. In a 1963 case brought by Dutch firm Van Gend en Loos, the ECJ confirmed that EU member states could not introduce new duties or increase existing ones under the European common market, going on to note that the Union constituted a new legal order in which its subjects were European nationals.[83] In the seminal 1979 Cassis de Dijon case, the Court ruled that there had to be mutual recognition by member states of each other's standards for the safety of products. Both cases helped to lay some of the foundations for the EU's Single Market of 1992.

In 1985 the ECJ also compelled the European Council to fulfil its 1968 treaty obligation to introduce a common European transport policy. By 2007 the Court had delivered about 7,200 judgements. Some national governments and the supreme courts of Germany and Italy have historically questioned what they saw as the ECJ's encroachment on domestic jurisdiction.[84] The supremacy of the Court over community law is, however, universally accepted by its members. This was evidenced in 1988 when the ECJ overturned a British act of parliament that sought to ban Spanish trawlers from British waters.[85] Due to its heavy caseload, the ECJ created a 'Court of First Instance' in 1989, with one judge from each of its twenty-seven member states, to help clear its backlog of cases by hearing mainly complaints brought by individuals and companies. The Court of First Instance is the first to hear cases involving appeals, damages, and failure to comply with decisions, and had decided over 4,000 cases by 2004.[86] An EU Civil Service Tribunal was set up in 2005 to hear cases relating to the European Commission's employees, as many such cases had clogged up the Court of First Instance.

The most significant difference between the European Court of Justice and Africa's legal bodies is that the ECJ's judgements have always been complied with by its member states, even though sometimes with delays. Unlike the EU judges, who are well compensated and work full-time, some of the ACHPR's judges have held more than one job. But one advantage of the African human rights charter is that it prioritises not only civil and political rights (the sole areas of focus of the ECJ), but also economic, social, and cultural rights, even if this is more aspiration than reality.

Concluding reflections

The material for transforming visions into concrete realities often requires large funds and technical capacity. Europe—despite the destruction of the Second World War—had these resources in abundance in the form of America's $100 billion (in 2011 money) Marshall Plan of 1947. Europe already possessed highly trained citizens in countries with established education systems who could take advantage of this 'aid'. Two Frenchmen, Jean Monnet and Jacques Delors, were thus able to fulfil their visions in contributing to a 'more united Europe'. Two Africans, Salim Ahmed Salim and Alpha Konaré, were in contrast unable to match their words with deeds and realised that the stuff of which dreams are made was in short supply in Africa: a continent in which leaders often pull the levers of power only to discover no effect on the situation on the ground. Small African economies often remain largely dependent on external markets; the continent also continues to suffer from a $290 billion external debt and chronic internal corruption, both of which have drained Africa's scarce resources; and the continent's marginalisation from the globalisation process is underlined by Africa accounting for less than 2 per cent of world trade.

European institutions like the Commission, the Council, the Parliament, and the Court of Justice evolved gradually over time and acquired increasing powers as they gained credibility and effectiveness. The EU has also provided 'public goods'[87] to its members—an international market, a single currency, international clout (particularly in the area of multilateral trade), and enhanced security—which they would have struggled to achieve individually. The AU's institutions, in contrast, do not appear to be evolving organically, and the appearance of the Commission, the Peace and Security Council, and the Pan-African Parliament all seem to be an unsynchronised process of a miraculous 'Big Bang'. The 'afro' has not followed the 'euro' as a pan-continental currency. Africa's new integrationists also do not appear to have learned from past lessons of weak, poorly funded, moribund institutions inherited from the OAU, while the much better-resourced EU, in contrast, was able to adapt and make institutional changes from the era of the EEC based on the needs of its member states.

European integration appears, in contrast to African integration, to have been more grounded in the politics, economics, and societies of that continent. It was pushed by the concrete interests of politicians, bureaucrats, big business, and farmers who derived material benefits from the process, as did their populations. African integration was derailed by external Cold War rivalries and proxy wars, as well as by African political misrule and economic mismanagement. It thus became delinked from resources and concrete interests, often degenerating into meaningless declarations and empty pledges that governments apparently had no concrete interest in implementing, nor any real power to do so. The sole, noble exception was the consistent commitment to decolonisation and the anti-apartheid struggle in South Africa, which eventually bore fruit by 1994. While European integration is often compared to a bicycle in which all members have to keep pedalling to avoid falling off the contraption, African integration has often resembled a bumpy ride on the back of a rickety mammy-wagon on potholed roads with failing brakes and lights, and the memorable sign 'No condition is permanent' inscribed on the vehicle.

Freedom fighter and founding president of Algeria Ben Bella—who was instrumental in creating the OAU's Liberation Committee at its inaugural summit in 1963—famously implored his fellow leaders during the founding of the OAU in Addis Ababa: 'So let us agree to die a little or even completely so that the peoples still under colonial domination may be free and African unity may not be a vain word'.[88] This expression underlines the huge sacrifices that Africans will have to make to achieve genuine regional integration. As observed at the beginning of this chapter, Africa was the birthplace of humankind and the site of the Garden of Eden. As the Kenyan scholar Ali Mazrui noted in 1980, this is now a 'Garden of Eden in Decay',[89] and contemporary Africa represents a Miltonian example of 'Paradise Lost'. If the American historian Robert Kagan's analysis is correct, Paradise has now moved from Africa to Europe.[90]

PART 2

POLITICAL, ECONOMIC, AND STRATEGIC DIMENSIONS

4

THE TRAVAILS OF REGIONAL INTEGRATION
IN AFRICA

Adebayo Adedeji

Introduction

On 29 July 2008, the death knell of the Doha round of world trade talks
was struck, seven years after the process was launched. The Doha round was
embarked upon primarily to make world trade pro-development. This was
due to the global consensus that the only way in which the poverty-stricken
countries of the global South (among which African countries loom large)
could exit from their poverty was to focus on the creation of wealth instead
of pursuing aid-dependent poverty alleviation schemes. As the Ugandan
leader Yoweri Museveni once lyrically put it: aid without trade is a lullaby,
a song you sing to children to get them to sleep. No wonder the record of
aid has been so dismal. It has failed to promote sustainable development as
well as the democratisation of the development process. It has also had little
impact on employment creation. Fortunately, there is now an emerging
international consensus that the focus of neoliberal economists on macroeconomic parameters under the guise of structural adjustment has only
resulted in economic growth to the neglect of holistic human-centred development, which alone can get to the root of large-scale structural underdevelopment and unemployment in Africa.

The Doha development agenda, which was drafted at the beginning of the process in 2001–2002, includes the abolition of food and agricultural subsidies in Europe and North America and acceptance of the need of developing countries to hold on to their tariffs to protect their infant industries. Since the economies of developing countries are unstable and their industries fledgling, tariffs are still needed to enable them to cope more effectively with external shocks, particularly for countries that have followed the 'Washington Consensus' in promoting International Monetary Fund (IMF) policies regarding free capital flows and liberal exchange regimes. In addition, tariffs provide revenue to meet development needs in order to create a level playing field in world trade that can guarantee developing countries fair and free access to the markets of rich countries.

Thus it was hoped that the Doha round would result in substantial improvements in market access in favour of developing countries; in the elimination of all forms of export subsidies; in substantial reduction in trade-distorting domestic support in industrialised countries; and in the reversal of the adverse terms of trade of agricultural products vis-à-vis industrial goods. In other words, the political commitment made in Doha was to foster a new spirit of international cooperation based on the principle of shared benefits, but differentiated responsibilities.

The Doha round and Eurafrique

Of course, the Doha round was global—it went beyond Africa and Europe. However, it is largely Europe that determines, in collaboration with North America, the course of international trade and the state of the global economy. Anytime European economies sneeze, the rest of the world catches pneumonia! Although it has been claimed that there is collective responsibility for the collapse of the Doha negotiations, there is no doubt that the lack of agreement on agricultural products sounded its death knell. The rich countries of Europe and North America have, as usual, been consistently inconsistent. In spite of their acclaimed commitment to neoliberalism, they insist on continuing to subsidise food and agricultural production while demanding that developing countries pursue an 'open door' policy on food through the abolition of, or severe reduction in, tariffs. (See chapter 12 in this volume.) And because of Western fears of competitive food and agricultural production in developing countries, the rich North has provided minimal direct private investment and aid to the productive sector of developing countries, especially food, agriculture, and industry. Between 1980 and 2010, multilateral donor institutions cut overseas development assistance on agriculture by 85 per cent, while bilateral donors reduced their support by about 40 per cent. At the same time, domestic investment in food and agriculture in poor countries has been parsimonious and niggardly. Consequently, the high level of food prices in 2009–2010 was detrimental to the world's poorest inhabitants: those referred to by the Martiniquan intellectual Frantz Fanon as the 'Wretched of the Earth'.[1] Hence, pervasive famine and poverty will persist, particularly in Africa, which has for centuries been Europe's perennial underdog. Many African countries that once were food exporters have regressed to becoming net food importers with extremely limited resources to fund such imports.[2]

Africa: Europe's perennial underdog

Despite half a century of political independence by 2010, Africa has remained its European neighbour's permanent underdog. No one will deny that Africa has borne the scars of a long history of spoliation and deprivation, of the ravages of the slave trade and foreign aggression, of both political and economic injustices and civil wars and conflicts.[3] Today the African situation remains dire. Africa's neighbour Western Europe, which is the richest continent in the world, has, over a period of 400 to 500 years, integrated Africa into the world economy on the basis of unequal exchange. Hence, sub-Saharan Africa now virtually constitutes a group of its own: the periphery of the periphery, the 'Fourth World'. Africa is probably the only continent that has failed to recognise and exploit the nexus between economic growth, on the one hand, and holistic human development, the elimination of large-scale structural unemployment, and the creation of wealth as the only way to eradicating poverty, on the other. In short, Africa has not fully grasped the imperative of socioeconomic and political deconstruction and transformation. Nor has Europe, which went through this process in the eighteenth, nineteenth, and early twentieth centuries, but is still contributing to diverting Africa's attention from development to growth.

In the decade of the 2000s, the relatively high macroeconomic growth achieved in African countries was due largely to the high prices of primary export commodities, the high rates of inflation, and some external debt relief. This effectively constituted 'growth without development'. It is important to note that Africa's contact with Eastern Europe (the former Soviet

Union and its allies) was a post-Second World War phenomenon after 1945. In fact, this contact became effective only during the Cold War era, when East European countries played a crucial role in assisting nationalist movements to win national liberation wars and achieve political independence.

Given Africa's antecedents, one cannot but agree with the American scholar Immanuel Wallerstein that *dependent development leads nowhere fast*.[4] Africa has failed woefully to deconstruct the colonial economy it inherited at independence.[5] And the continent's march towards its future without addressing its colonial inheritance is clearly unsustainable.

Even more inhibitive to the deconstruction and decolonisation of the African economy is the failure to seek and pursue alternative patterns of African development and lifestyles in place of those inherited from European colonial powers. For too long, the impression has been created that African development strategies and lifestyles are an imitation—indeed a poor imitation—of the strategies and lifestyles developed elsewhere for other societies with different historical, cultural, economic, and political backgrounds.

Five decades after political independence, not only is the African continent more dependent on the outside world economically than ever before, but its 800 million citizens have also become the 'mimic people', although they often claim to be original and to be preparing themselves and their countries for self-reliant development as well as for an authentically African lifestyle.[6] This is no doubt one of the unfortunate consequences of the method and technique of Africa's colonial dispossession—self-alienation, subordination, and loss of self-esteem and self-confidence. Together these consequences—aided by the forces of separatism and irredentism—resulted in four centuries of a dehumanising slave trade, and a century of degrading colonialism.

The era of separatism and irredentism in precolonial and postcolonial Africa

Pervasive interethnic conflicts have been the unfortunate plight of Africa. Indeed, these conflicts aided and abetted colonialism. The seafaring European adventurers and their nations exploited Africa's separatism and irredentism to their own advantage. They began with concluding 'treaties' with 'friendly' natives for ports of call, entrepôt trade, refuelling stations, and naval bases. Under competitive pressure among themselves, territorial authority and protectorates were established. (See chapter 2 in this volume.)

This led to the establishment of two basic types of settlement: *colonies de peuplement* and *colonies d'exploitation*.

The coming together of hitherto warring ethnic groups and nationalities under the same imperial *Raj* gave the promise of integration into larger political entities. Indeed, almost all fifty-four African states and territories are the product of some form of integration brought about by European colonial rule. Two colonial powers—the British and the French—attempted to establish higher levels of political organisation through the regrouping of their territories. For example, the British, under Frederick Lugard, amalgamated the colony of Lagos with the Protectorate of the Southern Provinces of Nigeria, and then amalgamated these with the Protectorate of Northern Nigeria in January 1914. London granted independence to the Federation of Nigeria in 1960, thus bequeathing to Africa its most populous country and the tenth most populous country in the world.

Initially, the French colonial administration did even better than the British. Paris grouped its twelve territories into two federations—the French West Africa Federation (Afrique Occidentale Française, AOF) and the French Equatorial Africa Federation (Afrique Equatoriale Française, AEF). The former consisted of eight territories—Côte d'Ivoire, Dahomey (now Benin), Guinea, Mauritania, Niger, Senegal, Soudan (now Mali), and Upper Volta (now Burkina Faso)—with Dakar as the capital of the federation. The AEF, made up of four territories—Chad, the Central African Republic, Congo-Brazzaville, and Gabon—had Brazzaville as its capital. Each federation had its own currency and possessed tremendous potential for political and economic development.

Unfortunately, as the demand for independence intensified, France reversed its policy. It aborted and dismantled the regional integration process and instead launched the process of Balkanisation as a punitive measure against African leaders who dared to seek independence. In 1958—a year after the Treaty of Rome, which established the European Economic Community (EEC), was signed—France formally abolished both the AOF and the AEF as political organisations. So in 1960, instead of granting independence to two federations, each of which had a high possibility of being viable and dynamic, France granted independence to all the minuscule territories—fifteen of them, including Togo and Cameroon, two UN trust territories. It was unfortunate that Paris, in an act of vengeance, unleashed the forces of separatism and irredentism as its parting shot and political legacy to Africa, while at the same time spearheading the transformation of Europe.[7] (See chapters 3 and 16 in this volume.) In other words, the separatism and irredentism that made colonial rule the plight of Africa was reenergised to pave the way for postcolonial domination at the very moment that Europe was embarking on its own integration process.

Indeed, the same French government that launched the process of Africa's Balkanisation, which culminated in the abolition of both the AOF and the AEF, established the Union Douanière de l'Afrique de l'Ouest (West African Customs Union) in June 1959, consisting of Côte d'Ivoire, Dahomey, Mali, Niger, Senegal, and Upper Volta—all members of the disbanded AOF. In spite of the opposition by these African countries to this French-induced and masterminded Balkanisation, the process continued relentlessly. The Conseil de l'Entente, consisting of Côte d'Ivoire, Dahomey, Niger, and Upper Volta, was also established in 1959.

This unfortunate inheritance of Francophone West African countries led them, during their first post-independence decade in the 1960s, to be overly focused on establishing various intergovernmental entities. By 1975, over twenty intergovernmental multisectoral economic cooperation organisations had been established and scores of single sectoral multinational and bilateral organisations had also been created to promote technical and economic cooperation. These games of musical chairs were carried out exclusively among the fourteen former French colonies in Africa. The heavy cost of the abolition of both the AOF and the AEF brutally confronted these countries immediately after independence and still remains with them today. All the efforts made to close the divide between them and their Anglophone neighbours have been consistently sabotaged by France.[8]

In Anglophone Africa, these countries kept rigidly apart from each other after having achieved independence. In West Africa, the regional research and educational institutions and West African Airways, as well as the common currency inherited at independence, were all abolished, at the instigation of Ghana's Kwame Nkrumah, who is more commonly seen as one of the titans of pan-Africanism. Even East Africa, which had inherited a customs union among the three countries of Kenya, Uganda, and Tanganyika (later Tanzania), had fallen apart by 1975, when the East African Community (EAC) was finally disbanded.

Extrapolating the relationship between France and its former colonies into EEC-Africa cooperation

In addition to the effort of overwhelming the fourteen Francophone countries with a network of cooperation entities at both bilateral and multilateral levels, the establishment of the European Economic Community by the Treaty of Rome in 1957 provided France with the great challenge of developing ways of keeping these countries closely tied to the Mother Country's apron strings while at the same time pushing other EEC countries into providing aid, technical assistance, and trade preferences to former French colonies. And the plan succeeded brilliantly. The EEC signed (with these countries) the Yaoundé Convention in 1963, followed by Yaoundé II in 1969, which lasted another six years.

Unfortunately, neither of the two agreements met the expectations of Francophone Africa. The disillusionment of these countries led them to seek an alternative arrangement. Fortunately, Britain's joining of the EEC in 1973 reinforced the urgent need to broaden the scope of EEC-Africa cooperation to include non-Francophone countries.

The UN's Economic Commission for Africa (ECA), which since its establishment in April 1958 had been looking for a broad-based, all-inclusive pan-African integration mandate, decided at its conference of ministers in Accra in April 1973 that Nigeria should convene a meeting of ministers of trade in Africa to decide on the nature and scope of the EEC-Africa cooperation agreement that would succeed Yaoundé II. The Caribbean and Pacific countries expressed interest in participating in such a meeting. The forty-six-member Africa, Caribbean, and Pacific (ACP) association was subsequently established in 1975 and the successor agreement to Yaoundé II was signed between the EEC (of nine countries) and the ACP association (of forty-six countries) in the Togolese capital of Lomé that same year. Between 1975 and 2000 three more Lomé Conventions were agreed upon in succession, with each one altering significantly the nature of the relationship between the parties concerned, to the detriment of the ACP countries, whose number had risen to seventy-eight, with forty-eight of them African. (See chapter 2 in this volume.)

The first Lomé Convention was very much a child of the strong geopolitical power of ACP countries vis-à-vis that of the West in the context of the Cold War, the oil crisis of 1973, and the demand by Third World countries for a 'New International Economic Order' in the 1970s. Not surprisingly, therefore, equal partnership between both parties—the EEC and the ACP—was the pillar on which the Lomé Convention was built. Not only did the first convention concede to the ACP countries responsibility for their own development, but it also gave them a leading role in managing the resources made available by the EEC, with Brussels mainly playing a supportive role. Predictable aid flows over the five-year period of the convention as well as nonreciprocal trade benefits were also readily guaranteed. Two major innovations were introduced on commodities—the Stabex scheme, intended to help stabilise export receipts on a wide range of agricultural products (cocoa, coffee, groundnuts, tea), was introduced under Lomé I, while the Sysmin mechanism, intended to stabilise export earnings from mineral resources, was introduced under Lomé II.

While continuity has been a key feature of successive Lomé Conventions, the shift in the international power structure during the 'lost decade' of the 1980s, to the detriment of developing countries, led to a dramatic shift in the nature of this cooperation to the disadvantage of the ACP countries. Specifically, successive Lomé Agreements came under growing negative pressure due to seven key factors: first, dwindling common interests and the disappearance of the perceived mutual interdependence between Europe, Africa, and other ACP countries; second, the insistence on inclusion of human rights and structural adjustment in Lomé IV; third, the downgrading of ACP countries on the European Union priority list in terms of geopolitical, economic, and security concerns; fourth, the erosion of the principle of equal partnership and its replacement by that of conditionality; fifth, despite preferential access to EU markets, the persistent decline of the products of ACP countries in the EU market from 6.7 per cent in 1976 to 3 per cent in 1998; sixth, the failure by ACP countries to achieve a breakthrough in diversification away from traditional exports; and finally, the falling share of EU aid to ACP countries. Whereas in 1986 ACP countries received 69 per cent of total EU aid, in 1990, 1994, and 1998 the ACP share had declined to 58, 44, and 29 per cent respectively. Overall, the ACP's share of EU aid between 1986 and 1998 was 44 per cent.

The successor agreement to Lomé IV was signed in Cotonou, capital of Benin, in June 2000. It was christened the 'ACP-EU Partnership Agreement' and poignantly reflected the contemporary geopolitical situation: the persistent worsening of the vulnerability of countries of the global South in general and of Africa in particular. Thus the Cotonou Agreement of 2000 set out four key provisions: first, a new conditionality of 'good governance'; second, direct dealing with nonstate actors and local authorities; third, the cessation by 31 December 2007 of the ACP nonreciprocal tariff preferences and their replacement by a set of reciprocal economic partnership agreements (EPAs); and fourth, the programming of aid resources as a strategic management tool aimed at ensuring that EU aid to any ACP country or region would be deployed in much more effective and coherent ways.

The negotiation of the EPAs began in 2001, when the EU's membership had increased to fifteen countries and the ACP's stood at seventy-eight. (See chapters 10 and 11 in this volume.) Since then, the EU has been enlarged to twenty-seven members. While the EU has always negotiated as one entity, through its European Commission in Brussels, it has fragmented the ACP states into six regions—Western Africa, Central Africa, Eastern Africa, Southern Africa, the Caribbean, and the Pacific. Although the African Union was established in 2002, the EU has not fully engaged the organisation as its appropriate negotiating partner. (See chapter 11 in this volume for another perspective.) Even Africa's long-established and long-recognised regional economic communities (RECs), such as the Southern African Development Community (SADC), the Economic Community of West African States (ECOWAS), the Intergovernmental Authority on Development (IGAD), and the Economic Community of Central African States (ECCAS), have been neglected by EU Commission negotiators in preference for negotiations with individual countries. It is increasingly felt in Africa that the EPAs are another example of how Brussels abuses its vast negotiating power and aid budget to isolate and exploit individual African states and coerce them to open their markets to unfair penetration by European farmers and manufacturers. As the British nongovernmental organisation Oxfam has argued in a briefing paper, this is not partnership but power play. Indeed, one cannot but agree with Oxfam that the EPAs are 'denying African countries the "ladder to development" used in the past by Europe, the US and the Asian tigers, all of which juggled tariffs to foster diversification into other sectors'.[9] In addition, the EU has created a 'spaghetti bowl' of overlapping bilateral and regional EPAs, operating at different liberalisation speeds and time frames that cut across existing regional blocks. This is history repeating itself again: the spectre of fragmentation and Balkanisation of the AOF and AEF by France in 1958–1960 is once again rearing its ugly head through the contemporary EPAs.

To make matters worse, individual African countries now have to enter into bilateral agreements with the EU. This development has been likened to the Berlin Conference of 1884–1885, at which European imperial powers sat with a map of Africa in the background and set the rules to carve up the continent among themselves. (See chapter 2 in this volume.) The difference is that whereas in 1884–1885 the imperial powers were competing with each other for Africa's resources, Europe, now united under the EU banner, is today in competition with the United States, China, India, and

Japan for Africa's riches. And most tragically ironic is the fact that African leaders—like African chiefs in colonial times—are at the table signing asymmetrical agreements under the compulsion of perceived circumstances that have led them to believe that they have no other choice.[10]

Old habits die hard indeed. The future relations that are being forged under EPAs are not different from the way that relations between Africa and Europe have evolved over the past two centuries: market access for European goods, especially for financial services, communications, and consultancies; a substantial slice of the market in government procurement (which in some countries can be as high as 50 per cent of the national budget); opportunities for investment for European corporations that are rapidly losing their comparative advantage in Africa; and a protected market for Europe in ACP countries by means of intellectual property rights.

One would have expected Europe to emulate the example of Japan towards East Asian countries. Through its 'flying geese' policy from the 1950s, Japan facilitated the spread of the industrialisation process to East Asia, thus laying the foundation for the 'Asian Miracle' of the 1980s. There is no doubt that by taking all measures to push through the EPAs, Brussels is determined to sustain the asymmetrical relationship that has existed since Europe first established contact with its 'sleeping giant' neighbour Africa, and particularly sub-Saharan Africa. There has been, for some years, a growing consensus in Africa and beyond that the ACP-Europe economic relationship has not been significantly different from what it was in the colonial era. With EPAs now being forced on Africa, relations have become much worse, and Africa seems doomed to remain Europe's perennial underdog.

The countries of Western Europe are incessantly urging Africa to forge its own future. Yet whenever African leaders have taken the initiative to craft their own indigenous strategies and policies, they have been ignored and frustrated. This was the fate of the Lagos Plan of Action and Final Act of 1980, as well as of the African alternative framework to the structural adjustment programme for socioeconomic recovery and transformation of 1989[11]—to mention just two initiatives, both of which I was closely involved in while serving as executive secretary of the UN's Economic Commission for Africa between 1975 and 1991.[12] The EPAs have severely undermined the 1991 Abuja Treaty on the establishment of an African Economic Community by 2028.

Since the beginning of this millennium, African leaders and peoples have again been vigorously pursuing the economic and political integration of their continent. Why is it at this critical juncture, when Africa's resurgence for freedom, dignity, and unity is again being pursued on all fronts, that the EU is looking back rather than looking forward? Why is it that in spite of the Sirte Declaration of 1999 and the adoption of the African Union's Constitutive Act of 2000, followed by the launch of the New Partnership for Africa's Development (NEPAD) in 2001, Europe has persistently failed to rise to the historical challenge that Africa has presented to it?

Europe has never fully grasped its unique position in relation to Africa as a whole. Some EU member states still prefer to cultivate their special ties with individual African countries—usually their former colonies—instead of promoting AU-EU collaboration based on coherent, sincere, and strong policy frameworks that every member state of the EU will be obliged to implement. (See chapters 6–7 and 16–18 in this volume.) Instead, what the Belgian former EU development commissioner Louis Michel called a 'rentier reflex' has led some powerful members of the EU (invariably former colonialists) to 'live off past glories and not take full measure of the competition in relation with Africa'.[13] Yet only the thirteen kilometres of the Straits of Gibraltar separate Europe from Africa. In spite of the painful past involving five centuries of slavery, dispossession, exploitation, and dependence, and despite the uncertain present and future, both sides of the straits have acquired a multifaceted common heritage, particularly shared languages, cultural ties, and trade—even if this has often produced unequal benefits. Michel said it all when he wrote that 'there are the thousand and one tenuous and close links woven by centuries of sometimes painful or sometimes promising cohabitation'.[14] Even more striking than these are the similarities in the histories of both continents. In order to move steadily towards true and sustainable partnership between Africa and Europe, there must be a change of attitude and strategy in Europe towards Africa. Europe must be weaned off its xenophobic mind-set towards Africa.

While the principal engagement of the African countries that became independent in the 1960s was to establish their independence firmly and control the resurgence of forces of separatism and irredentism as well as Balkanisation and fragmentation, tentative steps were being taken to search for larger and sustainable integration that would cut across the colonial boundaries. Unfortunately, the decolonisation process lasted too long. By the beginning of the 1970s, while forty-two African countries had achieved political independence, eleven were still struggling for freedom. It was not until 1994, when a majority-ruled South Africa emerged, that the whole of Africa became liberated from foreign rule and the continent was free at last.[15]

Not surprisingly, Africa has vigorously embarked on rising to the challenge of full exploitation of the opportunities that these defining moments pose. The continent has begun to develop a clear vision, an unambiguous path, and rejuvenated energy for the integration, unification, and transformation of Africa. While the domestic dysfunctionalities that have held African countries down for so long still remain to be confronted and eliminated, derailment of these efforts by outside pressure is an ever-present challenge. This is where Africa has been consistently let down by the international community, most particularly its neighbour Europe, whose support and cooperation have been niggardly. Instead of taking advantage of the poverty, economic dependence, and vulnerability of Africa to try to force through the imposition of EPAs, Europe should be cooperating constructively with Africa and, where necessary, lending a helping hand in exploiting, to the fullest, the opportunities of Africa's strategies and roadmaps. (See chapter 9 in this volume.) Africa needs urgently to establish a firm linkage between economic growth, development, productive employment, and the democratisation of the development process.

Africa's indefatigable freedom fighter and Nobel peace laureate Desmond Tutu, former Anglican archbishop of Cape Town, made a good attempt at drawing attention to some lessons from the histories of Africa and Europe on which a new partnership can be modelled. This was contained in a powerful speech that he delivered at the closing session of the 2006 European Development Days. Tutu reminded his audience that the West, so prosperous and so powerful in the present era, went through a period when suspected witches and heretics were burned at the stake and when many of its citizens were victims of grinding poverty. He noted that Europe's march to modern democracy was characterised by excesses—the excesses of the powerful—and considerable bloodletting.[16]

During the nineteenth and twentieth centuries, Europe was also conflict-ridden—two world wars and the Holocaust, which saw the death of 6 million Jews. Europe was devastated by the excesses of Fascism and Nazism. There were dictatorships in Spain and Portugal until the mid-1970s. Even Greece, the birthplace of democracy, was from 1967 to 1974 ruled by a military dictatorship. There was a time when one was not sure who was the government of Italy, for it changed so rapidly and so often. All of these events led to 'Euro-pessimism' and 'Eurosclerosis' in the 1970s. But in spite of these setbacks, Europe emerged to become the giant it is today. Africa can and should draw much encouragement and inspiration from Europe's ultimate triumph, considering what preceded it all. And Europe has been extremely lucky to have the generous support of the United States—in war and peace, in postwar reconstruction, and in long-term growth and development. The postwar Marshall Plan provided $100 billion (in today's money). Is it too much for Europe to do likewise for Africa?

For its part, since 1957 Africa has fought the forces of colonialism, neo-colonialism, and apartheid relentlessly. Now from Cape to Cairo, from Luanda to Lagos, from Praia to Port Louis, Africa is free. In spite of the inhumanity of slavery, the slave trade reinforced the sense of affinity and solidarity among Africans and thus laid the foundation for the movement of the African diaspora in the Americas, the Caribbean, and Europe. (See chapter 21 in this volume.) This was also the genesis of pan-Africanism, under which guise consultations regularly took place on the pursuit of the freedom of Africa from the shackles of European colonialism and the pursuit of African unity. (See chapter 3 in this volume.)

Drawing lessons from the history of Europe: Africa's institutional frameworks

Today, Europe has its Union of twenty-seven member states. This is indeed a remarkable development, this emergence from the ashes of a war-torn Europe after the First World War of 1914–1918, and from a devastated and ideologically divided one after the Second World War of 1939–1945. Six countries embarked on the long and uncertain journey of establishing a regional economic community for Europe in 1957 (France, Germany, Italy, Belgium, the Netherlands, and Luxembourg). The year 1992 was fixed by the Treaty of Rome of 1957 for realisation of the single European market through the elimination of all barriers to intracommunity flows of goods, services, and factors of production: a goal that was achieved. By 2007, owing to the end of the Cold War, the membership of the EU had been enlarged to twenty-seven and a common currency (the euro) had been adopted. However, the Union has not yet effectively pooled the sovereignty of its member states in the areas of foreign policy, aid policy, defence, and security. Nevertheless, the EU has today become a combination of regional institution and major global player. The body also represents a mixture of intergovernmentalism and supranationalism. However, the political integration of Europe is not yet part of this agenda.

Contrary to the belief of some people in both Africa and Europe, the African Union[17]—in terms of its overarching goals as opposed to its institutional structure—is not therefore modelled on the EU. As already indicated, there has never been any doubt or dispute about the desirability and even the eventual inevitability of pan-African political unity and economic integration, so determined were African political leaders and the African diasporas in the Americas, the Caribbean, and Europe to redress the divisive legacy of the Berlin Conference of 1884–1885. But the fact that political independence was not achieved by African states at the same time, but was rather attained between 1956 to 1994, made the search for new approaches to pan-Africanism inevitable.

Let me stress that the EU is more like what Africans call a regional economic community, while the AU is intended primarily to become a political and economic continental organisation—the 'United States of Africa'—with, eventually, a continental government to provide an umbrella for its multitude of RECs and, most especially, for the African Common Market to be established by 2028. Specifically, the African Union, under Article 3 of its Constitutive Act of 2000, has seven key objectives: first, achieve greater unity and solidarity among African countries and peoples; second, defend the sovereignty, territorial integrity, and independence of its member states; third, accelerate the political and socioeconomic integration of the continent; fourth, promote and defend African common positions on issues of interest to the continent and its 800 million people; fifth, achieve sustainable development at the economic, social, and cultural levels; sixth, promote peace, security, and stability on the continent; and seventh, establish the necessary conditions that will enable Africa to play its rightful role in the global economy and in international negotiations.[18]

Eight years before the Sirte Declaration of 1999 and eleven years before the establishment of the African Union, the treaty that established the African Economic Community was adopted in Abuja, Nigeria, in 1991. It was a very much delayed follow-up process to the Lagos Plan of Action and Final Act of 1980, both of which had called for the establishment of the Community using the RECs as the building blocks. At the time of the Lagos Plan of Action, only ECOWAS—established in 1975—existed and was functioning. Hence the Lagos Final Act called on all the other African subregions—Central, Eastern, Southern, and Northern—to establish their own RECs.

Through the efforts of the UN's Economic Commission for Africa, and the persistence of member states in their commitment to regional economic cooperation and integration, many African RECs were created in the 1980s.

These included the Preferential Trade Area of Eastern and Southern Africa (PTA), which later became the Common Market for Eastern and Southern Africa (COMESA, nineteen states); the Economic Community of Central African States (ECCAS, eleven states); the Intergovernmental Authority on Development (IGAD, seven states); the Southern African Development Community (SADC, fifteen states); and the Community of Sahel-Saharan States (CEN-SAD, twenty-four states). As earlier noted, the East African Community, comprising Kenya, Tanzania, and Uganda, which had been in existence even before independence, was dissolved in 1975. The EAC has now been revived and expanded with the addition of Burundi and Rwanda as member states.

These, along with the Arab Maghreb Union (AMU), are the eight RECs recognised by the AU Assembly of Heads of State. However, there are others, among which are the French government-sponsored West African Economic and Monetary Union (UEMOA) and the Central African Economic and Monetary Community (CEMAC), competing with and impeding the most rapid advancement to regional integration in West Africa by ECOWAS and, in Central Africa, by ECCAS.

Article 38(4) of the Abuja Treaty of 1991 stipulates that African governments should—through their respective regional economic communities—coordinate and harmonise their subregional organisations, with a view to rationalising the integration process at the level of each subregion. ECOWAS accordingly revised its treaty in 1993 so that it would be designated as the only REC for West Africa. When the ailing Francophone Communauté Économique de l'Afrique de l'Ouest (CEAO) was dissolved in March 1994, it was generally felt that the timing was exquisite, as the CEAO had been set up through France's prodding as a rival to the all-inclusive Nigerian-led ECOWAS.[19] However, the Union Monétaire Ouest Africaine (UMOA)—which was in charge of the Communauté Financière Africaine (CFA), the common currency of West African Francophone countries—was converted into a REC as the Union Économique et Monétaire Ouest-Africaine (UEMOA, now grouping seven Francophone states and Guinea-Bissau). Yet all sixteen member states of ECOWAS (now fifteen with the departure of Mauritania in 2000) became engaged in negotiating with the eight member states of UEMOA, which in turn also constitute the majority of ECOWAS's membership. This 'variable geometry' approach can easily become disintegrative. Without doubt, no integrative strategy is likely to succeed if the steam for the locomotive is not generated by all the member states forming each African REC.

Some analysts have suggested that the RECs, having been established during the Cold War era, are based on the tenets of an 'old regionalism' that was influenced by neofunctionalist assumptions.[20] Among the RECs that have been lumped into the so-called old regionalism category are the PTA (now COMESA, 1979), ECOWAS (1975), ECCAS (1983), and the Arab Maghreb Union (1989). On the other hand, post-1990 RECs fall under the 'new regionalism' terminology, and SADC is often cited as an example.

As the individual who spearheaded the establishment of all of these RECs (except for SADC)[21] while serving as executive secretary of the UN's Economic Commission for Africa between 1975 and 1991, I can confirm that the driving force for these efforts was neither ideological nor connected with the Cold War. It will be clear, from what I have said so far, that the experiences to which Africa was subjected by Europe—particularly the continent's partition and the century of colonialism; the persistence and pervasiveness of separatism and irredentism that made it easy for colonialism to exist and thrive as well as to divide and dominate Africa and deepen its Balkanisation; the pervasive underdevelopment of Africa; and the emergence of a large number of minuscule states, many of which are also landlocked—all rendered regionalism in Africa a strategic tool for survival, revival, and transformation. In any case, as long ago as 1945, the fifth Pan-African Congress, in Manchester in England, recommended the establishment of a West African Economic Union as a means of combating the exploitation of resources and ensuring the participation of indigenous peoples in the industrial development of West Africa.[22]

Furthermore, the treaties of the African RECs that I was involved in establishing have made it abundantly clear that economic cooperation must serve four key functions: the RECs must be, first, an instrument for national survival and socioeconomic transformation; second, a forum for forging common strategies and policies in the food and agriculture sector and in the fight against drought and desertification; third, a platform for concerted industrialisation strategies and programmes; and fourth, a platform for developing and implementing regionwide systems of transport and communication.

Thus the economic integration promoted in Africa is more than trade liberalisation and customs unions. We can never forget that trade relations between African and European countries are like a hub-and-spoke arrangement of a gigantic bicycle. The EU countries constitute the hub, while individual African countries are the spokes. The key feature of this arrangement is that trade between the hub and each spoke is dominated by the former to the detriment of the latter, unless the spokes can work in a concerted manner and their economies become dynamic.

Hence regionalism constitutes the overarching objective of the Lagos Plan of Action of 1980. Indeed, without regional integration, this plan collapses as a strategy. The basic philosophy underlying the plan is self-reliance at national and regional levels to formulate and apply autonomous decisions to generate and implement independent ideas, identify problems, and analyse and solve them in terms of domestic, intercountry, and extra-African requirements. The action plan has also aimed to develop capacities and capabilities at national and intercountry levels to meet, albeit progressively, the greater part of each subregion's needs in terms of factors of production and final goods and services.

The Lagos Plan of Action is based on the fundamental proposition that economic growth, though essential, will neither be sufficient nor indeed be possible without a fundamental transformation of the debilitating distortions in Africa's economic and social structures. Accordingly, the plan advocated the pursuit of three key goals: first, high and sustained economic growth; second, transformation of economic and social structures; and, third, maintenance of a sustainable resource base. In light of the Balkanisation of Africa into arbitrary, minuscule nation-states and the subsequent difficulties encountered in the task of nation-building, regional and subregional integration constitutes the principal impulse in restructuring the fragmented African continent into more coherent and stronger economic regional and subregional entities.

The Lagos Plan of Action further postulated that the regionalism sought by African states involved six mutually interdependent processes: first, integration of the physical, institutional, and social infrastructure; second, integration of the production structures; third, market integration; fourth, resolution of intercountry conflicts and prevention of acts of political destabilisation; fifth, ensuring stability and security, both at nation-state and intercountry levels; and finally, creation of an enabling environment for initiative and enterprise as well as facilitation of cross-border factor movements.[23]

Consequently, seven of the Lagos Plan of Action's thirteen chapters focus on Africa's seven strategic sectors—food and agriculture; industry; natural resources; human resources; transport and communications; trade and finance; and energy. The remaining chapters deal with crosscutting issues such as the environment; science and technology; gender; least-developed countries; creation and nurturing of institutions for technical cooperation among developing countries and economic cooperation among developing countries; and development planning, statistics, and population. Little wonder that the plan is acclaimed as the first continent-wide collective effort by African governments for forging a comprehensive unified approach to economic development.

It has also been suggested that the imagined 'old regionalism' is narrow and state-centred. By this I understand that the efforts to establish Africa's RECs largely involved government initiatives and that other stakeholders in the countries concerned were excluded from the process. This, of course, was not the reality. When the first-ever conference of West African ministers responsible for economic development and planning and commerce was convened in Lagos in April 1973, I urged each government to include representatives of the organised private sector in their respective national delegations. As Nigeria's minister for economic reconstruction and development, I included Henry Fajemirokun, the president of the Nigerian Association of Chambers of Commerce, Industry, Mines, and agriculture (NACCIMA), as well as some of its members, in my delegation, and all my colleagues acted similarly. These representatives of the private sector took advantage of our Lomé ministerial meeting to launch the process that led to creation of the Federation of West African Chambers of Commerce in 1974, which in turn organised the establishment of the private-owned ECOWAS Bank (Ecobank) after the ECOWAS treaty was signed and ratified in Lagos in May 1975. Ecobank was eventually founded in 1985, and by 2010 had branches in all fifteen ECOWAS countries, as well as in Burundi, Cameroon, the Central African Republic, Chad, Congo-Brazzaville, the Democratic Republic of the Congo, Gabon, Kenya, Malawi, Rwanda, Tanzania, Uganda, and Zambia, and well as in São Tomé and Príncipe and in France. Similarly, during the negotiations on the establishment of the PTA, not only was the private sector fully involved in the process, but so also were representatives of all the liberation movements in Southern Africa who took part in all the negotiations.

Bringing this story up-to-date, one clear picture that has emerged from the audit of the AU's organs, which I chaired in 2007, is the state of internal institutional incoherence, and of disarray and lack of effectiveness, of the various organs. There is thus an urgent need for institutional revamping and development at all levels. The AU's various organs are in dire need of the injection of necessary dynamism commensurate with meeting the challenges posed by the acceleration of the political and economic integration of the continent.

The AU, Africa's regional economic communities, and the EU

As already indicated, Africa's RECs are like the EU in their overarching objectives—to work towards establishing a free trade area and common market in each of their respective regions, and to work collectively towards the creation of an African Common Market and an African Economic Community. By so doing, these bodies also constitute the building blocks for achieving pan-African political integration. It is important to note, however, that the RECs are not organs of the AU. In fact, they are independent of the organisation. Each of them has its separate treaty and different institutional architecture, which predate the AU. The harmonisation and rationalisation of the RECs, which has been the raison d'être of the African Economic Community since 2002, has become the responsibility of the AU as the successor of the Organisation of African Unity (OAU). The 1998 protocol between the AEC and the RECs clearly identified the lead roles to be played by African governments in the configuration of the RECs and the AEC. A new protocol on the relationship between the AU and the RECs was accordingly adopted in July 2007. Two other organs of the AU—the Specialised Technical Committees and the Economic, Social, and Cultural Council (ECOSOCC)—have also been assigned specific responsibilities in the rationalisation, harmonisation, and acceleration of the progress of the RECs in their movement towards an African Common Market and an African Economic Community. The AU Commission is further mandated to establish mechanisms to coordinate regional and continental efforts, particularly in the area of international trade negotiations.

Unfortunately, as the 2007 AU audit panel concluded, the AU Commission has not been able to take firm charge of this responsibility, as the EPA negotiations clearly demonstrated. Accordingly, the audit panel strongly recommended that the AU Commission should develop the necessary internal mechanisms to strengthen its coordinating and harmonising role among Africa's RECs and assume full leadership responsibility vis-à-vis external actors.[24] But the question is: Will the EU Commission cooperate to enable such processes as the EPA negotiations to become truly AU-EU negotiations?

Furthermore, there is the problem of overlap that exists in the membership of Africa's RECs. Three countries—the Democratic Republic of the Congo, Burundi, and Rwanda—are members of four different RECs; twenty-two African countries are members of three RECs; while twenty-four countries belong to two RECs each. Only five African countries belong to only one REC. Whenever these RECs reach their goals of customs union and common market, virtually all African countries—except Algeria, Mauritania, Cape Verde, Namibia, and Guinea—will be members of two, three, and even four different regional customs unions and common markets. This situation will clearly result in much confusion unless urgently addressed.

As the 2007 audit panel rightly noted:

Countries belonging to more than one REC face contradictions and tensions with respect to tariff and non-tariff barriers, bureaucratic procedures and formalities in customs and immigration offices, fear of competition, corruption, and the perceived fear of sovereignty loss. In other cases, tariff harmonization for countries belonging to more than one REC has caused disruptions in their trade liberalization policies. This is best illustrated by those countries that belong to a preferential trade area such as COMESA and also a Customs Union such as the EAC. Countries belonging to RECs with divergent timelines for trade liberalization programmes aggravate the situation.[25]

It is therefore not surprising that, more than two decades after most of these RECs were established and the Abuja Treaty was adopted in 1991, none of them has gone beyond the first of the six stages that must be traversed to reach their overarching integration goal. Hence the urgent need for accelerating the process. Africa's RECs have not succeeded in effectively removing intra-REC tariff and nontariff barriers, owing to multiple memberships of governments in different RECs. It is this failure that has given Brussels the opportunity and audacity to create overlapping bilateral and regional EPAs operating at different liberalisation speeds and time frames that cut across existing regional blocs.

The institutional structure of Africa's RECs has no doubt been inspired by that of the EU, while the AU has copied wholesale the structure of the AEC as envisioned in the Abuja Treaty. Three of the RECs—ECOWAS, SADC, and the EAC—have parliaments; the executives of all the eight RECs recognised by the AU are at the highest level (heads of state and ministerial councils); all RECs except CEN-SAD and IGAD have judicial institutions (courts of justice/tribunals); while all of Africa's RECs except the Arab Maghreb Union have institutional frameworks and mechanisms for peace and security.

While the RECs should no doubt retain their independence, the AU Commission must assume fully and proactively the responsibility conferred upon it by the AU Assembly under the 2007 Accra Protocol—which all the RECs as well as the AU Commission have now signed—to streamline the work of these regional bodies, develop a consciously structured process of inter-REC interaction and exchange, and achieve effective synergies between them. The AU Commission must take over initiatives such as the EPA negotiations with the EU Commission, thus putting an end to hopelessly unequal situations like the 'David vs. Goliath' EPA encounter.

The 2007 AU audit panel further proposed eight principal benchmarks for monitoring how steadfastly and successfully Africa is moving towards political unity and economic integration: first, coherence and effectiveness of institutional frameworks; second, popularisation and internalisation of the core values underpinning the AU's Constitutive Act of 2000; third, engagement and mobilisation of the peoples of Africa for unity and integration; fourth, free movement of the peoples of Africa all over the continent; fifth, rationalisation of the RECs; sixth, fast-tracking of the movement towards an African Common Market and African Economic Community; seventh, establishment of continental financial and monetary institutions; and finally, orientation of the African entrepreneurial elite towards regional and continental investments that advance unity and integration.[26]

Fortunately, these principles were accepted by the AU Assembly of Heads of State in July 2008. The audit panel put forward these benchmarks because the steps that are required for integration are measurable and should therefore allow for registering incremental progress in a coherent and cohesive manner. No doubt, Europe can and should play a positive and proactive role in the achievement of these eight important benchmarks. In stark contrast, it could also play the more negative role of the 'dog in the manger'. Whatever role Europe decides to assume—through the EU or at national level or both—there is no doubt that Africa is determined to redress the pernicious deeds of the Berlin Conference of 1884–1885 and its terrible aftermath. The 'business as usual' approach in relations between these two continents must change if Africa is to avoid becoming 'a forgotten continent'.

Concluding reflections: developing a genuine partnership

In bringing this chapter to an end, let us focus on what needs to be done to facilitate the emergence of 'Afro-europa' and the disappearance of 'Euraf-

103

rique'. (See chapter 2 in this volume.) This will not happen as long as Africa remains a suppliant continent of Europe—even if it is a courted suppliant. A new and indispensable alliance must be born, in which the African road-map for achieving political unification and economic and market integration is fully supported by Europe, and in which the EU and its policy organs work collaboratively and closely with the AU and its organs.

The African roadmap, which has been evolving since independence in the 1960s, has now reached full maturity. The commissioning of the 2007 AU audit and its general approval, including the endorsement of the eight benchmarks proposed in the report for monitoring the movement towards implementation of African political unity and economic integration, demonstrate not only Africa's determination but also the collective sense of urgency attached to facing the future challenges of regional integration. No doubt, African countries and people will have to lead this long crusade for socioeconomic freedom. Regarding implementation of the roadmap, the 2007 audit panel argued strongly that the diversity and multiple players in African society must be harnessed as a whole. A new pan-Africanism must be based on the fulcrum of collective self-reliance and self-sustainment so that Africa's 800 million citizens will be motivated to participate fully in these efforts. A psychological paradigm shift must also be developed that will deliver the peoples of Africa from the naive belief that their salvation will somehow come from outside the continent.

Will the EU contribute optimally to the realisation of this paradigm shift? Will it do its utmost to refrain from blocking African initiatives, from undermining Africa's confidence and will to operationalise its own road-map? Will Europe learn to treat Africa as its neighbour and partner, and thus leave behind the mind-set and methods that have shaped relations between the two continents for over two centuries? This requires—as Louis Michel stated—Europe offering the men and women of Africa every means of shaping their own future. It also requires treating Africa as a player not a pawn, and as a partner not a prostitute.

5

EUROPE, AFRICA, AND AID

TOWARDS A GENUINE PARTNERSHIP

Rob de Vos

Introduction

The term 'partnership' has been used—but more often misused—in official documents, speeches, and other forms of communication to characterise the relationship between the European Union and Africa. In most cases, this 'partnership' has been unequal and represents more a state of coexistence than a harmonious reciprocal relationship involving mutual give-and-take by both partners.

A good example of this phenomenon was the creation of the EU's New Strategy for Africa of December 2005, to provide the framework for a new, comprehensive, integrated long-term relationship between Europe and Africa. The document was almost completely prepared by the European Commission in Brussels without any substantial input from African governments. The joint strategy that the EU and Africa agreed in Lisbon in December 2007 did not, however, have to change. The fundamental wisdoms relating to how to create an environment for sustainable and inclusive development in Africa remain valid. Yet the agreed priorities form a huge agenda. There are also plenty of opportunities for the multitude of partners to escape the complexities of multilateralism, and to pick and choose within their own structures (the European Union and the African Union), and continue to act bilaterally. This situation is not going to change quickly in the foreseeable future.

The academic world has not yet developed a model to analyse EU-Africa relations in all their aspects. 'Development cooperation' and 'international relations' are still treated as two separate subjects. Why not think the unusual and compare the EU-Africa partnership with the functioning of a business? There are many different types of enterprises, but to illustrate this comparison, the example of a company that aims at continuity will be used. A former Shell director, the Dutchman Arie de Geus, described such companies in explaining why they stayed in business much longer than others. The term that de Geus used was 'the living company'.[1] Corporate longevity has much more to do with 'living working communities' than with financial assets. Companies that have stayed in business for sometimes more than a century are financially conservative, and are more aware of what is happening in their environment. They are conscious of their identity, and make room for experiments and the acceptance of new ideas.

This chapter analyses EU-Africa economic relations in the background of the Washington Consensus; the role of leadership and institutions; the need for greater accountability on the part of external donors; the effectiveness of aid within the comparative context of the African Union and the European Union; and the need to improve mutual accountability and to promote results-based management. The chapter concludes with policy recommendations to guide future economic relations between Europe and Africa.

Europe-Africa economic relations in the age of the Washington Consensus

Nowadays there is a clear consensus on what makes management in private companies successful in securing the long-term future of the company: vision, leadership, patience and perseverance, as well as an environment for learning with proper feedback mechanisms. These four elements could also provide building blocks for a proper dialogue between the EU and Africa. This chapter analyses these factors in the real world of international cooperation, and makes suggestions for their improvement. Similarities rather than differences are emphasised, even though the subject of Europe-Africa economic relations is very broad and must be dealt with on the basis of often sharp generalisations.

The way forward in the dialogue between the EU and Africa was agreed in Lisbon in December 2007 and, in general aimed at realisation of the UN's Millennium Development Goals (MDGs), which sought, among other things, to halve poverty by 2015; establishment of an effective peace and security architecture in Africa; promotion of regional integration to stimulate growth; improvement of 'good governance' and human rights; and shaping of global governance through an open and multilateral framework.[2]

However, there was a need to dig deeper and for this strategy to become more operational. The agenda was clearly dominated by a wish to implement programmes aimed at the alleviation of poverty by stimulating growth, creating employment, and making Africa a serious partner in the globalisation process.

It has been fashionable of late to state that the recipes from the Bretton Woods institutions—the World Bank and the International Monetary Fund (IMF)—have not worked, and hence that 'the Washington Consensus is dead'. This, however, is much too simple. First, the Washington Consensus—involving an emphasis on marketisation and democratisation—was never fully applied across the board, because African decisionmakers were far too clever, and only worked with the consensus when it suited them. Second, this neoliberal approach did not do justice to the great progress that Africa had made by 2010, at its own pace, nor has it provided a sound basis for sustainable development in the coming decades. Examples cited by Trevor Manuel, South Africa's finance minister at the time, in addressing a group of British-based chartered accountants in 2008 underlined that most of Africa's macroeconomic fundamentals have been correct: inflation was on average 61 per cent in 1994 in sub-Saharan Africa, but fell to 8 per cent in 2006; in the same year, African budgets were largely balanced, and foreign direct investment rose to $31 billion from $18 billion in 2003.[3]

On a macroeconomic level, Africa has thus been doing quite well. Yet on a microeconomic, structural level, the conclusions are less straightforward. Here we have learned that there are no 'one size fits all' solutions. In a remarkably honest account of lessons learned, the World Bank admitted in 2004 that growth is more than simple efficiency in the use of resources: it is essentially a process of social transformation.[4] At the beginning of the 1990s, policy advice seemed fairly clear-cut. Developing countries, including governments in Africa, needed to pursue macroeconomic prudence, domestic liberalisation, market incentives to open up their economies, as well as a reduced role for the state, and preferably 'shock treatment' to set change in motion. These were the key tenets of the Washington Consensus.

These recipes, however, did not work in many developing countries, especially in sub-Saharan Africa, where, in general, economies stagnated. Why did this occur? The key lesson from the 1990s was that incentives to expand productive capacity were different from those that stimulated better utilisation of existing capacity. Both institutions and policies mattered, and it was particularly important to assess how vital institutions in particular were, and how difficult it was to make progress when they were absent, as well as how hard it was to improve their quality. The World Bank's 2004 report was a plea to look for country specificities and binding constraints for growth, advising itself not to fall into the trap of blueprints, to demonstrate greater humility, and to accept that there are diverse solutions to finding the best road to growth for individual countries. In 2008 the Growth Commission[5] further built on these lessons, and concluded in a rich and extensive piece of research by policymakers, academics, and private sector managers that there is no single creative doctrine of growth. All these experiences provided clear lessons for the EU-Africa dialogue and its agenda, which have sought to avoid precooked prescriptions. We have to accept alternative paths when addressing real and 'binding constraints'.[6] There is also a clear need for time to experiment and to invest in collecting more information on the ground in developing countries.

The intellectual contributions of the EU to this debate on lessons learned have been difficult to measure. European academics and policymakers have certainly made a contribution, but notwithstanding the enormous financial contributions from Europe's institutions (nowadays amounting to more than half of all aid flows), these contributions have been limited. The intellectual centres of these debates are in Washington (the World Bank), Paris (the Organisation for Economic Cooperation and Development, OECD), and maybe New York (the United Nations), but certainly not in the capital of the EU in Brussels.

There has been no decisive, alternative, African contribution outside the continent's inputs into the institutions of the big international players like the World Bank and the UN. (See chapter 4 in this volume for another perspective.) The work of institutions like the African Economic Research Council (AERC)[7] more or less follows mainstream economic theories and 'wisdoms' and gives the impression that there is no need for an 'alternative' African vision.

In summary, it is fair to say that, in recent times, there has no longer been a strong ideological divide between rich North and poor South. One important building block for the dialogue was available, which meant that there was a shared vision. This building block preached that, for the stimulation of economic growth, there remained a need for functioning markets with an actively engaged government crafting predictable policies and possessing well-functioning institutions as well as sound macroeconomic frameworks: low inflation, balanced budgets, stable currencies, and manageable trade deficits. All these elements listed in the aforementioned growth report of 2008 still continue to play a decisive role, but for structural policies geared towards the functioning of institutions, one needed to look to country specificities.

Leadership and institutions

There is an important role for leadership, and there are strong examples in the modern history of international cooperation showing that leadership really matters and can make a substantial difference to policy outcomes. The EU's internal market process received a strong boost thanks to the dynamic leadership of the Commission under its French president Jacques Delors in the period between 1985 and 1994. Appointing similarly visionary leaders to head the Commission is now a less popular approach among EU government leaders, and the job profile in 2011 seemed to be more aimed at finding an effective chairman of a 'board'.

Under the Australian-born American James Wolfensohn, the World Bank became a dominant force in international cooperation between 1995 and 2005. Although Wolfensohn pushed the Bank too far in simultaneously dealing with too many different issues,[8] his successor in 2005, Paul Wolfowitz, did not have the same visionary skills, and contrived to lead the Bank almost into a crisis. Some 10,000 respected professionals became an anxious, nearly paralysed group, and developed great doubts about their role in the world of international cooperation. In this sphere, there has been no institution or group of countries that could play the role of dominant leader. Biannual meetings of the World Bank thus became a fantastic platform for knowledge exchange, and in the end the conclusions of these meetings have often been noncommittal, relying on the lowest common denominator in reaching consensus. The UN and its specialised agencies in the meantime have covered every field, but have not been a dominant player in any one sector, thus achieving breadth rather than depth.

Since the end of the Second World War in 1945, there have been profound changes in the world of global development, but the structure and division of power within international institutions have not changed fundamentally. The architecture of international cooperation has in fact shown an enormous resistance to change. Much effort has been put into preparing plans for change, but similar energy has often appeared to be used to water down the same plans in order to reach a level of harmless, but also useless, compromise.

What role has Europe played in this field? The EU has clearly been a special case because it is neither a multilateral institution—in the sense of the UN or the Bretton Woods institutions, the Bank and the Fund—nor a federation of states. In the interplay with global institutions, Europe does not yet speak with one voice, with the exception of trade issues, as demonstrated particularly in the World Trade Organisation (WTO) negotiations of the Doha round since 1995. While the EU consists of twenty-seven member states and the European Commission, there is a slow but growing acceptance that a greater coordinating role should be given to the Commission in Brussels, especially in what has been regarded as 'technical affairs'. However, international cooperation has to be seen as not being a purely technical matter. One could even state that nontechnical aspects like historical ties, commercial interests, and even emotional aspects often continue to shape the Europe-Africa relationship. (See chapter 2 in this volume.)

The German scholar Hartmut Mayer has suggested that we need a 'more responsible rhetoric that would allow for a more realistic translation of ethical principles and political goals into successful practical solutions'. European policymakers need to realise that many important international players do not see Europe as the 'leading ethical and normative power', and yet 'Europe can contribute to responsible global governance in a fashion that is powerful yet based on soft power'.[9] (See also chapter 22 in this volume.)

The European Union has pretended to present a more or less integrated external relations policy. Furthermore, there has been a clear attempt by the EU Commission to develop a process of complementarity through a division of labour with member states, as well as through joint programming. European policies should not be internally counterproductive, which is why more and more emphasis has been placed on reaching coherence in different policy areas. Coherence can clearly be reached at three different levels: coherence within the EU institution itself (the departments for international cooperation and other departments of the European Commission); coherence within the policies of a national government and the European Commission as a whole; and coherence of policies with the national plans of recipient countries.

EU policies on trade, migration, peace, security, and aid also have to become more consistent. Moreover, the hierarchy of priorities remains unclear, and has to be negotiated from scratch nearly every time. Brussels's production of a biannual report on 'development policy coherence' could be a useful tool for monitoring future progress.

Ranking the donors

Benchmarking can provide an opportunity to rank and compare the aid contributions of European and other important players. Since 2003 the Washington-based Centre for Global Development (CGD) has ranked annually the quality of international cooperation by analysing aid, trade, investment, migration, security, and technology transfer. This ranking provides a rough indication of how integrated and coherent the policies of individual member states are. The Netherlands and Denmark have traditionally competed for first place in the rankings. In 2008 the rankings were also conducted by the CGD with respect to sub-Saharan Africa.[10]

In nearly all of these rankings, Europe came out best. In terms of aid (quality-adjusted aid plus charitable giving), the Netherlands, Norway, Ireland, Sweden, and Denmark scored highest. However, in the area of trade, Canada, New Zealand, Australia, and even the United States beat European countries, though by a small margin. In the promotion of direct investment (companies, legislation, antibribery activities, and multilateral insurance), apart from Canada, the top listings consisted of European countries—Germany, Britain, and the Netherlands. For migration (inflow of migrants, openness to students, assistance to asylum-seekers, and refugees), reliable data were limited, but surprisingly Portugal came out on top, with Ireland, Sweden, Britain, and New Zealand following close behind. In environment-related areas (greenhouse gas, ozone depletion, oil tax, biodiversity, and fisheries subsidies), Norway, Finland, and Sweden topped the list. In the sphere of security (contribution to peacekeeping, arms exports, and securing sea lanes), Ireland came out strongest ahead of Britain, Sweden, France, and Portugal. In the field of technology, the differences were small, and France received the most points. In the final rankings, European countries received the highest rankings (Sweden, Ireland, Britain, the Netherlands, and Denmark), but also the lowest scores (Austria, Spain, and Italy).

This type of academic work does not pretend to be highly scientific, but one hopes it can stimulate a debate on consistency of policymaking in

Western capitals. In general, it is fair to conclude that one group—the so-called Nordics, comprising mostly Scandinavian countries (see chapter 19 in this volume), as well as Britain, Ireland, and the Netherlands—have been seeking to invest in moving the agenda forward. The US and Japan, however, have complained that the process was moving too fast. France and Germany have very often sat on the fence. In truth, Washington has not always been the slowest member, and has sometimes introduced radical and stimulating new approaches, like the Millennium Challenge Account (MCA) under the administration of President George W. Bush between 2001 and 2008, though some critics have questioned the effectiveness of the MCA's implementation.[11] There is, however, no reason for complacency, though Europe has largely seemed to be moving in the right direction on these issues.

The AU, the EU, and aid effectiveness

Turning from the donors to the recipients, the role of Africa in this field has not been easy to assess. There have been no comparative studies in this area like those on the EU and its partners. Africa has organised itself into the African Union and into subregional institutions and the African Development Bank. Furthermore, the UN's Addis Ababa-based Economic Commission for Africa has been influential in the development field.[12] The difference between the EU and the AU is quite striking. As the French scholar Daniel Bach has insightfully noted, the AU has no sovereignty of powers in any field and no autonomous resources.[13] Furthermore, do AU members really share 'common values' as EU members do? (See also chapter 3 in this volume.)

The EU and the AU, however, have shared a high capabilities-expectations gap. The expectations of the population in each member state, often driven by internationally operating media, have been high. Yet the possibilities to act and the room to manoeuvre have so far remained limited on both sides. In Europe, this gap has been decreasing, owing to the attitude of European citizens who have shown less faith in the EU. Yet in Africa, the gap has appeared to be growing. Especially in the field of peace and security, the pressure on the AU to act independently has been enormous (as in Sudan's Darfur region and Somalia), but its capabilities and resources to do so have not grown commensurately. (See chapters 13–15 in this volume.)

One of the problems in the EU-Africa dialogue has been a lack of clear and strong leadership on the African side. African representatives have often left decisions until the last minute, and thus created the impression of being evasive, disinterested, and even unprepared. The debates on the economic partnership agreements have provided good examples of this problem. (See chapters 10 and 11 in this volume.) Time pressure could have been avoided, and these debates should have concentrated on the real issues of pros and cons of market liberalisation, the content of industrial policy, and support for regional integration in Africa, instead of emotional reactions by Africans expressing feelings of being bullied by Brussels.

The process of crafting the New Partnership for Africa's Development (NEPAD) of 2001 gave Europeans hope that a number of African leaders were ready to take the initiative themselves with the African Peer Review Mechanism (APRM) of 2003 and investment programmes aimed at stimulating regional economic development. NEPAD has remained alive, but with the departure of Nigerian president Olusegun Obasanjo in May 2007, and the premature end of the term of South African president Thabo Mbeki in September 2008, these initiatives have come to lack leaders to drive the agenda.

In the international discussion on the reform of the World Bank, the IMF, and the UN, Africa has played too modest a role, though there is so much for the continent to gain from these reforms. All parties agree that development in Africa has not been a question of a 'quick fix'. Partners have needed perseverance, patience, and reliability with regard to commitments made. Unfortunately, these qualities have not been displayed by either side in the past few decades. Africa has been the subject of 'donor fatigue' and competition from other regions such as Asia (see chapter 8 in this volume), and its interests have been diverted by the entry of new member states into the EU. Some important donors, including EU member states, have found it difficult to plan ahead in a multiannual way. They have also found it hard to present reliable figures of support on an annual basis. Despite these constraints, every African finance minister is still expected to balance his or her country's budget and to improve on service delivery. Fortunately, Africa has slowly been moving towards less dependence on aid.[14] The growth of locally collected revenue in sub-Saharan Africa was faster than the rise in overseas development assistance between 2001 and 2006. For the time being, however, aid continues to play an important role. The 2007 report of the OECD's Development Assistance Committee shows that, since 1999, aid has been in a clear upward swing, with more assistance being provided every year to least-developed countries, mostly in Africa. A larger portion of aid has also become untied, and more aid has been concentrated on achieving the UN's Millennium Development Goals.

In September 2008, donors and recipient countries met in Accra to evaluate progress on the 2005 Paris Declaration on Aid Effectiveness.[15] The Paris Declaration's key components are that development is driven by partner countries themselves; donors align with systems and priorities of partner countries; donors harmonise their activities among themselves; outcomes should become more important than inputs; and both parties must aim at a mutual accountability mechanism. In Accra in 2008, a monitoring survey regarding the Paris Declaration was presented on the basis of participation by fifty-five recipient countries (including twenty-five in Africa) and most of the important donors.

Viewing this situation positively, one could say that the picture is a mixed one, based on four key indicators: first, on the whole, public finance management systems in many countries have improved, but the use of these systems remains weak; second, less than half of recorded aid flows go through national budgets; third, less than 10 per cent of recipient countries have sound frameworks to monitor and assess development results; and fourth, only twelve of fifty-five participating countries have established a mechanism for mutual review of progress on aid effectiveness commitments.

It is strange that there has been no further advance in these areas, because they all lie within the control of donor (and recipient) governments themselves. The only explanation for the lack of progress must be that institutional interests have been prioritised over issues of quality. National institutions in the West have not wanted to give up their playgrounds, and no one has been correcting them except the mechanisms of peer pressure and benchmarking. In the world of Western international cooperation, hardly any organisation ever calls it a day. Older ones have sometimes changed their name or areas of specialisation, and new ones have continuously been created. Hence the number of institutions for African governments to deal with only grows, rendering harmonisation of interventions and divisions of labour more difficult.

Another reason why the harmonisation agenda has been advancing so slowly is the role of European national politics. International cooperation has been mostly the field of a small group of specialists. No vital interests have been at stake, and no life of a political party has been at risk in this area. This situation has often led to micromanagement in the various interventions. Another fundamental flaw in the world of international cooperation has been the lack of clear accountability mechanisms. Who is ultimately responsible for what? There are so many players to take the blame for failures or to claim success for progress. This has made results-based management complex, and has often led to a noncommittal attitude on the part of donors. This situation has been reinforced by the way in which interventions have been evaluated. Is there a role for Africa to play in accelerating implementation of the Paris agenda?

Four high-level meetings on aid effectiveness and harmonization—in Rome, Italy (2003), Paris, France (2005), Accra, Ghana (2008), and Busan, South Korea (2011)—have shown that African countries have still not sufficiently realised the importance of the Paris Declaration process. The lukewarm attitude of African governments to these processes has provided an escape route for certain important donors to remain 'noncommittal'. In an encouraging move, the government of Mozambique increased the level of peer pressure by grading its partners, but this has so far been the exception rather than the rule.

The period 2011–2012 will be vital for the Paris Declaration process. Notwithstanding the firm commitments made at the Accra conference, subsequent high-level forums may show insufficient progress, which could indicate that the Paris agenda is already running out of steam. Completely different approaches may be necessary, as suggested by Owen Barder, a research fellow at the Centre for Global Development in Washington. He advocates abandoning present efforts based on a planning mind-set and instead working out an alternative model to coordinate multiple actors with diverse interests: a model based on markets and networks.[16]

Improving mutual accountability and promoting results-based management

One sometimes has the impression that African governments prefer to have as many partners as possible, and to deal with them on a more direct, bilateral basis. However, this approach has been time-consuming and lacking in the necessary transparency. This attitude could be changed by introducing an honest, mutual, and inclusive accountability system. Such accountability would mean that there are institutions responsible for results and commitments on delivery. The international cooperation system has so far focused almost exclusively on financial accountability, which means analysing and proving that funds have been spent on intended interventions. This system has made great progress and been closely monitored by accounting offices and parliaments in recipient countries.

The development of a mutual accountability system has only slowly been evolving. This is a complicated process due to the imbalance in power between donor governments and recipient countries, the different levels of accountability, and the complexity of these issues, which require constant and close scrutiny of the environment, as well as rigorous questioning of the validity of previous assumptions. This is hard work, and national bureaucracies often have no inbuilt incentive mechanism to pursue this approach.

There also needs to be a clear understanding—a contract—about mutually agreed results. Accountability is not only a process of showing and taking responsibility; it is also a process of learning. Both parties have to realise that they can only gain from an attitude of adaptive learning,[17] which is clearly different from compliance learning or resistance learning. These last two forms of learning can often be an alibi to keep the relationship going on a familiar, beaten track, but rarely provide deeper insights into lessons learned.

One would expect the international cooperation sector to be eager and open to learning whether it has been doing the right things and to be aware of the obligation to 'do no harm'.[18] Unfortunately, this has not always been the case. Five reasons can be identified to explain this approach. First, there is the complexity of the problems ('there are so many actors involved, the world keeps on changing constantly, and results-based management is an illusion'). Second, there is the lack of a proper accountability *system*, and the absence of automatic incentives to provide convincing material on results and outcomes. Third, the executing agencies have their institutional interests (knowledge can be dangerous because of the need to explain and, if necessary, the need to change). Fourth, the electoral cycle in the West of three to five years often encourages politicians to look for new, 'original' ideas that can provide them with a 'brand' to sell to voters, but often does not force them to look back and reflect deeply (many politicians ask, 'Why invest in the evaluation of the ideas of my predecessor?'). Finally, recipient countries, especially in Africa, rarely have any independent think-tanks to evaluate government policies, while much research continues to be conducted in Washington and New York, in Western academic institutions, and by individual consultants financed by donors, and this has clearly created a certain bias in research output.

The results-based management approach has to be taken more seriously. In the private sector, this system was generally introduced in the 1950s, but essentially the development community did not discover it until the 2000s. Results-based management requires three key elements.

First, efforts should be made to try to manage on an 'outcome' and not an 'input' basis, and to bring results and resources (internal and external) together in order to improve the measurement of efficiency and effectiveness. The unproductive charade of consultative group meetings and round-tables in which donors pledge funds and then 'forget' to follow up, while recipients present general reports that are equally forgotten and are often prepared outside the country, should come to an end as soon as practicably possible. Available information should be used wisely, as indicators are meant to demonstrate what progress has been made and what lessons can be drawn from deviations from agreed plans. However, results-based management was never intended for settling scores.

Second, progress can only be measured properly when one knows what the starting point is. Baseline surveys at the beginning of policy interventions have been more the exception than the rule. The government of the Netherlands, which I have served for three decades, has often been praised for its work on evaluation. Yet after more than 2,000 reports, it is fair to say that the Dutch evaluation service for international cooperation has not, in most cases, been in a position to reach any firm conclusions about the impact of the government's interventions. Above all, this has been due to the lack of baseline surveys. Ultimately, one simply has to accept the imbalances in power between European and African partners. These imbalances should not be denied, but be recognised and incorporated into efforts to establish a mutual accountability system.

Third, the American analyst Stephen Covey explains in his bestselling book *The Seven Habits of Highly Effective People*[19] the difference between sympathy and empathy. Sympathy is a form of agreement, a form of judgement, and sometimes makes people dependent. Empathy is the highest form of listening: you learn to understand the other side emotionally as well as intellectually. This requires skills, but there should also be a sincere desire to understand the other side, otherwise the process cannot work.

Relations between Europe and Africa seem to be governed more by sympathy than by empathy. Apart from power imbalances and financial flows, this has often created another sense of dependency at the receiving (African) end. Furthermore, owing to a heavy emphasis on socioeconomic issues, the element of psychological dependence has always been neglected in the business of international cooperation. (See chapter 4 in this volume.) The available literature on the psychology of aid,[20] which emphasises the importance of the human factor and combines systems theory and psychological analysis, is rarely read by policymakers in the world of development.

Hence the idea that aid may be harmful and that, from the recipient's point of view, such assistance could become symbolically threatening is alien to most people in the field of development. As a consequence, the search for inbuilt reciprocity in the various interventions, which could develop self-esteem by the receiver, has often not been pursued. Still, this sense of reciprocity could be the key to developing a relationship in which both sides feel more equal, and in which empathic listening can thrive.

Empathy can also mean that Europeans invest more in understanding the developments on the African continent: first, without analysing the continent as a monolithic bloc, and second, without seeing it through 'Western eyes'. Fortunately, more and more literature is coming out of Africa that helps us to understand the continent's realities better.[21]

Some African governments and academics have been quite successful at impressing upon some soft-hearted Europeans the notion that most problems in Africa originate from slavery, colonialism, the effects of the Cold War, and other historical inheritances. The definitive cost-benefit analysis of colonialism has not yet been done and most probably will never be done. But I agree with the Ghanaian economist George Ayittey[22] that the slave trade and colonialism have little to do with present-day economic mismanagement in Africa. National governments in Africa that try to encourage a feeling of guilt on the part of Europeans may, in some situations and with some Europeans, have positive effects, but this approach will ultimately backfire. New and younger generations in Europe will definitely not buy this guilt-ridden approach anymore, and for Africans this tactic could lead to obscuring real problems in their societies and may prevent the development of an advanced local accountability system.

Concluding reflections

At the end of the road, we may conclude that it has been possible to use the suggested management model of a company aiming at continuity in order to analyse at least part of the relationship between the EU and Africa, the part dominated by so-called international cooperation. This is not too far-fetched a concept, but it does require another way of working and thinking for European bureaucracies. Five key recommendations are important in concluding this chapter.

First, Europe and Africa should become much more businesslike in their relations and stop fooling each other by drawing up grand scenarios, the outcomes of which cannot be objectively verified in practice. Both parties should not commit themselves to targets and objectives that they cannot reach in the foreseeable future.

Second, the relationship between Africa and Europe is much broader than a question of financial aid, which is often not the real solution to deep-seated problems. African governments should also be much more selective in accepting aid and its conditions. The attempts by donors to coordinate, harmonise, and pool resources (the Paris agenda) are especially beneficial to African countries. However, strangely enough, these countries often lack genuine ownership of this process. Pledging conferences with a preponderance of donor participation should be replaced by meetings that achieve concrete results (such as economic indicators, MDG progress, etc.) and generate collective resources both internally and externally. Donors must increasingly realise that aid money is not neutral, and that such assistance can have negatively perverse effects. They must thus find ways of developing mechanisms of reciprocity between giver and recipient.

Third, Europeans and Africans should be clear about what is working well and what is not. Some institutions have a great interest in stressing that things are not going well, but Africa has made impressive progress in the macroeconomic field, and democracy is on the increase on the continent, although there are some signs that these positive trends may not continue. There are also certain groups of individuals and institutions that tend to exaggerate every positive sign and blow it out of proportion. Socioeconomic and political development in Africa must be dealt with in an unemotional manner, based on facts and figures, which fortunately are becoming increasingly reliable.

Fourth, the international donor-recipient architecture has become very complex and wasteful due to the duplication of efforts. This trend is extremely difficult to change. Africans do not seem to realise that in the long run, this architecture is ultimately not in their interest. Short-term gains like the provision of international jobs and the continuous flow of funds seem to be favoured over the longer-term gains of more fundamental changes involving higher effectiveness in achieving the MDGs; a quicker and more coordinated reaction in humanitarian emergencies; and better adaptation to changing environments.

Finally, more knowledge is needed to understand how Africa functions, in order to guide European decisionmaking. If EU leaders understand how Africa 'works',[23] Europeans will be less quickly disappointed and more capable of prejudging power relations and their functioning in African societies. This should by no means lead to an acceptance of those relations and power structures that reduce mobility, block modernisation, and stimulate corruption. But an approach that values the impact of traditional leadership and African values and norms, placing them in their proper perspective and accepting that they are part of the starting point for change, is more likely to produce useful results in this relationship.

Africa, however, also needs its own capacity to think, to analyse, and to criticise. Most of this work is taking place outside the continent. But we also need independent African think-tanks that can match the quality of the work produced in Washington, New York, and Paris, but which are home-grown and can teach often oversensitive African policymakers to appreciate and accept constructive feedback.

It is also important to note that the modern evaluation sector is a multi-billion-euro industry with very little to show for itself. If we do not start measuring impact on the basis of a proper methodology with baseline surveys as a starting point, we will keep groping about in the dark. This approach is becoming less and less convincing for the bigger audience who pay for development interventions through taxes and membership fees (donors), as well as for the recipients who in the end, through their participation, must make the interventions a success.

Much has been left out in this chapter, such as the influence of China and India on EU-Africa relations. More competition, however, is not necessarily a bad thing, and Beijing and New Delhi are good at implementing activities (such as certain infrastructure projects) that are no longer the speciality of the EU.[24]

The role of local and international civil society, too, has not been dealt with. This chapter is primarily about states and markets, yet intercontinental civil society cooperation, including between churches and academic institutions, can potentially stimulate a more balanced and equitable EU-Africa relationship.

The final and overriding message of this chapter remains that Africa should organise itself better and be critical about its leaders who often misuse grandiose schemes of pan-Africanism for their own parochial purposes. Brussels should also be honest about its own commitments, and should not promise things that are impossible to deliver. European leaders must realise that aid money is only one of many elements in this important relationship. The sooner this dependence on aid funding vanishes, the better the EU-Africa relationship will become.

6

SOUTH AFRICA AND THE EU

WHERE LIES THE STRATEGIC PARTNERSHIP?

Talitha Bertelsmann-Scott

'Over the years, the EU, currently 27 nations strong, has expanded its network of friends and allies by negotiating "strategic partnership" agreements with key countries. EU policymakers hope that such deals—backed by European peacekeeping and humanitarian operations across the globe—will help dispel the long-standing and widespread view of the EU as an economic giant, but a political dwarf. Despite initial hopes, however, these accords remain little more than a catalogue of noble ambitions and unfulfilled goals.'[1]

Shada Islam

Introduction

The European Union-South Africa bilateral relationship dates back to precolonial times, when the first Europeans settled on South African soil in 1652. The relationship has evolved over many decades into a seemingly important political and economic relationship, which, on the surface, has deepened since South Africa's transition to democracy in 1994. The relationship has had many periods of strengthening and weakening, but the jury is currently still out on the ultimate direction of this partnership.

The EU has recently identified South Africa, alongside other emerging powers and longtime allies, as a strategic partner. The other nine countries in this elite group include the members of the BRIC alliance, comprising Brazil, Russia, India, and China (of which South Africa became a member in 2011), and the United States, Canada, Mexico, Japan, and South Korea. This seems an odd grouping of countries, and South Africa is the EU's only strategic partner on the African continent, with the omission of what may be other key economic and political powerhouses such as Egypt, Nigeria, and Kenya. What is more, there seems to be little understanding of what a 'strategic partner' is to the EU, not only in the South African case, but in most of the others as well.

An analysis of the strategic dimension of the EU-South Africa relationship must necessarily evaluate the nature of these ties. At first glance, this is a complicated relationship. On the one hand, South Africa is a major recipient of EU aid—total commitment for 2007–2013 is 980 million euros, not including EU member states' bilateral contributions—and benefits tremendously from European interest in its development; yet on the other hand, the relationship is highly fraught by the ongoing and seemingly endless negotiations surrounding the economic partnership agreements (EPAs). (See chapters 10 and 11 in this volume.) While there are synergies in terms of the foreign policies of Tshwane (Pretoria) and Brussels, especially towards the Southern African subregion, there are also as many divergent outlooks, especially when it comes to international processes such as the negotiations in the World Trade Organisation (WTO) and climate talks, where South Africa and the EU often sit on opposites sides of the table.

The British scholar Martin Holland argued in 1994 that the EU never had a 'normal' relationship with South Africa.[2] Whereas politically apartheid South Africa was condemned and ostracised, economically sanctions were enforced in some areas but trade volumes grew and expanded in other traditional export sectors. Brussels had strict policies in dealing with apartheid South Africa, including the code of conduct for European Community (EC) firms with subsidiaries operating in South Africa, and yet trade with South Africa between 1984 and 1988—arguably the height of apartheid rule—almost doubled from 8,825 to 12,515 million ECU. Today, the relationship remains 'abnormal' in that deep conflict arises at a regional level because of the EPA negotiations, while bilaterally the relationship could apparently not be stronger. The support that the EU gives South Africa in order to become a state of global importance, one that is able to play a lead role on the continent, is often undermined by Brussels's approach to trade negotiations in Southern Africa, with both the South Africa-EU Trade,

Development, and Cooperation Agreement (TDCA) and the Southern African Development Community (SADC) EPA causing rifts in already fragile regional integration endeavours.

This chapter examines the many aspects of this 'strategic' relationship and how it has evolved over the past few decades, assessing its actual content and rationale. It also analyses the EPA negotiations in the context of regional integration and the impact that the negativity surrounding these negotiations has had on the overall relationship between Tshwane and Brussels. In closing, the chapter examines the content and outcome of the most recent South Africa-EU summit, of 2010, in order to reach a conclusion on the true strategic nature of this partnership.

The early years

South Africa always stood out on the African continent as a country that was pivotal to any Europe-Africa strategy, from as far back as the British colonial interest in Southern Africa from 1795, with a deep focus on South Africa and its rich natural resources. Following the creation of the Union of South Africa in 1910 after the bitter Anglo-Boer War of 1899–1902, South Africa was entrusted with managing and giving direction to the Southern African Customs Union (SACU), within which the former British protectorates of modern-day Botswana, Swaziland, and Lesotho were—at least at an economic level—unified.

Writing in 1995, the South African scholar Adrian Guelke identified five phases in the EU-South Africa relationship, building on the four previously identified by Martin Holland: a phase of consensus, between 1974 and 1984; one of conflict, in 1985 and 1986; a phase of compromise, between 1987 and 1989; and finally, another of reformulation, beginning in 1990. Guelke's fifth phase was the beginning of the institutionalisation of the relationship on a long-term basis, with the signing of the interim framework agreement between the EU and South Africa in October 1994.[3]

One could, writing in 2012, identify a few more phases in the relationship: the phase during which the TDCA was negotiated (1994–2004), the phase during which the EPAs were negotiated (2004 to the present), and, slightly in parallel to this, the phase of establishing a strategic partnership between the EU and South Africa (with the signing of a memorandum of understanding in 2007). Many commentators have pointed to the fact that there is little substance to the strategic partnerships of the EU, and that, apart from promoting regular summits, the agendas of these meetings often remain too broad to have a real impact.[4] The summits, in addition, do not differ much from the way in which the relationships were structured prior to elevating their stature—artificially—to one of a 'strategic' nature. Delving a little into the history of the EU-South Africa relationship, however, shows that these have always been ties of pivotal importance, to South Africa at least.

The period 1945–1960—during which the European project of regional integration was launched among the economic and political powerhouses of Europe (see chapter 3 in this volume)—was mirrored by apartheid South Africa's ever-deepening policy of racial segregation and oppression. At this point, the European Economic Community was still far from being established as a common foreign policy forum among its member states. Therefore, there were a number of bilateral engagements with apartheid South Africa, obviously dominated by the relationship with its former colonial power, Britain. Whereas London had the depth of a comprehensive relationship with Pretoria, other European countries, such as the Scandinavians, emerged as leading voices in condemning racial segregation in South Africa (see chapter 19 in this volume), which was mostly lacking from Britain, France, and Germany.

During the 1960s, both South Africa and Europe enjoyed a period of economic growth, allowing for consolidation of the apartheid state and for trade links between the two parties to strengthen. However, South Africa's racial segregation policies increasingly transformed the state into a pariah in international forums. The 1970s and 1980s saw a period of deepening and broadening of the integration project in Europe, ultimately resulting in the establishment of the Single Market in the European Union in 1992, which spanned twelve countries.

The EC's 'foreign policy' at this point was still a loose mechanism of coordination among its member states. In relation to South Africa, the organisation established the 'Special Fund for the Victims of Apartheid' in 1986,[5] which funded projects and programmes in the areas of education, training, and humanitarian, social, and legal aid. In addition, most EC member states adopted some form of sanctions against South Africa—as did the European Council—and increasingly voiced their opposition to apartheid South Africa.

Holland argued that the EC policy towards apartheid South Africa at the time was loosely based on the British example, given that London had the most comprehensive relationship with Pretoria and the most experience in dealing with the apartheid government. According to Holland, 'the EU South African policy was not an amalgam of member-state bilateral positions; rather the existing British policy was adopted, marginally adapted and applied'.[6]

The end of apartheid and the birth of the EU

The 1990s saw significant political and economic change in both the EU and South Africa. For Brussels, in 1993, the Maastricht Treaty was finally ratified, which transformed the EC into the EU and changed its foreign policy making apparatus. The long-standing system of political cooperation between EU member countries was abandoned and replaced by the adoption of the Common Foreign and Security Policy (CFSP). Among the first 'joint actions' of the CFSP were the promotion of peace and stability in Europe, including in the former Yugoslavia and the Middle East; support for the Russian parliamentary elections; and, notably, support for the democratisation process in South Africa.[7]

To a certain extent, apartheid South Africa demonstrated, through the years, the inadequacies and poor implementation of the past loose arrangements in the EC's foreign policymaking apparatus. The 'new' South Africa now provided the opportunity to test the CFSP. Holland argued that 'South Africa was both topical and of international importance: politically, the Union could not ignore becoming involved. "Joint action" was appropriate, justified and demanded'.[8]

The 1990s saw the demise of apartheid South Africa and heralded a new era in 1994 when South Africa gained a democratic government under the leadership of the revered Nobel peace laureate and former political prisoner Nelson Mandela. Brussels was quick to respond, asking for the initiation of trade talks with South Africa. The negotiations towards a comprehensive trade and development agreement were protracted and the accord—the South Africa-EU Trade, Development, and Cooperation Agreement—was only signed in 2004.

The first EU ambassador to democratic South Africa (appointed in 1994), Ireland's Erwan Fouere, identified the EU's bilateral strategy towards the country as one of support to the newly emerging democracy. The broad principles of this approach would rest on the pillars of 'respect for human rights and democratic principles; support for balanced and sustainable social and economic development and cooperation; and freeing up trade by encouraging investment by European companies in South Africa and vice versa'.[9] This strategy increasingly took on a regional focus, and by 2000 the EU's Country Strategy Paper for South Africa (2000–2002) stated that 'the rationale for EU involvement is based on the assumption that South Africa is a pole for the development of peace, democracy and democratic growth for the entire Southern African region. If South Africa is to play this role, it must still overcome major social and economic challenges which have started to be addressed in the last five years'.[10]

Europe was consolidating its integration agenda and reaping the economic and political benefits thereof. Wanting to replicate its success in other areas, the EU started to encourage regional integration in Southern Africa. Thus, at the same time as engaging South Africa bilaterally in trade talks, Brussels stepped up its support to the Southern African Development Coordination Conference (SADCC). As soon as South Africa became a member of this body in August 1994 (SADCC had become SADC in 1992), EU support was further deepened. The adoption of a trade agenda through the protocol on trade for SADC of 1996 came about as a direct result of South Africa choosing SADC membership in preference to that of the Common Market for Eastern and Southern Africa (COMESA). In essence, therefore, the EU had a two-pronged approach: dealing with South Africa on a bilateral basis, and using the country's clout in the subregion to promote and strengthen the regional integration agenda in Southern Africa.

The EU and Southern Africa

Understanding the EU's vision for South Africa and its own strategic partnership in promoting regional integration is critical to understanding the driving force behind the EU-South Africa strategic relationship. In proposing a strategic partnership with South Africa, the European Commission argued that

the EU Strategy for Africa considers Regional Economic Communities as prime building blocks for EU-Africa relations. In the case of the Southern African region, the EU and South Africa, as strategic partners, must engage in more intense and substantive dialogue and political cooperation on the complex regional context and its political challenges. They must define more clearly their respective roles in the region, taking into account the emergence of new economic powers.[11]

The EU relationship with SADC dates back to the apartheid era, during which the neighbouring states of South Africa were united as frontline states in the Southern African Development Coordination Conference. The organisation's objectives were to provide a unified front against apartheid South Africa and to promote the economic development of its members. Brussels agreed at the time to support SADCC and to combine efforts to bring about the end of apartheid.

During the process of ending white supremacy, SADCC became SADC in 1992 and, as Anne Graumans argued, 'South Africa's accession increased SADC's international credibility and made it a sought-after partner to dialogue and cooperate with'.[12] In 1994 the SADC-EU dialogue was institutionalised in ministerial conferences, held every two years. South Africa joined SADC just before the first ministerial conference, in September 1994. There, the 'Berlin Initiative' was launched, setting out objectives and areas of cooperation.

The Berlin Initiative identified the overall objectives of this relationship in the areas of human rights, 'good governance', democracy, and the rule of law. In addition, the two parties agreed to cooperate in international forums, promote economic development and investment, promote trade with, and in, the region, encourage arms reductions, and promote interregional cooperation by fostering contacts in the fields of culture, education, sport, and sociocultural activities. Political dialogue between Brussels and Tshwane now focuses on general matters of foreign policy, especially promoting peace and long-term stability in the Southern African region.[13] (See chapter 13 in this volume.)

Subsequent ministerial conferences have built on the Berlin Initiative and progress has been measured against these objectives. Despite this progress, however, SADC is still far from being considered an effective regional economic community, and its relationship with its most important donor, the EU, has become fraught owing to the EPA negotiations. In order to understand the problems related to the EPAs in Southern Africa, one has to go back to the bilateral negotiations on free trade between the EU and South Africa.

Pursuing bilateral interests: the Trade, Development, and Cooperation Agreement

During the years of the TDCA negotiations (1994–2004), South Africa maintained the position that it could ill afford to be an island of prosperity in a sea of poverty. All foreign policy decisions and directions taken in

Pretoria thus had to take due cognizance of their effects on the rest of Southern Africa. Under the first democratic presidency, of Nelson Mandela, there was also a desire to extend the model of democracy followed in South Africa to other international organisations, key among which was the Southern African Customs Union. As noted earlier, SACU had been established in 1910 at the same time that the Union of South Africa came into being. The organisation was an instrument to allow Botswana, Lesotho, and Swaziland to remain independent while enjoying the economic benefits of South Africa's mineral wealth (Namibia would join SACU at independence in 1990, but had formed part of the territory of SACU as the South African-administered territory). From 1910 to 2002, South Africa dominated SACU and acted without any sanction from the BLNS countries (Botswana, Lesotho, Namibia, and Swaziland). A new, more democratic agreement in 2002 changed all that, and allowed for consensus decisionmaking and the express objective of unified negotiating positions for all future trade negotiations.[14]

Trade negotiations had become a sore case in point, as South Africa was negotiating a free trade agreement with the EU without the active participation of the BLNS countries and without expecting them eventually to become signatories to the deal or to implement its provisions. Of course, this was a technical impossibility, as all imports and exports from the SACU region travel through South Africa (except for a tiny proportion that goes through the Namibian port of Walvis Bay). As a customs union, the five countries should have maintained a common external tariff without any exceptions.

The fact that the BLNS states were not included in the TDCA talks came back to haunt both South Africa and the EU once it became clear that the Lomé Convention of 1975, agreed between Brussels and seventy-nine African, Caribbean, and Pacific (ACP) states, had to be replaced with a trade regime that allowed for reciprocal free trade agreements. (See chapter 2 in this volume.) This meant that the BLNS countries now had to conclude a separate trade agreement with the EU that ideally should have been retrofitted to the TDCA, given the relative weakness of the BLNS economies. This meant that, for the first time in global liberalisation history, tariffs would have to be increased, rather than liberalised. The EPA negotiations have been difficult, protracted, and inconclusive in most parts of the ACP region. They have split SADC and left a major fault line in SACU that could well lead to the collapse of the organisation. So, instead of promoting regional integration, currently EU policies are in fact hampering such integration.[15]

The fault line: the EPAs

With the end of the Lomé Convention in 2000, the EU had to search for alternative avenues towards aligning its trade relationship with the seventy-nine ACP states in relation to World Trade Organisation rules on reciprocity. Given its strong belief in the benefits of regional integration, Brussels seized the opportunity to encourage such integration in the ACP region through the economic partnership agreement negotiations. The EU mandate for the negotiations has focused exclusively on regional approaches to the EPAs. The preamble to Brussels's negotiating mandate refers to 'the commitment of the parties to support the regional integration process with the ACP Group of States and to foster regional integration as a key instrument for the integration of ACP countries into the world economy'.[16]

However, in reality, the negotiating configurations have been far from contributing to regional integration, and are at present rather threatening Southern Africa's regional integration agenda. This aspect of the EPAs alone has created great animosity within Southern Africa: particularly between South Africa and Namibia, on the one hand, and Botswana, Lesotho, and Swaziland, on the other. In addition, a number of public spats between South African and European negotiators have given the impression that the EU-South Africa relationship is on rocky ground.

The situation is extremely complex and has been aggravated by Southern African states belonging to more than one regional integration body. South Africa belongs to both SACU and SADC, while Tanzania belongs to SADC and the East African Community (EAC). Eight SADC member states also participate actively in COMESA. In Southern Africa, only Mozambique belongs to one regional organisation. This situation has been aggravated by the EPA configurations not dovetailing with the regional organisations in Southern Africa. The SADC EPA group contains only seven of the fifteen SADC states, with the remaining eight negotiating either in East and Southern Africa (ESA) or in the EAC configuration. (See chapter 11 in this volume.)

Let us consider this idea: one state can belong to more than one free trade agreement but not to more than one customs union, unless the common external tariff of both organisations is an exact match. A member of a customs union cannot enter into a bilateral free trade agreement, as this would jeopardise the common external tariff of the customs union. Southern Africa has the customs union, SACU, of which all members are part of SADC, which in turn is moving towards establishing a customs union. In addition, South Africa—despite its membership in SACU—has a bilateral free trade agreement with the EU. The SADC EPA configuration in conjunction with the East and Southern Africa EPA configuration, taken in the context of both SADC and COMESA moving towards establishing customs unions, would thus result in a multitude of bilateral EPAs with the EU, which would make it all but impossible to establish effective customs unions in Southern and East Africa.

The biggest challenge for the SADC EPA group has been the question of how to accommodate or be accommodated within the South Africa-EU Trade, Development, and Cooperation Agreement. The EU and South Africa undertook a review of the TDCA at the same time as the SADC-EPA negotiations in order to address some outstanding issues, and to explore ways in which the EPA could be better harmonised with the TDCA. Another challenge is that the group includes four least-developed countries and yet Brussels's relationship with the economic powerhouse of the region, South Africa, is dominating the debate, instead of a focus on the needs of the least-developed countries.

South Africa vehemently objected to the outcome of these negotiations and the draft text of an interim EPA. Although there were a number of concerns, the main objection was to the most-favoured-nation clause, which mandated the SADC EPA group to extend any new trade preferences granted to third parties to the EU.[17] Despite South Africa's clear wish that no SACU state should sign up to the interim EPA on these grounds, Botswana, Lesotho, and Swaziland proceeded to do so. The signing of the interim EPAs (rather than the content itself) enmeshed SACU in a crisis, with talk of the possible collapse of the Union. Furthermore, the interim EPAs and their fraught negotiations also delayed conclusion of the TDCA review beyond February 2011.[18]

Negotiations were continuing towards a full EPA for the SADC EPA group in 2011. Although tempers flared and insiders reported a South African threat to let SACU collapse following the signing of the interim EPA,[19] all parties eventually committed themselves to concluding the talks. A self-imposed deadline of December 2010 was missed, and lingering contentious issues included the most-favoured-nation clause and the rules of origin, according to which the EU still would not allow cumulation with South Africa for products for which Tshwane did not have duty-free and quota-free access to the EU market under the TDCA. Again, the real interests of the least-developed economies in the SADC EPA group were being overshadowed by the South Africa-EU relationship.

There seems, therefore, to be a rhetoric of 'strategic partnership' with regard to the Southern African region by South Africa and the EU, while in actuality, real economic concerns and the 'scramble' by Brussels for an advantageous economic position within the developing economies of Africa have clouded the South Africa-EU relationship, and cast a long shadow over the EU's stated intention to promote regional integration in Southern Africa. The entry of China into profitable trade relations with South Africa, Angola, Zambia, Zimbabwe, and other Southern African states has added another complication to Brussels's actions.[20]

The content of the strategic partnership

Since the adoption of the strategic partnership between South Africa and the EU in 2006, there has been regular dialogue between the two parties, as the table below illustrates (numerous meetings have taken place at the technical level, not captured here). A joint action plan also gives direction to the partnership, which has been reviewed to map progress.

Table 1: South Africa-EUropean Union dialogue, 2006–2011.

June 2006	'Towards a Strategic Partnership' communication from the EU Commission to the Council and Parliament arguing for a strategic partnership with South Africa
May 2007	South Africa-EU Strategic Partnership—Joint Action Plan
October 2007	Second Ministerial Troika
June 2008	Third Ministerial Troika
July 2008	First Summit
January 2009	Fourth Ministerial Troika
September 2009	Progress Report on Joint Action Plan
September 2009	Second Summit
May 2010	Fifth Ministerial Troika
September 2010	Third Summit
September 2011	Fourth Summit

At the third South Africa-EU summit, in Brussels, the two parties again discussed progress compared with the joint action plan and highlighted several agenda items, including development assistance, investment, 'global governance', the Millennium Development Goals (MDGs), climate change, EPAs, and peace and security in Sudan and Zimbabwe. These are all critical issues for South Africa, and they require the political and economic clout of the EU to promote a favourable outcome. A more detailed look at some of these agenda items illustrates the point.

Development assistance, investment, and the Millennium Development Goals

The EU committed 980 million euros to South Africa between 2007 and 2013, making the country the largest recipient of European aid in Southern Africa. In addition, the EU and its twenty-seven member states, in conjunction with the European Investment Bank, annually provide up to 6 million rand to South Africa in grants and loans. At a time when most other large donors are winding down their programmes in South Africa—which they argue is neither a least-developed country nor dependent on aid for its national budget—Brussels is increasing its own spending in line with its identification of South Africa as a strategic partner.

In 1991 the British scholar Christopher Coker argued strongly that 'Southern Africa in general will cease to be of any significant policy relevance for the West by the end of this century. Without apartheid as the rallying call, the region and South Africa itself, loses its significance economically, strategically and morally'.[21] The opposite, however, appears to be true today. Apart from the enormous support for South Africa on a bilateral level, the EU's development aid also accounted for roughly 60 per cent of SADC's budget in 2009. The tenth European Development Fund (EDF) has committed 160 million euros to SADC, which it is hoping to disburse through general budgetary support if the organisation's institutional systems can become effective enough for this.

The South Africa-EU summit held in Brussels in September 2010 discussed the outcome of the UN High-Level Plenary Meeting on the Millennium Development Goals held in New York on 20–22 September 2010 and reiterated the shared commitment of both sides to support the achievement of the MDGs by 2015. Concerns were raised that it is especially in Southern Africa that progress towards the MDG goals has been weakest. A collective approach was thus adopted to promote the MDGs. The summit also discussed the multiple and interrelated global crises, including the financial and economic crisis of 2008–2009, the volatility of energy prices, food insecurity, and the effects of climate change, poverty, and underdevelopment, all of which have had an adverse impact on development gains and threaten to slow down future progress on the MDGs.[22]

In terms of achieving the MDGs, the EU welcomed the establishment of the South African Development Partnership Agency in 2010 'as a platform for EU-South Africa cooperation in supporting the development of the African continent'.[23] Both sides suggested that Brussels and Tshwane would increasingly become involved in trilateral forms of development assistance to Southern Africa. This form of cooperation has recently been welcomed by developing countries, as it enables access to EU funding through an established partner—in this case South Africa—which eases the strict requirements for funding from Brussels.

As recognised during the South Africa-EU TDCA negotiations, Tshwane can ill afford Southern Africa not developing at a pace similar to that of South Africa itself. In this endeavour the South Africans have a strong ally in the Europeans, and their South Africa-EU strategic partnership is assisting in achieving mutual development goals in Southern Africa.

Peace, security, and global governance

In terms of the EU's peace and security agenda, SADC is a major consideration, with joint approaches in the Democratic Republic of the Congo (see chapter 14 in this volume), Swaziland, and Madagascar. Divergent policies and outlooks on Zimbabwe have hampered this cooperation. However, at the South Africa-EU summit in September 2010, Brussels committed itself to lifting sanctions on Zimbabwe 'in case of positive development',[24] indicating that Tshwane's request to Brussels to lift sanctions did not entirely fall on deaf ears. Both South Africa and the EU committed themselves to assisting South Sudan to undertake a successful self-determination referendum in January 2011.

Partners in international forums support each other on key points. Again, arguing for the strategic EU-South Africa partnership, the European Commission put its case thus in June 2006: 'South Africa occupies a unique position on the international scene. On many occasions, it speaks on behalf of the emerging and the developing world. Its authority in international forums is remarkable and surpasses its economic weight'.[25] One of South Africa's objectives is to secure a permanent seat on an expanded United Nations Security Council, an ambition for which it needs EU support, particularly as France and Britain are among the veto-wielding permanent members of the Council (along with the US, Russia, and China). In return, Brussels can rely on South Africa for support in a number of international processes.

At the end of the third bilateral summit, in September 2010, a large section of the communiqué was devoted to global governance with a focus on the UN and the Group of 20 (G20), as well as a focus on climate change negotiations (COP17), which took place in Durban, South Africa, in November–December 2011. Both parties committed themselves to collaborating towards a positive outcome for these global climate talks. This was in line with their original commitment in 2007 to coordinate their policies more effectively in international financial institutions and international forums, including the UN, the World Bank, and the International Monetary Fund (IMF).[26]

The 2011 South Africa-EU Summit

The South Africa-EU summit held on 15 September 2011 in the Kruger National Park saw the two parties drifting further apart on issues of foreign policy, most notably on Zimbabwe and Libya. South Africa pushed for an end to all sanctions imposed on Harare in order to show faith in the unity government, while the EU continued to insist on keeping the assets of President Robert Mugabe and his inner circle frozen, as well as on continuing the travel ban and arms embargo. Further north, South Africa delayed recognizing the new post-Muammar Qaddafi government in Libya while encouraging its AU partners to insist on an inclusive government. Qaddafi's subsequent assassination in October 2011 ended these ambitions and left South Africa wrong-footed as many AU members recognized the National Transitional Council (NTC).

On a more positive note, there was strong concurrence between South Africa and the EU at the September 2011 summit on a joint vision for global climate talks at the UN's COP17 conference, which was convened in Durban in November–December 2011. Whereas globally there was little hope for a strong result coming out of COP17, in terms of the South Africa-EU strategic partnership it was here that one saw most overlap and joint cooperation. In addition to the EU financing a large part of the COP17 conference and South Africa hosting the event, the two parties also committed to push the COP17 agenda at the Rio+20 conference in the Brazilian city of Rio de Janeiro in June 2012. The thrust of this approach was to promote the 'transformation of economies into resource-efficient, low-emission economies leading to the creation of new "green jobs" and further eradication of poverty'.[27]

Concluding reflections

It is difficult to evaluate whether the South Africa-EU 'strategic' partnership is of real strategic value without ever having been offered a working definition by Brussels of what such a partnership should entail. Is this partnership a catalogue of noble ambitions and unfulfilled goals? The term 'strategic partnership' is borrowed from the sphere of business where such partnerships are clearly understood to be formal alliances between two or more commercial enterprises, usually formalised by one or more business contracts, but falling short of forming a legal partnership. The aim of each partnership thus varies according to the needs and ambitions of the parties involved.

This chapter has assessed the evolution of the relationship between South Africa and the EU. Despite many doomsday prophecies about a relationship in decline, in practice the opposite seems to be occurring. There is increasing depth and breadth to the South Africa-EU relationship, with mutually enforcing agendas at the national, regional, and international levels. There have admittedly been a number of hiccups, especially with regard to the SADC EPA negotiations, but even here the two parties are moving closer to resolution with renewed commitments to concluding the negotiations. Differences of opinion on the different approaches by Tshwane and Brussels to the crisis in Zimbabwe have not hampered cooperation in other areas like the situation in South Sudan. With continued support, South Africa can provide regional and continental leadership towards development and stability, which ultimately is the EU's vision for Southern Africa. And this is a strategy worth pursuing.

7

THE EU, THE MAGHREB,
AND THE MEDITERRANEAN

George Joffé

Introduction

We are so accustomed to considering the Sahara desert as a vast and impenetrable expanse, separating North Africa from the rest of the African continent, that we have forgotten the extent to which trade and contact existed across and within the great desert in precolonial times. After all, the great annual pilgrimage to Mecca from West Africa began in Senegal and Mauritania, returning a full year later. The grim salt mines of Taoudenni satisfied demand both in the Sahel and in the Maghreb. From the sixteenth century, the Moroccan sultan claimed suzerainty over Timbuktu. Libyan 'tribes' from Tripolitania and the Fezzan were also to be found in northern Chad, while the Toubou of Tibesti transhumed to Kufra and Sebha.

The sinews of trade had long tied regions north and south of the desert together, as the coastal ports of North Africa provided Europe with both the threat of corsairing and the promise of access to the products of Africa south of the Sahara. For the Arabised and Berberophone populations of the Maghreb—Libya, Tunisia, Algeria, Morocco, and Mauritania (although this chapter does not really focus on Mauritania)—the Sahara was an inland 'sea', crossed by camel caravans bringing gold, salt, ostrich feathers, and slaves northwards. In Libya, at least, this was formalised in the nineteenth century by the proto-state created by the Sanusi Order, reaching from Cyrenaica down into Chad, while in Egypt the Nile provided ready access through Sudan to the Great Lakes.

This was one of the realities that colonialism was to change profoundly with the French invasion of what was to become Algeria in 1830, followed by France's occupation of Tunisia in 1881 and Britain's intervention in Egypt in 1882. Then Italy pushed the Ottomans out of Libya in 1911, starting a twenty-year anticolonial war, while France and Spain jointly took over Morocco in 1912, although their presence was challenged by indigenous resistance up to 1934. Yet although the colonial experience was relatively short, ending in 1951 in Libya, in 1952 in Egypt, in 1956 in Tunisia and Morocco, and in 1962 in Algeria, it had profound effects on both state and society.

One of the most fundamental effects of colonialism was the way in which it diverted the attention of all five North African states (Libya, Egypt, Tunisia, Morocco, and Algeria) onto the Mediterranean and away from the Sahara. Now trade and increasingly migration were directed northwards, and their Sahara dimension decayed. Apart from Egypt, which was to acquire a dominant Middle East role as the centre of its leader Gamal Abdel Nasser's 'Arab Nationalism'—Nasser argued that Egypt was at the centre of three intersecting worlds, the Middle East, Africa, and Islam[1]—the four other Maghrebi states found themselves economically tied to Europe in an ever-tighter embrace, despite their political successes in ending colonial occupation.

Europe and the Maghreb

This history was to prove crucial for the future relationships of Maghrebi states with the European continent, as the latter began to experiment with an innovative political project, the European Economic Community (EEC), later to evolve into the European Union by 1993. (See chapter 3 in this volume.) For former colonial powers, especially France, there remained the question of how their relations with former colonies should be managed within the new European structures that were emerging. Under French pressure, with backing from the Netherlands and Italy, the original Treaty of Rome in 1957 made provision for special relationships between the new Community and other territories that had been previously associated with EEC member states.[2] (See chapter 2 in this volume.)

Thus, under Part IV and Annex VI of the 1957 Treaty of Rome, France's sub-Saharan African and Pacific colonies, together with the Belgian Congo and Rwanda/Burundi as well as minor Dutch, Italian, and British territories, were able to enjoy the same trading relations with the EEC as its member states. This agreement was to lead eventually, in 1963 and 1969, to the six-year Yaoundé Accords for eighteen former African colonies and then, in 1975, to the Lomé Conventions for the African, Caribbean, and Pacific countries. The provisions for the Maghreb were quite different and came under Protocol VI of the Treaty of Rome. They also applied to the Benelux countries (Belgium, the Netherlands, and Luxembourg) as far as Surinam and the Dutch Antilles were concerned; to France's territories in Indochina and the New Hebrides; and to former Italian territories in Libya and Somaliland, although not all these instruments were brought into force.

These provisions ensured that the metropolitan customs arrangements previously in force for imports from colonies or former colonies to their former imperial rulers remained in force, despite the general provisions of the 1957 Treaty of Rome. Although former colonies maintained the preferences they had enjoyed, they were worse off than the future Lomé countries, since they were still excluded from the markets of other EEC states. It was clear that this situation would eventually become untenable. However, for the two major countries involved, Morocco and Tunisia, no action could be contemplated until France's colonial presence in Algeria had ended, which occurred in 1962.

Thus, in 1963, a few months after Algeria became independent, the Maghreb countries began to push for revised and more advantageous economic relations with Europe. By 1969 Brussels was ready to offer them five-year association agreements that largely corrected the discrimination inherent in the 1957 protocol. The new agreements allowed for industrial goods to enter the European economic space tariff-free, except for cork (to protect Sardinian production) and coal and steel (because of the provisions of the European Coal and Steel Community created in 1951). There was a similar reverse preference for European industrial goods not produced in North Africa, and agricultural exports were placed under a selective tariff regime for products not already produced in Europe under the EU's Common Agricultural Policy. (See chapter 12 in this volume.) Despite these restrictions, however, it was calculated that, during the 1970s, up to 50 per cent of Moroccan and 70 per cent of Tunisian agricultural exports still made their way into Europe.[3] Finally, France was able to retain all its preferential customs import regimes with the Maghreb, as laid down under the original 1957 protocol.[4] The association-agreement model was to last up to 1976, two years beyond the original time limit for the agreements.

Two features stood out as a result of the first two decades of the Community's relationships with North Africa, between 1963 and 1983. The first was that they followed directly from North Africa's colonial experience, thus entrenching the region's Mediterranean dimension and confirming its separateness from sub-Saharan Africa. Hence the agreements were exclusively economic in nature, reflecting the underlying principles of the EEC itself, as well as one aspect of the prevailing climate of international affairs with respect to economic development.

The second feature was that, at this stage, there appears to have been no attempt to create wider political or security links across the Mediterranean, even though the EEC was aggressively committed to the West in the Cold War through the parallel alliance of the North Atlantic Treaty Organisation (NATO), to which all of its members at the time belonged. Instead, what political links there were reflected France's own bilateral neopaternalist policies towards its former colonies, whether they were acknowledged pro-Western allies, such as Tunisia and Morocco, or leaders in the Non-Aligned Movement, such as Algeria. (See chapters 2 and 16 in this volume.)

Libya under the leadership of Muammar Qaddafi, in the aftermath of the 1969 'Great September Revolution', was already set on its course as a maverick Arab nationalist and anti-imperialist state increasingly at odds with the West, until the shock of the American attack under the regime of Ronald Reagan on Tripoli and Benghazi in April 1986 gradually redirected Tripoli towards revived diplomatic links with Europe and, eventually, the United States.[5] Yet Europe continued to be curiously indulgent towards Libya and Algeria, both of which spurned close links with their former European colonial powers, Italy and France. No doubt this was because both were also major oil producers, and in the case of Algeria a major gas producer too, with Europe as a significant market for both products. Although Tripoli and Algiers nationalised or partly nationalised their hydrocarbon industries in the 1970s, they were still important suppliers to European states such as France and Germany.

Europe's Mediterranean policies

By the beginning of the 1970s, however, Europe's attitudes towards its own external relations had begun to change. By 1970, European leaders had recognised the need for some form of forum over foreign policy, and built it into the process of European political cooperation, with a first meeting of foreign ministers held in November 1970.[6] In the Mediterranean, this was reflected in the gradual abandonment of bilateralism in defining north-south relations, and the adoption instead of a vision of the Mediterranean as a single unified region, codified as the Global Mediterranean Policy.

In parallel, after the 1973 Arab-Israeli War, the European Policy Cooperation instrument was used as the umbrella for the Euro-Arab Dialogue with the Arab world and in the Eastern Mediterranean—the Levant, together with Egypt and Turkey. For Europeans, the purpose of this forum was to regularise relations to avoid future perturbations in oil supply, although Arab states sought to politicise the dialogue as a platform for discussion of the Palestinian issue. As a result of the Global Mediterranean Policy, however, Brussels began to negotiate a new set of agreements with South Mediterranean states, all based on similar, generic provisions. By 1972, France, under the presidency of Georges Pompidou, was proposing the creation of a free trade area between Europe and all the South Mediterranean states.[7]

Although this was an idea ahead of its time, it did result in the negotiation of a new series of cooperation agreements with North African and Eastern Mediterranean states. The new agreements were similar to their predecessors, preserving the tariff-free access to the European market for manufactured goods, but now introduced annually reviewed quotas—North African textiles, in particular, were to benefit from this. In the agricultural sector, the same provisions were retained—to be renegotiated to North Africa's disadvantage, ten years later, when Spain and Portugal became members of the European Community (EC) in 1986, and the EC became self-sufficient in agricultural products. Unrestricted access for primary mineral exports continued unabated.

The new agreements, which were negotiated and signed in 1976, came into force in 1978, and were renewed in 1981 and 1986 for five-year periods each time. For the first time, too, the agreements were accompanied by financial protocols. These were intended to modernise and diversify the agricultural and industrial sectors of North African states in a positive initiative to stimulate economic growth there, rather than to preserve former colonial preferences that were now expanded to the whole of the European Community. This new objective of Brussels, tied already to the new European aim of reducing the threat of migration into Europe by stimulating

economic development in countries of origin, became increasingly important over time, as the four protocols in 1978, 1982, 1987, and 1992 were
to demonstrate.

By the end of the 1980s, it was evident that the tensions created by the
Cold War, both in Europe and in the Mediterranean region, were approaching their end. At the same time, European leaders, particularly in Germany
and France, were beginning to rethink what the European ideal should be,
and how the European project itself should evolve. Despite British prime
minister Margaret Thatcher's Euro-sceptic speech at the College of Europe
in Bruges in September 1988, decrying attempts at further integrating
Europe politically, this was the general trend in European policy planning.
It was to be reflected, five years later, in the 1992 Maastricht Treaty, which
came into force in 1993. Maastricht created the European Union and its
three integrated policy pillars—the Single Market, integrated Justice and
Home Affairs, and the Common Foreign and Security Policy (CFSP).

By that time, of course, the Cold War had ended, the Soviet Union had
disappeared from the map of the world, and, in 1991, the European Union's
Global Mediterranean Policy had been replaced by the Renovated Mediterranean Policy—which now, on the basis of European expansion to include
Spain and Portugal in 1986, provided for regional funding to the Mediterranean, alongside the bilateral funding initiated in 1976. This approach was
designed to improve regional infrastructure and thereby regional cooperation in the South. In the event, the new policy turned out to be an interim
measure on the way to a much more ambitious and comprehensive restate-
ment of relations between the two sides of the Mediterranean.

The Euro-Mediterranean Partnership

The new policy, which emerged in 1995 as the first major achievement of
the EU's Common Foreign and Security Policy, was the product of three
different developments on the international scene. One was that, with the
entry of Spain and Portugal into the European Community in 1986, alongside France and Italy and, to a lesser extent Greece, there was now a much
larger constituency anxious to push the importance of the Mediterranean
region as a foreign policy arena in Brussels. As the Italian scholar Frederica
Bicchi points out, this created tensions over Mediterranean policy as to
whether it was intended to encompass all of the European Union, or only
the subregion formed by the northern littoral states of the Mediterranean

itself.[8] Further tensions arose over whether the real object of European policy in the Mediterranean should be the whole of the southern littoral or merely the Maghreb: France's old colonial stomping ground.

Allied to these conceptual challenges were the consequences of the end of the Cold War itself and the collapse of the Soviet Union in 1991, which meant that security threats from the East began to subside markedly inside Europe. The Mediterranean, in contrast, rose significantly within the European perception of threats and partnerships. Allied to that was a new sense of potential for the European Union in a world dominated by a sole 'hyperpower', the United States, increasingly described in terms of 'geo-economics' and the global economy rather than the geopolitics of confrontation.[9] Europe, after all, had by then reified its self-image into that of a 'normative power' (see chapter 22 in this volume),[10] and issues such as 'good governance' and respect for human rights had joined economic development in the desiderata that now defined the conscious objectives of Brussels's common foreign policy.[11] (See chapter 13 in this volume.)

The new Mediterranean policy itself was therefore to be an amalgam of two previous policy initiatives. This was allied to a new concern caused by the increasingly fractious European internal discourse on 'social inclusion' as a result of the development of permanent 'minority' communities arising from migration into Europe, principally from North Africa and Turkey, over the previous four decades. (See chapter 20 in this volume.) The first of the two main drivers, however, was the construction of the European project itself—driven by a desire to end violent confrontation between France and Germany, which had poisoned the continent's history for at least a century—predicated on economic integration as the necessary first step.

The second catalyst of the new Mediterranean policy was the experience of the Helsinki conference in 1975—the Conference on Security and Cooperation in Europe (CSCE)—at the height of the period of détente between East and West, which had led to the adoption of principles of confidence-building and cooperation on governance and human rights, as a means of dissipating Cold War tensions in Europe. This was refashioned in 1990, in a famous Spanish and Italian 'non-paper', into Italian foreign minister Gianni de Michelis's ambitious project for a conference on cooperation and security in the Mediterranean.[12]

Although this initiative was soon overshadowed by Iraq's invasion of Kuwait in August 1990 and the subsequent Multinational Coalition's war to force Saddam Hussein to abandon his conquest by February 1991, the idea was to reemerge in a more restricted form five years later in the new European policy for the Mediterranean proposed at a conference held in the Spanish city of Barcelona in November 1995. This was to be the Euro-Mediterranean Partnership, better known, perhaps, as the Barcelona Process. Its proclaimed objective was to create 'an area of dialogue, exchange and cooperation guaranteeing peace, stability and prosperity' in the Mediterranean basin.[13] Its tools were to be bilateral free trade area agreements, set within two multilateral policy frames: one for political and security issues, and the other to address social and cultural matters.

As with previous agreements, the economic dimension predominated, with the new bilateral partnership agreements deriving from their predecessors. They, however, differed from past accords in that although they concentrated as in the past on the industrial sectors of the new partner countries, they now required reciprocal free trade in industrial goods, with tariff barriers removed progressively over a fifteen-year period. The rationale of this approach was that only in this way could real restructuring take place, as a result of unhindered market competition. The new Mesures d'Ajustement (MEDA) financial protocols were, in part, designed to help with financing of the process of restructuring, given that, for example, in Tunisia, up to two-thirds of all industrial enterprises faced extinction without such help. As it was, a third of Tunisia's industrial plant was expected to disappear under the new agreement, as was 60 per cent of the industrial sector in Morocco. Agriculture, as in the past, remained constricted, although promises were made to discuss a new regime after 2000.

The new economic regime of the decade of the 2000s was, of course, founded squarely on the neoliberal economic principles of the 'Washington Consensus', which had governed the process of economic restructuring worldwide for the previous fifteen years. This was paralleled by new demands for democratic governance and respect for human rights within the framework of the rule of law. One reason for this, quite apart from the new international climate on governance, was a belief held by the Bretton Woods institutions—the World Bank and the International Monetary Fund (IMF)—that political institution-building was an essential part of the process of economic restructuring in order to ensure accountability and transparency. Indeed, a statement of these demands headed every partnership agreement signed by Brussels with South Mediterranean states as the partnership process evolved.

Moreover, behind this complex and sophisticated politico-economic programme lay an acute European security concern: to impede the growing flood of economic migrants onto the continent, alongside an equally worrying growth in demands for political asylum in European states. (See chapter 20 in this volume.) Economic development, it was argued, would obviate the need for economic migration, while 'good governance' would render political asylum in Europe unnecessary. Allied to this thinking were other security concerns as far as the Mediterranean was concerned, such as terrorism, proliferation of weapons of mass destruction, people-smuggling and drug-smuggling, and other international crimes.

This approach formed the essence of the multilateral security basket of measures, and was partnered in the third basket of measures by attempts to counter xenophobia in Europe and to improve civil society in the Maghreb and the Mashrek—the countries of the Arab Middle East, the Levant, and the Gulf, as well as Egypt—through confidence-building measures. Sadly, none of these policies was to advance very far; the first set was blocked in 2000 when the Arab-Israeli dispute made it impossible for partner-states to agree on a charter for stability and security in the Mediterranean, and the second because North African states (except for Morocco) were not prepared to tolerate European interference in their domestic affairs.

Ten years later, by the time of the review conference in Barcelona in November 2005, it was clear that the ambitious process had run into the sand. There were three key reasons for this: first, the question of 'ownership'; second, the apparent failure of the economic dimension; and third, the terrorist attacks on New York and Washington, DC on 11 September 2001. Allied to these three factors was the fact that, in December 2002, the United States had produced its own version of partnership in the form of the US Middle East Partnership Initiative (USMEPI), which in 2004 was to be folded into the Broader Middle East Initiative proclaimed by President George W. Bush at the Sea Island Group of Eight (G8) meeting in the US that year. In addition, partly in response to this initiative, and partly due to the successful process of accession by Eastern European states into the European Union, the European Commission foisted a new bilateral policy—the European Neighbourhood Policy—onto the Euro-Mediterranean Partnership in May 2004, thereby hastening its virtual demise.

The issue of ownership is complex. It reflects the fact that the Euro-Mediterranean Partnership was an entirely European initiative to which the southern partners were not able to make any significant contribution. (This was not unlike the EU Africa Strategy of 2007 that had also been unilaterally dreamed up in Brussels—see chapters 1 and 5 in this volume.) The

Euro-Mediterranean plan was presented to the EU's 'partners' as a complete package, created largely through French and Spanish initiative with Italian backing,[14] thus underlining both the internal split within the European Union and the external East-West divide along the Mediterranean basin between the northern European littoral and the Maghreb. More than that, southern states felt, correctly, that they had little choice but to accept it—as Tunisia and Morocco did with enthusiasm, while Algeria was much less keen, regarding the policy as an implicit attack on its sovereignty.

This problem did not arise for Libya though, because it had been excluded from the process as a result of Western-led United Nations economic and travel sanctions against it in 1992 over the Lockerbie affair, in which an American airliner was destroyed by a bomb over the Scottish town of Lockerbie in December 1988. Yet by the time that Tripoli escaped from the sanctions regime in 1999, it was in no hurry to join the Euro-Mediterranean Partnership. Instead Libya had to be lured into the body by Brussels as an 'observer'. Muammar Qaddafi, however, continued to reject the policy because of the political interference it implied. Instead the European Commission agreed to negotiate a separate 'framework agreement' to overcome Libyan sensitivities.

There was another side to the question of ownership. Since the Euro-Mediterranean Partnership was an initiative from Brussels, it was managed by the European Commission. The result was that this became an intensely bureaucratic operation, controlled directly by Europeans in all respects. This paternalistic approach further alienated southern states from the initiative, particularly as they felt that the EU had little interest in what they regarded as key economic issues—agriculture, for instance—and did not appreciate the very real security dangers that they faced. Algeria, for example, had fought a veritable civil war throughout the 1990s in which over 100,000 people perished, and violence continued at a diminishing rate into the first decade of the twenty-first century. Libya had faced down an incipient rebellion in Cyrenaica in the latter part of the 1990s. These North African regimes felt that Europe did not appreciate the security challenges they faced, but instead criticised them over human rights and governance issues while protecting their enemies through granting them political asylum in Europe.[15]

European attitudes, however, changed dramatically in September 2001. As a result of the terrorist attacks on the United States, European external policy—particularly in the Mediterranean—was radically securitised, both at the level of the EU and by individual European states. In consequence, Europe's claims to be a 'normative power' (see chapter 22 in this volume) were implicitly abandoned, and the arguments of the South Mediterranean over the threat of transnational violence from Salafi-Jihadism were adopted instead. Rhetorical calls for 'good governance' and respect for human rights in the South were soon replaced by intensive intergovernmental and transgovernmental cooperation over security issues.[16] In effect, the European Union abandoned the political dimension of the Euro-Mediterranean Partnership, while the security dimension had been blocked by the Arab-Israeli dispute the year before.

The greatest failure of this development, however, arose from the most complex element within the partnership: the economic dimension. The bilateral free trade area agreements had been predicated on two key assumptions. The first was that through economic restructuring under the pressure of intense competition, South Mediterranean economies would become far more efficient; thus they would attract direct private foreign investment, which in turn would boost economic development. This failed to happen, largely because the South Mediterranean offered international investors little comparative advantage over regions such as the Far East and China. As a result, the expected foreign investment did not arrive in the amounts that had been anticipated, and there was thus no spurt of domestic growth.

Second, an essential objective of the free trade agreements was to persuade South Mediterranean states to amalgamate their economies and thus benefit from economies of scale and competivity (an old dream in the Maghreb)[17] while simultaneously overcoming European dominance in Mediterranean economic affairs. The attempt at a federation in the Arab Maghreb Union (AMU), which was created in the Moroccan city of Marrakesh in 1989, had been rendered moribund as a result of the Libyan and Western Sahara crises. However, it was hoped that new integrative structures would emerge, for example under the Agadir Agreement of 1997. This brought together Morocco, Tunisia, Egypt, and Jordan in a putative common market, but even this initiative was stillborn. Yet without market integration, the South Mediterranean would never escape from domination by the vast European market, while its own domestic markets remained too small for endogenous growth.

The European Neighbourhood and Partnership Instrument

Quite apart from these problems, however, the decision in 2004 to introduce the European Neighbourhood Policy began a process of marginalisation of the Euro-Mediterranean Partnership. As mentioned, this had occurred partly in response to European anxiety about the introduction of the Middle East Partnership Initiative by the United States, itself a response to Washington's exclusion from the Barcelona Process at French behest in 1995. The problem with the American initiative was simply that it now offered South Mediterranean states, given their sense of exclusion from the management and ownership of the Euro-Mediterranean Partnership, an alternative that could also be used as a lever against European domination. This was certainly a concern within the presidency of the European Commission, although the formal justification for the new policy was to create 'a circle of friends' in the wake of the 2004 Accession Process, situated around Europe's borders—both East and South—and made up of states that could not anticipate membership in the European Union, but sought close relations with it.

In essence, the European Neighbourhood Policy offered surrounding states the closest possible association with the European Union without them acquiring legislative or executive power, in a relationship akin to membership in the European Economic Area created for the old European Free Trade Area (EFTA) countries of Iceland, Norway, and Switzerland. These goals were to be achieved through a series of bilateral arrangements between the EU and each individual country, whereby a programme of measures would be jointly defined to enable the country concerned to align its policies and institutions with Brussels's *acquis*.[18] These measures, proposed by countries concerned with EU agreements in a kind of positive conditionality, would be contained in a three- to five-year action plan, which would be reviewed annually. Progress made in fulfilling the agreed measures would then determine the degree to which the country concerned could access the EU's institutions, particularly the Single Market.[19]

What was not clear was the relationship between the European Neighbourhood Policy and the Euro-Mediterranean Partnership. This was supposed to be clarified in 2007, when the two policies were combined into a new financial initiative—the European Neighbourhood and Partnership Instrument (ENPI)—which replaced the old MEDA funding programme. In part, this initiative was an attempt to unify policy concerning Europe's relations with the states along its eastern borders (Moldova, Ukraine, and the Transcaucasian states) with its Mediterranean policies, excluding the Balkans. However, it was based on the postulate that Europe would be the centre of policy attention in a hub-and-spokes arrangement, which the integrative and holistic dimension of the Euro-Mediterranean Partnership had been designed to avoid. It was also difficult to define the precise relationship between the partnership agreements, which were the economic dimension of the Euro-Mediterranean Partnership, and the new action plans. The former were to remain in force, being supplemented by the action plans, which also reached into the political and social arenas covering issues of governance, civil society, and human rights.

The Union for the Mediterranean

Even as the new European Neighbourhood and Partnership Instrument was being formulated, yet another policy for the Mediterranean was being developed. This initiative was the brainchild of French presidential candidate Nicolas Sarkozy and his speechwriter and special adviser, Henri Guaino, who proposed the creation of a Mediterranean Union. This scheme was supposed to bring together the littoral states of the Mediterranean, thereby reifying the long-standing tension within the European Union over the Mediterranean, between Europe's southern states and the northern states, which traditionally had been more concerned about threats and security in the east of the continent. The new initiative proposed that Europe's traditional Mediterranean dimension should become the driver of a new union of states designed to promote common economic and cultural objectives in a structure of 'co-ownership' in which states along both littorals would share the process of management and control.

Northern European states did not take kindly to their proposed exclusion from the new initiative and, at the founding conference of the Mediterranean Union in July 2008, a year after Sarkozy won France's presidential election, Germany made it clear that European unity was still the predominant feature of European policy. In an implicit rebuff to Paris's attempt to reassert its leadership against hegemony from Berlin, the German chancellor, Angela Merkel, insisted that the new policy—shorn of many of its features such as a Mediterranean development bank—should be folded into the Euro-Mediterranean Partnership, now to be known as the Union for the Mediterranean. The body would promote regional projects through private sector financing and avoid the normative language of the original policy that had so irritated South Mediterranean states. It would also ensure that the principle of 'co-ownership' was respected. As the European Commission website suggested:

Some of the most important innovations of the Union for the Mediterranean include the rotating co-presidency with one EU president and one president representing the Mediterranean partners, and a Secretariat based in Barcelona that is responsible for identifying and promoting projects of regional, sub-regional and transnational value across different sectors.[20]

The Union for the Mediterranean has also identified six priority projects that are at the heart of the of partnership's efforts: de-pollution of the Mediterranean Sea; the establishment of maritime and land highways; civil protection initiatives to combat natural and human-made disasters; a Mediterranean solar energy plan; the inauguration of the Euro-Mediterranean University in Slovenia; and the Mediterranean Business Development Initiative, which is to focus on micro, small, and medium-sized enterprises.[21]

Concluding reflections

So, what is one to make of the Euro-Mediterranean Partnership? In theory, the initiative is still in force, now buried below two other layers of policy with which it is, in theory, considered to be compatible. However, the survival of its underlying principles—the creation of an integrated southern market; the installation of normative values of 'good governance', civil society, and respect for human rights; and the creation of a shared zone of peace, prosperity, and stability, based on the principles of Helsinki and the normative power of the European Union—seems to be much less certain. In theory, the European Neighbourhood Policy preserves the normative values considered so important fifteen years earlier. But the action plans have been constructed by neighbouring states and reflect their priorities, not those of the EU. They are also reinforced by positive conditionality in terms of the degree to which the states concerned approach the European ideal, not by the negative conditionality implicit in the Euro-Mediterranean Partnership, where sanctions, in theory, awaited those who ignored their responsibility for political reform.

It is true, of course, that the principle of 'co-ownership' is now enshrined within the Union for the Mediterranean, albeit at the price of no mention of the body's normative values. However, the issue of co-ownership has already run up against the key problem that has bedevilled all previous European attempts to establish collective and cooperative security in the Mediterranean: the Arab-Israeli conflict. In effect, therefore, even the principle of co-ownership seems to be suspended because of the failure of the

Middle East peace process, just as occurred with the Euro-Mediterranean Partnership's attempt to develop a charter for security and stability in the Mediterranean in 2000. And that, of course, can only be unravelled by American intervention, a good demonstration—if one were needed—of the degree to which European external policy initiatives still depend on a trans-atlantic relationship in which Europe has often acquiesced in its junior role.

It is also true that the tensions inherent in the north-south divide in Europe appear to have been resolved by Germany's decisive intervention in July 2008. Now the EU will act with one voice towards the Mediterranean, even if the complexity of its policies may render them ultimately ineffective. It is true, too, that North African states have gained a degree of autonomy from their former colonial masters and from the more onerous aspects of Europe's normative power, as realism has reasserted itself in international affairs. But the possibility of a genuine partnership across the Mediterra-nean seems to have been lost in the welter of ill-thought-out policy initia-tives that have developed since 1995. However, given the dramatic events in the Middle East and North Africa since the beginning of 2011, there are already hints that change may be on its way.

The original situation reflected the problems between east and west among South Mediterranean states, as typified by the moribund Middle East peace process in 2011. The imperatives that drive the states of the Maghreb in this respect are very different from those that propel the coun-tries in the Middle East. It has therefore been suggested that European policy should reflect this difference. The potential for success in Euro-Maghribi relations should thus not be aborted by the problems of the Mid-dle East. It was, after all, this assumption that had driven the '5+5' talks in the 1990s, and there is a growing constituency in Southern Europe that continues to argue for the creation of a Western Mediterranean community. Such a body would bring together North Africa—the Maghreb together, possibly, with Egypt—and the EU, in which the principles of the Barcelona Process could be applied. The problem with this approach, of course, is that this would be very far from the original Barcelona ideal of an amalgamated security community[22] in the Mediterranean, guided by the principles of European normative power and economic prosperity.

In any case the sudden and unexpected explosions of popular anger in Tunisia, Egypt, and latterly Libya at the start of 2011 have challenged all the assumptions underlying Europe's regional policies. Although economic hardship sparked off a series of demonstrations at the end of 2010, it was the contempt and arrogance shown by North African regimes that transformed the demonstrations into veritable revolutions in Tunisia and Egypt, which toppled the thirty-year rule of Hosni Mubarak and the two-decade rule of Ben Ali. In Libya, this situation created a civil war that toppled the forty-two-year rule of Muammar Qaddafi, who was killed in Sirte in October 2011. Algeria and Morocco avoided similar outcomes only by astute compromises with their domestic oppositions and because, in the case of Morocco, the legitimacy of the monarchy protected it from popular anger. The problem for the European Union is that its normative policies have, in practice, been predicated on regime stability in the South Mediterranean, as a bulwark against political Islam, as well as on the appropriateness of neoliberal economic restructuring as a guarantee against labour migration to Europe.

Now both policies have been shown to have been misguided—political Islam played no part in the North African demonstrations, whether for economic or political change, and the entrenched poverty of the region demonstrated the ineffectiveness of Europe's economic vision as well. Even though European politicians, quite misguidedly and against all available evidence, persist in believing in the Islamic 'threat' and ignore the demand from youth throughout the region for employment, either through development or migration, they also know that they will have to rethink—yet again—their partnership with South Mediterranean states. The problem is that, so far, the EU lacks a coherent vision of what to do, and in that failure lies the danger of the instability that its members fear, with the threat of regional extremism born of massive frustration, and a renewed and intensified wave of migration directed at Europe's own shores. European policy towards the Mediterranean, in short, needs to be radically restructured and redefined. It remains to be seen if Europe's politicians are capable of meeting the demands now placed upon them.

8

THE EU AND ASIA

LESSONS FOR AFRICA?

Shada Islam

Introduction

The European Union has since 2000 engaged in a vigorous drive to expand and deepen political, security, and economic relations with countries in its immediate neighbourhood, but also further afield in Asia and Africa. The focus has been on forging partnerships with key nations—for example China, India, and South Africa—as well as building links with regional cooperation organisations such as the Association of Southeast Asian Nations (ASEAN)[1] and the African Union. Ties have also been expanded with African regional organisations such as the Economic Community of West African States (ECOWAS) and the Southern African Development Community (SADC). In Asia, the process of Asia-Europe Meetings (ASEM), launched in Bangkok, Thailand, in 1996, provides an even wider framework for developing stronger relations between the two continents.

While the period from 2000 to 2010 put the EU in the spotlight as a global player, with an extensive network of friends and allies across the world, the Union's international profile stretches back to the 1970s, when it negotiated the first Lomé Convention,[2] on trade and aid cooperation, with a group of African, Caribbean, and Pacific (ACP) states, originally forty-six in 1975, then sixty-nine by the time of Lomé IV in 1990, and seventy-nine by the time of the Cotonou Agreement in 2000 (see chapter 2 in this volume). Similar accords were sealed in the following years with ASEAN,[3] India,[4] and China.[5] These agreements were limited in both scope and content, however, with the focus essentially on trade cooperation and development aid. Political issues, including human rights and security concerns, either were excluded from the agreements or were not central to them.

In contrast, the new agreements negotiated with Asian and African countries in the new millennium reflect Europe's determination to take on an active diplomatic and political role in a rapidly transforming, multipolar world. These accords highlight a growing awareness on the EU's part of the need to anticipate and respond effectively to new security threats and dangers, including global terrorism. Many of the strategic partnership agreements concluded with Asia and Africa either preceded or followed the groundbreaking European Security Strategy,[6] adopted by EU governments in December 2003. In this blueprint, issued in the wake of deep differences in Europe over the United States-led invasion of Iraq in 2003, European leaders sought to highlight four key points: first, the EU's willingness to take on global responsibilities to tackle a range of problems, including global poverty and disease, terrorism, and the proliferation of weapons of mass destruction; second, a commitment to forging 'strategic partnerships' with key countries such as the United States, Canada, Japan, China, and India, as well as with the United Nations and other international and regional organisations to ensure peace and security and tackle both immediate and 'distant threats'; third, a determination to become an ethical and normative power striving to strengthen global governance by exporting its values—democracy, human rights, rule of law, and free markets—to other nations (see chapter 22 in this volume); and finally the use of 'soft power'[7] to spread these values—though the document also highlighted the need to develop a 'strategic culture that fosters early, rapid, and when necessary robust intervention', including the deployment of military operations, especially under a United Nations mandate.

An update of the EU security doctrine, in December 2008, carried the argument in favour of an expanded European global role even further. 'The EU carries greater responsibilities than at any time in history', the document insisted, adding: 'To ensure our security and meet the expectations of our citizens, we must be ready to shape events. That means becoming more strategic in our thinking and more effective and visible around the world'.[8]

This chapter takes a closer look at the EU's strategic partnership agreements with Asia, drawing attention to the political and economic reasons for Europe's interest in the region, key EU objectives in seeking closer relations with Asian countries and regional organisations, and the challenges and obstacles that could hamper the realisation of these goals. I argue that Europe's interest in Asia is due to the region's growing economic weight, as well as the realisation that the EU can not gain recognition as a global player without stronger engagement with countries such as China and India or in regional organisations such as ASEAN. Significantly also, Brussels's interest in Asia is due at least partly to transatlantic rivalries and a sentiment that Europe cannot allow its economic and political interests in Asia to be displaced by the US—or China. Finally, the chapter examines the lessons that African countries can draw from the EU-Asian strategic partnerships.

EU strategic partnerships: myths and realities

European governments, eager to give substance to the 2003 security doctrine, were quick to conclude strategic partnership agreements with China and India in the following year. At the same time, a strategic partnership pact was signed with South Africa in 2006 (see chapter 6 in this volume), and a year later, at the EU-Africa summit in Lisbon in 2007, European and African leaders adopted a strategic partnership setting out a shared vision between both continents and set of common principles. This document was reviewed at the Africa-EU summit in Tripoli in November 2010.

These agreements have sought to help dispel the long-standing worldview of the EU as an economic giant but a political dwarf. Meanwhile, countries 'chosen' as the organisation's strategic partners tend to view their new status with pride, believing that a pact with Brussels is a recognition of their growing global geostrategic clout and standing. However, although these accords have helped bolster the EU's global profile, the strategic partnerships have yet to fulfil their full potential as powerful multinational tools for tackling common challenges in practice. (See chapters 6 and 7 in this volume).

The EU's strategic partnerships suffer from several further weaknesses. For one, they are signed with countries that—depending on the issue at stake—can, at the same time, be partners, competitors, and even adversaries. European policymakers have therefore been torn between their desire to engage fully with these countries and fears about their role as economic and political rivals. As a result, one of the key aims of the partnerships—a rapprochement of views between Brussels and its strategic allies on crucial global challenges such as climate change—has not been achieved.

Second, despite some progress in recent years, the twenty-seven-member European Union remains constrained by its failure to speak with one voice on key political issues. The EU's repeated failures in the 1990s to broker peace between the warring parties as Yugoslavia disintegrated, followed by deep divisions within the Union over the war in Iraq in 2003, have been two potent reasons for Europe's reputation as a weak political actor. The EU's continuing inability to coordinate its stance on issues as diverse as the Middle East conflict and relations with Russia and China has further consolidated the image of the Union as a group of twenty-seven fractious and divided states.

Third, there still remains a vacuum at the top of the EU foreign policy hierarchy. The British politician Catherine Ashton was appointed as the first-ever EU foreign minister alongside the former Belgian prime minister Herman Van Rompuy, who assumed the three-year presidency of the European Council in January 2010.

Finally, despite slow and steady progress in building a defence and military identity independent of the North Atlantic Treaty Organisation (NATO), Europe's focus has largely remained on its 'soft power' tools of trade, aid, and diplomacy rather than on the use of 'hard' military power to project its influence. (A notable exception was the NATO intervention in Libya in 2011 led by France and Britain.) Many of the EU's foreign partners, more accustomed to dealing with 'real' military players, have therefore failed properly to understand Brussels's increasing 'strategic' security approach.

Asia tops EU list of priority strategic partners

The EU's first attempt to set a modern, strategic framework for its relations with Asia as a whole, rather than with individual Asian nations, dated back to 1994, when the European Commission, prodded by Germany, made a case for stronger engagement with the economically vibrant Asian continent.[9] The outcome represented an important reversal in EU perceptions of Asia, a continent once seen as too far, too big, and too poor. European leaders attempted to take a hard look at the benefits for the EU of participating in the economic transformation taking place in many Asian countries. The emphasis at the time was also on countering Japanese and American influence in the region, and a feeling that building closer bonds with Asia's 'Tiger' economies, such as South Korea, Singapore, Malaysia, Indonesia, and Taiwan, was important for consolidating Europe's leading role in the world.

Publication of the new EU strategy was followed two years later with the launch of the first Asia Europe Meeting[10] in Bangkok in 1996. This occurred at a first-ever Europe-Asia summit marked by pledges of cooperation on political, economic, and cultural issues. The euphoria, however, did not last long. Asian economies were soon hit by a devastating financial crisis in 1997, and many in the region expressed disappointment at the EU's failure to come to their rescue. ASEM did manage to survive the storm, but only just. Marking a new turning point in the relationship, and a new recognition of Europe-Asia interdependence, the ASEM summit held in the Chinese capital of Beijing in October 2008 was dominated by fears of global recession. This time, however, making a plea for joint action to rebuild global financial and economic structures, the president of the European Commission, José Manuel Barroso, noted: 'We swim together, or we sink together'.[11]

Key EU objectives in Asia

Taking the EU-Asia relationship to a higher, more intense level, the European Commission's 2001 document "Europe and Asia: A Strategic Framework for Enhanced Partnerships"[12] set out six key EU objectives in Asia: first, to contribute to peace and security in the region; second, to strengthen further mutual trade and investment flows with the region, and reinforce dialogue on economic and financial policies; third, to promote the development of the less prosperous countries of the region, and address the root causes of poverty; fourth, to contribute to the protection of human rights and to spreading democracy, 'good governance', and the rule of law; fifth, to build global partnerships and alliances with Asian countries in appropriate international forums, to help address both the challenges and the opportunities offered by globalisation, and to strengthen joint efforts on global environmental and security issues like climate change, migration, and terrorism; and finally, to help strengthen the awareness of Europe in Asia.

The 2001 document further stressed that the EU must focus on strengthening its political and economic presence across Asia with a view to 'raising this to a level commensurate with the growing global weight of an enlarged EU'. Brussels insisted that it was time to move from a strategy based on 'aid and trade' towards recognition of the importance of a rapidly developing Asia. Significantly, the European Commission also noted that Asian countries were crucial and political partners for the EU, but at the same time noted that the importance for Asia of a partnership of equality in addressing both opportunities and challenges arising from globalisation had to be underlined.[13]

In practical terms, EU efforts in Asia have focused on three priority areas: first, support to regional integration, in which the key dialogue partners have been identified as ASEM, ASEAN, the Asian Regional Forum (ARF), and the South Asian Association for Regional Cooperation (SAARC); second, cooperation in areas such as the environment, energy and climate change, higher education (including support for research institutes and cross-border cooperation in animal and human health); and third, aid for displaced and uprooted people.[14]

In addition, crosscutting issues—such as the promotion of human rights and democracy, gender equality, 'good governance', rights of children and indigenous peoples, environmental sustainability, and combating HIV/AIDS—are addressed in thematic programmes and instruments and streamlined in each component of the regional programme. Brussels allocated nearly €5.2 billion to Asia for the 2007–2013 period.

Focus on Europe-ASEAN cooperation

The first Europe-ASEAN cooperation agreement entered into force in 1980, highlighting Brussels's interest in forging closer ties with what many in the Union viewed as an organisation that best mirrored the regional cooperation objectives espoused by the EC. But this first treaty was limited in scope. It provided for most-favoured-nation treatment for trade between the two regions; a commitment to joint actions for improving commercial, investment, and scientific relations; and some provisions on development cooperation. By 2003, as Asia recuperated successfully from the 1997 financial crisis and once again became an increasingly important economic player, the European Commission published a strategy paper calling for stronger engagement with a region that it said represented 'one of the most dynamic growth engines of the world economy'.[15]

The 2003 paper set out six strategic priorities for revitalising EU-ASEAN ties: first, supporting regional stability and the fight against terrorism; second, promoting human rights, democratic principles, and 'good governance'; third, mainstreaming of justice and home affairs issues such as migration, human trafficking, money laundering, piracy, organised crime, and drugs; fourth, injecting a new dynamism into regional trade and investment relations; fifth, continuing support for the development of less prosperous countries; and finally, intensification of discussions on economic and trade issues, justice and home affairs, science and technology, higher education, culture, energy, the environment, and information technology.

In further expounding on the need for stronger EU-ASEAN ties, the European Commission pointed to the two regions' common economic, political, and security interests, highlighting that 'countries of both regions have realised that creating a regional entity is the best way to sustain economic development, to reinforce their security ... and to have a strong voice in world affairs'.[16] The 2003 paper also noted that the EU, with its experience and know-how in regional integration, should be ready fully to support ASEAN's integration efforts. At the same time, however, 'unrealistic expectations' and demands were not to be made of the ASEAN secretariat. 'Only ASEAN countries will determine the content and rhythm of the original process that they are keen to develop between themselves',[17] warned the paper.

Attempts to negotiate a new EU-ASEAN agreement were effectively abandoned owing to differences over how best to deal with the military junta in Myanmar (Burma). The EU imposed sanctions on the country in 1996, but ASEAN opened its doors to Myanmar a year later. Seeking to sidestep this disagreement, the EU attempted to negotiate bilateral agreements with several ASEAN members. Free trade agreements with several countries have also been under negotiation, following a decision by EU governments in May 2007. Brussels initially said it wanted a free trade area with ASEAN as a whole, but that initiative also ran into obstacles due to disagreements over Myanmar.

Although the 2003 strategy paper did not explicitly say so, the EU's focus on ASEAN reflected concern about America's dominating presence in Asia, and a growing realisation that Europe's failure to engage with the region effectively would result in reduced European clout in the region. ASEAN countries were equally worried about being locked into an American-dominated world, and shut out of a rapidly expanding and increasingly influential Europe, which represented a lucrative market for Asian exports and had created a single currency—the euro—by 2002. ASEAN was also impressed by Europe's tougher stance on North Korea and forays into global peacekeeping operations in places such as the Democratic Republic of the Congo and the Central African Republic and Chad. (See chapters 14 and 15 in this volume.)

Despite these efforts, the negotiation of a new and more ambitious EU-ASEAN pact—including talk of a free trade area—remained an elusive goal by 2011. Determined to overcome this obstacle in early 2009, Brussels announced a set of concrete actions to deepen its relations with ASEAN.[18] This followed the entry into force of the ASEAN Charter in December 2008, which aimed to deepen ASEAN member states' cooperation with the EU on political, economic, and social affairs. This action was focused on the following three concrete steps: the accreditation of ambassadors of all twenty-seven EU member states and the European Commission to ASEAN countries; the deepening of operational relations with the ASEAN secretariat in the Indonesian capital of Jakarta; and the nomination of a special EU adviser for ASEAN affairs to Jakarta.

China and India as key strategic partners

The EU's current priority has been to try to put flesh on the skeletal bones of the strategic partnership agreements signed with India in 2004,[19] and with China in 2006.[20] The focus on Asia's emerging economic powerhouses is not surprising: there are hopes that China and India, which are expected to keep notching up impressive economic growth rates, albeit at a slower pace, will be able to extend a helping hand to battered European and American economies.

These partnerships have been of mutual benefit. Both China and India have vested interests in forging ties with Europe. Policymakers in both countries remain anxious to draw closer to the EU in order to balance their ties with the US, and are attracted by the Union's huge market of 400 million people for their goods and services—and possibly also for the export of labour to Europe. Asians have further been impressed by the EU's successive and successful enlargements, as well as by the EU's growing reputation as a global security actor.

Signing the partnership agreements by 2006 has certainly led to increased EU interaction with China and India within the framework of the United Nations and at a bilateral level, thereby strengthening ties and expanding the array of subjects under discussion. Significantly, EU meetings with China and India have included a review of regional and global 'hotspots' and conflict zones (with both Beijing and New Delhi contributing significantly to UN peacekeeping missions, particularly in Africa), but also cooperation in the fields of energy, science and technology, maritime transport, and climate change. However, a closer look at the EU-India and the EU-China strategic partnerships reveals serious shortcomings and dashed expectations.

EU-India relations: unfulfilled aspirations. The EU's strategic partnership with India is marked by a mismatch of aspirations and goals. While New Delhi and Brussels share common values, including a commitment to democracy, the rule of law, and effective multilateralism, the two sides have very different views on what a strategic partnership would mean in practice. This divergence in outlook reflects differing geostrategic interests and different levels of economic development.

According to the European Security Strategy of 2003, the EU must use its strategic partnerships to share global responsibilities in order to meet twenty-first-century challenges, including terrorism, the proliferation of weapons of mass destruction, state failure, and regional conflicts. However, as an emerging power, India's immediate concerns are understandably very different from those of the EU and its member states. As it aspires to play a more forceful global role, as illustrated by its demand for a permanent seat on an expanded UN Security Council (which US president Barack Obama supported during a visit to India in November 2010) and active participation in international peacekeeping operations, India views its strategic partnership with the EU (and the US) as a vehicle for ensuring greater global visibility, prestige, and political clout.

While developing a strategic partnership with the EU is seen as important, New Delhi's primary focus is on its troubled neighbourhood. Rivalry with China and tensions with Pakistan as well as political turmoil in Bangladesh, Nepal, and Sri Lanka have tended to dominate the country's foreign policy agenda.[21]

The EU has made no secret of its disappointment at India's failure to stand up for democracy and human rights during Myanmar's military crackdown on dissidents since 1988. The EU-Indian strategic partnership has also failed to soften New Delhi's tough line in the World Trade Organisation's (WTO) Doha trade talks since 2005, with India continuing to resist American and European demands for further cuts in industrial tariffs. In addition, New Delhi has refused to accept Western calls for stricter binding commitments to reduce greenhouse gas emissions in order to combat climate change, arguing that a developing country cannot be expected to slow down the pace of its industrialisation to satisfy the environmental concerns of the rich world.

EU-China relations: Tibet and human rights cast a shadow over ties. Sparring over human rights and especially over Tibet has long cast a dark shadow over the strategic partnership between the EU and China, which by 2010 had become the world's second largest economy. Differences over Tibet came to a head in December 2008, when Beijing cancelled a planned summit with Brussels out of anger at French president Nicolas Sarkozy's decision to meet the Tibetan spiritual leader, the Dalai Lama. China's unprecedented move was a blow to EU governments that were hoping to use the summit to forge a new partnership under which Beijing, with its $2 trillion foreign reserves at the time, would extend a helping hand to Europe's battered economies.

Few in Brussels have had any doubt that China's decision to cancel the summit was a demonstration of the country's growing assertiveness and self-confidence, sentiments reinforced by Beijing's successful hosting of a lavish and successful Olympic Games in 2008. But Europeans have also been conscious that this approach leaves the impression that, as it gains more economic and financial clout, China will demand not only a stronger voice in the management of global financial affairs (more votes in the International Monetary Fund [IMF] for example), but also more international respect for its political stance on issues such as Tibet, Taiwan, and international human rights. At the Group of 20 (G20) summit in London in April 2009, China announced $40 billion to help support the IMF's lending.

EU-China trade relations have been fraught. Trade disputes between Brussels and Beijing have been on the rise as the EU's trade deficit with China has ballooned, reaching €160 billion ($207 billion) in 2007. Brussels has imposed antidumping duties on Chinese-made candles and nonalloy steel products, and added tariffs to imports of some citrus fruit products. Beijing has routinely denied that it breaks trade rules, and argued that Europe resorts to protectionism against China's low-cost products.

Overall, Brussels's relationship with Beijing has been bedevilled by the fact that European governments have never quite made up their minds over whether China is a rival or a partner. EU officials insist that the organisation's 'fundamental approach to China must remain one of engagement and partnership', but European governments have long struggled to reconcile their desire for lucrative business deals in China with ongoing public concern over the country's human rights record. EU attitudes towards Beijing have also become mixed up with public fears over globalisation and threats to European jobs and investments. Many in Europe increasingly view China as the symbol of such challenges, and believe that managing globalisation means taming the Chinese dragon's economic might.

EU-China and Africa: from envy and competition to cooperation. Europe's complex relationship with China has worked in Africa's favour. The expansion of Chinese engagement in Africa since 2000 has spurred European governments to take another look at their own often jaundiced relationship with Africa. Europe's initial reaction to China's growing trade, aid, and business engagement with Africa was one of resentment, irritation, and anger at being supplanted as one of Africa's main aid and trade partners. This resulted in EU complaints that China was favouring African dictators and condoning genocide (in Sudan's Darfur region) and was only interested in making deals to satisfy its thirst for energy and raw materials without any regard for Africa's future.

Striving to undertake a more realistic assessment of China's presence in Africa, a European Commission paper released in October 2008 recognised that both the EU and China have a 'strong shared interest in promoting stable and sustainable development in Africa'.[22] The Commission also proposed that Africa, China, and the EU should work together in a flexible and pragmatic way to identify and address a specific number of areas suitable for trilateral cooperation, and to link this cooperation, where possible, with existing commitments in multilateral forums, in particular at the UN.

The 2008 paper further stressed the importance of practical cooperation on the ground, with the focus on concrete projects and sectors, and noted that both sides should try to avoid duplication of efforts, ensure closer coordination of their activities in relation to African development strategies, facilitate the exchange of experience, including China's own development experience, and ensure 'best practice'. Such 'trilateral cooperation' in an initial phase is to centre on building peace and security in Africa by working with the African Union and the UN to strengthen the development of the African peace and security architecture and assist with AU peacekeeping operations; building capacity and training; supporting African infrastructure to enhance interconnectivity and regional integration; and improving conditions for sustainable development and economic growth (multimodal transport corridors, telecommunications, and energy, including renewables and sector approaches), as well as focusing on sustainable management of the environment and natural resources, agriculture, and food security.

How Africa can learn from the EU's strategic partnerships with Asia

The EU's drive to reach strategic partnership agreements with Asian and African countries has reflected a common, overarching objective: to mark the emergence of Europe as a global player, ready to assume political, economic, and cultural responsibilities. The decade of the 2000s also saw the EU emerge as an important security actor, prepared to deploy peacekeeping missions and humanitarian operations under a UN mandate.

Dating back to 1975, the EU's institutional links with African countries through the first Lomé Convention, followed by the Cotonou Agreement of 2000, predate Europe's more recent efforts to forge closer ties with Asian countries. Yet there has been little doubt that in recent years, EU-Asia relations have dominated Europe's foreign and security policy agenda, while relations with Africa have remained virtually stagnant or mired in controversy over EU attempts to negotiate economic partnership agreements with African states. (See chapters 10 and 11 in this volume.) Disagreements over human rights, and more specifically over how best to deal with Robert Mugabe's Zimbabwe, have also soured the EU-Africa relationship.

Can Asia provide any lessons to African countries seeking an upgrade of ties with Europe? While some of Asia's success in forging closer ties with the EU can certainly be emulated by African countries, the political and economic landscapes of the two continents are obviously very different. In addition, while Asia and Africa have strong historical links with Europe, Britain and France—as former European colonial powers—have been much more involved and active in setting EU policy towards Africa than in determining the course of EU-Asia relations. (See chapters 16 and 17 in this volume.) It was Germany (on of China's largest trading partners by 2012), rather than France or Britain, that insisted on the need for an EU strategy towards Asia in 1994.

However, there are eight key lessons that Africa can draw from Asia as it seeks to attract more European attention, funds, and investments. First, competition and rivalry with other international actors have played a major role in the EU's search for a stronger relationship with Asia. As noted earlier, the overriding American and Japanese presence in Asia helped to trigger

European interest in ASEAN, while EU relations with India were developed at least partly to counterbalance China's rising influence in the region and worldwide. ASEM was also created in 1996 partly in response to the US-led Asia Pacific Economic Cooperation (APEC) network, of which Europe was not a member. Africa has similarly been able to use growing Chinese and Indian interest on the continent to revive EU interest there. But Africa will have to ensure that the right kind of European engagement is maintained.

Second, the EU has made no secret of its desire to work with regional organisations that mirror its own aims and objectives. The EU and ASEAN have a cooperation agreement that dates back to 1980, and Brussels is working hard to ensure that ASEAN keeps on track for further integration. It is therefore no surprise that EU-Africa ties only really took off after the establishment of the African Union in 2002, which the EU also sees as a worthwhile regional organisation. (See chapter 3 in this volume.) The EU communication on trilateral EU-China-Africa cooperation underlined the 'real momentum for change' in Africa represented by the birth of the African Union, the reinforced role of Africa's regional economic communities, and the New Partnership for Africa's Development (NEPAD) of 2001, as well as the African Peer Review Mechanism (APRM) of 2003, which seeks to promote 'good governance' on the continent. These initiatives, according to the EU Commission, mark 'a fundamental break in the way Africa looks at itself and how it engages with its external partners'.[23] Third, there has been the issue of political confidence, relating to the power and prestige of countries in a globalised, multipolar world. Not surprisingly, therefore, the EU is drawn to countries and regions that project confidence and are assertive on the world stage. The organisation's 2001 strategy for Asia spotlights the continent's growing political clout, while the 2003 paper on ASEAN notes that Europe can ill afford to ignore a region that is becoming increasingly assertive in international forums. Similarly, the 2008 paper on EU-China-Africa trilateral cooperation emphasised the emergence of a 'new' Africa that is more democratic, more vibrant, and positioning itself better to benefit from the opportunities provided by globalisation. The EU Commission indicated that 'Africa is now determined to assert its international status and is becoming active on major global issues like food security, energy and climate change and changing economic environments'.[24]

Fourth, EU governments have long recognised Asia's strategic role and significance and also acknowledged the dangers of a spillover effect of tensions and conflicts on the continent. The 'strategic card' has also been slowly beginning to be played in Africa's favour, as Europe—prodded by China—has shown renewed interest in Africa's strategic importance for supplies of energy and raw materials. At the same time, there has been a growing realisation that the evolving human security paradigm requires further international efforts to fight poverty and disease in Africa and South Asia.

Fifth, there is the question of economic weight: the EU's focus on Asia has undoubtedly been driven by compelling business and trade interests. Asian members of the Asia-Europe Meeting are key trading partners of the EU, accounting for 30 per cent of Europe's trade with the world. EU exports to ASEM members in Asia were worth €208 billion in 2006. Asia also hosted about 15 per cent of the EU's foreign direct investment stock abroad in 2008. In contrast, in 2007, EU trade with the seventy-nine African, Caribbean, and Pacific countries totalled only €80 billion, with the EU importing goods to the value of nearly €40 billion from ACP countries.

Sixth, in terms of financial significance, Asian countries—particularly China and India—are seen as crucial players in the global economy, with many in Europe hoping that despite their own economic problems, Asian countries, which are still expected to record relatively robust growth rates, will be able to help ease the impact of the global financial crisis of 2008–2009 on both the EU and the US.

Seventh, disagreement over human rights has been a running sore in Europe's relations with Asian countries. Plans to negotiate a new EU-ASEAN cooperation agreement and a first-ever region-to-region free trade agreement had stalled by 2010 because of Europe's refusal to conclude any accord that included Myanmar. However, both sides agreed to set aside their differences over the military junta in Naypyidaw, and sought to upgrade relations through the conclusion of bilateral meetings. They also attempted to organise more frequent EU-ASEAN encounters outside a strict institutional framework. African countries, similarly at odds with the EU over how to deal with leaders such as Zimbabwe's Robert Mugabe and Sudan's Omar al-Bashir (indicted for war crimes by the International Criminal Court in 2009), could learn from the Asian example by agreeing to disagree while not allowing such differences to slow progress in other critical areas.

Finally, Europe's strategic partnership agreements with Asia have included a focus on joint efforts to fight global terrorism and extremism, which are recognised as common challenges facing both continents. A similar argument could be employed by African governments facing similar threats from violent radicalisation, particularly in North Africa, East Africa, West Africa and the Horn of Africa.

Concluding reflections

In its immediate neighbourhood as well as in continents farther away, the European Union has begun flexing its muscles as a global player. The negotiation of 'strategic partnership' agreements is a crucial 'soft power' tool used for the projection of EU influence and power in the world. Brussels is also increasingly deploying 'hard power' crisis management and peace-keeping missions within Europe and far beyond, with EU soldiers and police officers increasingly involved in conflict prevention, peacekeeping, and antiterrorism activities in Africa, the Middle East, and Afghanistan. An EU antipiracy naval operation had begun patrolling the waters off the coast of Somalia by 2008.

The EU's focus on Asia and Africa is part of the drive to build a stronger network of friends across the globe to tackle challenges to peace and security, but also to address questions relating to climate change and global terrorism. As this chapter has illustrated, however, Europe's foreign and security policy is still a work in progress. Brussels' 'strategic partnership' agreements are often about meetings, communiqués, and speeches rather than substance and content. The twenty-seven EU countries have also been frequently divided over how best to deal with international flashpoints.

Building stronger bonds with the EU is in the interest of Asian and African countries seeking to break away from the influence of one overarching power, whether the US, Japan, China, Britain, or France. Engaging Brussels, however, entails time, energy, and patience. This will also require the use of powerful strategic and economic arguments that can attract and sustain Europe's interest in Africa.

PART 3

TRADE, INVESTMENT, AND DEVELOPMENT

9

GLOBAL AFRICA

THE LAST INVESTMENT FRONTIER?

Liam Halligan

Introduction

Just a few years ago, the idea of investing in Africa was treated with derision by the vast majority of international financiers. In both Europe and the United States, impressions of the 'Dark Continent' were driven by intermittent, apocalyptic media coverage dominated by disease, famine, and war.

This view has now lately been tempered. Despite nervousness on international markets in 2011, Africa is a 'hot topic'. Much of this interest has, of course, been driven by strong oil, gas, and mineral valuations. Crude oil prices have risen threefold since 2001, and given the escalating demands of Asia's fast-growing 'emerging giants' (see chapter 8 in this volume), there is a growing consensus that commodity prices, while remaining volatile, are likely to stay firm for years to come. This bodes well for Africa, given the continent's world-class resource endowment.

This new interest in Africa, however, goes beyond commodities. Asset managers are increasingly eyeing the continent's growing need for consumer goods, financial services, and infrastructure. The world is gradually realising that Africa is the world's second most populous continent after Asia, with a market of up to 800 million consumers. Unless one believes in 'African exceptionalism', it seems inevitable that, sooner or later, the cradle of humankind will live up to the undoubted potential of its human and physical resources, and become a major part of the global economy. The case for investing in Africa has recently become stronger because of better policy-making, an improving political climate (despite some trouble-spots), and Africa's 'low correlation' (see chapter 5 in this volume). The continent, for now at least, tends to move in a cycle of its own, rather than following other global markets, possibly making it an attractive 'hedge' as rich markets in the West suffer.

Huge obstacles remain, of course. Even the most positive investors in Africa—both foreign and domestic—still swap stories of ghastly infrastructure and a severe lack of skilled labour, as well as mind-numbing red tape and corrupt officialdom. But none of that has stopped the recent development of specialised investment vehicles offering exposure to the African growth story. Such funds often combine portfolio holdings (shares listed on Africa's growing number of stock exchanges) with 'direct' investments in unlisted private and quasi-government projects.

Reflecting the capital that backs them, though, such vehicles are notoriously fickle. Unless Africa's business environment improves soon, this new investment wave, before generating serious momentum, could easily recede. Specifically, as long as corporate governance risks remain at their extremely high levels of 2011, Western regulatory authorities will ensure that Africa-themed funds remain the preserve mainly of a relatively small pool of highly specialised investors, thus preventing large-scale retail and institutional money from entering the continent and hindering the classification of many African countries as proper 'emerging markets'.

Were this to happen, Africa would remain chronically short of capital for the foreseeable future. For yet another generation, the continent's huge potential would remain largely untapped. While frustrating for global investors, the impact on Africa's general populace, in terms of lower incomes and lost opportunities, would be far more serious.

Stronger, more stable growth

Growth across the African continent as a whole averaged more than 5 per cent for most of the decade of 2000–2010: more than twice the average of Western economies. More strikingly still, the forty-eight countries of sub-Saharan Africa—which, as a whole, have traditionally lagged the generally

Fig. 9.1: Global growth in real GDP, 1991–2007.

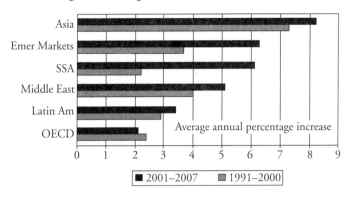

more economically advanced North African nations—have grown by more than 6 per cent annually since 2001 (see figure 9.1). This is almost three times the Western average—and considerably faster than Latin America and the Middle East.

Africa has now become one of the fastest-growing regions of the world, with some countries growing by 10 per cent or more annually—a performance matched only by China. The continent is currently enjoying its most sustained economic expansion since the early 1970s, driven by lower sovereign debts, better policymaking, and, of course, strong commodity prices.

Yet despite these developments, Africa remains systemically underinvested. Its entire free-float adjusted market capitalisation amounted to just $74 billion in 2008, or less than 2.5 per cent of the stock valuation of all countries typically classified as emerging markets.[1]

During the 1990s, sub-Saharan Africa was outpaced even by the relatively sluggish Organisation for Economic Cooperation and Development (OECD) countries. The continent is still growing more slowly than Asia and the emerging-market average. But Africa has no longer been left behind the rest of the world in this important area. Although the picture varies dramatically across the continent, the smaller African economies (excluding Nigeria and South Africa) have also fared well in terms of growth, in contrast to previous decades (see figure 9.2).

Africa has been growing faster, in part, because its constituent economies are being better managed. The continent has long been plagued by the impact of the colonial past, then by Cold War-related interference, and finally by ghastly domestic leadership. As the British writer Martin Mere-

Fig. 9.2: Subregional growth trends, 1999–2008.

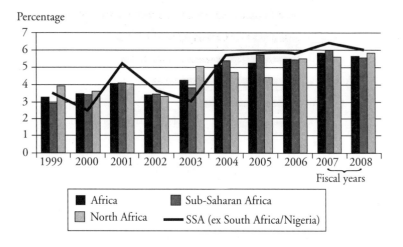

dith reminded us: 'By the end of the 1980s, not a single African Head of State in three decades had allowed himself to be voted out of office. Of some 150 leaders who had trodden the African stage, only six had voluntarily relinquished power'.[2]

The international financial community, for the most part, recognises that African politics is currently undergoing a dramatic sea-change. Despite flawed elections in Kenya, Nigeria, Zimbabwe, and Côte d'Ivoire between 2007 and 2010, the general trajectory is clear: a new generation of African leaders are now more likely to hold relatively free elections. The hope is that as democracy spreads, so corruption will wane and the business climate will improve.

There is also a deserved recognition that the standard of economic management in Africa has vastly improved. In the past, many of the continent's problems stemmed from weak institutions and poor policy design and execution, particularly on the fiscal side. Debt relief has helped ease the burden of Cold War-era liabilities, many of which were anyway wracked up by Western-backed despots like Zaire's Mobutu Sese Seko, Liberia's Samuel Doe, and Somalia's Siad Barre. But governments are now acting more responsibly, as shown by a marked improvement in internal balances among resource-intensive countries in sub-Saharan Africa, not only those with oil, but those with non-oil resources as well (see figure 9.3).

Fig 9.3: Fiscal balances in sub-Saharan Africa (resource-intensive), 2002–2007.

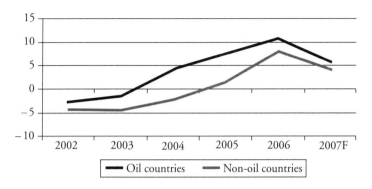

Oil-exporting countries in sub-Saharan Africa registered an aggregate fiscal surplus exceeding 10 per cent of gross domestic product (GDP) in the decade from 2000 to 2010. Countries exporting non-oil commodities also showed big fiscal gains during this period. At the other end of the spectrum, even African economies with few or no natural resources performed well from a fiscal point of view. Including grants and other overseas aid, non-resource-intensive sub-Saharan African governments registered a small surplus of 0.2 per cent of GDP during 2006, and a small deficit of 0.1 per cent during 2007. This shows that even in the very poorest African coun-

Fig 9.4: External balances in sub-Saharan Africa (resource-intensive), 2002–2007.

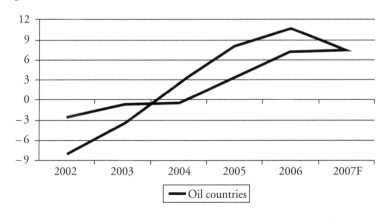

tries, fiscal management has been gradually improving. Many countries also showed progress in their external balances. Since 2003, sub-Saharan Africa's resource-intensive economies have registered a combined current account surplus, roughly coinciding with the long-term commodity price upswing (see figure 9.4). Non-oil-exporting resource-rich countries have, once again, also done well.

However, the poorest African countries—those with no resource endowments—have seen their current accounts spiral downward in recent years. These countries' combined deficit grew from 1.6 per cent of GDP in 2002 to 6.8 per cent in 2007—owing in part to the cost of importing more expensive fuel and other commodities. This further impoverishment of nations that are already extremely poor is a major problem, an aspect of Africa's commodity boom that has not received sufficient attention.

As policy has improved since 2000, with 'independent' central banking gaining favour, so inflation has moderated. Excluding the most extravagant 'hyperinflation' cases of Angola, the Democratic Republic of the Congo (DRC), and Zimbabwe, average African inflation remained below 8 per cent between 1997 and 2007. Inflation has also fallen because stronger fiscal positions, along with expanding reserves, mean that fewer governments are 'printing money' to engage in populist spending. Across Africa, lower inflation has also helped to boost macro-stability, while bolstering the development of local financial services and helping to drive recent investor interest in the continent.

Fig 9.5: Historical inflation rates in sub-Saharan Africa, 1980–2004.

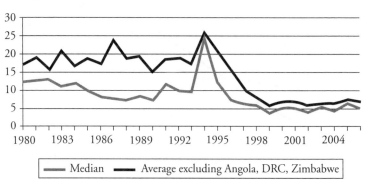

The opportunity

South Africa, with its modern infrastructure and highly developed legal system, has long been a 'honey-pot' for foreign and domestic investors. Its economy was worth about $346 billion in 2010: larger than that of Denmark or Thailand. The country boasts a world-class stock exchange and dozens of listed companies, and accounted for about a third of sub-Saharan Africa's economic might in 2010. While political flare-ups have generated Western headlines, international financiers have remained very interested in the continent's largest economy: not least in the run-up to, and aftermath of, the successful 2010 World Cup in South Africa, which gave tens of millions of visitors and viewers a more positive picture of a modern African industrialised state in stark contrast to the stereotypical 'Afro-pessimist' image of Africa that proliferates in the Western media.

It can also be argued that South Africa should not be classified as an investment frontier. The same can be said for much of North Africa, which is also already attracting extensive capital spending. The question really at issue is the extent to which the rest of the continent (sub-Saharan Africa, excluding South Africa) will generate investor interest over the coming years, not least from the West, the Middle East, and Asia.

Table 1 shows sub-Saharan Africa's top ten economies (excluding South Africa)—the focus of recent investor attention. Nigeria's economy was about $248 billion in 2010. For all the hype about Africa's 'emerging giant', this was smaller than the individual economies of both Austria and Malaysia. Nigeria is also dwarfed by South Africa's $346 billion economy. Thus, while sub-Saharan Africa is now being discussed by international investors, the economies concerned are still small compared with other emerging markets vying for investor attention. China's GDP was $6.4 billion in 2010, while India's was $1.8 billion and Russia's national income was $1.73 billion. Beyond the top-ranked emerging markets, Indonesia's economy was worth $806 million: more than three times that of Nigeria.

In terms of GDP per capita, also, Africa is also an interesting—although not yet breathtaking—investment opportunity. Per capita incomes indicate the revenue potential of retail and service investments, as well as of infrastructure projects reliant on user charges. Most of the top economies in sub-Saharan Africa in table 1 had a purchasing power parity (PPP) GDP per capita well below $2,000 in 2007, including Nigeria. China, in contrast, had a $5,345 GDP per capita—and with 1.4 billion people is the world's largest market and has the second largest economy in 2011. Russia's

Table 1: Sub-Saharan Africa's top ten economies (excluding South Africa), 2007.

	GDP PPP ($ billions)	Population (millions)	GDP per Capita (PPP $)	Life Expectancy (years)	Primary Exports	Primary Exports (percentage of total)
Nigeria	247.3	144.7	1,892	46.8	Crude petroleum	92.2
Angola	55.0	16.6	3,533	42.4	Crude petroleum	95.8
Sudan	79.5	37.7	2,249	58.1	Crude petroleum	89.2
Kenya	47.9	36.6	1,359	53.4	Tea	16.8
Ethiopia	42.5	77.2	591	52.5	Coffee	47.8
Tanzania	35.9	39.5	1,018	51.9	Gold	10.9
Cameroon	35.0	18.2	1,995	50.3	Crude petroleum	48.8
Côte d'Ivoire	30.1	18.9	1,575	48.1	Cocoa beans	38.2
Ghana	27.1	23.0	1,225	59.7	Cocoa beans	46.1
Uganda	26.3	29.9	991	50.7	Coffee	31.1

Sources: World Bank; UN database; Morgan Stanley.

GDP per capita in 2007 was $14,743, approaching Western levels, and the country remains less intimidating to most investors than sub-Saharan Africa. Even India's GDP per capita in 2007, at $2,818, was well above sub-Saharan Africa levels. India also has six times more people than Nigeria, and a better legal system, and is arguably an easier place to do business.

None of this is to say Africa will not become a large consumer market. The potential is there. Russia is now one of Europe's largest retail markets, but Nigeria's population, at about 150 million, is already larger than that of Russia (about 140 million people). Seeing that 44 per cent of Nigerians are younger than fifteen years old, the country is set to have a population of almost 200 million inhabitants by 2020.[3] The bottom line is that, while Africa has recently grown quickly, in most parts of the continent population growth has dampened the rise in spending power per capita. Africa's head-count is growing at 2.5 per cent per year, compared with 1.2 per cent in Asia and 1.5 per cent across the world. As a whole, Africa's GDP per capita is $2,905, similar to India's. But because South Africa and North Africa have such high relative wealth (GDP per head of $12,796 and $6,080 respectively in 2007), Africa's reasonable continent-wide income figure masks the reality that most regions are simply too poor to attract investment in utilities, roads, and retail infrastructure, which are the basic building blocks of modern economies.

Figure 9.6 shows the path of Africa's *nominal* GDP per capita in constant dollar terms since 1980. Though North Africa and Nigeria have clearly seen

Fig 9.6: Regional nominal per capita incomes, 1980–2008.

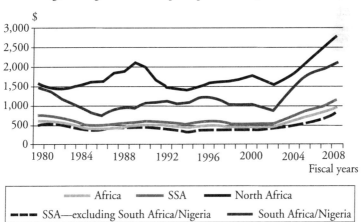

179

strong growth since 2003, their levels of spending power remain quite low by comparison with other emerging markets. More important, despite the recent expansion of the smaller sub-Saharan African economies, their spending power per capita remains extremely low, largely because of high population growth. So, for all the talk about 'the last true investment frontier', when it comes to attracting foreign investors, African officials and entrepreneurs still have relatively few cards to play.

The exception, of course, is in the area of commodities—not least oil, gas, and other minerals. Just as in previous centuries, Africa's natural resources remain the continent's biggest investment draw. After all, Africa boasts almost two-thirds of the world's known diamond deposits, two-fifths of its phosphates, and a sizeable share of its hydrocarbons.

As table 2 shows, Africa accounts for almost 10 per cent of the world's known oil reserves and about 8 per cent of the world's natural gas—with much of these resources in North Africa, rather than south of the Sahara. But still, as table 1 reminds us, three of the largest economies in sub-Saharan Africa outside South Africa are all oil-dominated, with crude accounting for at least 90 per cent of the export revenue generated by Nigeria, Angola, and Sudan.

Table 2: Africa's energy reserves.

	Proven Oil Reserves (percentage of world total)	Proven Gas Reserves (percentage of world total)
Libya	3.4	0.7
Nigeria	3.0	2.9
Algeria	1.0	2.5
Angola	0.7	–
Sudan	0.5	–
Egypt	0.3	1.1
Gabon	0.2	–
Congo-Brazzaville	0.2	–
Equatorial Guinea	0.1	–
Chad	0.1	–
Tunisia	0.1	–
Other Africa	0.1	0.7
Total Africa	9.7	7.9

Sources: British Petroleum; *World Energy Review;* Organisation of the Petroleum Exporting Countries (OPEC); UBS.

Fig 9.7: Africa's share of world energy reserves.

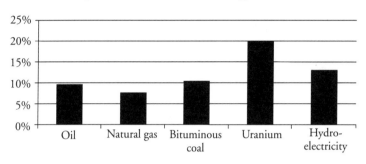

Figure 9.7 shows the extent of Africa's energy reserves in a global context, including uranium (as an essential component of atomic energy) and hydroelectricity. The continent's 10 per cent share of the world's proven oil reserves compares with 62 per cent in the Middle East, 12 per cent in Europe and Eurasia (including Russia), and 14 per cent in the Americas. And while the Middle East boasts 40 per cent of the world's natural gas and Europe/Eurasia has 36 per cent, Africa's 8 per cent share is still sizeable.[4] In general terms, most of this oil and gas is concentrated in North and West Africa, with the hydroelectric resources concentrated in Central and Eastern Africa, and much of the continent's coal concentrated in South Africa.

In terms of utilising these reserves, Africa accounted for 12 per cent of global oil output in 2008, at about 10 million barrels a day, and 6 per cent of the world's gas production, at about 147 million tonnes per day. These shares are similar to total reserves, indicating that the continent's primary energy sector is performing relatively well, with the outlook particularly promising for gas, given that Africa's total share of global supply is slightly below its share of world reserves.

In theory, Africa should be converting these energy sources into electrical power, which could then be harnessed to strengthen the continent's manufacturing and service sectors and thus promote economic diversification and, in particular, a broader range of export revenues. Unfortunately, this is barely happening. Despite its rich energy endowments, and although it accounts for 16 per cent of the world's population, Africa generated only 3 per cent of the world's total electricity production in 2010. This has major negative implications in terms of the continent's ability to attract non-energy investment, from both domestic and foreign sources.

By exporting such a large share of its oil and gas, Africa not only stymies its own development, but also increases dangerously its reliance on primary product exports. While most of the developing world has become less dependent on such exports in recent years, Africa has become more so. In 1990, primary products accounted for 27 per cent of Asia's exports, whereas by 2006 this measure had fallen to 22 per cent. In Latin America, primary products fell from 64 to 46 per cent of exports over the same period. Africa, in contrast, increased its reliance on primary products, from an export share of 70 per cent in 1990 to 77 per cent in 2006.[5]

Many investors find this an issue of serious concern, not least because of the phenomenon of 'Dutch disease': the situation in which an extremely dominant sector (such as oil or gas) attracts a large share of a country's resources, leading to higher wages and an overvalued exchange rate—in turn undermining the growth of other sectors, including manufacturing.

At the same time, many of Africa's resource-rich countries, given their 90 per cent or greater primary-product export share, remain sorely vulnerable to a fall in commodity prices. All these factors weigh on the minds of those trying to 'see beyond commodities' and invest in Africa's 'broader economy'. The trouble is that, unlike countries such as Sweden, Australia, Canada, and increasingly Russia, which have used their natural resource endowments to diversify their economies, Africa's 'broader economy' barely exists. In fact, the continent's economy is clearly becoming narrower.

Much of the new wave of investment into Africa is of course helping to drive this overreliance on commodities. The decade since 2000 has seen a renewed 'Scramble for Africa', with companies from the European Union, the United States, and Australia competing with Chinese and Russian firms for extractive industry concessions. And for some time to come, commodities and mining will be the sectors of most interest to foreign financiers.

For now, Africa is benefitting from the recent upswing in commodity prices, as China, India, and other large energy importers meet current needs and secure future supplies. But Africa's strong growth during the 1970s ended when commodity prices started to decline. The continent then entered what Adebayo Adedeji, the former Nigerian executive secretary of the United Nations Economic Commission for Africa (ECA), famously described as the 'lost decade' of the 1980s. Investors worry that the same thing could happen again.

On the other hand, Africa's latest growth resurgence began almost ten years before recent increases in commodity prices. Between 1995 and 2005, seventeen sub-Saharan African countries, representing almost two-fifths of the continent's population, grew by 5.5 per cent on average—without the benefit of sharp rises in commodity prices. That suggests that investors should view the continent as far more than 'just a play on raw material prices'.

However, a long-term commodity price 'super cycle' may in any case now be developing: the result of fast population growth and sharply rising fuel-use per capita in large emerging markets, coupled with a muted supply response from the global oil industry. Escalating demand could also drive demand for fossil fuels to such an extent that oil prices reach an annual average of $100 per barrel, and perhaps even higher, for several years to come.

This once heretical thesis is now emanating from highly credible sources.[6] Were it to happen, future investments in Africa could boom. But, at the same time, history suggests that strong commodity prices over a prolonged period would curtail the continent's ability to 'get over' its 'resource curse' and develop into a broad-based economy. That is why many foreign investors continue to view Africa's resources as a 'mixed blessing'.

While oil, gas, and other resources account for a huge part of Africa's export revenues, the continent may have an even bigger untapped comparative advantage in agriculture. Across Africa as a whole, agriculture accounts for 18 per cent of GDP—compared with 7 per cent in Asia and Latin America, just over 2 per cent in Europe, and around 1 per cent in the United States. In sub-Saharan Africa, the share of agriculture in the economy is particularly high—27 per cent of GDP. And Africa-wide, agriculture accounts for 70 per cent of all employment.

But Africa still generated only 3.5 per cent of global food exports in 2005—a mere 0.2 per cent of world exports overall (see figure 9.8). With the continent's share of total world food imports running at 3.6 per cent in 2005, Africa remained a net importer of farm produce—despite its enormous agricultural potential.

With the world population growing by 70 million a year, and the large emerging markets switching to high-protein diets, 'soft commodity' prices have been booming in recent years. That is why global investors have been pursuing agricultural opportunities, with many focusing on the 'black earth' regions of southern Russia and Ukraine. Yet some of the same investors see even more upside potential in Africa, given the extremely poor manner in which the continent currently uses its considerable agricultural resources.

As table 3 shows, Africa accounts for 20 per cent of the world's landmass and 12 per cent of the world's arable land. Compare that with Asia, which

Fig 9.8: Africa's Food Exports.

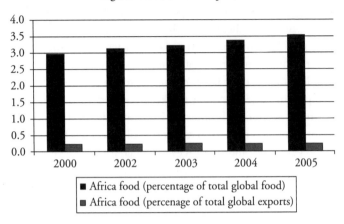

- Africa food (percentage of total global food)
- Africa food (percenage of total global exports)

has the same share of landmass, but has engaged in far more agricultural investment than Africa, and in 2006 boasted no less than 32 per cent of all arable land—almost three times more than Africa. Only 6 per cent of arable land in Africa as a whole is irrigated—and only 3 per cent in sub-Saharan Africa. This compares with 18 per cent globally and 34 per cent in Asia. Fertiliser use is also extremely low, particularly in Africa south of the Sahara, where only 9 kilogrammes of fertiliser are used per hectare per year, compared to 99 kilogrammes worldwide and 157 kilogrammes in Asia. Africa's pesticide use is also low.

This combination of minimal irrigation and low land husbandry represents a huge missed opportunity. In many African countries, poor land quality means that only low-grade crops are grown and in small quantities. This leaves vast swathes of people at the mercy of deficient rainfall. In 2006, Africa accounted for 62 per cent of all aid distributed by the World Food Programme (WFP), reflecting the continent's ongoing battles with malnutrition and famine. In that sense, Africa's inability to develop its agricultural sector substantially is nothing less than a human tragedy.[7]

But it is also a commercial tragedy. As table 3 shows, across Africa each hectare of cultivated land produced only $85 worth of value in 2006 (see table 3), as measured on international markets, and this figure was only $72 in sub-Saharan Africa. This compares with a value-yield of $260 across the world as a whole and a staggering $436 in Asia.

Table 3: Agriculture in Africa, 2006.

	Landmass (percentage)	Arable Land (percentage)	Irrigated Land (percentage of arable land)	Fertiliser Use (kilo-grammes per hectare)	Pesticide Use (kilogrammes per hectare)	Output Value ($ per hectare)
World	100	100	18	99	1.30	260
Sub-Saharan Africa	15	9	3	9	0.16	72
Africa	20	12	6	21	0.43	85
Latin America	14	10	11	80	2.24	185
Asia	20	32	34	157	0.78	436

Sources: Food and Agriculture Organisation (FAO); World Bank; Prosperity; UBS.

If Africa could approach even the $185 value-yield of Latin America, the potential upside—in both human and commercial terms—would be enormous. There are many reasons why this is not happening, including misguided domestic bulk-purchasing policies and lack of access to credit for African farmers. Many African leaders have also failed to channel resource windfalls into irrigation schemes and transport infrastructure, both of which could transform agricultural markets. Instead, valuable funds have often been diverted towards prestige projects and other 'white elephants'. Another huge impediment to Africa's agricultural development is the highly restrictive agricultural trading regime imposed by the West, not least the European Union.

Remaining barriers to development

After several 'false dawns', most global investors remain highly sceptical of Africa. Even positive press coverage of the continent's potential reflects some well-known realities. 'International monitors consistently place Africa in the lowest tier of rankings for business friendliness', one high-profile article in the American weekly *Newsweek* stated in 2007.[8] In 2000 the London-based *Economist* had also dismissed Africa, calling it 'the Hopeless Continent'.[9] Despite these 'Afro-pessimistic' perspectives, as Western markets have faltered, exacerbated by the 2008–2009 global financial crisis and the balance of global economic power increasingly shifting eastwards from the Atlantic towards Asia and the Pacific, financiers are becoming more broad-minded. In fact, there are now many Western investment funds, institutional investors, and high-net-worth individuals who actively eschew Western assets, having decided to place most or all of their wealth into emerging markets. Such investors are inevitably looking increasingly towards Africa.

The growing appetite of sovereign wealth funds based in the Middle East, China, and Russia also represents a huge opportunity for Africa. These funds have access to deep pools of long-term capital, and their own recent experiences of very basic economies developing rapidly make them more likely to consider capitalising Africa-based businesses.

But the barriers to investment remain extremely high. And the solutions are to be found both in Africa and in the West. Three areas desperately need improvement if the continent is to begin truly to develop its investment potential: infrastructure, trade regimes, and attitudes towards foreign aid.

Foreign investors in Africa bemoan many things, not least corruption, erratic policymaking, and political instability. But perhaps the most constant complaint, and the most important barrier to progress, is the continent's decrepit, and often nonexistent, infrastructure.

As a vast continent with fifteen landlocked countries,[10] Africa's future growth path will depend crucially on its transport infrastructure. Reasonably effective freight, road, and shipping installations are vital if African entrepreneurs are to gain access to national, regional, and international markets. And without such access, specialisation is likely to remain low and productivity gains muted, with the continent's growth and development paths being far shallower than they would otherwise have been.

Clearly, Africa's poor transport infrastructure translates into high costs for existing businesses. Across the continent as a whole, transport accounts for almost 15 per cent of total costs, far above the percentage on any other continent. This is clearly not only a serious barrier to the profitability, reinvestment, and growth of existing African businesses, but also a major constraint on the establishment of those businesses in the first place.

If Africa's transport infrastructure is to be more fully developed, then private finance will clearly need to play a major role in this process. Despite recent improvements, national tax bases remain fragile and subject to sharp deteriorations. State project-management skills are also generally weak. Many foreign investors are becoming interested in public-private partnership investments in Africa, including toll-model projects, land-value tie-ins, and other complex barter schemes.

Such public-private partnerships should be encouraged. But the extent to which they will prove sustainable in Africa, and be rolled out on a significant scale, remains highly uncertain. A major determinant will be the degree of even-handedness with which foreign-backed contractors are treated from a legal point of view. African officials and politicians should remember that bad experiences will become well known among major construction companies, severely hindering infrastructure development elsewhere in the country concerned.

For their part, Western construction and financial services industries need to practice restraint when negotiating and implementing such public-private partnerships. In Britain—the test-bed for many such schemes—perceptions are growing that some public-private deals represent extremely bad value for taxpayers' money.[11]

Clearly, the development of Africa's physical infrastructure is a major opportunity—one of the main nonresource sectors of interest to foreign investors. A rapid improvement in the continent's infrastructure is vital if investment in Africa is to increase. In some circumstances, overseas investors in extractive industries are granted concessions on condition that they build roads and other infrastructure: such a crude barter model is likely to apply only at the local level, and will not lead to the development of regional and countrywide infrastructure. But specific public-private partnership infrastructure schemes will only happen quickly, and spread, if both sides—African officialdom, and overseas industry and finance—do not squander the opportunity presented.

Perhaps the most important infrastructure gap is Africa's severe shortage of power generation capacity. As mentioned, despite its rich energy endowment, Africa generates only 3 per cent of the world's total electricity output (see figure 9.9). Russia, in contrast, produces 5 per cent of the global total, even though it has only a fifth of Africa's population. To diversify its export structure and thus strengthen its manufacturing and service base, a reliable electricity supply is a vital priority for Africa. Potential investors recoil in horror when considering that practically every kind of commercial activity, certainly in sub-Saharan Africa, requires multiple backup electricity generators. A passage from a recent research note from Renaissance Capital, an overseas investment bank already highly committed to Africa is perhaps instructive:

The Nigerian economy is roughly one sixth of the size of Russia's, and with a higher population, yet Nigeria has only 2 per cent of Russia's generation capacity. And demand for power in Nigeria is growing at 16 per cent a year. Almost everything outside the public sector is powered through privately-owned generators. For instance, each of the 8000 telegraph poles owned by MTN [Media Telecommunications Network], the country's largest mobile operator, has two individual generators (in case one breaks down). Imagine the logistics of supplying diesel to power 8000 telegraph poles in a country with no functioning transport network.[12]

The lack of power capacity does not hinder just the development of 'big-business'. The high costs of generators and fuel also act as an enormous barrier to entry for smaller firms. Investors with knowledge of other emerging markets know that small and medium-sized companies tend to play a leading role in driving forward the growth and development of such countries—making a disproportionate contribution to innovation, employment, and the rise in per capita incomes that form the basis of a sizeable consumer market.

So Africa's severe lack of power capacity looms extremely large—acting as a major roadblock against the continent's 'economic takeoff'. The situa-

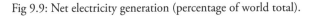

Fig 9.9: Net electricity generation (percentage of world total).

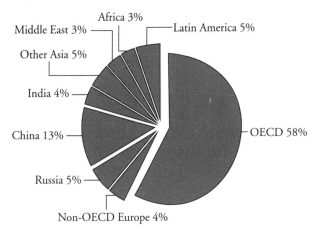

tion is even worse than figure 9.9 suggests, owing to Africa's significant electricity 'distribution losses' through inefficiencies and theft. Across the world, generators typically squander around 7 per cent of their output through such losses. Many African countries suffer losses well above 25 per cent, including Nigeria, Tanzania, Congo-Brazzaville, and Côte d'Ivoire.[13]

These power and transport deficiencies combine not only to hinder Africa's economic development, but also to make the continent much less attractive as a place for overseas financiers to invest their money. As figure 9.10 shows, such issues exist across other emerging markets. In China, power outages add around 1 per cent to the energy costs of companies over and above Western norms, and such outages add 0.4 per cent to energy costs in India. Transport bottlenecks and crime similarly add 1.6 per cent and 2 per cent respectively to Chinese and Indian costs. Given how fast these two markets are growing, and the scale of the commercial operations that foreign investors can become involved in, such inefficiencies can be absorbed. However, in many African countries, particularly south of the Sahara, the cost implications of the far greater power and transport deficiencies are much more serious. In Nigeria and Kenya—the most significant economies in West and East Africa respectively—power failures typically add more than 5 per cent to the costs of doing business in both countries. When start-up companies are likely to operate on extremely tight-margins, while having to engage in large-scale capital expenditure, such a burden is

Fig 9.10: Additional business costs.

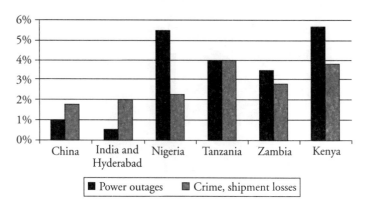

often crippling. Bureaucratic costs and losses from crime are also far more serious across Africa, with the same implications for foreign investors.

Along with infrastructure bottlenecks, another issue that desperately needs to be addressed if Africa is to fulfil its potential as the world's 'last investment frontier' is the trading regime, both between African countries themselves and between the continent and the rest of the world. This is an area in which the European Union needs to play a significant role. Africa's share of world trade has fallen dramatically in recent decades. The continent's contribution to global trade flows is now minuscule, the result not only of a lack of economic diversity but also of restrictive trade policies both within and beyond Africa. (See chapters 10 and 11 in this volume.)

In 1948, Africa accounted for around 7 per cent of total world exports, but by 2003 this share had fallen to 2 per cent (see figure 9.11). During the same period, Asia increased its global export share from 14 to 23 per cent, with Europe's proportion rising from 40 to 45 per cent. The US share also grew during this time—from 20 to 22 per cent. Clearly, Africa has enormous scope to trade more with the rest of the world.

It is striking, though, that a significant reason for Africa's trade weakness is the low and declining amount of trade between African countries themselves. In 2000, only 9.8 per cent of African exports were sold on the continent itself, a share that by 2005 had fallen to 8.9 per cent.[14] Within the European Union, in contrast, intra-EU sales account for 67 per cent of all member states' exports. So there is significant scope for trade between Afri-

Fig 9.11: Africa's imports/exports, 1948–2005 (percentage of world total).

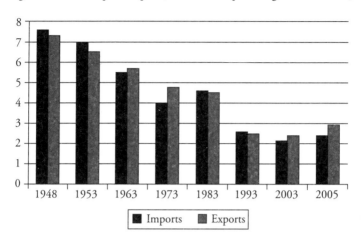

can states—trade that would have positive effects on growth and, in turn, overseas investment.

Intra-African trade is low not only because of the continent's severe transport bottlenecks, but also because of the complex web of local trade restrictions. Such regional trade agreements add high bureaucratic barriers, hinder specialisation, and undermine the gains from trade—leading to lower efficiency and a much lower rate of economic expansion. According to the International Monetary Fund (IMF), there are about thirty regional trade agreements currently operating in Africa, with each country belonging to an average of four regional trade bodies.[15] (See chapter 4 in this volume.) Almost all of these regional economic communities appear to be not only poorly administered, but also conceptually flawed. The point of most of them seems to be to allow certain countries to undermine the growth of others through the restrictive use of high taxes and duties, as well as complex administrative procedures. On a continent in which growth is so sorely needed, and in which the fate of nations are so closely intertwined, this approach seems incredibly shortsighted.

Many foreign investors also find Africa's intracontinental trade laws deeply frustrating, as they often prevent the import of raw materials and capital goods to one country from another. The huge administrative burden of maintaining the regional trade agreements also puts additional pressure on public sector administrative staff, leading to even bigger delays in other parts of state bureaucracies.

There is a widespread recognition, in addition, that the current regime of international trade rules is stacked against Africa. Given the constraints of the regional trade agreements, the continent seems to do little to help itself when it comes to facilitating trade. But many overseas investors accept that the global trading system also gives Africa a raw deal, particularly when it comes to agriculture. Europe remains Africa's largest trading partner, but this dominance is shrinking. In 2000 the European Union accounted for 50 per cent of African trade, but by 2005 this share had fallen to 43 per cent. The US share of African trade grew from 17 to 20 per cent during the same period. China also ramped up its trade with Africa in the decade of the 2000s. During the first half of 2009 China overtook the US as the biggest export destination of South Africa, the continent's largest economy, and in 2011 China was South Africa's most profitable bilateral trading partner. Trade between Africa as a whole and China increased tenfold between 2000 and 2010, hitting $107 billion in 2009.

However, the EU remains, by far, Africa's largest regional trading partner, with the US also significant. In general terms, both the EU and the US still maintain very high tariff protection against agricultural goods from elsewhere in the world, which seriously hampers Africa's development. The EU's Common Agricultural Policy (CAP) distributed subsidies amounting to $52 billion in 2008. (See chapter 12 in this volume.) In the US, agricultural subsidies reached $115 billion in 2006. Such payouts lead to considerable overproduction, generating a severe disincentive to the development of agro-business in Africa. With more than two-thirds of the African population working in agriculture, this is a profoundly disturbing situation.

In recent years there appears to have been a shift in political emphasis, with leading Western voices stressing that Brussels and Washington could soon give ground and curtail their agricultural subsidies that do so much damage to peasant farmers in Africa and elsewhere in the developing world. In 2006 Pascal Lamy, the former EU trade commissioner turned director-general of the World Trade Organisation (WTO), issued a clarion call for change: 'It is a reality', he said, 'that the global trading system disfavours the developing world. On agriculture, on coffee, on footwear, there remains in the system rules that work against poor countries'. Lamy employed some extremely tough language in a bid to push Western powers into a deal with the developing world, in completing the Doha 'trade round' that had begun in 2001. The Frenchman realised that a new overarching trade agreement would provide a boon not only to the global economy, but also to global political stability, given that the Western powers launched the Doha 'development round' with the explicit pledge of reaching out to the rest of the world. In the spring of 2006 he said:

Fifty years ago, the process of political decolonisation began. But the process of economic decolonisation is not yet complete. And the Doha trade round is about getting rid of those features of the global trading rules that are remnants of colonisation. If all the Millennium Development Goals are going in the right direction but the most important one—trade—isn't, then we have a very serious problem. If this round fails, I am sure there will be a backlash from the developing world.[16]

Another respected senior Western voice—Robert Zoellick, a former US trade representative and, between 2007 and 2012, president of the World Bank—also weighed in: 'A fairer and more global trading system for agriculture will give more opportunities—and confidence—to African and other developing country farmers to expand production', he said in the spring of 2008. 'But the world's agricultural system is stuck in the past. If ever there was a time to cut distorting agricultural subsidies and open markets for food, it is now.... This is the moment of decision for the Doha round. It's now or never'.[17]

As it turned out, the Doha trade round has since floundered. Considering that the Uruguay round of 1986–1994 took eight years to agree and Doha was put on ice after seven years, it is not impossible that the talks could be concluded. However, with protectionist sentiments rising in both the US and Europe in 2010, it may be that the world has just witnessed the first outright failure of a multilateral trade negotiation since the 1930s.

This has been a major setback for the global trade regime overall, but is of particular disappointment to Africa. Given the continent's agro-industrial potential, a significant reduction in farm protectionism would have been hugely beneficial to Africa, not only in commercial terms, but in humanitarian terms as well. It appears, however, that Western farm lobbies have prevailed and, as the 'Scramble' for Africa's resource wealth intensifies, enthusiasm for granting the continent's agricultural produce access to Western markets has diminished. This is a shameful situation and the European Union must acknowledge that it has played a central role in failing to resolve it. So, along with the resolution of infrastructure bottlenecks, it is crucial that the global trade regime is altered to give developing countries a fairer crack of the whip. Unless this happens, it is difficult to see how Africa's share of world trade can increase significantly, which is also bad news for the continent's prospects as a viable investment destination.

Another aspect of Western relations with Africa that requires urgent change is aid. By 2008, Africa had received an estimated $625 billion of foreign aid since 1960. Yet per capita incomes in sub-Saharan Africa (excluding South Africa) have risen only very slowly in constant dollar terms over this period.[18] At the same time, the UN's scale of human development—which includes health, education, and economic well-being—ranks thirty-four African countries among the world's forty lowest performers. Aid seems to have been spectacularly ineffective in promoting socioeconomic development on the continent.

Aid flows can be of vital importance in extreme circumstances, such as famine and other humanitarian crises. Such aid should, of course, continue to flow. Having said that, one can argue that most development assistance extended to Africa between 1960 and 2010 has been counterproductive. In the eyes of this author and many foreign investors, aid flows can undermine 'good governance' and distort political accountability. Governments that are highly dependent on aid are often more interested in pleasing foreign donors than in serving their own citizens. And all donors have some non-developmental motives and their own priorities, often resulting in confused and shifting policies and priorities as well as erratic spending.

Adrian Wood, professor of international development at Oxford University, proposed an upper limit on the aid that donors can give to any specific country (outside emergency situations). This figure was set at 50 per cent of the amount of tax revenues that aid-recipient governments raise from their own citizens, excluding oil and mineral revenues. 'This would keep the governments of non-mineral countries dependent for revenue mainly on their citizens', argued Wood, 'thus giving them incentives to pay attention mainly to what their citizens want, not donors. It would also encourage governments to raise more taxes from their citizens, since every extra dollar of tax raised would attract a matching increase of 50 cents of aid'.[19] (See chapter 5 in this volume.)

This approach seems sensible. Apart from some perilously poor countries, nonemergency development assistance, with its related 'tied aid' and 'conditionality', should be phased out. Africa needs new, commercial relationships with the West, built on investment flows and equity ownership, rather than on aid. Such investments could emerge. It is one of the ironies of the global situation in 2011 that, while short-term liquidity had dried up, there was abundant long-term cash available for the right investments. Several emerging market funds are starting to invest long-term in Africa, not least the large sovereign wealth funds.

More than a dozen countries in sub-Saharan Africa had stock markets of their own by 2011. The trouble is, however, that while such markets have been gaining attention, they remain extremely small and often illiquid, making it difficult for most investors to gain exposure to them. This explains why 'private equity' is increasingly popular, with financiers spotting their own opportunities to fund commercial projects away from stock markets. While stakes in such investments are difficult to sell until projects are complete, they usually do not suffer from the valuation swings connected with nascent stock markets.

Money is now flowing into African portfolio investments beyond North Africa and South Africa, even though many of the banks and other financial services companies offering such investment vehicles are, in fact, South African. By 2010, South Africa's Standard Bank had unveiled several pan-African funds in response to demand from investors in the US, Europe, and the Middle East. The country's Investec has launched similar opportunities for investments in sub-Saharan Africa. A slew of funds have also been listed on the Alternative Investment Market—London's 'junior stock exchange'—allowing even the smallest Western investors to gain some exposure to Africa. In addition, Britain's private equity industry has raised several billion pounds for Africa.

It must be noted, however, that there is still a reluctance to invest in Africa, given the continent's institutional weaknesses and chronically low levels of per capita income. That is why many investors interested in the continent's potential, instead of investing in Africa-based companies themselves, tend to use proxy holdings. Examples might include South African companies with their own operations in Africa, such as Sasol, MTN, Standard Bank, and Naspers. Other proxies include Western-based companies with a heavy 'footprint' in sub-Saharan Africa, such as Total, Nestlé, Vodaphone, Anglo-American, Tullow, and Standard Chartered. For now, such companies have been perceived as offering global investors exposure to Africa at cheaper valuations and with less endemic risk.

Concluding reflections

It is important to note that large parts of Africa cannot be described as 'the last investment frontier', as they are already well-developed destinations for a wide range of international capital, or rapidly on their way to becoming so. The business communities in South Africa and North Africa would not accept the 'last frontier' label, for fear of underselling their markets. They would probably be right. But sub-Saharan Africa truly is the world's last investment frontier. The region deserves this moniker, not because it remains for the most part so underdeveloped, but because its potential is so great, despite the current lack of socioeconomic development.

Africa's macroeconomic stability has improved markedly in recent years, not least because of the commodity price boom of the decade of the 2000s. This general improvement has been seen not only among the relatively large oil- and gas-exporting countries, but also among many smaller nations. Some very poor African countries, though, are still suffering from extremely fragile budget positions, and, in fact, their fiscal position has weakened in recent years as a by-product of more expensive fuel imports.

Across sub-Saharan Africa, lower inflation and growing real incomes (albeit from a very low base) will continue to encourage foreign investors to take the plunge. But much of the continent still suffers from extremely serious infrastructure deficiencies, particularly when it comes to power generation. This lack of generation capacity should be seriously and urgently addressed. Without an expansion in sub-Saharan Africa's power supply off the back of an influx of foreign capital and expertise, it is impossible for the region to diversify its export base and take the next steps towards sustained growth, economic modernisation, and poverty reduction.

While many of Africa's problems need to be solved by Africans themselves, many foreign investors also acknowledge that the current international trading regime penalises the continent. Effective political leadership is therefore needed to resolve this immoral situation—from Europe, the US, and a few large emerging markets. These countries between them failed to make the concessions required to reap the benefits represented by the Doha trade round. This has been unfortunate for the world economy, but particularly so for Africa, setting the continent back on its journey to fulfilling its vast investment potential.

The renowned Kenyan scholar Ali Mazrui ended his famous 1986 documentary *The Africans: A Triple Heritage* by noting that Africans are 'the people of the day before yesterday, potentially the people of the day after tomorrow'. While this is true, 'Africa's Renaissance'—an expression popularised by Thabo Mbeki, South Africa's president between 1999 and 2008—could happen even sooner than is generally expected. The potential is most certainly there. But such a renaissance will only happen with sustained domestic and foreign investment, and the economic progress that this brings.

10

AN ANATOMY OF THE ECONOMIC
PARTNERSHIP AGREEMENTS

Mareike Meyn

Introduction

The 2000 Cotonou Agreement established the basis for a new trading regime between the European Union and the seventy-nine-member African, Caribbean, and Pacific (ACP) group of countries by providing for reciprocal trade relations in conformity with the trade rules of the World Trade Organisation (WTO) from 2008 onwards. Economic partnership agreements (EPAs) are supposed to be asymmetrical trade agreements that foster sustainable economic and social development in the ACP, and promote their smooth and gradual integration into the world economy. This should first be achieved through economic and trade cooperation with the EU, which aims to address supply-side constraints, enhance production capacities and competitiveness, and attract investment.[1]

While the objectives of EPAs are clear, the tools for achieving them are disputed between the negotiating parties. The European Commission in Brussels aims to negotiate comprehensive free trade agreements including trade in goods and services and also addressing 'behind the border measures' such as competition policy and public procurement, which it believes will stimulate structural reforms. African countries, for their part, argue that institutional and administrative capacity at the national and regional levels needs to be built first before tackling such reforms.

The battle about what the 'development component' of the EPAs should entail continued throughout the five-year negotiation process (2002–2007) without being satisfactorily resolved. African countries became increasingly disappointed with the lack of financial commitments accompanying the EPAs as well as with the negotiation process, which they felt was largely dominated by the European Commission without sufficient input from them. Brussels was pushing hard to reach agreement before the start of the EU-Africa summit of December 2007 in Lisbon. Indeed, about half of the ACP countries initialled the EPAs in early December 2007, just before the Lisbon summit started.

What do the EPAs actually involve and what do they mean for African countries? By reviewing comprehensive research undertaken by the London-based Overseas Development Institute (ODI) on EPAs in 2007–2008, this chapter aims to provide an initial review of a set of very complex documents and their development implications.

The European Union is the major trading partner for most African countries. Its special relationship with sub-Saharan Africa as well as with the countries of the Caribbean and the Pacific dates back to 1963, when the European Economic Community (EEC), as it was known at the time, entered into a trade and development relationship with former European colonies (the Yaoundé Convention). Beginning in 1975, Brussels granted the ACP countries unilateral preferences under the Lomé Conventions (I–IV). The unilateral character of EU-ACP preferences was outlawed by WTO rules as discriminating against other developing countries. Since there are no homogeneous groups among the ACP countries, which rather consist of developing countries and least-developed countries (LDCs), this preferential treatment was said to discriminate against other developing countries and LDCs.

In the late 1990s, with the expiry of the last Lomé Convention (IV) imminent, the European Community proposed a new trade and development regime. The Cotonou Agreement, which came into force in 2000, envisaged the creation of reciprocal trade agreements between the EU and regional blocs of ACP countries by establishing economic partnership agreements, which were to take effect by the beginning of 2008. EPAs, as reciprocal trade agreements liberalising 'substantially all trade' in a 'reasonable length of time' between the EU and regional groupings of ACP states, appear to fall within the scope of Article XXIV of the General Agreement on Tariffs and Trade (GATT), the forerunner of the WTO (see box 1). To cover its ability to discriminate legally against non-ACP countries during this transition period, the EU obtained a waiver at the WTO, which expired in 2007. (For background on EU-ACP relations, see chapter 2 in this volume.)

Box 1: What must a WTO-compatible EPA look like?

EPAs are negotiated under Article XXIV of GATT, which requires in essence that 'the duties and other restrictive regulations of commerce … are eliminated on substantially all the trade between the constituent territories in products originating in such territories', with establishment of 'a plan and schedule for the formation … of such a free-trade area within a reasonable length of time'.[2]

The interpretation of Article XXIV remains disputed, since it does not define what is required to attain the liberalisation of 'substantially all' trade.[3] The EU's view on this relates to the share of trade that is liberalised, considering about 90 per cent of bilateral trade liberalisation to be WTO-compatible. Since the EU liberalises 100 per cent of trade, it requires the ACP to liberalise about 80 per cent of EU imports.

Regarding the interpretation of the term 'reasonable length of time', the 'Understanding on the Interpretation of Art. XXIV' states that the time frame for liberalisation should exceed ten years only in exceptional cases. Since Article XXIV was not conceptualised to govern North-South free trade areas (FTAs) between regional blocs but to regulate the conditions of FTAs and customs unions vis-à-vis the multilateral trading regime, EPAs are often interpreted as an 'exceptional case'. The European Community followed this argument in parts, agreeing to transitional periods for the full implementation of EPAs up to twenty-five years in 'exceptional cases'.[4]

The negotiation process

EPA negotiations started in 2002 on an all-ACP level. Two years later, these talks were devolved to the regional level. Although the EU Commission in

Brussels knew exactly what it wanted—comprehensive, WTO-compatible trade deals with the six ACP regions—it did not have a clear idea of how to align these objectives with ACP realities. The three main pitfalls in the process were: differing interpretations of the development component; failure to agree on 'WTO plus' components; and application of the regional components of EPAs.

Differing interpretations of the development component. While the ACP countries wanted to tie import liberalisation commitments to development aid, arguing that guaranteed access to long-term funds is crucial to overcoming supply-side constraints and diversifying the productive base of national economies, the European Commission insisted that EPA negotiations and talks on development finance were two separate issues. In any case, the EU Directorate-General for Trade (responsible for the EPA negotiations) argued that funds had been made available under the tenth European Development Fund (EDF) programme, administered by the Directorate-General for Development, to implement the EPAs. The ACP countries countered that it was unacceptable to limit guaranteed funding to 2013, given that the implementation process would extend beyond this date, and that the full effects of major liberalisation and regulatory reform would only be felt thereafter. The EU Commission retorted that multilateral and bilateral funds would be made available for the implementation of the EPAs if and when needed.

Failure to agree on 'WTO plus' components. Only a few ACP regions (and very few countries in Africa) wanted to include services, investment, and trade-related aspects (such as competition and public procurement) in the EPA negotiations. Rather, the focus of the ACP countries was on trade facilitation and technical support, with the aim of improving access to higher-value segments of the EU market. Brussels, however, insisted that binding rules on services and 'some' related issues represented the real development component of EPAs.

Application of the regional component of EPAs. Regional integration is considered to be a key element in EPAs. Larger markets can reduce the economic and political risk premium, offering opportunities to attract more investment. Because of the potential welfare effects of regional integration that have been experienced by the EU, the Cotonou Agreement of 2000 regards regional integration as a 'key instrument for the integration of ACP countries into the world economy'.[5] However, Brussels's seemingly relentless promotion of regional integration among ACP countries betrays an inherently Eurocentric view of the world and neglects the unique difficulties faced by ACP countries.[6]

It would have been desirable for each ACP region to negotiate a common external tariff regime with the EU, as well as, ideally, through a joint negotiation mechanism. However, when negotiations began on a regional level in 2004, only three regions, covering just eighteen of the seventy-five qualified ACP countries,[7] had established a customs union or were in the process of doing so. In the absence of sufficiently well-developed regional entities, six EPA configurations were eventually established, which either incorporated nonmembers into existing regional groups (as was the case in the Caribbean and the Pacific) or merged subregions to create larger entities (as was the case with the Southern African Customs Union/Southern African Development Community [SACU/SADC] and the East African Community/Eastern and Southern Africa region [EAC/ESA]).[8] This approach profoundly underestimated the importance of economic integration, and the fact that these new associations had yet to reach a sufficient level of integration.

Though negotiations started in 2002, five years before the deadline elapsed, the process and outcome of EPAs remained disputed throughout the negotiations. Many African countries were not overly concerned about the slow progress of discussions, but relied on what they regarded as the EU's obligation to provide a suitable fallback position.

The alternatives

According to Article 37.6 of the Cotonou Agreement of 2000, those ACP countries that did not find themselves in a position to enter into EPAs were to be provided by the EU with a trading alternative that was 'equivalent' to their existing situation and in conformity with WTO rules. However, Brussels failed to come up with an 'equivalent' to Cotonou, and instead insisted that its General System of Preferences (GSP) was the only available alternative. The GSP has three different preference levels: the standard GSP, which applies to most developing countries and all ACP countries; the 'Everything but Arms' initiative, which has applied to the world's least-developed countries since 2001; and the GSP+ regime, which grants enhanced terms to a range of countries that have ratified and implemented a list of international conventions on core labour and human rights principles (by 2011, no ACP country had qualified for the GSP+ regime). In this scheme, the standard GSP is the only alternative available for all ACP countries, while countries in the group classified as 'least-developed' have, additionally, the option to export under the 'Everything but Arms' initiative. Do these alternatives provide 'equivalent' market access to the Cotonou trading regime?

The standard GSP. Research by the Overseas Development Institute found that the standard GSP is much less favourable than Cotonou for many ACP exports. All non-LDC ACP members would experience a jump in the EU tariff applied to some of their exports if they were subject to the standard GSP. Although many of the increases would be relatively small, for 267 goods exported to the EU in 2005 the tariff jump would be 10 per cent or more, and would result in new or increased duties, some of them very high. Nearly two-thirds of non-LDC ACP countries would see their tariffs jump by over 25 per cent of the value of their current exports to the EU. For just over one-quarter of those countries, the proportion affected would be over 50 per cent of their exports. The countries most affected would be exporters of the EU's most protected agricultural products: sugar, beef, bananas, citrus fruits, fish, and horticultural products.

Taking the example of the only African beef exporters to the EU—Botswana and Namibia—ODI research found that the taxes imposed on their exports would have exceeded their annual EU aid fund contributions by more than four times. In both cases, the taxes would have been prohibitive, and would in all likelihood have resulted in the immediate cessation of beef exports to Europe. In the case of diamond-rich Botswana, the loss of EU preferences could have turned the country into a mono-export economy.[9]

The 'Everything but Arms' initiative. The 'Everything but Arms' initiative is the only available trading alternative that provides equivalent market access to Cotonou. It is, however, only available for the ACP countries that are LDCs. The incentive for LDC ACP countries to enter into an EPA was therefore limited—and most of them have exported under this initiative since January 2008.

The GSP+ regime. The GSP+ regime has been available to fifteen countries (mainly in Central America) that applied by December 2005 and met the EU's criterion of having ratified twenty-seven conventions on core labour standards and human rights. When the GSP+ regime was first introduced, not one of the ACP countries applied. Given the impending deadline for the WTO waiver as well as limited progress in the EPA negotiations, however, two ACP countries, Seychelles and Nigeria, applied to become GSP+ beneficiaries in the course of 2007. The EU Commission rejected both applications on the basis that neither country could meet the labour, human rights, and environmental conditions necessary to benefit from GSP+ treatment and that, in any case, a decision on whether or not to renew the GSP+ regime was not due to take place until December 2008. Both countries were also refused GSP+ treatment in December 2008, because they had not ratified all the relevant conventions. However, beneficiaries of the EU's previous GSP regimes automatically qualified for GSP+ when the initiative was launched in 2005, despite the fact that not all countries had complied with the conditions at the time of its introduction.[10] Moreover, at the time of applying for GSP+, Seychelles had ratified all twenty-seven relevant conventions, while Nigeria had ratified all but one. The EU Commission also determines unilaterally how and when to revise the regime and the degree to which it should be made available to ACP countries at any given point in time.

The Commission was equally reluctant to extend the WTO waiver beyond 31 December 2007, arguing that it would be too costly, particularly given that other developing countries would inevitably seek similar concessions. The option of 'stopping the clock' and allowing the expiry of the WTO waiver to pass while granting ACP countries Cotonou preference even as EPA negotiations continued, was similarly turned down. Brussels argued that such a policy would not only detract from EPA negotiations, but also breach WTO rules—something the Commission said that it could ill afford to do.

Although the 2007 deadline presented a very substantial challenge for a 'normal' trade agreement, it would not necessarily have been unattainable for an accord that established the key principles and left the details for a later stage. This was why some ODI analysts[11] recommended the creation of 'framework agreements'—a proposal that differed fundamentally from the 'interim EPAs' that were finally concluded by the end of 2007. The basic idea of these framework accords was to take advantage of the shallow WTO provisions (liberalising 'substantially all trade' in a 'reasonable length of time') by creating a number of liberalisation tranches over twenty-five years. Under this approach, only the first tranche would have needed to be specified by the end of 2007, while the details of the other tranches could be determined at a later stage. Such an accord could have been WTO-compatible. Provided that it represented a genuine commitment and was implemented according to its timetable, it was certainly not clearly incompatible with WTO rules.

The advantage of such an approach would have been to buy time to harmonise ACP schedules on a regional basis in a way that reflected the genuine interests of these countries in regional trade. Additionally, such 'framework agreements' would not have borne the risk of losing momentum by simply extending the negotiations for two to three years, as some ACP members had requested.

The EU Commission decided, however, to create facts on the ground by demanding national liberalisation schedules, which ACP countries provided at the last minute. Between 2004 and 2010, Brussels negotiated with six regional ACP groups: West Africa, Central Africa, Eastern and Southern Africa, Southern Africa (SADC-minus), the Caribbean, and the Pacific. During the second half of 2007, the five countries of the East African Community (Kenya, Tanzania, Uganda, Rwanda, and Burundi) intimated that they were considering negotiating as a separate region, but this was not confirmed until December 2007, when they created a seventh group (taking four members from ESA and Tanzania from SADC-minus).

At the end of the negotiations, only two regional EPAs had been created: one for the Caribbean Forum (CARIFORUM) and one for the EAC. All other regions 'lost' members (opting for the above-mentioned 'alternatives'). Only the EAC region agreed on a joint liberalisation schedule. For CARIFORUM, the EPA appears to include a single regional liberalisation schedule, but in fact comprises fifteen country-specific schedules with a certain level of overlap.[12] Thus it appears that only the EAC has reinforced regional integration through the EPA process.

At the other end of the spectrum is West and Central Africa. Only two West African countries (Ghana and Côte d'Ivoire) had, by 2011, signed an EPA with two separate liberalisation schedules. In Central Africa only one country (Cameroon) had signed an EPA by 2010. This means that over four-fifths of the West and Central African members had yet to sign EPAs in 2011.

The other regions—ESA, SADC-minus, and the Pacific—were in a midway position. Each of the signatories within the group had agreed on an identical text, but their liberalisation schedules differed. Owing to the last-minute creation of the East African Community EPA, there have been substantial changes to the composition of the 'Eastern and Southern Africa EPA', which consists of just four island states (Comoros, Madagascar, Mauritius, and Seychelles) plus Zimbabwe and Zambia (which submitted liberalisation schedules only in July 2008). (See also chapter 11 in this volume, on EPA negotiations.)

The signatories

Thirty-five African countries had initialled EPAs by the end of 2007. Most of the nonsignatory countries were classified as LDCs and had, with the 'Everything but Arms' initiative, an equitable fallback position. The same applies to South Africa, which has had a WTO-compatible 'trade, development, and cooperation agreement' with the EU since 1996, and therefore was not under the threat of losing EU market access. (See chapter 6 in this volume.)

Only three non-LDC African countries did not initial the EPAs: Congo-Brazzaville, Gabon, and Nigeria. These three oil-producing countries export few agricultural products to the EU, and were therefore in a comparably comfortable position. As can be seen from Table 1, less than 2 per cent of Nigeria's exports to the EU, accounting for 1 per cent or more of its total exports, faced tariff increases in 2007—compared with more than 56 per cent in the case of Kenya.

Table 1: From Cotonou to GSP: costs of preference loss for selected African countries.

	Number of Items with Change of				Items Accounting for 1% or More of Total That Would Experience a Change in Access (percentage)
	10 to < 20%	*≥ 20%+*	*Specific Duty*	*Total*	
Nigeria	32	1	24	57	1.7
Congo Republic	5	–	4	9	3.3
Gabon	5	–	1	6	4.1
Ghana	28	6	33	67	16.3
Kenya	42	4	16	62	56.5

Sources: Eurostat COMEXT; UNCTAD TRAINS; UK Tariff 2007.

It appears therefore that in the main, 'push' factors were decisive for the decision by non-LDCs to initial EPAs. Facing the real risk of being downgraded to the GSP (and subsequently losing market access for some of their most valuable export products, such as sugar, beef, bananas, and horticultural products), most non-LDC ACP countries agreed to the deal. However, the fact that a number of LDCs signed the EPAs indicated that there were also some 'pull' factors, which leads us to the question: How did market access for non-LDCs and LDCs improve as a result of the EPAs?

The EU's liberalisation offer

In January 2008 the EU removed all remaining tariffs and quotas on imports from EPA signatories except for sugar and rice, for which duty-free quota-free (DFQF) market access was being phased in. DFQF for the rice varieties exported by ACP countries faced a transition period, but they could still be exported duty- and quota-free from the beginning of 2010. The transition for sugar involves three phases for non-LDCs: (1) January 2008 to September 2009: continuation of the Sugar Protocol, with 'additional market access' (180,000 tonnes) for beneficiaries;[13] (2) October 2009 to September 2015: DFQF for non-LDC ACP countries subject to an 'automatic volume safeguard clause' (3.5 tonnes for all ACP countries) and, for processed agricultural products with high sugar content, an 'enhanced surveillance mechanism in order to prevent circumvention of the sugar import regime'; and (3) October 2015 onwards: DFQF for non-LDC sugar exports, subject to a 'special safeguard clause'.[14] In absolute terms, the immediate gains from duty-free quota access have been relatively small, but this is because the status quo ante was already liberal. For some ACP countries, the principal export benefit of EPAs with the new opportunities offered by DFQF is less than the retention of previous levels of access.

DFQF has four types of actual or potential effect. First, and most immediate, is the redistribution of the import tax that Brussels previously levied on imports. This has now been transferred from the EU to elements in the ACP export supply chain (retailers, importers, shippers, exporters, and producers). To the extent that any benefits accrue to ACP exporters or producers, exports have been made more profitable. Second, if the revenue transfer induces importers to shift purchases away from less preferred sources towards the ACP, this could result in an increase in the volume of ACP exports. This may also enable them to increase their supply of competitive products without substantial new investments. Third, by removing some very high tariff barriers, DFQF might make it commercially feasible, for the first time, for ACP countries to export products to the EU market that they already supply competitively to other markets. The fourth effect of duty-free quota access could be the most substantial, but is also the most difficult to predict. If DFQF induces increased supply from ACP states (for example, as a result of new investments or shifts between products), there could be wide-ranging political effects both in terms of foreign exchange earned and in knock-on effects for the rest of the economy.

The greatest change resulting from the EPAs has been for the twenty-six states that are not LDCs, some of their EU imports (valued at €1.4 billion in 2006) have been immediately affected. Although this is equivalent to a very small percentage of total EU imports from all non-LDC ACP states (just 2 per cent in 2006), the immediate gains for some items, such as rice, grapes, beef, citrus fruits, and vegetables, could be extremely large.

By 2010, no comprehensive analysis on the development implication of DFQF for ACP economies had been undertaken, and it was unclear whether DFQF has provoked an increase in export supply from the ACP countries or increased investment in the most lucrative sectors, such as meat, grapes, rice, and citrus.

Exports of processed food have not been positively affected by DFQF as a result of the EU's onerous rules-of-origin regime. Previously these concerns were primarily raised in relation to manufactures, but now DFQF extends them into processed foods. In many cases, the current rules do not allow an ACP state to process raw materials that are imported, unless they have been produced in another member of the same EPA or within the EU.

Still, there have been some improvements on the rules of origin under the EPAs, notably on clothing, for which the EU has adopted a rule similar to the US African Growth and Opportunity Act (AGOA) initiative of 2000,[15] which might have provided an incentive for some clothing-exporting LDCs such as Madagascar to initial EPAs.

Another reason for some LDCs to initial EPAs might have been their trading dependence on the 'hub economy' with which they coexist in a regional integration framework. In light of these regional integration processes, some LDCs apparently judged the costs of remaining outside the EPAs to be higher than the costs of joining them. Indeed, most LDCs that signed EPAs are part of functioning regional integration schemes (Lesotho of SACU; Burundi, Rwanda, Tanzania, and Uganda of the EAC). Since these LDCs import, to a large extent, through their regional partners (South Africa and Kenya respectively), which both have free trade agreements with the EU,[16] they would have needed to impose intra-regional trade barriers if they had not joined the EPAs.

The implications of EPAs for regional integration in Africa

The EU Commission argued that interim EPAs had to be negotiated with individual countries to avoid disruption of trade for non-LDC ACP countries. Since all interim EPAs provide for a review of tariff concessions, building regional markets would not have been a problem while negotiating comprehensive EPAs.[17]

However, low levels of economic integration and huge disparities among countries in terms of their protectionist tendencies (reflected in their wildly divergent tariff levels) have inhibited a joint approach to regional EPA negotiations once they have been initiated. These problems have not suddenly disappeared—if anything, they have multiplied and become even more complex with the introduction of the EPAs (see chapter 4 in this volume). Four years after signing the 'interim EPAs', Brussels had not yet succeeded in agreeing on 'comprehensive EPAs'—neither on scope nor on content.

The country-specific interim EPAs allowed each ACP country to exclude about 20 per cent of its national EU imports from its liberalisation commitments. On a regional basis, an individual country could only keep this exclusion basket if it mirrored exactly the priorities of its neighbours. This is, however, far from being the case.

In the case of SADC-minus, only one-fifth of the items excluded by the BLNS states (Botswana, Lesotho, Namibia, and Swaziland) match the exclusion basket of Mozambique. For the ESA, the situation is even more complex. Not a single item is in the exclusion basket of all five countries, and over three-quarters of items are excluded by just one country.[18] To align these individual schedules on a regional basis would require comprehensive reviews of national exclusion baskets—and the liberalisation of hitherto excluded items in order to keep the regional exclusion baskets under the 20 per cent threshold (see box 1). This mammoth task has been undertaken since 2008 but has not yet succeeded in any region.

While the revision of schedules might be a minor problem in Central and West Africa, since only single country EPAs exists in each subregion and very few countries are likely to sign up to the EPAs, this is a major problem in Southern and Eastern Africa. Hence the degree to which regional integration can continue within the current COMESA (Common Market for Eastern and Southern Africa)[19] and SADC frameworks must be questioned, given that, first, the ESA/COMESA has split with the emergence of the East African Community EPA, which leaves the region with mainly least-developed countries and island states, none of which are likely to champion regional integration strongly; and second, SADC has lost most of its members during the EPA negotiation process, so that economic integration is now centred on SACU (plus Mozambique), with the other SADC countries either having tied their external tariffs to a different framework (Tanzania in the EAC, and Madagascar, Mauritius, and Zimbabwe in the ESA) or having hardly any involvement in regional economic integration.

It is very difficult to imagine how this 'spaghetti bowl' of different national and subregional commitments can be knitted into two regional integration groupings comprising all Southern and Eastern African countries (see figure 10.1).

The fact that SACU—the only fully implemented customs union in Africa—has been split up during EPA negotiations has added another challenging dimension to the regional integration debate.[20] Since the 2004 SACU agreement[21] requires the consent of all members to enter into external trade relations (Article 31), the EPA obligations entered into by Botswana, Lesotho, and Swaziland are not enforceable. Whether South Africa will accept the changes that have to be made in SACU's common external tariff as a result of the interim EPAs remains to be seen. Given the fact that South Africa collects 98.6 per cent of SACU's customs duties,[22] it is doubtful that Botswana, Lesotho, and Swaziland have the capacity to enforce a separate external tariff with the EU. If South Africa were to decline to join the SADC EPA, it would be up to the EU Commission's discretion to judge whether or not the BLNS states have fulfilled their tariff liberalisation commitments under the EPA.

Namibia initialled the SADC EPA in December 2007 but refused to sign it, arguing like South Africa and Angola (the other SADC states that did not sign) that the EPA would not sufficiently address Namibia's development interests. However, in contrast to Angola (which is classified as an LDC and benefits from DFQF to the EU) and South Africa (which, as earlier noted, has a separate trade agreement with the EU), Namibia does not have a fallback position. As of December 2011, Namibia continued to enjoy DFQF in the EU market without having signed the EPA—a clear violation of WTO rules and a discrimination against other non-EPA signatories such as Nigeria and Gabon.

Figure 10.1: Regional integration and EPAs in Southern and Eastern Africa.

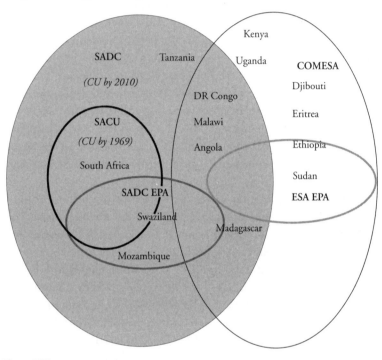

Notes: CU = customs union.

In sum, it appears that the EPA negotiation process facilitated and accelerated economic integration in the EAC while adding additional challenges for deeper integration in Southern Africa. On the other hand, it is fair to point out that economic integration in the SADC and COMESA regions had been inconsistent before the debate over the EPAs. For West and Central Africa as well as the Pacific, the implications of the EPAs for regional integration appear to represent largely 'unfinished business', since only very few countries in both regions have initialled the EPAs.

African liberalisation commitments in the EPAs

As a comparative analysis carried out in 2008 by the ODI with the Maastricht-based European Centre for Development Policy Management (ECDPM) showed, African countries have been very differently affected by their liberalisation commitments under the EPAs. No clear pattern could be identified to show that poorer countries have longer to adjust than richer ones or that the EPAs had been tailored to meet development needs (however defined). Some of the richer countries among the list have to adjust quickly—but so do some of the poorest.

It is important to note that the 2008 study analysed a 'moving target': African EPA texts and liberalisation schedules that were initialled in December 2007. Several changes had been made by 2008: Ghana submitted a new schedule, Zambia joined the ESA EPA, Mozambique revised its schedule, Namibia refused to sign the EPA, and the ESA countries were busy aligning their individual schedules on a regional level. However, not much has happened. As of December 2011, no more countries have joined the EPAs, nor have countries succeeded in aligning national EPAs at a regional level.

So, what do the schedules say? Côte d'Ivoire and Mozambique will face adjustment challenges that are among the largest that will occur soonest. Abidjan, for example, is set to have removed tariffs on 60 per cent of its imports from the EU completely, two years before Kenya even begins to start reducing its tariffs as part of the EPA; Ghana should have liberalised 71 per cent of its imports from the EU completely by the time Kenya is three years into this process, which, after a further six years, is set to result in just 39 per cent of its imports being duty-free.

A similar controversial picture emerges in the analysis of ACP agricultural liberalisation commitments. While Côte d'Ivoire's and Ghana's agricultural liberalisation schedules have been front-loaded, Cameroon has largely back-loaded its agricultural liberalisation (in effect it has had to liberalise most of its agricultural imports at the end of the implementation period, and has therefore had more time to adjust). Cameroon, and also Mozambique, the BLS states (Botswana, Lesotho, and Swaziland), and Mauritius, have liberalised hardly any agricultural items that appear to compete with domestic production. Agricultural liberalisation for Côte d'Ivoire and Ghana, on the other hand, has included many items that appear to be competing with domestic production, such as poultry, tomatoes, potatoes, eggs, and grains. (See chapter 12 in this volume.)

One interesting aspect that was observed in analyses of ACP liberalisation commitments in the EAC and ESA frameworks (and in comparing them with the current tariff being applied) is that the biggest adjustment costs are likely to occur when bringing applied tariffs down to the agreed regional level. While these adjustment costs can be contributed as a 'customs effect' and not as an EPA effect, they might well be perceived to be harsh measures by domestic producers. In this context, it also needs to be considered that a maximum protection level of 25 per cent (EAC and COMESA common external tariffs) might be insufficient to protect this region from agricultural import surges.

The picture that emerges from the analysis of the EPA liberalisation schedules also confirms the hypothesis that African countries that were able to negotiate in a firm manner and with awareness of their interests, obtained a better deal. Comparing African liberalisation commitments with those of Caribbean and Pacific countries shows further that the latter had more political leverage than most African countries. The reason for this is that the Caribbean and Pacific countries source considerably less products from the EU than do African countries. Hence these countries were largely in a position to exclude high-revenue-earning and sensitive agricultural products from EPAs without exceeding the totally allowable threshold of 20 per cent of EU imports.

Key legal provisions in the EPAs

The ODI/ECDPM 2008 study also analysed the implications of the main legal provisions in the EPA texts in an issue-by-issue summary and compared them with other EU-developing countries' free trade agreements according to their restrictiveness. The study differentiated between 'actionable' and 'non-actionable' provisions. Actionable provisions set clear rules for the action of parties, such as the prohibition on increasing the level of applied customs tariffs. Breaches of actionable provisions by either party can be brought to the dispute settlement body, and may result in sanctions (such as the temporary termination of preferences). Non-actionable provisions are not enforceable, and include such issues as the intention of parties to cooperate in various fields.

The 2008 report highlighted the difficulties in assessing the implications of the EPA texts for different ACP countries. While some actionable provisions (such as export bans and intra-regional quantitative restrictions) might be unproblematic for some countries in a specific region, other provisions might well be in contradiction with the practice of other countries in the same region. To give three examples: first, export bans (which are used by several countries in case of food emergencies) are prohibited in all EPA texts except that of the EAC; second, intra-regional charges and duties (which are, for example, used by the small SACU countries) are equally prohibited in all texts; and finally, all economic partnership agreements in Africa envisage the free circulation of goods in their configurations. However, except for the EAC, the members of the EPAs do not mirror the members of the joint customs regimes.

There might be several other areas in which ACP countries' policies have been in contradiction to EPA provisions, and some countries might not yet be aware that this is the case. EPAs are complex documents and the implications of their implementation will only become fully apparent over time. These agreements cover a comprehensive set of commitments that apply not only to ACP trade with the EU, but also to intra-regional ACP trade. It therefore appears to be important for all EPA signatories in Africa to undertake country-specific studies in order to identify possible concerns and to accommodate these in comprehensive EPAs. All EPAs show so-called rendezvous clauses that provide for continued negotiations on selected trade-related topics as well as the alignment of national (or subregional) EPAs at the regional level. However, although negotiations continued in 2008–2009, no further major achievements had been made by December 2011.

The dispute avoidance and settlement provisions in the EPAs are extensive and rigid. The procedures for consultations—seeking advice from a mediator and establishing an arbitration panel—are detailed and the time frames are very strict. The application of temporary trade remedies is envisaged in cases of noncompliance with an arbitration decision.

All EPAs in Africa have comprehensive but wholly nonbinding provisions for development cooperation. However, to date, the European Commission has limited its financial commitments to the funds provided under the tenth European Development Fund (2007–2013). Additionally, the Commission and its member states have pledged to raise €2 billion of aid for trade annually from 2010 onwards—half of which would be reserved for the ACP. However, by 2011, the funds for aid for trade had not been agreed. Nor had it been agreed how the money will be spent. Infrastructure support and the expansion and modernisation of production capacities have been regarded as a priority by African countries, but donors prefer supporting trade policy and development. Thus the EU's commitment relates only to support for trade policy and regulation (trade facilitation, and institutional and technical support) and trade development (investment and trade promotion, as well as trade finance). Support for trade-related infrastructure and productive capacities would have to be covered through additional funds. (See chapter 13 in this volume.)

Have EPAs in Africa been implemented in a credible manner?

The power imbalances and biased negotiating capacities between the European Commission and African governments contributed to the fact that African countries have not been able to set out and carry through their development ideas within the EPA discussions. The result is that most ACP members feel dissatisfied with the results achieved hitherto and distrust Brussels's intentions in these negotiations. However, should the comprehensive EPAs not provide an outcome regarded as being mutually beneficial by both sides, the ACP will only implement the EPAs if the sanctions in case of nonimplementation exceed the costs of implementation.

Most EPAs in Africa defer, for some years, the reduction of tariffs. During these years, African preferences in the EU market will be eroded further, by both external trade liberalisation and internal reform. Although the erosion of preferences is generally undesirable for African exporters, this has the positive side effect of shifting the 'balance of power' from Brussels to African countries by reducing the sanction ability of the EU to remove preferences in cases of noncompliance with EPA obligations. The capacity of the EU to enforce implementation is linked to four key factors: the ability of the European Commission to obtain evidence that the implementation of EPAs is not occurring sufficiently; the Commission's inclination to monitor the implementation sufficiently closely to notice this evidence (by collecting and analysing data to back up the evidence); the availability of sufficiently strong sanctions to enforce change; and a willingness and ability to use sanctions.[23]

Judging whether an EPA is being implemented effectively is not as straightforward as might at first appear. Since product codes can change over time, it will be very difficult and time-consuming for the EU to check whether the items that a country liberalises in 2013 or 2015 are those it agreed to liberalise in 2007. Additionally, Brussels's ability to sanction defaulting countries is likely to decline with the decreasing attractiveness of its preferences. Thus, the more time that elapses before African countries must implement EPAs, the more unlikely that the agreements are to be implemented in a credible manner. While the process of tariff liberalisation started very early for some African countries (notably the SADC EPA countries in 2008 and the West African EPA countries in 2009), others have until 2013 (ESA) and 2015 (EAC) before having to remove positive tariffs from EU imports.

Most important, even if the EU Commission is, despite all caveats, able to demonstrate that an African country is not implementing its EPA obligations effectively, it does not have the power to remove DFQF preferences. To do that, a majority vote by the European Council of heads of state is required.[24] Since the diversity of opinions is most pronounced among the EU's twenty-seven leaders (see chapter 3 in this volume), this decisionmaking process provides a certain level of security to (alleged) noncompliant EPA countries—and even to nonsignatory EPA countries such as Namibia.

Concluding reflections

'Ownership', joint accountability, and equal partnership are the three fundamental values of the EU's Strategy for Africa of 2007. The EPAs form the heart of the 'trade, growth, and development component' of this strategy, but most African countries would probably respond negatively if asked whether EPAs meet the values of the Strategy for Africa. These governments did not sign the EPAs because they were believed to be 'pro-development', but because not signing them would certainly have been construed as 'anti-development'—implying the immediate loss of their most valuable EU preferences.

EPAs were supposed to be comprehensive trade and development agreements, but the results attained after five years of negotiations were poor: the EPAs in Africa are hardly more than standardised European Commission templates to which African governments' country-specific liberalisation schedules have been annexed. Brussels is to blame for not having provided guidance throughout the negotiation process and—after years of a laissez-faire approach—for having imposed accelerated pressure on the ACP in 2007 (in light of the approaching deadline of the expiry of the WTO waiver), without considering any other alternatives. African countries were largely ill-prepared throughout the negotiations and have, in contrast to the Caribbean countries, failed to articulate their own concrete interests and to come up with joint regional positions.

Negotiations towards comprehensive EPAs have continued since 2008, but have failed so far to offer the chance of revising some of the mistakes made in the past. The divergent protective interests of African countries, mirrored in the small overlap of exclusion baskets, have presented serious challenges particularly in drawing up regionally coherent schedules that comply with WTO requirements. Moreover, Brussels failed to convince new countries to sign the EPAs. It is therefore highly unlikely that 'comprehensive EPAs' will be established in future.

To make EPAs more attractive to African countries, they would need to be broadened through supportive policies that are covered by binding financial commitments. More generous rules of origin that have the potential to stimulate investment in African countries, as well as technical support that assists African countries to comply with EU standards, could help them to take full advantage of DFQF. Trade in services, competition policies, and intellectual property rights should be discussed in a flexible manner with no obligations beyond WTO rules, if they are found to be unacceptable by African governments. The final objective should be to devise a compromise that satisfies both sides and is, if implemented, likely to promote trade and development in Africa.

11

AFRICA AND EUROPE

ENDING A DIALOGUE OF THE DEAF?

Gilbert M. Khadiagala

Afro-pessimism is still too prevalent in Europe, not just in the circles of power, but in public opinion too. Africa continues to be regarded as a 'problem'. In counterpoint to this perception is the moralising, charitable approach that ultimately provides a blinkered view of the relationship with Africa.

Louis Michel, EU Commissioner for Development
and Humanitarian Aid, 2004–2009[1]

Introduction

In March 2007, Europe celebrated fifty years since the signing of the Treaty of Rome, which ushered in the continent's momentous process of regional integration. The anniversary marked the maturing of the political and economic integration that stemmed from the steady and incremental process towards a common and united European Union. The Treaty of Rome also marked the beginning of a new phase in Europe's relations with Africa, captured in political and economic arrangements such as the Yaoundé (1963) and Lomé (1975) Conventions, and the Cotonou Agreement (2000). These treaties helped to underwrite a wide range of integration schemes in Africa, including its current regional economic communities (RECs) and the African Union.[2]

To meet the challenges of the future, a summit of African and EU heads of state and government in Lisbon in December 2007 established a new framework, a joint EU-Africa strategic partnership, which put the African Union at the centre of EU engagement with the continent. Although this framework underscored the significance of regionalism in Africa and Europe as the core avenue for cooperation, questions linger about the solidity of this engagement, as evidenced by continuing disagreements at the Africa-EU summit in the Libyan capital of Tripoli in November 2010. European integration has flourished over the past half century, but there are profound questions about the strength of regionalism in Africa. Moreover, as Louis Michel, EU development commissioner, noted (quoted at the start of this chapter), Africa-Europe relations are still marked by profound pessimism in attitudes, and by structural asymmetries of power, reflected in anxieties over new trade negotiations, migration, and Europe's role in conflict resolution in Africa.

I argue in this chapter that regionalism in Africa and Europe has embraced the goals of building multilateral institutions to enhance political, security, and economic interaction. Although sturdy regional institutions are founded on functional states, regionalism also invariably seeks to create structures that gradually reduce the salience of nation-states. Yet, while European integration propelled African integration in the initial decades of African independence from the 1960s, there has been growing divergence between the two continental experiences in regionalism, since, over the years, the expansion of European integration eroded its ties with Africa.[3] (See chapter 4 in this volume.) The decline of the 'special relationship' between Africa and Europe has placed relations between both continents on an uncertain path. Alongside this decline has been the absence of coherent European voices to articulate African issues and interests, resulting in a 'dialogue of the deaf' between the two continents. Unlike in previous years, Europe has ceded its Africa policy primarily to multilateral institutions, notably the Group of Eight (G8) industrialised countries and subsequently the Group of 20 (G20).[4]

Current invocations of new 'partnerships' obscure the irreversible changes that have emanated from contrasting efforts to construct regional institutions. As deepening regionalism has given Europe the means to disengage from its myriad relations with Africa, the latter has been slow in building regional institutions that can promote prosperity, security, and identity, while also seeking more equal relationships with Europe. The result is the persistence of paternalistic relationships clothed in the rhetorical garbs of 'reciprocity' and 'partnerships'. Ultimately, the major task for Africa lies in building collective institutions for integration and development that can manage the dual challenges of proliferation of fragile states on the continent, and Africa's weakened position vis-à-vis Europe and the rest of the world.

Negotiating the economic partnership agreements

The Cotonou Partnership Agreement (CPA) of 2000 was an attempt by Europe to manage its economic relationships with the seventy-nine African, Caribbean, and Pacific (ACP) states, in light of mounting multilateral pressures for the reduction of special privileges. As European integration expanded over four decades to incorporate new members, it became difficult to sustain the postcolonial privileges embedded in the Lomé Conventions, which held sway from 1975 to 2000.[5] (See chapter 2 in this volume.) Thus the CPA was a reappraisal of the forty-year relationship that took into account the accession to the EU of countries that had no historical ties with Africa. Moreover, the multilateral pressures brought about by the World Trade Organisation (WTO)—which had succeeded the General Agreement on Tariffs and Trade (GATT) in 1995—forced the changes that would eliminate the generous trade preferences of the Lomé Conventions. In June 2005 the EU and ACP signed the revised text of the Cotonou Partnership Agreement (CPA II), broadening the areas of cooperation to include security, political dialogue, transparency, and increased social responsibility.[6] A third revision, CPA III, was signed in June 2010.

The Cotonou Partnership Agreement anticipated the phasing out of the trade preferences between the EU and ACP members by December 2007 and their replacement by economic partnership agreements (EPAs) that would meet the stringent requirements of the WTO. A decade after the signing of the Cotonou Agreement, however, the negotiations of EPAs had only yielded interim agreements. Acrimonious bargaining over EPAs has been interspersed by civic mobilisation in Africa and Europe against the deleterious impact of these agreements on African economies and regional integration schemes. In conception, the EPAs had three key objectives: removal of the previous nonreciprocal clause whereby African states gained free access to European markets for their nonagricultural and most agricultural products, without Europe gaining similar access to African markets for its own products; the establishment of new trading blocs among African states that could negotiate free trade areas (FTAs) with Europe; and better coordination of EU aid programmes with the EPAs.[7] (See chapter 10 in this volume.)

The other major objective of the EPAs has been to rationalise African regionalism, which has been characterised by overlapping membership of various regional economic communities, incompatible goals, and unwieldy mandates. In regions with many overlapping memberships, some countries have been reluctantly forced to negotiate EPAs in organisations of their second choice. For example, Tanzania campaigned vigorously, beginning in 2003, to negotiate an EPA in one of the Southern African Development Community (SADC) subregion's configurations, but the EU insisted on Dar-es-Salaam negotiating under the East African Customs Union (EACU), covering Kenya, Tanzania, Uganda, Burundi, and Rwanda. Similarly, although Kenya wanted to negotiate its EPA through the Eastern and Southern Africa (ESA) configuration, which represents countries in the Common Market for Eastern and Southern Africa (COMESA), pressure from Brussels, along with Tanzania and Uganda, forced Kenya to join the EACU configuration.[8]

In August 2007, heads of states of the East African Community (EAC) agreed that its five members would collectively sign one EPA with the EU by the end of 2007. But in November 2008, Kenya broke ranks with its neighbours and signed an interim agreement, the Framework Economic Partnership Agreement (FEPA), covering trade in goods, market access, and development cooperation. Negotiations, however, continued with the EAC on services, investment, and cooperation in other trade-related areas such as competition and government procurement. Although the negotiators established a new deadline of July 2009 to complete the talks, disagreements on nontariff barriers such as rules of origin, the scope of trade in services, and development assistance continued to cause deep rifts between the two sides.[9]

By December 2009, the EU was showing impatience with the pace of the negotiations; Peter Thompson, the key EU negotiator, warned that the situation in which interim economic partnership agreements (IEPAs) remained unsigned was 'untenable'. He further charged that 'EAC countries, despite not signing the EPA, have been enjoying free access to EU markets in the same way [as] other ACP countries that took legally binding commitments by signing [an] IEPA', and maintained that 'the current situation is contrary to both EU law and WTO rules'.[10] As a result, Brussels resorted to the strategy of putting more pressure on Nairobi to force its partners to sign the IEPA. Unlike the other four members of the EAC, Kenya is categorised as a non-least-developed country (non-LDC) that would not be eligible for duty-free, quota-free access under the EU's 'Everything but Arms' initiative of March 2001. In the absence of an EPA, the EU would reimpose import duties on major categories of Kenyan exports.

Although Nairobi reiterated its willingness to maintain regional solidarity with its EAC partners and pledged continued support to the resolution of outstanding issues, the Kenyan government was anxious for a speedy conclusion of the negotiations in order to avoid its exporters losing their preferential concessions to the EU. The Kenyan government estimated that exports to Europe were essential to its economic development, creating more than 1.5 million jobs and 70 billion Kenyan shillings worth of investment in the horticulture and fisheries sectors in 2006–2008. In a poignant reminder of this vulnerability, the European Commission (EC) delegation in Nairobi warned that failure by the EAC to sign a new trade agreement would lead to the introduction of taxes on Kenyan exports to Europe. According to Jacques Wunenburger, the head of the EPA unit in the European Commission, 'the discussion about the costs of an EPA should now move towards discussion about the cost of non-EPA'.[11]

Following the announcement of new EU concessions in February 2010 that included progressive liberalisation in trade and services and financing for priority development programmes in the EAC, both sides indicated their determination to conclude an interim EPA by June 2010 and the conclusion of a comprehensive EPA by December 2010. Uganda, however, noted that although it would sign an agreement on market access and development aid, it was unwilling to conclude a comprehensive agreement that included provisions on trade in services, investment rules, and government procurement.[12] After a fourteen-month hiatus, the EAC-EU EPA negotiations restarted in September 2011 in Zanzibar with a focus on economic development cooperation, rules of origin, and agriculture. The talks remained deadlocked in March 2012.[13]

Sorting out the issue of membership configurations has also led to confusion in negotiations for EPAs in Southern Africa, where countries are divided among three negotiating blocs: East and Southern Africa (ESA), the Southern African Development Community, and the Southern African

Customs Union (SACU). South Africa—a dominant actor in SADC and SACU—signed a bilateral free trade agreement with the EU in 2000, the Trade, Development, and Cooperation Agreement (TDCA), under which 95 per cent of South African goods exported to the EU were fully liberalised.[14] (See chapter 6 in this volume.) The TDCA was a precursor to the South Africa-EU strategic partnership that was initiated in 2006 and provided a framework for intensified relations and dialogue between the two sides. Despite Tshwane's (Pretoria) concern that negotiating many EPAs would have dire consequences on the future of regional integration in Southern Africa, the SADC region was forced to negotiate EPAs under four different configurations: Botswana, Lesotho, Mozambique, Namibia, and Swaziland decided to negotiate an EPA under the SADC configuration; Madagascar, Mauritius, Zambia, and Zimbabwe chose to negotiate as part of the ESA configuration; Tanzania negotiated as part of the EAC configuration; and the Democratic Republic of the Congo and Malawi opted to negotiate as part of the Central African configuration. Only Angola chose not to join any of the negotiating blocs.[15]

The SADC-EU EPA negotiations were launched in July 2004, with both sides agreeing on a joint roadmap setting out the principles, organisation, main stages, and timeframe of the negotiations. Substantive negotiations commenced in January 2005 and continued until June 2009, when Botswana, Lesotho, Swaziland, and Mozambique signed an interim EPA, with the agreement with Namibia pending. Although South Africa expressed its dissatisfaction with these developments, the SADC-EU IEPA came about after Brussels agreed to favourable terms for infant-industry protection, which would exclude from liberalisation in the SADC configuration sectors that were earmarked for development. The EU also made concessions by allowing the continuation of existing export taxes by the SADC group. Brussels further modified its demand on quantitative restrictions of exports in favour of the SADC group, and the parties agreed on the free circulation of goods to facilitate trade in the subregion.[16] Since 2009, negotiations have continued over services, investment, and trade-related rules for Botswana, Lesotho, Swaziland, and Mozambique. Namibia opted out of these commitments. A deal on these issues is supposed to constitute the steppingstone to a comprehensive SADC-EU EPA.

In August 2009, negotiations under the ESA configuration led to an IEPA signed by Mauritius, Seychelles, Zimbabwe, and Madagascar. The British EU trade commissioner at the time, Catherine Ashton (who became

EU High Representative for Foreign Affairs and Security Policy in December 2009), lauded this agreement as 'the foundation to build a more comprehensive trade partnership that will support the ESA region's work to build diverse and sustainable economies.... [T]his agreement brings a diverse region together under a single trade arrangement with the EU, tailored to the specific needs of the region and recognizing its diversity'.[17] After the signing of the accord, Brussels noted that the main impact of the IEPA would be the start of implementation of tariff reductions on EU exports to the signatory countries.[18]

Negotiations for EPAs in West Africa have been equally marred by controversies and countless delays. In contrast to other subregions that have been characterised by fragmentation, in West Africa two regional organisations—the Economic Community of West African States (ECOWAS) and the Francophone West African Economic and Monetary Union (UEMOA)—decided to join forces in negotiating an ECOWAS EPA. But like the EAC, West Africa has had to deal with the problem of differences between non-LDCs—Nigeria, Ghana, and Côte d'Ivoire—and other countries categorised as LDCs. Conducted through a ministerial monitoring committee, the negotiations in West Africa commenced in 2006, with ECOWAS requesting a three-year extension of the 2007 deadline for the conclusion of negotiations. Anxious to insulate their economies from disruption of their exports following the December 2007 expiry of the preferential trade terms, Côte d'Ivoire and Ghana broke ranks with ECOWAS and signed interim EPAs with Brussels. In mid-2009, both parties agreed to take a two-stage approach by signing an agreement on market access, development cooperation, and trade-related issues by December 2009, while continuing negotiations on other subjects into 2010.[19]

Throughout the negotiations, the major bone of contention was the ECOWAS demand that Brussels should make firm and specific commitments on financing of the costs of fiscal and economic adjustments to the EPA, through the creation of a regional fund to provide direct support for the specific needs of each member state. The fund would serve as a compensatory mechanism for revenue losses for countries that rely almost exclusively on import duties as a major source of government revenue. ECOWAS members also demanded increased EU investment to remove supply-related constraints in the subregion, including the upgrading of West Africa's infrastructure to enable subregional industries to benefit from the agreement and enhance their competitiveness. In April 2010, the subregion requested €9.5

billion from the EU to finance a five-year development programme covering the infrastructure, agriculture, tourism, and textile sectors, in order to neutralise the shocks that would result from liberalisation of goods under the EPA.[20]

EPA negotiations in West Africa have been participatory and broad-based, encompassing parliamentarians, business groups, and civil society activists.[21] In a joint West Africa-EU ministerial meeting in Mali in May 2010 to review the progress in EPA negotiations, the West African negotiating position was that, although the subregion would be willing to exercise some flexibility in areas such as rules of origin and market access, EPAs must support regional development and also act as a strong catalyst for development of the industrial base of individual countries. In this regard, the West Africans sought to prioritise the finalisation of the subregional common external tariff (CET) concurrently with a new protocol on rules of origin. The CET would consolidate regional integration and guarantee that West Africa would not be short-changed in its access to the EU market after the signing of the EPA. Because of the multiplicity of issues under negotiations, Brussels agreed to delay the signing of the EPA with the West African subregion until 2011, to allow time to address the range of outstanding issues.[22] By the time of the ECOWAS Ministerial Monitoring Committee (MMC) meeting in the Ghanaian capital of Accra in November 2011, differences between ECOWAS and the EU had been reduced to a few key issues, with development funding being the main outstanding one. Amid growing anxiety that the talks were taking too long to conclude, Gbenga Obideyi, director of trade for ECOWAS, noted that West Africa was looking for a 'a quality agreement' and was not willing 'to sacrifice a good agreement on the altar of time'.[23]

In the Central African configuration, negotiations have been conducted under the framework of the Economic and Monetary Community of Central Africa (Communauté Economique et Monétaire de l'Afrique Centrale, CEMAC)—comprising Cameroon, the Central African Republic, Congo-Brazzaville, Gabon, Equatorial Guinea, and Chad—as well as the Democratic Republic of the Congo and São Tomé and Príncipe. Three of these countries—Cameroon, Congo-Brazzaville, and Gabon—have non-LDC status. Negotiations started in 2004 and by December 2007 only Cameroon had opted to sign an IEPA to protect its access to the EU market.[24] Subsequently, difficult negotiations ensued over the degree of liberalisation, the transition period for trade in goods and services, and the amount of development assistance to be made available by Brussels. Like other subregions, Central Africa has insisted on stressing the development of subregional infrastructure for trade before it can proceed with the EPA negotiations. Initially, Central Africa proposed the liberalisation of 60 per cent of its imports over twenty years, but Brussels rejected this suggestion, claiming that it would be incompatible with the WTO's market-access liberalisation of 80 per cent of trade over fifteen years. France and the European Parliament appealed to the European Commission to adopt a more flexible approach to the negotiations, but EU negotiators were unwilling to budge.[25] Thus, although Central African governments requested an extension of the Cotonou preferences for two years in October 2007, Brussels rejected this idea. As a result, Gabon and Congo-Brazzaville were subjected to trade restrictions from 2008, while the other countries in the subregion, being LDCs, continued to benefit from the 2001 'Everything but Arms' initiative.[26] (See chapter 10 in this volume.)

In the February 2009 round of negotiations, CEMAC made concessions to Brussels on market access liberalisation, accepting an increase from 60 to 71 per cent liberalisation over twenty years, but the EU remained inflexible on all issues. Owing to these differences, in addition to the institutional restructuring of CEMAC, and elections in Gabon, Equatorial Guinea and Congo-Brazzaville, no substantial progress was made in EPA negotiations during 2009. At their meeting in January 2010, CEMAC leaders instructed the subregion's negotiators to conclude a regional EPA with Brussels expeditiously, given the importance of the EU to the subregion's overall trade and economic relations. In addition, they requested the European Commission to grant them an EPA-related financial support programme of €12.5 billion. Although the negotiations resumed in early 2010, the difficulties faced by the Central Africa-EC EPA negotiations were similar to those confronting other African configurations.

Most critics of EPAs have focused on their potential distortions of trade initiatives, charging that Africa would become a dumping ground for Europe's cheap imports. Since 2004, several African and European civil society organisations have rallied under the banner of 'Stop EPAs' campaigns to raise awareness of threats to African agriculture that would result from the liberalisation of Africa's markets for EU goods. These critics further contend that African countries are unlikely to gain better access to European markets through EPAs. On the contrary, their local industries would be put under severe strain by competition from cheap European imports.[27] Oxfam International released a study in 2008 showing that EPAs were likely to deny African countries a favourable foothold in the global economy. Specifically, it noted that the rules on liberalisation of services had the potential to drive local firms out of business, reduce competition, and extend the monopoly power of large companies in African markets. The new rules in the EPAs, it was also argued, posed a threat to poor people's access to essential services, since African countries would be committed to allowing foreign investors into public utilities when these sectors were opened up to private companies. In addition, new investment rules would prevent African states from requiring foreign companies to transfer technology, train local workers, and source local inputs. According to Oxfam, 'the overall effect of these changes in the rules is to progressively undermine economic governance, transferring power from governments to largely unaccountable multinationals firms, robbing developing countries of the tools they need to develop their economies and gain a favourable foothold in global markets'.[28]

Critics have also decried the impact of EPAs on regional integration in Africa. Although these agreements can be widely justified for their potential contribution to the expansion of intraregional trade and trade links with Europe, many questions have been raised about whether EPAs will facilitate or hamper regionalism in Africa. Brussels has often championed EPAs as vehicles to improve the business environment for African entrepreneurs by promoting regional integration and tackling supply-side constraints that often impede regional integration. The British economist Christopher Stevens has observed, however, that EPAs may erect new trade barriers among African countries, and defeat the objective of regional integration. As he noted: 'By increasing the stakes, EPAs may make regional liberalisation less likely. Some countries willing to remove barriers to imports from their neighbours with similar economies may be unwilling to offer the same terms to highly competitive (and possibly dumped) EU imports. Regional groups may splinter between those willing to liberalise towards the EU and the others'.[29] As acknowledged by the EU in a 2007 appraisal of the effects of multiple EPAs on integration efforts in Southern Africa:

The implication of FTAs being established with the EU (ensuring compatibility under Article XXVI, GATT) will have serious implications for SADC's own integration agenda under the RISDP [Regional Indicative Strategic Development Plan]. There will be difficult technical issues with respect to overlapping membership and the costs connected to the implementation of these various EPAs. One of the objectives behind the EPAs is the promotion of deeper integration among ACP countries. In order for that to be possible, suitable and effective institutional and legal arrangements must be established and they must make sense in terms of geographical, historical, and economic factors. The jury is still out on the future of deeper integration in sub-Saharan Africa.[30]

Undoubtedly, as the preceding discussion of the negotiations for various EPA configurations has revealed, African countries have reluctantly embraced these agreements, because the pace of negotiations has been forced by Brussels, though the new arrangements are clearly undermining the work of existing subregional bodies on the continent. The Ugandan academic Yash Tandon wrote:

What we have on the ground is a mish-mash of countries grouped incongruously without economic or political logic. They do not have even the historical logic any more.... Nothing seems to make sense anymore. Everything is higgledy-piggledy. Old regional boundaries are torn away. Years of regional integration efforts under bodies such as SADC and EAC are under strain and indeed in peril. Is Africa back again to 1884 when Europe sat around a table in Berlin carving out Africa's border?[31]

Despite the widespread scepticism about EPAs across Africa, opposition to the agreements has essentially been dissipated in the face of EU pressures and concessions on some issues. Through the creation of an EPA template for use by all African countries, Brussels has been able to frame the terms of partnership, as African governments have scrambled to manage the economic uncertainties caused by these agreements. Shorn of its diplomatic niceties, 'partnership' fundamentally reflects the continuities in the asymmetrical power relations between Africa and Europe. These asymmetries have only been strengthened by the gradual fragmentation of the once-solid African bloc within the seventy-nine-member group of African, Caribbean, and Pacific countries. One of the outcomes of the EPA negotiations has been the radical realignment of African regional organisations, as individual countries have struggled to decide where they belong. Despite Europe's claims that EPAs will rationalise African regionalism, these agreements have created new subregional configurations among African countries without eliminating the existing institutions, thus resulting in subregional incoherence.

Africa and Europe in a multilateral world

Negotiations on EPAs have occurred alongside Europe's bid to cede the burdens of coping with Africa's economic plight to multilateral bodies, notably the annual summits of the Group of Eight industrialised countries. Since the mid-2000s, the G8 has assumed significance in charting the course of debates about Africa's economic future. In addition to the six-month rotational leadership within the EU, the growing importance of the G8 forum has led to sporadic attention being focused on African issues. Targeted invitation of a few selected African leaders to G8 gatherings has further deepened the fragmentation of African voices, while sustaining the illusion of inclusiveness in decisionmaking. In recent years, the G8 has been dwarfed by the G20 (in which South Africa is the only African representative), but this has not improved Africa's position.

Former British prime minister Tony Blair's 2005 'Commission for Africa' (CfA) report exemplified his country's leadership efforts in seeking a multilateral consensus on African development issues.[32] Coinciding with British chairmanship of the G8 and presidency of the EU in 2005, the report tried to galvanise major donors to refocus on a host of African economic challenges.[33] Presented as the most serious analysis of Africa's problems for generations, the report invoked global common interests and collective responsibilities in the search for a coherent policy towards Africa. The CfA report recommended, among other suggestions, the tripling of aid flows to Africa to $50 billion a year by 2015, an additional $10 billion annually to fight the HIV/AIDS pandemic, complete debt forgiveness, an extra $10 billion in aid annually for vital infrastructure, and the repatriation by banks in the rich world of money stolen by corrupt African leaders. The report also recommended a greater voice for Africa in the councils of the World Bank and the International Monetary Fund (IMF), and argued that appointments for heads of international institutions should be based on merit rather than on nationality. The CfA further revisited the old issues of 'good governance' and capacity-building, reiterating the importance of the creation of socioeconomic and legal frameworks to promote growth and development.[34]

At the G8 summit at Gleneagles, Scotland, in July 2005, Blair attempted to convince his colleagues to embrace the recommendations, and provide funding to meet its policy objectives. In the run-up to the Gleneagles summit, Britain had endorsed all the recommendations of the report and mobilised considerable diplomatic efforts to obtain support from the rest of the G8 countries. Most of these countries were sceptical about London's African activism. However, they agreed to increase official development assistance by $25 billion per year by 2010, and the most significant concession was debt forgiveness, to the amount of $40 billion owed by eighteen countries (most of them in Africa).[35] Blair also obtained a commitment from G8 countries to ratify the UN convention against corruption and to take action to recover and confiscate stolen assets and return them to their legitimate owners, to deny entry to corrupt officials found guilty of misdeeds, and to enforce laws against the bribery of foreign public officials.[36]

Although the CfA report anticipated increased scaling up of resources to tackle the HIV/AIDS epidemic, during the conference on the replenishment for the Global Fund to Fight AIDS, Tuberculosis, and Malaria in September 2005 Britain doubled its share of the fund, but other donors pledged only $3.8 billion: $3.3 billion short of the target. Similarly, despite Blair's campaign for fairer trade terms for Africa, neither the G8 countries nor the WTO Doha development-round trade talks in Hong Kong in December 2005 made any breakthroughs on trade issues. Overall, what Blair described as his 'Africa 2005' agenda fell well short of expectations. (See chapter 17 in this volume.) As Penny Jackson explained:

Counterbalancing the Blair campaigns, however, were considerable political and economic obstacles. To begin with, it seems that some G-8 members thought the diplomatic drive was an attempt by Britain to steal the high moral ground and that it gave an insufficient recognition to their own increased commitments to the continent. The Canadians and the French had already used their chairmanships to talk about African issues, and the [George W.] Bush administration [in the US] has taken increased interest in Africa.[37]

Britain's presidency of the EU produced a landmark review of Euro-African relations to coincide with the momentum unleashed by the CfA report. In October 2005 the European Commission produced a report, 'EU Strategy for Africa: Towards a Euro-African Pact to Accelerate African Development', that was endorsed by the EU Council of Ministers in December 2005. While rehashing some of the issues raised in previous policy statements on Africa, the report brought new topics to the fore. Among the economic components of the EU strategy was the establishment of the European-African Business Forum (EBF), a body that aimed to forge dialogue and closer ties between private and public investors in Africa and Europe. As part of this initiative, Brussels made a commitment to support African chambers of commerce in exploring business and trade opportunities in Europe. Related to the notion of the EBF was the proposal of twinning partnerships in business, industry, and trade unions. Similarly, the EU strategy gave new prominence to assisting African countries in diversifying products exported to Europe.[38]

The EU strategy of 2005 also sought to provide a template for resolving the vexing question of migration. (See chapter 20 in this volume.) Promising to make migration between Africa and Europe a positive force for development, the strategy proposed finding mechanisms that would ease the sending of remittances from Europe to Africa. Additionally, the document outlined ways of transforming 'brain drain' into 'brain gain' for Africa through innovative programmes such as 'helping African countries to tap into the potential available in their diasporas in Europe and by facilitating various forms of brain circulation, including return migration and temporary or virtual return by which African migrants can make their skills available to their home countries'.[39]

On political issues, the EU's 2005 strategy was less innovative, reiterating concerns about democracy, governance, and human rights that had formed the bulk of the donor conditionality regimes since the late 1980s.[40] These governance initiatives, however, sought to better align Europe with local African initiatives, notably the African Peer Review Mechanism (APRM) of 2003, the flagship programme of the New Partnership for Africa's Development (NEPAD) of 2001.[41] By backing the APRM, Europe has tried to underscore the 'domestication' of NEPAD's principles of political, economic, and corporate governance. The more innovative component of the strategy was the establishment of the North African Governance Facility to promote democratisation in Egypt, Libya, Tunisia, and Mauritania. (See chapter 7 in this volume.) The strategy also went beyond the rhetorical fealty to human rights, proposing the establishment of an EU-Africa human rights forum with the objective of encouraging the sharing of resources and expertise on human rights issues.

On African conflicts, the EU strategy of 2005 built strongly on previous documents detailing Europe's role in conflict resolution. Since Brussels's 1999 'Communication on EU Cooperation with African Countries Involved in Armed Conflicts', Europe had emphasised the importance of conflict prevention as the key to its Africa policies. In April 2000, through the Cairo Declaration and Cairo Plan of Action, adopted jointly by the EU and the Organisation of African Unity (OAU)—forerunner of the African Union—Brussels developed a conflict management and resolution strategy dealing with common guidelines for arms exports, postconflict reconstruction, conflict diamonds, and small arms proliferation. In November 2002 in a follow-up to the Cairo summit, EU and African ministers agreed to four key goals: first, the exchange of information on a regular basis; second, the establishment of an inventory of institutions dealing with conflicts; third, the strengthening of the institutional capacity of early warning and preventive diplomacy; and fourth, the fostering of 'good governance' and the rule of law as essential elements in conflict prevention. Towards these objectives, the EU also provided €10 million to the African Union's Peace Fund.[42]

Subsequently, as part of the EU-Africa dialogue on conflict prevention, Brussels established the African Peace Facility in 2004. A €250 million allocation was hived from the European Development Fund to foster peace and enhance early warning and conflict prevention efforts. The facility specifically funds peacekeeping operations in Africa that are carried out and staffed by African militaries. Funds from the facility have been used in support of the African Union Mission in Sudan (AMIS) in the country's Darfur region between 2004 and 2007, and the European Union Force (EUFOR) to support the electoral process, police training, and security sector reform in the Democratic Republic of the Congo in 2006.[43] (See chapter 14 in this volume.) When the AU peacekeeping force in Darfur formally became a hybrid UN-AU force known as UNAMID in July 2007, the EU continued to support the mission financially through the African Peace Facility, but phased out the role of European advisers to UNAMID in December 2007. The AU and its external donors, including the G8 countries, also agreed to set up a fund to support underfunded peacekeeping missions on the continent. Financed as part of the AU's Complementary Peace Facility, this mechanism augments the existing European Union-African Peace Facility (EU-APF) and increased resources available for Africa-led peace support operations. Under a different framework, the EU has earmarked battle-ready groups of its own soldiers for limited peace operations in Africa.[44] (See chapter 13 in this volume.)

In addition to being the largest donor to AU peacekeeping missions, and engaging in long-term peacekeeping capacity-building through the Peace Facility, the EU intervened with a military mission in Chad and the Central African Republic in 2008–2009. Approved by the EU Council in October 2007 as a one-year bridging operation under UN Security Council Resolution 1778 (2007), the 4,000-strong EUFOR mission to Chad and the Central African Republic was the largest EU military mission in Africa.[45] (See chapter 15 in this volume.) The 2005 strategy sought to concretise most of the policy positions on conflict prevention and peacekeeping in Africa within the framework of Europe's Common Security and Defence Identity (ESDI) and its Common Foreign and Security Policy (CFSP).

Tony Blair's activism raised Africa's global profile, but dependence on the new multilateral institutional leadership for agenda-setting also raised profound questions of continuity. Thus, in 2006, when the G8 presidency passed on to Russia—a non-EU member—there was less focus on Africa. A year after the unprecedented international focus on Africa at Gleneagles, African issues barely made it onto the G8 agenda at its St. Petersburg summit in July 2006.[46] It was left to the perennial African attendees at the G8 summits (South Africa's Thabo Mbeki and Nigeria's Olusegun Obasanjo) to chastise Europe and the world for 'ignoring' African issues and failing to live up to their promises at Gleneagles. Under the presidency of German chancellor Angela Merkel, G8 leaders reconfirmed their commitment to double official development assistance to Africa by 2010 in June 2007. Berlin also proposed that each G8 member sign a partnership agreement with one African country that was abiding by the expectation of global governance standards, a proposal that irked many Africans who regarded this suggestion as paternalistic and a departure from the policy of geographical coherence.[47]

Although the G8 summit in Hokkaido, Japan, in July 2008 reconfirmed the pledge to increase annual aid to Africa by $25 billion from the 2005 level by 2010, G8 members met none of these pledges, citing as reasons the global financial crisis of 2008–2009 and other pressing domestic priorities. Promises of doubling aid to Africa have thus not been met by G8 members. At the G8 summit in Muskoka, Canada, in June 2010, the Gleneagles promises were not even on the agenda, which signalled a radical shift in Africa's relations with this group of rich countries. The Muskoka Declaration at the end of the summit only noted that 'support for development, based on mutual responsibility, and a strong partnership with developing countries, particularly in Africa, remains a cornerstone of the G8's approach'.[48]

When Portugal assumed the EU presidency in June 2007, there were heightened expectations that its long history in Africa would help refocus attention on African issues. (See chapter 18 in this volume.) As part of these efforts, Lisbon announced an EU-Africa summit in December 2007, the first Europe-Africa summit in seven years. Although overshadowed by conflicts over the attendance of Zimbabwe's President Robert Mugabe, the December 2007 summit adopted a new strategy, an EU-Africa joint partnership, that committed both sides to a renewed long-term political partnership based on Euro-African consensus on values, common interests, and strategic objectives for the future. Negotiations between the EU and the AU on the joint strategy started in February 2007 and culminated in the Lisbon summit.[49] (See chapter 2 in this volume.)

The joint strategy of 2007 sought to provide a long-term framework for Africa-EU relations to be implemented through successive short-term action plans and political dialogue at all levels in a bid to achieve outcomes in specific areas of this partnership. Key to the first action plan (2008–2010) were eight 'priority partnerships' on key issues: peace and security; democratic governance and human rights; trade, regional integration, and infrastructure; the UN Millennium Development Goals; energy; climate change; migration, mobility, and employment; and science, information society, and space.[50] In the implementation and monitoring of these objectives, the joint strategy envisaged the active participation of Africa's regional economic communities, civil society, private sector, and local stakeholders.

In conception, the 2007 joint strategy built on the initiatives launched since the first Africa-EU summit, in Cairo in 2000, and captured most of the questions elaborated in the 2005 EU strategy for Africa, particularly recognition of the importance of emerging issues such as security, migration, and the environment. What is different, however, is the joint strategy's delineation of the AU as the central interlocutor between Africa and Europe. In a departure from the tradition established since the 1950s of dealing with distinct regional groupings in Africa, Brussels earmarked the AU largely because of its renewed mission to be the comprehensive security, economic, and political framework for regionalism in Africa. This was underscored by the appointment of the first EU ambassador to the AU Commission in Addis Ababa, Belgium's Koen Vervaeke, in December 2007, to manage both the political relations between Brussels and Addis Ababa, and the financial and other support provided by the EU to the AU Commission. As part of these efforts, the EU has devoted resources to building the capacity of the AU Commission in the belief that a stronger AU was one of the conditions for the successful implementation of the joint strategy of 2007. In addition, during the G20 summit in London in March 2009 to discuss measures to deal with the global financial crisis of 2008–2009, the AU was invited, alongside Ethiopia (representing NEPAD), to join South Africa in placing Africa's concerns on the global agenda. The EU-Africa Tripoli summit in November 2010, however, saw continuing disagreements over 'good governance', immigration, and climate change.

Proponents of the 2007 joint strategy have lauded it as an important instrument offering a framework that is potentially able to overcome fragmentation and foster continent-to-continent relationships. However, 'treating Africa as one' will require a significant organisational and attitudinal shift within the EU, as well as the creation of new funding institutions.[51] Besides, the pan-African approach embedded in the 2007 joint strategy seems to run counter to the prevailing fragmentation and *diktat* embodied in the EPAs. Furthermore, despite their envisaged role in the implementation phase, Africa's RECs have not been accorded significant attention in the new rhetorical commitment in Brussels to support the AU and NEPAD frameworks. Given that the AU has designated the RECs as the building blocks for the African Economic Community (AEC), to be established by 2028, their limited role in the new joint strategy raises serious questions about the EU's commitment to regionalism in Africa.

On the African side, the credibility of the AU as the overarching institution for African security and prosperity has been damaged by the ongoing contests over its institutional reach, particularly between opponents and proponents of a grandiose 'Union Government of African States'. (See chapter 3 in this volume.) AU leadership of the African agenda and engagement with the EU presupposes the emergence of consistent voices on the continent about the pace and timing of creating continental institutions. The power contest between an AU faction led by Muammar Qaddafi (who was killed in October 2011) to fast-track the Union Government, and one guided by the gradualist approach preferred by most African countries, further compounded the problems of forging African unity at the very moment when the EU and other external actors were seeking such unity. Leadership contests in Africa over the scale and scope of regionalism have exacerbated perceptions of continental disunity.

Concluding reflections

Regionalism in Africa has evolved as a mirror image of Europe, attempting to overcome the flaws of fragmentation in a competitive world. Through its own integrative architecture, Europe has contributed ideas and resources to strengthening the basis for African regionalism. Throughout the five decades of European regionalism, however, one of its fundamental objectives has been to build a common European framework that reduces Brussels's engagement with its former colonies and dependents. As a result, a more integrated Europe is now seeking to disengage from its previous African ties, largely through the multilateralisation and globalisation of its relations with Africa. The current dynamic of multilateralisation has whittled down the extent of Euro-African relations. Through new ideas and structures encompassed under the rubric of 'partnership', Europe has tried to manage the enormous transitional challenges occasioned by multilaterisation, but partnership has not fundamentally altered the inequities that have dominated Euro-African relations, and the 'dialogue of the deaf' between both continents has continued.

However, despite structural weaknesses, African regionalism has come of age, surviving the turmoil of botched and competitive schemes, multiple memberships and mandates, and underachieving and underresourced institutions. As before, the key driver of integration has remained consistent in its objective: the pooling of sovereignty to broaden the space for resolving myriad economic and political problems. The new impetus for integration that has been captured in the AU and NEPAD, and in the reinvigoration of Africa's RECs, underscores the abiding significance of collective African approaches to problem-solving on the continent. European regionalism has, on occasion, played a vital part in this enterprise, but durable regionalism in Africa remains the responsibility of local actors who are imbued with a sense of collective vision and responsibility.

12

A CRITIQUE OF THE EU'S COMMON AGRICULTURAL POLICY

Charles Mutasa

Introduction

In a rapidly changing world, Europe's Common Agricultural Policy (CAP) faces steep challenges, in conditions different from the post-Second World War era when it was established. The CAP began operating in 1962 as a system of European Economic Community (EEC)—later European Union—agricultural subsidies and programmes, with the Community intervening to buy farm output when the market price fell below an agreed target level.[1] There is no doubt that at the time the CAP was born, it represented an ambitious and innovative agenda in terms of political and economic dialogue, regional integration, and trade and development. The aim of the Common Agricultural Policy is to provide European farmers with a reasonable standard of living and consumers with quality food at fair prices, as well as to preserve the 'rural heritage' of European countries. In several of these areas, major progress has been achieved, while in others the CAP has not yet been able to live up to the high expectations of its founders. In recent years, some controversy and the call for fundamental reforms in the policy have cast a cloud over its future. This chapter seeks to provide a critique of the CAP with a view to stimulating a constructive debate on its concept and practice and, in the process, tries to ascertain the future orientation of EU policies in this area and determine the nature of Brussels's developmental relations with the rest of the world and, in particular, the Third World, within the context of the CAP.

The chapter begins by defining the CAP's objectives and parameters, providing its historical origins and background. It then proceeds to appraise critically the CAP in terms of its reform agenda, offering a critique of the programme's concept and practice by examining its implications within Europe and beyond. The chapter concludes with some final reflections and recommendations on how to reform the CAP in ways that could be beneficial for Africa.

The objectives of the CAP

Agriculture has always had a special place in Europe's economic and social structure. This is a sector with unique characteristics, which means that agricultural policy is more developed than policies for other sectors. The Common Agricultural Policy is a system of European Union agricultural subsidies and programmes. The EU's trade policy in this area has been largely shaped by the CAP. Over about half a century, the policy has developed an elaborate system of support for agriculture that has taken many forms. The basic characteristics have involved market price support, bolstered by import protection and export subsidies. The CAP has its roots in the Western Europe of the 1950s, in which societies had been destroyed by six years of war in the previous decade, at a time when agriculture had been crippled and food supplies could not be guaranteed.

The CAP is funded by the European Commission's Agricultural Guidance and Guarantee Fund (EAGGF). The policy accounted for 64 per cent of the EU budget in 1990, 49 per cent in 2003, and 31 per cent in 2010.[2] The subsidies worked by guaranteeing a minimum price to producers and by direct payment of a subsidy for crops planted. The CAP provided an incentive to European farmers to increase their agricultural productivity and to make use of the factors of production: capital, enterprise, land, and labour. The policy also provided EU producers with market preference by imposing a common external tariff on imports from outside the common market.

Among the European Union's policies, the CAP is regarded as one of the most important sectors. A further 7 million farmers have been added to the EU's existing farming population of 6 million in the former fifteen member states, making a total of 13 million farmers in twenty-seven states by 2007. The twelve new member states also added about 55 million hectares of agricultural land to the 130 million hectares in the old EU of fifteen members, an increase of 40 per cent, although production in the EU of twenty-seven members will only expand by about 10–20 per cent for most products.[3]

The policy has been justified because of the share of agriculture in the EU budget, the vast number of people involved in the sector, and the extent of the territory directly affected. The CAP has also enjoyed support due to the symbolic significance of agriculture and the extent of sovereignty transferred from the national to the European level through this sector.[4] It is important to note that CAP price interventions cover only certain agricultural products. According to Chapter 39 of the 1957 Treaty of Rome, which created the EEC, the CAP's five initial objectives were first, to increase productivity by promoting technical progress and ensuring the optimum use of the factors of production, particularly labour; second, to ensure a fair standard of living for the agricultural community; third, to stabilise markets; fourth, to secure availability of supplies; and finally, to provide consumers with food at reasonable prices. These objectives were pursued by implementing European Economic Community instruments, in line with three key principles: first, market unity, which requires European products to be able to move freely within the Community, with regional integration being used to provide a larger internal market for producers; second, community preference, which means that food supplies must be purchased first within the Community before imports from third countries can be considered (this principle was responsible for the high customs duties and restrictive quotas applied to 'sensitive' products); and finally, financial solidarity, which spreads the costs inherent in the CAP to the creation of common market organisations between the members of the Community through the European Agricultural Guidance and Guarantee Fund.

The CAP stabilised agricultural markets in Europe and regulated prices so that farmers could be assured that there would be a market without huge fluctuations in the prices they received for their annual output. The programme has also allowed the EU to intervene in the normal workings of the market in relation to forces of demand and supply. When products are scarce relative to demand, they command a higher price. However, when there is a glut—an oversupply—prices generally fall. The CAP was so successful at increasing agricultural productivity in Europe that by the 1980s the European Community had to contend with almost permanent surpluses. Some of the surplus produce was exported with the help of subsidies, while the rest had to be stored or disposed of within the Community.[5] Surplus stocks of produce kept in storage became known as beef and butter 'mountains' and milk and wine 'lakes'. In another sense, the CAP is often explained as the result of a political compromise between France and Germany: German industry would have access to the French market; in exchange, Germany would help subsidise French farmers. Germany is still the largest net payer into the EU budget; however, by 2005, France had also become a net payer, and the poorer and more agricultural-based Spain, Greece, and Portugal were the largest beneficiaries of the EU budget.

As Alan Matthews noted in 2008, the CAP has evolved to meet society's changing needs, so that food safety, preservation of the environment, value for money, and agriculture as a source of crops to convert to fuel have all acquired steadily growing importance.[6] The current biggest beneficiaries of the CAP, each gaining more than €1 billion, are Greece, Poland, and Spain, followed by France, Ireland, and Hungary. All these countries have consistently defended a large CAP budget.[7] In recent years, France has benefitted the most from these agricultural subsidies. The new accession countries from Eastern and Central Europe that joined the EU in 2004 and 2007 have large farm sectors and would have overtaken France as the largest beneficiaries of the EU budget had it not been for transitional regulations limiting the subsidies that these countries receive. Every wheat farmer in the EU currently receives a subsidy of approximately £35 per tonne. The distribution of farm subsidies from Brussels means that the larger the farm, the greater the subsidy. In Britain, the Duke of Westminster, for example, with farm holdings of about 55,000 hectares, received almost £300,000 a year in farm subsidies from European taxpayers in 2008.[8]

Background and developments within the CAP

The CAP came into existence at a time when the members of the European Community had emerged from over a decade of food shortages from the mid-1940s to the 1950s. They thus resolved that it was essential to establish a common market in which tariffs on agricultural products would be removed. The principles of the Common Agricultural Policy were set out at the Community's Stresa Conference in July 1958. Two years later, the CAP mechanisms were adopted by the six EEC founding member states (France, Germany, Italy, Belgium, the Netherlands, and Luxembourg), and in 1962 the CAP came into force. The Treaty of Rome of 1957, which created the EEC, had defined the general objectives of a common European agricultural policy. In order to guide the CAP, three further principles were established in 1962: market unity, community preference, and financial solidarity.[9] Since then, the CAP has been a central element in the EU's institutional system. The programme's affairs have since been placed under the custody of an Agricultural Council in Brussels.

There has been some criticism of the CAP expressed by members of the European Union: Sweden and Britain both called on the EU to cut the budget and subsidies for the programme and redirect spending to other priorities such as climate change.[10] Some lobby groups,[11] both within and outside Europe, have also voiced similar criticisms. However, the CAP still remains strong and well-funded. The programme has even stalemated World Trade Organisation (WTO) talks under the Doha development round, which began in 2001. The European Environmental Bureau (EEB),[12] a think-tank, has been very critical of the CAP given Brussels's claim to be working for fair trade, especially for developing countries. The policy has survived for five decades, disadvantaging the marketing of developing countries' agricultural produce. One of the major reasons for the CAP's survival has been the fact that farming is regarded as a 'heritage' and a special livelihood activity in parts of Europe, particularly in France. Of key importance seems to be a shared nostalgia for a rural past, and concern to avoid a return to the traumatic post-1945 era's food crisis by ensuring self-sufficiency in food production and consumption. The CAP has been altered several times. Each reform has stressed three key factors: the need to shift the emphasis from agricultural policy to rural policy (so that rural industrialisation, forestry, and tourism would also fall within the policy's remit); the recognition of regional variations in the rural problem throughout the Community; and a push for dismantling of price support systems in order to curb overproduction.[13]

The current three key areas that constitute issues of reform in EU agriculture are lowering prices, ensuring food safety and quality, and guaranteeing the stability of farmers' incomes. Three other important issues include environmental pollution, animal welfare, and finding alternative income opportunities for farmers. Some of these issues are the responsibility of EU member states. In May 2008 the European Commission published proposals for the 'Health Check' reforms of the EU Common Agricultural Policy. This is seen as an important review of the CAP that could potentially have significant implications for the programme—particularly for farmers across the EU—as well as for enhancing the delivery of environmental benefits through farming for the environment and cutting prices for consumers. A 2013 review is also expected to usher in some changes to the CAP.

Reforms and challenges within the CAP

Calls for CAP reform were caused by a number of problems and weaknesses in the policy.[14] Since the mid-1980s, policy emphasis has shifted somewhat in response to three key factors. First, the budgetary costs of maintaining open-ended CAP support became unacceptably high. This led, for example, to the imposition of milk quotas and grain co-responsibility levies during the 1980s. Second, the consequences of the subsidised export of Europe's growing farm surpluses ensured that agricultural trade became a subject of intense scrutiny during the Uruguay round (1986–1994) of the General Agreement on Tariffs and Trade (GATT), which became the World Trade Organisation in 1995. This, together with continuing budgetary pressures, led to a general—but phased—lowering of price support and protection measures under the 'MacSharry reforms' of the CAP initiated in 1992 by Ray MacSharry, the Irish EU commissioner for agriculture from 1989 to 1992. Third, the environmental impact of agriculture gained in importance as a political issue. This led to the introduction of agri-environmental measures under the CAP, starting with Article 19 of Structures Regulation 797/85 (which established 'environmentally sensitive areas') and broadening out to Agri-Environment Regulation 2078/92, one of three 'accompanying measures' to the MacSharry reforms.[15]

Some modifications were made to the CAP, including the introduction of a quota on dairy production in 1984 (milk quotas), and a ceiling on EU payments to farmers in 1988.[16] In 1992, the reforms by the EU commissioner for agriculture at the time, MacSharry, addressed renewed upward trends in intervention stocks of surplus produce. These changes also met insistent demands from GATT to mitigate the effects of EU subsidies on world markets. These reforms were the first step away from a system of market support to a system of direct payment to farmers.[17] Substantial cuts were made in the level of support prices for the main agricultural products, while income support payments linked to production were made directly to farmers to compensate them for the price cuts. The implementation of the 1992 CAP reforms was phased in over a period of three to four years and coincided with other major events that greatly affected the economic climate for agriculture. These reforms also included measures to encourage less intensive farming in the interests of the environment, to aid afforestation of agricultural land, and to provide a more attractive early retirement scheme for farmers over fifty-five years of age. In November 1997 the EU Agriculture Council defined Europe's 'model of agriculture' as having a multifunctional role that included maintaining the European countryside, conserving nature, contributing to the vitality of rural life, responding to consumer demands and concerns regarding food quality and safety, protecting the environment, and safeguarding animal welfare.

The second reform of the CAP—the Agenda 2000 Agreement of March 1999—reinforced the move from market support to direct payment. The Agenda 2000 Agreement also intensified the emphasis on food safety and the environment. In June 2003 EU farm ministers adopted a fundamental reform of the CAP, completely changing the way that Brussels supported its farm sector. The CAP was geared more towards consumers and taxpayers, while giving European farmers the freedom to produce what the market wanted. In future, the vast majority of subsidies would be paid independently of the volume of production. To avoid abandonment of production, EU member states could choose to maintain a limited link between subsidy and production under well-defined conditions and within clear limits.[18] These new 'single farm payments' were linked to respect for environmental, food safety, and animal welfare standards. Severing the link between subsidies and production made European farmers more competitive and market-oriented, while providing the necessary income stability. More money was made available to farmers for environmental, food safety, and animal welfare programmes by reducing direct payments for larger farms. The EU Council also revised the milk, rice, cereals, durum wheat, dried fodder, and nut sectors. In order to respect the tight budgetary ceiling for the EU until 2013, the CAP cost about €55 billion per year in 2010. This currently represents 31 per cent of the EU's total budget, less than 0.5 per cent of the gross domestic product of EU governments.[19] European ministers also agreed to introduce a financial discipline mechanism into the CAP.

The communication on the Health Check of 2008 identified a number of new, and ongoing, challenges for the CAP (risk management, climate change, bio-energy, water management, and biodiversity), and considered the Rural Development Policy as one of the possible tools with which to deal with these challenges. The enlargement of the EU by 2007, the assertion of its trade interests at the WTO, a series of food crises, and the need for a sustainable development strategy all continue to highlight the need for a robust and fundamental review of the CAP beyond its financing aspects.

Box 1: What the 2002 CAP Proposals Do Not Do

- Give consideration to developing-country concerns
- Reduce the overall level of EU support to agriculture
- Radically change the two CAP 'untouchables': dairy and sugar
- Provide any scope for large reductions in price support or export refunds
- Decrease inequalities in the distribution of subsidies by providing a sufficiently low subsidy cap on payments going to any one farm

Source: Adopted from Action Aid, http://www.ukfg.org.uk/docs/AAFarmgate%20briefing.pdf

---

With limited reforms in farm subsidies, the EU continues to move in the wrong direction. European countries agreed to limited reforms in 2003, reducing import controls and transferring subsidies to land stewardship rather than specific crop production (these measures were phased in between 2005 and 2012). Detailed implementation of the scheme varied among different member countries, as there was no common consensus on the issue. At the first EU Agriculture Council under the Slovenian presidency in January 2008, a press statement was issued:

The Member States welcomed the Communication of the Commission and are of the opinion that it correctly assesses the main movements by the implemented reforms adopted in 2003 and 2004, as well as the main challenges for the CAP in the following years. As expected, opinions about the level of ambitiousness and scope of the adjustments defined in the Communication are divided.[20]

By decoupling payments to farmers from what they actually produce, EU member states reduced the incentives of European farmers to overproduce particular commodities—at least in theory. In reality, the reforms were likely to have little impact on production, because European countries can still link farm subsidies to production of up to 25 per cent for cereals and up to 40 per cent for beef.[21] Furthermore, the EU reforms completely ignored the issue of market access, and did not address the equally important issue of export subsidies. In other words, the agreement covered only one of the three main problems, and without really resolving it.

A critique of the CAP

One of the things that EU member states and European civil society organisations have failed to agree on, in terms of evaluation or policy change, is the CAP. Some farming and environmental nongovernmental organisations (see the list in 2009 calling for a new CAP proposal),[22] by linking the CAP to both domestic and international development debates, seek a complete overhaul of the entire policy rather than piecemeal changes.[23] Three schools of thought seem to have emerged among EU member states on the issue of the CAP. In the first two groups there is a relatively broad consensus on the need for continued reform of the programme, although opinions remain divided on the extent of reform required. This broad conclusion was largely

---

Box 2: The CAP Budget for 2007–2013[24]

The proportion of the EU budget spent on agriculture has declined since the 1980s, from a peak of almost 70 per cent to around 40 per cent of the total budget in 2008. Over the 2007–2013 period, about €377 billion is set to be spent on the CAP from the EU budget. When national co-financing of the rural development fund, the European Agricultural Fund for Rural Development (EAFRD), is accounted for, this sum rises to €434 billion.

---

expected, given that the CAP accounts for the greatest proportion of EU expenditure (see box 2).

Of the three schools of thought among member states, the first group questions the added value of continuing to support the existence of such an anachronistic programme and is keen to see Brussels cut the budget allocation to the CAP. This group is also pushing for reduced expenditure in the CAP and redeploying resources elsewhere. Leading this group are the British and Czech governments.[25] Through its Department for International Development (DFID), London called for the EU to cut the funding budget on CAP subsidies in December 2007. At the British Department for Environment, Food, and Rural Affairs, Lord Rooker, minister for sustainable food and farming and animal welfare at the time, called for further cuts in the trade-distorting nature of the CAP and a reduction in regulatory burdens, giving European farmers greater control over their business decisions, and directing more public spending towards the delivery of targeted public benefits.[26]

There is no doubt that since its inception, a number of countries have benefitted from the CAP. For example, France received 20 per cent of the total budget in 2006, and in later years shared the largest amounts, along with Poland, Hungary, Spain, and Greece.[27] However, the key question must be asked as to whether the old wine of CAP can still fit into today's new bottle of globalisation and multilateralism.

The second school of opposition to CAP among EU member states came from governments that were sceptical about, and opposed to, the continued belief in the programme's ability to continue boosting agricultural production without radical reforms. This group was led by Sweden, which in May 2007 became the first EU country to call for the abolition of all farm subsidies except those related to environmental protection.[28] Another related group of non-EU member states, led by the European Parliament's Environment Committee, has emphasised reforming aspects of the CAP, but excluding public health, environmental, and food safety issues.[29] The majority of EU member states—almost three quarters[30]—seem to support this idea, backing some selected reforms within the CAP.

The third and perhaps most radical school of thought on the CAP seems to be composed of those governments that wish to see the CAP status quo maintained without much reform. These countries include EU members with large farming populations, such as Bulgaria, Greece, Hungary, and Poland.[31]

The WTO, global trade, and the CAP

The EU's Common Agricultural Policy is widely known in developing countries, and in international trade negotiations, for its excesses and abuses, particularly its export subsidies and their pernicious consequences for producers in poor countries. Since some 70 per cent of Africans are involved in agriculture, this programme is particularly harmful to the continent. At the global level, the impact of the CAP and other EU policies on agriculture has attracted much criticism. First are the issues around the preferential access to EU markets for developing countries, provided under a variety of measures, including the 'Everything but Arms' initiative of 2001, which grants duty-free access to the EU for imports of all products, including agricultural products, for the world's forty-nine least-developed countries.[32]

CAP subsidies also add to the problem of what is sometimes called 'Fortress Europe', in which the EU, just like the United States, spends large amounts on agricultural subsidies each year, which effectively amounts to unfair competition. By 2008, Washington was paying about $20 billion per year to farmers in direct subsidies as 'farm income stabilization'. The justifications for this transfer and its effects are complex and often controversial.[33] The internal subsidies that EU countries pay their farmers skew international trade in favour of farmers from rich countries to the detriment of those in developing countries. This creates unfair competition, demotivating African farmers and, at the same time, threatening the structure of agriculture in sub-Saharan Africa. By encouraging surplus production within the EU, the CAP has also encouraged the sale of farm produce to poor countries, which to a large extent can put local farmers in developing countries out of business. The dumping of cheap CAP agricultural surpluses (such as dairy products, cereals, and beef) on poor countries also damages the viability of agriculture and agricultural processing industries, particularly for the small-scale farming sector, which does not receive state support. As Akin Adesina, the Nigerian vice president of the Alliance for a Green Revolution in Africa, observed: 'Today the small farmers in developing countries are not being supported.... The critical issue is that international development institutions and multilateral finance institutions have pursued policies of abandonment over the last 20/30 years and what we need today are policies of support for farmers'.[34]

Europe remains Africa's most important trading and development partner. The Lomé trade regime (and, under constraints, that of Cotonou) granted nonreciprocal tariff preferences for exports from African, Caribbean, and Pacific countries to the EU. (See chapters 2 and 4 in this volume.) However, this preferential access did not extend to certain agricultural products falling under the Common Agricultural Policy, including cereals, milk, beef, rum, bananas, and sugar, which are defined as 'sensitive' products for European farmers.

Increased competition from the EU's highly subsidised agricultural products, such as maize, milk, tomatoes, and meat, could also mean the loss of domestic and regional markets for millions of African smallholder farmers. Loss of markets means loss of livelihoods, which in Africa can lead to loss of life. The far-reaching effects of this situation could result in the collapse of rural economies, rising poverty, and a threat to food security for rural small-holder farmers, particularly among women, who are the backbone of the agricultural sector in Africa. Owing to long-established regional trade rela-tionships, EU policies tend to have a greater impact on Africa. In fact, if trade-distorting policies were eliminated worldwide, almost 70 per cent of the increase in the value of exports for sub-Saharan Africa would come from liberalisation policies within the European Union. The CAP continues to support major unproductive sectors of European agriculture, notably through high levels of border protection. This has helped to frustrate the WTO's Doha development agenda and to obstruct the EU's broader com-mercial policy agenda. European countries have generally spent less on pro-moting agriculture in developing countries. For example, Britain's DFID has neglected agriculture for many years, with bilateral spending on agriculture programmes in sub-Saharan Africa amounting to little more than £20 mil-lion, or 0.35 per cent of its total budget of £5.7 billion, in 2008–2009. Of this amount, just £13.7 million was spent on least-developed countries.[35]

As a result of policies such as the CAP, in order to obtain the money to pay for $290 billion of external debt in 2011, African governments have been forced to skew their agricultural policies towards the growth of export crops, which for many countries are their only source of foreign currency.[36] Forced to produce cash crops, Africa is now heavily dependent on imports to meet its basic food needs. The fact that poor producers frequently have only incomplete markets—or none at all—in which to sell their products, obtain inputs for production, and sell their labour, results in increased food insecurity. The absence of markets can fundamentally alter the behaviour of economic agents, whose activity becomes their only means of subsistence. Poor countries in Africa cannot afford to lavish subsidies on their farmers as their wealthier counterparts in Europe do. Being economically vulnera-ble, these countries need simplified and streamlined means to confront unfair trade practices and import surges—through dumping—that may irreparably damage the livelihoods of their small-scale farmers. That does not mean, however, that increasing agricultural protection in developing countries, as some argue, is the right approach to remedy this problem. Some of the claims that more protection is necessary to shelter small-scale farmers will continue to ring hollow if current underinvestment by African governments in rural development and poverty alleviation continues. In 2008 the World Bank rightly noted that 'agriculture has served as a basis for growth and reduced poverty in many countries, but more countries could benefit if governments and donors were to reverse years of policy neglect and remedy their underinvestment and misinvestment in agriculture'.[37]

Thus, protectionism and subsidies by the CAP cost developing countries dearly in lost agricultural and agro-industrial income. The thirty-four countries of the Organisation for Economic Cooperation and Development (OECD) perversely spent $265 billion on farm subsidies in 2008, compared with $4 billion on aid contributed to agriculture in developing countries. Currently, agriculture is estimated to be 31 per cent of the EU budget, and in 2009 it accounted for more than 40 per cent (€129 billion, or £115 billion).[38] The CAP remains controversial in terms of the EU's trading relationships with developing countries. If Brussels were to pursue a more sensible agricultural policy, much of the money that is now ineffectively spent on development aid could be saved. European taxpayers are currently financing this profligate agricultural policy that amounts to about €50 billion per year and costs each tax payer about €100 annually. OECD analysts have estimated that cutting agricultural tariffs and subsidies by 50 per cent would add an extra $26 billion to annual world income, equivalent to just over four dollars a year for every person on the planet.[39] In addition to causing real harm to poor farmers in developing countries, the CAP and its related policies hurt taxpayers and consumers in rich countries. These programmes mostly benefit large-scale producers at the expense of food-buying populations in wealthy countries, and eliminate production opportunities in poor countries.

The 2007–2009 world food crisis has renewed calls for farm subsidies to be removed in light of evidence that these subsidies have contributed to rapidly increasing food prices, which have had a particularly detrimental impact on developing countries. Despite amendments to the Common Agricultural Policy and skyrocketing food prices worldwide, Europe's farm subsidies in 2010 still amounted to $85 billion.[40]

In their rhetoric, EU governments continually stress their commitment to poverty reduction in the global South, particularly in sub-Saharan Africa. Yet the same governments have used their CAP and trade policies to conduct what amounts to blatant daylight robbery against the world's poor. While European countries continue to protect their agriculture through the CAP, they ask poor countries to liberalise their agricultural sectors. Similarly, while EU agriculture markets remain firmly closed, poor countries have been pres-

FIG 12.1: Agriculture in percentage of EU total budget.

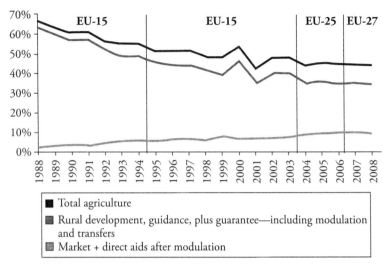

Source: EU Commission, Agriculture and Rural Development, Brussels, 2009.

sured by the International Monetary Fund (IMF) and the World Bank to open their own food markets at breakneck speed, often with damaging consequences to poor communities. As Oxfam noted in 2002, EU agricultural subsidies have destroyed millions of livelihoods in developing countries. By encouraging overproduction and export dumping, these subsidies have driven down world prices of key commodities such as sugar, dairy products, and cereals. Reforming a system in which Europe's 15 million landowners and agribusinesses are provided €55 billion of CAP subsidies per year, while smallholder farmers in developing countries suffer the consequences of these perverse policies, is an essential step towards ensuring global fair trade.[41]

The CAP and criticisms within the EU

Criticisms of the European Union's CAP have been wide-ranging, to the extent of convincing the European Commission in Brussels of the policy's numerous defects. In comparing the key issues emerging in the various debates on the future of the CAP, it is striking that divergent issues have been put forward by EU member states, and there is rarely a consistent view on the primary purpose of the policy.[42] The overall impression is that the issues at stake tend to reflect country-specific concerns. The governments of Denmark, Finland, Sweden, Britain, and Latvia have advocated further liberalisation and more market orientation within the CAP, including elimination of price support, export refunds, production quotas, and other interventionist market support measures. This position is linked to support for full decoupling of the Single Payment Scheme. David Miliband, the former British foreign secretary, in a June 2010 Parliament debate, said: 'The previous Government set out a clear plan for how the CAP should be reformed, so that there was spending on rural development and rural support, notably with an environmental, green and climate change focus'.[43]

Austria, France, Portugal, and Spain can be characterized as being much more resistant to the idea of further liberalisation. Within these countries, the CAP is mainly seen as an instrument for supporting the functions and structure of European agriculture. However, in other member states, such as Italy, the Netherlands, and Sweden, a more broad-based territorial approach is emphasised, taking account of the needs of the entire rural population.

The concern here for the CAP seems to be the need to shift from subsidies and concentrate on protecting the environment, encouraging farmers to manage their land in a more environmentally beneficial way, and taking concrete measures to improve Europe's landscape and biodiversity. Although a number of reforms have been made to the CAP, it should be noted that the programme itself has long been criticised as a good example of policy incoherence in relation to development objectives.

Many economists believe that the CAP is unsustainable within an enlarged EU of twenty-seven members. The large agricultural production potential of the new member states is still far from being fully utilised. The inclusion of twelve additional EU countries—Cyprus, the Czech Republic, Estonia, Hungary, Latvia, Lithuania, Malta, Poland, Slovakia, and Slovenia in 2004, and Bulgaria and Romania in 2007—has forced bureaucrats in Brussels to take measures to limit the CAP's expenditure. Poland is the largest new member state, and has 2 million smallholder farmers. Taken together, the new states represent a significant increase in the number of CAP recipients. Even before the EU's 2004 expansion, the CAP consumed a large proportion of its budget, upwards of 90 per cent in the late 1980s. The CAP budget has been falling as a proportion of the total EU budget since 1985, as European collaboration has steadily extended into other areas.

In recent years, EU agricultural protectionism has come under heavy fire as some critics have argued that the setting of 'artificial' prices inevitably leads to distortions in production, with overproduction being the usual result.[44] Subsidies allowed many small, outdated, or inefficient European farms to continue to operate when they would not otherwise have remained in business. A straightforward economic model would suggest that it would be better to allow the market to find its own price levels, and for uneconomic farming in Europe to cease. Resources used in farming could then be used for more productive operations such as infrastructure, education, and healthcare.

The CAP has also been criticised for allowing farmers to employ unecological ways of increasing production, such as the indiscriminate use of fertilisers and pesticides, with serious environmental consequences.[45] Domestically, the CAP continues to impose substantial costs on European consumers and taxpayers and is inefficient in delivering support to farmers and promoting an attractive rural environment. Indeed, much of the programme still has a negative impact on the environment. One of the criticisms of the CAP concerned the way its surpluses were managed.[46] The measures taken to deal with these surpluses had a high budgetary cost, in terms of both storage costs on the internal market and subsidised exports. Although the CAP reforms did put a ceiling on the EU budget to reassure taxpayers that the programme's costs would not run out of control, on average each EU citizen contributes around two euros a week to finance the CAP. This is hardly a high price to pay for a healthy supply of food and a living countryside,[47] but these measures have not always served the best interests of European farmers and consumers, and have become unpopular with taxpayers. Some prominent European farmers have also criticised the CAP's policy implementation for not funding primary producers sufficiently.

Because the CAP has traditionally rewarded farmers who produce more, larger European farms have benefitted much more from agricultural subsidies than smaller ones. In 2011 the vast majority of aid to farmers was paid independently of how much they produced. Severing the link between subsidies and production (usually termed 'decoupling') will enable EU farmers to be more market-oriented. They will thus be free to produce according to what is most profitable to them while still enjoying a required stability of income. In addition, farmers have to respect environmental, food safety, phytosanitary, and animal welfare standards. Farmers who fail to meet these standards will face reductions in their direct payments (a condition known as 'cross-compliance').[48] Since the 1992 MacSharry reforms, CAP subsidies have made their way to large-scale farmers, as subsidies have been linked increasingly to the size of farms. Often the programme has not distributed support equally between large and small producers, and the development of excessively intensive farming practices in some EU member states has had an extremely negative impact on the environment and on animal welfare.[49]

Concluding reflections

Agriculture is of particular importance to the economic prospects of many developing countries, particularly in Africa. Reforming the current unfair practices in the global farm trade holds perhaps the most immediate scope for improving the livelihoods of the world's poorest inhabitants. Although some important progress has been achieved in reforming the EU's Common Agricultural Policy, this programme remains the most visible and wasteful policy of the Union, and is increasingly out of step with the needs of Europe to respond to the challenges of globalisation and development. Internationally, the CAP continues to attract criticism, to create tensions in the EU's relations with its trading partners in the global South, and to impose significant costs on developing countries. Furthermore, economic partnership agreements proposed by the EU (see chapters 10 and 11 in this volume) will further restrict the possibility of using tariffs to protect locally grown crops from foreign imports, thereby placing small farmers in further jeopardy.

There are six key ways to alleviate the adverse effects of the CAP on African agriculture. First, EU governments must overcome their short-sighted reticence in providing substantial development assistance to African countries. Not only should they invest more resources in Africa, but they should also focus more of the existing aid on agriculture and human development. Beyond providing aid, European governments must agree to significant reductions in their own CAP protectionism and subsidies.

Second, field experts and nongovernmental organisations in Europe must advocate that rules of origin should be applied with more flexibility where needed, in order to benefit developing countries. Improving the development coherence of the EU's agricultural policies will require more liberal market access for food imports from developing countries than currently exists.

Third, the EU must craft policies to protect and assist developing countries that are unable to take advantage of improved market access, or lose out in cases where lower trade barriers lead to preference erosion. The interests of the millions of people in Africa and elsewhere in the global South who depend on agriculture must properly and sensitively be taken into account, and sudden shocks to economies and livelihoods must be avoided.

Fourth, European governments must phase out, as soon as possible, agricultural subsidies in the rich world that distort production and trade and lead to pernicious dumping of agricultural products on African and other developing markets. Fifth, the European Commission must redirect the remaining subsidies in the rich world towards conserving the environment, promoting rural development, and targeting these funds instead at small-scale European farmers and more sustainable agricultural practices. And finally, African and other developing countries must vastly increase their investments in agriculture, eliminate biases against their agricultural sectors, and maintain a neutral, effective trade policy that reduces protection over this vital sector.

PART 4

SECURITY AND GOVERNANCE

13

AU-EU SECURITY
AND GOVERNANCE COOPERATION

Garth le Pere

Introduction

In 2005 the British prime minister at the time, Tony Blair, declared that it would be the 'Year of Africa'. This was perhaps emblematic of the continent's rise to an important place on the international agenda after years of relative neglect as a consequence of risk-aversion and general apathy by a West at first heady with a post-Cold War triumphalism, and then shell-shocked by the terrorist attacks of 11 September 2001. It is not only the sheer scale of the economic, governance, and security challenges in Africa that has prompted Western governments and institutions to renew and review their commitments to the continent: Africa is also a place of boundless opportunities. As has been argued by the French scholar Jean-François Bayart, 'more than ever before, the discourse on Africa's marginality is a nonsense'.[1] This reflects the post-11 September 2001 shift in Western priorities, a shift that has been marked and indeed propelled by a paradigmatic redefinition of the nexus between security, governance, and development. More than before, this reorientation is a direct result of an acknowledgement by the West that it now needs to pursue a strategic engagement with Africa on account of the continent's natural resource abundance—a consideration that has introduced a delicate calculus of rivalry and cooperation between the European Union and the United States on the one hand, and China on the other.

Owing to Beijing's increasing hold over Africa's extractive sectors[2] and, moreover, the continent's importance as an alternative source for energy and raw materials, the quest for mutually beneficial cooperation has become an urgent imperative for external actors. Even Washington has weighed in on the resource 'race', since it imported more of its oil from Africa (22 per cent by 2010) than it did from the entire Middle East (17 per cent). The US has even tried to establish a strange hybrid structure in the Pentagon—the African Command—which is meant to promote democracy, peace, development, and stability on the continent but which, stripped of its embroidery, appears to be more of a military instrument to combat terrorism and secure future energy sources. More discerning observers have thus rejected this 'Africom' idea with the contempt that it deserves.[3]

Framing the context

Among the differing dynamics that have shaped Africa's changing landscape stands the European Union, whose ambitions towards global power status have subtly altered international dynamics since the end of the Cold War.[4] Although the contemporary EU-Africa relationship can trace its origins to the very beginnings of the European Economic Community (EEC) in 1957, the relationship has changed over time, reflecting the political and economic shifts in international relations, the emergence of independence and liberation movements on the continent, and the advances that have characterised the different thresholds and accelerating pace of European integration (see chapter 3 in this volume). The European Community's early incarnation as an external actor was directly aimed at Africa, with Brussels eventually emerging to play a key role in areas such as aid and trade, a posture that culminated in a series of preferential agreements embedded and codified in frameworks such as the Yaoundé Conventions (1963–1975), the Lomé Conventions (1975–2000), and the Cotonou Agreement (since 2000). (See chapter 2 in this volume.)

These frameworks brought seventy-seven (currently seventy-nine) African, Caribbean, and Pacific (ACP) countries into a 'special' relationship with the EU. But critics argue that these frameworks essentially set the basis for ongoing asymmetric, highly dependent, and unequal relations that violated and made a mockery of the spirit of mutual benefit and common interests that was supposed to underpin them.[5] The same critique has been levelled at the EU's economic partnership agreements (EPAs), which anticipate fully reciprocal trade relations between the EU and the ACP.[6] (See chapters 10 and 11 in this volume.) Brussels's rhetorical commitment to 'partnership' has rung hollow when viewed within the context of the dialectic between expectations and capacities: both sides have seen demands colliding with the ability to meet them.[7] However, the balance has swung decidedly in Brussels's favour, since the cooperation frameworks have served more to entrench and maintain particular EU interests than to promote trade and development in Africa. More often than not, Africa has had to bear the more onerous burden of its growing marginalisation in global markets, although this situation is changing rapidly.

Recently, Africa has come to occupy a more strategic place on the EU agenda, occasioned by a mix of structural and policy factors. This development includes the conceptual and normative linkages between security, governance, and development; changes within the EU and the African Union's institutional architecture; the emergence of China and, more recently, India as new actors on the African stage; and a growing focus on natural resources, energy, and food security. Ghana's Kofi Annan, the UN's Secretary-General between 1997 and 2006, perhaps best articulated the need for a different and new moral enterprise in the West when he noted in 2005: 'We will not enjoy development without security, we will not enjoy security without development, and we will not enjoy either without respect for human rights'.[8] The link between security, governance, and development has provided the basis for widening the ambit of areas for cooperation between Africa and the EU, and hence donor countries have become more emboldened in attaching conditions and requirements for trade and aid, insisting especially that African countries must observe norms and practices that encourage 'good governance' and democracy.[9] (See chapter 4 in this volume.)

The 2005 UN World Summit made an explicit reference to the development and security link, with an emphasis on principles of human security and 'freedom from fear' and 'freedom from want'. The Group of Eight (G8) industrialised countries, at their Gleneagles summit in 2005, integrated this theme into their concerns and sought—albeit somewhat patronisingly—to put Africa 'back' on the international agenda. Three other international compacts have also exerted significant gravitational pull on EU-Africa relations.

First, the Millennium Development Goals (MDGs) commit signatories to meeting eight development targets by 2015, the most important being halving poverty. Individual EU member states have, for example, pledged to contribute 0.7 per cent of their gross national products to aid each year, doubling the 2008 average of 0.34 per cent, to help developing countries, especially those in Africa, meet the ambitious MDG targets. By 2010, EU member states were still struggling to meet their dedicated benchmark of 0.59 per cent.[10] Then there is the 2005 Paris Declaration, augmented by the 2008 Accra Agenda for Action, on effective development aid, alignment, and coordination, which sought—under the auspices of the Organisation for Economic Cooperation and Development (OECD)—to improve the volume, quality, and effectiveness of aid. Brussels has drawn up a 'European Consensus for Development' which is a de facto code of conduct for observing the letter and spirit of the declaration.

The codes of the World Trade Organisation (WTO) have also influenced the dynamics of EU-Africa relations. The special bilateral trade arrangements, based on protocols that have underpinned the different framework agreements between Brussels and Africa, were found to be incompatible with the WTO's multilateral rules and the orthodoxy of free trade agreements. The controversial and divisive EPAs have emerged against this backdrop and, with the expiry of the WTO waiver by December 2007, the EU has aggressively sought to forge ahead with their implementation in ACP countries. The Balkanising effects of EPAs have been especially evident in Africa because of the different contours they have assumed across its subregional economic formations. EPAs have thereby served to undermine the confidence that came with expectations in Africa that Brussels would craft a new trade deal that was more sensitive to the continent's development needs and challenges.[11] (See chapters 10 and 11 in this volume.)

The institutional environments of Africa and Europe have also undergone fundamental changes in the post-Cold War era. The overall stability of the continent has demonstrated a remarkable improvement, although some intractable conflicts persist, such as those in Somalia, Sudan, and the Democratic Republic of the Congo. The new continental equivalent of a social contract has been enshrined in the African Union's Constitutive Act of 2000, which stresses important values of democracy, peace, security, and development. Among the AU's key organs, a fifteen-member Peace and Security Council has been established to develop an operational mechanism for promoting and keeping peace, and establishing a continent-wide African Standby Force. In addition, democratic participation has been broadened with the establishment of the Pan-African Parliament as well as the Economic, Social, and Cultural Council (ECOSOCC), while the 2001 New Partnership for Africa's Development (NEPAD) has sought to promote an 'African approach' to development and, as the continent's own socioeconomic blueprint, to address important governance and development deficits.[12] An important milestone was reached by African heads of state at their summit in Accra in 2007, where a firm commitment was made by AU member states to move the continent inexorably towards incremental integration and unity on the basis of strengthening their subregional economic communities. The cold realities of African politics, however, could still prove antithetical to this level of ambition.

For its part, the EU's external relations and policy instruments have also evolved in line with the changes in the international context. Its competences in the areas of foreign policy, diplomacy, defence, and security matters are embodied in its Common Foreign and Security Policy (CFSP), which was consolidated and refined in the Maastricht Treaty of 1992 and the Lisbon Treaty of 2007. The European Security Strategy (ESS) was introduced in 2003 to achieve greater doctrinal coherence in foreign policy for the benefit of Brussels's international partnerships and to bring greater clarity to CFSP objectives. The strategy also brings other key threats such as terrorism, weapons proliferation, regional conflicts, state failure, and organised crime within the CSFP purview. The ESS further defines more active policies, and attempts to create stronger synergies between EU institutions and member states through the development of diplomatic, civil, and military capabilities.

The strategy's philosophy is strong on promoting development as a precondition for security, and stresses the importance of this premise for shaping the EU's continued commitment to Africa. Complementing the ESS is the Common Security and Defence Policy (CSDP). The CSDP was formulated and integrated into the Lisbon Treaty—which came into force in 2009—and includes the 'Petersberg tasks', which were adopted in 1992. These promote humanitarian and rescue efforts, peacekeeping, and the role of combat forces in crisis management, including peacemaking. The CDSP thus provides the operational platform for assisting with peacebuilding initiatives in Africa and elsewhere.[13] The broadening of EU-Africa cooperation has led to the creation of special funds in the area of security promotion and support, the most visible being the Africa Peace Facility, which was allocated €300 million for 2008–2010 (a further commitment of €230 million was made for the next three year cycle, 2010–2012). Brussels also actively supports AU efforts in many parts of Africa, and has provided direct support, such as €242 million to assist the AU Mission in Sudan (AMIS). Plans were also set out to appoint an EU Special Representative for Africa who will wear two hats by representing the Council and the Commission.[14] Koen Vervaeke, a Belgian national, was appointed to this position in December 2007. Also important, a French general, Pierre-Michel Joana, was appointed Special Adviser for African Peacekeeping and has worked closely with the EU Special Representative for Africa.

This is the overall picture that has helped to set the stage for a more focused and deeper relationship between the EU and Africa. It takes into account a growing consensus in the EU on aid and development policy, the need for more frequent and intense CFSP initiatives, and the altered governance and institutional dynamics of the AU and its enhanced role in Africa. Quite critically, Brussels felt a need to draw together the different strands of the evolving cooperation architecture into a more streamlined agenda that was guided by a broad strategic compass.

The EU's policy management dilemmas

The European Union's efforts to promote democracy, security, and development have progressively become both objectives and conditions for development aid, but have been criticised for their lack of coherence, consistency, and effectiveness. The technocratic mode determines aid and is the cause of the opacity of Brussels's bureaucratic procedures. This has ipso facto obliged the EU's administrative arm—the European Commission (EC) and its 24,000 staff, spread over twenty-four directorates-general—to address political problems with technical solutions in the straitjacket of complex decisionmaking processes, often driven by Byzantine management procedures. An administrative labyrinth, a technocratic approach to management of aid, and burdensome *ex ante* financial controls further compound the absence of an overarching strategy for promoting security, governance, and development. This is best demonstrated with regard to the two directorates-general responsible for implementing the EU's Africa strategy.

The Directorate-General for Development is responsible for those parts of the strategy related to development and humanitarian aid in sub-Saharan Africa and other developing countries. The Directorate-General for External

Relations (RELEX) is responsible more broadly for the foreign policy aspects of the European Neighbourhood Policy as well as relations with North Africa. (See chapter 7 in this volume.) The Directorate-General for Trade was split in 2000 and its development focus has been commensurately reduced. This separation of decisionmaking meant that the EU's trade regime was no longer considered an aspect of development aid. That might help to explain the incongruence and contradictory impulses behind the neo-mercantilism of the EPAs and the seeming altruism of the EU development strategy. There are thus certain thematic areas that cut across directorates-general within the strategy, rendering Brussels's clarion call for policy coherence and better coordination even more tendentious.[15]

Despite good intentions, altruistic aims, and genuine commitment by the EU, aid has been a case of perverse institutional incentives. The acerbic Clare Short, when she was Britain's secretary for international development, remarked in June 2000 that 'the Commission is the worst development agency in the world. The poor quality and reputation of its aid brings Europe into disrepute'.[16] The proliferation of budget lines and a thicket of regulations and declarations have hampered the definition of sectorwide strategies, which in turn have affected the coordination of EU security, governance, and development promotion efforts. This has meant that, over time, the aid provided by Brussels has often lacked identity and effectiveness, with the European Commission being perceived more as a funding agency than as a partner in development with clearly demarcated aid strategies. Hence Brussels's political influence continues to be disproportionate in relation to its financial muscle, and weakens EU leverage in the global aid regime that attempts to promote security, governance, and development.

These programming, coordination, and implementation pathologies are brought into sharper relief when considering the vast levels of aid that the EU provides. For 2002, the European Commission's budget allocated an impressive €8.3 billion for financing its external relations activities (including foreign policy, pre-accession assistance, and development aid). By 2007, this figure had increased to nearly €15.5 billion. Combined, the European Commission and EU member states are the largest providers of official development assistance globally, mainly in the form of grants. This represents 55 per cent of all overseas development assistance and was worth €47 billion in 2006. In 2000 the European Commission alone provided $4.9 billion in development assistance, and in 2001 this figure rose by 21.1 per cent, to $5.9 billion. The figure for 2007 almost doubled, reaching $11.7 billion, and in 2010 increased to $12.2 billion.[17]

Brussels's foreign aid programme combines elements of a bilateral donor and a multilateral institution, which makes the EU unique among development cooperation organisations. In 2008 the European Commission had financial responsibility for almost 10 per cent of total overseas development assistance, and was the world's largest donor of humanitarian aid. Brussels is directly responsible for development cooperation programmes with the ACP countries, Latin America, Asia, the Mediterranean, East and Central Asia, the Western Balkans, and East and Central Europe. The Commission's external assistance programmes total almost €5 billion per year, in addition to the European Development Fund (EDF), which is dedicated to the ACP countries. Under the ninth EDF, €13.5 billion was provided to cover 2000–2007; for the tenth EDF, €22.6 billion has been allocated for 2008–2013.[18]

The European Community

The provision of these significant resources is grounded in the 1992 Maastricht Treaty, which for the first time codified development cooperation as an autonomous field of policy with specific objectives (Title XVIII, Article 130). The 1997 Amsterdam Treaty reaffirmed that European Community policy is to contribute to the 'general objective to developing and consolidating democracy and the rule of law, and to that of respecting human rights and fundamental freedoms' (Title XX, Article 177.2). Respect for democracy and human rights was thus made a general principle of EU law, and this in turn has informed other derivatives such as 'good governance', security, and development.[19] In the 1990s, Brussels was challenged to respond to recurrent crises of democratic governance that were destabilising politically fragile countries, especially in Africa.

Standard European approaches for promoting democracy and governance, including governance conditionality, tend to fall flat in crisis situations and can sometimes compound the problems that prompted the crisis in the first place. The cases of Zimbabwe and Kenya are instructive in this regard. Western pressure and demands for democratic and constitutional reform as *quid pro quo*s for aid served only to exacerbate the repressive and authoritarian tendencies of Zimbabwe's Robert Mugabe and Kenya's Daniel Arap Moi. Democratisation does not typically follow a natural, orderly, and linear sequence of positive and progressive transformation. More often than not, it is irregular, erratic, and sometimes reversible, occurring as it does in highly fluid and volatile environments. The EU approach recognises the multifaceted links between postconflict peacebuilding and conflict prevention, as well as between relief, rehabilitation, and development. In particular, it recognises that preventing the occurrence or recurrence of conflict in 'dysfunctional' states entails rebuilding the administrative capacities of countries, strengthening democratic institutions, and improving systems of governance and accountability. The promotion of security and governance therefore becomes an important tool for preventing, managing, and resolving political crises and, in extreme cases of political instability and uncertainty, for preventing violent conflict.

There are thus inherent tensions between positive and negative measures to promote governance, security, and development. The enduring question is how conditionality can best further these objectives. Punitive routes have largely proved ineffective and remain controversial. Indeed, it has been established that there is no direct relationship between aid flows and policy reform or the ability of aid to induce policy change. Positive approaches, or what has been described as 'allocative conditionality', attempt to increase the effectiveness of aid by concentrating assistance in those countries that demonstrate a genuine commitment to improving the environment in which governance, security, and development can take root and flourish. However, in EU policy, political considerations still remain important in determining aid flows: better policies and improved performance too often lead to decreasing levels of development aid.[20] For example, once Ghana had become the 'poster child' for the efficacy of structural adjustment programmes in Africa in the 1990s, it started to experience declining levels of aid. Tanzania, on the other hand—with development indices showing a steady decline, especially over the decade of the 1990s—continued to receive generous amounts of external assistance.[21] Governance performance is thus often delinked from incentives to obtain greater external aid.

A central thrust of successive EU-ACP agreements has been the attempt to strengthen their political foundations. This has been accomplished by introducing democracy clauses and governance conditionality mechanisms in the cooperation framework. For example, the fourth Lomé Convention was revised in 1995 to include democratic principles, human rights, and the rule of law as 'essential elements' of the partnership. 'Good governance' was cited as an objective of this renewed cooperation. In the case of sub-Saharan Africa, Brussels focused its attention on the need to address 'state failure' in order to strengthen 'good governance' and the rule of law, especially in conflict-ridden countries. Hence, progressively, a link was being forged between security, governance, and development. In this formulation, state-building and reform were seen as critical, especially for meeting the challenges of improving the effective functioning of institutions and building administrative capacity. This is in marked contrast to the 1990s, when the European Commission tended to avoid these issues by focusing instead on 'nonstate actors' and promoting decentralisation. The role of African civil society is still recognised, but Brussels—with its subsidiarity principle—now stresses the need to strengthen and enhance the capacities of states, as well as subregional and regional bodies, as important pivots of security, governance, and development on the basis of enhanced political dialogue.[22]

This background is instructive, for it helps to explain the bases and modalities of the EU's changing posture with regard to security, governance, and development. It also points to the normative dimensions of Brussels's policy of improving the efficiency and effectiveness of aid on the basis of attributes such as transparency, accountability, and responsiveness. The obvious irony is that while the EU insists on these values, its own practices tend to represent the archetype of bureaucratic opacity, technocratic over-kill, and political hubris.

EU-Africa strategic summitry

Since the late 1990s the EU has attempted to develop a more specific relationship with Africa, outside the parameters of the ACP countries. This was the impulse that drove the first EU-Africa summit, in Cairo in April 2000. The result was a comprehensive framework for political dialogue based on a plan of action and priority areas. The Cairo agenda set the priorities that would assist with the development of the EU-Africa dialogue and partnership. This has been translated into an increasing convergence of interests, although emphases and accents differ: the EU regarded peace and security as more consequential for Africa's development; Africans stressed the importance of the trade and economic dimensions of the partnership, including the urgency of addressing the $290 billion external debt problem. Thus four areas converged to define the priority areas of cooperation: first, the integration of Africa into the world economy, including trade, private sector development, development resources, industrial infrastructure, research and technology, debt relief, and cooperation in international forums; second, the promotion of human rights, democratic principles and institutions, 'good governance', and the rule of law; third, support for peacebuilding and conflict prevention, management, and resolution, including disarmament, demobilisation, and rehabilitation (DDR) as well as combating terrorism and eliminating small arms and land mines; and fourth, a focus on development, including poverty eradication and addressing challenges of health, environment, food security, drug trafficking, and illegal migration.[23]

A second EU-Africa summit was supposed to be held in Lisbon in April 2003 in order to further consolidate the Cairo platform. The meeting was indefinitely postponed because of acrimonious disputes and differing interpretations in the EU and Africa about the attendance of Zimbabwe's President Mugabe, following that country's slide into autocracy and Mugabe's increasingly despotic behaviour. African heads of state were unwilling to agree to a summit at which all African states would not be given the opportunity to be represented, while those in Europe, with Britain (against) and Portugal (for) at the helm of opposite factions, were divided on this issue. Notwithstanding this impasse, dialogue outside the summit process continued on the basis of the European Commission's 2003 'EU-Africa Dialogue' document. Accordingly the Ministerial Troika,[24] established in 2000, continued to hold high-level annual meetings to assess progress and to help clear the way for the next EU-Africa summit.

An important product of this process was the joint development of the modalities for a strategic partnership, which culminated in the 2007 'Joint Africa-EU Strategy'. This document's broad context, vision, and principles were expected to inform the deliberations as well as the focus of the next summit. The strategy had four main objectives: to improve the political partnership over the long term; to promote peace, security, democratic governance and human rights, and sustainable economic development; to enhance regional and continental integration; and to ensure progress towards meeting the MDGs in Africa by 2015. These were brought together in the strategy's first action plan, for 2008–2010, which proposed eight themes for supporting deeper and wider cooperation between Africa and the EU: peace and security; democratic governance and human rights; trade, regional integration, and infrastructure; the MDGs; energy; climate change; migration, mobility, and employment; and science, information, and space technology.

The summit eventually took place in Lisbon in December 2007—hosted by Portugal—albeit under a controversial cloud, since Mugabe was allowed to attend and Britain's premier, Gordon Brown, stayed away in protest. This notwithstanding, and as a measure of its importance, the Lisbon summit was very well attended. Present were fifty-two African heads of state and leaders of twenty-seven EU member states, representing 1.5 billion people. Also attending was Morocco (not an AU member), the African Union Commission, the EU Commission, and the General Secretariat of the EU Council. An important normative shift at the summit, which is also engrained in the joint strategy, was the move away from past practices of developing strategies *for* Africa and towards crafting a political partnership *with* Africa. This long-term strategic partnership is predicated on 'going beyond development cooperation, beyond Africa, beyond fragmentation and beyond institution'.[25] The partnership anticipates that African states and regional and subregional bodies will have primary responsibility for their political future and development, while the EU will continue to provide development support in critical areas of peace and security, governance and human rights, trade, regional and continental integration, energy, and climate change. Brussels will further work towards expanding the ambit of the relationship so that it becomes more political, global, and equitable in scope and function. The third Africa-EU summit took place in the Libyan capital of Tripoli in November 2010 and offered an opportunity to assess the key deliverables of the 2008–2010 action plan and lay the basis for the plan's next phase.

The EU-Africa strategic partnership

After the conclusion of the Cairo summit in 2000, it would take a gestation period of five years for the EU and Africa to evolve a joint strategy that brought together the Cairo priorities into a single policy framework. This 'EU-Africa Strategic Partnership' of 2005 summarises commitments previously made by Brussels but, quite importantly, integrates the voice of the AU in framing the partnership's vision and principles. (Some critics, however, noted that the document was unilaterally developed in Brussels; see chapter 2 in this volume.) The primary value of the EU-Africa strategy is its scope and political status, since it was approved at the highest levels by the European Council and the AU Assembly of Heads of State. This approach is meant to govern *all* EU-AU relations, including those of their member states as well as their commissions and associated organs; and, crucially, it is meant to improve the complementarity of their actions and policies so as to engage effectively with the new institutional context of Africa, especially the EU's interface with the AU and NEPAD. The strategic framework therefore focuses on four key areas: peace and security, governance and human rights, trade and regional integration, and key development issues including aid, social development, gender, energy, climate change, migration, and food security.

Both sides are committed to developing an institutional architecture and implementation modalities that give life to the agreed principles and identified priorities, as well as to addressing the legion of administrative and bureaucratic inefficiencies. This approach was to be based on more frequent contact between the political leadership of the AU and the EU, complemented by biannual Troika meetings. Other actors would also have key roles to play in these evolving arrangements. Closer cooperation and dialogue are encouraged between the Pan-African and European Parliaments (see chapter 3 in this volume) as well as between the AU's Economic, Social, and Cultural Council and the European Economic and Social Committee. More focused upstream preparation and agenda-setting, and better priority management and operational continuity, are to be enhanced by annual meetings of the AU and EU Commissions and biannual meetings of a joint AU-EU task force. Nonstate actors such as civil society networks, research institutes, and think-tanks are also to be brought into this process. In order to manage the AU interface and the coherence of EU action more effectively and to improve its own implementation competence, in December 2007 Brussels opened an EU delegation in Addis Ababa exclusively dedicated to the AU.[26]

Peace and security dimensions

The primary aim of cooperation is to build the African Peace and Security Architecture (APSA) so as to improve stability, conflict management and prevention, peacekeeping, and peacebuilding at all levels. This includes support for a continental early warning system, the Panel of the Wise (a panel of special envoys and advisers established under the fifteen-member Peace and Security Council [PSC]), the AU Special Fund (for peace and security), and the African Standby Force (to comprise at least 25,000 rapid reaction troops and 980 military observers, as well as African training centres).[27] These are the essential components of the APSA, for which the EU had provided €1 billion by June 2010.[28] A key principle will be to empower the Peace and Security Council to take the lead role in these initiatives by ensuring that the capacity-building component of the African Peace Facility

(APF) complements and reinforces the work of the PSC. The AU's Peace and Security Council has been conceived as the 'standing decision-making organ for the prevention, management and resolution of conflicts and a collective security and early-warning arrangement to facilitate timely and efficient response to conflict and crisis situations in Africa'.[29] Brussels's support for the PSC will also include mobilisation of other funds, especially from the Group of Eight and other potential donors. The EU will further contribute to improving UN mechanisms, under Chapter VIII of the UN Charter, in order to provide more predictable, flexible, and sustained funding for AU peacekeeping operations. Other areas of cooperation will address the proliferation of small arms, light weapons, and antipersonnel mines.

Assessment of the EU's role. The European Union's 'Common Position on the Prevention, Management, and Resolution of Violent Conflicts in Africa' states that 'the EU shall support, over the long term, the enhancement of African peace support operations capabilities, at regional, sub-regional and bilateral levels as well as the capacity of African States to contribute to regional integration, peace, security and development'.[30] This resulted in two initiatives. First, in November 2004, an action plan for the CFSP in Africa was developed, which seeks to determine practical ways of implementing EU support for the AU and for building the latter's conflict prevention and management capacities. Beside this capacity-building aspect, the plan further seeks to encompass DDR activities, security sector reform (SSR), training, provision of equipment, operational support, and possibly the launching of CFSP advisory or executive missions in the context of African-led or UN-supported peacekeeping missions. The second initiative was the adoption in November 2006 of the 'EU Concept for Strengthening African Capabilities for the Prevention, Management, and Resolution of Conflicts', which aims to 'provide a coherent and comprehensive EU framework for the implementation of key aspects of the Peace and Security cluster of the EU Strategy for Africa'.[31] This is to be implemented through concrete measures that directly support the APSA, including the establishment of the African Standby Force, which was launched in 2010. These developments are perhaps indicative of the extent to which Brussels has so far been able to contribute to peace and security efforts in Africa.

Since 2003 the EU has been able to conduct several civilian and military operations not only in Africa but also in Asia, the Middle East, the South Caucasus, and the Western Balkans. These operations certainly enhance the profile of the ESDP and are a manifestation of Brussels's early 'hands-on' security and defence experiences. The tasks have ranged from support for the rule of law and law enforcement to ceasefire monitoring, security and humanitarian management, SSR advice and assistance, and building political institutions. As additional measures to support Africa's peace and security agenda, the EU has included more assistance for postconflict reconstruction in Africa's fragile states, as well as for counterterrorism. And as part of an APSA strategic needs assessment, Brussels has also decided to provide more coherent and comprehensive support for the 'AU-Regional Economic Community Roadmap' to assist with making the continent's peace and security architecture more effective.

In the UN context and on the basis of the December 2008 report of the joint AU-UN panel on modalities for supporting AU peacekeeping operations,[32] the EU has been promoting bilateral dialogue with the G8, the US, and China to help improve Africa's crisis response management. Equally critical for Africa's capacities, the European Defence Agency was established in July 2004 to help member states improve their military capabilities in terms of the CSDP. Under the agency, there are political and military bodies that directly support the EU's peace and security efforts in Africa and have been approved by the European Council: the Political and Security Committee, the EU's Military Committee, its Military Staff Committee, its Committee for Civilian Aspects of Crisis Management (CIVCOM), and the EU Satellite Centre. In January 2007 the EU Operations Centre began work in Brussels and can command battle groups of up to 2,000 troops. The centre is further supported by five operational headquarters. The EU has undertaken over twenty-four missions spread across three continents; some have been completed, while others were still ongoing in 2012.

Support for the African Peace Facility. Established in November 2003, the European Union's African Peace Facility has become an important mechanism in Brussels's support for the APSA based on principles of ownership, solidarity, and partnership. It exists within the framework of the EDF, under which, in March 2004, financing of €250 million was provided to the programme. In April 2006 the EU Council extended the duration of the APF for three years (2008–2010), increasing funds by €50 million and providing it with replenishment support of €300 million under the tenth EDF. This sum was rather negligible considering Africa's enormous peace and security challenges and the fact that the total tenth EDF budget was €22.6 billion.

The APF rests on two pillars. First, it seeks to develop African military and civilian capacities for prevention, management, and resolution of conflicts and to support peace operations run by African organisations. Second, it aims to build the capacity of the AU in areas of planning and developing organisational skills for peace support missions. AMIS has received the bulk of the funds (€242 million) dedicated to peace support operations. A mid-term review was undertaken in 2005 and concluded that the APF 'has been a very positive initiative which has allowed the EU to support African work on peace and security in a practical, flexible and highly relevant manner that has respected the principle of African ownership'.[33]

Governance and democracy dimensions

Article 6 of the EU Treaty of 1957 emphasises the founding principles of liberty, democracy, respect for human rights, and the rule of law. The EU-Africa relationship thus has a strong focus on the promotion of democratic governance and human rights as a central component of dialogue and partnership. Brussels does not have an institutional model for governance and has therefore insisted that this should evolve organically as part of a 'home-grown' process.[34] In practical terms, the entire spectrum of aspects and concepts—such as children's rights, gender equality, the rule of law, local governance, natural resource management, transparent use of public funds, institutional development and reform, human security, security sector reform, and anticorruption and corporate social responsibility—has been included under this umbrella. Given a range of other challenges relating to conflict, crisis, instability, and authoritarian tendencies, 'situations of fragility' also form part of this dialogue.[35]

At the institutional levels and in order to give effect to human rights and other concerns, regular interactions occur between the European Court of Human Rights, the African Court on Human and Peoples' Rights, the African Commission on Human and Peoples' Rights, and African and European human rights advocacy groups. (See chapter 3 in this volume.) The partnership is also expected to assist with enhancing the efficacy of the UN Human Rights Council, especially through effective implementation of international and regional human rights instruments. Equal attention must be paid to cooperating in preventing crimes against humanity, war crimes, and genocide, and in this regard the EU and the AU are expected to work to ensure that the intervention capacity of the Hague-based International Criminal Court is strongly supported and endorsed.

At the continental level and flowing through the AU, NEPAD, and sub-regional bodies, the pan-African governance architecture that has been put in place represents a potentially important innovation for shaping norms, practices, and institutions and for ensuring progress towards achieving the Millennium Development Goals. This will be supported by the EU's Governance Initiative on the basis of a special programming line for this purpose in the EDF. Hence €2.7 billion has been made available as an 'incentive tranche' within the tenth EDF in order to encourage commitments to credible and relevant governance measures and democratic reforms.[36] Brussels also contributes €2 million to the United Nations Development Programme's (UNDP) Trust Fund to support the secretariat of the African Peer Review Mechanism (APRM) as well as national APRM structures. The EU has further allocated €1 million for an AU Electoral Assistance Fund. Another Brussels-based initiative is the Africa-EU Civil Society Human Rights Dialogue.

Assessment of the EU's role. Governance is a contested concept, lacking consensus over definition and riddled with fundamental conceptual and practical problems. Most egregious in the EU-Africa context has been the application of governance principles as a condition for obtaining development aid in terms of the equally contested concept of 'mutual accountability' between donor and recipient (see chapter 5 in this volume). The logic of 'aid governance' has been to ensure transparent criteria for resource allocation, which helps to explain the excruciatingly cumbersome procedures in ACP-EU cooperation. This was further complicated by a shift from a technical focus, for example fighting corruption, to include clear decision-making procedures, legally correct resource distribution, and institutional development, in order to ensure proper implementation.

In the new formulation, and building on the lessons learned from the Lomé and Cotonou conventions between 1975 and 2000, the emergent EU-Africa strategy of 2005 sought to avoid the 'conditionality trap' by stressing the importance of dialogue, ownership, and negotiation for arriving at shared governance agendas. Much of the EU's assistance for enhancing governance capacity has taken place within the context of NEPAD's African Peer Review Mechanism, in which thirty countries were participating by 2011. Individual member states' participation in this area has been supported by the European Initiative for Democracy and Human Rights. Other enabling AU mechanisms for revitalising governance that have been consequential for mobilising EU resources include the Lomé Declaration on Unconstitutional Changes of Government (2000), the NEPAD/APRM Declaration on Democracy, Political, Economic, and Corporate Governance (2002), the AU Protocol on the Rights of Women (2003), and the African Common Position on the Review of the MDGs (2005).

Brussels also considers election assistance and monitoring to be an integral element of its efforts to support the African Charter on Democracy, Elections, and Governance of 2004. Strengthening of the rule of law is intended to take place on the basis of enhanced support for Africa's national human rights commissions, parliaments, subregional bodies such as the Southern African Development Community (SADC) and the Economic Community of West African States (ECOWAS), independent electoral commissions, and civil society organisations. There is also a commitment to work together to support international initiatives to combat illicit trade in natural resources and to encourage more equitable and transparent management of these resources. In this regard, cooperation has been framed by the 2003 Kimberley Process, which regulates certification for the diamond trade; the 2003 Forest Law Enforcement Governance and Trade, which regulates trade in timber; and the 2002 Extractive Industry Transparency Initiative, which seeks to improve transparency and accountability in the extractive sector. The EU and the AU have also expressed the need for greater cooperation in the fight against corruption, counterfeiting, money laundering, and tax fraud.

Notwithstanding EU goodwill and progress in seeking to develop a governance architecture, the imperative to embed African ownership of democratic governance and human rights will be particularly challenging for the AU. Africa's pan-continental body still suffers from weak institutional and financial capabilities, which will continue to be a major impediment in its efforts to implement, monitor, and evaluate its governance functions. (See chapter 3 in this volume.)

Concluding reflections

The challenges of security, governance, and development will prove to be the crucible to test the changed ideological and institutional context defined by the EU-Africa strategic partnership and bolstered by the political heft from the Lisbon summit of 2007 and the Tripoli meeting of 2010. This is because, as has been argued by Adrian Hyde-Price, 'there is a fundamental contradiction at the heart of the EU's identity and role as international actor.... The pursuit of an ethical agenda for any actor in international politics is an inherently problematic undertaking'.[37] While the EU serves as the main platform for pursuing a pan-European agenda of common and shared interests that have led it to become more of a global actor, the Union also sees itself as an ethical power and a 'force for good in the world', seeking to champion values and principles that have universal applicability and reflect its own cosmopolitan norms. (See chapter 22 in this volume.) Nowhere is this contradiction clearer than in the axioms of Brussels's neo-mercantilist trade policies and the normative thrust of its development strategies. As the American high priest of realism, Hans Morgenthau, noted: 'How often have statesmen been motivated by the desire to improve the world, and ended up making it worse? And how often have they sought one goal, and ended up by achieving something they neither expected nor desired?'[38]

Hence, any sanguine reading of the prospects for consolidating the relationship between the EU and Africa on the basis of equality and mutual benefit will inevitably come up against a history of good intentions sacrificed on the altar of expediency and European self-interest, a history characterised by a litany of broken promises, policy ambiguity, lack of commitment, tensions, and implementation shortcomings. It is important to remember that EU-Africa relations have fundamentally been shaped by colonialism and that, for better or for worse, this has had a determining and formative effect on how political and economic frameworks have evolved, even if they have retained the ethos of giving the relationship a rhetorical 'special' attribute (see chapter 2 in this volume). Or put another way, in British historian E.H. Carr's formulation, a harmony of interests 'thus serves as an ingenious moral device invoked, in perfect sincerity, by privileged groups in order to justify and maintain their dominant position'.[39]

The Africa-EU joint strategy of 2007 certainly defines a new frontier for cooperation in areas of critical importance for both continents—governance and security. However, it remains to be seen whether Brussels has the necessary political will to turn this initiative from simply an instrumental project into a moral enterprise.

14

THE EU SECURITY ROLE IN
THE GREAT LAKES REGION

Aldo Ajello

Introduction: the burden of good intentions

It is widely recognised that peace, security, and stability are preconditions for development. The European Union and its twenty-seven member states have accepted this concept, which now appears quite often in their official declarations. In the ponderous document known as the 'EU Strategy for Africa', adopted by the European Commission in October 2005, it is clearly stated that 'without peace there can be no lasting development. Without African leadership to end African conflicts there can be no lasting peace'.[1] In the same document, the European Union solemnly declares its commitment to 'work with the African Union, sub-regional organizations and African countries to predict, prevent and mediate conflict, including by addressing its root causes and to keep peace in their own continent'. The strategy further stresses Brussels's commitment to 'strengthen the African peace facility with substantial, long-term, flexible, sustainable funding' and 'to develop African capabilities such as the African Union's standby force'. Finally, through its Common Foreign and Security Policy (CFSP) and the European Security and Defence Policy (ESPD), the European Union pledges its commitment to 'provide direct support to African Union, subregional or UN efforts to promote peace and stability', and its preparedness to send 'military and civilian crisis management missions, including potential deployment of the EU battle-groups'.

This 2005 EU strategy document is ambitious and innovative, covering all areas of possible cooperation between Africa and Europe over a period of ten years (2005–2015). Declarations of intentions and firm commitments in the area of peace and security are explicit and unambiguous. Is there any chance that these declarations of intentions will be translated into concrete action? The experience of the past, including the period from 2006 to 2009, is not entirely reassuring in this regard.

In the area of conflict prevention, very little has been done by the EU to prevent African crises. The case of the Rwanda genocide in 1994 (in which an estimated 800,000 people were killed) is only the most conspicuous. Before the genocide, when it was already clear that the massacres were in preparation, nothing was done to prevent them.[2] During the genocide, when it was necessary to strengthen the UN's peacekeeping mission to stop it, the UN Security Council took the opposite decision, and most of the 2,500-strong UN military contingent was withdrawn from the country, giving a de facto green light to the killers. After the genocide, when the masterminds of the mass killings were trying to destabilise the new Rwandan government in pursuit of revenge, nothing was done to disarm these criminal groups that had transformed the refugee camps in the Democratic Republic of the Congo's (DRC) Kivu provinces into military sanctuaries, in violation of all the rules of the Office of the UN High Commissioner for Refugees (UNHCR). This passive attitude by the international community, including the European Union, left the door open for two wars that have devastated the Congo for a decade and a half, and still wreak massive devastation and death in the eastern DRC. At least 3 million people have been killed and over 3 million internally displaced in the Congo since 1997.[3]

The problem is that the EU, and more generally the international donor community, is prepared to spend a large amount of financial resources on facing the devastating effects of crises, but very little in preventing them. Humanitarian aid is much easier to obtain than development aid, and development aid is much easier to obtain than aid for improving long-term security and stability. Millions of euros are spent each month assisting the victims of crises that could have been avoided with appropriate preventive actions, even though these preventive actions would have cost much less in terms of money and misery.

There are several reasons for this irrational behaviour. The first derives from the perverse link between the media and the decisionmaking process in donor countries. In Western democracies, decisionmakers must face elections every four or five years. Politicians are thus largely driven by opinion polls, which are in turn driven by the media. Political leaders are typically more reactive than proactive, and more prepared to address the effects of crises than their root causes. In addition, politicians are often interested in short-term projects that can be concluded within their tenure of office, and can have a positive influence on their reelection. Very few leaders are therefore prepared to become involved in long-term projects whose uncertain results will be known only after the end of their terms in office.

Humanitarian catastrophes are immediately reported by the media and have a strong emotional impact on public opinion (the idea is to force immediate decisions), while preventive action should ideally be decided upon without any pressure from domestic public opinion. Furthermore, this preventive action may be perceived by public opinion as a waste of resources, since nobody can prove definitively that anything wrong would have happened without this action.

When we move from crisis prevention to peace and stability in a post-conflict situation, it appears obvious that armies and police forces that are well trained, disciplined, and loyal to democratic institutions are essential instruments in ensuring peace and stability. Building such security forces should be the first priority of postconflict governments and the international community.

However, when we try to mobilise resources for reforming and improving the security sector, we have to face another serious obstacle. An old ideological approach—akin to a dogma—dictates that aid should be addressed exclusively to poor people and vulnerable groups such as women and children. To provide financial and human resources for the security sector, especially the army, from development budgets, is considered politically incorrect and even immoral. In addition, such funding is typically not included in official development assistance.

In fact, while the Paris-based Organisation for Economic Cooperation and Development (OECD) recognises peace, security, and stability as preconditions for development, the body refuses to consider any money spent in the security sector as part of ODA. As a result, very few donors are prepared to assist in security sector reform (SSR) by providing financial resources from their ODA. Changing this shortsighted approach will require a profound modification of entrenched cultural assumptions. Doing so will also require courage, determination, and a genuine interest in stability, especially in the case of Africa, a continent that, despite the frequent solemn declarations of good intentions, continues to be of low priority on the international agenda. There is no sign that the international community is moving in this direction.

Security sector reform in the DRC

The dichotomy between declarations and actions is well illustrated by the example of the Democratic Republic of the Congo, where I served as EU special representative from 1996 to 2007. In the DRC, the army, and to a certain extent the police, was the main source of insecurity and instability. The Congolese army was badly and irregularly paid, badly fed, badly equipped, ill trained, and often living in squalid, subhuman conditions. The concept of discipline has been unknown to many of these soldiers. Under these conditions, they have often survived by harassing civilian populations in areas in which they are deployed. They have looted, raped, and killed with impunity, since the judicial system has been inefficient and seriously corrupt. It is often noted that the worst job in the Congo is that of a lawyer, for as is often repeated: 'Why would you pay a lawyer when you can buy a judge?'

The declared number of soldiers in the DRC has also been heavily inflated. This figure has included many elder people well over the age of retirement, a number of soldiers seriously wounded or affected by chronic illnesses, and a very large number of 'ghost soldiers', who continue to receive regular salaries. In fact the ghost soldiers have often been the only ones who have 'received' a regular salary! The salaries of the real soldiers have often disappeared in a chain of payment that coincides with the chain of command. The envelope with the full amount of the salaries for the entire army is delivered by the central bank to the chief of staff of the army. This money is then moved through the various levels of command, and by the time it reaches the level of the brigade, the pay-sack is almost empty.

It is obvious that in order to move from a situation of short-term precarious stability, supported by a 20,000-strong UN peacekeeping force in 2011, to lasting security, it will be essential to invest in security sector reform. This process has mainly involved setting up a viable and effective police force and creating and maintaining well-trained, well-equipped, and well-disciplined armed forces who are properly fed and regularly paid. This reform should have been combined with an effective programme of disarmament, demobilisation, and reintegration (DDR) of soldiers and armed groups who were not willing or eligible to join the integrated national army.

Unfortunately the military brass, accustomed to taking advantage of the ongoing situation for its own selfish ends, has strongly resisted any reform that would kill the goose that lays the golden eggs. The obstructionist tactics of the Congolese military hierarchy have been visible at every step of the security sector reform process.

The first step—including a census of the army—proved to be very difficult, because it implied the identification of real soldiers and the end of the profitable system of ghost soldiers. This would have resulted in the reduction of the salary package and elimination of the illicit gains of the high-ranking top brass. Under these conditions, it is not surprising that it took almost five years, from 2004 to 2008, to complete the process; and when the identification was completed, it was necessary to start again, since there was a serious suspicion that many men could have deserted while others, including children, could have been recruited again by armed factions. The World Bank's programme update of September 2009 noted that the European Union Security Sector Reform Advisory Mission (EUSEC) and the Integrated Military Structure (SMI) attempted to carry out a new census. However, in 2008, the size of the Congolese army was reduced from 340,000 to 150,000 and the salary of each soldier was increased from $5 to $40 per month. But this inventory was never properly used, and as of 2010 only a few soldiers received their pay on a regular basis. No decision had been taken on the actions of the military commanders, and the reform of the army was still entrusted to the same people who had created the problem in the first place.

Despite its absolute and proven inefficiency, the military top brass in the DRC is very powerful. It is unable to protect the country against foreign enemies, but is efficient at blocking any decision that would imply a serious reform of the Congolese army. Under these conditions, it was clear from the start that it would be impossible to make any significant progress in security sector reform in the DRC without strong commitment and support from the international community, including the significant provision of human and financial resources. But this strong support and commitment were not forthcoming, since following the UN's deployment of peacekeepers in the Congo from 1999 until July 2010, the mission was transformed into the UN Organization Stabilization Mission in the DRC (MONUSCO), at the request of the government in Kinshasa for phased withdrawal of the peacekeepers.

The role of the EU in security sector reform

The European Union and some of its member states did much more in the DRC than the rest of the international community, with the exception of African countries such as South Africa and Angola, but they did not do enough. Brussels recognised the importance of prioritising security sector reform and decided to establish two units to support the Congolese government in this endeavour: the European Union Police Mission (EUPOL), for training and monitoring the Integrated Police Unit (IPU) in Kinshasa, and the European Union Security Sector Reform Advisory Mission, to assist in the reform of the army, starting from the chain of payment, which had to be disconnected from the chain of command.

Unfortunately, both units, but especially EUSEC, were understaffed and underequipped from the start. Because of this severe lack of resources, Congolese police and military units benefitting from EUPOL and EUSEC support were very few, and the EU's contribution to security sector reform in the Congo was a drop in a vast ocean, given the enormous challenges in this sector.

The genesis of EUPOL and EUSEC is worth briefly recalling. In October 2003 the government of the DRC, led by Joseph Kabila, sent an official request to the EU for assistance in setting up the Integrated Police Unit, which was supposed to reinforce the internal security apparatus in Kinshasa and contribute to the protection of state institutions. In December 2003 the EU's Political and Security Committee (PSC) agreed that Brussels should support the establishment of the IPU following a three-pronged approach: first, rehabilitating and refurbishing a training centre and providing basic equipment; second, training the IPU; and third, following up and monitoring the concrete implementation of the mandate of the IPU after the initial training phase.

The establishment of this project revealed a serious weakness in European institutions. The project was launched by the Council of the European Union within the framework of its Common Foreign and Security Policy, but the financial resources of the Council under the CFSP were insufficient to finance the entire project. Thus the project was divided into two parts.

The first part, which included rehabilitation, refurbishing the training centre, providing nonlethal equipment, and training the units, was entrusted to the European Commission, while the part concerning monitoring was left under the responsibility of the European Council.

The problem, however, was that at that time, the CFSP was little more than an empty shell. The EU was given an ambitious mandate, but left with very modest financial resources by its member states, which were largely unwilling to allow the Common Foreign and Security Policy to gain force. In 2004, when the IPU project was launched, the total budget of the CFSP was €62.6 million. As a result of this lackadaisical approach, the European Council had a mandate for the execution of the entire project, but lacked the resources, while the European Commission had the resources, but lacked the mandate.

Each of the two EU institutions had to operate separately, sometimes in competition with each other, in a 'creative' combination of mandate and resources. Human energy and financial resources were thus wasted in this time-consuming exercise. The IPU nevertheless started becoming operational in March 2005, and performed well during the Congolese electoral process of 2005–2006.

The third phase of the project was an interesting and effective innovation. The IPU was not simply trained and then left to operate on its own. EUPOL continued to monitor and advise the IPU, even after it had been trained and became operational under a Congolese chain of command. This ensured that the IPU was acting according to international 'best practice' in its field.

EUSEC pursued a similar approach: following an official request by Kinshasa, the EU decided to establish an advisory and assistance mission for security sector reform in the DRC. The purpose of this mission was to provide advice and assistance to the Congolese authorities in charge of army reform, while ensuring the promotion of policies compatible with human rights and international humanitarian law, democratic standards, principles of good public management, transparency, and observance of the rule of law.

The mission was officially launched in June 2005 for a period of twelve months, and was subsequently renewed. It comprised eight experts seconded by EU member states. Within the framework of its mandate, experts were assigned to key posts within the Congolese administration: the office of the minister of defence; the general military staff, including the Integrated Military Structure; staff of the land forces; the National Commission for Disarmament, Demobilisation, and Reintegration (CONADER); and the Joint Operational Committee.

Three additional experts were sent to the mission, for a period of one month, with the specific task of analysing and changing the existing chain of payment within the military structure. The objective was to set up, together with the Congolese authorities, a mechanism that would radically reform the current system, a process prone to corruption and mismanagement.

Within the limits of the scarce resources available, EUSEC was a success. A new chain of payment, disconnected from the chain of command, was designed and applied to the first integrated brigades. To implement the new system and ensure that it was working properly, EUSEC was mandated to deploy two European officers with expertise in army administration to each integrated brigade. However, two major problems reduced the impact of this programme. First, EU member states were unwilling or unable to provide the requested number of officers to EUSEC; second, the United Nations was extremely reluctant to provide security and logistical support to the European officers. Rivalry between the two institutions was not unusual. The new system of payment, in the absence of guidance and control, was as a result much more limited and less effective than it could have been.

In addition to EUSEC, some European Union member states—Belgium, Britain, France, the Netherlands, and Germany—provided assistance to security sector reform. In order to coordinate the efforts of these countries a contact group was established, which was later joined by the United Nations, the African Union, the United States, Angola, and South Africa. EUSEC was required to coordinate the group in Kinshasa. This task, however, proved harder than expected, since every country wanted to retain its specific identity, and to pursue its own bilateral agenda.

Disarmament, demobilisation, and reintegration in the DRC

Before security sector reform could begin in the DRC, the parallel programme of disarmament, demobilisation, and reintegration had to be implemented. Soldiers and combatants had to be gathered in preestablished assembly areas (*centres d'orientation*), where they were identified, disarmed, and registered. Then some of them were selected, on a voluntary basis, to join the new army, before being sent to training centres (*centres de brassage*). The others, who were either unsuitable or unwilling to join the army, were integrated into the demobilisation and reintegration programme.

In 2002 the World Bank, in partnership with several donors, was identified as the leading agency for an ambitious regional DDR programme, the Multi-Donor Reintegration Programme (MDRP). The European Union was the main contributor of funds to this programme. Of the thirteen donors, eleven were EU member states, together with the European Commission.[4] By July 2008 the contribution of the European Commission and the EU member states to the MDRP trust fund was about $223 million. The World Bank and International Development Association contributed $213 million, Norway provided about $7 million, and Canada $19.5 million. Some serious structural problems were identified from the beginning, but nothing serious was done to resolve them. These problems were related to the basic principles of the World Bank and its rules and procedures.

In accordance with these basic principles, the World Bank had to apply the concept of 'national ownership' to all its programmes. Unfortunately, while this concept is universally accepted in development programmes, it is hardly applicable to postconflict demobilisation initiatives. Furthermore, because of its rules and procedures, the World Bank could not cover any expenditure related to the military component of the DDR process. Hence the Bank could not finance the disarmament of soldiers and combatants. For an organisation playing the lead role in the DDR programme, this was a major handicap.

As a consequence of this limitation, additional resources for disarmament had to be provided from other sources. The programme, therefore, lost coherence, which led to many delays. Since disarmament was the first step of the operation, the programme could not start until these resources were found and made available. While the World Bank could finance the setting up of the *centres d'orientation*, it could not allow any soldier or combatant who carried a weapon to join these centres. The Bank excluded even the possibility of collecting weapons at the entrance of the centres.

To resolve this problem, it was suggested that mobile units be used to disarm soldiers and combatants in other areas before they reached the *centres d'orientation*. This required setting up an additional step in this already long and complex process, just for the collection of weapons. The World Bank did not make available any funding for this operation. In a country lacking basic infrastructure and logistical facilities, this additional step in the DDR process implied further serious delays and unjustified additional costs.

But this was not the end of the story. In any peace process, DDR requires an impartial leading force to make it move forward at reasonable speed.

This force can hardly be the government, since it is composed of competing groups and includes 'spoilers' whose agenda is to obstruct the peace process. In the DRC, these 'negative forces' were present in every sector of the political and military establishment. The 'Cinderella syndrome' was the formula that I used as EU special representative to define the attitude of these forces: they viewed the day of election as the midnight of Cinderella, when all the magic would disappear. Since these spoilers had very little chance of being elected, they did everything they could to avoid or at least delay elections in the DRC.

These negative forces were especially active in the area of DDR and SSR, where high-ranking officers of the army had two good reasons to obstruct the process. The first was to avoid, or at least delay, the counting and identification of soldiers, since this would have revealed a large number of ghost soldiers. The second was to keep their best forces in reserve, in order to retain bargaining power for future negotiations, in case the result of the elections was not satisfactory. This was also the approach employed by the parties in Angola between 1991 and 2002.

The World Bank's approach to DDR, based on the principle of national ownership, was a gift to these negative forces. In accordance with this principle, the Bank gave full power for the implementation of the DDR programme to the transitional government, and consequently to the army. A gigantic bureaucratic machine with various commissions and subcommissions was set up to manage the programme. Every Congolese ministry with even a distant connection to DDR wanted to have representatives in these commissions, assuming that there would be some money to be distributed. The size of this machinery was in itself a perfect instrument for causing further delays in the process.

Predictably, the army representatives in this bureaucracy used the power given to them by the World Bank to obstruct and paralyse the entire process. Over a year after the beginning of the national plan of DDR in 2004, not a single *centre d'orientation* had been established. The absence of *centres d'orientation* consequently prevented the start of the SSR programme. Soldiers and combatants could therefore not be selected for the new army and join the *centres de brassage* to be trained.

The lack of progress in the DDR/SSR programme in the DRC had an extremely negative impact on the UN peacekeeping operation, whose presence in the Congo was costing about $3 million a day. Completion of the DDR/SSR programme was an essential component of the UN's 'exit strategy', since the UN Organisation Mission in the DRC (MONUC) could not withdraw its troops from the country until a critical mass of the unified and integrated army had been created and trained. Furthermore, the integrated brigades were poorly trained and equipped. They were unable to disarm the Rwandan militias of the old regime, the Forces Démocratiques de Libération du Rwanda (FDLR), and cope with the militias of General Laurent Nkunda's Congrès National pour la Défense du Peuple (CNDP), in order to put an end to the devastating war in eastern Congo. The poor performance of his army eventually convinced President Joseph Kabila to seek an agreement with the Rwandan leader, Paul Kagame, in December 2008. As a result of this agreement, a joint military operation (Rwando-Congolese) was launched against the FDLR in eastern Congo and the CNDP militia was neutralised. Kigali placed General Nkunda under house arrest, and his combatants were integrated into the Congolese army. The process is still ongoing and will take a long time to be completed, but its impact on the effectiveness of security sector reform may be marginal. However, by April 2010, Kabila's government was calling for the withdrawal of UN peacekeepers from the DRC. The UN devised a plan to reduce its peacekeepers and withdraw from the Congo by 2013.

Lessons not learned from DDR

With the EUPOL and EUSEC missions, and various bilateral initiatives by some EU member states, the European Union was the most committed and active external donor providing assistance to the DRC in the area of security. However, despite these efforts, it was clear that the needs largely surpassed the assistance offered. The limitation of resources was the most serious problem. But even within the scarce resources available, better results could have been achieved if the actions of the European Union had been more consistent with its commitments in at least two areas.

First, there could have been more coordination between EU member states. The lack of a common approach to SSR and DDR led to a patchwork approach in the activities undertaken in army integration and police training. It would have been in the interest of all to combine efforts and exploit comparative advantages.

Second, Brussels and EU member states could have taken a more proactive role in questioning the World Bank's strategy on DDR, especially the rigidity of its rules, including the dogmatic application of the concept of 'national ownership'. The EU, in its capacity as a major contributor to the Multi-Donor Reintegration Programme, should have been in a position to ask the World Bank to adopt an ad hoc strategy for the DDR process with an appropriate set of rules and procedures, or to pull out of the process and let another, more nimble organisation with more flexibility undertake all aspects of the process. Unfortunately, even when it was obvious that the Bank's strategy on DDR had a negative impact on the entire programme, including SSR, the European Union was unwilling to question the intimidating authority of the World Bank and the untouchable concept of 'national ownership'. The result of this lack of action is that, eight years after the creation of the transitional government in 2003 and six years after the establishment of EUSEC in 2005, the DDR/SSR process in the Congo had yet to be completed and a large amount of time and money had already been wasted.

It is worth recalling that between 1992 and 1994 in Mozambique, with a much simpler mechanism under the direct responsibility of the UN mission there (ONUMOZ), in which I served as the Special Representative of the Secretary-General (SRSG), 90,000 soldiers and combatants were successfully demobilised and reintegrated into civil life in less than nine months.[5] The secret of this success was a flexible approach in setting up and applying rules and procedures, and the replacement of the concept of 'ownership' with the more appropriate concept of 'partnership'.

The EU military support in the DRC

In addition to the presence of EUPOL and EUSEC in the Democratic Republic of the Congo, direct military assistance was provided by the European Union to the country on two occasions. In 2003, an interim European multinational force (Artémis) was deployed to keep the peace process on track by preventing a further escalation of violence in the volatile northeastern Ituri region.[6] Its purpose was to fill the vacuum until the UN could identify and deploy a more suitable military force. Subsequently, in 2006, another interim military operation (EUFOR) was deployed by the European Union to assist MONUC during the electoral process in selected areas of the DRC, mainly in Kinshasa. Both of these missions operated under a UN Security Council mandate and were deployed at the request of the United Nations for a limited time and in limited areas where the UN military forces were unable to cope with the situation on the ground.

Artémis was a rapid response operation. The joint action was adopted by the European Council on 5 June 2003, five days after the approval of UN Security Council Resolution 1484, and the military operation was launched seven days later, on 12 June 2003. 'Force enablers' were immediately deployed to the town of Bunia in Ituri, and all key military tasks were performed from that date, even though it took a further four weeks to deploy the entire force. Neighbouring countries, mainly Uganda and Rwanda, were informed and their support for Artémis was obtained.

The EU military force was intended to put an end to the ethnic massacres and reduce the possibility that local militias and 'negative political forces' in Kinshasa could use the Ituri crisis as an excuse to derail the final stages of the peace process. All these objectives were achieved: massacres were significantly reduced, and the peace process was given a new impulse with the signature of the final agreement on military issues and the formation of the transitional government in June 2003.

The rapid and efficient deployment of the French-led Artémis operation was impressive considering that this was the first operation of this nature set up by the European Union in an African country under the umbrella of the CFSP. The secret of the success of this operation was the fact that the entire deployment had been planned in advance in Paris. France was committed to giving a positive response to the request of the United Nations, and was prepared to provide as large a force as it could, while maintaining Artémis as a European operation and not a bilateral one. Thus, while France led the military aspect of the operation, the EU's Political and Security Committee in Brussels led the political management of the mission. The French military force was complemented by additional contingents provided mainly by other EU member states—Britain and Sweden—while Germany and Belgium provided noncombat soldiers. The EU's military institutions were involved in the last phase of the planning and the execution of the mission.[7]

For the CFSP, Artémis was an important learning exercise that proved to be very useful for setting up EUFOR, the second operation in the DRC deployed in 2006. In contrast to the French-led Artémis, EUFOR was an entirely European operation. It was planned in Brussels by the EU's military institutions, and Germany was selected to be the lead country. EUFOR was a complex operation, with a contingent of 800 soldiers pre-deployed in Kinshasa under the command of a division general, a full battalion 'over the horizon' in Libreville, capital of Gabon, and another battalion on reserve in Potsdam in Germany, where the operational commander was based.

Extensive diplomatic efforts were made to seek the support of the DRC's neighbours (mainly Uganda, Rwanda, and Congo-Brazzaville) and other relevant countries (Gabon, Angola, and South Africa) for the mission. EUFOR proved to be a strong deterrent against potential troublemakers at the time of the 2006 elections, and was considered a successful operation.

Critique of EUFOR

Even before EUFOR became operational, the international media, including the *International Herald Tribune*,[8] raised several criticisms about the mission. The force generation process was described as 'slow and constraining', with the implicit conclusion that the European Union was incapable of providing a quick response to an emergency as a strategic actor.

This, however, was grossly inaccurate. The concept of battle groups established by the European Union to intervene rapidly in emergency situations was not applicable to the case of EUFOR, which was supposed to be deployed many months after the UN's request, just before elections in the DRC, and only for the duration of the electoral process. Since there was enough time available, the decisionmaking process followed the normal rules and procedures, in accordance with the legislation of EU member states. The process was definitely long, but it did not generate any delay in the agreed timetable. Even if the final decision had been taken five months earlier, the force was deployed at the right time, just before elections.

Criticisms were also made about the scope, format, mandate, and duration of the force. In fact, the EUFOR operation was mandated by the European Union in response to a specific request by the United Nations. The UN asked for one battalion to be kept 'over the horizon' for four months during the electoral period, in order to support MONUC in areas in which it felt that the peacekeepers were not strong enough to deal with possible problems, mainly in Kinshasa. In eastern Congo, where MONUC had the strongest concentration of its military force, EUFOR was excluded by the UN, and not by the European Union.

EUFOR's mandate included the extraction of populations in danger, stabilisation of areas affected by crises, and additional protection of Kinshasa's airport. Other assistance such as mapping, intelligence, and assistance to the Congolese police was included in the mission's mandate, and was provided by other European institutions or projects like the EU Satellite Centre and EUPOL.

The only point on which criticisms of EUFOR were accurate was the rigid date established for the termination of the operation. Germany and a few other EU member states in the Political and Security Committee had been extremely reluctant to approve the mission and were determined to set up a firm and credible 'exit strategy'. They eventually agreed to approve the mission, but imposed a precise termination date just after the elections in the DRC, leaving no flexibility for prolonging the operation. As a consequence of this decision, if the losing party in the polls had refused to accept the results of the elections, EUFOR would have had to withdraw just at the moment when its very presence was needed. Fortunately, all parties accepted the election results after a long and painful exercise of persuasion, and no major incidents occurred to destabilise the process. The quick departure of EUFOR did not therefore produce any negative consequences. But there is no doubt that the decision to set such a rigid deadline was wrong and dangerous, and should never be repeated in the future.

Finally, additional criticisms of EUFOR came from several Congolese journalists and politicians when the mission was announced at a press conference in June 2006. Many questions were asked about the duration of the mission. The insinuation was that the European troops had a hidden agenda to stay in the DRC long past their need in order to influence the outcome of the elections in favour of President Joseph Kabila. Vice President Jean-Pierre Bemba's supporters were particularly vociferous on this issue, accusing the European Union of 'neocolonialist temptations'. This atmosphere changed dramatically when a heavy attack launched by the presidential guard against the office of Vice President Bemba, in Kinshasa in August 2006, was halted with the help of EUFOR.

A few weeks later, when the departure of EUFOR was announced at another press conference, the same Congolese journalists who had accused the EU of 'neocolonialist temptations', and insinuated that the European troops would extend their presence in the DRC, expressed disappointment at the departure of the force, which was perceived to have contributed to stability during and after the elections. But EUFOR's mandate was limited, and the European Union had no intention of prolonging its military presence in the DRC.

The perception of EUFOR held by sections of the Congolese media and political leaders was therefore wrong. The problem is that the idea of a 'neocolonialist' conspiracy is so deeply rooted in the minds of many Africans that they do not sometimes realise that the real problem is not how to prevent European countries and institutions from interfering in African affairs, but how to convince them and the rest of the international community to become more seriously involved in prevention, management, and resolution of African crises in a spirit of genuine political and economic partnership. Unfortunately, this spirit was not always present in the Congo.

Concluding reflections

In 1995, after the failure of UN peacekeeping operations in Angola, Rwanda, and Somalia, the UN decided to give up on African crises and pass the responsibility for their management and resolution to African regional and subregional organisations. At that time, the international community was very generous in giving a large mandate to what was then the Organisation of African Unity (OAU) and to subregional organisations, but very stingy in providing them with financial resources and technical assistance.[9] All the stereotypes of the politically correct dictionary were used—'African Ownership' and 'African Solutions to African Problems'—but no funding mechanism was established and no logistical support was provided. In fact, the rich countries just wanted to get rid of African crises, which were considered to be too difficult and too expensive.

Unfortunately, the solution to this problem is not so easy, and it soon became evident that, under these conditions, neither the OAU (later the African Union from 2002) nor Africa's subregional organisations could manage crises on the continent effectively. Nevertheless, the international community did not take any action. Only the European Union decided to intervene, establishing a special fund—the €250 million-yearly Peace Facility—in 2003 to allow the African Union to set up a functioning peace and security mechanism. Through this instrument, the African Union was able to deploy a peacekeeping operation in Burundi and subsequently in Sudan's Darfur region. (See chapter 13 in this volume.)

It is worth recognising that, while the commitments of the European Union, reiterated in its 2005 Africa strategy, have not always been followed by adequate action in such areas as crisis prevention, postconflict security building, and assistance to security sector reform, its performance in supporting the peacekeeping role of the African Union and Africa's subregional organisations has been quite remarkable. The EU's commitment was followed by immediate action despite the existence of serious difficulties. Convincing EU members that financial resources from the European

Development Fund could be used for peace and security activities was not easy. Some member states, especially the Nordic countries, were hostile on grounds of principle to the use of any development funds—even money not used because of a lack of absorption capacity on the part of recipients—for peace and security purposes. Under these conditions, it is impressive that the European Peace Facility was approved so quickly, and was replenished a year later.

Nonetheless, it is evident that the EU's Peace Facility cannot provide a permanent solution to Africa's security challenges, for two key reasons. First, money provided by the Peace Facility has been insufficient to fund long-term missions. In Burundi, African Union peacekeepers were replaced fifteen months later, in 2004, by a United Nations mission, while in Darfur, the AU operation was replaced after three years, in 2007, with a hybrid UN-AU mission. Second, continuing the European Peace Facility as the sole funding mechanism for African military operations would place on the EU's shoulders a burden that should be carried by the entire international community. A substantial, long-term, flexible, sustainable, and reliable mechanism—including funding and political support, as well as technical and logistical assistance—should therefore be set up within the framework of the United Nations under the umbrella of its powerful Security Council for this purpose.

15

THE EU SECURITY ROLE IN CHAD AND THE CENTRAL AFRICAN REPUBLIC[1]

Winrich Kühne

Introduction

Since the early 1990s the European Union has progressively stepped up its crisis prevention and peacekeeping involvement in sub-Saharan Africa, not only in civilian and police missions, but also in military ones. Three of the latter have received particular international attention: Operation Artémis in the Democratic Republic of the Congo (DRC) in 2003, the European Union Force (EUFOR) in the DRC in 2006 (see chapter 14 in this volume), and EUFOR in Chad and the Central African Republic (CAR) in 2007–2009, which this chapter focuses on. All three EU missions were launched in support of UN missions.

The EU mission in Chad and the CAR has been the biggest of the three European military mission in Africa. It was authorised in October 2007 by the UN Security Council and the European Council, and was declared operational in March 2008.[2] Designed as a one-year 'bridging mission', it came to a conclusion in March 2009. Its tasks were then taken over by a UN force as part of the UN Mission in the Central African Republic and Chad (MINURCAT). An earlier effort to field a bigger and better-mandated UN-led military mission failed in 2007 because the Idriss Déby government in Chad refused to agree to it.

The need for an international presence in parts of Chad and the Central African Republic was mainly triggered by humanitarian demands. Violence against local civilians was rampant, and the number of unprotected internally displaced persons (IDPs) and refugees had reached unacceptable levels. In his first report to the Security Council, in February 2007, the UN Secretary-General, Ban Ki-moon, reported that the 'refugee population' in Chad had risen to more than 230,000, and that of IDPs to more than 120,000. In the CAR, the number of IDPs had reached 70,000, and there was a sizeable number of refugees.[3] In early 2009 the Office of the UN High Commissioner for Refugees (UNHCR) noted that the number of IDPs and refugees in the CAR had reached levels of more than 190,000 and 125,000 respectively.[4]

Assessing the impact and problems of EUFOR Chad/CAR is not an easy task. There was a complicated division of labour and cooperation in the field between the UN secretariat in New York and MINURCAT, established in 2007. EUFOR also had a complex decisionmaking process for its own planning and command. In addition, there was a volatile theatre of sand, dust, and violence in the Darfur-Chad-CAR triangle, which was, and still is, extremely difficult to disentangle fully.

It is hard to come to any definite assessment of the success of EUFOR Chad/CAR. The mission's deployment for a mere one year as a 'bridging force' adds to the difficulty of such an assessment. EUFOR's impact cannot be evaluated separately from that of the UN presence in MINURCAT, which ended by December 2010, as well as other missions in the region, such as the United Nations-African Union Hybrid Mission in Darfur (UNAMID), which was deployed by 2007. However, three general conclusions can be reached with sufficient certainty.

First, the presence of EUFOR Chad/CAR, in conjunction with MINURCAT, led to some improved sense of security in the region. However, this was limited to the refugee and IDP camps in EUFOR's areas of deployment. Being a military force, EUFOR was not able to cope with the upsurge of banditry and criminality in both countries. Even worse, there was no significant indication that the deployment of EUFOR and MINURCAT improved the overall outlook for peace and security in either Chad or the CAR. Indeed, EUFOR's presence may have given both countries' regimes—which are, above all, busy securing their survival using all available means—a false sense of support and security. It was not the promotion of democratisation and the rule of law, but this quest for survival that was driving the agenda of both presidents, Idriss Déby of Chad and François Bozizé of the CAR.

Second, at the strategic level, the deployment of EUFOR and MINUR-CAT was a positive example of improved UN-EU cooperation. There is no denying that, at lower levels, both sides tried their best to cooperate. However, the differences between the two organisations regarding their decision-making, planning, financing, headquarters arrangements, and other bureaucratic structures and procedures were immense, and made coordination between EUFOR and MINURCAT as well as with other international and local actors in the field very cumbersome. Mission personnel were often busier coping with these structures than with the task for which they were primarily deployed: managing and resolving the conflicts in the region.

Finally, conflict, violence, and instability in Chad and the CAR have been closely intertwined with the developments in Sudan and its volatile Darfur region, as well as the wider region of the Greater Horn of Africa. Apart from the difficulties in substituting EUFOR with a credible UN-led force in support of MINURCAT, three other international peacekeeping missions in the region have faced serious security challenges: the United Nations Mission in Sudan (UNMIS), deployed in 2005 to oversee the Comprehensive Peace Agreement between Khartoum and the government of South Sudan; UNAMID, deployed in 2007 in Sudan's Darfur region (the AU had earlier deployed a force in 2004); and the African Union Mission in Somalia (AMISOM), deployed in 2007. There is a real danger that the entire region will be plunged into more conflict and violence, resulting in humanitarian disaster if these missions falter.

Profound rethinking is thus needed by Africa, Europe, the US, and the broader international community on how the decline of this huge region into more violence, conflict, banditry, refugees, and IDPs can be stemmed.

This chapter assesses the EUFOR mission in Chad and the CAR by explaining its mandate, examining issues of troop contributions, financing, and relations with its headquarters in France, and analysing the complicated relationship between EUFOR and the UN, including the transition from EUFOR to MINURCAT. The chapter concludes with some lessons learned from this mission.

EUFOR and MINURCAT: mandate and division of labour

On 25 September 2007 the UN Security Council—with EU members France and Britain as two of its five veto-wielding permanent members—

agreed on the mandate for a joint EUFOR-MINURCAT mission in Chad and the CAR. A difficult process of negotiations between the UN secretariat in New York and the Idriss Déby government in Chad had finally come to an end. In this process, the world body had to make substantial concessions to N'Djamena. In the report preceding this resolution, the UN Secretary-General, Ban Ki-moon, had noted that the mandate given to the international mission was far from what he had envisaged. In an earlier report to the Security Council in February 2007, Ban had submitted a very different proposal regarding the mandate and structure of the planned international presence, requiring

a Chadian and United Nations police presence to be complemented by the deployment of a mobile and well-equipped UN military force, which would be capable of taking robust action to protect civilians at risk, deter conflict, facilitate the delivery of humanitarian assistance, reduce tension and contribute to the establishment of a more secure environment in its area of operation. The size of the force needed was estimated to be upwards of 11,000 to be able also to provide wide-area security, in particular as a prerequisite for the deployment of a police presence.[5]

In other words, Ban Ki-moon had envisaged a much more comprehensive mission originally under the exclusive command of the UN.

However, in the course of informal discussions held in March 2007 by the UN Secretary-General with the Chadian foreign minister, Ahmad Allam-Mi, it became clear that N'Djamena had no intention of agreeing to a UN mission with such a wide-ranging mandate. Obviously, Déby did not consider such a mission to be favourable for his kind of autocratic rule. He therefore ordered his ministers to counter with a significantly different proposal that, most importantly, did not include a UN military component. The ensuing deadlock between the Chadian government and the UN brought the French foreign minister, Bernard Kouchner, into the negotiations. In June 2007, Kouchner travelled to N'Djamena to discuss the situation with Déby. Subsequently, the UN was informed by Ahmad Allam-Mi that Kouchner and Déby had agreed on the deployment of an international military presence in eastern Chad composed not of UN but of French and other European Union forces. Ban Ki-moon immediately dispatched another UN delegation to Chad and the CAR to consult with the authorities of both countries and to clarify the options for such an international presence.

The results of these consultations were contained in the Secretary-General's September 2007 report to the Security Council. In this report, Ban Ki-moon did not fail to point out, although in a diplomatic manner, the significant concessions the UN had been forced to make to the Déby government to reach an agreement. The UN Secretary-General explicitly noted that the revised concept therefore included three significant adjustments to the proposals made in his report of 23 February 2007. First, the tasks and functions of the military component, which were required for the effective functioning of the international presence, would be *performed by a European Union military force* that had been accepted by President Déby. This arrangement would be in place for a period of twelve months from the time of deployment of the force, after which an appropriate follow-on arrangement, including a possible United Nations successor operation, would be put in place. Second, there would be *no direct involvement* of the multidimensional international presence in the border area, and this presence would not be directly involved with security in the refugee camps; in particular, EUFOR soldiers would have no mandate to enter these camps. And third, the Chadian police and gendarmes selected to maintain law and order in the refugee camps and internally displaced person sites would *continue to serve under national authority;* however, they would be trained, monitored, and mentored by the UN police component and provided with direct logistical support from the United Nations.[6]

The UN Security Council finally adopted the mandate for the international presence in September 2007. Determining that the situation in the border area between Sudan, Chad, and the Central African Republic constituted a 'threat to international peace and security', the Council approved the establishment in Chad and the CAR of a 'multidimensional presence' to help create the security conditions conducive to a voluntary, secure, and sustainable return of refugees and internally displaced persons; facilitate the provision of humanitarian assistance in eastern Chad and the northeastern Central African Republic; and create favourable conditions for the reconstruction and economic and social development of those areas.

A distinguishing feature of this mandate was that it resulted in the deployment of an operation with a unique structure, consisting of three distinct elements. The first was MINURCAT, a multidimensional UN presence in Chad and the CAR consisting of civilian staff, including in the areas of civil affairs, human rights, rule of law, and mission support, as well as UN police and a number of UN military liaison officers. The key responsibility of MINURCAT was to select, train, advise, and support the Police Tchadienne pour la Protection Humanitaire (PTPH). But MINURCAT was also encouraged by the UN Security Council to assist the governments of Chad and the CAR in the promotion of the rule of law. (One might argue that this was nothing more than a fig-leaf covering the significant concessions directly made by the UN to the Déby government.) To fulfil this task, the Security Council authorised a maximum strength of 300 international police, 50 military liaison officers, and an appropriate number of civilian staff.

Second was the PTPH, the Chadian police component, serving under the authority of the Chadian government but comprising police officers and gendarmes who would be screened, selected, trained, and supported logistically and materially by the United Nations presence. This special Chadian police contingent would be established exclusively to maintain law and order in the refugee camps, key towns, and surrounding areas associated with concentrations of internally displaced persons, as well as to conduct humanitarian activities in eastern Chad.

The third and final element of the international presence was EUFOR Chad/CAR, the European Union's military force. Unlike MINURCAT, this force was explicitly authorised to act under the UN Charter's Chapter VII peace enforcement powers for a period of one year (from the date when its initial 'operating capability' was declared) in supporting MINURCAT and the PTPH. EUFOR was authorised to take 'all necessary measures, within its capabilities and its area of operation in eastern Chad and the northeastern Central African Republic', to fulfil three tasks: to contribute to the protection of civilians in danger, particularly refugees and displaced persons; to facilitate the delivery of humanitarian aid and the free movement of humanitarian personnel by helping to improve security in the area of operations; and to contribute to protecting UN personnel, facilities, installations, and equipment, and to ensuring the security and freedom of movement of EU and UN staff and associated personnel.

EUFOR: joint action, troop contributors, financing, and headquarters

The fact that the European Council in Brussels did not take long to follow up the UN Security Council decision in New York, agreeing in October 2007 on a joint action to authorise EUFOR on behalf of the EU, proves that UN-EU cooperation can work on the strategic-political level if both sides have the will to act.[7] A month earlier, the EU Council had already accepted the concept of operations for the planned European military operation. In terms of overall strength, about 3,700 troops were to be deployed, with France taking the lead by providing up to 2,000 troops. An additional strategic reserve of 600 would be kept in Europe, bringing the overall authorised strength of EUFOR to 4,300.

Although EUFOR faced considerable deployment problems in its start-up phase, its initial operational capability in terms of the UN Security Council mandate was declared in March 2008 by the European Council. According to this mandate, the force was designed to serve only as a 'bridging mission' for one year. Its mandate therefore would be terminated in March 2009. A UN force was subsequently 'envisaged' to take over from the EU mission. EUFOR reached its full strength only six months later, in September 2008, with a troop strength of about 3,400. As well as the issue of troop strength, the joint action also addressed financing as well as headquarters issues. The overall cost of the mission, initially estimated to be €99.2 million (later reaching €150 million), included 50 per cent of common EU costs, administered by the EU's Athena mechanism. For all other costs the principle of 'costs fall where they lie' applied: these had to be carried by contributing states.[8]

The headquarters and the command and control issues were dealt with in the joint action plan more concretely. The EU's operational headquarters was to be located in Mont Valérien in northern France, with Ireland's General Patrick Nash as operation commander. Command of the field headquarters in Chad was given to a French general, Jean-Philippe Ganascia, as in the two previous EUFOR missions in Africa (both in the Democratic Republic of the Congo; see chapter 14 in this volume). In view of France's overall dominance in troop contributions, and its special interests in Chad and the CAR (see chapter 16 in this volume), this came as a surprise to nobody.

However, these commanders had to act under the close supervision of Brussels. The overall political and strategic direction lay with the EU's Political and Security Committee (PSC). The PSC was the only body with the right to change the planning documents, such as the operation plan, the chain of command, and the rules of engagement. Under the PSC, the Brussels-based EU Military Command (EUMC) was to monitor the 'proper execution of the military operation' and receive reports from the EU operation commander 'at regular intervals'. It was the chair of this EUMC who then regularly reported to the PSC regarding the conduct of the mission, and not the operation commander, General Nash himself. Surprisingly (at least for those unfamiliar with the Byzantine workings of the EU), there was in the joint action plan no reference to any obligation of the operation commander or his superiors in Brussels to report directly to the UN Security

Council or its Department of Peacekeeping Operations (DPKO) in New York, despite the fact that EUFOR had been authorised by the UN Security Council. The Council had merely 'requested' the EU to 'report to the Security Council, in the middle and at the end' of its one-year deployment.[9]

The EU and UN in Chad and the CAR: a complicated liaison and cooperation partnership

Those who had to run the joint EUFOR-MINURCAT mission did not have an easy job. Even though both missions operated under one mandate authorised by the UN Security Council, they had to cope with a multitude of governmental and nongovernmental actors in the field as well as outside, in particular in Brussels and New York. The UN Security Council acknowledged this complex partnership structure and therefore noted a list of key actors with which MINURCAT was obliged to 'liaise'. These included the national army of Chad, the gendarmerie and police forces, the nomad national guard, the judicial authorities and prison officials in Chad as well as in the Central African Republic; the Chadian government and the UNHCR in support of their efforts to relocate refugee camps; the Sudanese government, the African Union, UNAMID, and the United Nations Peacebuilding Support Office in the Central African Republic (BONUCA); the Mission de Consolidation de la Paix en Centrafrique (MICOPAX) and the Community of Sahel-Saharan States (CEN-SAD), which were to exchange information on emerging threats to humanitarian activities in the region; and the UN Country Team, with its numerous participants.

In addition, in his report of August 2007, Ban Ki-moon was quite explicit on the extensive need for liaison and co-location between EUFOR and MINURCAT to 'ensure full coordination and to maximise the integration of the operations'.[10] For the theatre, the UN Secretary-General recommended at least a coordination and liaison office in N'Djamena and co-location of the EUFOR and MINURCAT headquarters in Abéché, as well as in the regional headquarters. Regarding the EU, Ban recommended the deployment of UN liaison officers to the Council secretariat as well as to the operational headquarters in Mont Valérien in France.

The European Council seemed to have worried less than the UN about coordination and the need to liaise. In their joint action plan, Europe's leaders did not spend much time on these issues. However, like the UN Security Council, the European Council recognised that EUFOR was part of a wider effort of regional stabilisation by explicitly linking the mission to the need for 'regional security' and, in particular, to the existence of UNAMID.[11] The European Council also asked the key actors and persons involved on the side of the EU to 'ensure close coordination of their respective activities'. This required the EUFOR force commander, in addition to his reporting obligations with regard to Brussels, to 'consult and take into account political guidance from the EU Special Representative (EUSR) in the region, in particular on issues with a regional dimension'.[12] The European Council, however, did not provide a clear delineation of the rights and duties of the EU special representative nor of those of the operation commander.

There was another important EU actor in the field, of which the EUFOR commander, the EU special representative, as well as those in charge of MINURCAT had to be aware: the powerful European Commission in Brussels. The Commission was mandated to contribute about €50 million to the joint UN-EU initiative. Among other things, it was to support the UN police mission financially. In total, the Commission was due to spend about €299 million in Chad and €137 million in the CAR over a five-year period.[13] Again, the European Council remained rather silent on the details of this cooperation, although it was well known that cooperation between the European Commission and its actors in the field was often not easy.

Altogether, the call for the 'coherence of the EU response' sounded somewhat hollow. Surprisingly, the European Council was more specific when it came to the need for liaison by the EU force commander with New York: he was asked to liaise with the UN Department of Peacekeeping Operations; to maintain close contacts with MINURCAT, local actors, and other international actors; and to enter into the necessary arrangements with the UN regarding the modalities for mutual assistance and cooperation.[14]

Taken together, the joint EUFOR-MINURCAT operation was a busy mission in terms of coordination and liaison. Numerous liaison personnel were needed, triggering additional coordination demands. The notion that the EU and UN, in their joint effort to contain more human suffering and conflict in Chad and the CAR, had produced a 'coordination and cooperation hydra' did not seem too far-fetched. Much of the coordination burden remained with the EUFOR operation commander and his staff. In addition to all these liaison and cooperation needs, the EUFOR commander had to ensure that EU member states (and 'third states') were supportive, in particular those that had contributed troops.

EUFOR/MINURCAT: deploying into a volatile theatre of sand, dust, and violence

A vast environment. In an exchange with the press in January 2008, the EUFOR operation commander, General Patrick Nash, left no doubt that he was aware of the difficult theatre into which EUFOR would deploy.[15] He identified some of the particular challenges: the vastness of the region (unpopulated areas), the severe landscape and climate (rainy season and heat), the lack of viable infrastructure and low economic development in Chad and the CAR, the endemic political instability, and the presence of transiting rebel groups and bandits.[16] To be able to cope with this environment and the different requirements of the displaced civilian population, Nash explained that the activities of the operation would be split into three strategic areas. First, in the northern area, where most of the refugees from Darfur were concentrated, EUFOR would maintain a general presence for security operations if necessary; second, a more robust security presence would be stationed at the centre of this area, which contained considerable numbers of both refugees and internally displaced persons; and third, in the south, special operation forces would be deployed in the border area between Chad and the Central African Republic to deter rebel attacks.

As noted earlier, it took EUFOR six months to move from its initial operational capability in March 2008 to its full operational capability of about 3,400 troops in September 2008. About twenty-five European states actively participated in the mission in one way or the other, with nineteen countries deploying troops in the field. France (1,177), Ireland (447), Poland (421), Austria (169), Italy (104), the Netherlands (71), and Sweden (about 10) were the main troop contributors. Germany and Britain, unenthusiastic about this mission, posted only a few liaison officers to EUFOR headquarters, as did a few other EU member states.[17] With twenty-five member states participating at headquarters level and nineteen with troops in the theatre, EUFOR Chad/CAR could be qualified as the most pan-European force ever deployed in Africa, despite the clear dominance of France.

From the very beginning, it had been a feature of ESDP missions to be open to the participation of non-EU states: the so-called third countries. In the case of EUFOR Chad/CAR, this became very important, as it helped Brussels to resolve a key problem of the mission: the lack of helicopters. In the beginning, the mission was far from being able to obtain the planned number of transport and combat helicopters. Eight French and two Irish helicopters were the first in place, but this was insufficient. Three Polish helicopters followed in July 2008, after being adapted for desert conditions. Calls for more helicopters, in particular to EU member states, fell on deaf ears. After long negotiations, Russia finally provided four additional helicopters. In November 2008, around a hundred military personnel from the Russian air force and four MI-8 helicopters arrived aboard an Antonov cargo plane and became operational in December 2008. Albania had already sent about sixty soldiers in the early phase of the mission, and Croatia later sent fifteen soldiers.

Headquarters and logistical challenges. The Abéché region in eastern Chad had been chosen as EUFOR's local force headquarters. In Abéché town, EUFOR deployed its special forces unit, consisting of elite specialists from Austria, Sweden, Ireland, Finland, and Belgium. EUFOR's three forward bases, in Goz Beida (south), Forchana (centre), and Iriba (north), were supported from Abéché. A fourth camp was run by a small contingent of French troops in Birao in the CAR. The mission's operational headquarters was based outside the theatre, in Mont Valérien in France.

Organising EUFOR's logistics was extremely demanding.[18] The operating area covered about 280,000 square kilometres—larger than the size of France. The long distances created particular logistical challenges.[19] Most of the heavy equipment and supplies had to be shipped by sea to Douala in Cameroon, a two-week journey from Europe. From there, the containers, trucks, and other vehicles faced an overland journey of almost 2,000 kilometres, a distance similar to the Rome-Stockholm distance by road. The distance between N'Djamena and Abéché was 760 kilometres by air, but by road it would take five days during the dry season to travel 1,380 kilometres, and possibly a good deal longer during the rainy season.

Water was another logistical nightmare that EUFOR had to cope with. Even if consumption were reduced to sixty litres of water per person a day, supplying a daily amount of 204,000 litres, or 1,428,000 litres weekly, would be a tremendous challenge given these long supply routes. EUFOR knew, from the beginning, that this would be a major problem. A huge Russian Antonov cargo plane—the second largest transport aircraft in the world—was chartered to haul bottled water to Chad. Then the French tried to drill their own wells, so as not to infringe too much on the resources of the local population. This was not a completely satisfactory solution, and EUFOR ultimately had to take water from the local wells, causing a lot of resentment among the local population. By digging ditches at every EUFOR camp that could handle substantial amounts of rainwater, the EUFOR command tried to ease this problem. Camp Europe, near N'Djamena, was thus nicknamed 'little Venice' because of the network of ditches that permeated the site.[20]

Mandate and problems of impartiality. EUFOR struggled not only with the lack of helicopters and difficult logistics, but also with the limitations of its mandate. When an international peacekeeping mission deploys into a war-torn country, local populations expect protection and improvement, whatever the fine print of a mandate says. Reading and understanding complicated limitations of mandates negotiated in Brussels and New York is beyond the daily challenges of survival for local populations. EUFOR therefore had a difficult time in explaining to local populations, as well as to international nongovernmental organisations (NGOs), the narrowness of its mandate. The same was true regarding the complex and confusing setup of the EUFOR-MINURCAT architecture. Soon after reaching its preliminary operational capability, the mission undertook a series of information campaigns to clarify its role and the limitations of its mandate. How successful these campaigns were in convincing the population and international NGOs is debatable. During a visit by Javier Solana, the Spanish EU High Representative for the Common and Foreign Security Policy (CFSP), in May 2008, many aid workers wore black armbands and placed black flags on their vehicles to demonstrate their conviction, and that of the local population, that EUFOR should have been doing more in this region.[21]

Given the concessions made to the Déby government, and in view of the French dominance of the mission, EUFOR's impartiality was questioned from the very beginning. Both among the local population and in the view of many African analysts, the French-led EUFOR had come to save the Déby regime.

This suspicion was not surprising in view of France's past history in Chad and its dominant role in EUFOR. Only a few months before the arrival of the European mission, Paris had felt compelled once more to save the Déby regime from a rebel attack, this one launched against N'Djamena in February 2008. About 2,000 Khartoum-backed Chadian rebels entered the capital after a three-day advance from the east, with more than 250 armed four-wheel-drive pickup trucks and Toyota Land Cruisers. (It is not fully clear whether the rationale for this attack was to preempt the arrival of EUFOR by achieving a forced regime change in N'Djamena.)

The rebel force was initially successful, taking a large part of the capital and attacking the presidential palace. The latter, however, never fell, because of a last-minute intervention by the French air force, which played a decisive role in the turn of events. Within a few days, Déby's troops had pushed the rebels out of the city. Paris, probably in agreement with Washington, had at the last moment come to the conclusion that a regime change in Chad, one that would bring Khartoum-supported rebels to power, was intolerable.

In an effort to counteract the impression that EUFOR was merely a French puppet sent to support Déby, the European Parliament explicitly asked EUFOR to remain strictly neutral and to stay clearly separated from the existing French force, Operation Epervier,[22] which had been in Chad since 1986. General Nash and Javier Solana also spared no effort in declaring that EUFOR would maintain strict neutrality and impartiality with respect to Chad's domestic and foreign policies.

Still, a number of observers continued to wonder how such impartiality would be possible in practice, considering the obvious attempt of the regimes in both N'Djamena and Bangui to hide behind the French-led international presence in order to ensure their survival.[23] Chadian rebel movements immediately dismissed EU claims of neutrality and threatened that they would attack the European force if it stood in their way. However, only minor incidents occurred between EUFOR and the rebels. This, in turn, angered Déby, who started accusing the force of aiding rebel groups, thereby sparking a diplomatic row between Brussels and EUFOR. Members of his government later appeared to back away from Déby's accusations.[24] Indeed, in the end, Déby's anti-EUFOR rhetoric turned out to enhance EUFOR's credibility as an impartial force.

EUFOR: transition to a UN force and preliminary assessment

Almost at the same time that EUFOR was reaching its full operational strength, Ban Ki-moon had to start thinking about the follow-up force to EUFOR, which was, as earlier noted, only a one-year 'bridging force' to be terminated in March 2009. In September 2008 the UN Secretary-General outlined to the Security Council the concept of a new UN-led force, MINURCAT, and highlighted seven key elements for bringing it into operation.

First, the area of operations of the new MINURCAT force would be enlarged to include the Ennedi Est department and the Wadi Fira, Ouaddai, and Salamat regions in eastern Chad. Second, acting under Chapter VII of the UN Charter, the force would provide the security necessary to protect civilians at risk, enhance the delivery of humanitarian assistance and the implementation of the MINURCAT mandate, and protect UN personnel and installations; these objectives would be achieved through a concept of deterrence based on force presence. Third, an information, surveillance, and reconnaissance capability would also be required, to gather situational awareness, demonstrate presence, and provide deterrence. Fourth, to ensure its freedom of movement, the force would require mobility assets, integral to the military component. Owing to the terrain and distances involved, this could only be achieved through a robust military helicopter fleet (a military air component of eighteen utility helicopters and an armed aerial reconnaissance unit would, in the UN Secretary-General's view, provide the necessary aviation assets). Fifth, owing to the volatility of the security situation, the force would require an 'over the horizon' capability of about one battalion, with appropriate support requirements. Sixth, in deploying MINURCAT, the UN would continue to support the establishment of what was now called the Détachement Intégré de Sécurité (DIS), the former PTHP; the government of Chad had requested that the total strength of the DIS should be increased from 850 to 1,700. And finally, the force would need to remain impartial in order to succeed.[25]

UN Secretary-General Ban Ki-moon argued forcefully that an increased number of well-equipped troops would be needed to ensure the credibility of this concept. He asked for at least 6,000 troops, not including the 'over the horizon' force that would be needed to support them. In defence of this number, he reminded the UN Security Council that it was not much larger than that of EUFOR if the latter were realistically counted to include all the logistical and aerial support that it received on a bilateral basis. The new force would also need to cover a larger area than had EUFOR. The number of additional troops required for the CAR was left open by the UN Secretary-General.

It was obvious that, with this concept, the UN Department of Peacekeeping Operations tried to revive elements of its original proposal for a more comprehensive, more extended, and truly impartial mission, as contained in the UN Secretary-General's February 2007 report. This endeavour, however, was not met with much enthusiasm, either in the Security Council or from N'Djamena. Although the UN Security Council welcomed the Secretary-General's proposal 'in principle' in September 2008, several members of the Council later signalled that they considered the number of troops and helicopters he was asking for to be unrealistic. The reaction of the Déby government was even blunter. In October 2008 the permanent representative of Chad at the UN, Ahmad Allam-Mi, sent a letter to the president of the Security Council and the Secretary-General in which N'Djamena demanded that the operation to be undertaken by the UN force 'should not be a conventional peacekeeping one implying some kind of "neutrality", "impartiality" or "good offices" within the framework of any type of peace agreement', and that the force should not exceed 3,000 troops and should be better equipped compared to EUFOR.[26]

Déby's refusal to accept a 'non-neutral, non-impartial' UN force challenged the very basis of UN peacekeeping, and once more revealed the true intensions of his regime. The Chadian autocrat sought to use the international presence for his own political survival. Again, the UN Department of Peacekeeping Operations had to bend over backwards to accommodate N'Djamena. This required three visits—one by the UN Undersecretary-General of the Department of Field Support, Argentina's Susana Malcorra; one by the military adviser of the Department of Peacekeeping Operations, Nigeria's Chikadibia Obiakor; and one by the UN Secretary-General himself, to work out a more 'refined' concept—before N'Djamena finally agreed to a force of 4,900.[27]

It was this number that the UN Secretary-General finally proposed in his December 2008 report to the Security Council, signalling the painful compromises that the UN had to make while noting that 'in developing this concept, careful consideration has been given to the continued concerns expressed by the government of Chad'.[28] Ban Ki-moon also did not hesitate to voice his concerns regarding the minimum strength of the proposed force: 'The refined force concept reflects adjustments to the helicopter support troops, signals units, special forces and reconnaissance units, as well as some logistical elements. They are deemed operationally achievable, although not ideal, as they reduce the logistical support and enablers to the minimum. Any further reduction in the force would significantly impact on its effectiveness and situational awareness'.[29] Altogether, the history of negotiating a mandate first for the joint EUFOR-MINURCAT mission and then for the new MINURCAT force represented a demonstration of the degree to which 'political' considerations took precedence over the need for effectiveness in international peacekeeping.[30] It was particularly surprising to realise the extent to which the 'representatives' of the international community—above all, the members of the Security Council—were ready to accede to the demands of the Déby regime.

The fact that the design of the concept did not engender a systematic, thorough, and honest assessment of the failures as well as the successes of the joint EUFOR-MINURCAT mission fits well into this picture.[31] Of course, the time frame of less than one year during which EUFOR and MINURCAT were truly operational would have made such a thorough assessment difficult. Most likely, such a review would have come to the conclusion that only a highly improved mandate and mission, similar to that proposed by the UN Secretary-General in February 2007, would have really made sense. The results of the cursory evaluation undertaken by a joint EU-UN team and presented to the Security Council by the UN Sec-retary-General in his September 2008 report support this assumption.[32] They show how limited the impact of the joint EUFOR-MINURCAT mission had been in improving the situation on the ground. Five of the key results regarding Chad were presented by the UN Secretary-General in his December 2008 report.[33]

First, the security situation, particularly in eastern Chad, remained vola-tile. Over the preceding few months, both the Chadian armed forces and the country's rebel groups had strengthened their positions on their respec-tive sides of the Chad-Sudan border in anticipation of a possible offensive. Second, car-jacking, armed robberies, and crimes targeting national and international humanitarian staff continued during the reporting period. With the end of the rainy season, the possibility of renewed rebel attacks increased. Third, eastern Chad hosted over 290,000 refugees and more than 180,000 internally displaced persons, who continued to rely on humanitar-ian aid for their survival. Up to 700,000 individuals among the host com-munities were also estimated to require humanitarian assistance. The security situation continued to seriously undermine the capacity of humani-tarian workers to deliver assistance. Over $1.5 million worth of nonfood items and vehicles had been lost. Fourth, investigations into criminal acts by the local authorities—if they took place at all—were usually not com-pleted. Following an attack on one of its staff members in July 2008, the International Committee of the Red Cross (ICRC) suspended its activities in IDP sites pending an investigation into the incident by national authori-ties. And fifth, in October 2008 in the Am Nabak refugee camp in Wadi Fira region, a group of women had forcibly entered an area where staff of the UNHCR were registering refugees, and the incident had degenerated into a violent attack against UNHCR and NGO workers. Gendarmes from the Commission Nationale pour l'Accueil et la Réinsertion des Réfugiés eventually restored order with the help of EUFOR, and evacuated the humanitarian workers.

Ban Ki-moon did not hide his concerns regarding political developments in Chad, particularly in relation to the organisation of elections and the need for electoral reforms. In his September 2008 report to the UN Security Council, he cautiously acknowledged 'some progress' regarding these reforms. Three months later, in his December 2008 report to the Council, his language became even more cautious, noting that only 'some limited progress' had been made.[34]

Regarding the assessment of EUFOR, there was no denying that there were some positive developments. A report published by Oxfam in September 2008 noted that 'EUFOR has made many feel safer by patrolling the main roads, destroying unexploded ordnances, and by positioning battalions around camps during rebel and government fighting'.[35] But the sense of increased security that EUFOR was able to generate was unfortunately limited mostly to areas close to its camps. As a military force, the EU mission had been unable to deal with the upsurge in banditry and other crimes (in addition, this was not being dealt with by the new Chadian police force, the DIS, since its responsibility had been limited to the refugee and IDP camps).

Regarding MINURCAT, its main achievement was that the total number of trained officers for the DIS was increased to 418 by 2009. Another training course, for 222 officers, started in November 2008. In January 2009 the mission started to deploy more than 140 police officers throughout the operational area, and 525 DIS officers were deployed to a number of duty stations in eastern Chad.[36] MINURCAT finally withdrew from Chad and the Central African Republic by December 2010, with the Chad-Sudan border, in particular, remaining volatile.

In view of the limited achievements of the joint EUFOR-MINURCAT mission and the dubious mandate of the MINURCAT mission, it was not surprising that Ban Ki-moon had great difficulty finding the 4,900 troops for the UN force. In his December 2008 report, the UN Secretary-General summed up what he had been able to achieve thus far: sixteen countries 'indicated' a willingness to consider contributing troops to the mission, while one potential contributor indicated a wish to contribute to the helicopter requirement.[37] This was a meagre result, indeed, if one takes into account that at the time the report was written, only three months were left until the takeover of the force in March 2009. In January 2009 the UN Security Council approved a maximum force of 5,500 peacekeepers (4,900 for Chad and 600 for the CAR). UN member states did not rush to provide troops and equipment to MINURCAT.[38] The danger of a security vacuum caused by the transition from an EU to a UN force was real. Ban Ki-moon sought to prevent this scenario by convincing as many EUFOR troop contributors as possible to agree to 're-hatting' their contingents as MINUR-CAT peacekeepers. A handful of countries, such as Ireland, Poland, Austria, Finland, Romania, Portugal, and Spain, also joined MINURCAT.[39]

Concluding reflections

Aside from the difficulties of substituting EUFOR Chad/CAR with a credible UN force from 2009, three other international peacekeeping missions in the region were in serious trouble. First, in neighbouring Darfur, UNAMID continued to struggle to keep the peace with the slow deployment of its 26,000 troops. Helicopters were still lacking, although the mission had been approved in July 2007. The security situation in Darfur in 2011 remained volatile as fighting continued and UN peacekeepers and humanitarian workers continued to be attacked. The prospect for a successfully negotiated peace in Darfur remained dim in March 2012.

Second, regarding the North-South peace process in Sudan, the indictment of Sudanese president Omar al-Bashir by the Hague-based International Criminal Court—announced in 2009—complicated the work of UNMIS, while the January 2011 referendum in South Sudan resulted in an overwhelming vote in favour of secession from the North.

Finally, Somalia continued its two-decade downward spiral into violence, conflict, and destruction. In January 2009 the transitional federal government fell apart, but a new 'moderate' Islamist president, Shaikh Sharif Ahmad, was appointed that month. More significant, Ethiopian troops left the country in 2009. They had provided some modicum of stability, despite being deeply resented by the majority of Somalis and facing constant attacks by Islamist groups. AMISOM, the African Union peacekeeping mission to Somalia, consisting mostly of Ugandan and Burundian troops, continued to experience difficulties in stabilising the country. Kenyan troops also became embroiled in a military intervention into Somalia in October 2011, which came under the AU force in the country.

In sum, there is a very real danger that the entire region of the Greater Horn of Africa—extending from the Chad-Darfur-CAR triangle of conflict, violence, and destabilisation to Sudan and Somalia, as well as Ethiopia and Eritrea on its eastern side—may escalate into more conflict, violence, and humanitarian disaster. Neither Africa, Europe, nor the broader international community seems to be able to halt this slide into conflict.

Four key conclusions can be drawn from this analysis. First, the mandates of the existing missions have been far too restricted and weak. Second, the capabilities of peacekeepers in terms of troops, policy, and other kinds of personnel as well as military hardware—in particular helicopters and other high-value elements—have been insufficient. Third, the regimes as well as the armed groups and rebel movements in this region have learned how to abuse and manipulate the different kinds of international presence to their advantage. And finally, the hope that the creation of 'peacekeeping partnerships' between multilateral organisations such as the UN, the EU, and the AU would lead to more effective and better-equipped peacekeeping missions in Africa has not yet materialised. On the contrary, these partnerships seem to have bred cumbersome, bureaucratic cooperation and coordination monstrosities.[40]

Obviously, profound rethinking has been needed, by Africa as well as Europe, the US, and the broader international community, on how the decline of this huge region into more violence, conflict, banditry, and streams of refugees and internally displaced persons can be halted. By 2011 there were more than 10 million IDPs and an estimated 2.5 million refugees living in camps in the Greater Horn of Africa and adjacent states. The international community, in particular Africa, Europe, and the US, was caught in a profound dilemma between the moral call for preventing further humanitarian catastrophes in the region and the realistic insight that the external world has provided neither convincing strategies nor the necessary means to implement such ideas.

PART 5

THE EU-AFRICA POLICIES OF FRANCE,
BRITAIN, PORTUGAL, AND THE NORDICS

16

FRANCE, THE EU, AND AFRICA

Douglas A. Yates

Introduction: a lasting colonial legacy

The French empire in Africa was a vast geographical space inhabited by culturally diverse populations who, with a few exceptions, were conquered during the 'Scramble for Africa' between 1880 and 1910 (see chapter 2 in this volume). For purely administrative purposes, these African territories were aggregated into two large federations—French Equatorial Africa (AEF), with its federation capital in Brazzaville, and French West Africa (AOF), with its federal capital in Dakar. The African subjects of the AEF and AOF were dominated by models of colonialism known as 'direct rule' and cultural 'assimilation'. It is best to think of these two components of French colonial rule as separate parts of a single system, rather than as synonymous terms each interchangeably referring to one and the same phenomenon.

Unlike the British empire in Africa, which used a model of *indirect* rule that employed 'native' rulers as intermediaries in the power structure, dominating African subjects indirectly through African traditional elites, the French colonial federations established administrative apparatus that *directly* ruled subject peoples. African subjects were dominated by French colonial officers. Of course, this was only a model and an ideal.[1] Realities on the ground were never quite so clear-cut. When the French first expanded their conquests into the hinterland, they signed treaties of protection with traditional rulers who acknowledged French sovereignty and, in exchange for their cooperation, continued to rule over their people with only loose supervision by French officials. But as time went on, the French administration in the two federations turned gradually to a form of direct administration. 'Lines of decision flowed from the colonies to Dakar or Brazzaville and through these centres to Paris'.[2]

The concept of *assimilation* refers to a process through which Africans were assumed into the body of the French nation, taught its language, and indoctrinated in its culture. Unlike the British colonial officers, whose aloofness from their subjects was reflected in the official policy of 'association', the French embraced what they considered to be a *mission civilisatrice*.[3] For the British, there had been no desire to create a population of 'black Englishmen' and so the process of education, when it occurred at all, was usually left to the British missionaries. For the French, however, there was a strong universalist belief in the ability of their language and culture to transform individuals, so education was officially promoted by the government in the capital cities of the colonies, creating an assimilated class of educated 'black French'. The contribution of this class to future French influence was an important colonial legacy.

When combined, these systems of direct rule and cultural assimilation merged to shape francophone Africa into a sphere of influence in which French politicians and businessmen in the metropolitan capital made decisions that were implemented by white expatriates living in the colonies along with their black 'collaborators'. By directly ruling over their African subjects, the French cultivated a political culture of dependency and 'extraversion'.[4] By transforming Africans into 'black Frenchmen', they managed to create a class of African elites who often proved to be more loyal to the interests of France than of Africa.

One of the most perplexing questions for francophone Africans is why their two large federations were broken up. It is clear that some of the Africans themselves wanted their federal structures to survive, and it is also clear that France had worked for decades to centralize its administrative authority and services in Dakar and Brazzaville. So why, then, did France, in the closing days of its empire, decide to break up the AEF and AOF into twelve separate sovereign states? An underlying goal of this policy was surely the perpetuation of strong Franco-African links. 'Indeed, what better way to perpetuate close relations than to split the empire into many dependent mini-states?' asks Francis Terry McNamara. 'Dealt with individually by France, these weak, financially strapped countries were likely to be less adventurous and to possess far less bargaining power than would two large, more financially secure federations'.[5]

In order to perpetuate a dominance-dependence relationship with its former colonies in which real decisionmaking and capital accumulation would be monopolized by the French, President Charles de Gaulle created the post of secretary-general for African affairs in 1958 and appointed to it the notorious Jacques Foccart, who became responsible for maintaining contact with African heads of state. Foccart and his staff prepared all presidential decision papers on issues that involved Africa. He organised all visits by African dignitaries and heads of state to France, as well as all visits to Africa by the French president. But more important, Foccart created a clandestine network of agents and spies, placed in every port and capital city of the former French empire in Africa—the infamous *réseau Foccart* ('Foccart network')—to report disturbing developments that might challenge French supremacy in these countries, and promising discoveries that might enrich French businesses.

De Gaulle succeeded in preventing decolonization from automatically breaking the close links that had been forged with the Gallic African empire. But formal independence was the price that he had to pay in order to preserve all the close cultural and economic ties that had been forged over the previous century. Granting independence to these countries was also a means of avoiding long and bloody wars of independence, which France had already experienced in Indochina and North Africa. So de Gaulle embarked on an ingenious system of bilateral agreements that became the basis of relations between France and its former African possessions. These bilateral treaties were called 'cooperation accords', and they included a full range of diplomatic, defence, economic, monetary, financial, commercial, and technical assistance agreements. 'These cooperation accords remain something of a taboo subject', laments Grégoire Biyogo, a Gabonese scholar now living in exile in France. 'One finds very little university-level work, or even essays on the matter, doubtless because of the extreme confidentiality of the texts and of the information in this particularly sensitive domain'.[6] These accords established, among other things, permanent bases for French military forces in five former colonies: Côte d'Ivoire (550 troops), Djibouti (3,000), Gabon (600), Senegal (1,100), and

Chad (700). The military accords signed with Côte d'Ivoire, Gabon, and Chad were secret, and remained the cornerstone of France's military strategy of pre-positioned troops in the region. The secret accords enabled Paris to intervene militarily in signatory states under three circumstances: for the defence of the country if threatened by foreign aggression, for humanitarian missions, and for 'stabilization of internal politics'.[7] This last condition was invoked by France to prop up friendly political puppets whenever they were threatened by popular uprisings.

Military interventions in Africa became something of a French specialty during the Cold War. It used its troops in Gabon to put down a popular uprising against the pro-French puppet Léon Mba in 1964. Paris used its troops in Chad to fight the Tibesti rebellion between 1968 and 1972. It sent troops into Zaire (now the Democratic Republic of the Congo [DRC]) to put down the Shaba rebellion in 1977. France sent troops into Western Sahara to fight the Algerian-backed Polisario Front liberation movement on behalf of Mauritania in 1977. It deployed soldiers in the Central African Republic (CAR) to support the overthrow of the tyrannical Jean-Bédel Bokassa in 1979. France sent troops into Chad to fight Muammar Qaddafi's Libya between 1983 and 1984. It sent its troops into Togo to buttress the pro-French dictator Gnassingbé Eyadéma in 1984, and deployed troops into the Comoros in 1989. These are only a few of the over forty military interventions that France undertook on the African continent, many of them facilitated by the cooperation accords. The list continued to grow after the Cold War, with French troops being sent into Rwanda (1990–1994), Zaire-DRC (1991), Comoros (1995), the Central African Republic (1996), Congo-Brazzaville (1997), Côte d'Ivoire (2002–present), the DRC (2003), and Chad (2006 and 2008), not to mention frequent military incursions into the Sahel region for humanitarian purposes and to combat terrorism.

Following debacles in Rwanda (1994) and the DRC (1997) in which former French clients lost power, Paris has been attempting to Europeanise its military presence in sub-Saharan Africa, while preserving its traditional sphere of influence in the region. This chapter focuses specifically on the administration of Nicolas Sarkozy between 2007 and 2011, which symbolises the increasing shift from a unilateral to a multilateral approach in promoting France's security interests in Africa. The chapter does not focus on the economic dimensions of this relationship (aspects of which are covered in chapter 2 in this volume).

President Sarkozy's promise of a 'rupture' with the neocolonial practices of the past remains a pious vow, while institutional reforms of the French military system have evolved from a policy of 'Africanisation' to one of 'Europeanisation'. An examination of Gallic military interventions in Africa suggest that France uses the European Union when it serves French interests, but when it does not, will go it alone.

Françafrique, mon amour

On 14 July 2010, twelve African leaders and some of their troops were invited to join Nicolas Sarkozy on the traditional Bastille Day military parade down Paris's famous Champs Elysées. The event was meant to mark the fiftieth anniversary of the decolonisation of Francophone Africa, but many African and French observers wondered aloud what they were supposed to be celebrating. Was this not an incomplete decolonisation process? A formal independence that was at best partial? A postcolonial status that was perversely neocolonial? The French African empire south of the Sahara (which after 1944 was renamed the French Union, just as colonies were renamed 'overseas territories') had been fourteen times the size of France, comprising fourteen sub-Saharan African territories, twelve colonies, and two protectorates. French-style decolonisation in 1960, far from completely tearing down this empire, consisted of building a new system on its ruins.[8]

After their independence, the former African colonies formed a bloc with the former colonial metropole that came to be known as *Françafrique*. From a constitutional standpoint there was no legal foundation for such an alliance. But on the ground, it was referred to as the *coopération* system, which succeeded the old colonial one just as the CFA (Communauté Financière Africaine) franc of the African Financial Community succeeded the old franc of the French African colonies. In four years, between 1959 and 1963, France signed 138 aid agreements, putting in place collaborative regimes that Frederick Cooper has called 'gatekeeper states'.[9] The old French colonial ministries were replaced by a new Ministry of Cooperation, and official diplomacy with newly independent states was handled by the Ministry of Foreign Affairs at the Quai d'Orsay. Yet behind this façade, a dominance-dependence relationship survived.

The term *Françafrique* describes the neocolonial enmeshment of France with its former African colonies.[10] Because this term is used in many different ways, and because it is almost impossible to interpret in a way that allows for scientific debate, another idea, coined by the French anthropologist Jean-Pierre Dozon, has emerged to describe the half-French, half-African hybrid system: the 'Franco-African State'.[11] People made their careers in this hybrid regime, moving from French administration to the African bureaucracy and vice versa, without losing their seniority or their retirement benefits. French ambassadors in former African colonies remained in their posts so many years that they were more like 'proconsuls'. Men like Jacques Raphaël-Leygues (1963–1979) and Michel Dupuch (1979–1993), for example, both served in Côte d'Ivoire. French officers were regularly 'detached' to serve in African armies, still wearing their French uniforms. In fact, there were more French coopérants in Africa after decolonisation than during the colonial era itself: an increase from 125,000 in 1960 to 250,000 in 1970. There were 50,000 coopérants in Côte d'Ivoire in 1970, triple the number at independence.[12]

This was coopération de substitution, in which French agents substituted for Africans who held official posts of responsibility. 'In that era', notes Stephen Smith, who for many years reported on Africa for Libération and then Le Monde, 'interviewing a minister [in francophone Africa] meant shaking his hand and exchanging a few courteous words before he excused himself and left his technical adviser, invariably French, to take care of answering the reporter's questions'.[13] French soldiers wore the uniforms of African armies in which they served. Substitution was practised in all domains: political, diplomatic, economic, and military. Because the system survived for so long, many people believe that it still exists as a permanent structure. 'But the Franco-African State today has become a shadow of its former self', claims Smith, repeating the message of decline that he and the French journalist Antoine Glaser had famously argued in their 2005 best-seller Comment la France a Perdu l'Afrique. For Glaser and Smith, 'Françafrique is dead'.[14]

The main cause of this death is demographic. France no longer has great weight south of the Sahara. For example, at the time of its independence in 1960, Côte d'Ivoire had 3 million inhabitants, while France had 45 million. Since then, the Ivorian population has multiplied six times, while that of France has only grown by 0.3 per cent. After the end of the Cold War, the number of French technical assistants in Africa fell from 6,464 in 1992 to 1,325 in 2008, and that of its military assistants from 925 to 264. The number of 'pre-positioned' troops dwindled in the same period, from 30,000 in 1960 to 5,300 in 2008.[15] The French army, which used to conduct pacification missions in Africa, 'now specialises in evacuation operations'.[16]

A second cause of the demise of *Françafrique* was due to ·increasing democratisation processes in Africa. After the Cold War, when a 'third wave of democratisation'[17] swept across the continent, and old pro-French puppets found themselves challenged through the ballot box by free polls, conducted for the first time, in many cases, in Francophone Africa. As Stephen Smith noted, 'Victim of demography and democracy, the Franco-African State only survives in dark niches, like a secret affair only for the initiated…. *This* is what *Françafrique* refers to'.[18] Lamenting that the 'privatisation of the state' in postcolonial Africa has degraded the old intergovernmental relations into 'a little arrangement between men of power' who 'no longer have any political project',[19] Smith nevertheless rejected using the term *Françafrique* as an analytical tool for understanding Francophone Africa:

I hate *Françafrique*, the word as much as the thing. The word has an ugliness which the puns cannot hide. It designates a seedy world of parallel diplomacy, a world of intermediaries with deep pockets, and an elite pact degenerated into a collusion of the powerful. The Franco-African State is dead, but its zombie, *la Françafrique*, continues to haunt the minds in both France and the postcolonies.[20]

'What does the new Franco-African world resemble? … Not *la Françafrique*.'[21] For Smith, the French neocolonial empire is dead. If I have cited him so extensively, it is because he typifies a kind of 'end of empire' writing found in the scholarly literature. But not everyone agrees with this analysis. In fact, there are two competing viewpoints on the evolving Franco-African relationship: according to the first view, advocated by Glaser and Smith, what we are seeing is 'a real French disengagement from francophone Africa and a simultaneous redeployment of French politico-diplomatic, strategic and economic interests away from francophone Africa'.[22] The second view, more militant in perspective and typified here by the Malian author Guy Martin, argues that French policies of 'reform' are really 'a mere smoke screen behind which the traditional status quo policy of *Françafrique* is maintained'.[23] Not only is the French empire still alive in spirit, but France also has tangible vested interests that are protected by its government (traditionally through the African affairs *cellule* in the Elysée palace); through its powerful global businesses (such as Total and Areva); and through its occult *réseaux* (networks, such as the Freemasons), who all continue to play a major role in the region. Evidence of this continuity is not hard to find for the radical critics who recite the old French adage *Plus ça change, plus c'est la même chose.*[24]

Sarko Africanus

The loss of empire torments France's concept of its own identity, because it means the end of French *grandeur*. As Smith satirised: 'France pretends to care about Africa, but really it is only contemplating itself in front of the mirror of *its* Africa ... to ask itself: "Tell me, am I still the prettiest or ugliest one there? Am I still a great power, or only a middle-level one?"'[25] Ever since the French Third Republic, from 1870 to 1914, an idea of 'greater France' has been an essential component of national identity, one that 'Sarkozy has turned into a political portfolio to get an electoral return on his investment'.[26]

The French president was elected on a promise of a 'rupture' with the past, but since his election in 2007, Nicolas Sarkozy's promise to break with *Françafrique* has been reduced to the rank of a pious vow, belied by his unconditional economic, diplomatic, and military support for the historical dictators of the French *pré-carré* (backyard). This has also been evidenced in the French president's active support for military putsches in Mauritania and Madagascar in 2008, and his validation of fraudulent elections in Congo-Brazzaville and Gabon in 2009 as well as of the failed constitutional coup in Niger in 2009. This is not very astonishing for a man who wants to preserve the economic and strategic influence of France in Africa and the world.

Sarkozy's atavistic outlook is also present in improvised speeches on Africa and Africans, in which he has suggested the criminality of immigrants, refused to repent for French colonial sins, and displayed a paternalistic regard with latent racism that seems to blame African imperial victims for their own sorrows. As Sarkozy put it in a much criticised speech in the Senegalese capital of Dakar in July 2007: 'One cannot blame everything on colonisation—the corruption, the dictators, the genocide, those are not colonisation.... Africans have never really entered history. They have never really launched themselves into the future. In a world where nature controls everything, man has remained immobile in the middle of an unshakable order where everything is determined. There is no room either for human endeavour or for the idea of progress'.[27] All of these themes are at the very heart of Sarkozy's rhetoric. What is new about his Africa policy is its uninhibited style. Whether he is decorating new Gabonese leader Ali Bongo with the *Légion d'Honneur*, publicly undermining the trial of 'Angolagate' to facilitate Total's access to Angolan oil,[28] or holding a family reunion of

African dictators to celebrate the fiftieth anniversary of their independence on Bastille Day, Sarkozy's style is totally 'uninhibited' (*décomplexée*).[29]

So, who shapes Sarkozy's Africa policy? First there has been his chief of staff, Claude Guéant, Sarkozy's right-hand man, who shares a common mentor: Charles Pasqua, a former hard-line interior minister under Jacques Chirac between 1986 and 1988, then under Edouard Balladur between 1993 and 1995. In addition to being a minister, Pasqua was the head of an influential network of politicians, administrators, and businessmen—known as *la maison Pasqua*—that conducted shadowy operations in the Mediterranean and sub-Saharan Africa during his heyday.[30] In the 1990s, Guéant served on Pasqua's staff in the Interior Ministry, then as general director of the national police, before being called back to the Interior Ministry by Sarkozy, upon Pasqua's recommendation, in 2002. Since then, Guéant has never left Sarkozy's side, obtaining the strategic post of secretary-general of the Elysée in 2007. He became omnipresent in the small world of French foreign policy, multiplying his Parisian meetings with African heads of state and their emissaries, to the point that French diplomats started complaining that they had no role to play. As the key driver of French Africa policy during the hyper-presidency of Nicolas Sarkozy, Claude Guéant has directly intervened to negotiate with the former Libyan leader Muammar Qaddafi (killed in October 2011 following a Franco-British North Atlantic Treaty Organisation [NATO]-led rebellion), for the release of imprisoned Bulgarian nurses from Libya; made amends with the Angolan leader José Eduardo dos Santos in the wake of the Angolagate scandal (coordinating French arms sales); shuttled back and forth to maintain 'friendship' with the Bongo family in Gabon; reestablished diplomatic relations with Rwanda; and maintained permanent contact with coup leaders in Mauritania and Madagascar to ensure diplomatic support for them from Paris.

When journalists expressed surprise to see him making French Africa policy from inside the Elysée, Guéant replied, without any inhibitions: 'What? Isn't that how things always worked?'[31] In February 2011, Guéant was made interior minister in a return to his old portfolio.

Also influential in the making of French Africa policy under Sarkozy was Robert Bourgi. The son of a rich Lebanese merchant, Bourgi is a Senegalese-born lawyer who joined the closed circle of African rulers cultivated by Jacques Foccart, the *éminence grise* of French Africa policy, presidential adviser, and confidant of African dictators for three decades.[32] Bourgi also served as an adviser to Jacques Chirac in the mayor's office in Paris in the 1980s, then in the Cooperation Ministry during the *cohabitation* of Socialist and Gaullist parties between 1993 and 1995. When Foccart died in 1997, President Chirac gave Bourgi the task of initiating his idealistic chief of staff, Dominique de Villepin (later foreign minister and prime minister, and a deadly political foe of Sarkozy) into the hidden system of African affairs. When later, during the presidential elections of 2007, Bourgi abandoned the Chiraquiens to join candidate Sarkozy, and thereby gained entry into the 'family' circle of the new president, he played the role of intermediary between Sarkozy and Francophone African heads of state.

For example, when Sarkozy evicted Jean-Marie Bockel, a Socialist, from the Cooperation Ministry in 2008 (because of the latter's efforts to reform *Françafrique*), Bourgi narrated to reporters how he went to see Sarkozy, carrying a firm but threatening message from the Gabonese autocrat Omar Bongo: 'He said to me, "Listen, tell Omar and the other heads of state that Mr Bockel is leaving soon and will be replaced by one of my friends. This new minister will carry your attaché cases, and you will initiate him to our Africa."'[33]

The 'friend' that Sarkozy named as the new cooperation minister was Alain Joyandet, a media businessman who had no particular links with Africa before being named to the post. Joyandet was a local politician—a mayor, then a National Assembly member, running the federation of the presidential majority. His lack of knowledge about Africa surprised reporters. But he quickly adopted Sarkozy's uninhibited *Françafricain* style: 'We need to reinforce the influence of France, its market share, and its businesses', the new minister of cooperation told reporters. 'We should not be afraid to tell Africans that, while we do want to help them, we also want it to pay off'.[34] While minister, Joyandet served as a kind of Sherpa for French businesses. He was the only representative of a Western country present in Libya to celebrate the fortieth anniversary of Colonel Qaddafi's coup in 2009. His principal innovation was a project for 'African Bingo', probably inspired by Pasqua's gambling network. Before being forced to resign in July 2010 (in the wake of a real-estate scandal), Joyandet's role had been to demonstrate Sarkozy's continual support of African rulers, and to reduce the anger of those who saw in Bockel someone prepared to break with the past.

Another key player in Sarkozy's government was the former interior minister, Brice Hortefeux, whose 'tough-on-immigrants' persona reflected the domestic face of France's Africa policy. Through visits to police *commissariats*, morning helicopter landings in 'troubled' neighbourhoods accompanied by journalists and cameras, meetings with prefects on the ground after harsh dismantling of gypsy camps—an act condemned by the European Commission in Brussels, which threatened legal action against Paris—Hortefeux, since being named interior minister in 2009, and all through 2010, applied to the letter a formula invented by Sarkozy: a 'presentist' strategy of 'being present' on the ground for television journalists from the evening news. Endless multiplication of images in the mass media of the minister visiting the 'battlefield' was supposed to produce a placebo effect on French audiences: 'Rather than lowering their actual insecurity', explained French analyst Denis Muzet, 'these lowered their *feeling* of insecurity'.[35]

This strategy functioned well between 2007 and 2008. It produced effects because the man who implemented it—Sarkozy—represented a break with the disappearance of the older generation of the French political class symbolised by Chirac. It should be remembered that one of the French president's major political achievements in 2007 was to capture far-right voters from the racist, anti-immigration National Front. Sarkozy's government went on to enact restrictive immigration policies specifically targeting Africans, north and south of the Sahara: from drastic reductions in delivery of entry visas, to multiplication of administrative obstacles and bureaucratisation of the visa process, to forced expulsion on chartered planes under degrading and humiliating conditions. Following a series of gaffes, one of which had serious racial overtones (undiplomatic in a minister already perceived as anti-immigrant), Sarkozy removed Hortefeux in February 2011 in what was the tenth reshuffle of his first term of office.

All of this has succeeded in antagonising many Francophone Africans, and has contributed to a significant deterioration in France's image in Africa. If it seems contradictory for Sarkozy to be promoting *la Francophonie* while expelling Francophones from France, this is how foreign and domestic policies have become entangled. 'Sarkozy the African' is a rightist politician who promises domestic security through tighter immigration and border controls. Even so, the French president did not see any contradiction. 'No country in the world can allow itself to receive a quantity of migrants which exceeds its capacity to welcome them with dignity, work, housing, education and healthcare. Imbalance of this equilibrium leads to phenomena like mass unemployment, exclusion and ghettos'.[36] Sarkozy claimed that his policy of 'co-development', designed to 'mobilise migrant populations to develop their countries of origin', is supposed to be 'part of a package of policies promoted at the Lisbon EU-Africa Summit [of 2007]'.[37] Controlling illegal immigration, Sarkozy explained, is in the interests of both Europe and Africa. For, he claimed, uncontrolled immigration resulted in an African 'brain drain' and illegal smuggling networks, which also hindered development in Africa. (See chapter 20 in this volume).

Not surprisingly, many now question whether or not Sarkozy is really prepared to implement the changes he promised in his February 2008 speech in Cape Town. 'We must change the Africa-France summits, change the methods, and change the objectives', he declared.[38] He promised, for example, to adjust the timing of Franco-African summits to coincide with 'other meetings in the framework of the European Union'.[39] But two years later, when the Africa-France summit in Nice was held in May 2010, no special effort had been made to synchronise its timing with the Africa-Europe summit in Libya in November 2010. The Africa-France summit, like the Bastille Day military parade, is still a French exception that remains unique, at least among Western powers.

It is strange to watch a repeating pattern unfold. First, every new president promises change in Franco-African relations, but once in office he pursues continuity, with the same old clichés. In one of his many dramatic declarations of 'rupture', Sarkozy announced that he would renegotiate France's military cooperation accords. These are secret agreements drafted at independence in the 1960s containing the essentials of French defence policy in Africa. As the French president noted:

This change must be pursued because the French military presence in Africa is still based on accords that were concluded on the eve of decolonisation ... 50 years ago! I am not saying that those accords were not justified in their time. But I do affirm that what was done in 1960 does not make the same sense today. Their writing is obsolete. It is no longer conceivable, for example, that France's army should get mixed up in internal conflicts. Africa of 2008 is not Africa of 1960![40]

In his Cape Town speech of 2008, Sarkozy made four proposals to change his country's Africa policy. First, he would engage in dialogue with African heads of state to adapt the old cooperation accords to 'the realities of the present'. Second, he would re-create bilateral relations on the principle of transparency. Third, he would use the French military presence in Africa to help Africans to build their own collective security system. 'Finally, my last proposition seeks to make Europe a major African partner in the matter of peace and security. That is the sense of the partnership concluded between our two continents at Lisbon last December [2007]. It is in all of our interests, because a strong Europe needs a strong Africa'.[41] The French president's emphasis on 'Europe' merits closer examination, as it indicates a larger Gallic strategy in Africa and the world. As Sarkozy noted: 'I want to affirm before you that the security and prosperity of France and Europe are indivisible from the security and prosperity of Africa. To not understand that our fates are linked is to misinterpret history with dramatic consequences'.[42]

The Europeanisation strategy

France sought to shift its burden onto the shoulders of the European Union for more than two decades. Its Africa policy is only one part of that burden-shifting effort. French armed forces number 251,750 and are the largest military in the EU in terms of personnel,[43] and were the third largest in the North Atlantic Treaty Organisation. France has the fourth highest expenditure of any military in the world ($67 billion in 2010)[44] as well as the third largest nuclear force in the world. This massive military machine comes with a heavy price tag, which Nicolas Sarkozy has sought to reduce. For example, since 2009 the French armed forces have been going through one of the most wide-ranging reforms in their history, with a forecast abolition of 54,000 (out of 320,000) civilian jobs by 2014, the closure of eighty-three bases stationed on its national territory, and the relocation of thirty-three other bases by 2016.[45] A strategic think-tank in Paris, the Centre d'Étude et Prospective Stratégique (CEPS), published a report in 2002 about France's efforts to Europeanise its national defence.[46] This report raised the following questions: What was French national defence policy? Did it still aim to ensure the integrity of the territory, the survival of the population, the power of the nation? Or was it destined to install in Europe and the world a new international order? 'Rare are those who still believe that France is big enough to bring together by itself the means that are necessary for its defence', concluded the report. 'In fact, nobody with the slightest knowledge of the subject even professes such a doctrine. The only question is whether national defence can conserve some kind of autonomy in a vaster military ensemble'.[47]

The French military's traditional focus on territorial defence has now begun to be redirected to meet new global challenges: the identification and destruction of terrorist networks in metropolitan France and Francophone Africa. Arguably, this provides a new rationale for maintaining a strong military presence in Africa, with blessing from both the European Union and the United States. France's 2010 military adventures against Al-Qaeda of the Islamic Maghreb (AQIM) in Mauritania, Mali, and Niger are emblematic of its new 'War on Terror' and the shift of strategic priorities. The minister of defence since November 2010, Alain Juppé (later appointed foreign minister by Sarkozy in February 2011), announced the 'Plan Sahel', which is supposed to help three countries targeted by AQIM—Mauritania, Mali, and Niger—to build a regional response, including military coopera- tion on antiterrorist capacities: 'The action of France is aimed at reinforcing their capacities when faced with this challenge thanks to a cooperation that is at once political, military and civilian. The European Union will make its contribution'.[48]

But it would be wrong to conclude that Paris's restructuring of defence policy is something new, or something that started with Nicolas Sarkozy. The original restructuring of the French military had started ten years ear- lier, in 1997, during the period of *cohabitation* between the Gaullist presi- dent Jacques Chirac and the Socialist prime minister Lionel Jospin. Until then, for purposes of military cooperation, France's former African colonies were treated differently from the rest of the world. *Missions militaires de coopération* had been attached, since 1965, to the Ministry of Cooperation, but by 1997, Jospin—who enjoyed a reputation for being 'Mr Clean'— wanted to break with the Gaullist institutional legacy. There was also con- cern in the French military that the Operation Turquoise intervention in Rwanda at the time of the 1994 genocide—widely seen as a cover for the retreat of Hutu *génocidaires*—had been a political disaster for France, and a measure of retrenchment was therefore required. Jospin downgraded his cooperation minister to the rank of secretary of state, rationally reassigned the military cooperation mission to the Ministry of Defence, and imple- mented a drastic reduction and redeployment of pre-positioned French troops in Africa. The strategic thinking back then was that France could substitute its 44,500-strong rapid reaction force, located in France, for its old 'pre-positioned' troops stationed in Africa. Military planners also argued that it was possible to reduce troops in Africa from 8,000 (in 1997) to 5,600 (in 2002) without losing any operational capacity.[49]

Another French military reform initiative involved the creation of the Direction de la Coopération Militaire et de Défense (DCMD) within the Quai d'Orsay (Ministry of Foreign Affairs), with the task of managing mili- tary cooperation by collaborating closely with other military directorates while making Africans share the burden. 'The aim', explained the head of the DCMD, General Emmanuel Beth, 'has been to transform a policy of substitution into one based on partnership and empowerment, leaving operational cooperation like the training and equipment to be implemented by the Ministry of Defence and the general staff'.[50] The old distinction between countries inside and outside the old African sphere of influence was officially abolished. However, cooperation with Francophone Africa still represented 96.4 per cent of personnel, and two-thirds of the total military cooperation budget. In 2006, 80 per cent of the DCMD budget was earmarked for Africa.[51]

Back in 1997, the vogue was not 'Europeanisation' but 'Africanisation' of the French forces. A new French policy of assistance to multinational and subregional peacekeeping forces in Africa, the Renforcement des Capacités Africaines de Maintien de la Paix (RECAMP), created black African contingents who were armed, equipped, trained, and managed by France. Paris provided support to African troops deployed on UN missions in the Central African Republic between 1998 and 2000, and in Côte d'Ivoire between 2003 and 2004. What characterised French military cooperation in Africa, claimed DCMD head General Beth, was 'a determination to equip African states with the instruments they need to build and control their defence resources within the limits set by the rule of law, to help the continent put in place structures at regional and sub-regional levels for planning, command and intervention enabling it to manage and respond to crises'.[52]

According to General Beth, the DCMD acts to strengthen defence and security capacities of states that request its help through training, advice, and technical support. This new thinking was based on the logic of empowerment and 'ownership' by African countries of their own defence systems. No longer would *substitution* be the policy. For example, the number of Africans trained in France remained substantial, but the DCMD also sought to provide African countries with the means to conduct their own training at regionally oriented schools in countries such as Mali, Ghana, Nigeria, and Zimbabwe, covering specialisations such as peacekeeping, mine-clearance, infantry, aeronautics, gendarmerie, healthcare, signal transmission, and applied military engineering. Alas, 'Africanisation' had its limits, and so the DCMD became more involved in multilateral frameworks, notably through the European Union.

In the eyes of many in France, the European Union provides the ideal solution to its military dilemmas in Africa. Europe permits France to exercise an influence corresponding fairly well to its geostrategic ambitions. As a small world power but a large European power, France can hope to find in the EU a relay, a way of accessing an international role that it refuses to renounce. The ending of obligatory military service in 2001 has placed a great distance between French citizens and the defence of their country, and this distance will only grow over the course of the coming decades. Since Europe benefits from a fairly favourable French public opinion, the notion of 'European defence' is often put forward to define French policy on the matter. European defence has the double advantage of not arousing passions—positive or negative—as much as a national policy (or one that is openly geared towards supporting the United States), while also permitting public authorities in Paris to avoid rendering any account for the numerous deficiencies that are present in the incoherent, spotty, and poorly defined national defence system since the disappearance of the Soviet threat in 1991.

Notwithstanding its double advantage, the European Union may not be ready to provide France with the necessary means to conduct a common foreign and defence policy, for Brussels may just not have the will. The countries that compose the EU seem largely to be satisfied with an American hegemony that assures them, at the lowest possible cost, a degree of security to which they aspire in the short to medium term through NATO. While the EU has well-established institutions for a common foreign policy, the challenge of a deeper integration will require the establishment of common defence institutions. If, in the past, European diplomacy was able to distinguish itself from France's Africa policy, this appears no longer to be the case. The EU seems to have aligned itself with French positions in crises in Togo (2005), Guinea (2007), and even Chad (2008), under the influence of its Belgian development commissioner, Louis Michel.

In December 2005 the European Union adopted a strategy that made Africa a priority region. Paris claimed to have been the initiator of this Africa strategy. According to the French general Henri Bentegeat, in an interview published by an intelligence review, 'France has been able to transmit its interests for Africa to other European states'.[53] For many decades, France has been reticent about letting other countries into its privileged *chasse gardée* (private hunting-ground). However, in the present context of liberal globalisation and acute competition, not to mention growing criticism of French imperialism, 'only the inscription of French interventions in Africa *within the framework of the European security and defence policy* will permit France to remain engaged on the African continent without exposing itself to accusations of paternalism and neo-colonial aims'.[54] According to General Jean-Claude Thomann, 'Today it is at the European level that we must henceforth find the multiplier of force indispensable to confront and act with necessary legitimacy'.[55]

To summarise, the first reason for the Europeanisation of France's Africa policy is the need for renewed legitimacy, as its unilateral military interventions became discredited in the aftermath of the Rwandan genocide in 1994, in which about 800,000 people were killed.[56] A second reason is financial, with other European countries being forced to share the costs of French military interventions in Africa. Third, this policy created a pole that was independent of the Americans (at least in terms of African issues) and capable of standing up to Chinese influence, with France preserving its traditional leadership role in Africa. Since the defence of European territory is guaranteed by NATO, the EU can dedicate itself entirely to the protection of its interests within the larger hemispheric environment. But France's willingness to 'Europeanise' its military presence in Africa has met some resistance among some of its European partners like Britain and Germany, either because of their strong attachment to NATO, or because they suspect France of wanting to maintain undue influence in Africa while simultaneously using EU resources to subsidise this role.

Congo, Chad and the Central African Republic, and Côte d'Ivoire

So far, France has succeeded in undertaking three military operations in Africa under the EU flag. The first was the French-led EU intervention in the Democratic Republic of the Congo at the end of the second Congo war in 2003. (See chapter 14 in this volume.) This followed the negotiation of the Sun City accords to set up a transitional government with Joseph Kabila as president, the withdrawal of Rwandan and Ugandan troops, and the creation of the United Nations Organization Mission in the DRC (MONUC) to oversee a ceasefire. The Ghanaian UN Secretary-General, Kofi Annan, turned to Paris for assistance when MONUC was in need of reinforcements, part of an appeal to the international community to help avoid a humanitarian catastrophe. At that time, France was not directly participating in MONUC, but President Chirac proposed a European operation in the form of an interim emergency force to support the UN troops while they waited for reinforcements. Operation Artémis in 2003 was the first time in its history that the EU had acted as an autonomous military force outside its

European theatre, setting a precedent for later missions. This was also the first time that France had succeeded in convincing its European partners to intervene militarily in Africa.

Artémis also permitted a concrete application of the 2002 EU 'framework-nation' principle that allowed a mission to be called 'European' even if it was run by a small group of EU states or just one single nation. France played the dominant role in the operation. As noted by the American scholar Eric Miller, 'President Chirac wanted to demonstrate that the EU common foreign and security policy was not dead because of divisions over the war in Iraq. He also wanted to reassert France's influence in the region. The mission served both of these purposes'.[57] In fact, Artémis grew out of a French operation that had started in 2003, called Operation Mamba, to which other EU states then made contributions. Comprising 1,800 troops—the majority of them French—the mission deployed to reach the capital of the DRC's Ituri province of Bunia, and was 90 per cent funded by France.[58]

Artémis remained in place until it was replaced by a UN force, MONUC, which managed to secure the regional capital of Bunia, and to stop several massacres as they were unfolding. Congolese militias were outgunned by this French-led force, and fled when they heard the sound of approaching EU helicopters. They were chased into the forest, but were not pursued. However, this force never ventured more than a hundred kilometres beyond Bunia, and stayed for only three months.[59] The limited mission helped the first EU intervention force to accomplish its objectives, but the failure of UN peacekeeping to stabilise the eastern Congo left some analysts sceptical. The only real accomplishment of Artémis may have been that France reasserted its role in the Great Lakes region. This mission also allegedly enabled Paris to supply arms to the Hutu rebel group Forces Démocratiques de Libération du Rwanda (FDLR), and for French secret services to exfiltrate Abdul Ruzibiza, the principal witness of Judge Jean-Louis Bruguière, who accused Rwanda's President Paul Kagame of being responsible for shooting down the aircraft carrying the late Rwandan president Juvénal Habyarimana in 1994, the prelude of the genocide. This theory assigns some share of blame for the genocide to Kagame, and can thus be used to support the dubious French 'double-genocide' theory.[60]

The second French-led EU intervention in Africa took place three years later—also in the DRC—when presidential and legislative elections were held in the large Central African state in July 2006 after a long power-sharing arrangement between the belligerent parties. Since all observers believed the outbreak of violence to be a distinct possibility, the UN authorised the deployment of another mission, the EU Force (EUFOR-RDC), whose mandate was limited to four months to support MONUC during the period of elections. The pan-European dimension of EUFOR was clearly stronger than in the first intervention in Bunia in 2003, as only one-third of the soldiers in 2006 were provided by France, one-third by Germany, and another third by other European countries. German participation—a condition of any real pan-European dimension—was only obtained after limiting the time and the mandate of the operation requested by France.

The French were reported to have twisted the Germans' arms to get them to accept Gallic command of the operation.[61] EUFOR deployment in the field was ultimately under the authority of the French general Henri Bentegeat, who took control of the EU's highest military organ in May 2007. It is important to remember that this operation was not a UN initiative, but had been proposed by Jean-Marie Guéhenno, the French Undersecretary-General for Peacekeeping at the UN secretariat in New York, who in his zeal to launch the operation forgot first to contact either the Congolese government or the African Union.[62] Rather than reinforcing the existing MONUC mission, France created an independent EU military force operating under UN cover. 'This military operation was thus a French initiative, draped in a European cloak and camouflaged with a "request" from the UN'.[63]

The third EU operation in Africa was EUFOR Chad/CAR, a military adventure in Chad and the Central African Republic whose annual mission costs have been estimated at about €150 million, covered largely by the EU (see chapter 15 in this volume). This mission raised some eyebrows in Berlin. By pursuing a multilateral framework, and engaging EUFOR in a mission in Chad and the Central African Republic, France was able to defray some of the costs of an expensive military intervention, while maintaining important operational control. With twenty-five member states participating at EUFOR's headquarters level (nineteen of which had troops in the theatre),[64] the mission has been described as the most pan-European force ever to be deployed in Africa. Is this mission the beginning of a true European military force? Perhaps. But EUFOR headquarters were located in Paris, command of the field headquarters in Chad was given to a French general, and French troops outnumbered those of all the other European countries combined.

Thus, in the eyes of many observers, 'European' peacekeeping forces are really 'French' and serve largely Gallic national interests. Sarkozy's ability to paint this *trompe l'œil* in such a way as to create an optical illusion of a European dimension for what was in reality a French military operation in Chad, is perhaps one of the greatest public relations stunts of a theatrical showman. France intervened twice to save the autocratic regime of Idriss Déby, in 2006 and 2008, again exposing the parochial interests at play in this 'peacekeeping' mission. The EUFOR mission in Chad, in other words, combined evidence of both continuity and change. Although it operated under the aegis of an EU mission (change), French policy in Chad has consistently involved using its own troops in the country (continuity). The EUFOR mission arrived in eastern Chad in March 2008 with an official role of protecting civilians, refugees, and displaced people. The aim of the force was to prevent Sudan's Darfur conflict from spreading across the border, but the main problem faced by people in eastern Chad was common banditry. EUFOR, not being a police force, had no mandate to arrest bandits. Many Chadians and humanitarian workers thus noted that its mandate has not been adapted to the real problems on the ground.

When it serves French interests, therefore, France uses Europe. When it does not, the French are willing to go it alone. Consider the French intervention in Côte d'Ivoire, Operation Licorne, a military operation under French command stationed in Port-Bouët, whose main mission has been to support the 8,000-strong United Nations Operation in Côte d'Ivoire (UNOCI)—deployed in 2004—with troops who could be rapidly dispatched to support the Ivorian army. Licorne was also used to ensure the security of French nationals and their business enterprises, at an estimated cost of about €200 million a year. This entirely French military operation started in 2002, upon the outbreak of the Ivorian civil war, effectively independent of any UN resolution, based largely upon the old 1961 bilateral defence agreements between Paris and Abidjan. However, this intervention was different from earlier ones in that it was not intended to prop up the government in power. In fact, since it involved an impartial interposing force, Licorne's presence angered the government of then-president Laurent Gbagbo.

Sarkozy did not invent this mission, but inherited it from his political rival, Dominique de Villepin, who as President Chirac's foreign minister had sent Licorne to separate the belligerents after a ceasefire agreement among all the Ivorian political forces was signed at a French château in

Marcoussis in 2003. The UN eventually took over responsibility for a French-funded, largely Francophone force deployed between 2003 and 2004 under the auspices of the Economic Community of West African States (ECOWAS). The 4,600-troop Operation Licorne force remained under French command, its numbers dwindling to around 900 by 2010. According to Paris, the force was supported by a UN resolution, had stopped a civil war, and had prevented massacres of civilians. According to its critics, however, Licorne was just another case of France sending in troops to 'pacify the natives', as the former colonial power had important investments to protect in the country—human, material, and symbolic. Critics regard Licorne as another case study of old-fashioned French military intervention.

The emblematic event of such French-style peacekeeping occurred in 2004 when, after the Ivorian air force was accused of carrying out an attack on the French position in Bouaké, causing the deaths of nine French soldiers and wounding thirty-seven others, President Jacques Chirac ordered Licorne to destroy the entire Ivorian air force. This was ostensibly done to prevent any further attacks by the Ivorian army against the rebel Forces Nouvelles, but was probably done to prevent any further possible attacks against French military positions. After this incident, a crowd of anti-French protestors was fired upon at the Hôtel Ivoire in Abidjan by French troops, resulting in 67 Ivorian deaths and 1,256 wounded.[65] The events of November 2004 placed Licorne in an invidious position vis-à-vis the civilian population. It would have been extremely difficult for EU forces to have acted in this manner, and all but impossible for UNOCI. France's use of decisive military force in 2004 meant that it was more difficult for the conflict between northerners and southerners to be resolved. This ethnoregional conflict, by itself, has helped to perpetuate the continued justification for a military presence of French troops in its former colony. It was no secret that Sarkozy did not like Gbagbo, and that the French would prefer someone else in the presidency.

This hostility, which had been inherited from Chirac, eventually found expression in the crisis after the October–November 2010 Ivorian presidential election, which ECOWAS, AU, and UN observers felt that Alassane Ouattara had won. However, Laurent Gbagbo claimed victory and refused to step down. After three months of mounting tension and confusion, the Forces Nouvelles—the rebel troops supporting Ouattara—moved on Abidjan and overthrew Gbagbo, an exercise that only happened with substantial support from the French military presence. Sarkozy unwisely could not stop himself from claiming this as a French victory.

Concluding reflections: burial of the un-dead

The death of the founding Ivorian president, Félix Houphouët-Boigny, in 1993 was used as a symbol to mark the end of an era in Franco-African relations. This seems now to have been a premature verdict. When Houphouët expired, his French-backed regime had lasted for thirty-three years. He had been the *doyen* of Francophone Africa, and a key ally of France. As Guy Martin noted, 'His close personal ties with several generations of French leaders were reflected in the level and size of the French delegation to his state funeral, which included the late president Mitterrand, Prime Minister [Edouard] Balladur, former president Giscard d'Estaing, six former prime ministers, and more than 70 other dignitaries'.[66] But despite the potent symbolic meaning assigned to it, and the fact that Ivorians now openly defy their former coloniser, Houphouët's funeral did not bring an end to French domination of its neocolonial empire.

There appears to be a very hard core of states that remain under the jackboot of French imperialism. Gabon is at the centre of this core. The death of Omar Bongo in June 2009 did not receive the same attention as that of Houphouët-Boigny, although it should have. Many members of the closely knit Franco-Gabonese elite feared the collapse of the system that had made them rich. There was definite unease among the ruling class in Libreville that, with Omar Bongo dead, the system would fall apart. This was a very real fear that, after forty-three years of uninterrupted rule by Bongo, the Gabonese people would rise up in the streets, as they had done in 1964 and 1991, when symbols of French power had been targeted.[67] Indeed, so important was Gabon to France that the projected withdrawal of French troops from the country, announced prior to Bongo's death, was reversed, with Senegal substituted as a target for withdrawal, to the great irritation of President Abdoulaye Wade.

Omar Bongo's official state funeral on 18 June 2009 brought together the whole dysfunctional family of Francophone Africa. Those who think that *Françafrique* is dead should examine the guest list at the official ceremonies marking Bongo's funeral. They had not come to bury *Françafrique*, but to praise it. There, before Omar Bongo's rich coffin, were more than a dozen African heads of state and government, not only rulers of former French colonies in Africa like Yayi Boni (Benin), Abdoulaye Wade (Senegal), Amadou Toumani Touré (Mali), Blaise Compaoré (Burkina Faso), Denis Sassou-Nguesso (Congo-Brazzaville), Idriss Déby (Chad), and Paul Biya (Cameroon), together with Simone Gbagbo (the then president's wife) and Guillaume Soro (Côte d'Ivoire), and François Bozizé (the CAR), but also rulers from other states who have entered into the family, like Teodoro Obiang (Equatorial Guinea), Joseph Kabila (the DRC), Fradique de Menezès (São Tomé and Príncipe), as well as former heads of state like Nicéphore Soglo (Benin), Alpha Oumar Konaré (Mali), and Abdou Diouf (Senegal), now head of the Paris-based Francophonie organisation, as well as the former French president Jacques Chirac.

Nicolas Sarkozy, whose personal gestures towards the Gabonese patriarch the previous year had deeply compromised his image as the president of 'rupture', was also in attendance. In fact, as earlier noted, Omar Bongo had personally lobbied Sarkozy to fire Jean-Marie Bockel after that Socialist cooperation minister had questioned the cosy, corrupt relationship between the African dictator and his French sponsors. When Bongo's body was flown from the capital, Libreville, to Franceville for the private ceremony, the global media captured images of Gabonese crowds hissing and booing Sarkozy's motorcade. What was the meaning of this? People wondered. Was this the end of the discredited system of *Françafrique*? On the contrary, those Gabonese citizens jeering Sarkozy were Bongo loyalists who were angry that the French president had not done enough to protect their patriarch from criminal investigations into his ill-gotten fortune, reported to include dozens of multimillion-dollar properties in France and the principality of Monaco.[68] Little did they realise how much Sarkozy could reportedly do. After Bongo's death, the charges were dropped.

A few months later, when the defunct ruler's eldest son, Ali Ben Bongo, ran for president, Sarkozy supported him. Not only did Paris congratulate Ali for his victory and legitimise the results of his dubious election in February 2010, but Sarkozy also personally promoted the new leader to the rank of grand officer in the *Légion d'Honneur*. Those who announce that French hegemony in Africa is over must consider the counterevidence, be it the influence of French Freemasonry, the continued presence of 5,000 French troops, the large, ubiquitous French corporations, and the hereditary presidencies of pro-French puppets' sons in places like Gabon and Togo. These all suggest a persistence of neocolonial patterns. However, those who proclaim that Francophone Africa can be reduced to a cliché of *Françafrique* must also consider the counterevidence, be it anti-French sentiment in Côte d'Ivoire, the reduction of French bases and civilian expatriates, the increasing penetration of Africa by China,[69] or even the Europeanisation of formerly French forces: all striking counterexamples that change is under way.

The French role in initiating (with support from the British) the NATO-led intervention in Libya in 2011 gave new ammunition to those who saw Paris as continuing to pursue a policy of *grandeur* in Africa. President Sarkozy sought to put a new shine on his tarnished image by this action, especially as it could mean pickings for French business in the post-Muammar Qaddafi regime. Joint action with the British can almost be seen as a substitute for the EU, many of whose member states had much less enthusiasm for the NATO involvement in Libya.

Paris's Europeanisation strategy is therefore important, not just for Africa, but also for France. The stated gains of the European Union have always been economic and political, but the deeper truth is that the European project has always been about French geopolitical fears and ambitions. The fears have sought the reassurance that, so long as Germany is subsumed into an alliance that it does not control, then Paris need not fear another German invasion, or any other invasion for that matter. A France that can harness German strength is a France that does not need to burn resources protecting itself against Germany, and is therefore a France that hopes to become, once again, a global Great Power. This had been a solid plan that took advantage of the American occupation of Germany after the Second World War ended in 1945, and it worked well for many decades. During the Cold War, Paris was able to chart a middle course between Washington and Moscow, and focus on deepening economic links to both Europe and its former African colonies.

But this situation did not last. Eventually the Cold War ended, and the collapse of the Soviet Union was perceived very differently in France. While most of the 'free world' celebrated, France had not been a 'front-line' state during the Cold War, so Paris had never felt Moscow's threat as profoundly as other states like Germany. After the Soviet collapse led to the reunification of Germany in 1990, Paris could no longer consider Berlin to be a nonentity content to be harnessed for someone else's ends. The French feared that Germany would claw back its position as the premier power in Europe and attempt to remake Europe in its own image—with more resources and thus more success. The Gallic solution was thus to ensure that continued German membership in European institutions remained in Berlin's interest.

When it became apparent that German reunification was imminent, France rushed forward on negotiations for monetary union. Twenty years later, by 2012, Berlin could not abandon the European Union without triggering massive internal economic dislocations. Paris today is faced with a Germany that is still tied to France (mostly by the EU but, indirectly, also through NATO), but Berlin is beginning to think for itself. It will take all of France's diplomatic flexibility, acumen, and influence to maintain its influence as one of the world's major powers. Paris will have to make itself indispensable to Berlin's control of Europe, while making sure that Germany is outmanoeuvred on the global stage. As George Friedman noted: 'It is a difficult challenge, but France has a 1,000-year history of diplomatic intrigue and Machiavellian politics from which to draw'.[70]

Jean-Baptise Duroselle, a French scholar, noted in his famous 1981 book, *Tout Empire Périra*,[71] that 'all empires perish'—and this is a good thing. For empire, the fruit of conquest and the will-to-power carries within it government by force, the subjugation of peoples, their submission, and their terror. From these dark constructions, born out of excess, the only promised destiny is collapse. Perhaps that is what the French emperor Napoleon Bonaparte imagined on Saint Helena, after Europe in its entirety allied against him and condemned him to exile between 1815 and 1821. Unlike Alexander, at least, death did not take the conqueror in his full glory before undoing his life work; nor, like Hitler in his bunker, did it deliver an apocalypse born of his own delirium. Whatever the case, empire is fated to shipwreck, with ordinary people often paying the price.

Yet there is another image that rises up, the Roman Empire, a regime of universal reference invented by Augustus to dilate the power of Rome to the scale of the known world and that, up until a certain point, managed its excesses, granting the rights of the city to all 'free men' and opening for decades an era of peace around the Mediterranean. This is an imperial dream that the West has never renounced. It travelled across the Middle Ages. It was carried by Charlemagne across the Rhine to pave the way for the German Holy Roman Empire. It was revived by Napoleon, exhumed by Otto von Bismarck for Kaiser Wilhelm I, and rivalled by all of the Russian tsars who claimed the Byzantine heritage.

The rest is history. All the old European empires eventually died in the trenches of the First World War of 1914–1918. The Versailles Treaty of 1919 sanctioned their end, even if their final demise only came after the Second World War of 1939–1945. These 'prisons of peoples' were dynamited for good with the benediction of the world's new superpowers. There were still some dreamers who nourished nostalgia for these defunct empires, looking for what the famous British historian Edward Gibbon had sought at the end of the eighteenth century: the true causes of the decline of empires. Gibbon observed along the way the political agonies of Rome, Byzantium, and Vienna.[72] We now know that nations are no more innocent than empires, that they exclude and shut themselves off, and that their triumph sometimes assumes a sinister allure of settling accounts by ethnocide. Disappointed, some begin to dream again of those lost multinational empires. This dream requires that former imperial powers like France forget about the constraints, the humiliations, and the oppressions of their conquered cultures for whom this experience is a nightmare. It is a dream of perpetual peace and civic equality. In other words, it is a dream.

17

BRITAIN, THE EU, AND AFRICA

Paul D. Williams

Introduction

Although successive Labour governments in Britain have traditionally paid more attention to African affairs than their Conservative predecessors, the continent is clearly not a top priority for foreign policymakers in Whitehall.[1] Not only are other regions of the world considered more important in a geostrategic sense, but British governments also increasingly define their international priorities in thematic rather than explicitly geographical terms. The country's Foreign and Commonwealth Office (FCO), in its strategic framework of 2008, for example, identified four policy priorities: countering terrorism and weapons proliferation, preventing armed conflict, promoting a low carbon, high-growth economy, and developing effective international institutions.[2] British foreign policymakers thus traditionally do not develop priorities based on geographical regions, but rather focus on those parts of the world that are most relevant to these strategic priorities. While the legacy of empire continues to influence the allocation of London's attention and resources in Africa, increased engagement with states previously outside the Commonwealth—notably Rwanda, the Democratic Republic of the Congo (DRC), Mozambique, and Angola—suggests that thematic priorities are becoming increasingly influential in Britain's foreign policy.

For the purposes of this chapter, it is significant that along with the United Nations, Prime Minister Gordon Brown's government (2007–2010) consistently stressed the need to make the European Union 'effective'. The Conservative-led Coalition government of David Cameron since 2010 has also expressed a wish to engage the EU and promoted burden-sharing among its members as a way of maintaining influence on the African continent. Substantial divisions over Europe, however, remain evident between the Conservatives and the Liberal Democrats in the ruling coalition. After the Labour Party took office in May 1997, Britain became a more proactive player in EU politics. Over time, this intensified the 'EU-isation' of Britain's foreign policymaking process. It also generated unprecedented British support for developing the Common Foreign and Security Policy (CFSP) for the EU, complete with the capabilities required to conduct expeditionary missions under the European Security and Defence Policy (ESDP) framework. While London has been generally supportive of these ventures, it has not had a major presence in ESDP operations in Africa. This is unlikely to change in future unless the situations in Kosovo, the Middle East, and especially Afghanistan improve dramatically. While these problem areas persist, London is likely to continue to focus on training and assistance packages to enhance 'African' crisis management capabilities. As a consequence, the likelihood of Britain playing a leading role in African affairs is dwindling. Consequently, the country is likely to try to develop influential niche roles in the areas of peace and security and international development and focus more on boosting its own national interests in Africa, defined primarily in terms of increasing British trade with the continent.

In order to explore these issues in more depth, this chapter proceeds in five parts. First, I provide a brief overview of some of the major themes in Britain's postcolonial relations with Africa. The second section extends the analysis to Britain's strategic priorities under Gordon Brown's premiership (2007–2010) and how they relate to African affairs, while highlighting continuity and change from the Tony Blair administration (1997–2007). I then briefly analyse the extent to which the EU has influenced London's Africa policies. The fourth and fifth sections discuss Britain's policies for promoting peace and security in Africa, as well as trade, aid, and development, and briefly highlight the emerging trends in the premiership of David Cameron's Coalition government since 2010.

Britain and independent Africa: A brief history

It is impossible to summarize British relations with independent African states and peoples without descending into sweeping generalizations and caricature. Nevertheless, several broad themes are apparent in the way successive British governments organised their policies towards Africa. Despite the different context for contemporary British-Africa relations, the legacies of these themes have not altogether disappeared.

The first theme is that ever since London's retreat from empire in Africa got under way in earnest in the late 1950s, the primary concern of successive governments towards the continent has been aptly summarized by James Mayall as one of 'damage limitation'.[3] This stemmed from what Christopher Clapham described as the traditional postcolonial British mind-set that saw Africa as 'a source of trouble rather than opportunity'.[4] During the Cold War, between 1945 and 1990, therefore, Britain's Africa policy was largely preoccupied with how to turn its imperial legacies 'from liabilities into assets'.[5] This was thought to require the creation of 'a network of low key, but still special, relationships between Britain and her former colonies'.[6] And as what Mayall—after French emperor Napoleon Bonaparte—described as 'a nation of shopkeepers', it was not surprising that during this period Britain's bilateral relations with African states were often preoccupied with the protection of trade and investment.[7] This focus was also energetically pushed by the major British corporations active in Africa, including Lonrho, Unilever, ICI, British Petroleum, Marconi, and British banks such as Standard Chartered and Barclays.

A second theme was selectivity, inasmuch as Britain has never really had a 'whole of Africa' policy but has instead focused its activities on particular parts of the continent while neglecting others. At the most general level, British policy traditionally split the continent into two parts, with separate concerns and ministerial structures for dealing with North Africa and the Mahgreb, and Africa south of the Sahara. Within policymaking circles in Whitehall, Britain's Africa policy was usually taken as shorthand for policy towards sub-Saharan Africa. Within sub-Saharan Africa, London also engaged selectively, largely because its aid, trade, investment, and political interests were concentrated—at times almost exclusively—on Commonwealth Africa. Indeed, even within the Commonwealth, and with the exceptions of Nigeria and to a lesser extent Ghana, British policy has focused on Southern and East Africa, particularly South Africa, Kenya, Zimbabwe, and Uganda. The most startling example of this tendency was the almost total indifference displayed by John Major's government to the massacres in the Great Lakes region during the mid-1990s. In the case of the 1994 Rwandan genocide, for instance, the country was deemed to lie outside Britain's traditional sphere of interest. Consequently, the few signals from London to British diplomats in the region were that Rwanda was a 'country of which we knew little and cared less'.[8]

A third theme of traditional British policy towards Africa was that despite sometimes lofty rhetoric, Africa was only ever a marginal concern to Britain's policymaking elite. There were some differences in emphasis between Labour and Conservative administrations. The former, for instance, generally displayed a greater degree of support for 'liberal internationalism' and from 1964 established a separate ministry for international development, while the latter folded the development ministry back into the FCO and generally placed more emphasis on promoting Britain's 'national interests', usually defined in primarily economic terms.

Thus two broad phases of African engagement emerged during the Conservative years of government, 1979 until 1997. From 1979 until 1989, parts of the continent were seen as important in the struggle against communism, most notably South Africa. However, the general objective was to 'muddle through' without courting major crises, while actively promoting British commercial interests on the continent. With the end of the Cold War by 1990, successive Conservative governments emphasized the importance of democracy and 'good governance' in their rhetoric, but the reality was one of further disengagement from Africa.[9] Between 1989 and 1997, Britain's overall aid budget was reduced from 0.31 per cent of gross national income (GNI) to 0.26 per cent.[10] Diplomatically, British attention focused on eastern European and successor states of the Soviet Union while cutting the number and size of its diplomatic missions in Africa—five were closed in 1991 alone. Even so, London's Africa policy became almost solely the concern of the Overseas Development Administration (ODA), which encouraged a tendency within Whitehall to view Africa policy as being synonymous with the British aid programme, and for policy to be heavily influenced by the former de facto 'minister of Africa', Lynda Chalker at the head of the ODA.[11]

In 1995, Chalker had presented Britain's Africa policy as having five main objectives: the promotion of 'good governance', economic reform, and the alleviation of poverty; support for the peaceful resolution of conflicts; international cooperation over criminal activities in Africa (notably drugs, terrorism, and illegal immigration); support for the new democratic order in South Africa; and the furthering of British commercial interests.[12] In practice, economic growth, the commercial interests of British trade and investment, and bilateral relations with South Africa attracted the lion's share of official attention; conflict resolution and combating criminal activities were far less of a priority. In similar fashion, the subject of Britain-Africa relations did not stimulate any significant debate among scholars. As David Styan correctly noted in 1996, 'Africans and students of Africa will search in vain for sustained debates or literature on contemporary British policy in Africa'.[13]

With the arrival in office of Tony Blair's New Labour government in 1997, African issues gained a much higher degree of attention and were articulated in terms of promoting peace, prosperity, and democracy on the continent.[14] According to Tom Porteous, a seasoned commentator and one-time British official, four main elements stood out in Blair's approach to Africa: the idea of 'enhanced partnership' with African governments that were committed to 'good governance', conflict prevention, and poverty reduction; a big push for a massive increase in aid, debt relief, trade, and investment as the primary means of stimulating economic development; efforts to strengthen British networking and relations with nonstate actors, including celebrities, to increase the country's leverage in Africa; and efforts to protect and promote British national interests in Africa.[15] Other interests soon emerged as well, the most crucial being counterterrorism, energy security, commerce, migration, and climate change.

Britain's recent international priorities: where does Africa fit in?

Under Gordon Brown's leadership, between 2007 and 2010, the British treasury continued to devise targets to measure the impact and monetary value of the country's policies. In an attempt to promote 'joined-up' government, the 2007 Comprehensive Spending Review set thirty public service agreements for 2008–2011 across the British government as a whole rather than on a department-by-department basis. The FCO was named as having a role in the delivery of eight of these agreements and a prominent role in five of them: ensuring controlled and fair migration, reducing the risk from international terrorism, leading the global effort on climate change,[16] reducing poverty through quicker progress towards meeting the UN Millennium Development Goals (MDGs) by 2015, and reducing the impact of conflicts.

While these targets are clearly too broad to serve as a usable guide for designing specific policies, Africa was an important venue for all of these issues. In relation to migration, the continent has been the source of 'economic migrants' as well as a considerable number of people seeking asylum in Britain (see table 1). Chief among the latter have been people looking to escape from wars and repression in Somalia, Zimbabwe, the DRC, Sierra Leone, Eritrea, Sudan, and Angola.[17] On the question of armed conflicts, although the number of state-based conflicts in Africa more than halved between 1999 and 2006 and the combat death toll dropped by some 98 per cent, armed conflicts remained a huge problem, by any measure, especially in the Greater Horn and Central Africa.[18]

Table 1: Asylum applications to the UK from African applicants, 2001–2010.[19]

	2001	2002	2003	2004	2005	2006	2007	2008	2009	2010
Total Applications	20,839	29,711	20,604	15,043	10,885	10,502	8,628	10,269	11,162	6,601

Source: United Kingdom Home Office, London.

In relation to poverty alleviation, many African states remain firmly trapped on the bottom rungs of the international development league tables. The UN Development Programme's (UNDP) 2007–2008 Human Development Index, for example, suggested that Africa contained thirty-four of the world's forty most underdeveloped states, the least-developed being Sierra Leone.[20] It also became apparent that many Africans would be hit hard by the negative consequences of global climate change.[21] In relation to terrorism, it is important to remember that very few African states export terrorism. Rather, London's counterterror and anti-weapons proliferation initiatives stemmed from the fear that many of the continent's weak governments might not be able to prevent transnational terror networks from exploiting uncontrolled areas of territory. Finally, contemporary interest in Africa's energy and other natural resources—especially oil, gas, diamonds, coltan, timber, and fish—suggests that the continent had at least the potential to attract significant British business interests as part of an attempt to promote a high-growth global economy.[22] The energy sector witnessed a substantial increase in interest, with African oil attracting British business in North Africa, Angola, Equatorial Guinea, and elsewhere. In 2003, for example, British exports to Equatorial Guinea—hardly a model of 'good governance'—were worth £109 million, far greater than British exports to, say, Ethiopia.[23]

In January 2008, Gordon Brown's foreign secretary, David Miliband, set out a new strategic framework to guide the future work of the FCO for the period 2008–2011.[24] This was described as a 'smarter and leaner' framework for foreign policy than those elaborated during Blair's premiership between 1997 and 2007.[25] The framework had three elements that reflected Miliband's vision of the FCO's main roles: providing a flexible global network servicing the British government as a whole, delivering essential services to the British public and business, and shaping and delivering the government's foreign policy. The strategic framework also identified four policy priorities for the FCO: countering terrorism and weapons proliferation, reducing and preventing conflict, promoting a low-carbon, high-growth global economy, and developing effective international institutions, especially the EU and the UN. The new framework came into effect in April 2008, thereby replacing the FCO's existing ten strategic priorities, which Miliband considered to be too many.[26] In light of this framework, the FCO published a list of eight departmental strategic objectives (see Box 1).

Box 1: The FCO's strategic objectives, 2008–2011

1. Flexible global network serving the whole of the British government.

Three essential services:

2. Support the British economy.
3. Support British nationals abroad.
4. Support managed migration to Britain.

Four new policy goals:

5. Counter terrorism, weapons proliferation, and their causes.
6. Prevent and resolve conflict.
7. Promote a low carbon, high-growth, global economy.
8. Develop effective international institutions, above all the UN and the EU.

Britain, the EU, and Africa

The relationship between British and EU foreign policies is complex, inter-related, and variable depending on the issue and part of the world in question. In general, however, Brussels has arguably had a greater impact on the process of London's foreign policy making than on its substantive goals.[27] This process is commonly referred to as the 'EU-isation' of British policy. The context for it was provided by the 'Step Change' programme. Initiated by Tony Blair's government in September 1998, this was a ten-year project to develop a more proactive British approach towards the EU and thereby enhance London's influence within it. It involved government departments, the cabinet, ministers, and officials all intensifying contacts with their counterparts within the EU and its applicant states. Within the FCO, this prompted reforms in which all EU-related matters were brought into one management structure known as the EU Directorate.[28] More generally, the 'constant participation of British officials and ministers in EU-level discussion' was said to have built 'a new fabric of instinctive EU consultation at the heart of British foreign policy-making'.[29]

At the substantive level, London's strategic priorities and other foreign policy objectives have generally been consistent with those espoused by the EU as a whole. For example, the European Security Strategy of 2003, titled 'A Secure Europe in a Better World', reflected a victory for Britain's vision of the ESDP, particularly, between the document's first and final drafts, in the greater emphasis placed on the North Atlantic Treaty Organisation (NATO) and the relationship with the United States. This was hardly surprising given that the main drafter of the strategy in Javier Solana's office was Tony Blair's former foreign policy adviser, Robert Cooper.[30]

Within the EU, Britain is clearly more interested in African affairs than many others in the twenty-seven-member Union, especially those members from Central and Eastern Europe. London has tended to turn to Brussels as a source of collective legitimisation, burden-sharing, and, when the EU's support might provide extra leverage, implementation of British policies. One example of this was the Union's targeted sanctions imposed on about a hundred members of the Robert Mugabe regime in Zimbabwe in 2002. However, London has also largely ignored EU mechanisms when it was thought that these might complicate the political dynamics in question or prove unduly cumbersome. The British military operations Palliser and Barras, in support of the UN Mission in Sierra Leone (UNAMSIL) in 2000, for example, were conducted outside the CFSP framework.[31]

After Gordon Brown assumed the premiership in 2007, he confirmed his reputation for being less overtly pro-EU than Blair. He also tended to adopt a more awkward negotiating style in Brussels that created friction with the give-and-take characteristic of the EU's intense process of bargaining or compromise politics. In addition, Brown viewed Brussels in largely economic terms, and hence emphasised the political economy dimensions of the EU more than its actions in the military-security sphere. Specifically, Brown spoke pejoratively of 'trade bloc Europe' as an inward-looking and protectionist entity. Instead, he called for a more outward-looking Europe, one that would be 'flexible, reforming, open and globally-oriented'.[32]

Peace and security

Under Brown's premiership, between 2007 and 2010, peace and security issues in Africa were not a priority for London. In spite of the rhetorical hype, this had also been the case during the Blair years of 1997 to 2007: the exception was the highly unusual British operation Palliser in Sierra Leone in 2000.[33] As a result, Britain has attempted to promote peace and security primarily by funding training and assistance programmes for certain African states and regional organisations rather than through deploying large numbers of its own personnel to peace support operations on the continent. This pattern has applied to both ESDP and UN operations, in which Britain has had at best a meagre presence (see table 2). Beyond the usual concern with 'body bags' being brought home, common justifications for this stance revolve around anxieties about command, control, and competence within UN peace operations, and the claim that Britain regularly places personnel in key strategic management positions within these missions. The main reason, however, is that London's strategic priorities have been outside Africa: specifically in the Balkans, Iraq, and Afghanistan.

Since the mid-1990s and the wars of Yugoslav secession, Britain has deployed a considerable number of troops to the Balkans, particularly in Bosnia and Kosovo.[34] By 2009, however, Gordon Brown retained only a small presence, of less than 200 troops, in the Balkans. The next set of large-scale operations came in Afghanistan after Britain contributed to the US-led mission to topple the Taliban regime in 2001, and in Iraq, following the American-led invasion to topple Saddam Hussein's regime in 2003. In Iraq, the number of British troops peaked at 46,000 for the initial invasion in March 2003, but dropped to about 18,000 after the end of major com-

Table 2: British uniformed personnel in UN peacekeeping operations in Africa, 2001–2010 (31 December annually).[35]

Mission	2001	2002	2003	2004	2005	2006	2007	2008	2009	2010
MINURCAT	–	–	–	–	–	–	0	0	0	0
UNAMID	–	–	–	–	–	–	1	6	0	0
UNMIS	–	–	–	–	3	3	5	3	3	5
UNOCI	–	–	–	0	0	0	0	0	0	0
UNMIL	–	–	3	3	2	3	3	3	0	0
ONUB	–	–	–	0	0	–	–	–	–	–
UNAMSIL	22	21	32	21	–	–	–	–	–	–
MONUC	5	6	5	5	6	6	6	5	5	4
UNMEE	0	3	3	0	0	0	0	–	–	–
MINURSO	0	0	0	0	0	0	0	0	0	0
British Total	27	30	43	29	11	12	15	17	8	9

Source: UN Department of Peacekeeping Operations, New York.

Figure 17.1: Troop levels in major British military operations Abroad, 2000–2010.[36]

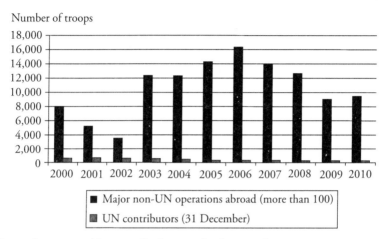

Number of troops

■ Major non-UN operations abroad (more than 100)
▨ UN contributors (31 December)

Source: International Institute for Strategic Studies, London.

bat operations several months later. Figure 17.1 illustrates the number of British troops on operational deployments abroad, excluding the invasion of Iraq. Post-invasion stabilization and counterinsurgency operations in Iraq and Afghanistan were responsible for the vast majority of these figures. Whereas British forces had officially withdrawn from Iraq by June 2009, they are not scheduled to withdraw from Afghanistan until 2014.

The operations in Afghanistan and Iraq placed a serious strain on Britain's armed forces. In such circumstances, missions in Africa were unlikely to receive serious consideration. Nevertheless, it is important to remember that some senior British military figures believed that although overstretched, Britain's armed forces could cope with additional operations. For example, in light of the massacres in Sudan's Darfur region in June 2004, which had resulted in an estimated 300,000 deaths by 2010, General Sir Mike Jackson, the chief of General Staff of the British army, told the BBC that 'if need be, we will be able to go to Sudan. I suspect we could put a brigade [about 5,000 troops] together very quickly indeed'.[37] In fact, London did not send combat troops to Darfur. Indeed, apart from its operations in Sierra Leone, arguably the only significant military mission in sub-Saharan Africa in recent years was Operation Phillis—the evacuation mission that took British nationals and other evacuees out of Côte d'Ivoire

353

and into Ghana in November 2004. The military intervention in Libya from March until October 2011 primarily involved the use of British aviation and maritime assets rather than ground troops. Although both Blair and Brown sought to bolster the EU's ability to conduct foreign and security policies, they stressed that this should not be done at the cost of jeopardising NATO's primary position. Despite the obvious progress in the security realm, the EU remains suited to conducting only relatively small-scale crisis management operations (the higher end of the spectrum being represented by the EU force in Bosnia, and the lower end by the type of rule of law and security sector reform operations seen in the DRC and elsewhere). David Miliband acknowledged these limitations when he noted:

It's embarrassing when European nations—with almost 2 million men and women under arms—are only able, at a stretch, to deploy around 100,000 at any one time. EU countries have around 1,200 transport helicopters, yet only about 35 are deployed in Afghanistan. And EU member states haven't provided any helicopters in Darfur despite the desperate need there.[38]

The limited scale of the EU's crisis management capabilities was also reflected by the way in which the idea of operationalising the Union's Helsinki Headline Goal (a 60,000-strong rapid reaction force), which was paramount in public debates between 2000 and 2003, was jettisoned thereafter. In its place, the debate has focused on operationalising the significantly smaller EU battle groups, consisting of about 1,500 troops capable of conducting the sort of temporary and geographically focused missions exemplified by the 2003 Operation Artémis in the DRC (see chapter 14 in this volume).[39]

For London, therefore, Brussels is viewed as a relatively limited option for crisis management. Unlike France, which has been the primary driving force behind ESDP operations in Africa (see chapter 16 in this volume), Britain has deployed only token numbers of its personnel to these missions.[40] At least in relation to the EU's policing and rule of law missions, London's lack of a gendarmerie and the existence of over forty local police forces mean that it is not particularly well-suited to participate in these operations. This does not, however, hold for operations such as Artémis (2003) or the EU Force (EUFOR) missions in the DRC (2006) and Chad and the Central African Republic (2008) (see chapters 14 and 15 in this volume). In 2008, London was reported to have 'pushed back hard against MONUC's calls (in 2003) for an EU force to buttress its forces in the east [of the DRC], despite considerable evidence that MONUC will continue to struggle unless it has a very robust modern military backbone'.[41] Specifically, it was suggested that while the FCO saw some merit in deploying British troops as part of an EU bridging force in eastern Congo, the British Ministry of Defence (MOD) was much less keen on such a mission, given the prospect of additional commitments in Afghanistan.[42]

Despite the low level of strategic priority accorded to Africa, a number of changes to Britain's relevant institutional architecture have taken place. This reflected the Labour government's emphasis on the idea of a 'joined-up' foreign policy. One innovative development was the establishment of the Africa Conflict Prevention Pool in 2001 (which was quickly followed by a Global Conflict Prevention Pool). While these represented welcome attempts at bureaucratic coordination between the FCO, the MOD, and the Department for International Development (DFID), the Africa Conflict Pool budget was so small that, in its first few years, about half of it was swallowed up by the Sierra Leone operations (mostly in training the country's army and police).[43] In April 2008 the Africa and Global Conflict Prevention Pools were merged into a single prevention pool. This was perhaps another example of Africa losing some of the special status it had gained under Blair's government. Other innovations in British policy included the Africa Conflict and Humanitarian Unit, established in 2003; the Joint FCO/DFID/MOD Post-Conflict Reconstruction Unit, established in 2004;[44] and the appointment of a handful of regional conflict advisers. Operating out of Tshwane-Pretoria (Southern Africa), Addis Ababa (Eastern Africa), Nairobi (Central Africa), and Abuja (West Africa), the advisers monitored their special regions, providing London with up-to-date analysis of what was happening in states where there was no official British presence, and helping regional teams to enhance their conflict prevention activities. While the advisers encountered significant difficulties in transcending the different bureaucratic cultures within DFID, the FCO, and the MOD, they reflected the need to adopt a regional rather than a parochially national approach to conflict management. Moreover, the British government decided to deploy similar regional advisers to other parts of the world in light of the relative success of the African model.[45]

In May 2007, after Blair announced his resignation, there was speculation by 'some MOD insiders' that under Gordon Brown's leadership Britain might 'become more militarily involved in humanitarian and peace support operations in Africa'.[46] This did not happen, for several reasons. First,

Brown was often perceived as not being particularly in favour of the armed forces: his critics suggested that he never gave the military enough budget support either as chancellor of the Exchequer or as prime minister. There were also significant debates in Westminster and Whitehall about 'over-stretch' and the fraying military covenant. These encouraged the opposition Liberal Democrats to make calls for a new defence review, which the Brown government ignored. In March 2008 the government published its first national security strategy. In relation to Africa, this document highlighted the usual issues of armed conflict, 'extremism' (especially in North Africa), disease, and drug trafficking (especially in West Africa). It also identified 'parts of Africa' that were experiencing conflicts and 'extremism' as one of its priority areas (the other priority areas being Pakistan and Afghanistan, the Middle East, and Eastern Europe).[47]

Second, although Brown indicated his support for the 'responsibility to protect'[48] idea—that the UN's member states have a duty to protect populations at risk if their governments are unable or unwilling to do so—and spoke about what he called 'hard-headed intervention', he more often prioritised the much vaguer notion of reforming 'our international rules and institutions'.[49] Clearly, Brown did not renounce the use of military force as an instrument of British policy, but he emphasised the nonmilitary dimensions of engagement as well as the importance of long-term peacebuilding efforts to avoid further conflicts. Interestingly, in February 2008, David Miliband floated the idea of 'security guarantees', whereby external powers might offer a security guarantee 'to a new but fragile government, conditional upon them abiding by democratic rules'. The hope was that this 'could create a strong incentive for them to abide by the democratic process'.[50] Even if any such British guarantee were to be taken seriously, it would raise awkward questions about the merits of reverting to the type of clientelistic relationships that characterised the early postcolonial Cold War era, and for which France, in particular, has endured significant criticism (see chapter 16 in this volume).[51]

A third factor was that some of the most high-profile ministers who championed Africa's cause within Blair's administration (including Blair himself, as well as Clare Short and Peter Hain) resigned or moved to positions unrelated to African affairs. In the case of Blair, he focused relatively little attention on following through on the recommendations developed by his 2005 Commission for Africa (discussed later), choosing instead to devote his political energies largely to the Middle East peace process and certain consulting and bilateral relationships. In June 2007, Brown appointed Mark Malloch-Brown, the former deputy UN secretary-general and former head of the UN Development Programme, as his minister for Africa, Asia, and the UN. Malloch-Brown attended cabinet meetings, but it was notable that neither Africa nor Asia was given its own dedicated minister, and Malloch-Brown resigned in June 2009 during Brown's premiership. In sum, there is little evidence to suggest that London will divert from its previous policies of attempting to keep the peace by funding and training Africans to do the job themselves. It is also worth mentioning that in three years as prime minister, Brown visited Africa only once, and that was for the Commonwealth heads of government meeting in the Ugandan capital of Kampala in November 2007 (this contrasts starkly with Nicolas Sarkozy's four separate visits to nine African countries in a two-year period).

Trade, aid, and development

By comparison with issues of peace and security, Britain devoted considerable attention to issues of trade, aid, and development in Africa. While British-Africa trade patterns have remained roughly stable, under Labour, DFID's prominent place in the machinery of London's Africa policies meant that the development agenda often took centre stage.[52] (There are signs that this is changing under the Conservative-led Coalition government, as discussed later.) After supporting large increases in Britain's aid budget under Blair, the debate subsequently revolved around the pros and cons of direct budget support to 'enhanced partnership' countries. While Britain's former colonies continued to account for most of its resources, the country welcomed some newcomers to the fold. Symbolically, the biggest British push on these issues came in 2005 with Blair's Commission for Africa and the British presidency of the Group of Eight (G8) in the same year. (See chapter 11 in this volume.) In the years that followed, however, the commission failed to stimulate the changes that the British government had hoped it would.

Since 1997 DFID's development agenda has played a central role in Britain's Africa policies. Indeed, during the Blair era, the department was often dubbed 'the Ministry for Sub-Saharan Africa'.[53] This was made possible by the confluence of several factors: an influential minister in the form of Clare Short; a large number of new civil servants, many of them activists whose forte was development and not diplomacy; and, in contrast to the

FCO, a budget that consistently increased, courtesy of the prime minister and the chancellor. In both relative and absolute terms, DFID's bilateral and regional programmes in sub-Saharan Africa increased dramatically, from £300 million in 1997–1998 to £1.25 billion in 2006–2007.[54] Nevertheless, even with these large budget increases, British expenditure on overseas development assistance is not set to reach the UN's recommended target of 0.7 per cent of GNI until 2013. By 2005, nearly 90 per cent of these funds were going to sixteen priority countries, only four of which were not former British colonies (the DRC, Rwanda, Ethiopia, and Mozambique).[55] By 2007 DFID was apparently so flush with cash that it was 'struggling to find good ways of spending all the extra money it had been given by the Treasury'.[56] The main African recipients of DFID's bilateral programmes in 2006–2007 are set out in table 3. In light of the global financial crisis of 2008–2009, it is also worth noting that all three of Britain's largest political parties—Labour, the Conservatives, and the Liberal Democrats—pledged to 'ring-fence' development aid from the impending cuts that the Coalition government announced after winning power in May 2010. Once in office, however, the Coalition began to bring more of its overseas aid budget under FCO supervision.

Table 3: DFID bilateral expenditure in top-ten African states, 2006–2007.[57]

Bilateral Aid		Net Bilateral Overseas Development Assistance		Bilateral Aid Excluding Humanitarian Assistance	
Tanzania	£112m	Nigeria	£1,731m	Tanzania	£111m
Sudan	£110m	Tanzania	£119m	Ethiopia	£88m
Ethiopia	£90m	Sudan	£117m	Nigeria	£81m
Nigeria	£82m	Uganda	£117m	Ghana	£68m
Uganda	£78m	Malawi	£93m	Zambia	£61m
DRC	£75m	Cameroon	£92m	Malawi	£61m
Ghana	£69m	Ghana	£91m	Uganda	£60m
Kenya	£65m	Ethiopia	£89m	Mozambique	£56m
Malawi	£63m	DRC	£76m	Kenya	£52m
Zambia	£61m	Kenya	£59m	Sierra Leone	£38m

Source: Department for International Development, London.

As DFID's role strengthened, so Britain's Africa policies came increasingly to resemble its development policies.[58] This had several effects. First, it led to London aligning itself more with the Nordic European countries within the EU and the UN (see chapter 19 in this volume).[59] Second, because DFID sometimes lacked a sophisticated appraisal of the political dimensions of, and context for, its activities in Africa, it often worked within a relatively narrow view of the continent. As a result, as British analyst and former government official Tom Porteous has argued, DFID's 'resources and staff were deployed only in those countries where it had a major aid programme, and it therefore had little institutional understanding of what was going on in the rest of Africa'.[60] This gave rise to the conditions that had sparked the creation of the regional conflict advisers.

By Blair's second term, after 2001, DFID was certainly seeking to build its own capacity for historical and political analysis, for example through the 'Drivers of Change' project.[61] Yet despite all the official talk of devoting greater attention to African affairs since 1997, London actually reduced the number of its diplomatic missions on the continent. This arguably made it more difficult to build a comprehensive analysis of events in Africa (see tables 4 and 5). These cuts occurred in a broader context in which Britain's global network of government posts increased from 242 in 1997 to 261 in 2007.[62] Although Africa did not suffer as many cuts as European posts (officially this has been in recognition that much European business is carried out in Brussels), the big increases occurred in South and East Asia and the Middle East, and not in Africa. By early 2011, eight other states had more embassies across sub-Saharan Africa than Britain (the US, Russia, China, France, South Africa, Nigeria, Germany, Brazil, and Japan).[63] In spite of these figures, David Miliband continued to insist in January 2008 that, 'by no stretch of the imagination is it possible to argue that the UK's [United Kingdom] influence in Africa is lower today than it was 10 years ago. In fact, it is massively enhanced'.[64] Given that Kenya's post-election crisis in December 2007 is said to have prompted anguished reflection in London about why DFID failed to anticipate the eruption, the problem of analysis clearly runs deeper than merely ensuring the presence of British missions across Africa.[65]

The third consequence of defining development as the primary objective of British policy in Africa was that the primary problem was quickly identified as 'bad governance'—'a polite way of saying that African governments were themselves at the heart of the problem'.[66] In essence, London sought to tackle this problem by offering favourable treatment for African governments that it regarded as being committed to 'good governance', conflict prevention, and poverty reduction. This idea came to be known as 'enhanced partnership'. In such cases, London stopped providing its development assistance through programmes managed by development agencies and nongovernmental organisations (NGOs), and instead provided African governments with direct budget support. By 2005 DFID was channelling direct budget support to seventeen African countries and focusing more attention on 'larger and longer term programmes'.[67] As the department acknowledged, this meant that 'understanding how the UK's money is used therefore means understanding the way in which the recipient government allocates and uses all its funds'.[68]

Table 4: British missions in Africa closed since 1997–1998.[69]

April to March	Country	Post Name	Status
2003–2004	Mali	Bamako	Embassy
2004–2005	Cameroon	Douala	Consulate
2005–2006	Lesotho	Maseru	High Commission
2005–2006	Madagascar	Antananarivo	Embassy
2005–2006	Swaziland	Mbabane	High Commission
2005–2006	Côte d'Ivoire	Abidjan	Embassy

Table 5: British missions in Africa opened since 1997–1998.[70]

April to March	Country	Post Name	Status
2000–2001	Guinea	Conakry	Consulate
2000–2001	Mali	Bamako*	Consulate
2000–2001	Libya	Tripoli	Embassy
2007–2008	DRC	Goma	'unEmbassy'#

Notes: * Post opened and closed during this period.
Comprising a single staff member working from a hotel room.

This, in turn, raised some important questions: not least, what should happen if the recipient state turned out not to be committed to 'good governance' and poverty reduction, and what Britain was to do about the many African states that were not committed to these goals but also needed development assistance.[71] One prominent example of the first scenario came in Ethiopia after violence erupted in the aftermath of the disputed 2005 elections. Here, London initially suspended a planned increase of £20 million in budget support assistance to Addis Ababa. After a sustained period of intense pressure, primarily from NGOs, in January 2006, Britain announced that it was stopping direct budget support to Ethiopia because of the 'breach of trust' following the disputed elections.[72] However, the Meles Zenawi government in Addis Ababa continued to remain one of the largest recipients of British aid (see table 3). In light of these dilemmas, by 2007 DFID had explicitly recognised that its search to promote development meant that it could not remain detached from the continent's power struggles. As its 2007 policy paper on government, development, and democratic politics suggested:

The focus is now about how power is used, and on whose behalf. Governance work has moved away from asking 'What is wrong and how can we fix it?' to asking 'What are the incentives to which political elites respond and how can they be changed?' Asking these sorts of questions makes our work both more relevant but also more challenging. It takes us into the heart of politics and how political systems work, and whether or not they benefit poor people.[73]

It is not clear how the British government has resolved this challenge in either theory or practice. The pinnacle of British efforts to devise a coordinated approach to the issues of trade, aid, and development as well as conflict prevention and management came in 2005 with Tony Blair's Commission for Africa, which called for international donor countries—especially the G8—to provide a massive increase in aid, debt relief, trade, and investment to Africa as the primary means of stimulating economic development in return for promises of good behaviour from African governments.[74] As the commission put it, what was required was 'a big push on many fronts at once'.[75] In particular, the commission argued that three changes were needed immediately: 'continued improvements in governance in Africa, a substantial increase in aid from the international community, and a significant change in the way donors do business in Africa'.[76]

While this approach generated a good dose of media attention, some increased aid, and more debt relief, the Commission for Africa's substantive results in relation to trade and investment have been disappointing.[77] In four respects, the commission has exemplified some of the problems and limitations of Britain's approach to Africa. First of all, the way the commission's report was put together was problematic. Not only did the commission sideline the FCO and rely far too heavily on econometric studies, but it was also, as Christopher Clapham observed, 'far too dominated by the British government to have any credibility as an independent assessment of Africa's needs'.[78] In hindsight, it was also rather unfortunate that the commission included Ethiopian prime minister Meles Zenawi—touted by Blair as one of Africa's 'new breed of leaders'—at the same time as his troops were shooting civilians on the streets of Addis Ababa.

Second, Britain's leaders were unable to ensure at Gleneagles, Scotland, in 2005 that the other G8 members lived up to their part of the bargain, especially when the photo opportunities were over and the difficult job of implementation began. This was the commission's third problem: a lack of sustained follow-up on the many recommendations and commitments made in its report. This should not have been a problem for the British given that Gordon Brown was one of the commissioners and since one of his top economic advisers, Nicholas Stern, had been the commission's director of policy and research. While British aid flows did increase following the commission's report, there was much less success with regard to improving Africa's terms of trade with the West. This was at least partly because Britain's EU presidency in July 2005 failed to secure substantial reform of the EU's $50 billion-yearly Common Agricultural Policy (CAP), which has had a significantly negative impact on Africa's agricultural sector (see chapter 12 in this volume).

The fourth problem was that the Commission for Africa failed to spell out a strategy for how to tackle the central problem of bad governance. Nowhere did the commission's report go into detail about how badly governed states might be reformed. Britain's prevarications with Robert Mugabe's regime in Zimbabwe suggested that there were no obvious answers, at least in the short term. Nor did the commission address the central contradiction at the heart of its approach: how to ensure accountability without undermining 'African ownership' of the reform process.[79] Nor did the body question whether massive external assistance was really the only route to development. The case of Somaliland, for example, suggests that external assistance is not the crucial component in building effective systems of governance.[80] The net result was that, for all its good intentions, Blair's Commission for Africa represented a misguided push for 'big aid' rather than 'smart aid'.[81]

As Tom Cargill has observed, the arrival of a Conservative-led coalition government in 2010 has changed the emphasis of Britain's Africa policies in four principal ways.[82] First, the government has reverted to giving the FCO the leading role on African issues over DFID, and channelled an increasing portion of British overseas development aid through the Foreign Office. Second, the government's discourse on Africa has given more prominence to the idea of securing the country's national interests on the continent, primarily through boosting British trade as part of the Coalition's 'Prosperity Agenda'. There is little evidence of a concerted push on this front, however, given that UK Trade and Investment (UKTI) has offices in only nine sub-Saharan African countries compared to seventeen in South America and the Caribbean. This is despite the fact that British exports to the top twenty sub-Saharan African states are nearly 30 per cent larger than to the top twenty South American and Caribbean importers. The third trend since 2010 stems from the lack of a widespread party-political hinterland of interest in Africa within the Conservative-led Coalition, as was evident in sections of the Labour Party—the partial exception being Zimbabwe. This has produced a general reluctance to engage deeply with African issues and may generate some hostility from British advocacy groups who work in this area, and gained a significant hearing in the corridors of power during the Labour years. Fourth, in the era of financial austerity under the Coalition government, burden-sharing—particularly with EU partners—is thought to offer the surest route to maintaining influence in Africa. To some extent, this was borne out during 2011, when despite the focus on traditional national interests and commercial diplomacy, David Cameron's Coalition—in tandem with his French counterparts—was at the forefront of the political push to undertake a humanitarian military intervention in Libya authorized by UN Security Council Resolution 1973 in March 2011.

Concluding reflections

Labour governments under both Tony Blair and Gordon Brown (1997–2010) devoted greater attention to African affairs than their Conservative predecessors. However, despite this attention, Africa was clearly not a strategic priority for Britain. The exception to this rule was in the area of development assistance, where London devoted about half of its rapidly increasing aid budget to the continent from 1997 onward. Here the problems encountered by British policymakers had less to do with limited resources and more to do with the way in which they conceptualised the central policy problems and attempted to implement the solutions. Although there is some evidence that London is thinking more seriously about how to reform Africa's neopatrimonial regimes, the government has clearly not overcome this challenge in practice.

In relation to peace and security issues, however, the Labour governments and the Conservative-led Coalition have sought to continue Britain's long-standing strategy of helping Africans to help themselves by funding various training and assistance programmes, rather than deploying their own personnel to peace operations on the continent. The exception here is Britain's participation in the UN-authorized invasion of Libya in 2011. While British membership of the EU has significantly influenced the policymaking process within Whitehall, it has had far less impact in setting London's strategic priorities or its more specific objectives in Africa. While British objectives on the continent have been broadly consistent with those of Brussels, neither Blair nor Brown regarded EU frameworks as being the only, or most important, means for implementing their Africa policies. Operating alone, however, there were clear limits to the amount of leverage the British government could generate on the continent. This was highlighted most starkly in the cases of Zimbabwe and Sudan's Darfur region, where London could not achieve its key objectives. On the other hand, there were occasions when British power significantly affected outcomes on the ground. This was most evident in the country's role in stabilising the situation in Sierra Leone after the near collapse of a UN peacekeeping mission in May 2000. In this sense, London has sometimes regarded the EU as a useful source of legitimisation and leverage, but in general has avoided making a major contribution to its military operations in Africa.

18

PORTUGAL, THE EU, AND AFRICA

Alex Vines

Introduction

The decolonisation of Portuguese-speaking Africa was the outcome of two interrelated historical processes: protracted anticolonial wars in three of Portugal's five African colonies (Angola, Guinea-Bissau, and Mozambique), and the overthrow of the country's Salazar-Caetano dictatorship and the transition to democratic rule. The years 1974–1975 were traumatic for Portugal, as among the former European powers in Africa, Lisbon had been the first to arrive and the last to leave the continent.[1]

Shorn of its African colonies in the chaotic period following the coup d'état of junior military officers in 1974, Portugal was forced to focus on obtaining European Union membership and pursuing a successful European destiny. It was under Prime Minister Mário Soares's Socialist government that Lisbon made its formal application for European Community (EC) membership in March 1977. As Soares argued at the time: 'Portugal according to the understanding of the Government is a European country and can only benefit from European integration, including for improving relations with its ex-colonies'.[2] With Guinea-Bissau already signed up to the Lomé Convention of 1975 and other African Lusophone states expected to follow, Mário Soares emphasised the advantages of joining Lomé (not to be excluded from privileged links with ex-colonies) to overcome domestic resistance to EC accession.[3] (On the Lomé Conventions, see chapter 2 in this volume.)

Portugal eventually joined the European Union in 1986 and its former African colonies had all joined the Lomé Convention by this stage.[4] The years since 1975 have seen rapid material and social transformation in Portugal, from a backward and authoritarian past associated with the colonial period, to its contemporary social and economic achievements. The country had adapted to its postcolonial reality by defining a new relationship between itself and the world. However, there was also continuity in its foreign policy, as Lisbon's continued independence and survival were linked to an international role of overcoming the limitations imposed by the country's size and economic development.

Since 2011, Portugal has been experiencing its greatest challenge since decolonising from Africa in 1974–1975. The country faces a period of heightened political instability following an economic crisis that required a financial bailout by the EU and the International Monetary Fund (IMF), which foresees severe budget cuts and tough structural reforms over the next few years. President Anibal Cavaco Silva was reelected for a second term in January 2011, and a new majority government of the Social Democratic Party (PSD) and the Popular Party (PP) was elected in June 2011. The Eurozone crisis has increased Portugal's efforts to deepen its political and economic ties with its former colonies, particularly Angola. Angolan investments into Portugal continued to grow, taking stakes in Portuguese banks, supermarkets, and even a cable-television provider. Such investments rose to €116 million in 2009, and by December 2010 Angolan investments comprised 3.8 per cent of Portugal's stock market, amounting to a significant €2.18 billion. No other European power has become so economically dependent on a single former African colony.

Portugal also sought a new role for itself in relation to Africa. Intermediaries like this Iberian country were viewed by the two superpowers—the United States and the Soviet Union—at the end of the Cold War as useful instruments in the final disengagement from conflicts in countries such as Angola and Mozambique, by masking the responsibility that fell to Washington or Moscow in resolving hostilities that they had actively encouraged and fuelled.

This chapter assesses Portugal's relations with its former African colonies in Angola, Cape Verde, Guinea-Bissau, Mozambique, as well as the Communidade dos Países de Língua Portuguesa (CPLP)—the Community of Portuguese-Speaking Countries. I further examine EU-Africa ties, Portugal's aid and trade policies on the continent, and the presence of Africans in Portugal.

Angola: an internal issue

When Cavaco Silva first became prime minister of Portugal in 1985, he resolved to end friction between Angola and his country.[5] These tensions stemmed from the controversial Alvor Agreement of January 1975, which had established the terms and date of Angolan independence for 11 November 1975, and the events that followed. Portugal was the last country to recognise an independent Angola (except for Israel and the US), and this led to severe tensions between Luanda and Lisbon. Diplomatic relations were severed between Angola and Portugal between February and July 1976. The resentment was targeted at the governing Socialist Party and Prime Minister Soares, whom the ruling Movimento Popular de Libertação de Angola (MPLA) blamed for encouraging Washington's nonrecognition of the MPLA government and support of Jonas Savimbi's União Nacional para a Independência Total de Angola (UNITA). UNITA was also granted permission to use Lisbon as a second base for its diplomatic activities, causing further ruptures between both governments.[6]

The relationship between Luanda and Lisbon began to improve through then-president General António Eanes, which led to a meeting in Bissau between General Eanes and Angola's first president, Agostinho Neto, in an attempt to develop a cordial postcolonial relationship. Relations improved further from 1979 to 1982, with the arrival of two right-wing governments in power in Lisbon. President Eanes's visit to Angola in 1981 sought to encourage the MPLA not to deal with Portugal through the Portuguese Communist Party. However, the return of Socialist governments in Lisbon from 1983 to 1985 soured relations once more.[7]

Cavaco Silva (prime minister between 1985 and 1995, and president since 2006) encountered many challenges to his policy of establishing friendlier relations with the five former African colonies—Angola, Mozambique, Cape Verde, São Tomé and Príncipe, and Guinea-Bissau (collectively known as the Países Africanos de Língua Oficial Portuguesa, PALOP)—especially over Angola, where rapprochement with the MPLA regime was strongly opposed by powerful sectors of Portuguese society. These challenges had their roots in the process of decolonisation. The fact that Portuguese interests had not been safeguarded during the decolonisation process was especially unpopular with the *retornados:* Portuguese citizens who had fled to Portugal from the colonies. They sought compensation or return of properties expropriated by nationalist governments in the newly independent Lusophone African states.

During the late 1980s and early 1990s, the *retornados* allied with sympathisers in Portuguese military intelligence to support counter-revolutionary rebel groups in Mozambique (the Resistência Nacional Moçambicana, RENAMO) and Angola (UNITA).[8] Despite official policy, the activities of these groups, combined with the presence of sympathisers and official representatives of the two main rebel groups in Portugal, tended to complicate relations with governments in Lisbon and their former colonies. A further complication was that some among the 300,000-strong Portuguese community in South Africa were active in aiding and abetting the rebels, with the encouragement of the apartheid-era South African Defence Force (SADF).[9]

Cavaco Silva's rapprochement strategy between 1985 and 1990 was much criticised at the time for being devoid of morality and based on naked economic self-interest. Yet Silva's *Realpolitik* of good state-to-state relations allowed him to maximise the economic advantages of these good relations, while also adapting Portugal to Africa's post-revolutionary and postcolonial reality.

Portuguese businesspeople acted as political brokers and messengers between Cavaco Silva and Angolan president José Eduardo dos Santos in the late 1980s, which resulted in a visit by the latter to Lisbon in 1987. This trip marked the start of a new relationship between Portugal and Angola, with Luanda targeting Lisbon as the core of its European policy, while Portugal moved closer to Africa once more. This development also reflected the MPLA's judgement that continued Soviet economic and military aid could no longer be assumed. Other former African colonies had also realigned themselves geostrategically in the 1980s, including Mozambique after the rejection of its application to join the Soviet-led Council for Economic Cooperation (Comecon) in 1983.

The Angolans viewed Portugal as an instrument for forging new links with the European Community, and also as a vehicle for seeking rapprochement with the Americans, since Portugal was a member of the North Atlantic Treaty Organisation (NATO). This approach was also aimed at eroding support for UNITA. In March 1988, a few months after dos Santos's visit to Lisbon, the Portuguese formulated plans to seek a resolution of the conflicts in Angola and Mozambique.[10] These plans were crafted in the office of then-secretary of state for foreign affairs and cooperation José Manuel Barroso, who later became president of the EU Commission in July 2004.[11]

Despite a strong UNITA lobby in Lisbon led by João Soares (son of ex-president Mário Soares), who followed his father in supporting the pro-UNITA group and later became mayor of Lisbon, Cavaco Silva improved his standing with the MPLA. Following the failed Gbadolite talks in Zaire (now the Democratic Republic of the Congo) in June 1989 between the MPLA and UNITA, it became clear to Lisbon that negotiations between the Angolan government and the UNITA rebel group were possible. After Gbadolite, Portugal engaged in 'shuttle diplomacy' aimed at seeking African support for a possible Portuguese-led peace initiative. This included direct contact with UNITA by Cavaco Silva. Rebel leader Jonas Savimbi was also allowed to visit Portugal, in January 1990.

Following a number of other initiatives, secret talks between UNITA and the MPLA began in April 1990 in a Catholic convent near the Portuguese city of Evora. José Manuel Barroso was the official mediator. Four more inconclusive rounds of talks took place, until international pressure forced both sides to reach an agreement using 'deadline diplomacy' in April 1991. President José Eduardo dos Santos and Jonas Savimbi signed the Estoril Accords in March 1991, and all the church bells rang out across Lisbon in celebration of the peace agreement. Portugal, along with Russia and the US, became officially part of the observing 'Troika' for the implementation of what became known as the Bicesse Accords.

Lisbon's involvement in the 1991 Bicesse Accords in Angola provided a first, and significant, diplomatic breakthrough, signalling that former Lusophone colonies were prepared to accept the 'mother country' as an intermediary to end postcolonial civil conflicts. For the Portuguese, the conclusion of a peace agreement and achieving stability in Angola were important goals of its foreign policy. The collapse of Bicesse and return to war in Angola in October 1992, following elections, was therefore a major setback.[12]

Angola remained a deeply divisive issue in Portugal through the 1994–1999 Lusaka peace process, although the UNITA lobby in Lisbon began to weaken following the rebel movement's isolation under a raft of UN sanctions that followed Savimbi's return to war. It took the terrorist attacks of 11 September 2001 in New York and Washington to push Portuguese officials to move against UNITA bank accounts and assets in Lisbon, although they had been obliged to do so under UN sanctions for several years. However, as part of the Troika on Angola (with Russia and the US), Portugal had supported sanctions at the UN and, in April 2002, officially witnessed the signing of the Luena Memorandum, which finally ended the Angolan civil war following the killing of Savimbi by Angolan government forces. Efforts to reach a common EU position on human rights issues in Angola were frustrated in the 1990s, however, by the consistent Portuguese decision to block any reference to Luanda's shortcomings.

Only after the death of Jonas Savimbi in February 2002 could the Portuguese government finally draw up a coherent policy paper on Angola, based on broader consultation with other political forces. The end of the Angolan civil war had at long last buried this neocolonial hangover, and cleared the way for a more coherent policy towards Africa based on Lisbon's long-standing objectives.[13] In November 2002, Portugal and Angola finally established a joint commission to find ways to pay off Angola's debt to Portugal. Following a visit to Angola by then-prime minister Durão Barroso in October 2003, a repayment schedule was reached in August 2004 for an immediate reimbursement by Angola of $258 million followed by repayment over twenty-five years of the remaining $698 million, with an interest rate of 1 per cent. Three visits to Angola by then-prime minister José Socrates, in 2006, 2008, and 2010, further signalled the rapid improvement of bilateral relations.

In April 2009 the Angolan president, dos Santos—who had visited Lisbon in 1987—made his first official state visit to Portugal (the first such visit by an Angolan leader in thirty years), hoping to boost bilateral trade. Portugal's ambassador to Angola, Francisco Telles, commented prior to President Cavaco Silva's state visit to Angola in July 2010: 'If we look back to the past, we have never had so good relations as they are now. The visit ... by the Angolan head of state, José Eduardo dos Santos to Lisbon, in April 2009, can be regarded also as an historical moment in the relations of our countries'.[14]

Using Africa to have a stronger voice in Europe

Following the decolonisation process in 1975, Europe had become the key focus of Portuguese foreign policy. However, from the mid-1980s, Lisbon developed a new synthesis between the old and the new in order to maximise the advantages of its membership of the European Community. Painfully aware of its peripheral position in Europe, Portugal has attempted to follow a strategy that allows it to pursue its own parochial national interests in Brussels. European issues and the relationship with EU partners, especially Spain, have remained central to Portuguese policy, as have relations with Algeria and Morocco due to the politics of proximity and migration. (See chapters 7 and 20 in this volume.) Seeking consensus for European policies such as the EU Common Security and Defence Policy (CSDP), which has been pursued since 1999, in order to 'ensure consistency, between European positions and what we ourselves support, particularly in Africa'.[15] (See chapter 13 in this volume.) In support of the Common Foreign and Security Policy, Portugal's army joined the EU's peacekeeping mission in Chad and the Central African Republic in February 2008 by sending thirty soldiers and a C-130 military plane to Chad for a two-month mission. (See chapter 15 in this volume.)

Portugal sees itself as an intermediary between Africa and the EU. The decision by the European Council in November 1989 to open the Europe Centre for Global Interdependence and Solidarity (better known as the North/South Centre) in Lisbon was further recognition of this new role. With the expansion of the European Union to Eastern Europe in the 1990s, Portugal sought to retain its continental voice by positioning itself as an intermediary with African governments. The desire to have an overseas presence of some kind has been an enduring foreign policy ambition for Lisbon. As a small, weak, and peripheral European state, Portugal has long perceived that these disadvantages can be overcome through international links, of which those in Africa are a key component. Hosting of the headquarters of the CPLP in Lisbon, and Portuguese efforts to help draw up a common EU strategy towards Africa between 2005 and 2007, are a key part of this approach.

The CPLP. During the Portuguese presidential election of January 2006, the five left-leaning candidates—including Communists and Socialists—refrained from making any reference to African issues. Cavaco Silva, however, eventually once more made these issues central to his message. After being elected, Silva ended his first presidential address by recalling that Portugal's greatest and most durable achievement could be the fact that Portuguese is a language spoken by the CPLP, a cultural community already comprising more than 220 million people, 80 per cent of them in Brazil.

The CPLP comprises Portugal and its five former African colonies—Angola, Cape Verde, Guinea-Bissau, Mozambique, and São Tomé and

Príncipe—as well as Brazil and East Timor. The CPLP was not formed until July 1996, as Lisbon's desire to create a Lusophone bloc had previously been frustrated by suspicion from its former African colonies, as well as rivalry with Brasilia over influence in the Portuguese-speaking world.

The CPLP has a permanent secretariat located in Lisbon and is headed by an executive secretary (Bissau Guinean national Domingos Simões Pereira, in December 2011) who is elected for renewable two-year terms. Its objectives are to promote the Portuguese language and cooperation between CPLP members in international diplomacy, economic affairs, culture, justice, and science. The organisation also aims to increase the influence of the group in multilateral organisations and to promote stronger ties between Europe and Africa as well as between the EU and Mercosur (Mercado Común del Sur), the South American trade bloc comprising Brazil, Argentina, Uruguay, and Paraguay. All of the CPLP's decisions are reached by consensus. Mozambique's decision to join the English-speaking Commonwealth in 1995 had an immediate effect in galvanising Portugal's efforts to promote the creation of the CPLP a year later. The creation of the CPLP has underlined the importance that Lisbon places on its relationship with its former colonies, and has also helped to manage its rivalries, such as those with Brazil over strategy toward the situation in Guinea-Bissau after instability erupted in the country in June 1998. It is also interesting to note that, in 2011, Portugal was supporting Equatorial Guinea's efforts to become a full member of the CPLP.

The EU-Africa summit. In Luanda in 1996, the Portuguese foreign minister at the time, Jaime Gama, made a speech calling for an EU-Africa summit to help make Brussels's policy towards Africa more coherent. Four years later, in April 2000, an EU-Africa summit of heads of state was held in the Egyptian capital of Cairo—during the Portuguese presidency of the EU— as a demonstration that Lisbon was prepared to use its influence in European institutions to promote African interests. A second EU-Africa summit in Lisbon, planned for 2003, was called off, as some European governments—particularly Britain—opposed the presence of Zimbabwe's President Robert Mugabe on human rights grounds (see chapter 17 in this volume), while the African Union insisted that all of its fifty-three members should be represented at the meeting. A couple of months later in Benin, all Lusophone African countries signed the Cotonou Agreement, between the EU and seventy-nine African, Caribbean, and Pacific (ACP) countries, in June 2000 (see chapter 2 in this volume). Portugal has also actively used its position within the EU to try to leverage the European Development Fund (EDF) financing for these countries.

Although Zimbabwe continued to be a live issue, a third EU-Africa summit was held in Lisbon under the Portuguese presidency in December 2007. On this occasion, Portugal was helped by the presence of José Manuel Barroso as EU Commission president, as well as a network of Portuguese in influential positions in Brussels. This injected a Portuguese perspective into the decisionmaking processes of the EU Commission. According to Manuel Lobo Antunes, Portugal's secretary of state for European affairs at the time, this summit 'underscores the importance of the commitment that Portugal has to African issues. We will do everything in our power for Europe as a whole to engage with Africa and, of course, for Africa to engage in a structured dialogue with Europe'.[16]

The outcome of the EU-Africa summit in Lisbon in 2007 was a strategy, an action plan, and a commitment to hold a follow-up summit in three years (held in the Libyan capital of Tripoli in November 2010). During the Portuguese EU presidency, a series of meetings on Africa were held in Lisbon, but they seemed to have been mostly for mood-setting. Portugal's secretary of state for foreign affairs and cooperation, João Cravinho, embarked on regular 'shuttle diplomacy' to Africa in the run-up to the summit.[17] He also sought tangible outcomes from the meeting, including some sort of monitoring and verification effort of the action plan. The launch of the Europe-Africa Research Network (EARN) in December 2007 was part of this Portuguese effort, and the mandate was subcontracted through the Lisbon-based Instituto de Estudos Estratégicos e Internacionais.[18]

Portuguese trade with Africa

Manuel Lobo Antunes, the Portuguese secretary of state for European affairs at the time, underlined the commercial logic of Lisbon's efforts to achieve a more coherent EU policy in Africa:

In Portugal, our businesses turn to Africa rather than China. There is an obligation for us to do everything we can to ensure that these long-established links that are so close and so human between Europe and Africa are preserved and developed. It is natural for Africa to diversify its relations and engage new partners, but beyond that, Africa must continue to consider Europe as an essential partner.... Perhaps it is because of a degree of indifference that Africa is looking for other partners, or that others are focusing on Africa. There has been a sort of vacuum, which can only be filled with a firmer commitment from Europe. It is our intention to draw our partners' attention to that, as this oversight must not continue.[19]

The Portuguese business community has also encouraged this strategy, viewing its former colonies as offering new opportunities, but also fearing increasing global competition. As a weak colonial power, Portugal historically lacked the means fully to exploit its African territories. Instead, these territories were generally seen as a means to acquire investment and resources to promote Portugal's own development. In the post-independence period, former African colonies have also been used by Lisbon as a means to achieve broader foreign policy ambitions. Portugal has sought to establish privileged economic relations with its five former African colonies, and to establish a role for itself as a European intermediary on African issues.

Contemporary Portuguese policy has also operated through a network of informal instruments of foreign policy—including cultural, political, and commercial ties with former colonies—to overcome Lisbon's own lack of financial resources. However, the strength of these ties, and the influence of powerful domestic lobbies, are responsible for the disproportionate prominence of Portugal's Africa policy in its broader foreign policy. The influence of such lobbies has been a force for both good and ill, depending on their congruence or otherwise with official objectives. Luso-African countries have attracted, unprompted, an increasing number of private Portuguese citizens in recent years. The 300,000-strong community of Portuguese in South Africa is well established, but up to 100,000 Portuguese are estimated to reside in Angola, while numbers are much smaller elsewhere, such as 500 recorded in Guinea-Bissau.[20]

In material terms at least, Africa should matter less and less to Portugal. Trade with Lisbon's five former African colonies is now dwarfed by trade with the EU and the rest of Europe. Import trade with former colonies is even more meagre, accounting for 0.18 per cent of total imports. However, in 2010, Portugal was importing significant amounts of oil and gas from Angola, Algeria, Libya, Nigeria, and Equatorial Guinea.

Table 1 shows the value and percentage of PALOP-Portuguese trade in 1999, while figure 18.1 below shows Portuguese exports to PALOP countries between 2000 and 2009. These figures demonstrate the increasing importance of Angola for Portugal as an export market. Angola is by far the most important export market for Portugal in Africa, dwarfing its other African interests with the exception of South Africa and Morocco.

Table 1: Portuguese trade with PALOP, 1999.

	Exports		Imports	
	$ millions	Percentage of Total	$ millions	Percentage of Total
Angola	294	1.26	11	0.03
Cape Verde	148	0.64	10	0.03
Mozambique	72	0.31	42	0.11
São Tomé and Príncipe	20	0.09	4	0.01
Guinea-Bissau	18	0.08	0	0.00

Source: International Monetary Fund, Direction of Trade Statistics.

Angola was the sixth largest export market for Portugal in 2007, accounting for 4.5 per cent of total exports and growing in 2008 by 35 per cent to become Portugal's fourth largest export market, accounting for 17 per cent of imports of almost $16 billion in 2009. For Angola, Portuguese imports in 2007 represented 18.2 per cent of total imports, followed by the United

Figure 18.1: Portuguese total exports of goods to PALOP, 2000–2009 (in € millions),

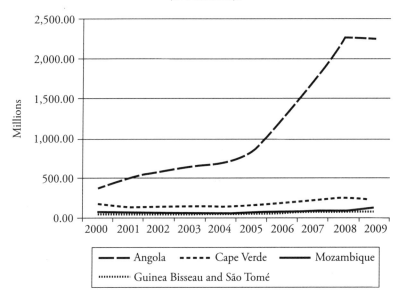

Source: Instituto Nacional de Estatística, Portugal.

375

States (10.1 per cent), South Korea (9.6 per cent), and China (9.5 per cent). These figures peaked in 2009 because of the global economic downturn of 2008–2009, but have not declined, helped by high levels of Angolan consumption. For example, Angola became the biggest overseas market for Portuguese winemakers in 2009, accounting for €57 million out of €246 million worth of exports.[21]

As demand falters in Portugal's main export markets, led by Spain, Germany, and France, local Portuguese companies are seeking to expand outside traditional European markets, particularly into Angola and Brazil. Some 10,000 Portuguese companies are estimated to be doing business with Lusophone Africa. Helped by the weaker euro since 2009, these companies are looking beyond the EU. Common language, direct transport links, shared legal frameworks, and long-standing business ties have also assisted. By 2010, TAP-Air Portugal was making twenty direct weekly flights between Lisbon and Luanda and fourteen weekly flights to Cape Verde. As discussed in more detail later in this chapter, by 2009 Portugal had become the main supplier of imports into Cape Verde and São Tomé and Príncipe (43 percent).

Leading Portuguese companies including Sonae (manufacturing and services), Pestana (tourism), Millennium BCP (banking), Mota Engil and Teixara Duarte (construction), and Galp (oil) are rapidly expanding their operations in Africa. These groups invested more than $1 billion into Angola between 2007 and 2010. For example, Unicer, Portugal's largest drinks group, decided to build a €100 million brewery in Luanda.

However, by 2010, Portuguese construction firms were encountering payment problems from the Angolan government amounting to about $3 billion. In April 2010, Luanda pledged to pay the most important companies, such as Mota Engil and Teixeira Duarte, in order that construction could continue. These repayments will be partly financed by Angola's €500 million credit line from Portugal, agreed in April 2010. The Angolan press has also reported that Portugal will extend a further €1.1 billion in loans to help the Angolan government to pay off its domestic arrears. According to Luanda, $850 million was repaid to seventy-eight construction companies, many of them Portuguese, between April and August 2010.[22]

Foreign banks were allowed back into the Angolan market in 1992. Since then, Portuguese banks have been particularly dominant, controlling 40 per cent of assets in 2005, and using historical connections in Angola to limit competition from other foreign banks, in particular from South Africa.

Banco Espírito Santo, Banco Português de Investimento (BPI), and Banco Millennium BCP together have 170-odd branches in Angola, and made $440 million profit in 2009. In return, all three banks had to ensure that at least 49 per cent of their operations were owned by Angolans.[23] Angolans also acquired stakes in Portuguese banks in Portugal, such as the private Banco Fomento de Angola (BFA), which is owned by Portugal's Banco BPI. Angola's Banco BIC plans to buy Portugal's Banco Português de Negócios (BPN) for $58 million: about a fifth of the original asking price of $260 million. The IMF made the sale of BPN a condition for its bailout of Portugal in 2011. The newly elected government in Lisbon immediately turned to its former colonies—particularly Angola—to encourage further investments in the 'mother country'. In July 2011, Portuguese foreign minister Paulo Portas began his first official visit abroad by visiting Angola, before going on to Mozambique and Brazil. In Angola, he pushed for 'excellent and mutually beneficial relations', noting that Lisbon's ties with Luanda were 'a truly special case' within Portugal's foreign policy priorities.

Only two other African countries feature significantly as export markets for Portugal: Morocco and South Africa. South Africa's main exports to Portugal are coal, steel products, frozen fish, fruit juices, fruit, vegetables, wood, and granite. (See table two below for volume of trade). Its main imports from Portugal are cork, machinery, textile fibres, cables, and electronic equipment.

Table 2: Portuguese exports to South Africa and Morocco, May 2008.
(in € millions)

South Africa	4,478.049
Morocco	27,280.966
Total	*31,759.015*

Source: Instituto Nacional de Estatística, Portugal.

Portuguese aid policy

Unlike former colonial powers France and Britain, Portugal has not had the economic means to pursue a more traditional 'neocolonial' policy, based on aid, investment, and political and military intervention, owing to its weak economic base. In 2011 Portugal maintained eighteen embassies in Africa: one in each former colony, one in each North African country, and others in key hubs like Addis Ababa, Nairobi, Abuja, Kinshasa, and

Tshwane/Pretoria (the other three embassies are located in Dakar, Windhoek, and Harare).

Responsibility for Portugal's foreign policy, including development cooperation, lies with the Ministry of Foreign Affairs. In 2010 the minister of foreign affairs was assisted by three state secretaries: one responsible for European affairs, another for foreign affairs and cooperation, and a third for Portuguese communities (Portuguese citizens living abroad). The state secretary for foreign affairs and cooperation determines the strategic vision and oversees the Portuguese Institute for Development Support (IPAD). Parliamentary oversight over IPAD, however, is weak, according to the Paris-based Organisation for Economic Cooperation and Development (OECD).[24]

IPAD was created in 2003 as the central planning, supervisory, and coordinating body for Portuguese aid.[25] In November 2005 the Portuguese Council of Ministers approved a new strategy for development cooperation titled 'A Strategic Vision for Portuguese Cooperation'. The strategy committed Portugal to achieving the United Nations Millennium Development Goals (MDGs), which aim to halve poverty by 2015 as one of five key principles, while maintaining the geographical focus on the PALOP countries in Africa and East Timor in Southeast Asia.[26]

Table 3: Net official Portuguese development assistance to PALOP, 2001–2005. (in $ millions)

	2001	2002	2003	2004	2005
Angola	11.9	14.4	19.5	15.5	20.9
Cape Verde	23.0	10.9	40.2	30.8	45.4
Mozambique	34.3	23.9	19.1	24.3	22.6
São Tomé and Príncipe	14.0	13.0	11.1	12.8	11.5
Guinea-Bissau	13.9	6.7	8.3	9.9	12.2

Source: OECD, *Geographical Distribution of Financial Flows to Aid Recipients*.

Debt relief and technical cooperation have dominated Portuguese cooperation with Africa, with technical cooperation representing about 32 per cent of total gross disbursements on average between 2000 and 2004 (such as scholarships and imputed student costs). An estimated 67 per cent of Portugal's gross bilateral aid in 2004 was accounted for by debt rescheduling to Angola. Project and programme aid has remained small, while aid to, and through, nongovernmental organisations has been negligible since the

Figure 18.2: Portuguese aid by region (in $ millions).

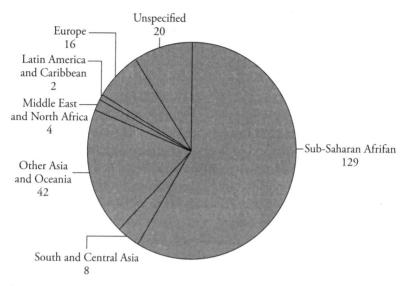

Source: OECD-DAC.

1990s. Although Portugal has associated itself with the EU's collective undertaking to attain a target of 0.33 per cent of gross national income by 2006, 0.51 per cent by 2010, and 0.7 per cent by 2015, Lisbon is falling short of these targets as the Portuguese economy lags behind the average growth in the eurozone. Portuguese aid disbursement is predominately focused on Africa, and goes mostly to PALOP countries, as figure 18.2 and table 3 illustrate.

Like France's Africa policy (see chapters 2 and 16 in this volume), Portugal's relations in Africa have an emotive and cultural component that is intimately connected to national conceptions of identity and Portugal's role in the world. The Portuguese language and the depth of Lisbon's cultural and historical ties with its former colonies, as well as similar institutional arrangements, continue to condition Portugal's geographic allocation of aid. The Portuguese also maintain Camões Institutes to promote Portuguese culture in all five PALOP countries in Africa.

A 2006 study of the role of external actors in Angola and Mozambique found that, in Angola, the US, China, and Brazil had the most perceived influence. Portugal figured seventh and eighth respectively in Angola and

Mozambique, but came second after the US in both countries when Angolans were asked which country they would most wish to strengthen relations with. The EU hardly featured in these responses.[27] This poll shows the continued pull of Portugal for Angolans, especially those who own property and seek to travel to the rest of Europe through Portugal.

Africans in Portugal

The reverse side of the overseas Portuguese presence in Africa is the large African community in Portugal itself, and the attraction that the former metropolitan power continues to retain in these countries in the areas of culture, education, tourism, and exile politics. In 1974–1975, some 700,000 Portuguese fled their former colonies and returned to Portugal, many retaining links with, and an interest in, Africa. By 2010, in addition, 150,000–200,000 Africans were estimated to be living in Portugal.

Africans living in Portugal have also increasingly found a voice, and their impact is visible in sports and music, as well as in the amount of PALOP news, debate, and discussion available in the country. Statistics of foreigners with residence permits from 2000 to 2005 show how residents from Cape Verde, Angola, and Guinea-Bissau dominate the exile African community. A similar pattern was found in Portugal's prison population in 2009: out of 11,535 recorded inmates, 727 were from Cape Verde, 229 from Guinea-Bissau, and 192 from Angola. A Portuguese customs survey estimated that there were 16,557 Angolans resident in Portugal in 2009: the fifth largest foreign population in the country. Informal figures are higher, and the Portuguese media have estimated that 60,000 Angolans reside in Portugal. These figures are difficult to assess, as dual nationality is common and because, until recently, fraudulent access to Portuguese passports has been relatively easy.

Portugal's relations with Cape Verde, Guinea-Bissau, and Mozambique

Cape Verde. Over 56,000 Cape Verdeans on residence permits resided in Portugal in 2005, as shown in table 4. Portugal's relationship with Cape Verde has traditionally been stronger than that with its other former African colonies, owing to the country's more advanced economic development and longer historical association. Cape Verdeans had full Portuguese citizenship before independence in July 1975, in contrast to the assimilado system of the other former colonies, in which this was granted as a privilege to educated Africans. To some extent, independence in Cape Verde was regarded as accidental, in that, under different circumstances, associate status with Portugal as an overseas territory could have been easily negotiated. Relations with Lisbon were relatively stable during the immediate post-independence period, when Cape Verde's policy was generally pragmatic. Bilateral links improved from the mid-1980s following economic and political liberalisation, and have since deepened further.

Table 4: Foreigners with residence permits in Portugal, 2000–2005.

Nationality	2000	2001	2002	2003	2004	2005
Cape Verde	47,093	49,845	52,223	53,434	54,806	56,433
Brazil	22,202	23,422	24,762	26,508	28,732	31,546
Angola	20,146	22,751	24,782	25,616	26,520	27,697
Guinea Bissau	15,941	17,791	19,227	20,041	20,583	21,258
UK	14,096	14,953	15,903	16,860	17,977	18,966
Spain	12,229	13,645	14 599	15,281	15,874	16,383
Germany	10,385	11,167	11,878	12,539	13,098	13,571
France	7,193	7,817	8,377	8,841	9,249	9,602
São Tomé and Príncipe	5,437	6,304	6,968	7,279	7,829	8,274
US	8,022	8,023	8,000	7,998	7,992	8,003

Source: Serviço de Estrangeiros e Fronteiras, Lisbon.

The defeat of the former ruling African Party for the Independence of Cape Verde (PAICV) in 1991 brought to power the Movement for Democracy (MpD), a party dominated by civil society and professionals including former exiles from Portugal. Competent economic management and extensive investment in social capital have since then underpinned a broad rise in living standards, which are now among the highest in Africa. Portuguese investment in Cape Verde has increased sharply through privatisation and increased opportunities in tourism. Lisbon has also moved to promote economic stability and integration: in July 1998, the Cape Verdean currency, the escudo, was fixed to the Portuguese escudo and later to the euro, backed by a $50 million Portuguese reserve fund.[28] Policymakers in Lisbon regard Cape Verde as the most successful of its former colonies.

Trade links between Cape Verde and Portugal have strengthened since 1990, and accounted for 23 per cent of exports and 41 per cent of imports in 2006. Spain, however, has become the main market for Cape Verde's exports, owing to the proximity of the country to the Spanish-controlled Canary Islands, followed by Portugal (62 per cent of exports of $36.7 million went to Spain and 34 per cent to Portugal in 2009). Portuguese tourism is also growing, with the country accounting for 12 per cent of 2.2 million tourist arrivals in Cape Verde in 2009, and Portugal remains the island's main foreign supplier, with 48 per cent of a total of $746.3 million in goods in 2008. Cape Verde has traditionally courted aid and investment from a variety of countries. The ruling MpD has significantly strengthened economic and political ties with Lisbon, as well as with the rest of the EU. After years of lobbying, in November 2007 the EU agreed, in principle, to grant Cape Verde special partnership status, under which the island and the EU would cooperate in key areas.

In Cape Verde, intermunicipal cooperation is also an important part of Portugal's development efforts. Building on links created through the Cape Verdean community living in Portugal, many of the country's seventeen municipalities have direct relationships with Portuguese cities covering such fields as education, culture, local institution-building, conservation of heritage sites, and social welfare. This approach could provide a quick means of financing local projects by Cape Verdean municipalities, which could contact their partner cities in Portugal directly.[29]

Guinea-Bissau. Also in West Africa, Portugal remains Guinea-Bissau's key development partner despite the country's small size, lack of resource wealth, and stagnant economic performance. Historical ties ensured that Portugal was the dominant foreign influence in the country and the leading source of imported goods (24.5 per cent in 2008). Portugal is one of only two Western countries to maintain an embassy in Bissau (the other being France), while Portuguese companies are active in banking and shipping. There is a small resident Portuguese population of about 500 in Guinea-Bissau and an expatriate Bissau Guinean community of about 25,000 living in Portugal, driven out by the instability that followed the onset of civil war in June 1998. The war also underlined the marginalisation of Guinea-Bissau. The country remained an active arena for Portuguese diplomacy as a mediator: the civil war ended in May 1999, after Portugal agreed to provide asylum for former dictator João Bernardo Vieira, but Lisbon also suspended its disbursement of bilateral aid to the country in 1999–2000 owing to the conflict.

In April 2008 an EU security sector reform mission was deployed to Guinea-Bissau. This small mission sought to help kick-start the government's stalled strategy to restructure and modernise its volatile security sector. But following a mutiny within the Bissau Guinean military in April 2010, Brussels argued that it could not continue this assistance and pulled out of the country in September 2010.[30] In March 2008, Lisbon had provided the government in Bissau with $3.1 million in budget support. However, Bissau announced that it was taking back control of national telecoms operator Guiné Telecom (GT) and its mobile service, Guinetel, because Portugal Telecom managers had fled the country during the 1998–1999 civil war and failed to return, leaving debts and deteriorating infrastructure. Portugal Telecom, in turn, refused to return to the country until the Bissau government had settled $50 million of debts to GT.

Mozambique. The unfinished business of decolonisation is also drawing to a close in regard to Portuguese business interests in countries such as Mozambique. Its hydroelectric mega-dam, Cahora Bassa, was completed in 1974, just as the colonial war was reaching its peak. The dam was primarily exporting energy to apartheid South Africa. During most of the Mozambican civil war of 1975–1992, such exports ceased due to the destruction of power lines by RENAMO rebels. Exports resumed in 1997 after a second line was built connecting the dam to Zimbabwe. In 2006 the exports of the electricity company operating the dam, Hidroelectrica de Cahora Bassa (HCB), were worth $184 million.[31]

Following years of negotiations, in November 2007 the Mozambican government finally assumed majority ownership of HCB. Maputo increased its shareholding to 85 per cent, with the former owner—the Portuguese government—holding the balance. Mozambique also agreed to pay Portugal $950 million, much of it from a loan arranged by a consortium including Banco Portugûes de Investimento. This loan was repayable over fifteen years. Portugal's remaining share in HCB may fall again, to 5 per cent, if the Mozambican government decides to increase its stake further.[32]

President Armando Guebuza of Mozambique has since 2007 adopted a more antagonistic approach towards Lisbon than that of his predecessor, Joaquim Chissano. He has used past hostilities as a means of exerting leverage, yet Portugal remained one of the top five exporters to Mozambique in 2009.

Concluding reflections

The trauma of forced decolonisation for Portugal in 1974 is gradually receding. Since the country joined the European Community in 1986, Portuguese policy has focused on Europe. But as a small member of the EU, Lisbon has also sought to 'punch above its weight' on issues of interest to it. PALOP countries in Africa remain emotionally important for Lisbon, while Angola is becoming a strategic export market for Portuguese goods.

Portugal's official objectives appear, on the surface, to be moving towards convergence with those of other Western powers with fewer economic or historical interests in PALOP countries. Lisbon's goals in Africa are primarily to promote 'good governance', democratic development, economic growth, and poverty reduction, as well as bilateral cooperation and trade. The constraints to achieving these objectives are similar to those affecting the aid programmes of most other Western countries. (See, for example, chapter 19 in this volume.) To protect its interests and strengthen its voice, Portugal has used the EU-Africa summits, the European Development Fund, and the creation of the CPLP to maintain its influence in PALOP states, as well as to encourage a common EU strategy towards Africa as an overarching framework within which to place its relationship with PALOP. Lisbon's relationship with Angola is truly strategic for its economy, and this distinguishes Portugal from other European states and their former African colonies.

It is also important to separate policy towards Portugal's five former African colonies from ties with the rest of sub-Saharan Africa, where influence and interest are marginal, with the exception of South Africa, which hosts a 300,000-strong Portuguese community. Policy towards Algeria and Morocco is also increasingly driven by the politics of proximity, migration, and energy security. Portugal's relations with Africa thus reflect elements of both continuity and change.

19

THE NORDICS, THE EU, AND AFRICA

Anne Hammerstad

Introduction

The Nordic countries (Denmark, Norway, Sweden, Finland, and Iceland) are often seen by outsiders as a united group. This is due to the similarities in their socioeconomic models and foreign policy approaches. The common model has acquired its own name, the 'Nordic Model', while the foreign policy approaches consist of a range of 'middle-power' attributes and ambitions. The aim of this chapter is twofold: first, to investigate what this social-democratic middle-power approach consists of and how it has affected the Nordic countries' policies towards, and relationships with, the African continent; and second, to ask whether the many strong ties and affinities between the Nordic countries have resulted in a common and coordinated Nordic approach to Africa.

I begin the chapter by discussing what the concepts of 'middle power' and 'Nordic Model' entail, and justify the choice of focusing mostly on three of the five Nordic countries: Sweden, Denmark, and Norway. Next I adopt a historical approach to describe how a common stance against apartheid, white minority rule, and colonialism in Southern Africa brought the Africa policies of these three countries closely together. Turning to contemporary Nordic-Africa relations, I then outline and compare the three countries' newly (and individually) launched Africa strategies, and conclude that, although there are numerous instances of informal consultation and commonalities of interest, there is in 2012 not much concrete and institutional Nordic cooperation on African issues.

The myth and realities of Nordic unity

The Nordic region in northern Europe, consisting of Sweden, Denmark, Norway, Finland, and Iceland, is often presented as a paragon for the rest of the international community. The Nordic countries are among the richest nations in the world. They are at the same time among the world's most equal societies, where wealth and opportunity are spread widely among their populations. These countries continually rank at the top of the United Nations Development Programme's (UNDP) Human Development Index. In the 2010 index, Norway ranked first, Sweden ninth, Finland sixteenth, Iceland seventeenth, and Denmark nineteenth.[1] While the situation changed dramatically for Iceland after its banking system collapsed in 2008, the other Nordic countries seem to have weathered the global financial crisis of 2008–2009 better than most rich countries.

The Nordic countries are also among the most peaceful countries in the world, both in terms of communal cohesion and harmony within their borders, and in their relationships with other states and the international community. Sharing a long common history (some of which entailed colonial ties between Denmark and Sweden on the one hand, and their weaker neighbours on the other), the Nordic region is closely integrated: culturally, linguistically (especially in the case of the three Scandinavian countries of Denmark, Norway, and Sweden), economically, and politically. The Nordic governments introduced a passport union as early as 1954, decades before the European Union signed its own Schengen Agreement in 1985.[2]

At the same time, Nordic unity should not be overstated. During the Second World War of 1939–1945, Sweden was neutral; Finland fought on the side of Germany against the Soviet Union; Norway and Denmark were occupied by Germany (having tried to remain neutral); while Iceland was under Allied occupation. After the war, Denmark, Norway, and Iceland joined the United States-led North Atlantic Treaty Organisation (NATO), while Sweden and Finland remained neutral. When the collapse of the Soviet Union in 1991 removed the Cold War's icy constraints on Swedish and, particularly, Finnish foreign policy options, the two countries quickly joined Denmark as members of the EU in 1995. Norway and Iceland, not spurred by the same urge to reorient westwards, declined membership of the EU and opted instead for a thick web of political and economic ties with Brussels, including membership in the Schengen Agreement.

Despite such differences, the Nordic countries are almost routinely viewed as a united group by the outside world. It is commonplace to talk about a 'Nordic model' of social democracy characterised by a combination of capitalism, welfare, and social inclusion.[3] Some would also argue that there is a particular Nordic approach to foreign policy—perhaps not so strong as to be described as a 'model', but significant nevertheless. The traits usually deemed to characterise this foreign policy approach are: an activist but consensus-seeking multilateralism; a strong ethical dimension reflecting the urge to spread the ideals of the 'Nordic model' of equality, redistribution, and peaceful resolution of conflicts to the rest of the world; support for the United Nations and its agencies; and generous aid and assistance to the developing world.

There is also a presumed lack of geostrategic calculations in the aid policies of Nordic countries. Camelia Minoiu and Sanjay Reddy have argued that Nordic aid is mostly driven by developmental aims, and not by considerations of national interest.[4] Scott Gates and Anke Hoeffler have similarly suggested that 'Nordic aid allocation seems remarkably free from self-interest and, indeed, more orientated towards their stated objectives of poverty alleviation, the promotion of democracy and human rights. Norway and Sweden serve as leaders in these regards'.[5] (See chapter 5 in this volume, on EU aid policies towards Africa.) Finally, the Nordic countries' standing in international society ranks above what a proponent of the realist school in international relations would expect from studying the size of their small populations, middle-sized economies, and unthreatening armed forces. All in all, then, the Nordic region is a bastion of middle-power attributes. As described by Jack Spence, the Nordic countries are

economically well-developed and democratic states in political structure and process, the governments of which aspire to a role in international politics. Such states seek to use their standing as good citizens to influence outcomes in areas such as the protection and assertion of human rights; peacekeeping; mediation …; the promotion of good governance in the Third World; relief of debt; and support for African development programmes such as the New Partnership for Africa's Development (NEPAD).[6]

A further characteristic of middle powers is that they limit their foreign policy ambitions to certain niches within which they can play a particularly powerful role. In the case of the Nordic countries, Spence's categories are a fairly accurate description of the middle-power agendas of the Nordics: humanitarian and development assistance, 'good governance', human rights advocacy, and conflict resolution. However, the author misses a more recent but central dimension of Nordic middle-power politics: environmentalism and concerns over climate change. The geographical focus for this middle-power agenda has been the developing world, and in particular sub-Saharan Africa.

The Scandinavian core of Nordic Africa relations

This chapter principally focuses on the three Scandinavian countries—Sweden, Denmark, and Norway—rather than on the Nordic region as a whole. The four key reasons for this approach are simple. First, covering the relations of all five countries with Africa is too big a task for this short chapter. Since Sweden, Denmark, and Norway all launched new Africa strategies between 2007 and 2010, it is natural to focus on them. Second, the choice of two Nordic EU members (Denmark and Sweden) and one nonmember (Norway) also allows discussion of how EU membership affects Nordic cooperation on Africa policies.

Third, the three Scandinavian countries have a long history of cooperating on, and with, Africa. They also have strong reputations in Southern Africa due to their sustained contributions to the subregion's anti-apartheid and liberation struggles, an engagement that started in the 1960s and lasted until the last bastions of white minority rule fell with Namibia's independence in 1990 and South Africa held its first democratic election in 1994. The level and nature of official and unofficial aid and support from Nordic governments to Angolan, Mozambican, South African, and Zimbabwean liberation movements have been thoroughly documented.[7] If there is such a thing as a Nordic approach to Africa, it has been particularly pronounced within Scandinavia.

Fourth, the Scandinavian countries have been particularly active in Africa. Sweden and Norway are almost always listed (along with Canada) as typical middle powers that have, through their activist and generous assistance policies, become influential players in North-South relations. Denmark has a slightly lower profile, but is also a strong international player in Africa. Finland, however, is more of an emerging middle power, whose foreign policy has been released in recent decades from its delicate

Cold War balancing act in the shadow of its Soviet neighbour. Its level of engagement with Africa, although growing, is lower than that of the three Scandinavian countries. Iceland is too small, and in 2010 was too economically troubled, to be a fully fledged middle power. It had no ambassadorial-level representation left in sub-Saharan Africa after it closed its embassy in South Africa in 2009. The country's capacity to participate in Nordic initiatives and meetings on Africa has also been reduced. In contrast, Norway has expanded its diplomatic representation and in 2010 had fifteen embassies in sub-Saharan Africa,[8] while Sweden had thirteen[9] and Denmark eleven.[10] Finland, catching up, had eight.[11]

Historical ties: the struggle against apartheid and colonialism

Are the Nordic countries sufficiently similar in their outlook and priorities towards Africa to claim the existence of an identifiable *Nordic* approach to Africa? A brief examination of the history of the relations of Denmark, Sweden, and Norway with Africa during the Cold War suggests that a relatively cohesive and recognisably Nordic approach did exist in this period. This section sets out the basis for this cohesion, while the following section discusses whether the present period is characterised by a similar unity of purpose and policy.

Starting in the early 1960s, a joint Nordic approach took shape against colonialism, apartheid, and white minority rule in Southern Africa.[12] Sweden took an early lead in these efforts and in 1969 became the 'first—and for several years the only—industrialised Western country to extend direct official assistance to the Southern African liberation movements'.[13] In stark contrast to British and American policies, Stockholm supplied 40 per cent of all its official development assistance in Southern Africa directly to the subregion's liberation movements. The movements benefiting from this aid were the African National Congress (ANC), the South West Africa People's Organisation (SWAPO), the Zimbabwe African National Union (ZANU), the Zimbabwe African People's Union (ZAPU), the Frente de Libertação de Moçambique (FRELIMO), and the Movimento Popular de Libertação de Angola (MPLA).[14] In addition, Sweden provided large amounts of development assistance to anti-apartheid nongovernmental organisations (NGOs) and movements within Namibia and South Africa in the 1980s.[15]

Norway soon followed Sweden's example, spurred on by pressure from its own influential nongovernmental sector. Tore Linné Eriksen argues that 'although the support given [by Norway] to the liberation movements in Namibia and South Africa in the main belong to the period after 1975, there is no other Western country—apart from Sweden—which had such close relations to the struggle for liberation in Southern Africa'.[16] This economic support was offered both indirectly (through humanitarian aid to apartheid victims and refugees) and, gradually from 1973 onwards, directly to the liberation movements.[17] In the 1980s, Norwegian consuls-general in Cape Town even had their own substantial 'emergency funds', which were distributed clandestinely to pro-democracy groups in South Africa without too many financial questions being asked by Oslo.[18]

Denmark never contributed official aid directly to armed liberation movements, but provided humanitarian aid to victims and refugees through the United Nations and NGOs, allowing Danish aid money to be distributed indirectly through the country's civil society groups to liberation movements in Southern Africa. Denmark was the first Western country to introduce full political and economic sanctions against South Africa, in 1986.[19]

It is easy to forget, two decades after the end of the Cold War, that the Nordic governments' engagement in the struggle against white minority rule in Southern Africa was quite remarkable. Southern Africa was one of the regions of the world where the Cold War was at its hottest. In this climate, the Nordic countries went against the Western grain and decided that the liberation struggles were a matter of fighting colonialism, racism, and human rights abuses, and not an issue of 'communism versus the free world'. This principled stand made the Nordic group unique among Western governments. These countries talked to, collaborated with, and financially supported armed liberation movements condemned by the United States and Britain as 'Soviet-backed'. In the case of NATO members, Norway and Denmark, this collaboration even extended to liberation movements engaged in armed struggle against their NATO ally, Portugal.[20] While anti-apartheid movements became more and more vociferous in many Western countries, it was only in the Nordic region that this public sentiment gained government recognition and support from an early stage.

This support still resonates among Africa's political elite, particularly in Southern Africa. For example, on her arrival in Oslo, South Africa's ambassador to Norway, Beryl Rose Sisulu (who took up her post in January 2009), made the pertinent point—which was well received by the Norwegian media—that she and her siblings had been supported by Norwegian money while her father, Walter Sisulu, had been incarcerated on Robben Island.[21]

Although its impact on contemporary Nordic-Africa relations should not be overstated, the Nordic stance against white minority rule had a twofold effect. First, it strengthened Nordic diplomatic, political, and economic cooperation on Africa, confirming the Nordic region's sense of shared values and ideals. Second, it built enduring ties of solidarity between elites in the Nordic and Southern African regions. But do these ties within the Nordic region, and between the three countries and Africa, remain as strong today, nearly two decades after the end of apartheid?

Current Scandinavian approaches to Africa

Between 2007 and 2008, Sweden, Norway, and Denmark all published major white papers setting out their Africa strategies. Although there are many similarities in aims, and some concrete forms of cooperation, among these documents, there is somewhat less convergence and coordination between the Nordic countries than history would lead us to expect. One reason for this development is a change in foreign policy outlook in Stockholm, Oslo, and Copenhagen, with a stronger focus on national interests and a more strategic approach to aid policy.

Sweden: partnerships, holistic approaches, and national interest. In 2009, Sweden spent about 4.6 billion Swedish kronen (SEK) on development aid to Africa.[22] Stockholm announced its new Africa policy in a government communication to parliament titled 'Sweden and Africa: A Policy to Address Common Challenges and Opportunities' in March 2008. On a close reading of this policy paper, three concepts stand out: 'equal partnership', 'holistic approach', and 'national interests'. The emphasis on partnerships involves two steps. First, Sweden places its policy firmly within the EU's approach to Africa. The Africa policy paper tends to talk about 'Sweden's and the EU's policies' in the same breath,[23] in order to underline the harmony between the two. The second step is that of forging a strong strategic partnership between the EU and Africa, one in which African and European countries are equal partners and where African countries assume ownership of, and provide more active contributions to, issues of their own development, peace, and security.

Turning to the concept of a 'holistic' or integrated approach, the Swedish 2008 policy paper spells out how key issues are related to each other in a complex and globalised world. The press release in March 2008[24] that announced Stockholm's new Africa policy made a point of providing quotations from three different ministers, from the Ministries of International Development Cooperation, Trade, and Foreign Affairs. Each minister approached the question of Africa's sustainable development from the particular perspective of his or her own ministry. Both the press release and the policy paper emphasise that aid alone, although important, will do little to foster sustainable development in Africa, and that poverty alleviation, economic growth, climate change, human rights, and peace and security on the continent are all intertwined and must be addressed in a coherent and integrated manner. In addition, these African issues are also inextricably linked to Stockholm's foreign policy:

Sweden's development is closely interwoven with that of the rest of the world. Thus development, security, stability, democracy and human rights in Africa are also matters of concern for Sweden. Distance is of little significance when it comes to climate change, environmental threats, epidemics, international terrorism and war.[25]

This quotation brings us to another important concept in the Swedish policy paper: 'national interests'. This emphasis on Swedish interests is a departure from earlier development discourses on Africa, which tended to be exempt from the dictates of narrow national interests. Instead, Africa policy was mostly part of the turf of the Ministry of Development and the Swedish NGO community, and was allowed to be dominated by principled norms of equality and justice. As we will see, the same shift towards interests ('What is in it for us?') is evident, indeed more pronounced, in the Africa discourses of the Danish and Norwegian governments.

It should be noted, however, that the emphasis on national interests is not as hard-nosed and realist as it may sound. First, the Swedish policy paper continues to refer to many development goals as good in themselves, regardless of Stockholm's interests. For example, in the discussion of the impact of globalisation, the paper states categorically that 'the benefits of globalisation should be made available to more people'.[26] It also makes clear that the traditional Swedish emphasis on human rights and aiding the very poorest in society remains intact.[27] Second, the document suggests an Africa strategy whereby Stockholm seeks cooperation with African countries and organisations in areas in which they have common interests. For example, it is noted that economic ties and efforts to improve African trade with the rest of the world can be good for African economies *and* Swedish commercial interests.[28] Finally, and linked to the integrated approach, the 2008 paper makes it clear that 'Africa's development is a common global concern'.[29] It is thus clearly in the interest of Sweden to aid Africa's development, because an African continent marred by underdevelopment, conflict, and frail and 'failed' states may have repercussions as far away as Sweden, manifested through problems such as migration control (see chapter 20 in this volume), international terrorism, and global warming.

The broad 2008 'Sweden and Africa' policy paper was complemented by a regional strategy paper specifically about *aid* to Africa in the period 2010–1015. Building on the priorities discussed, the newer aid strategy displays stronger concern with tackling corruption and climate change than the 'Sweden and Africa' document. This recent trend is also noticeable in Norway's aid policy towards Africa.

Norway: climate, conflict, and capital. Norway spent almost 5.7 billion Norwegian kroner (NKR) on development assistance to Africa in 2009.[30] The Norwegian Foreign Office published its *Platform for an Integrated Africa Policy* in October 2008. This document was part of a larger overhaul of Norwegian foreign and development policy goals, evidenced by a flurry of white papers, propositions, and reports published in 2008–2009. Apart from the platform, most important for Oslo's relations with Africa are two reports to parliament, one on foreign policy, titled *Interests, Responsibility, and Possibilities*, and the other on development policy, titled *Climate, Conflict, and Capital*.[31] The title of the former provides a clue to the increased focus on Norway's interests in its relations with other countries, while the title of the latter illustrates the central position that climate change and the exploitation of natural resources now have in Norwegian development policy. The link between development and climate has been further enhanced by the establishment of a minister for the environment and development in Oslo.

Norway's Africa platform of 2008 sets out, in a similar vein to Sweden's Africa policy statement in the same year, an integrated approach to Africa, in which foreign policy, trade, aid, climate, and development issues are dealt with as interlinked parts of a whole. Like their Swedish colleagues, the authors of the Norwegian platform note that aid is only a small part of Oslo's relations with Africa. But Norway has moved further away than Sweden from a traditional focus on aid. A new buzzword in Norwegian Foreign Office thinking on development is 'capital'. This is shorthand for policies to strengthen foreign direct investment; improve Africa's terms of, and participation in, international trade; combat illegal capital flows; harness migrant remittances for development; and deal with Third World debt (Africa's external debt was about $290 billion in 2011). The platform notes that trade and investment are worth far more than aid, both in monetary terms and in their potential for supporting sustainable development. To take the most extreme example: in 2008, the taxes paid by the Norwegian oil company Statoil to the government of Angola were worth more than twice the entire official Norwegian aid budget for sub-Saharan Africa that year.[32]

As an oil-exporting and resource-rich country, Norway has decided to link its expertise on resource management to its development assistance strategy. Thus the platform stresses ways in which Oslo can help resource-rich African countries to avoid, or escape from, the 'resource curse' and harness their resources to sustainable development. This can, for example, take the form of assisting African governments in renegotiating privatisation deals, so that more of the profits and taxes from resource extraction are channelled into state coffers. There is also a link in Norway's Africa platform between resource management and climate change: Norwegian expertise, money, and technology are offered to help African states extract their resources in a more environmentally friendly manner, and to counteract the potentially dramatic effects of global warming on the African continent.

This emphasis on resources is inescapably linked to the closer alignment of Norway's aid policies with its national interests. It is no coincidence that Angola and Nigeria have become two of Norway's closest African cooperation partners, considering the vast investments by Norwegian oil companies in both countries. The emphasis on climate change can also be seen through the more self-serving lens of Oslo paying to reduce global warming—inducing emissions in the developing world, while continuing to pump up oil and gas from the North Sea at an unrelenting pace. On the other hand, Norwegian policymakers note the common interests between Oslo and African countries in dealing with climate change. They argue that although Norway (like the rest of the world) will be affected by global warming, climate research suggests that the impact will potentially be more severe for the African continent than anywhere else in the world.

After capital and climate, the third 'C' in Norway's Africa approach is a strong conflict resolution and peacebuilding element. Norway is strongly engaged, for example, in Sudan, Ethiopia, Eritrea, the Great Lakes region, and Zimbabwe. Finally, Oslo has, of course, not abandoned its traditional development aid goals of poverty alleviation and support for the weakest members in society. Nevertheless, the issue of climate also makes its way onto the list of the top three priority areas of the official Norwegian international aid agency, NORAD, in its strategy for combating poverty. These goals were spelled out as, first, sustainable use of natural resources; second, gender equality; and third, conflict-sensitive assistance and peacebuilding.[33]

The emphasis on climate change and energy security has become more pronounced since the publication of the 2008 Africa platform. For 2012, Norway dedicated a further 800 million kroner of aid money to energy and climate change related projects, with Africa as the prioritised region.[34] As in Sweden, anticorruption efforts have also made their way onto Norway's aid agenda in recent years. After revelations of the corrupt uses of Norwegian aid money, direct budget support to African governments has been reduced by 48 per cent since 2008.[35]

Denmark: geographically narrow, thematically broad. To a greater degree than Sweden and Norway, Denmark has gone through phases of waxing and waning interest in the African continent, with a period in the early 2000s when it scaled back its Africa aid and struck Malawi and Zimbabwe from its list of core aid recipients. The remaining African partner countries had their aid tied to strong conditionalities regarding economic liberalisation, democratisation, and human rights. These conditionalities were accompanied by threats of removal of 'programme country' status if progress in these areas was not satisfactory.[36] (See chapter 13 in this volume, on broader governance issues.) This led to greater divergence between Denmark and its Scandinavian neighbours, which can go some way in explaining the gradual reduction in concrete Nordic cooperation on their respective Africa policies. With the publication of its new Africa strategy in a white paper in August 2007,[37] Copenhagen seemed to return to the Nordic fold. This strategy promised considerable increases in aid to Africa: about two-thirds of Denmark's bilateral aid budget was now earmarked for the continent.[38] Copenhagen continues to target its bilateral aid at a small selection of 'programme countries': Benin, Burkina Faso, Ghana, Kenya, Mali, Mozambique, Tanzania, Uganda, and Zambia. Almost three quarters ($607 million out of $847 million) of all Danish bilateral aid to Africa in 2009 went to these nine countries.[39]

Another sign of the renewed importance placed on Africa was the creation in 2008 of the Africa Commission (not to be confused with former British prime minister Tony Blair's Commission for Africa of 2005, on which see chapters 11 and 17 in this volume). Denmark's commission was chaired by its prime minister, Lars Røkke Rasmussen, and consisted of eminent Danish, African, and international experts, politicians, and businesspeople. The commission launched its final report in June 2009. The document had relatively little to say about traditional aid. Instead, the focus was on private-led growth, especially facilitating African entrepreneurship and small and medium-sized enterprises.[40] As we have seen, Oslo, and to a lesser extent Stockholm, now also emphasise the crucial role of the private sector for growth and poverty alleviation. In that sense, recent years may have seen less of a return to the fold of Denmark, and more of a coming around to Danish ideas by Norway and Sweden. Even the idea of conditionalities, in the form of demanding anticorruption measures in recipient states, has made a partial return to Norwegian and Swedish aid policy in recent years.

Denmark's 2007 Africa strategy had many similarities to the strategies of Norway and Sweden. It emphasised the importance of Africa for the rest of the world in an age of globalisation, in which climate change, epidemics, sustainable extraction of natural resources, migration, and 'radicalisation' would all have global consequences.[41] The document also noted that Copenhagen's ties with Africa consisted of more than the donor-recipient relationship, and that Denmark's Africa strategy must be coordinated over a range of spheres. Unlike Oslo and Stockholm, however, Copenhagen stipulates strict conditions for its cooperation with particular African countries. The introduction to its 2007 Africa strategy, *Afrika på Vej* (Africa on Its Way), notes that central to the foundations for such cooperation are 'demands for responsible governance that fights poverty through the promotion of democracy and respect for human rights'.[42] Conditionalities—although the document does not use that discredited term—still flow through Denmark's aid strategy. Its 2007 Africa document stipulated considerable increases in Danish aid to its strategic cooperation partners, but only if these partners display 'continued progress' on Danish-defined goals.[43] The focus of Denmark's Africa strategy was geographically narrow, confined to a few partner countries, but thematically broad, although with an emphasis on democracy and 'good governance'. Copenhagen has also shown a sustained and specific interest in security sector reform in African countries.

Like Sweden and Norway, Denmark wishes to see Africa fully integrated within and benefitting from globalisation, both economically and politically. Thus, many of the targets of the Danish strategy relate to strengthening African participation in international forums such as the UN Security

Council and the World Trade Organisation (WTO). As a route to such increased international participation, Denmark wishes to strengthen regional integration and cooperation within Africa through support for regional organisations such as the African Union and the Southern African Development Community (SADC). (See chapters 3 and 4 in this volume.) This is yet another interest shared with Norway and Sweden.

One area in which Denmark differs from its Scandinavian neighbours is in its emphasis on migration. Copenhagen has had a marked anti-immigration dimension to its domestic politics since 2000. This is also reflected in its 2007 Africa strategy, which aimed to strengthen the administrative capacity of African migrant-sending countries to manage the movement of people; to achieve closer cooperation between African migrant-sending and European destination countries; and to reduce the consequences of 'brain drain' on African countries. Most controversially, but in line with EU thinking on the subject,[44] *Afrika på Vej* noted that Denmark wished to maintain a 'marked effort in [refugee] regions of origin'.[45] Containing African refugee flows within the continent, of course, would reduce the flow of asylum-seekers to 'Fortress Europe'. (See chapter 20 in this volume.)

Despite a rather long list of 'priorities', and the strong focus on migration, it is clear from a close reading of the 2007 Danish Africa document that the most important aim of the strategy was to deal with climate change—to slow it as well as counteract its negative consequences. There are similarities here with Norway's priorities, but Denmark's ambitions, due partly to its role as host of the stalemated global climate negotiations in Copenhagen in December 2009, have been broader than Norway's focus on energy.

In 2010, Denmark followed up its Africa strategy (*Afrika på Vej*) with a new strategy for development cooperation titled 'Freedom from Poverty, Freedom to Change'.[46] It continued the priorities of the Africa strategy, but with emphasis on 'freedom' in all its aspects. The new development strategy also confirmed in no uncertain terms the Danish insistence on control and conditionalities, including threats of withdrawing aid to recipients who are not compliant with Danish goals. As stated in the 2011 implementation document to the new strategy:

Denmark's multilateral development assistance will be further focused [on fewer recipient countries] with emphasis on efficiency and results. Denmark can achieve greater impact by focusing on organisations that deliver results and where Denmark can gain influence.[47]

The Nordic approach to Africa: converging over the pursuit of national interests? To what extent do these largely unilaterally developed strategies—although certainly with some exchanges and cross-fertilisation of ideas[48]—translate into a common *Nordic* approach to Africa?

First, there are many points of convergence in the Scandinavian strategies, as all three countries want their aid policies to reflect their *comparative advantage*, a currently popular term in the development assistance community.[49] This is particularly pronounced for Norway, with its prioritisation of energy, natural resources, and climate change. Both Copenhagen and Oslo, which have been strong advocates of international climate cooperation, have placed environmental policies at the top of their Africa agendas, with Stockholm also taking a close interest in this topic. Thus comparative advantage and national interests converge in the case of the unprecedented emphasis on climate-related problems in the Africa strategies of all three Scandinavian countries, and ensure a degree of alignment and commonality of interest between them.

Another example of convergence is the focus on conflict resolution and peacebuilding activities. Norway has a particularly strong self-identification as a global peacemaker, but the Nordic countries have in common their belief in the benefits of exporting their consensual and peaceful sociopolitical models to the rest of the world. Thus, exporting the 'Nordic model' as a way of promoting both peace and development in the global South is viewed as another comparative advantage shared by all five Nordic countries.

There is a degree of practical cooperation between the three Scandinavian countries in the area of peace and security. For example, in the Horn of Africa, Sweden and Norway have created an informal division of labour, but no strategic partnership: they keep each other closely informed, and try not to duplicate each other's work. In Somalia, there is also some direct cooperation between Stockholm and Oslo on particular projects.[50] In Zimbabwe, the Nordic countries have maintained a common stance, and issued several joint statements on the crisis. After the creation of a government of national unity in Zimbabwe in February 2009, the five governments were the most responsive among Western donors to Prime Minister Morgan Tsvangirai's efforts to convince the international donor community to give this troubled and flawed coalition a chance. In March 2009, Denmark, with Norway fast on its heels, became the first Western donor to send a development minister to Zimbabwe after the inauguration of Tsvangirai as prime minister, despite apparent British objections. These visits led to more

Nordic aid to Zimbabwe,[51] channelled through civil society groups and the United Nations, rather than through state actors and institutions. It is nevertheless fair to say that the Nordic countries have been particularly proactive in their support for Tsvangirai's reconstruction efforts.

In addition to common features in their understanding of what constitutes the Nordic region's 'comparative advantages' as donors, the Scandinavian countries also share the holistic assumption that issues of aid, trade, politics, and security in Africa are intrinsically linked, and must therefore be addressed in a concerted manner for sustainable peace *and* development to take root. One aspect of this belief is that the private sector and trade-related issues are given much higher prominence in the Africa strategies of these countries, pushing traditional aid topics down the list of priorities.

A second aspect of this holistic approach is the Scandinavian countries' desire to support Africa's own regional integration efforts. Much Scandinavian hope and resources have been invested in Africa's regional organisations, especially the AU, but also in subregional organisations such as SADC in Southern Africa. For Denmark and Sweden, there is a strong additional reason for supporting African regional institution-building and integration: both countries emphasise the centrality of the EU's role in their own Africa strategies, and Brussels needs the AU to be institutionally strong if the EU-Africa partnership is to become meaningful. (See chapter 3 in this volume.)

Dearth of institutional ties. Considering the strong commonality of these interests, combined with the historical Nordic engagement in the anti-apartheid and anti-colonial struggles, there were surprisingly few formal institutional ties between the Nordic countries on African issues in 2011. Norway, Denmark, and Sweden have shared embassy complexes in some African countries, such as South Africa and Mozambique, but diplomats question how much difference this physical proximity makes in terms of actual collaboration. However, this practice does at least make the informal exchange of information easy, and projects an image of Nordic unity and coherence.

However, the Nordic Development Fund (NDF) was so inactive that Nordic ministers almost closed it down in 2005. Instead, after four moribund years, the NDF was finally relaunched in May 2009 with a narrow mandate of funding 'climate-related interventions in poor developing countries' to help these states tackle the impact of climate change.[52] Whether this new mandate will lead to the NDF becoming an important development actor remains to be seen.

The only formal political institution for Nordic cooperation with Africa is the Nordic-African Foreign Ministers Meeting, where the foreign ministers from the five Nordic countries meet annually with their counterparts from ten African countries.[53] These meetings have been described by Nordic ministers as a 'unique opportunity to engage in a dialogue on critical issues affecting not only our two regions, but the entire international community'[54] in an informal, open, and frank manner. The deliberations take place behind closed doors, and are hosted every other year by an African or Nordic country.

There was talk of abolishing this forum after a lack of high-level participation at the Benin meeting in 2006. But the process was resuscitated in 2007 by Norway, which managed to persuade most of the participating countries to send smaller but higher-level delegations to the Oslo meeting. Since then, the level of participation, including of foreign ministers, has been good, but questions remain whether the Nordic-Africa meetings have been able to live up to their aim of being more open and less confrontational than the atmosphere that has characterised EU-Africa meetings in Cairo (2000), Lisbon (2007), and Tripoli (2010). According to Nordic diplomats present at the eighth meeting, hosted by Denmark in March 2009, things did not go according to plan. Nordic ministers, who had tried to set an agenda dominated by climate change and preparations for the then-upcoming Durban II Racism Conference, were taken aback by the direction that the dialogue took. The main topic of debate instead became the indictment of Sudan's President Omar al-Bashir by the Hague-based International Criminal Court (ICC), with venting of anger by African foreign ministers against an alleged Western-sponsored ICC bias against Africa. The official agenda was thus not covered in an in-depth manner.[55]

This puts a question mark on the notion that the Nordic region, owing to its anticolonial history, is somewhat immune from traditional African distrust of Western motivations that have often hampered the EU-Africa strategic partnership. (See chapter 2 in this volume.) The Nordic countries also have a number of agenda items that they wish to push with African countries, with climate change being particularly high on this list. It is not clear that the Nordics are managing better than other European countries in pursuing their agenda within the framework of a real partnership of equals with African countries. The focus of this chapter has been on the

Nordic half of the Nordic-Africa relationship, and I have not attempted to discuss the factors shaping African approaches to their Nordic counterparts. However, it does seem a wasted opportunity by Africans to use the Nordic-Africa meetings as a 'soap box' for defending Sudan's leader. A more constructive approach would have focused the dialogue on the many areas in which Nordic and African countries clearly share interests and can deepen their cooperation.

EU membership: a help or hindrance for Nordic-Africa relations?

One reason for the low level of institutional cooperation between the Nordic countries on African issues is the membership of Sweden, Denmark, and Finland of the EU, a body to which Norway and Iceland do not belong. The Africa strategies of Sweden and Denmark enthusiastically embrace the idea of a common EU platform on Africa. While this may have hampered the construction of formal Nordic cooperation channels, it has led to much informal consultation and divisions of labour between Sweden and Denmark on the one hand, and non-EU member Norway on the other.

The most obvious way in which this works is that Sweden and Denmark function as Norway's ear into the EU's internal deliberations, and keep their Scandinavian neighbour informed about issues affecting its interests. But the benefits also flow the other way. Sometimes Oslo is able to make statements or act in cases in which Copenhagen or Stockholm are bound by joint EU positions, for example on the political crisis in Zimbabwe. Norway's nonmembership in the EU can thus be a strength, not only for its own ability to form and pursue a distinct African agenda, but also in terms of the ability of the Nordic region as a whole to provide flexible responses to challenges on the African continent.

Concluding reflections: back to geopolitics?

Camelia Minoiu and Sanjay Reddy have argued that the Nordic (or middle-power) approach to aid provides better long-term growth in receiving countries than the geostrategic approaches of, for example, the United States.[56] The basis for this conclusion is that Nordic aid policies are remarkably free from narrowly self-interested motivations. This chapter has, to some degree, raised questions about this notion. I have found that the Africa strategies of Denmark, Sweden, and Norway have moved towards a stronger concern with national interests, even if these interests remain defined in quite generous and inclusive terms. The emphasis on 'comparative advantage' can also be read in this light: it is in the interests of the Nordic countries to play to their strengths and construct an aid and cooperation agenda around services and technologies that their own industries and societies are best placed to provide. Future research will be necessary to gauge whether this shift towards interests will affect the successes of the Nordic model.

In conclusion, although Africa is relatively high on the foreign policy agendas of all three Scandinavian countries, the continent's concerns are not particularly high on the Nordic cooperation agenda. Nordic foreign ministers commissioned a report on Nordic cooperation on foreign and security policy, submitted by former Norwegian foreign minister Thorvald Stoltenberg in February 2009, but it had little to say about Africa.[57] In light of the increased assertiveness of Russia's foreign policy in the Arctic region, the document's main focus was on the geostrategic importance of the Nordic region itself, its oceans, and its resources. The Arctic region was given particular attention, since global warming is opening up new shipping routes and new opportunities for the exploitation of natural resources in this area. As the competition between the Arctic nations for these opportunities gathers pace, Nordic cooperation in this region has become particularly attractive.

While the Stoltenberg report of 2009 begins with a chapter on peacebuilding, suggesting the creation of a Nordic stabilisation task force to support the UN's peacekeeping efforts to stabilise weak and failing states, most of the report concentrates on a national interest-led agenda for political, intelligence, and military cooperation within the boundaries of the Nordic region itself. The Stoltenberg report's focus on challenges within the Nordic region and its immediate neighbourhood is symptomatic of current thinking on Nordic cooperation among the region's governments.

A December 2006 policy paper published by the Maastricht-based European Centre for Development Policy Management (ECDPM) on EU-Africa relations had posed the question: 'How can [a] fragmented Europe-Africa relationship be overcome to enter into a continent to continent relationship as desired by the African Union?'[58] This chapter has underlined the pertinence of this question. If even the five Nordic countries—with their shared history and culture, common political values, and strong, well-established regional links—are not investing the time and resources necessary to enable strong institutional cooperation on Africa, imagine how difficult this task will be for the twenty-seven member states of the European Union.

PART 6

MIGRATION AND IDENTITY

20

MIGRATION AND 'FORTRESS EUROPE'

Andrew Geddes

Introduction

The European Union cannot be an island entire of itself. There is no more profound example of this fact than the tragic loss of life in the waters that separate countries such as Italy, Greece, and Spain from North African countries such as Algeria, Morocco, and Tunisia. These waters constitute a huge international border of inequality between the extremely wealthy European space and less economically developed African countries. Regional integration in Europe has important consequences for non-European countries. Thus, while we can discuss the 'Europeanisation' of the twenty-seven EU member states, we can also analyse the ways in which the effects of European integration spread to nonmember states in Africa.

This chapter explores the development of European Union migration and asylum policy and its implications for Africa. It asks why these international migration relations have intensified, what forms they have taken, and what effects they have had. Migration is a key issue in international politics, one that has enormous practical and ethical implications. Indeed, analysing the content of European action on migration can tell us interesting things about the EU as an international organisation and the kinds of power it wields, while allowing us to reflect on the consequences of the global imbalances of wealth and power that drive international migration.

EU action on migration and asylum and the search for dialogue

The EU claims to seek 'migration dialogue' with African countries. During the decade of 2000–2010 the 'external' dimension of European action on migration and asylum became a much more prominent component of policy development, shaping the behaviour of nonmember states. These states include countries in the process of joining the EU (such as Croatia, which will join in 2012), those with a more distant membership prospect (such as Albania), and even those countries that will not become EU member states (such as Algeria, Libya, Morocco, and Tunisia) but have important bilateral migration relations with the EU and its members. (See chapter 7 in this volume.) It is important to emphasise that none of this migration can be understood as a simple South-North movement. In fact, relations between Africa and Europe are based on a far more complex setting, as countries can be sending, receiving, or acting as transit countries, or more often a combination of all three. In addition, there are complex processes of issue-framing. For example, the actions of the EU and its member states in the area of migration have tended to focus on security concerns. This has been a cause of irritation to African countries that have been keen to extend this relationship to include aid, trade, development, and human rights. This situation has also led to tensions in issue-framing as EU members focused on 'threats' have dwelt on the 'threat' of migration, while African countries have sought to broaden this frame, in order to address more fully the root causes of migration.

These developments have highlighted the basic issue in international migration relations between the EU and African countries: the necessity for any agreement on migration to be broad, and to encompass a range of issues including aid, trade, development, and human rights, as well as peace and security. Any attempt by Brussels to impose its priorities on nonmember states is unlikely to succeed. EU states have recognised this, and the 'migration and development' agenda has become far more prominent in Africa-Europe relations. But there is still a tension derived from the strong security-oriented focus in the domestic migration policies of most EU member states.

Before exploring Europe-Africa migration relations further, it is important to note that the EU is a unique, supranational organisation. The Union is not a state, in the sense that it has not acquired statelike qualities. It has, though, become a political system in its own right, within which there is a migration and asylum policy. The particular focus of this chapter is on the external dimension of EU action on migration—in other words, the ways in which Brussels's migration policies have impacted surrounding states and regions both within what the EU calls its 'neighbourhood' of fourteen proximate states—from Belarus to Morocco—and beyond. This means a focus on non-EU member states and on migration flows from and across them, and a need for a closer examination of the relationship between these and EU approaches to migration, development, and security.[1]

The result is the development of new forms of 'international migration relations' centred on the EU as a regional organisation with twenty-seven member states that has migration relations with a large number of non-EU states. Some of these states may eventually become EU members, but the important point regarding African states is that they will never become EU member states. This changes the nature of the political game in the sense that incentive structures differ, depending on whether or not there is a membership perspective. If a country is able to join the EU (such as non-member states in the western Balkans), then different dynamics drive relations with Brussels, and may give the EU more leverage. If a state does not have the prospect of membership, then one may ask what kind of incentives and leverage exist within this migration relationship. The answer to this question, so far as can be seen from current action, is the creation of 'migration dialogue'. In this sense, 'dialogue' seeks to develop channels of communication and discussion on migration between EU and non-EU states. These channels are nested within broader patterns of relations.

The international political drama that this chapter explores is played out on Europe's borders. These are what Rob Walker terms the 'dangerous edges—the awful discriminations between us and them—that constitute our spheres of domestic comfort and external distress'.[2] These borders can be seen as lines of territory, as points of demarcation, but are actually more symbolic than that, in the sense that they also go very much to the heart of debates about the meaning of Europe: both as an economic bloc and as some kind of community. The centrality of borders is more than just a debate about border security, although that is, of course, important. It is also a debate about the identity of the EU and its member states and how they relate to other states. European integration changes the location of borders, their meaning, and associated notions of territoriality, territorial management, and population control.[3] International relations scholar James Rosenau has characterised the domestic-foreign frontier as an arena where domestic and foreign issues 'converge, intermesh or otherwise become indistinguishable within a seamless web'.[4] This insight is particularly important, because it helps us to understand how responses to international migration necessarily involve both domestic and international politics.

When we apply this approach more specifically to migration relations with African countries, we find that there are significant processes of what Joseph Nevins has called 'boundary build-up' at the EU's borders.[5] Nevins analysed the United States-Mexico border, but his findings have some resonance for Europe and Africa as well. He showed that 'boundary build-up' imparts a spatial dimension to debates about borders and to the relationship between various types of flow across these borders. This is because concerns about the 'thinning out' of place as a result of global flows have led to

complex interchanges between state actors and groups of citizens [and] produced a set of deep concerns about the ethno-cultural, socio-economic, and bio-physical security of the nation, all of which are inherently geographical given their inextricable relationship to a particular territory. Boundary build-up is thus a territorial strategy to achieve that security and assuage those concerns.[6]

A rationale for European boundary build-up can be found in a body of work on the 'securitisation' of migration, within which security is understood to be

a practice, a specific way of framing an issue. Security discourse is characterised by dramatising an issue as having absolute priority.... 'Security' is thus a self-referential practice, not a question of measuring the seriousness of various threats and deciding when they 'really' are dangerous to some object.... It is self-referential because it is *in* this practice that the issue becomes a security issue. What we can study is the practice that makes this issue into a security issue.[7]

The 'securitisation' of migration emphasises the links between market relations embodied within the free movement framework and the control of population.

The 'targeting' of population acquired an EU dimension through the development of the Justice and Home Affairs (JHA) 'pillar' after the Maastricht Treaty of 1992 and the designation of the EU as an 'Area of Freedom, Security, and Justice' after the Amsterdam Treaty of 1997. Both treaties contributed to intensified cooperation between security specialists and other officials as well as to a European-level representation of threats. In the multilevel EU field, the implication of these developments is that relationships within and between states, and between states and nonstate actors, are better viewed as heterarchical rather than hierarchical.[8]

In 2005, EU member states issued a strategy for the external dimension of JHA departments in the context of terrorist attacks, organised crime, and global migration flows (the issue-'frame' for migration is not too difficult to detect). Such attacks and threats provide institutional opportunities and impel cooperation and integration, but 'security policy is never compelled by external events'.[9] A security 'frame' has thus been well established at the EU level, and has been a key driver of cooperation since well before the terror attacks of the decade of the 2000s, including those on New York, Washington, Madrid, and London.

The European Union therefore seems to use enlargement and its external relations to align its objectives. This brings us to the content of Brussels's migration relations with African countries, or—put another way—to the quest for dialogue between both continents.

The content of the dialogue

The most developed statement of the principles underlying migration partnership can be found in the Cotonou Agreement of June 2000 between seventy-eight African, Caribbean, and Pacific (ACP) states and the EU. (See chapter 2 in this volume.) Article 13 of Cotonou specifies that migration partnership involves in-depth dialogue, consonant with commitments in international law to respect human rights and to eliminate all forms of discrimination based particularly on origin, sex, race, language, and religion. The EU approach to building migration dialogue has three key elements.

First, residence and employment, including fair treatment of third-country nationals; integration policy that grants rights and obligations comparable to those of citizens; enhancement of nondiscrimination in economic, social, and cultural life; and the development of measures against racism and xenophobia. In employment, treatment by each member state of legally employed workers is to be free from discrimination based on nationality as regards working conditions, remuneration, and dismissal, relative to EU member states' own nationals. The EU's June and November 2000 directives on antidiscrimination and its November 2003 directive on the rights of long-term residents covered most of these areas, but labour migration rules remain a national competence, and Brussels's actions to shape migration opportunities for nationals of nonmember states remain very limited.

The second element of the EU approach to building migration dialogue is addressing 'root causes', which includes efforts to 'normalise' migration flows through strategies aimed at poverty reduction, improving living and working conditions, creating employment, and developing training. Partnership should also include provision for training and education, such as schemes to facilitate access to higher education. And the final element is the 'fight against illegal immigration' through return and readmission policies with bilateral agreements governing specific obligations for readmission and return.[10] In 2010 the EU had readmission agreements with Hong Kong, Sri Lanka, Macao, and Albania, and was negotiating accords with Morocco, Russia, Pakistan, Ukraine, and Algeria.[11]

The European approach to migration and asylum has developed around two main elements. First, there is an important internal element of EU migration policy that focuses on conditions for the entry, residence, and status of third-country nationals, measures to tackle irregular migration, and conditions for the reception and processing of asylum claims. These are the classic domains of migration policy.

An external element focuses on relations with third countries and measures to tackle the root causes of migration. Here we see clear evidence of the external dimension of EU action on migration, as well as the blurring of the distinction between internal and external security.[12] The implication of this blurring of lines is that the location of responsibility for migration within national and EU political systems also becomes more complex.

At EU level, the European Commission's Directorate-General for Freedom, Security, and Justice has the lead responsibility, but must also deal with the Directorate-General for External Relations (RELEX) and with other interested directorates-general in Brussels, such as those dealing with social policy, employment, and development. As far back as 1994, the Commission's communication on immigration had registered the need for cooperation with non-EU states and recognised the growing 'foreign policy' dimension of migration policies.[13] This external dimension raised what are known in EU jargon as 'cross-pillar issues'—issues that bridge 'external' and 'internal' security and render visible both the domestic and international politics of migration, as well as the links between them.[14]

This necessarily raises 'issue linkages' whereby action in one policy area has important implications for action in other areas. A key factor in discussion of migration as 'danger' and as 'potential' is the link between migration and development. There is now a growing body of evidence pointing to the importance of migration as a development tool.[15] Research also suggests that, if international migration relations between the EU and African countries are to contribute to successful poverty reduction strategies, then one short- to medium-term effect might be an increase in migration as a result of boosting the motives and resources necessary for movement and creating a 'migration hump'.[16] Put another way, 'poverty reduction is not in itself a migration-reducing strategy'.[17] For sending states, emigration can relieve labour-market and political pressures, provide education and training, generate remittances, and lead to eventual return by successful migrants. The downside can include 'brain drain' and 'brain waste', the difficulty of establishing voluntary return programmes, and the relatively unproductive channelling of remittances towards inflation and inequality-generating consumption.

Until economic recession hit Europe hard in 2008 and 2009 following the global financial crisis, the demand for migrant workers in EU member states had been fuelled by labour-market and skills shortages, as well as by the effects of population change, low fertility rates, and ageing populations across Europe. There are, however, major differences among the policies of EU states towards labour migration (particularly by the highly skilled), which is largely welcomed, and towards asylum-seeking and irregular migration flows, which generally are not. There has also been the major effect on migration of EU enlargement in May 2004 and January 2007, which brought in ten new member states from Central and Eastern Europe.[18] One effect of this situation is some substitution in the labour market of migrants from African countries with those from Central and Eastern Europe, particularly in new migrant-receiving countries such as Spain and Italy.[19]

The strategic context

The strategic context at the regional level for EU relations with North African states is provided by the Barcelona Process[20] (see chapter 7 in this volume). The instigation of the Barcelona Process in 1995 placed relations with the countries of the Middle East and North Africa (MENA) on a sounder footing, with political and financial structures in places that could sustain a broad dialogue about migration. This relationship has matured, but has thus far largely reflected EU concerns about migration and asylum flows from and across MENA countries, with an emphasis on return and readmission. This could be seen as positive for EU states, at least in the short term. The benefits for MENA countries are more questionable. There are three main aspects to this process: the Euro-Mediterranean framework for discussion, the association agreements, and aid provided by the EU to Mediterranean partners through the EU's MEDA programme. The MEDA programme, for example, is funding a €2 million migration observatory, coordinated from the European University Institute in Florence, that will bring together information, develop migration scenarios, offer training, and analyse the policy implications of these initiatives.

The launch of the Barcelona Process in 1995 was driven by European concerns about migration, but migration only began to rise up the agenda as the drive towards formalisation of EU competencies was consolidated after the European Council meeting at Tampere, Finland, in October 1999.

The external dimension of EU action on migration has become particularly apparent in recent EU policies and initiatives. There are five key issues involved: the High-Level Working Group on Migration and Asylum; the Tampere conclusions of October 1999; the EU Council's summit in the Spanish city of Seville of June 2002; the EU Commission's communication of December 2002 on integrating migration issues in relations with third countries; and the EU Council's conclusions of May 2003 on integrating migration issues in relations with third countries.

The High-Level Working Group on Migration and Asylum. Migration management has become a 'cross-pillar' issue within the EU, with implications for foreign and security policy, justice and home affairs, and trade and development, as well as for the units and departments that must manage these policies.[21] The cross-pillar dimensions of migration and asylum policies have been evident within the EU's High-Level Working Group on Migration and Asylum. This working group was established in June 1999 on an initiative of the Dutch government. In The Hague, responsibility for international migration and refugee strategies rests with the Ministry of Foreign Affairs rather than the Ministry of Justice, which largely shapes international migration and refugee strategies. The EU approach thus reflected this Dutch attempt to 'integrate' the internal and external dimensions of migration policy.

The working group produced action plans in 1999 for Morocco, Somalia, Afghanistan, Albania, Iraq, and Sri Lanka. These plans sought to coordinate the EU's response to migration and to bring the interests of security, foreign policy, and development to bear on the protection of human rights; democratisation and constitutional governance; social and development issues; combating poverty; conflict prevention and resolution; asylum; and irregular migration. The working group was composed mainly of Justice and Home Affairs officials who had relatively little experience in dealing with third countries or with issues of development aid. These reports were criticised for disproportionately reflecting EU priorities about migration control, readmission, and return, rather than pursuing bilateral partnerships based on genuine dialogue with the countries in question.

The Morocco action plan of 1999 attracted four specific criticisms. First, the proposal for the use of MEDA funds to analyse migration patterns and instruments led to tensions between the High-Level Working Group on Migration and Asylum and EU Commission officials working in the areas of development and external relations. Second, Rabat was not consulted about the action plan and initially refused to discuss the document with Brussels. Third, there was a lack of coordination between Justice and Home Affairs, external relations, and development within the EU, although one effect of the High-Level Working Group on Migration and Asylum has been stimulation of agenda-setting activities by Commission officials working on development and external relations. And finally, the working group historically lacked a sound financial basis, although this has changed with the allocation of €15 million for its work in 2003. For example, the working group has funded a programme encouraging Moroccan migrants to set up businesses in their country, and another project to establish a savings bank for the remittances of Moroccan migrants.

The Tampere conclusions. These developments emphasised, among other things, a 'root causes' approach to migration and the importance of migration relations with third countries. The Tampere conclusions of October 1999 outlined components of a 'common migration and asylum policy' that would include a 'comprehensive approach to migration addressing political, human rights and development issues in countries and regions of origin and transit'. Member states were further invited 'to contribute ... to a greater coherence of internal and external policies of the Union. Partnership with third countries concerned will also be a key element for the success of such a policy, with a view to promoting co-development'.[22] Since Tampere, the European Commission has pursued a two-phase approach: first, creating a basic legal framework centred on the development of minimum standards in those Treaty articles introduced at Amsterdam in 1997; and second, the employment of the open method of coordination to promote gradual convergence of legislation, policy, and practice. The concerns

413

of EU member states have particularly focused on asylum, irregular migration, readmission, and return.

The Seville European Council summit. The conclusions of the European Council's summit in Seville in June 2002 called for a targeted approach using all EU foreign policy instruments: 'an integrated, comprehensive and balanced approach to tackle the root causes of irregular immigration must remain the EU's constant long-term objective.... [C]loser economic cooperation, trade expansion, development assistance and conflict prevention are all means of promoting prosperity in the countries concerned and thereby reducing the underlying causes of migration flows'. It was further concluded at Seville that 'any future co-operation, association or equivalent agreement which the EU or the EC [European Commission] concludes with any country should include a clause on joint management of migration flows and on compulsory readmission in the event of irregular immigration'.[23]

The EU Commission's communication on relations with third countries. In response to the conclusions of the June 2002 Seville summit, the EU Commission in Brussels produced a communication in December 2002 that sought to integrate migration into relations with third countries. The document outlined four key principles: first, maintain the coherence of external policies and actions through a comprehensive approach, of which a part is migration and which is differentiated by country; second, address the root causes of migration; third, include migration within regional and country strategy papers; and finally, extend additional funding.[24] The latter, extension of additional funding, was undertaken initially through an allocated sum of money within the EU budget labelled as 'Co-operation with Third Countries in the Field of Migration', which has since been replaced for 2004–2008 by the budget line 'Financial and Technical Assistance to Third Countries in the Areas of Migration and Asylum' (AENEAS).[25]

The European Council's conclusions on integrating migration issues in relations with third countries. The EU Council's conclusions of May 2003 set the agenda in the area of integrating migration issues into relations with third countries. The conclusions identified migration as a major strategic priority for Brussels; highlighted the importance of addressing root causes; established the strategic framework for North African countries; and stressed the importance of including dialogue on migration within current and future cooperation and association agreements. Four priorities were further identified: managing migration and combating trafficking; improving national legislation; offering migration-related assistance; and facilitating 'sustainable return'.

The EU Council's conclusions of 2003 also focused on action in five key areas: first, facilitating 'brain circulation' and encouraging voluntary return, in order to encourage migrants to contribute to their countries of origin; second, encouraging more efficient use of remittances from diaspora communities in Europe; third, better integrating legally-resident third-country nationals living in EU member states with rights and obligations comparable to those of other EU citizens; fourth, dealing with tensions between high-skilled recruitment and development; and finally, calling for readmission agreements.

The facilitation of 'brain circulation' and encouragement of return is a response to the basic problem that migrants are likely to be concerned that if they leave the EU, then they will not be allowed to reenter 'Fortress Europe'. In its 2007 communication 'Circular Migration and Mobility Partnerships', Brussels raised the possibility of creating routes for migrants to enter, leave, and reenter the EU, and linked this to tougher border-control enforcement in sending states.[26]

The second key action area—more efficient use of remittances with cheaper and more reliable transmission and efforts to channel their use towards productive investment—is important because remittances from migrants that often flow to 'kith and kin' in countries of origin far exceed development aid as a source of funding for developing countries. Although these are private flows, and their uses cannot easily be controlled or necessarily channelled towards productive investment, remittances have generally tended to have a positive impact on development. Governments, international organisations, and nongovernmental organisations can thus encourage remitting behaviour through incentive schemes and improved financial infrastructure. These actors can also seek to channel remittances towards productive investment in African countries.

The third key action area—better integration of legally-resident third-country nationals living in EU member states with rights and obligations comparable to those of other EU citizens—entails providing opportunities for migrants to participate in education and vocational training in EU countries.[27]

The subject of the fourth key action area—possible tensions between high-skilled recruitment and development—can arise if EU member states cherry-pick skilled migrants. An EU approach to labour migration may then not be in the interests of developing countries, as they may lose their 'best and brightest' professionals to Europe. However, it has been argued that wider channels for migrants who work in lower-skilled occupations can choke off some of the demand for irregular migration.

Finally, as the fifth key action area, admission agreements have been called for by the EU Council, which urged the Commission to step up negotiation of such agreements and to consider ways in which financial and technical assistance can be used to develop reception capacity and 'durable solutions' to asylum in developing countries. This issue of readmission is right at the top of the EU agenda.

The budget for EU actions in these five key action areas was initially made within the budget line regarding a multiannual programme to assist third countries in managing migration flows and implementing readmission agreements. The budget line focused on improving national legislation and management of migration and asylum; more effective legislation to combat illegal immigration, linked to the fight against organised crime and corruption; institution-building and technical assistance to combat people smuggling and human trafficking; and capacity-building for customs and law enforcement, including technical assistance. As earlier noted, the budget line 'Co-operation with Third Countries in the Field of Migration' was replaced for the period 2004–2008 by the budget line known as AENEAS with an allocation of €250 million, of which €120 million was for the period until the end of 2006. The EU 2007–2013 budget settlement allocated €4 billion to 'Solidarity and Management of Migration Flows'. This includes €1.82 billion to external borders, €676 million to a return fund, €699 million to the European Refugee Fund, and €825 million to the Integration Fund. The EU's agency for operational cooperation on management of the external borders of its member states, or FRONTEX as it is better known, also operates a fund for the development of programmes to increase border-control capacity within the EU.

The attempt to build partnerships between Brussels and Africa is evident in various forums, including dialogue with and between Africa's regional and subregional organisations, among them the Economic Community of West African States (ECOWAS) and the African Union, as well as in specific regional initiatives, such as the EU-Africa Ministerial Conference meeting of fifty-eight African and European states that convened in the Moroccan capital of Rabat in July 2006.

The ambitions of EU member states in these areas remain bold. In December 2006 the European Council called for strengthening and deepening of cooperation and dialogue with third countries of origin and transit through specific EU delegations to African countries in 2007; closer integration of migration and development policies; coherent follow-up by Brussels to the UN High-Level Dialogue on Migration and Development; measures on return and readmission; actions against smuggling and trafficking; and new thinking on legal migration, though this latter area is recognised as remaining a member state competence.

Concluding reflections

There is an evident tension in the European Union between understandings of migration as a danger and migration as a potential, with the former leading to security-driven approaches and the latter leading to attempts to 'manage' migration, create 'dialogue' and establish 'partnerships' with other concerned governments. These processes thus lead to different relations and issues that are linked to migration, particularly security and development. Boundary build-up and boundary shift have also been key aspects of recent European integration as border controls have been intensified, but also as the EU has grown from fifteen to twenty-seven member states in only three years, between 2004 and 2007.

The external dimension of EU migration and asylum policy can be seen to represent a new phase in the pursuit of territorially focused strategies to achieve security. The relationship between Brussels and Africa regarding migration consists of four main elements. First, there has been intense activity in these areas within a multilevel polity, which has changed the nature and form of migration politics in Europe in important ways. Second, there are asymmetries and imbalances in migration relations between the EU and North African and Middle Eastern states, which have led to a perception that European actions are driven more by the concerns of EU member states to inhibit 'unwanted' flows of asylum-seekers and 'illegal' immigrants, than by the desire to establish genuine dialogue with these states.

Third, a rebalancing of priorities has been difficult to establish. EU efforts have been particularly focused on border controls and the 'export' of these controls to neighbouring nonmember states. This has been done at the expense, so far, of measures to facilitate circular migration, which research suggests could possess significant development potential. Finally, tensions between 'migration as a threat' and 'migration dialogue' are clearly apparent in European actions. This is not a surprise, since these are the tensions apparent within the domestic politics of migration in many EU member states. These tensions have now acquired resonance in the EU, and any serious analysis of migration and asylum policies in Europe must factor in the impact of the developing EU migration and asylum framework on African countries.

21

THE BLACK ATLANTIC FROM OTHELLO TO OBAMA

IN SEARCH OF A POST-RACIAL SOCIETY

Ali A. Mazrui

Introduction

Eurafrique is usually interpreted as relations between African and European *political organisations*. But for historical accuracy, we need to recognise that relations between both continents were between the *peoples* of the two continents long before they were about states and regional organisations. For centuries, Europeans saw Africans in racial terms long before colonial and post-colonial states came into being. It is because of these considerations that I have offered a chapter primarily about the racial experience of *Eurafrique*, and re-designated the region as the 'Black Atlantic'. Let us set the historical stage for this broad racial drama. (See introduction and chapter 2 in this volume.)

In the discourse about modernity and the role of the people of colour, a new idea was tabled in a book published in 1993, *The Black Atlantic*, which unleashed a fierce debate about Anglo-Guyanese scholar Paul Gilroy's conceptualisation of the dispersal of African people, from the continent's shores to North and South America, to the Caribbean, to Britain, and to Western Europe, originally triggered by the trans-Atlantic slave trade. Gilroy traverses the cultural variations of the Black Atlantic, paying special attention to both uniqueness and diversity. Central to his thesis is that modernity is a phenomenon of hybridity that was partly created by the Black dispersal.[1]

My own definition of the Black Atlantic is more purely a political geography of race. 'Global Africa' in this chapter is divided between the Black Atlantic and the Black Indian Ocean. The Black Atlantic combines the African continent with the part of the African Diaspora that is located in Europe and the Western hemisphere. The African Diaspora in Europe and the Americas was initially a product of the slave trade involving Europeans. Four continents thus constitute the Black Atlantic—Africa, Europe, North America, and South America, accompanied by neighbouring islands, especially the islands of the Caribbean.

The Black Indian Ocean, on the other hand, consists mainly of Africa and Asia, the two largest continents on Planet Earth. The African Diaspora in Asia is mainly a product of the Arab slave trade. That trade was much older than the Atlantic traffic, but much smaller in scale. In addition to Africa itself, there has been a significant African presence in the history of the Middle East, South Asia, and farther east. The Black Indian Ocean encompasses what used to be known as Africa's Eastern Diaspora, but combines it with Africa itself.

Because the concepts of 'Black Atlantic' and 'Black Indian Ocean' are products of the political geography of race, this chapter also addresses the political periodisation of race. Are we approaching a post-racial age? Our focus here will be on the Black Atlantic, paying little attention to the Black Indian Ocean. I have addressed the political geography of 'Afrabia' elsewhere.[2]

From pre-racial to post-racial Africa?

Can there be such a phenomenon as a post-racial society? Here we need to distinguish between a post-racial society and a post-racism age. Outgrowing racism, though difficult, can nevertheless be attained sooner than the disappearance of race as a demographic category. South Africa will outgrow racism as a form of prejudice by about the middle of this twenty-first century, but it may take the country at least one additional full century to outgrow race-consciousness. A post-racial society is one that has not only abandoned racism as a form of bigotry, but also shed race-consciousness as a residual mode of defining a group.

In post-colonial Africa it may be easier to imagine a post-'tribal' society than a post-racial society. While many African societies were still basically 'tribal' at the time of independence, there has been a genuine effort to get beyond 'tribalism' as a form of intolerance while still accepting boundaries of 'tribal' identities. As a verse from the Qur'an put it: 'We have created you from a male and female, and forged you into nations and tribes that you may know each other [and learn from each other]. Verily the best among you are those who are the most pious'.

The Qu'ran seems to be arguing that 'tribalism' and nationalism can create a wrong sense of who is superior to whom. But instead of 'tribalism', 'tribal' and national consciousness can be a beneficial resource if it leads to learning from each other and getting to know each other better. In pre-feudal days, Western society was at one time pre-tribal. Then most Western European countries became tribal and feudal. And from the Treaty of West-phalia of 1648 onwards, Western Europe became more national and post-tribal, except in places like Scotland where clan loyalties are still powerful and compelling.

If periods of national history can be pre-tribal, tribal, or post-tribal, why cannot periods of continental history also be either pre-racial, racial, or post-racial? It is possible to argue that while much of pre-colonial Africa was basically 'tribal', the continent south of the Sahara was still essentially *pre-racial*. It is almost certain that much of pre-colonial Africa knew very little about either race or racism before large-scale penetration by the Arabs, and especially before the even more spectacular arrival of Europeans. To the present day, most African languages have no word for 'race', which is different from the word for 'tribe'. In Kiswahili, both 'race' and 'tribe' are referred to as *kabila*, which is itself a word borrowed from the Arabic language.

In this chapter, we have indeed conceded that sub-Saharan Africa was once pre-racial. European penetration—even more than the impact of the Arabs—racialised the quality of political life in colonial Africa. The big question since the end of political apartheid in 1994, which resulted in the liberation of South Africa, is whether we are slowly heading for a world that not only is post-racism, but may eventually become post-racial.

In the context of the Black Atlantic world, there is a transition from the pre-racism world of William Shakespeare's *Othello* to the potentially post-racism America of Barack Obama. In the Venice of Othello, race-conscious-ness was widely manifest from time to time. What was indeed still underdeveloped and obviously rare was the kind of racism that could lynch a black man for engaging in inter-racial sex.

Of all the countries with a white majority population, the one that was earliest in allowing a man of colour to be the absolute best in cultural creativity was Czarist Russia, rather than the Soviet Communists. Indeed, Russia's supreme literary hero has continued to be Aleksandr Pushkin (1799–1837), who is still widely regarded as more than that country's Shakespeare. Pushkin remains not only Russia's greatest poet, but also a great novelist, dramatist, and short-story writer. His importance to Russian literature exceeded Shakespeare's significance to English literature. In his versatile genius, Pushkin is widely acknowledged to be the founder of modern Russian literature. But how is this related to the debate about Europe before racism? It would be an exaggeration to portray Aleksandr Pushkin as a symbol of pre-racial Russia. But there is no doubt that by American definitions of a black person, Pushkin was indeed a man of colour. Pushkin's mother was the granddaughter of Abram Hannibal, an Abyssinian princeling who was bought as a slave from Constantinople. Tradition has it that Hannibal was adopted by Peter the Great as one of his favoured generals.[3] Pushkin immortalised his great grandfather and his links with Peter the Great in his unfinished novel *Arap Petra Velikogo* (The Negro of Peter the Great), which was published in 1837.

Across the Atlantic in North America, it took much longer than a century before such upward racial mobility was even conceivable. But in 1968, Senator Robert F. Kennedy was startlingly prophetic when he envisaged a black president of the United States by 2008. In a talk broadcast on the *Voice of America* radio station in 1968—the year of his own assassination—Bobby Kennedy prophesied as follows: '[Things are] moving so fast in race relations, a Negro could be president in 40 years…. There is no question about it. In the next 40 years a Negro can achieve the same position that my brother had'.[4]

In the white part of the Black Atlantic, Barack Obama has indeed attained the highest pinnacle of political power ever reached by a man of colour in a primarily white society by being elected president of the United States in November 2008. What we already know is that Aleksandr Pushkin did indeed successfully rise to the pinnacle of cultural power in a society with a white majority. Was this possible only in a Russia, which had yet to evolve into a more racist society? It was certainly a Russia that recognised supreme genius, regardless of race.

In the wider Black Atlantic, the best examples of a Europe before racism may be found more in the creative literature or drama of the period than in official documents or solemn records. A particularly compelling illustration is afforded by a comparison of two plays by William Shakespeare—*Othello* and *The Merchant of Venice*—both plays being set mainly in Venice. But here we must distinguish between prejudice based mainly on differences in skin *colour*, and prejudice based on differences in *culture*. Religious bigotry is prejudice rooted in cultural variations, while racial intolerance is usually a derivative of differences in colour.

During the era of William Shakespeare (1564–1616), religion was a much bigger cause of conflict within and between societies than was skin colour. It is partly because of this contrast between religion and race that there is more anti-Semitism in Shakespeare's *The Merchant of Venice* than there is colour prejudice in *Othello*. While the Moor, Othello, does trigger race consciousness among the Venetian aristocracy, he is highly respected as a military hero. The play does highlight consciousness of physical differences, but minimises outright racism and intolerance.

Othello as a character emerges as a tragic hero in spite of his marrying a white woman and, indeed, despite his killing the woman in a fit of unjustified jealousy. In the centuries that followed Shakespeare, inter-racial sexual mating became repugnant to mainstream British and Anglo-Saxon culture. This trend culminated in Jim Crow, a model of American apartheid.

Between Othello and Shylock

In *Othello* we have a Black man addressed as 'My Lord' by a white woman in the bedroom. We see him kissing her after murdering her. Yet the play's villain is Iago, a scheming white man who succeeded in transforming Othello's tender love for Desdemona into a murderous jealous rage. This became Shakespeare's most memorable portrayal of domestic violence. Yet we pity Othello, rather than hating him. And we admire his decisiveness when he kills himself as soon as he discovers his monumental injustice to Desdemona. He says to her dead body:

I kissed thee ere I killed thee.
No way but this,
Killing myself, to die upon a kiss.

Before he dies, Othello also calls upon the rest of us:

When you shall these unlucky deeds relate,
Speak of me as I am. Nothing extenuate.

Nor set down ought in malice. Then must you speak,
Of one that loved not wisely, but too well.

[Act V, Scene II][5]

Shakespeare even makes Othello more prejudiced against another culture than against another race. Here is a black man who is not against white people, but against Muslims. In Shakespeare's day, Islam was almost synonymous with the Ottoman Empire; the words 'Turk' and 'Muslim' were practically interchangeable. And the last words uttered by Othello before he stabs himself are essentially Islamophobic. Othello tells us about a man he killed in Aleppo (Syria). He describes the victim as a 'turbaned Turk'. He also knows that Muslims are circumcised, and uses this as a term of Islamophobic abuse:

> ... *in Aleppo once,*
> *Where a malignant and turbaned Turk*
> *Beat a Venetian and traduced the state,*
> *I took him by th' throat the circumcised dog*
> *And smote him—thus*
>
> *[Othello stabs himself.]*

Othello is clearly much more culture conscious than colour conscious. The skin of the Turk was probably white, but Othello is more offended by the Turk's culture—turban, circumcision, and all. We are back to the Shakespearean rank order of prejudice. We are witnessing culture prejudice in Othello, rather than colour bias. The culture of Venice at the time, as depicted by Shakespeare, manifested colour consciousness, but fell short of outright racism.

In contrast to this sympathetic treatment of Othello, the Moor of Venice, Shakespeare is fundamentally unsympathetic to the Jew of Venice. Shylock is portrayed stereotypically as a greedy Jewish money-lender, constantly worried about *ducats* rather than dignity. (*Ducats* were the Venetian currency, the 'bottom line' in Shakespeare's day.) Shylock is also portrayed as almost literally blood-thirsty, as he insists on getting the literal 'pound of flesh' from a fellow human being. Demanding a pound of flesh is horrid, but as a crime it is far less horrid than Othello's strangulation of his innocent wife. Yet Othello emerges as, at worst, a foolish but tragic hero, whereas Shylock is obsessed with gruesome greed. Once again, we see in Shakespeare a greater aversion to a man from a different culture (Shylock) than to a man of a different colour (Othello).

But does not Shakespeare assign to Shylock great lines of defence of racial and cultural equality? Was Shakespeare ambivalent about the Jew? Was he torn between the apartheid of colour and the apartheid of culture? It is indeed true that one of the great speeches in *The Merchant of Venice* is Shylock's eloquent assertion that Jews were no less human than Christians. The former Tanzanian leader 'Mwalimu' (Teacher) Julius Nyerere loved that speech when he was translating the play into Kiswahili for publication by Oxford University Press in 1969:

... I am a Jew. Hath not a Jew eyes? Hath not a Jew hands, organs, dimensions, senses, affections, passions?—fed with the same food, hurt with the same weapons, subject to the same diseases, healed by the same means, warmed and cooled by the same winter and summer, as a Christian? If you prick us, do we not bleed? If you tickle us, do we not laugh? If you poison us, do we not die?

But Shylock soon disappoints us about his real motives. As he continues, it becomes clear that he is not using a shared humanity as a reason for tolerance, but as a reason for vengeance. When wronged by somebody else, a Christian may at least consider turning the other cheek. But Shylock says instead:

And if you wrong us, shall we not revenge? ... If a Christian wrongs a Jew, what should his sufferance be by Christian example? Why revenge! The villainy you teach me, I will execute.[6]

The conclusion to be drawn regarding Shylock and Othello is that, in Shakespeare's era, culture prejudice (such as anti-Semitism) was much stronger than colour prejudice (such as Negrophobia). The apartheid of values overshadowed the apartheid of skin-colour. Venice represented a Europe that was yet to be truly consumed by outright racism or the bigotry of skin-colour.

However, in the succeeding centuries, the English people and their overseas descendants became more and more averse to Blackness and less and less hostile to Jewishness. Among Anglo-Saxon prejudices, colour eventually overshadowed culture decisively for several centuries. The Europe of institutionalised racism was asserting and consolidating itself in this new phase of the Black Atlantic.

But the phenomenon of Barack Obama now poses new challenges. The central question that our own twenty-first century poses is whether, at the global level, we are returning to a kind of Shakespearean scale of values. Of course colour racism is still alive and well, but is it losing salience in human behaviour? Culture conflict goes back to the Crusades of the eleventh century, and further back to 'tribal' societies. Are we now witnessing a resurgence of cultural belligerence in human affairs in the wake of globalisation and unprecedented inter-continental migratory patterns?

In his successful campaign to win the White House in 2008, Barack Obama was sometimes less threatened by his obvious black skin colour than by the obstinate suspicion that he might be a closet Muslim. A hypothetical Obama friendship with a Muslim imam would have destroyed Obama more decisively than did his twenty-year friendship with the Christian reverend Jeremiah Wright. Is the shaikh of Islam the next Shylock of culture prejudice? Is this culture line slowly superseding the colour line as the dominant foundation of inter-group prejudice?

There may be far more racist American voters than the polls indicated before the 2008 presidential election. It may be too early to reach definite conclusions, but the fellow Nobel Peace Prize winners Barack Obama and Nelson Mandela—South Africa's president between 1994 and 1999—together may nevertheless be pioneering icons of a newly unfolding post-racial age. Let us look more closely at this historic juxtaposition.

Paradoxes of a broken home

Are Nelson Mandela and Barack Obama really icons of the post-racial age that is still unfolding? If they are, they are very different post-racial icons. Mandela was very much a child of the struggle against racism at its height, whereas Obama attained maturity when racism was on the decline and the civil rights movement in the United States had already attained some of its most important achievements.

Indeed, Obama was born in 1961, nearly a decade after the US Supreme Court decision *Brown v. Board of Education* in 1954, which struck down school segregation in the United States. Barack was born in Hawaii during the 1960s, when the civil rights struggle was at its most earnest, and voting rights for black people were expanded. The racial system of Jim Crow was under sustained attack, but the country was not yet dreaming about a post-racial America.

Obama's parents—Ann Dunham, the white woman from Kansas, and the senior Obama, a black man from Kenya—were married during the final decade of an America that still had laws against inter-racial marriage, or what the laws described as 'miscegenation'. By a strange coincidence, young

Barack saw his father for the last time at just about the time that the US Supreme Court had just struck down anti-miscegenation laws as unconstitutional. The seminal case was between the State of Virginia and an interracial couple coincidentally with the surname Loving (*Virginia v. Loving*). Young Barack was ten years old when he saw his father for the last time—eight years after their previous encounter.

The racial infrastructure of the United States was being dismantled brick by brick. The deracialisation of America had begun. A post-racial America awaited Obama's potential leadership as conceivably the first black president of the United States. A major precondition of his preparation for the American presidency was being abandoned by his African father. Being brought up by a single white mother, instead of by a biracial couple, turned out to be a political blessing in disguise for Barack.

His parents' divorce must be counted by historians as one of the most significant matrimonial break-ups in history, with Obama winning the US presidency in November 2008. Why? Had Barack Obama Senior remained married to his wife from Kansas, and had the boy been brought up by both parents, the child would have become more of an African and less of a full-blooded American. His credentials for being an attractive candidate for the US presidency would have been drastically reduced.

Ann Dunham's divorce from the elder Obama has turned out to be almost as historic as the brutal so-called divorce of Anne Boleyn from Henry VIII. Anne Boleyn was, of course, executed. The king's obsession with divorce or annulment set the stage for the birth of the Church of England (the Anglican and Episcopalian legacy).

If young Barack had been brought up by his father, and become a member of the black Diaspora of post-coloniality, he would have been a case of another African sending remittances back home to Kenya. If Obama was prepared to serve in the poor areas of Chicago as a matter of conscience, he would also have been tempted to serve in Africa—a case of 'brain gain'. Since Barack was one of the most brilliant black students ever to graduate from Harvard Law School, this brilliance could have been mobilised to serve Africa as 'brain gain'. There is another great *might-have-been:* if Barack Obama's mother had been black, but his wife white, it is unlikely he would have been chosen as the Democratic nominee for US president in 2008. American culture accepts a white mother of a black child more easily than it does a white wife of a black man. An African American married to a white woman could have been less attractive to African American voters—

as well as less politically attractive to blue-collar white voters. A white first lady married to a black president would have been a bleak prospect to many race-conscious voters, both black and white. Many African American women sometimes feel offended when a highly eligible black male turns to a white female and proposes marriage. An Obama married to a white woman would not have made it even halfway.

From race-conscious DuBois to post-racial Obama?

Let us now compare Barack Obama, as a child of the twentieth century, with W.E.B. DuBois, who was born in the nineteenth century. By a strange destiny, DuBois died in August 1963 at about the time that Barack was born. But this was not a case of the torch being passed to a new generation of African Americans. It was also certainly not a case of reincarnation. On the contrary, the two historical figures turned out to symbolise two entirely different paradigms of inter-group relations in American history.

But let us begin with what DuBois and Obama had in common. Both were products of intermarriage between black and white. Both carried names that betrayed their bicultural descent. Barack Obama's name betrayed his Luo ancestry on the side of his Kenyan father; William Edward Burghardt DuBois's name betrayed his French legacy on his father's side. Both suffered from a crisis of identity in their earlier years. In personal appearance, DuBois was much fairer in skin colour than Obama. However, over time, DuBois identified himself with black identity more passionately than did Obama. Indeed, DuBois came to see himself as first and foremost an African: he eventually naturalised as a citizen of Ghana, and died and was buried in that country in 1963. Obama, on the other hand, saw himself as less and less of an African, despite the fact that his father was born an African and died as a citizen of Kenya. In terms of preferred policy, W.E.B. DuBois was a Black Atlanticist: he dreamed of the unification of the African Diaspora in the Americas with Black Africa as a new racial Commonwealth in the world system. Barack Obama sees himself as fundamentally an American, and forever a citizen of the United States.

In 1895, DuBois became the first African American to receive a doctorate in history from Harvard University. His pre-doctoral degree was from Fisk University in Nashville, Tennessee. In 1990, Obama became the first African American to be elected president of the *Harvard Law Review* in Cambridge, Massachusetts. Obama's pre-law degree was from Columbia University in

New York. In his younger years, DuBois was often regarded as 'not Negro enough', partly because he was fair-skinned, and partly because of his upper social class demeanour. Throughout much of his career, Barack Obama was demeaned by some fellow African Americans as 'not Black enough', more because he was brought up in a white family by his grandmother than simply because his Kansas mother was white. In later years, Obama's brilliant Harvard career earned him the political stigma of 'elitist'.

DuBois's vision of the proper destiny for African Americans had two contemporary rivals. Booker T. Washington wanted African Americans to forego—for a while—political power, civil liberties, and higher education in the liberal arts and the liberal professions. His 'Tuskegee Machine' recommended 'industrial education' for black youth instead. Washington was at the peak of his influence from 1895 to 1910. In contrast, DuBois's vision of education for America's black youth focused on cultivating what he called 'the Talented Tenth' in preparation for black entry into 'modern civilization'.

Another rival black vision in DuBois's era was that championed by Marcus Garvey, a Jamaican immigrant to the United States who succeeded in mobilising many thousands of African Americans in the 1920s to pursue private enterprise, and to aspire to migrate back to Africa en masse. W.E.B. DuBois and Marcus Garvey debated with each other in abusive terms and even exchanged racial epithets. In their different ways, both DuBois and Marcus Garvey were Black Atlanticists. But while DuBois aspired to send to Africa some members of the 'Talented Tenth' of the Black Diaspora to help develop and even 'civilise' Africa, Marcus Garvey believed in a kind of 'Black Zionism'. For Garvey, all African peoples in the Diaspora were entitled to the right of returning to Africa. But since most of Africa was still colonised in the first half of the twentieth century, Garvey's dream was even more remote than DuBois's 'Talented Tenth' vision.

While in policy terms W.E.B. DuBois limited himself to the unity of the Black Atlantic, his own de facto concept of 'Global Africa' included a version of the Black Indian Ocean. Indeed, DuBois went to the extent of claiming that black-skinned South Asians like Tamils of India and Sri Lanka were descended from black Africans of pre-recorded history.

Barack Obama's dream of a post-racial America also had rival paradigms among African Americans. Prominent civil rights leaders Jesse Jackson and Andrew Young believed in the integration of African Americans into mainstream American culture, but still retained and defended black race-consciousness. Jackson and Young sought to promote a *multi-racial* America, while Obama championed a *non-racial* America.

The third black school of thought in Barack Obama's life was that represented by his pastor for twenty years, the Reverend Jeremiah Wright of Trinity United Church of Christ in Chicago. The Reverend Wright's America was far from being *non-racial* like Obama's dream. Nor was Wright's preferred America *multi-racial* like that of Andrew Young and Jesse Jackson. Essentially, the Reverend Jeremiah Wright was *racially separatist*, although the wider church to which he belonged was committed to *multi-racialism* and racial integration.

But a more fundamental shift that was taking place from the world of DuBois early in the twentieth century to the world of Barack Obama early in the twenty-first century was a shift from prejudice based on differences in colour to prejudice based on differences in culture. It is to this massive paradigm-shift that we must now turn.

From the colour line to the culture line

At the beginning of the twentieth century, W.E.B. DuBois, the great African American thinker and leader, predicted that the central problem of the twentieth century would be 'the problem of the colour line'. DuBois prophetically foresaw the century engulfed by racism, lynching, the 'white man's burden', and what came to be known as apartheid. The twentieth century was overwhelmed by refugees on the run from racially and nationalistically instigated conflicts.[7]

Now that we are in the twenty-first century, the question has arisen of whether its central problem is going to be the problem of 'the culture line'. Has a transition occurred between a 'clash of identities' (such as races) to a 'clash of values' (such as cultural norms in conflict)? Are refugees in the twenty-first century already disproportionately *cultural* refugees?

The late American political scientist Samuel Huntington was not, of course, a latter-day W.E.B. DuBois. But, on the eve of the twenty-first century, Huntington famously forecast in 1993 that the twenty-first century was headed for a 'Clash of Civilizations'.[8] He argued that, with the Cold War having ended, future conflicts in the world would be less and less between states and ideological blocs, and more and more between civilisations and cultural coalitions. Huntington launched this debate with his famous 1993 article in the journal *Foreign Affairs*—an article that reverberated around the world. He followed this up with a major book on the same subject.[9]

While another distinguished African American scholar, William Julius Wilson, had earlier predicted the declining significance of race[10]—as race was increasingly overshadowed by class and economics—Huntington predicted the rising salience of culture, overshadowing both race and class. Wilson, once a professor at the University of Chicago, later moved to Harvard University, where Huntington had also taught.

Worldwide, there was evidence in the last years of the twentieth century that the salience of race was on the decline. There was also evidence that the salience of culture was on the rise. However, today, this balance varies from country to country. South Africa is a less racist society than it was in the 1980s. But the Netherlands and Norway may be more racist in 2012 than twenty years before.

Overt discrimination was ending in Africa and the United States: black folks have had the vote and influenced outcomes. In the US, the House of Representatives has had multiple black members. But by 2008 the Senate had had only six black members in 200 years.[11] Yet the freshman black senator Barack Obama became a superstar and was elected president of the United States in November 2008.

Old-style race-based European colonialism has ended in Africa. Political apartheid has collapsed in South Africa. Overt racism is on the defensive, in spite of rearguard actions in Britain, Germany, France, the United States, and indeed the law enforcement system in Norway. At the global level, there is more Islamophobia than Negrophobia. But there are a few countries in which Negrophobia is increasing rather than diminishing.

Globalisation has generated international migration. And these migratory patterns, in the short run, continue to trigger racist challenges and responses. (See chapter 20 in this volume.) But over the long run, migration is eroding prejudice based on skin colour and increasing prejudice based on conflicting values. In what sense is this rise in culture-conflict threatening to erode Africa's ecumenical spirit?

A major area of the salience of culture is the confrontation between political Islam, on one hand, and the American anti-terrorist alliance, on the other. Since the end of the Cold War and the collapse of apartheid in 1994, far more Muslims than blacks have perished in conflicts with white folks. The natural enemy of the white man is now perceived to be less and less a person with a different skin colour, and more and more a person with a different religion and values. The salience of culture continues to rise. As earlier noted, Barack Obama's prospects for the United States presidency in 2008 were threatened less by his being black (which is self-evident) than by the widespread rumours that he was a closet Muslim in disguise. His African name of 'Obama' has been less of a handicap than his Muslim middle name of 'Hussein'.

Inter-racial wars of black versus white have almost disappeared. But inter-cultural and inter-religious wars in the decade of the 2000s raged mostly in Iraq, Afghanistan, Kosovo, and Chechnya, between Israelis and Palestinians—and between Al-Qaeda and its enemies in Africa and across the world. On the whole, these conflicts produced cultural refugees rather than racial asylum-seekers. Africa has often been caught in the crossfire.

The worst terrorist acts in sub-Saharan Africa in recent years have not been between races, but between civilisations. These include the 1998 bombing of the US embassies in Nairobi (Kenya) and Dar-es-Salaam (Tanzania), and the 2002 suicide bombing of an Israeli-owned hotel in the Kenyan port city of Mombasa. In order to kill 12 Americans, Arab militants massacred over 200 Kenyans in the embassy atrocity in Nairobi. The Kenyans were caught in the crossfire in 1998.[12] And the number of Kenyans who were killed at the Paradise Hotel in Mombasa was three times the number of Israeli casualties.[13] In confrontations between antagonistic cultures, many cultural bystanders are often annihilated by default.

The jails of the United States are still full of black people in disproportionate members.[14] But black prisoners have been convicted for violating the civil code, and are in jail for such alleged offences as robbery, rape, murder, assault, and drug abuse.[15] But overwhelmingly the political prisoners under American jurisdiction are culturally distinct. They are Muslims suspected of terrorist intent—whether the suspicions are validated or not.[16] Many of these individuals are African members of the Muslim world. Most prisoners were denied access to a lawyer, and were seldom told of the evidence against them. Both the Black Atlantic and the Black Indian Ocean have become major theatres of culturally inspired terrorism and counterterrorism.

As for the 'extraordinary rendition' through which the United States sent terrorist suspects for interrogation in countries with a history of torture, unfortunately many of those receiving countries were in Africa—both north of the Sahara and in the Horn. African countries inhabited by both Muslims and Christians were reported to be doing America's dirty work. Good relations between Africa's own Christians and Muslims have been endangered by this policy of 'extraordinary rendition'.

From 'triple heritage' to globalisation

It is not often realised that the globalisation of Pan-Africanism has also been—almost unconsciously—a transition from solidarity based on skin colour to a new solidarity based on shared cultural experience. The 'Founding Fathers' of Pan-Africanism were almost unaware of this remarkable transition. By a strange twist of destiny, Pan-Africanism led the way from the politics of colour-identity to the politics of the identity of shared cultural experience.

Within the Black Atlantic, this began with the ultimate contradiction of W.E.B. DuBois: a man whose family name was French, whose actual physical appearance was virtually white, but whose allegiance was indisputably African. DuBois was the reverse of the Englishman William Blake's poem about the African child. For Blake (1757–1827), the child was black, but 'Oh good Lord, his soul was white' ('The Little Black Boy').[17] For W.E.B. DuBois, one could proclaim the reverse—that this man was white, but 'Oh good Lord, his soul was black'. As we intimated earlier, DuBois's actual skin-colour defied his real cultural allegiance. What the DuBois paradox taught us was that 'Blackness' could be a cultural identity rather than a physical appearance. As for Barack Obama, he was culturally brought up in a white home under his maternal grandmother. Even in multi-racial Hawaii, he went to a school that was disproportionately white. For quite a while, Barack was psychologically caught between a black skin and a white culture.

Then there was the phenomenon of another Father of Pan-Africanism, the Trinidadian George Padmore, in his fascination with Marxism, alongside the response of W.E.B. DuBois to historical materialism. Here were two major Pan-African thinkers who were involved in the politics of black identity, while at the same time being drawn towards the ideas of an ethnic German Jew named Karl Marx. Padmore's most influential book, published in 1956, was indeed originally titled *Pan-Africanism or Communism? The Coming Struggle for Africa*.[18] This was an illustration of a huge ideological ambivalence between the politics of Blackness on the one hand, and the politics of class—regardless of race—on the other. The Black Atlantic was particularly exposed to the ideological winds of Western civilisation. (See chapter 3 in this volume on Pan-Africanism.)

On the whole, almost without realising it, W.E.B. DuBois and George Padmore were products of the 'dual heritage': two converging civilisations. Both were Pan-African titans and products of left-wing Western civilisation on the one hand, and left-wing Pan-Africanists on the other. Without fully realising it, DuBois and Padmore constituted a transition from the politics of Black identity to the politics of multicultural ideologies.

Then came Ghana's Kwame Nkrumah. He constituted the next stage of transition from the 'dual heritage' of leftist Westernism and leftist African-ism to the new 'triple heritage' of Africanity, Islam, and Western civilisation. Kwame Nkrumah called this convergence *Consciencism*[19]—identifying it as a synthesis of African tradition, Islamic heritage, and what he called 'Euro-Christian values'. Barack Obama, when he was very young, was briefly influenced by both Islam and Westernism.

The concept of 'Global Africa' did not emerge until the 1980s. Was this concept first proclaimed in the ninth programme of my 1986 television series *The Africans: A Triple Heritage*? I titled this concluding programme 'Global Africa', and promoted a synthesis of three cultures—Africanity, Islam, and Westernism. Was this a prelude to cultural globalisation? Had his Kenyan father not abandoned Obama, he might have become a product of this 'triple heritage'.

The concept of 'Africa's triple heritage' came with me in the 1980s. But the fusion of three civilisations originated with Americo-Liberian intellectual Edward Blyden's *Christianity, Islam, and the Negro Race*, which was published in 1887.[20] This was then reincorporated in Kwame Nkrumah's *Consciencism* in 1964, and consummated in my *Triple Heritage* series in 1986.

Obviously this was a transition from the politics of colour to the politics of culture. Kwame Nkrumah reconfirmed this approach in his marriage to a white-skinned Egyptian woman, Fathia Rizk. The bride was Arab linguistically, Christian by religion, and fair-skinned in colour. Nkrumah's Pan-Africanism had gone both multicultural and multiracial.

The brain drain and Global Africa

It is widely understood that two interactive forces cause a 'brain drain' from Africa to the West—the 'push-out' factors in weak countries in Africa and the 'pull-in' factors in stronger Western countries, which serve as magnets. The 'push-out' factors in Africa include political instability, economic uncertainty, the pendulum between too much government (tyranny) and too little government (anarchy), and the resulting dilution of occupational opportunities and professional recognition. The 'pull-in' factors in stronger and more stable countries include higher professional rewards, greater political openness, and the reassurance of stability and better prospects for one's children and grandchildren.

But are African conditions always a 'push-out' force? And is the Western world always a 'pull-in' magnetic force? There are changes at work that are likely to affect the balance between the 'brain drain' and the 'brain gain'. The senior Barack Obama (the father) resisted the 'pull-in' factors of the United States: he returned to Kenya, leaving his young son behind. Inadvertently, the father permitted his son to become American enough to become a credible candidate for the US presidency.

A distinction needs to be made between *Africans of the blood* and *Africans of the soil*. Those of the blood belong to the African race, but not necessarily to the African continent. Africans of the soil, on the other hand, belong to the African continent but not necessarily to the Black race. By being left behind in America by his father, young Barack Obama was prevented from becoming an African of the soil and became only an African of the blood. Most Algerians, Tunisians, and Egyptians are Africans of the soil but not of the blood. Most African Americans, Afro-Brazilians, and Afro-Jamaicans are Africans of the blood—belonging to the Black race, but no longer to the African continent. However, most black people who reside south of the Sahara are Africans of both the blood and the soil.

Boutros Boutros-Ghali, Egypt's former UN Secretary-General (1992–1996), was an African of the soil by ancestry. F.W. De Klerk, former president of South Africa (1989–1994), was an African of the soil by adoption. On the other hand, Ghana's Kofi Annan, the UN Secretary-General between 1997 and 2006, was an African of both the blood and the soil. There are Africans of the blood objectively who may not subjectively regard themselves as Africans at all. These would include Saudi or Kuwaiti princes with black mothers. The longtime Saudi ambassador to the United States, Prince Bandar bin Sultan (who held the post between 1983 and 2005), was objectively an African of the blood, but subjectively in denial about his Africanity. The late President Anwar Sadat of Egypt (in power between 1970 and 1981) was African of the soil both objectively and subjectively. Because his mother was black, Anwar Sadat was also an African of the blood, but only objectively. He did not, however, regard himself as a black African at all.

When Africans of the blood rise higher and higher in national and international positions, that is one more measurement of declining racism in the global equation. It is no longer uncommon to see black cabinet officials, legislators, judges, and businessmen and women in countries in the Middle East, Europe, and the Western Hemisphere. This is a very important development. In the United States, for example, the George W. Bush administration (2001–2008) had three blacks in top government positions: the secretary of state, Colin Powell; the national security adviser (and later secretary of state), Condoleezza Rice; and the secretary of education, Rod Paige. Also, the 110th Congress of the United States, which took office in January 2007, had 43 black members, which included 42 members (nearly 10 per cent) of the 435 total members in the House of Representatives, and one black Senator (the Kenyan-Kansan Barack Obama).[21] The Congress of 2007 even included two Muslim black members in the House of Representatives. In addition, there was a black man, Clarence Thomas, among the nine members of the US Supreme Court in 2012. In Brazil, Raymond Colitt reported in the *Financial Times* in May 2003 that, for the first time, a black man—Barbosa Gomes—had been appointed to the Brazilian Supreme Court.[22] Does a black president of the United States represent the pinnacle of black ascent and upward mobility?

When individual Africans rise higher, collective racism is on notice. In Britain, under Tony Blair (1997–2007), there were two black cabinet ministers in the Labour government: Paul Boateng as Treasury minister became the first black cabinet minister in the country's history in 2002, while Baroness Amos, the first black woman cabinet minister, was appointed International Development secretary in 2003. In Gordon Brown's government, between 2007 and 2010, the attorney general, Baroness Scotland, was a black woman. In the United States, Barack Obama retained his African names and even his culturally Muslim middle name (Hussein). Unlike Prince Bandar of Saudi Arabia, Obama retained a conscious African connection; Barack, unlike Bandar, was not in denial.

Even before the two African Secretaries-General of the United Nations (Egypt's Boutros Boutros-Ghali and Ghana's Kofi Annan), Africa had already produced a black director-general of the Paris-based United Nations Educational, Scientific, and Cultural Organisation (UNESCO). Senegal's Amadou Mahtar M'Bow (in office between 1974 and 1987) was an African of both the blood and the soil. His openly pro-Third World policies infuriated the United States, which withdrew from UNESCO in 1985, followed by its compliant British ally a year later. London returned to UNESCO in 1997 after the sweeping victory of the Labour Party in the national elections.[23]

The International Court of Justice (ICJ) at The Hague elected an African of both the blood and the soil, Nigeria's T.O. Elias, as its first African president, between 1982 and 1985. An African of the soil, Algeria's Mohammed

Medjauni, was elected as the ICJ's president in 1994. The World Bank in the 1990s had two African vice presidents—Callisto Madivo, an African of both the blood and the soil from Zimbabwe, and Ismail Serageldin, an African of the soil from Egypt. In 1999, Serageldin was also a serious candidate in an unsuccessful bid to become the first UNESCO director-general of the new millennium.[24]

The Commonwealth (former British Commonwealth) had Third World secretaries-general for two and a half decades—Shridath Ramphal of Guyana (1975–1990) and Emeka Anyaoku of Nigeria (1990–1999). Both were only partially diverted by the 'brain drain'.

Ralph Bunche and Martin Luther King Jr. were, of course, African American Nobel peace laureates, Africans of the blood in our sense, but not of the soil. Anwar Sadat and F.W. De Klerk, also Nobel peace laureates, were Africans of the soil but not of the blood. Albert Luthuli, Desmond Tutu, and Nelson Mandela were Africans of both the soil and the blood. All three were South Africans, as was F.W. De Klerk. But we should note that De Klerk is an 'African of the soil' by adoption rather than by indigenous roots to the continent. Kofi Annan, Kenya's environmental activist Wangari Maathai, and two Liberian gender activists, Ellen Johnson-Sirleaf and Leymah Gbowee, as Nobel peace laureates, are Africans of both the soil and the blood. Another Nobel peace laureate—Egypt's Mohamed El Baradei, director-general of the International Atomic Energy Agency (IAEA) between 1997 and 2009—is an African of the soil. Obama himself, another Nobel peace laureate, is an African of the blood but not of the soil.

As the twentieth century was drawing to a close, Nelson Mandela achieved a unique status. He became the first truly universal black moral leader in the world in his own lifetime after spending twenty-seven years in prison. Martin Luther King Jr. achieved universal status after his own martyrdom in April 1968. King and Jesus Christ are the only two religious figures whose birthdays are federal holidays in the United States.

Positive globalisation needs new legal and moral standards. The shadows in Africa itself are not yet fully lifting. Poverty, underdevelopment, disease, and instability are still rampant across the continent. The 'brain drain' continues in an unrelenting manner. But the shadows of Africa's role in world affairs are indeed more clearly lifting. As US secretary of state Colin Powell—the son of Jamaican immigrants—was an African of the blood and a compatriot of Martin Luther King Jr. As UN Secretary-General Kofi Annan was an African of both the soil and the blood—and a compatriot of Kwame

Nkrumah. As for W.E.B. DuBois, he represented a reverse 'brain drain' from America to Africa. DuBois was also a compatriot of both Colin Powell (fellow African American) and Kwame Nkrumah (fellow Ghanaian).

The first African woman to win the Nobel Peace Prize, Wangari Maathai in 2004, was also the first black woman of any country to win that prize. And Liberia has led the way with the first elected woman president in Africa's history, Ellen Johnson-Sirleaf, who assumed office in January 2006, and won the Nobel Peace Prize in 2011 along with her compatriot Leymah Gbowee. Johnson-Sirleaf also happened to be a returnee from the Diaspora. A former member of Africa's 'brain drain' thus returned to Liberia to make gender history. With his election as US president in November 2008, Barack Obama may well be the final fulfilment of upward political mobility.

Concluding reflections

While W.E.B. DuBois's famous prophecy about the 'colour line' was indeed vindicated for the twentieth century, longer-term prophetic indications of the 'culture line' had begun to manifest themselves on the eve of the twenty-first century. Globalisation as a planetary phenomenon had been preceded by the cultural globalisation of Africa itself.

We have defined the Black Atlantic as a combination of Africa with the Black Diaspora scattered in the Western world. We have defined the Black Indian Ocean as a combination of Africa with the Black Diaspora scattered in the Middle East and Asia. Ironically, the Black Indian Ocean has had a longer history of racial intermarriage than has the Black Atlantic. Therefore, the African Diaspora in the Middle East and Asia started the process of deracialisation and declining race-consciousness sooner than did the Western world.

However, the age of post-racism has been more dramatic in the Black Atlantic, especially in the aftermath of decolonisation and the more recent dismantling of political apartheid in South Africa by 1994. But the era of post-racism is not the same thing as the post-racial age. Post-racism implies declining racism, which is more easily achieved than the end of race-consciousness. Barack Obama's dream is of an America that has not only transcended Jim Crow laws and racist attitudes, but has also become less and less conscious of racial differences. Booker T. Washington championed a black consciousness of humility, encouraging African Americans to learn basic skills without pursuing basic rights. W.E.B. DuBois championed a black consciousness of dignity and racial assertiveness, under the leadership of the 'Talented Tenth'. Marcus Garvey championed black separatism even to the extent of promoting African American migration back to Africa. Martin Luther King Jr. and Jesse Jackson both championed multi-racialism, or what Jesse Jackson called 'a rainbow coalition'.

What is distinctive about Barack Obama is a quest for non-racialism, rather than multi-racialism or a 'rainbow coalition'. Obama represents a new stage in the long odyssey of inter-racial relations. His quest for a post-racial America is being helped by a major shift in global patterns of prejudice. Race prejudices of the old kind are on the decline. On the other hand, culture prejudice is on the rise. The scale of values that had characterised Shakespeare's plays is now being revived. After all, Shakespeare's *Othello* was less racist than Shakespeare's *Merchant of Venice* was anti-Semitic.

Since the birth of this twenty-first century, far more people have died in militarised cultural conflicts than have died in militarised racial confrontations. Al-Qaeda as a movement of religious militancy has become much more relevant to world politics than has the Ku Klux Klan as a movement of racial arrogance.

With his election as US president in November 2008, Barack Obama became the most powerful black man in the history of civilisation. A post-racial world may continue to be elusive for at least another century. But 'Global Africa' is already feeling the vibrations of racism in retreat—and the rumblings of cultural forces on the ascent. Historians of the future have already been forewarned by a repentant Othello, hereby paraphrased:

> *When you shall these unlucky deeds relate,*
> *Speak of us as we are. Nothing extenuate.*
> *Nor set down ought in malice.*
> *Then must you speak,*
> *Of men that loved not wisely, but too well.*

22

EUROPE'S POSTCOLONIAL ROLE AND IDENTITY

Hartmut Mayer

Introduction

A final chapter in a comprehensive volume on Euro-African relations, provided by a German scholar of the European Union, requires careful positioning from the outset. This contribution is no doubt a beginner's approach to the world of 'Eurafrique' or 'Afro-europa' or whatever name is used for the new phase in the relations between two neighbouring continents in a fast-changing global environment (see introduction to this volume). In terms of scholarship, this is a continuation and a different application of my previous research on the EU's broad role in global governance.[1] As far as policymaking is concerned, it is a call first and foremost to Europeans to change the EU's global role and identity in order to reflect the actual shifts in global trends and to enable Brussels to play a more realistic, responsible, and constructive role in its engagement with Africa. In a book on Europe and Africa, this author suffers from asymmetrical knowledge: a fair amount of understanding about the EU is contrasted with a frightening amount of ignorance with regard to African affairs. For a scholar, this might be problematic. For a European citizen, it might be symptomatic. However, for the EU as such, it might be symbolic indeed. This author might represent a standard European policymaker, civil servant,

441

or politician who still embraces a *Weltanschauung* that puts Europe and the wider West at its centre and believes that European standards and modes of operation ought to be the universal norm. Here is where the chapter stands: it has certainly left the old world of 'Eurafrique' behind, but has not yet arrived at a notion of 'Afro-europa'.

Nevertheless, the clear starting assumption of this chapter is that Europe's influence and standing in the world of the twenty-first century can best be enhanced if Europe recognises the fact that it is nowadays embedded but not swallowed up in a 'non-European world'. Europe needs to acknowledge an increasingly peripheral place in world affairs, and must therefore design and implement a new general narrative for all its external engagements. (See chapter 8 in this volume, on EU-Asia relations.) Creating a new External Action Service as envisaged by the Lisbon Treaty of December 2007 and implemented since 2010, and presenting two new figureheads—Herman van Rompuy as Council president and Catherine Ashton as a 'quasi-foreign minister'—will not be sufficient. This institutional innovation, welcome as it may be, must be underpinned by a new rhetoric and etiquette. This applies to Africa and all other regions of the world. It would leave colonial attitudes and missions far behind, and focus on truly shared responsibilities with Europe's partners for all of the major global challenges that they confront. The European Union can only remain credible and effective if it shifts its mind-set from Europe's promises and ambitions to its global obligations. The chapter also calls for a more modest EU, which avoids the customary mistake of raising unrealistic and exaggerated expectations.[2] Instead of assuming more tasks by chance or by choice, Brussels must have a clearer sense of what it should do either alone or—better and more realistically—through inter-institutional cooperation. A responsible and capable EU would overcome Eurocentric notions of self-importance and serve the global community better through its very considerable economic and political means. Under this new approach, traditional missions without effective policies would be replaced by effective policies without traditional missions. This is particularly relevant for relations between Europe and Africa, where the colonial heritage is likely to continue to shape mutual perceptions and common projects.

Europe's global role and identity

The potential for further strategic engagement between Africa and Europe rests not only on the intertwined history and identity of the two continents as well as the web of political and economic partnership agreements. It also rests on both continents' relative position and self-perception in a rapidly changing world order. African and European countries and regional organisations have been forced to adapt to tectonic shifts in the post-Cold War order since 1990, with each continent individually and jointly adjusting to the newly enhanced partnership that has developed in the new millennium.

In the changing balance of relevant power in world affairs, economic globalisation, emerging regional powers, new security risks, and cultural diversity all contribute to an increasing marginalisation of Europe as a driver in world affairs. I argue here that, as a prerequisite for fostering new, stable, and mutually beneficial partnerships as envisaged with Africa[3] and other regions of the world, Europe must overcome its Eurocentric self-image and rhetoric and initiate a serious dialogue on its wider global responsibilities.

It is vital that Europe 'de-Europeanises' in order to remain a significant player in the emerging global order.[4] Policy discourses about the future of European external relations with Africa and other regions remain too self-absorbed on both sides. Europe still defines its outlook vis-à-vis Africa through self-interest: in different versions of the same mind-set, it sees Africa mainly as a supplier of raw materials, as an opportunity for business, as a competition playground with other global powers such as China and the United States, and as a potential threat to European stability.[5] African perceptions of Europe, on the other hand, are still often shaped by the colonial past, with notions of dependency, resistance, and requests for compensation for past wrongdoings. (See chapters 4 and 5 in this volume.)

However, when reflecting on the future direction of the EU's role in Africa and beyond, one must not draw a completely gloomy picture. Europe's role and responsibility in the world, in general, will remain important, and might even be revitalised if the EU quickly adopts a distinctly non-European perspective. In the decade of the 2000s in European-African relations, the highly institutionalised web of summits, joint actions plans, and strategies has on the whole been positive—even if these have often fallen far short of ambitions, failed tests of coherence and consistency, confirmed the famous 'capability-expectations' gap, reaffirmed mutual stereotypes, and witnessed rhetoric sometimes unrelated to reality and naked interests that have sometimes been presented as 'common goodwill'. However, what will be important for future progress in this relationship is the need to free Euro-African relations from the classic traps of tunnel vision and navel-gazing. Africa-Europe relations remain embedded in joint global responsibilities, and any future cooperation must be based on shared notions of global tasks. The real missing link remains between regionalism, inter-regionalism, bi-regionalism, and global governance: not Europe, not Africa, not Euro-African relations alone, but global concerns must always be the benchmark when assessing the future of EU-African relations.

This chapter makes a general case for how Europe should engage in world affairs, and applies this argument to the specific relationship between Africa and Europe. Within this general context, the chapter offers three main contributions to the debate. First, it elaborates why Europe needs a new narrative for its role in the world. Second, it analyses, more theoretically—based on six principles of institutional responsibility—how and why a proper understanding of global responsibility should become the guideline for any reflection on the future of EU-African relations. Third, it suggests practical implications for policymakers resulting from previous reflections on global responsibility, offering nine global priorities on which the EU must focus attention. The chapter then concludes with a few general reflections on how the EU should urgently redefine its global role towards Africa and other parts of the world if it is to remain a relevant power.

Why Europe needs a new narrative for its role in the world

A new narrative for Europe's international role is urgently needed. This is not to say that in the past Europe and the EU have been static in their conceptions of their global role. However, their current state of mind has not yet reached a level appropriate for the changes of the twenty-first-century world. The new narrative for Europe in the world needs to satisfy two different demands: first, it must recognise and accept the widely held external perceptions that Europe's future place in the global order is bound to be more peripheral; second, it must be squared with Europe's internal demand and ambition to remain an important force in the world and its desire to enhance this role at the international level. In essence, the question is how Europe can become smaller and bigger at the same time. A consistent narrative that combines global demands—originating from Africa, Asia, Russia, or America—with domestic expectations and adjustments, is the only route through which the EU can regain support at home and trust abroad. Only a convincing narrative of 'Europe in a non-European world' will provide the context for a narrative of 'EU-Africa in a world of common global challenges'. A reference to global challenges first and foremost can provide the legitimacy needed to allow the EU to act towards Africa as an equal and responsible partner, but no longer a dominant and overbearing one.

The external rationale

At the beginning of the twenty-first century, European and African nations live in a state of transition and uncertainty. Ever since the end of the Cold War in 1990, global order is constantly being reshaped[6] in ways that affect all states and regions. Finding one's place in a world of many worlds is becoming ever harder for all regional players.[7] As discussed in detail elsewhere,[8] ten key visions of global order seem to compete in the current international relations literature, including, most prominently, concepts of American unipolarity,[9] antagonistic and cooperative multipolarity, and notions of a transpolar order in which economic rather than political power is decisive. Visions of nonpolarity[10] have also proliferated in the intellectual debates. Different theoretical paradigms such as 'neorealist instability', 'unipolar or multipolar stability', and the notion of 'deep and divisive cultural friction', as well as more optimistic scenarios based on 'rules-based multilateralism', have been the conflicting parameters of the global debate in the post-Cold War era. As far as the EU is concerned, generally overlapping eclecticism or nonawareness of theoretical contradictions have characterised the rhetoric emanating from Brussels and national capitals across Europe. In its various publications, the EU has, for example, promoted first, a multipolar world with strategic partnerships at the heart of it; second, a world of integrated regions and inter-regionalism; and third, a world order based on 'effective multilateralism'. Brussels generally lacks a consistent strategic vision and has failed to explain whether all three visions are possible to pursue at once, whether one trumps another, or whether different rationales apply to different policy fields.[11] Leaving these debates aside for the moment, any reflections on EU-Africa relations must naturally be part of the crucial larger debates on general global order, the political dimensions of globalisation, and the place of Europe and Africa within a world of different worlds.

Scholars and policymakers who work on Europe's external relations have broadly failed to integrate themselves sufficiently with thinkers on globalisation, global order, development studies, and non-Western approaches to international affairs. With this in mind, Europe's new identity as a basis for revived and mutually beneficial Africa-Europe relations should at least consider the following six missing links in the standard research agendas: first, the relationship between globalisation and regionalisation; second, a realistic assessment of Europe's actual place in a de-Westernising world and Europe's contribution to global governance; third, the general tension between universal value systems and regional interpretations of universality; fourth, the obvious discrepancy between the EU's rhetoric and its actions in world affairs; fifth, the mutual interplay between Europe's confident self-image and the very diverging outside perceptions of 'Fortress Europe'; and finally, the intellectual merger of the postcolonial perspective with European debates on its own global role.

While this chapter does not address all of these issues, it highlights a general reference point: shared 'global responsibility'. This offers a way of integrating some of these concerns, and becomes the litmus test for constructive Africa-European engagement.

The EU's global responsibilities

In the ears of African citizens and policymakers, defining notions of 'global responsibility' might once again sound like the oldest feature of colonial rule: Europe once again defining values on its owns terms and in its own interests, and then declaring them to be global necessities. Offering moral principles and ethical values as a guideline for a new narrative of the EU in the world and Brussels's external actions might not appear to be a significant departure from traditional thinking in the field. Most writing on the EU as a global actor, from the very beginning of this research, such as that undertaken by Swedish scholar Gunnar Sjöstedt in the mid-1970s,[12] has perceived shared values and principles as the prerequisite for European action. Scholarship on EU external 'actorness' normally analyses overarching values alongside limited capacity to mobilise common policies as one of the principal pillars of Brussels's external relations.[13] Furthermore, all popular theoretical labels—such as 'civilian power',[14] 'normative power',[15] 'soft empire',[16] 'transformative power',[17] 'ambiguous power',[18] 'conflicted trade power',[19] 'green normative power',[20] or even 'metrosexual superpower'[21]—are based on the notion of the EU as a uniquely norm-promoting force.

With this plethora of concepts, why would one need another norm-based approach? I simply advocate a change of perspective: Europe's self-image of a force that is 'doing good for the whole world', and most other normative approaches, so far, start off from a European departure point—the continent's own desires, missions, and convictions. This is essentially an 'inside-out' perspective. Europe is seen as the transmitter of global norms and voluntarily assumes global responsibilities. For our subject, this traditional notion would mean that Europe alone could determine what to do with, for, and about Africa, as well as when and how. The basic assumption tended to be that 'what is good for Europe must be good for the world'. What is instead needed is a perspective acknowledging that Europe is nowadays the receiver of global obligations that are allocated to the EU by general global moral considerations.

The discourse of such global obligations must be shaped by non-European thinkers as well: by African, Asian, Latin American, Russian, and Muslim voices, as well as whoever else wishes to engage in this dialogue. However, these agents must also be bound by global public goods and necessities rather than solely by their own perceived interests. It means that there is no more 'Eurafrique', maybe no 'Afro-europa' either, but possibly that there is, in the end, a 'Globafricopa'. Only an 'outside-in' perspective can make sense for Europe and most likely for Africa as well. One needs to define global responsibility first and then ask what Europe as a whole, and the EU in particular—with its unique set of instruments, values, and capacities—ought to do to qualify as a responsible actor in world affairs. The same should apply to Africa, with its own unique set of opportunities and instruments.

My previous work defined an initial set of general moral principles, admittedly shaped by Western thinking, that one ought to apply when distributing such responsibilities to different actors and regions.[22] The six principles of global responsibility are the following:

1. *The contribution principle.* An actor has a duty to mitigate harmful consequences of action to which it has contributed. If it has caused and contributed to a situation of harm or loss, it is clearly responsible.
2. *The beneficiary principle.* If an actor has benefitted from a situation whereby others suffered harm or loss, it has a duty to alleviate the harm or reduce the loss.
3. *The community principle.* Membership in a community or group means incurring certain duties. If one is part of a community, one has a responsibility to obey the law, rules, and customs of that community.
4. *The capacity principle.* If there is a valid obligation to perform a particular duty, then all actors who are capable of fulfilling that duty must act.

5. *The legitimate expectation principle.* An actor is obligated to perform a particular duty if others legitimately expect the actor to perform that duty. This principle is very difficult to put into practice. However, the clearest obligation arises if an institution has repeatedly stated an intent to perform a particular duty.

6. *The consent principle.* An actor is obliged to do something once it has voluntarily consented to do so.

Before addressing the potential implications for Europe-Africa relations of these six principles, one further qualification needs to be made when applying these ideals to the EU: an adverse actor with overlapping responsibilities among its twenty-seven member states and its own institutions. (See chapter 3 in this volume.) How much responsibility would rest with the EU, and how much with its member states? Since Brussels's external relations are a combination of those of the EU as a whole and those of its individual member states, this implies that, with shared agency, there is also shared responsibility. For example, if one takes the 'contribution principle' seriously, would the EU in its entirety be responsible for historical wrongdoings such as colonial crimes committed by Britain and France in Africa, India, and elsewhere, or even for Germany's Nazi Holocaust? Surely not, as these national historical responsibilities must rest with each member state. But what if—as for example in the case of the seventy-nine-member Africa, Caribbean, and Pacific (ACP) group in its agreements with the EU and, in fact, in the case of most relations with African countries and regional bodies—colonial heritages and patterns were simply transformed and translated into European preferences and privileged policies? Then, surely, the EU as a whole must bear some responsibility for perceived injustices that flow from its own policies. These examples show that the distinctions remain somewhat blurred, and that determining the moral obligations to specific actors—be they nation-states, the EU, or any other actor—is an extremely difficult task.

In relations between Africa and Europe, some guilt stemming from colonial wrongdoings of EU member states must be taken aboard by Brussels. (See chapter 2 in this volume.) The reason is that such colonial misdeeds became part of the EU's heritage as member states transferred and translated them into the organisation's early development policies. With regard to Africa, the EU's responsibility to engage with the continent and to fulfil its duties is considerably higher than for other actors as a direct result of the 'contribution principle' defined earlier.

Another problem arises from overlapping and conflicting sources of responsibility. Any real political decision may have very different consequences for different communities. An illustrative and important example for Europe-Africa relations is the EU's external trade policy. The confusion and contradiction of the EU's economic partnership agreements is discussed elsewhere in this volume. (See chapters 10 and 11.) What should be clear here is that the general principles of global responsibility can send confusing messages when it comes to implementing them in practice.

A major question that thus arises is: To whom should the EU be responsible when it makes and implements its trade policies? One can distinguish between five different responsibilities: first, to the 500 million European citizens who would be directly and adversely affected by the EU's international trade decisions or by the lowering of subsidies for its industries; second, to EU residents in general; third, to people in former European colonies (including the seventy-nine ACP countries); fourth, to the functioning of the existing international trading system; and, fifth, to people in the world at large. Studies have shown that the EU tended to give priority in the past to one of the first four constituencies over the fifth. However, one cannot conclude that any of the first four priorities would always trump the others.[23] If global responsibility—that is, concerns for all residents of the world at large, and in our particular case, non-ACP citizens in Africa—was the first priority, the EU would clearly be judged as not having fulfilled its duties. If, however, the community principle were to be highlighted, then Brussels's record would look better. This example, which is highly relevant for future discourses between Europe and Africa, indicates an important problem that emerges when asking about the general practical relevance of abstract moral principles: What is their use for practical decisionmaking, and how does one translate such principles into policies?

Let me try to provide some answers. Five general practical functions of a 'globally responsible Europe' can be identified. I have elaborated on each of these in turn elsewhere,[24] but present a brief summary here:

1. The normative origins of EU policies towards Africa in the context of global policy goals provide a check on what Brussels should and should not do. They also generate better policy-relevant questions, although they do not provide all the answers. This is particularly relevant for the relationship between Europe and Africa, a relationship historically more charged than any other.

2. A justification of origins of responsibility allows for a better sense of priorities when deciding what Europe should do first and foremost in light of its overall limited capacities. Assessing European-African relations in an isolated prism would deprive this dialogue of that crucial global checklist.

3. European foreign policy making still very much depends on national (French, British, Portuguese, Nordic, and other) preferences, legacies, and practices (see chapters 16–19 in this volume). Thinking about common European responsibilities helps to overcome purely national perspectives. As far as approaches to Africa are concerned, a better convergence of perceived interests or even a guideline for responsible European responses to neocolonial tendencies by some EU member states seems possible.

4. In light of Europe's colonial past and its legacy of *mission civilisatrice*, a normative and global EU must make the principles of ethical claims available to others. In our case, Europe has to persuade Africa that it promotes common ideas rather than prescribing and promoting its own parochial interests. Brussels can shape the direction of the Euro-African dialogue only through a two-way discourse and not through unilateral imposition of its own preferences. Transparency about the legitimacy of Europe's global tasks and shared responsibilities reduces the problem of 'asymmetrical discourses', of which the EU has so often been accused.

5. After having identified and made transparent the underlying principles that guide Europe's global actions, Brussels could reasonably ask its partners in Africa and elsewhere to offer a similarly coherent justification for their claims at the global table. A mature EU-Africa partnership that shares global responsibilities would certainly need such a mutually enriching debate.

The EU's global priorities

On the whole, the key to success in the EU's engagement with Africa will not rest only on abstract formulations of global obligations derived from general principles of morality. It is also important to place EU-Africa relations into a perspective of priority within the overall set of global tasks. For African observers who might suffer from tunnel vision and might therefore exaggerate the weight of EU-Africa relations in Brussels's overall set of global responsibilities, I provide a list of policy priorities for the EU that was originally drawn up for a larger study on Europe's global role. The rationale for the list is explained in detail elsewhere.[25] This is by no means a general list of global priorities, but a list of *EU responsibilities* that are based on the organisation's actual capacities and primary obligations when considered in light of our six foundations of global obligations. The nine priorities are:

1. Internal EU consolidation (to include a unified view in external affairs).
2. A new transatlantic understanding—the rescue of the West—and the joint project of managing multipolarity in the twenty-first century.
3. Engaging with Russia as a uniquely European responsibility.
4. Advancement of the EU's Neighbourhood Policy.
5. Comprehensive reflection on inter-institutional burden-sharing: new cooperation with the United Nations, the North Atlantic Treaty Organisation (NATO), the World Trade Organisation (WTO), the Organisation for Security and Cooperation in Europe (OSCE), the Association of Southeast Asian Nations (ASEAN), the Council of Europe, and many other regional organisations.
6. Constructive and realistic engagement in the Middle East.
7. Global development policy within and beyond the current preferential focus on the seventy-nine ACP states.
8. Contribution to the larger sustainable development agenda.
9. Cooperative inter-regionalism and larger EU regional strategies for Asia, Latin America, and Africa.

This list might look particularly strange in the context of a book on Africa-European relations. However, it is important that Africans are cognisant about their place in the EU's global priorities. Many of Africa's concerns—which are at the heart of this volume—are also implicit in some of these priorities, such as 'internal consolidation' (for example, coherence and consistency in development policy) and 'reviving a Western position', particularly 'institutional burden-sharing'. In addition, many of the actual problems facing Africa cannot be addressed principally by Europe, and must be achieved through common efforts in various multilateral forums such as the UN and the WTO.

The first four items on my list represent the EU's primary responsibilities. Ever since the inception of a common foreign policy in the early 1970s, internal institutional consolidation has been needed to overcome the oldest of the EU's problems: not being able to speak with one voice. The second oldest theme concerns cohesion and consistency of the various branches of Brussels's external relations, trade, development aid, conditionality, and foreign policy coordination. Internal cohesion and external influence are inherently intertwined. This, of course, also concerns the various dimensions of the EU's relations with Africa, where inconsistency and hypocrisy have sometimes been evident.

Within the next circle of responsibilities are transatlantic relations, relations with Russia, and the European Neighbourhood Policy. These three areas must be seen as 'core responsibilities'. The Neighbourhood Policy, in this context, would include recent initiatives in the Union for the Mediterranean, which includes the EU's relations with North Africa. (See chapter 7 in this volume.) It remains debatable whether the EU's three-tier approach to the African continent—North Africa, sub-Saharan Africa, and South Africa (see chapter 6 in this volume, on South Africa)—and its different policy instruments, make sense.

The high priority given to transatlantic cooperation might also surprise some in light of what has been argued throughout this chapter. However, I have elaborated elsewhere why a new transatlantic alliance, based on a triple notion of responsibility—that is, a 'mutual', 'shared' and 'dual' responsibility of the EU and the US—would define the most prudent and most responsible route for Brussels.[26] The next priority—the need for the EU to engage closely with Russia—is self-evident, since all principles of prudence suggest developing a special relationship, not a full community, with the big bear on the EU's eastern borders.

Geographical proximity is no doubt a legitimate justification for special commitments. Hence the EU's Neighbourhood Policy can be classified as the fourth priority. Brussels's official ambitions[27] are not well matched in its ambiguous institutional design,[28] its lumping together of different regions under similar policies, and the actual results of these approaches. However, transforming and stabilising the EU's neighbourhood through the promotion of democracy, human rights, a functioning market economy, 'good governance', rule of law, and sustainable development must clearly remain high on the EU's list of priorities.

The fifth priority, inter-institutional cooperation, is structurally different and opens up all regions and policy areas that the EU cannot shoulder alone. Recognising that the capacities of Brussels are seriously limited, with natural ceilings far below the official rhetoric, requires a more serious debate on inter-institutional burden-sharing. Following the general argument that global rather than European interests and responsibilities must guide EU debates, one identifies alarming deficits in this area. Inter-institutional cooperation is one of the less developed aspirations in Brussels, even though many of the EU's official documents suggest otherwise. With regard to Africa, the clearest sign of a serious commitment to meeting European obligations would involve enhanced engagement with African regional bodies and listening to their perspectives before deciding on EU action towards the continent. (See chapter 4 in this volume.)

However, in general terms, inter-institutional competition, rivalry, and self-centred notions of importance prevail in most EU discussions. Most prominent are ongoing, often counterproductive debates over relations between the EU and NATO. Generally speaking, a commitment to collective burden-sharing would certainly enable Europe to tackle most global problems that are listed further down my table of priorities, including, of course, relations with Africa and its various regional bodies. The UN, the Group of 20 (G20), the WTO, the World Bank, the International Monetary Fund (IMF), and many global nongovernmental organisations must be seen as natural partners for the EU in jointly addressing global concerns. So far, owing to its typical self-centredness, there have been legal limitations of the capacity of Brussels to participate in international organisations and to act in tandem with others: the EU has, in the past, often been very reluctant when it comes to international cooperation. The real problem is a lack of political will and direction. Suggestions have been made to use the doctrine of 'human security'[29] as a strategic compass for EU global engagement. This is an admirable concept, but owing to its origin and scope, primacy on human security should probably rest with the UN, and not with the EU. Instead, the EU's hijacking of a popular concept, a shared vision, and original vision of 'global responsibility' should be the primary reference point and must become the basis for serious debate about institutional burden-sharing with many other institutions.

This general request for inter-institutional cooperation also explains why regions such as Africa, the Middle East, and Asia rank lower on my list of priorities. This is by no means a judgement on the relative importance of these regions and the policy challenges they pose; it is only a reflection on the limitations of the EU as an independent actor. Even though ambitions in Brussels, mostly unfounded, might suggest otherwise, a modest assessment of the real capacities of the EU has become a moral and practical necessity.

Better EU public diplomacy

Having established and justified the virtues of 'global responsibility' as a guide for future EU engagement with all regions of the world, one can see that a different public diplomacy is also needed in Brussels. Civil servants in EU delegations worldwide tend to believe that the EU has, so far, not fully succeeded in selling its beneficial global role convincingly. Early studies on outside perceptions of the EU[30] reveal a wide gap between Brussels's self-perception and external views. Overcoming this gap will require a successful establishment of the new European External Action Service—currently under way in 2012—as much international misunderstanding results from insufficient institutional support for the EU's Common Foreign and Security Policy (CFSP), European Security and Defence Policy (ESDP), and Brussels's various other forms of external engagement. It is clear that a truly common European diplomacy would represent a major step forward. The second urgent step required is an understanding of the real causes and consequences of this widespread misperception and the often very negative image of the EU's role in the world. The interplay between the messages sent by Brussels and the way they are received outside the EU is a much under-researched area. We are beginning to understand the EU's external images, but conceptualisation of the impact of outside perceptions on Brussels's identity and policymaking remains a rather blank sheet of paper.[31] The third pillar of EU public diplomacy should be the new narrative described earlier, in which 'global responsibility' becomes the overriding story. Europe would then possibly be able to influence its partners in Africa and elsewhere through persuasion rather than through prescription, and engage in more fruitful dialogue with its strategic partners across the world.

Concluding reflections

Returning to the main theme of this volume, the question arises as to how the concept of a 'responsible Europe' can help to improve EU-Africa relations. In particular, how does the work of a European scholar aimed primarily at European decisionmakers contribute to a volume on Africa and Europe, in particular when it criticises 'Euro-centrism' as an obstacle to the EU playing a globally responsible role?

The chapter has attempted to provide a larger framework for conducting principled discussions on the future of the European position in global governance. Based on the recognition that Europe's place in the world will become increasingly peripheral, I have called for a shift of perspective. This would apply to Europe's general role in a changing world, as well as to European-African relations specifically. The principles of global responsibility could become the starting point for a new European postcolonial identity. The core idea would then be that global responsibilities override European interests or any such narrowly defined obligation that might result from historical guilt. What is relevant is not what Europe—in its old missionary mode—can and wants to offer to other regions like Africa, but what general global requirements would demand of Europe. The cosmopolitan should ideally trump the communitarian rationale. The external demand—and not parochial national interests—should guide the EU's external policies. The new identity should recognise that the world no longer serves European needs, but that Europe serves global necessities.

When it comes to relations with Africa, European decisionmakers must therefore ask, as a first step: What is expected of Europe and the European Union? What sort of European behaviour is considered by Africans to be responsible and appropriate? A notion of global responsibility, based on a dialogue about the principles of such responsibility, would be a good starting point for this debate. Considering the past decade of EU-Africa relations, with its new intensification analysed in its various aspects by the contributions in this book, the picture is not completely bleak. Even though Brussels has always had a highly institutionalised relationship with African countries since the very beginning of the integration process, the 2005 European Council's 'Strategy for Africa' was the first comprehensive and long-term strategy for Africa as a whole. (See the introduction to this volume.) The language of the strategy, of the various EU-Africa summit communiqués in 2000, 2007, and 2010, and of the joint EU-Africa action plans, mostly strike an appropriate tone. However, as in most EU foreign policy fields, rhetoric and action are somewhat far apart. The need for coherence and consistency remains as much of a challenge as ever, and the perennial competition between member states' foreign policies and the common EU policy instruments plays a significant part in explaining Brussels's mixed record vis-à-vis Africa since 2000.

In divergence with this chapter's recommendation advocating abandonment of an approach that starts from the 'European model' as anchor of the EU's external relations, much of Europe's initiatives have resulted from the desire to promote regional integration institutions in the European image to address questions of security, economic development, and environmental protection in Africa.

In a balanced and comprehensive 2010 study of EU-African relations, Daniela Sicurelli concluded that the EU remains unique as a significant partner and sponsor for African states and institutions. However, Brussels's reputation has suffered once again through contradictory ways of promoting its own model and inconsistencies in various policy areas. Sicurelli notes that 'the European attempt at promoting regional integration can be read as a result of institutional isomorphism. The EU is building its own identity on the basis of its ability to promote its constitutive norms'.[32]

There is a clear element of self-centredness in this approach, as opposed to serving global or African needs. The promotion of regional integration in Africa, and the financial and technical weight behind the EU's programmes in this respect, have been helpful and patronising at the same time. There is still the notion in Brussels's stance towards African states and institutions that 'doing it your own way actually somehow means doing it in our own way'.

Stark contradictions in the EU's policy implementation are also evident. With regard to peacekeeping, the EU has advocated African 'ownership', but has also intervened on various occasions with ESDP missions—in the Democratic Republic of the Congo in 2003 and 2006 and in Chad and the Central African Republic between 2007 and 2009 (see chapters 14 and 15 in this volume)—without African requests and with the intention of first and foremost promoting itself as a capable 'security actor' in the world. African security needs have been incidental to this agenda. In the area of trade, the EU presents regional integration as a path towards a free trade area, but has signed different economic partnership agreements with groups of African states belonging to the same geographical area, which has sometimes distorted their own regional integration efforts. The commitment to a full liberalisation of African markets is lukewarm at best. With regard to climate talks, the EU has played an occasional two-faced game: claiming to treat the African Union as an equal partner, while simultaneously promoting the UN as a strong player in Africa against the desires of the AU. Such contradictions and lapses have clearly been noticed everywhere in Africa and have rendered an equal dialogue between both regions more difficult.[33]

As a result of the EU's action and rhetoric, African leaders have confirmed their perceptions that Brussels, although an important partner and occasional source of inspiration, essentially remains a self-centred, self-interested, divided, and impotent actor when it comes to addressing the larger challenges facing the African continent. In order to overcome this problem, EU institutional consolidation and a shift of perspective from Eurocentrism to global responsibility will be essential.

However, Europe should not stop there. In fact, Europeans should invite Africans to conduct a similar exercise: shifting their perspective from an inward-looking and dependent Africa to one that places the continent firmly within a global context (see chapter 9 in this volume). A confident and realistic assessment by Africans of their capacities and contributions to global governance would then shape African contributions to a fruitful EU-Africa dialogue.

Meanwhile, Europe is not in a position to criticise Africa, as it has not yet woken up from its deep slumber to confront the full extent of its own challenges to become a truly responsible and capable global actor. If EU foreign policy does not engage in a dialogue along the lines advocated in this chapter, it could forever lose its capacity to shape global dialogues and policies. The old continent would then be forced to react to discourses imposed on Europe rather than developed by constructive engagement with its global partners. If the EU wants to remain any power at all, it must become a 'modest and persuasive power' as well as the 'globe's most responsible servant'. The vision for Africa and Europe must be neither *Eurafrique* nor *Afro-europa*, but rather *Globafricopa*.

ANNEX A

Table 1: European Community aid to the Maghrib, 1978–1996.
(in ECU millions)

	Commission budget grants	European Investment Bank loans	Total
MOROCCO			
1978–1981	56	74	130
1982–1986	90	109	199
1987–1991	151	173	324
1992–1996	218	220	438
Total	515	576	1,091
ALGERIA			
1978–1981	70	44	114
1982–1986	107	44	151
1987–1991	183	56	239
1992–1996	70	280	350
Total	430	424	854
TUNISIA			
1978–1981	41	54	95
1982–1986	78	61	139
1987–1991	131	93	224
1992–1996	116	168	284
Total	366	376	742
Total	*1,311*	*1,376*	*2,686*

Source: European Institute for Research on Mediterranean and Euro-Arab Cooperation, http://www.medea.be/index.html?page=2&lang=en&doc=369.

Table 2: European Union Meda Support, 1995–2004 (in € millions).

	MEDA I (1995–1999)	MEDA II (2000–2004)	MEDA I and II (1995–2004)
Bilateral funding			
Algeria	164.0	232.8	396.8
Palestine	111.0	350,3	461.3
Egypt	686.0	353.5	1,039.5
Jordan	254.0	204.4	458.4
Lebanon	182.0	73.7	255.7
Morocco	660.0	677.1	1,337.1
Syria	101.0	135.7	236.7
Tunisia	428.0	328.6	756.6
Total bilateral	2,586.0	2,358.8	4,942.1
Regional funding	471.0	739.8	1,210.9
Total funding	3,057.0	3,095.9	6,153

Source: Europe Aid.
Note: According to the MEDA budget projections, funding under MEDA I (1995–1999) was set at €3,435 million, with an additional €4,808 million in soft loans from the European Investment Bank. Funding under MEDA II (2000–2006) was set at €5,350 million, with European Investment Bank loan funding up to 2007 of €6,700 million.

Table 3: ENPI Funding, 2007–2013 (in constant € millions).

2007	2008	2009	2010	2011	2012	2013	Total
1,433	1,569	1,877	2,083	2,322	2,642	3,003	14,929

Source: Karen E. Smith, 'The Outsiders: The European Neighbourhood Policy', *International Affairs* 81(4) (2005), p. 760.
Note: These figures combine funds for both the Mediterranean and the East and are therefore not comparable with MEDA funding. They can be compared instead with the budgets for the East and for the Mediterranean in 2004 (€1,420 million for the East, with €953 million for the Mediterranean).

Table 4: ENPI Country Allocations, 2011–2013 (in € millions).

Country Programmes	Total
Algeria*	172.0
Armenia	157.3
Azerbaijan	122.5

Egypt*	449.3
Georgia	180.3
Israel*	6.0
Jordan*	223.0
Lebanon*	150.0
Libya*	60.0
Moldova	273.1
Morocco*	580.5
Syria*	129.0
Tunisia*	240.0
Ukraine	470.1
Country programmes total	3,213.1
Multi-Country programmes	
Regional Programme—East	262.3
Inter-Regional Programme	757.7
Multi-country programmes total	1,020.0
Overall total	4,233.1

Source: http://europa.eu/rapid/pressReleasesAction.do?reference=IP/10/221&.
Note: * = Euro-Mediterranean Partnership member.

Table 5: American Usmepi Financial Support, 2002–2005 (in $ millions).

	2002	*2003*	*2004*	*2005*
Economic development	6	38	32	23
Political development	10	25	20	22
Educational development	8	25	22	14.4
Women's empowerment	5	12	15.5	15
Total	29	100	89.5	74.4

Source: http://mepi.state.gov/mepi.

NOTES

1. INTRODUCTION

1. Kwame Nkrumah described the Yaoundé Association as 'collective neo-colonialism' in *Neo-Colonialism: The Last Stage of Imperialism* (London: Nelson, 1965), p. 19.

2. 'What France wants to do with Africa is to prepare the future of Eurafrique, this great common destiny which awaits Europe and Africa'. Report of speech by President Nicolas Sarkozy at Cheikh Anta Diop University, Dakar, *Reuters*, 27 July 2007.

3. There was an imbalance in the academic studies of the early pre-1973 period, when there was an abundance of literature in French, specifically from the point of view of the much criticised concept of *Eurafrique*, much of it of limited value to scholars (see chapter 2 in this volume). A typical example was C. Lucron, 'Les Orientations Nouvelles de l'Association Entre la Communauté Economique Européenne et les Etats Africains et Malgaches Associés', in *Chronique de Politique Etrangère* 22(6) (Brussels: Institut Royal des Relations Internationales, Centre Inter-Universitaire de Recherche, 1965). An exception at this time, however, was William Zartman's dispassionate study *The Politics of Trade Negotiations Between Africa and the European Community: The Weak Confront the Strong* (Princeton: Princeton University Press, 1971).

4. This dearth has increasingly been rectified by a number of research bodies. For example, the Overseas Development Institute in London was one of the few institutions that provided enlightenment at this time (in such works as David Jones's damning analysis of the Yaoundé Conventions, *Europe's Chosen Few*, (London: Overseas Development Institute, 1965). Since then, over the years a number of writers such as Chris Stevens have established a substantial body of work on EU development policy issues. Stevens's work has always been trenchantly to the point. One recent example was a paper to an international symposium held

in Glasgow in December 2009 on EU-Africa relations in the twenty-first century, titled 'EU Trade Policy and Africa: Losing Friends and Failing to Influence'. The European Centre for Development Policy Management (ECDPM) in Maastricht since 1986 has also produced a series of well-considered widely ranging studies, although from a position of greater closeness to European institutions. The *EU-ACP Courier*, produced from the European Commission and funded mainly from the European Development Fund, has a long pedigree, going all the way back to the Yaoundé Convention, of producing literature on aspects of the Europe-ACP relationship that can be valuable to researchers, but was discontinued in 2011. For a recent study, see Daniela Sicurelli, *The European Union's Africa Policies: Norms, Interests, and Impact* (Farnham: Ashgate 2010). See also Olu Sanu and Ralph Onwuka, *Nigeria, Africa, and the European Union Beyond 2000* (Ibadan: Dokun, 1997).

5. Pius Okigbo, *Africa and the Common Market* (Evanston: Northwestern University Press, 1967).

6. John Ravenhill *Collective Clientelism: The Lomé Conventions and North-South Relations* (New York: Columbia University Press, 1985). See also M.R. Lister, *The European Community and the Developing World* (Aldershot: Avebury, 1988); and E. Grilli, *The European Community and the Developing Countries* (Cambridge: Cambridge University Press, 1993).

7. Kunibert Raffer, 'Cotonou: Slowly Undoing Lome's Concept of Partnership', DSA European Development Policy Study Group, Discussion Paper no. 21 (2001).

8. See also James Mackie, Henrike Klavert, and Faten Aggad, 'Bridging the Credibility Gap: Challenges for the ACP/EU Relations in 2011', *Policy Management Insights* no. 2 (December 2010) (Maastricht: European Centre for Development Policy Management).

9. Commission of the European Communities, 'Development Aid: Fresco of Community Action Tomorrow', supplement to the *Bulletin of the European Communities, 1974*.

10. Ibid.

11. After Lomé was signed in 1975 there had been a number of more positive appreciations, especially from English-speaking academia, such as Carol Cosgrove Twitchett, *Europe and Africa: From Association to Partnership* (London: Saxon, 1978); and Frans A.M. Alting von Geusau (ed.), *The Lomé Convention and a New International Economic Order* (Alphen Aan den Rijn, Netherlands: Stjthoff and Noordhoff, 1976). The winning over of African leaders such as Sekou Touré and Julius Nyerere to the cause also meant that former academic critics often adopted positions of modified approval. See, for example, the papers in Frank Long (ed.), *The Political Economy of EEC Relations with African Caribbean and Pacific States* (Oxford: Pergamon, 1980). In particular there is a chapter (pp. 3–31) by Marxist economist Reginald Herbold Green providing a pertinent

quote from Nyerere, who saw the ACP as the trade union of the poor: 'The truth is that we need power to negotiate, just as we need power to go on strike. So far we have been negotiating as noisy and importunate supplicants. We need to negotiate from a position of steadily increasing power', p. 3.

12. See Adebayo Adedeji, 'ECOWAS: A Retrospective Journey', in Adekeye Adebajo and Ismail Rashid (eds.), *West Africa's Security Challenges: Building Peace in a Troubled Region* (Boulder: Lynne Rienner, 2004), pp. 21–49.

13. See S.K.B. Asante, *Europe's Brand of a Trojan Horse? Africa and the Economic Partnership Agreements* (Tema, Ghana: Digibooks Ghana, 2010).

14. European Commission, *Green Paper on Relations Between the European Union and the ACP Countries on the Eve of the 21st Century: Challenges and Options for a New Partnership* (Luxembourg: Office of Official Publication of the European Union, 1997).

15. *Lisbon Declaration and Joint EU Africa Strategy*, EU-Africa Summit, Lisbon, 9 December 2007 available at http://www.ec.europa.eu/development/geographical/regionscountries/eurafrica.

16. See Stephen Castle, 'Trade Deals Stymied at Lisbon Meeting', *New York Times*, 10 December 2007. The report quotes Senegal's President Abdoulaye Wade as saying, 'It's clear that Africa rejects EPAs'.

17. Jean-Pierre Stroobants, 'L'Union Africaine et l'Union Européenne Tentent de Dessiner un "Partenariat"', *Le Monde*, 2 December 2010, p. 6.

18. Keynote address by Ambassador John Shinkaiye at the conference on 'Ensuring Peace and Security in Africa'. Chatham House, London, October 2010.

19. Ibid.

20. Confidential interview.

21. Adrian Hewitt and Kaye Whiteman, 'The Commission and Development Policy: From the Lomé Leap Forward to the Difficulties of Adapting to the 21st Century', in Karin Arts and Anna K. Dickson (eds.), *EU Development Cooperation: From Model to Symbol* (Manchester: Manchester University Press, 2004), pp. 133–148.

22. Karen E. Smith, 'The ACP in the European Network's Network of Regional Relationships: Still Unique or Just One in the Crowd?' in Arts and Dickson, *EU Development Cooperation*, pp. 60–79.

23. Alex Vines, 'Rhetoric from Brussels and Reality on the Ground: The EU and Security in Africa', *International Affairs* 86(5) (September 2010), pp. 1091–1108.

2. THE RISE AND FALL OF *EURAFRIQUE*: FROM THE BERLIN CONFERENCE OF 1884–1885 TO THE TRIPOLI EU-AFRICA SUMMIT OF 2010

1. See the CCR seminar reports 'Eurafrique? Africa and Europe in a New Century', Cape Town, 31 October–1 November 2007, and 'From Eurafrique to Afro-

Europa: Africa and Europe in a New Century', Stellenbosch, 11–13 September 2008, available at http://www.ccr.org.za.

2. Daniel G. Brinton, *Races and Peoples: Lectures on the Science of Ethnography* (New York: NDC Hodges, 1890).

3. Guernier used the term in a number of articles on North Africa. Born in Tunisia, he was an enthusiastic advocate of the notion of a 'Mediterranean Lake' that joined Europe and Africa together as one geographical unit. He claimed to have coined the expression *Eurafrique* as far back as 1923, but set his ideas out in a book in *Le Destin des Continents: Trois Continents, Trois Civilisations, Trois Destins* (Paris: Librairie Felix Alcan, 1936).

4. The Latin Library is one of many websites to have a full English translation of the text of the General Act of the Berlin Conference of 28 February 1985. See http://www.thelatinlibrary.com/imperialism/readings/berlinconference.html.

5. See, for example, Stig Förster, Wolfgang J. Mommsen, and Ronald Robinson (eds.), *Bismarck, Europe, and Africa: The British Africa Conference, 1884–1885, and the Onset of Partition* (Oxford: Oxford University Press, 1988); and Wm. Roger Louis, *Ends of British Imperialism: The Scramble for Empire, Suez, and Decolonization* (London: Tauris, 2006).

6. Thomas Pakenham, *The Scramble for Africa* (London: Weidenfeld and Nicolson, 1991).

7. General Gordon died on 26 January 1885, one month before the General Act of the Berlin Conference.

8. Adam Hochschild's *King Leopold's Ghost* (Boston: Houghton Mifflin, 1999) is a devastating account of Leopold's rule in the Congo.

9. Pakenham, *The Scramble for Africa*, p. 114.

10. A.J.P. Taylor, *The Struggle for Mastery in Europe, 1848–1918* (Oxford: Oxford University Press, 1954). Although the book is concerned with European politics, with very little mention of Africa, Taylor does note, with his characteristic eye for paradox, that Berlin had been designed by Bismarck as anti-British but failed in this objective and 'even threatened to bring them together' (p. 297).

11. Kaye Whiteman, 'The Entente Cordiale and Africa, 1904–2004', *African Geopolitics/Géopolitique Africaine* (Paris) no. 15 (Summer 2004), pp. 105–120.

12. On the impact of the Berlin Conference on contemporary Africa, see Adekeye Adebajo, *The Curse of Berlin: Africa After the Cold War* (London: Hurst, 2010); and A.I. Asiwaju, *Artificial Boundaries* (New York: Civiletis International, 1990).

13. David Levering Lewis, *The Race to Fashoda: European Colonialism and African Resistance in the Scramble for Africa* (London: Bloomsbury, 1988).

14. Pa'gan Amum Okiech, secretary-general of the Sudan People's Liberation Movement (SPLM), in conversation with the author (July 2010), said he actually came from the village of Fashoda, and drew attention to the historical fact that

if Colonel Marchand had not withdrawn from confrontation at Fashoda in 1898, he (Pa'gan) might very well have grown up speaking French.

15. Kaye Whiteman, *Chad* (London: Minority Rights Group, 1989), p. 4.

16. Judith Diane Trunzo, 'Eurafrica Counterpart? Counterpoint? A Study of French Views on Regional Integration', PhD dissertation presented to the Graduate Faculty of the University of Virginia in Candidacy, 1973.

17. Trunzo, 'Eurafrica Counterpart', pp. 49–52.

18. General Meynier continued to campaign in favour of *Eurafrique* into the 1950s.

19. Hjalmar Schacht, 'Germany's Colonial Demands', *Foreign Affairs* 1(2) (January 1937).

20. René Viard, in *L'Eurafrique: Pour une Nouvelle Économie Européenne* (Paris: Fernand Sorlot, 1942), argued at the height of the Vichy regime that Europe and Africa should be a 'coherent economic unit'.

21. See Adekeye Adebajo (ed.), *From Global Apartheid to Global Village: Africa and the United Nations* (Scottsville: University of Kwazulu-Natal Press, 2009).

22. François-Xavier Verschave, *La Françafrique: Le Plus Longue Scandale de la République* (Paris: Editions Stock, 1998). This is representative of a much wider body of literature on the subject, almost entirely critical of the concept.

23. See John Chipman, *French Power in Africa* (Oxford: Blackwell, 1989); Paul Gifford and W.R. Lewis (eds.), *The Transfer of Power in Africa: Decolonization 1940–1960* (New Haven: Yale University Press, 1982); Guy Martin, *Africa in World Politics: A Pan-African Perspective* (Asmara: Africa World Press, 2002); and Victor T. Le Vine, *Politics in Francophone Africa* (Boulder: Lynne Rienner, 2007).

24. Léopold Sédar Senghor, 'L'Eurafrique: Unité Economique de l'Avenir', essay in *Liberté* (Paris: Editions Seuil, 1971).

25. The eighteen signatories of the two Yaoundé Conventions were Burundi, Central African Republic, Cameroon, Chad, Congo-Brazzaville, Congo-Kinshasa, Côte d'Ivoire, Dahomey (now Benin), Gabon, Madagascar, Mali, Mauritania, Niger, Rwanda, Senegal, Somalia, Togo, and Upper Volta (now Burkina Faso).

26. David Jones, *Europe's Chosen Few* (London: Overseas Development Institute, 1965).

27. Kaye Whiteman, 'Ramphal and Lomé', in Richard Bourne (ed.), *Shridath Ramphal: The Commonwealth and the World: Essays in Honour of his 80th Birthday* (London: Hansib, 2008), pp. 156–163.

28. *Declaration on Cooperation, Development, and Economic Independence*, resolution at the 10th Ordinary Session of the OAU Assembly of Heads of State and Government, Addis Ababa, 28 May 1973, AHG Res. 69.

29. See, for example, Olujimi Adesina, Yao Graham, and Adebayo Olukoshi (eds.), *Africa and Development Challenges in the New Millennium: The NEPAD Debate* (Dakar: CODESRIA, 2006); John Akokpari, Angela Ndinga-Muvumba, and Tim Murithi (eds.), *The African Union and Its Institutions* (Johannesburg: Jacana,

2008); and Patrick Bond (ed.), *Fanon's Warning: A Civil Society Reader on the New Partnership for Africa's Development*, 2nd ed. (Asmara: Africa World Press, 2005).

30. *ACP-EU Partnership Agreement*, signed in Cotonou on 23 June 2000, special issue of *The ACP-EU Courier*, September 2000 (Brussels: EC Directorate General for Development).

31. Guy Martin, 'Africa and the Ideology of Eurafrica: Neo-Colonialism or Pan-Africanism?' *Journal of Modern African Studies* 2(2) (1982), pp. 221–258.

32. See obituary of Maurice Foley by Kaye Whiteman in *The Guardian* (London), 22 February 2002, p. 43.

33. Olu Sanu and Ralph Onwuka, *Nigeria, Africa, and the European Union Beyond 2000* (Ibadan: Dokun, 1997).

34. General Gowon, head of state of Nigeria, speech at Commonwealth Heads of Government Meeting, Ottawa, Canada, 2–10 August 1973, available at http://www.thecommonwealth.org.files.

35. John Ravenhill, *Collective Clientelism: The Lomé Conventions and North-South Relations* (New York: Columbia University Press, 1985). This is one of the most probing analyses of how disillusionment set into the Lomé relationship.

36. Adebayo Adedeji owns this famous phrase, uttered while serving as executive director of the United Nations Economic Commission for Africa between 1975 and 1991.

37. Trevor Parfitt, 'The Decline of Eurafrica? Lomé's Mid-Term Review', *Review of African Political Economy* 23(67) (March 1996), pp. 53–66.

38. European Commission, *Green Paper on Relations Between the European Union and the ACP Countries on the Eve of the 21st Century: Challenges and Options for a New Partnership* (Luxembourg: Office for Official Publications of the European Communities, 1997). See also Kunibert Raffer, 'Rolling Back Partnership: An Analysis of the Commission's Green Paper on the Future of Lomé', DSA European Development Policy Study Group, Discussion Paper no. 9 (1998).

39. Jane Kennan and Christopher Stevens, 'From Lomé to the GSP: Implications for the ACP of Losing Lomé Trade Preferences', DSA European Development Policy Study Group, Discussion Paper no. 8 (February 1998).

40. Kunibert Raffer, 'Cotonou: Slowly Undoing Lomé's Concept of Partnership', DSA European Development Policy Study Group, Discussion Paper no. 21 (2001).

41. Tom Porteous, *The British and Africa* (London: Zed, 2007).

42. Porteous, *The British and Africa*, p. 6.

43. *Lisbon Declaration and Joint EU Africa Strategy*, EU-Africa Summit, Lisbon, 9 December 2007, available at http://www.ec.europa.eu/development/geographical/regionscountries/eurafrica.

44. *Declaration of the ACP Council of Ministers at Its 86th Session Expressing Serious*

Concern on the Status of the Negotiations of the Economic Partnership Agreements, Brussels, 13 December 2007, ACP/25/013/07. See also James Mackie, Henrike Klavert, and Faten Aggad, 'Bridging the Credibility Gap: Challenges for the ACP/EU Relations in 2011', *Policy Management Insights* no. 2 (December 2010) (Maastricht: European Centre for Development Policy Management).

45. Jean-Pierre Stroobants, 'L'Union Africaine et l'Union Européenne Tentent de Dessiner un "Partenariat"', *Le Monde*, 2 December 2010, p. 6.
46. Louis Michel, commissioner for development, 'Europe-Africa: The Indispensable Partnership', speech to the European Policy Centre, Brussels, 30 November 2007.
47. President Nicolas Sarkozy, speech to the South African Parliament, Cape Town, 28 February 2008.
48. Ibid.

3. PARADISE LOST AND FOUND: THE AFRICAN UNION AND THE EUROPEAN UNION

1. This chapter builds on Adekeye Adebajo, 'Towers of Babel? The African Union and the European Union', in Adekeye Adebajo, *The Curse of Berlin: Africa After the Cold War* (London: Hurst, 2010), pp. 261–285.
2. See John Leonard, introduction to John Milton, *Paradise Lost* (Johannesburg: Penguin, 2000). Milton's book was first published in 1667.
3. See Ali A. Mazrui, *The African Condition* (Cambridge: Cambridge University Press, 1980), pp. 1–22.
4. See, for example, Adekeye Adebajo, 'An Axis of Evil? China, the US, and France in Africa', in Kweku Ampiah and Sanusha Naidu (eds.), *Crouching Tiger, Hidden Dragon? Africa and China* (Scottsville: University of Kwazulu-Natal Press, 2008).
5. See Adebajo, *The Curse of Berlin*.
6. I thank Chris Hill for reminding me to make more explicit this important fact.
7. See, for example, Francis Kornegay, 'The AU and Africa's Three Diasporas', in John Akokpari, Angela Ndinga-Muvumba, and Tim Murithi (eds.), *The African Union and Its Institutions* (Johannesburg: Jacana, 2008), pp. 333–352.
8. This section builds on Adekeye Adebajo, 'Towards a New *Pax Africana:* Three Decades of the OAU', *Praxis*, Spring 1993, pp. 59–71.
9. Quoted in Geoffrey Barraclough, 'The Revolt Against the West', in Prasenjit Duara (ed.), *Decolonization: Perspectives from Now and Then* (London: Routledge, 2004), p. 118.
10. See, for example, Kwame Nkrumah, *Africa Must Unite* (London: Panaf, 1963).
11. See Tajudeen Abdul-Raheem, 'Introduction: Reclaiming Africa for Africans— Pan-Africanism, 1900–1994', in Tajudeen Abdul-Raheem (ed.), *Pan-African-*

ism: Politics, Economy, and Social Change in the Twenty-First Century (London: Pluto, 1996), pp. 1–30.

12. Immanuel Wallerstein, *Africa: The Politics of Unity* (New York: Vintage, 1967), p. 15.

13. See, for example, Wole Soyinka, *The Burden of Memory: The Muse of Forgiveness* (Cape Town and Oxford: Oxford University Press, 1999), pp. 93–194.

14. Quoted in Ali Mazrui, 'Africa Entrapped: Between the Protestant Ethic and the Legacy of Westphalia', in Hedley Bull and Adam Watson (eds.), *The Expansion of International Society* (Oxford: Clarendon, 1984), p. 296.

15. Quoted in Ubang P. Ugor, 'Reparation, Reconciliation, and Negritude Poetics in Soyinka's *The Burden of Memory, the Muse of Forgiveness*', in Onookome Okome (ed.), *Ogun's Children: The Literature and Politics of Wole Soyinka Since the Nobel* (Asmara: Africa World Press, 2004), p. 273.

16. Wikipedia, 'Caliban', http://en.wikipedia.org/wiki/Caliban_(character). See also Aimé Césaire, *Une Tempête* (Paris: Seuil, 1969).

17. Wallerstein, *Africa*, p. 17.

18. The Brazzaville group consisted of twelve Francophone African states: Benin (then Dahomey), Burkina Faso (then Upper Volta), Cameroon, Central African Republic, Chad, Congo-Brazzaville, Côte d'Ivoire, Gabon, Madagascar, Mauritania, Niger, and Senegal. The Monrovia group consisted of Liberia, Ethiopia, Libya, Nigeria, Sierra Leone, Somalia, and Togo. The Monrovia group eventually incorporated the Brazzaville group. Members of the Casablanca group included the Algerian provisional government, Egypt, Ghana, Guinea, Mali, and Morocco. The blocs were named after cities where conferences forming them were held.

19. See Georges Abi-Saab, *The United Nations Operation in the Congo, 1960–1964* (Oxford: Oxford University Press, 1978); Catherine Hoskyns, *The Congo Since Independence, January 1960–December 1961* (London: Oxford University Press, 1965); Conor Cruise O'Brien, *To Katanga and Back: A UN Case History* (London: Hutchinson, 1962).

20. Ali A. Mazrui, *Towards a Pax Africana* (Chicago: University of Chicago Press, 1967).

21. I am grateful for my analysis in this paragraph to Zdenek Cervenka, *The Unfinished Quest for Unity: Africa and the OAU* (London: Friedmann, 1977); Domenico Mazzeo (ed.), *African Regional Organizations* (Cambridge: Cambridge University Press, 1984); Gino Naldi, *The Organization of African Unity* (London: Mansell, 1989); and Wallerstein, *Africa*.

22. See, for example, Adebajo, 'An Axis of Evil?'; John Chipman, *French Power in Africa* (Oxford: Blackwell, 1989); Paul Gifford and W.R. Lewis (eds.), *The Transfer of Power in Africa: Decolonization 1940–1960* (New Haven: Yale University Press, 1982); Guy Martin, *Africa in World Politics: A Pan-African Perspective*

(Asmara: Africa World Press, 2002); and Victor T. Le Vine, *Politics in Francophone Africa* (Boulder: Lynne Rienner, 2007).

23. See Dominique Jacquin-Berdal and Aida Mengistu, 'Nationalism and Identity in Ethiopia and Eritrea: Building Multiethnic States', in Dorina A. Bekoe (ed.), *East Africa and the Horn: Confronting Challenges to Good Governance* (Boulder: Lynne Rienner, 2006), pp. 81–100; Tekeste Negash and Kjetil Tronvoll, *Brothers at War: Making Sense of the Eritrean-Ethiopian War* (Oxford: Currey, 2000); David Pool, 'The Eritrean People's Liberation Front', in Christopher Clapham (ed.), *African Guerrillas* (Bloomington: Indiana University Press, 1998), pp. 19–35; Peter Woodward, *The Horn of Africa: Politics and International Relations* (London: Tauris, 2003); John Young, 'The Tigray People's Liberation Front', in Clapham, *African Guerrillas*, pp. 36–52.

24. See Yassin El-Ayouty (ed.), *The Organization of African Unity After Thirty Years* (New York: Praeger, 1994); Solomon Gomes, 'The Peacemaking Role of the OAU and the AU: A Comparative Analysis', in Akokpari, Ndinga-Muvumba, and Murithi, *The African Union and Its Institutions*, pp. 113–130; Salim Ahmed Salim, 'The OAU Role in Conflict Management', in Olara Otunnu and Michael Doyle (eds.), *Peacemaking and Peacekeeping for the New Century* (Lanham: Rowman and Littlefield, 1998), pp. 245–253; Amadu Sesay, Olusola Ojo, and Orobola Fasehun, *The OAU After Twenty Years* (Boulder: Westview, 1984).

25. Naldi, *The Organization of African Unity*, p. 123.

26. See, for example, Adekeye Adebajo (ed.), *From Global Apartheid to Global Village: Africa and the United Nations* (Scottsville: University of Kwazulu-Natal Press, 2009).

27. Quoted in *Africa Report*, September–October 1992, pp. 22–23.

28. Quoted in Solomon Gomes, 'The OAU, State Sovereignty, and Regional Security', in Edmond Keller and Donald Rothchild (eds.), *Africa in the New International Order: Rethinking State Sovereignty* (Boulder: Lynne Rienner, 1996), p. 41.

29. Salim, 'The OAU Role in Conflict Management', pp. 245–253.

30. Cited in Francis M. Deng, *Protecting the Dispossessed: A Challenge for the International Community* (Washington, DC: Brookings Institution, 1993), p. 17.

31. See, for example, Monde Muyangwa and Margaret A. Vogt, *An Assessment of the OAU Mechanism for Conflict Prevention, Management, and Resolution* (New York: International Peace Institute, 2000).

32. See Adekeye Adebajo, 'Africa's Quest for El Dorado', *Mail and Guardian*, 29 June 2007. For another perspective, see Kwesi Kwaa Prah, 'Without Unity There Is No Future for Africa', *Mail and Guardian*, 29 June 2007.

33. Gordon Kerr, *A Short History of Europe: From Charlemagne to the Treaty of Lisbon* (Harpenden: Pocket Essentials, 2009), pp. 13–16; Lucidcafé Library, 'Charlemagne', http://www.lucidcafe.com/library/96apr/charlemagne.html.

34. Jean Monnet, *Memoirs* (London: Collins, 1978), pp. 318–335.
35. For a background, see Anne Deighton, 'The Remaking of Europe', in Michael Howard and Wm. Roger Louis (eds.), *The Oxford History of the Twentieth Century* (Oxford: Oxford University Press, 1998), pp. 190–202; Chris Hill and Michael Smith, *International Relations and the European Union* (London: Oxford University Press, 2005); Anand Menon, *Europe: The State of the Union* (London: Atlantic, 2008); Brent F. Nelsen and Alexander Stubb (eds.), *The European Union: Readings on the Theory and Practice of European Integration*, 3rd ed. (Boulder: Lynne Rienner, 2003); Loukas Tsoukalis, *What Kind of Europe?* (London: Oxford University Press, 2005).
36. I thank Chris Hill for this nuance.
37. Quoted in Nicholas Atkin, *The Fifth French Republic* (Basingstoke: Palgrave Macmillan, 2005, p. 90).
38. This information is gleaned from Stephen Martin, 'Building on Coal and Steel: European Integration in the 1950s and 1960s', in Desmond Dinan (ed.), *Origins and Evolution of the European Union* (Oxford: Oxford University Press, 2006), pp. 126–140.
39. Richard T. Griffiths, 'A Dismal Decade? European Integration in the 1970s', in Dinan, *Origins and Evolution of the European Union*, pp. 169–190.
40. Cited in Charles Grant, *Delors: The House That Jacques Built* (London: Nicholas Brealey, 1994), p. 88.
41. I have relied here on the excellent chapter by N. Piers Ludlow, 'From Deadlock to Dynamism: The EC in the 1980s', in Dinan, *Origins and Evolution of the European Union*, pp. 218–232.
42. I have relied in this section on Dorothee Heisenberg, 'From Single Market to the Single Currency', in Dinan, *Origins and Evolution of the European Union*, pp. 233–252.
43. The countries were Bulgaria, Romania, Poland, the Czech Republic, Hungary, Estonia, Latvia, Lithuania, Slovenia, Slovakia, Cyprus, and Malta.
44. The information from this paragraph and on the Amsterdam and Nice treaties is gleaned from John Pinder and Simon Usherwood, *The European Union: A Very Short Introduction* (Oxford: Oxford University Press, 2007), pp. 9–35.
45. See, for example, Charlemagne, 'We Are All Belgians Now', *The Economist*, 28 November 2009, p. 39; Peter H. Koepf, 'This Is Europe Speaking', *The African Times* 2(12) (December 2009), pp. 1, p. 4.
46. See AU Commission, *Audit of the African Union: Towards a People-Centred Political and Socio-Economic Integration and Transformation of Africa* (Addis Ababa, 2007), pp. 44–45.
47. See ibid., pp. 42–77.
48. Ibid., pp. 147–152.

49. Andreas Staab, *The European Union Explained* (Bloomington: Indiana University Press, 2008), p. 51.

50. John Paterson and Michael Shackleton, 'The EU's Institutions', in John Paterson and Michael Shackleton (eds.), *The Institutions of the European Union*, 2nd ed. (Oxford: Oxford University Press, 2006), p. 9.

51. Staab, *The European Union Explained*, p. 45; Clive Archer, *The European Union* (London: Routledge, 2008), p. 37.

52. Pinder and Usherwood, *The European Union*, pp. 54–55.

53. AU Commission, *Audit of the African Union*, pp. 24–31, 57–58.

54. These countries were Algeria, Botswana, Burkina Faso, Ethiopia, Ghana, Liberia, Nigeria, South Africa, and Zambia.

55. *The Economist*, 'Short of Cash and Teeth', 20 January 2011, p. 36.

56. Daniel Bach, 'The AU and the EU', in Akokpari, Ndinga-Muvumba, and Murithi, *The African Union and Its Institutions*, p. 358.

57. Staab, *The European Union Explained*, p. 48.

58. Ibid., p. 50.

59. AU Commission, *Audit of the African Union*, p. 35.

60. Ibid., p. 34.

61. Ibid., pp. 36–38.

62. Ibid., pp. 58–60.

63. Staab, *The European Union Explained*, p. 52.

64. See Gerhard Hugo, *The Pan-African Parliament: Is the Glass Half-Full or Half-Empty?* Paper no. 168 (Tshwane: Institute for Security Studies, September 2008); Saki Mpanyane, *Transformation of the Pan-African Parliament: A Path to a Legislative Body?* Paper no. 181 (Tshwane: Institute for Security Studies, March 2009); and Baleka Mbete, 'The Pan-African Parliament: Progress and Prospects', in Akokpari, Ndinga-Muvumba, and Murithi, *The African Union and Its Institutions*, pp. 307–315.

65. AU Commission, *Audit of the African Union*, p. 79.

66. Ibid., pp. 78–81.

67. Staab, *The European Union Explained*, p. 64.

68. Ibid., p. 62.

69. Pinder and Usherwood, *The European Union*, p. 49.

70. See European Parliament, 'Motion for a Resolution on the Future of the Africa/EU Strategic Partnership on the Eve of the 3rd Africa/EU Summit', 8 December 2010, Plenary Sitting, B7–0696/2010.

71. Paterson and Shackleton, 'The EU's Institutions', p. 7.

72. Staab, *The European Union Explained*, p. 65.

73. Paterson and Shackleton, 'The EU's Institutions', p. 13.

74. AU Commission, *Audit of the African Union*, p. 83.

75. Muna Ndulo, 'The African Commission and Court Under the African Human

Rights System', in John Akokpari and Daniel Shea Zimbler (eds.), *Africa's Human Rights Architecture* (Johannesburg: Jacana, 2008), p. 187. See also Ahmed Motala, 'The African Court on Human and Peoples' Rights: Origins and Prospects', in Akokpari, Ndinga-Muvumba, and Murithi, *The African Union and Its Institutions*, pp. 271–289.

76. AU Commission, *Audit of the African Union*, pp. 82–85.
77. Ndulo, 'The African Commission and Court', pp. 188–191.
78. Sonya Sceats, 'Africa's New Human Rights Court: Whistling in the Wind?' briefing paper (London: Chatham House, March 2009), p. 5, available at http://www.chathamhouse.org.uk.
79. AU Commission, *Audit of the African Union*, pp. 86–88.
80. Sceats, 'Africa's New Human Rights Court', p. 6.
81. Ibid., pp. 9–10.
82. See A.H.M. Kirk-Greene, 'His Eternity, His Eccentricity, or His Exemplarity? A Further Contribution to the Study of H.E. the African Head of State', *African Affairs* 90(359) (April 1991), p. 182.
83. Staab, *The European Union Explained*, p. 70.
84. Ibid.
85. Ibid., p. 72.
86. Archer, *The European Union*, p. 39.
87. See Paterson and Shackleton, 'The EU's Institutions', p. 2.
88. Quoted in Wallerstein, *Africa*, p. 67.
89. See Mazrui, *The African Condition*, pp. 1–22.
90. See Robert Kagan, *Of Paradise and Power: America and Europe in the New World Order* (New York: Knopf, 2003).

4. THE TRAVAILS OF REGIONAL INTEGRATION IN AFRICA

1. See Frantz Fanon, *The Wretched of the Earth* (New York: Grove, 1963).
2. See, for example, René Verduijn, 'The Food and Agriculture Organisation and the World Food Programme', in Adekeye Adebajo (ed.), *From Global Apartheid to Global Village: Africa and the United Nations* (Scottsville: University of Kwazulu-Natal Press 2009), pp. 437–462.
3. See, for example, Adekeye Adebajo, *The Curse of Berlin: Africa After the Cold War* (London: Hurst, 2010).
4. Peter C. Gutkind and Immanuel Wallerstein (eds.), *The Political Economy of Contemporary Africa* (Beverley Hills: Sage 1976), pp. 30–57.
5. See, for example, Adebayo Adedeji, 'South Africa and Africa's Political Economy: Looking Inside from the Outside', in Adekeye Adebajo, Adebayo Adedeji, and Chris Landsberg (eds.), *South Africa in Africa: The Post-Apartheid Era* (Scottsville: University of Kwazulu-Natal Press, 2007), pp. 40–62.

6. Jeggan C. Senghor and Adebayo Adedeji, *Towards a Dynamic African Economy: Selected Speeches and Lectures, 1975–1986* (London: Cass, 1989), pp. 321–322.

7. It is worth recalling that although France had joined much of Upper Volta (Burkina Faso) with Côte d'Ivoire in 1932 for the purpose of strengthening its colonial political and economic base, the two territories were separated in 1947 in order to reduce the political weight of Ivorian leader Félix Houphouet-Boigny, because his political party, established in 1946, was dedicated to the anticolonial struggle.

8. See Bola Akinterinwa, *Nigeria and France, 1960–1995: The Dilemma of Thirty-Five Years of Relationship* (Ibadan: Vintage, 1999); Bassey E. Ate and Bola Akinterinwa (eds.), *Nigeria and Its Immediate Neighbours: Constraints and Prospects of Sub-Regional Security in the 1990s* (Lagos: Nigerian Institute of International Affairs, 1992); and Jean-François Médard, 'Crisis, Change, and Continuity: Nigeria/France Relations', in Adekeye Adebajo and Raufu Mustapha (eds.), *Gulliver's Troubles: Nigeria's Foreign Policy After the Cold War* (Scottsville: University of Kwazulu-Natal Press, 2008), pp. 314–333.

9. Michael Griffin, 'No Salvation in EPAs: The EU Is Changing Its Trading Relations with Africa, but Not Everybody Is Sure It Is for the Better', cited in *New African*, 1 August 2008, available at http://www.thefreelibrary.com/No+salvation+in+EPAs%3b+The+EU+is+changing+its+trading+relations+with+...-a0183 750385.

10. 'EPAs Will Benefit Europe at the Cost of Both ACP and Latin America', *South Bulletin Reflections and Foresights Editorial* no. 17 (16 June 2008).

11. Organisation of African Unity (OAU), *Lagos Plan of Action for the Economic Development of Africa, 1980–2000* (Geneva: International Institute for Labour Studies, 1981). See also World Bank, *Accelerated Development in Sub-Saharan Africa: An Agenda for Action* (Washington, DC, 1981).

12. Adebayo Adedeji, 'The UN Economic Commission for Africa', in Adebajo, *From Global Apartheid to Global Village*, pp. 373–398.

13. Louis Michel, *Africa-Europe: The Indispensable Alliance* (Brussels: European Commission, n.d.), p. 31.

14. Ibid., p. 28.

15. African Union, foreword to *Audit of the African Union: Towards a People-Centred and Socio-Economic Integration and Transformation of Africa* (Addis Ababa, September 2007), pp. iii–iv. I chaired the High-Level Panel of thirteen eminent persons from twelve African countries.

16. Desmond Tutu, speech at the 2006 European Development Days.

17. See John Akokpari, Angela Ndunga-Mavumba, and Tim Murithi (eds.), *The African Union and Its Institutions* (Johannesburg: Jacana, 2008).

18. See *Constitutive Act of the African Union* (Addis Ababa: Organisation of African Unity, 2000).

19. See Adebayo Adedeji, 'ECOWAS: A Retrospective Journey', in Adekeye Ade-bajo and Ismail Rashid (eds.), *Building Peace in a Troubled Region: West Africa's Security Challenges* (Boulder: Lynne Rienner, 2004), pp. 21–49.

20. John Akokpari, 'Dilemmas of Regional Integration and Development in Africa', in Akokpari, Ndunga-Muvumba, and Murithi, *The African Union and Its Institutions*, pp. 88–90.

21. I was the leader of the ministerial group that negotiated the establishment of ECOWAS from 1972 to 1975. I vacated my post as the federal minister responsible for integration five days after the signing of the ECOWAS treaty on 28 May 1975 to become executive secretary of the UN's Economic Commission for Africa, where I embarked on similar initiatives.

22. Adebayo Adedeji, 'Comparative Strategies of Economic Decolonisation in Africa', in Ali A. Mazrui (ed.), *General History of Africa: Africa since 1935* Volume VIII, (Oxford: James Currey, and Berkeley: University of California Press, 1993), p. 408.

23. OAU, *Lagos Plan of Action*.

24. *Audit of the African Union*.

25. Ibid.

26. Ibid.

5. EUROPE, AFRICA, AND AID: TOWARDS A GENUINE PARTNERSHIP

1. Arie de Geus, *Living Company: Habits for Survival in a Turbulent Business Environment* (Cambridge, MA: Harvard Business Press Books, 2002).

2. See EU-Africa Summit, Lisbon, December 2007.

3. Cited in *Business Day* (South Africa), 13 July 2008.

4. World Bank, *Growth Experience: What We Learned from the Nineties* (Washington, DC, June 2004).

5. World Bank, *The Growth Report: Strategies for Sustained Growth and Inclusive Development* (Washington, DC, 2008).

6. This is a term used by the economist Dani Rodrik, who advocates a 'second best' mind-set instead of the search for an ideal world that drove the Bretton Woods institutions. See Dani Rodrik, 'Second Best Institutions', *American Economic Review* 98(2), pp. 100–104; and Dani Rodrik, *One Economics Many Recipes* (Princeton: Princeton University Press, 2007).

7. The African Economic Research Consortium, based in Nairobi, provides master's and doctorate fellowships to African economists and commissions for joint research activities. See the consortium's website at http://www.aercafrica.org.

8. Sebastian Mallaby, *The World's Banker* (London: Penguin, 2004).

9. Hartmut Mayer, 'Is It Still Called "Chinese Whispers"? The EU's Rhetoric and Action As a Responsible Global Institution', *International Affairs* 84(1) (January

2008), pp. 61–79. On the notion of 'soft power', see Joseph Nye Jr., *Soft Power: The Means to Success in the World of Politics* (New York: PublicAffairs, 2004); and Robert Kagan, *Of Paradise and Power: America and Europe in the New World Order* (New York: Knopf, 2003).

10. David Roodman, *The Commitment to Development Index for Africa* (Washington, DC: Centre for Global Development, May 2008).

11. See, for example, R.W. Copson, *The United States in Africa* (London: Zed, 2007).

12. See, for example, Adebayo Adedeji, 'The UN Economic Commission for Africa', in Adekeye Adebajo (ed.), *From Global Apartheid to Global Village: Africa and the United Nations* (Scottsville: University of Kwazulu-Natal Press, 2009), pp. 373–398.

13. Daniel Bach, 'The AU and the EU', in John Akokpari, Angela Ndinga-Muvumba, and Tim Murithi (eds.), *The African Union and Its Institutions* (Johannesburg: Jacana, 2008), pp. 355–370.

14. See Development Assistance Committee, *Development Reports* (Paris: Organisation for Economic Cooperation and Development, 2006).

15. Accra Agenda for Action, Third High-Level Forum on Aid Effectiveness, 2–4 September 2008.

16. Owen Barder, *Beyond Planning: Markets and Networks for Better Aid*, Working Paper no. 185 (Washington, DC: Centre for Global Development, October 2009).

17. Rosalind Eyben, *Power and Mutual Accountability* (Sussex: University of Sussex, Institute of Development Studies, February 2007).

18. See Mary B. Anderson, *Do No Harm: How Aid Can Support Peace—or War* (Boulder: Lynne Rienner, 1999).

19. Stephen Covey, *The Seven Habits of Highly Effective People* (New York: Free Press, 2004).

20. See, for example, Stuart Carr, Eilish McAuliffe, and Malcolm MacLachlan, *Psychology of Aid* (Abingdon: Routledge, 1998).

21. Some examples include Wangari Maathai, *The Challenge for Africa* (London: Heinemann, 2009), on leadership, culture, identity, land, and the like; Moeletsi Mbeki, *Architects of Poverty* (Johannesburg: Picador, 2009), on the origins of the lack of a real entrepreneurial class in Africa; Michaela Wrong, *It's Our Turn to Eat* (London: HarperCollins, 2009), on the systems of corruption in Africa through a case study of Kenya; and Patrick Chabal, *Africa: The Politics of Suffering and Smiling* (London: Zed, 2009), which offers a new analysis of postcolonial African politics 'from below'.

22. George Ayittey, *Africa Unchained* (New York: Palgrave MacMillan, 2005).

23. See Patrick Chabal and Jean-Pascal Daloz, *Africa Works: Disorder as Political Instrument* (Oxford: Currey, 1999).

24. See, for example, Chris Alden, Daniel Large, and Ricardo Soares De Oliveira (eds.), *China Returns to Africa: A Rising Power and a Continent Embrace* (London: Hurst, 2008); Kweku Ampiah and Sanusha Naidu (eds.), *Crouching Tiger, Hidden Dragon? Africa and China* (Scottsville: University of Kwazulu-Natal Press, 2008); Garth le Pere (ed.), *China in Africa: Mercantilist Predator or Partner in Development?* (Johannesburg: Institute for Global Dialogue and SAIIA, 2006); Robert I. Rotberg (ed.), *China Into Africa: Trade, Aid, and Influence* (Washington, DC: Brookings Institution, 2008); and Ian Taylor, *China's New Role in Africa* (Boulder: Lynne Rienner, 2009).

6. SOUTH AFRICA AND THE EU: WHERE LIES THE STRATEGIC PARTNERSHIP?

1. Shada Islam, *Strategic Partnerships: The European Union's Quest for Global Clout*, EU-Africa Project, Occasional Paper no. 33 (Johannesburg: South Africa Institute of International Affairs [SAIIA], 2009).

2. Martin Holland, 'From Pariah to Partner: Relations with the EU', in Greg Mills, *From Pariah to Participant: South Africa's Evolving Foreign Relations, 1990–1994* (Johannesburg: SAIIA, 1994).

3. Adrian Guelke, 'The European Union: A Most Important Trading Partner?', in SAIIA, *South Africa in the Global Economy* (Johannesburg, 1995).

4. Sven Biscop and Tomas Renard, *EU's Strategic Partnerships Lack Content* (Brussels: Egmont Royal Institute of International Relations, 2009).

5. The EU Delegation to South Africa, *The European Union and South Africa: Development Partners, A Progress Report 2010*, available at http://www.eusa.org.za.

6. Martin Holland, *European Common Foreign Policy: From EPC to CFSP—Joint Action and South Africa* (Basingstoke: Macmillan, 1995).

7. Dani Venter and Ernst Neuland (eds.), *The European Union and South Africa* (Johannesburg: Richard Havenga, 2004).

8. Holland, *European Common Foreign Policy*.

9. Venter and Neuland, *The European Union and South Africa*.

10. Ibid.

11. Commission of the European Communities, *Communication from the Commission to the Council and the European Parliament: Towards an EU-South Africa Strategic Partnership* (Brussels, 2006).

12. Anne Graumans, *Political Dialogue Between the EU and SADC: Insights for ACP-EU Dialogue*, Working Paper no. 61 (Maastricht: European Centre for Development Policy Management).

13. Ibid.

14. See, for example, Richard Gibb, 'The New Southern African Customs Union Agreement: Dependence with Democracy', *Journal of Southern African Studies* 32(3) (September 2006), pp. 583–603.

15. In order to avoid the collapse of SACU and to find a way around the difficulties being experienced in the organisation, SACU held its first summit ever in July 2010 in Windhoek, Namibia, followed closely by another two in a one-year time frame.

16. European Union, *Directives for the Negotiations of Economic Partnership Agreements with ACP Countries and Regions* available at http://www.europa.eu.

17. E. Bursvik, 'South Africa and the "More Favourable Nation" Clause in the SADC-EU Economic Partnership Agreement (EPA) Negotiations', in *Supporting Regional Integration in East and Southern Africa: Review of Select Issues* (Stellenbosch: Trade Law Center [Tralac], 2010), available at http://www.tralac.org/cgi-bin/giga.cgi?cmd=cause_dir_news_item&cause_id=1694&news_id=86141&cat_id=1033.

18. Talitha Bertelsmann-Scott, *SACU: One Hundred Not Out—What Future for the Customs Union?* Occasional Paper no. 68 (Johannesburg: SAIIA, 2010).

19. Author's interview notes with Neil Cole, South African Treasury.

20. See, for example, Kweku Ampiah and Sanusha Naidu (eds.), *Crouching Tiger, Hidden Dragon? Africa and China* (Scottsville: University of Kwazulu-Natal Press, 2008); Garth le Pere and Garth Shelton, *China, Africa, and South Africa: South-South Co-operation in a Global Era* (Midrand: Institute for Global Dialogue, 2007); and Chris Alden, Daniel Large, and Ricardo Soares De Oliveira (eds.), *China Returns to Africa: A Rising Power and a Continent Embrace* (London: Hurst, 2008).

21. Holland, 'From Pariah to Partner', p. 128.

22. *South Africa-EU Joint Communiqué*, Third South Africa-EU Summit, Brussels, 28 September 2010.

23. Ibid.

24. 'EU Ready for Fresh Look at Zimbabwe Sanctions?' *Business Day* (South Africa), 29 September 2010.

25. Commission of the European Communities, *Communication from the Commission to the Council and the European Parliament: Towards an EU-South Africa Strategic Partnership*, Brussels, 2006, COM (2006) 347 Final.

26. Chris Landsberg, *The Diplomacy of Transformation: South African Foreign Policy and Statecraft* (Johannesburg: Macmillan, 2010).

27. Council of the European Union, 'Fourth South Africa-European Union Summit Joint Communiqué', press release, South Africa, 15 September 2011, 14292/11 PRESSE 311.

7. THE EU, THE MAGHREB, AND THE MEDITERRANEAN

1. See Ali Mazrui, 'Africa and Egypt's Four Circles', *African Affairs* 63(251) (April 1964).

2. See *Treaty of Rome* (1957), Part IV, Annex IV and Protocol 6.

3. Gregory White, *A Comparative Political Economy of Tunisia and Morocco: On the Outside of Europe Looking In* (Albany: State University of New York Press, 2001), pp. 56–58.

4. *Treaty of Rome.*

5. George Joffé, 'Prodigal or Pariah? Foreign Policy in Libya', in Dirk Vandewalle (ed.), *Libya Since 1969: Qadhafi's Revolution Revisited* (New York: Palgrave, 2008), pp. 202–204.

6. George Joffé, 'Israel, Palestine, and the European Union', in Aslam Farouk-Ali (ed.), *The Future of Palestine and Israel: From Colonial Roots to Post-Colonial Realities* (Midrand: Institute for Global Dialogue, 2007), p. 304.

7. Federica Bicchi, *The European Origins of Euro-Mediterranean Practices* (Berkeley: Institute of European Studies, University of California, 2004), pp. 3–5.

8. Ibid., p. 5.

9. The original use of the term 'hyper-power' was by Peregrine Worsthorne in the *Daily Telegraph* in 1991. However, it was revived in 1998 and then popularised by Hubert Védrine, then—French foreign minister, in a speech to the Association France-Amériques in Paris in February 1999. 'Geo-economics' was very much an American vision, pushed by the Bill Clinton administration (1993–2000), and reflected the argument that factors related to economic globalisation would determine international relations, with the United States seeking to dominate the globalised world economy. Allied to this, of course, was American scholar Francis Fukuyama's argument that, in the great ideological battle of the Cold War, Western concepts of democratic governance within free market economies had won a definitive victory. See Francis Fukuyama, 'The End of History?', *The National Interest*, Summer 1989.

10. Ian Manners relates the values that define Europe as a 'normative power' to key principles enshrined in the Union's *acquis*—peace, liberty, democracy, the rule of law, and respect for fundamental individual rights and freedoms, together with a more implicit concept that is of some importance here, 'good governance'. See Ian Manners, 'Normative Power Europe: The International Role of the EU', presentation to the European Communities Studies Association Panel, Madison, 31 May 2001; and Ian Manners, 'Normative Power Reconsidered', presentation at the CIDEL workshop 'From Civilian to Military Power: The European Union Reconsidered', Oslo, 22–23 October 2004. Helen Sjursen and Karen Smith argued that these are best represented by the EU's Copenhagen Principles, which determine the criteria for membership. Helen Sjursen and Karen E. Smith, *Justifying EU Foreign Policy: The Logics Underpinning EU Enlargement*, Arena Working Paper no. WP1/01 (Oslo: Centre of European Studies, University of Oslo, 2001).

11. In 1987 the European Parliament had initially refused to ratify the financial protocol with Morocco because of Rabat's alleged abuses of human rights—a

decision that shocked the Moroccan government into reviewing its domestic policies, and contributed to the liberalisation process that began in the country in 1990.

12. George Joffé, 'Europe and North Africa', *Cambridge Review of International Affairs* 10(2) (Summer 1997).

13. *Barcelona Declaration* (28 November 1995), Preamble.

14. Frederica Bicchi describes these countries as the 'entrepreneurs' of a new normative vision of the Mediterranean as a region. See Frederica Bicchi, *Defining European Interests in Foreign Policy: Insights from the Mediterranean Case*, Arena Working Paper no. WP 13/03 (Oslo: Centre of European Studies, University of Oslo).

15. London, for instance, was known in the Francophone Algerian press as 'Londonistan', in ironic reference to the shelter accorded to Algerian dissidents there.

16. George Joffé, 'The European Union, Democracy, and Counter-Terrorism in the Maghrib', *Journal of Common Market Studies* 46(1) (January 2008), pp. 166–167.

17. See Abderrahman Robena, *The Prospects for an Economic Community in North Africa* (New York: Praeger, 1973).

18. The *acquis* is the corpus of the Union's legislation that defines its institutions and activities.

19. See http://ec.europa.eu/world/enp/policy_en.htm.

20. See http://ec.europa.eu/contact/index_en.htm.

21. See http://ec.europa.eu/external_relations/euromed/index_en.htm.

22. Karl Deutsch et al., *Political Community in the North Atlantic Area* (Princeton: Princeton University Press, 1957).

8. THE EU AND ASIA: LESSONS FOR AFRICA?

1. ASEAN members include Brunei, Cambodia, Indonesia, Laos, Malaysia, Myanmar, the Philippines, Singapore, Thailand, and Vietnam.

2. The first Lomé Convention was signed in the Togolese capital of Lomé in 1975.

3. The EU-ASEAN Cooperation Agreement was signed in 1980.

4. The EU-India Cooperation Agreement was signed in 1994.

5. EU relations with China were established in 1975 and were governed by the EU-China Trade and Cooperation Agreement of 1985.

6. 'A Secure Europe in a Better World' European Security Strategy, 12 December 2003.

7. Joseph S. Nye, *Soft Power: The Means to Success in World Politics* (New York: PublicAffairs, 2004).

8. 'Providing Security in a Changing World', report on implementation of the European Security Strategy, 11 December 2008.

9. 'Towards a New Asia Strategy', communication from the European Commission to the European Council, 13 July 1994, COM (1994) 314 Final.

10. The Asia-Europe Meetings comprise forty-eight members, including the twenty-seven EU states and the European Commission. On the Asian side, ASEM includes the ten member states of ASEAN, China, Japan, South Korea, India, Mongolia, Pakistan, and the ASEAN secretariat, with Australia, New Zealand, and Russia joining the Asian side of ASEM in 2010.

11. José Manuel Barroso, president of the European Commission, speech at the opening of the EU-China summit in Beijing, 24 October 2008.

12. 'Europe and Asia: A Strategic Framework for Enhanced Partnerships', communication from the European Commission, 4 September 2001, COM (2001) 469 Final.

13. Ibid.

14. 'Regional Programming for Asia: Strategy Document 2007–2013', European Commission, 31 May 2007.

15. 'A New Partnership with South-East Asia', communication from the European Commission, 9 July 2003, COM (2003) 399 Final.

16. Ibid.

17. Ibid.

18. 'The European Union Deepens Relations with ASEAN', press release no. 2009/D/241, Delegation of the European Commission to Indonesia and Brunei Darussalam, 12 February 2009.

19. 'An EU-India Strategic Partnership', communication from the European Commission, 16 June 2004, COM (2004) 430 Final.

20. 'EU-China: Closer Partners, Growing Responsibilities', communication from the European Commission, 14 October 2006, COM (2006) 631 Final.

21. See, for example, David M. Malone, *Does the Elephant Dance? Contemporary Indian Foreign Policy* (Oxford: Oxford University Press, 2011).

22. Communication from the Commission: The EU, Africa and China: Towards trilateral dialogue and cooperation, European Commission, COM (2008) 654, 17 October.

23. Communication from the Commission: The EU, Africa and China: Towards trilateral dialogue and cooperation, European Commission, COM (2008) 654, 17 October, p. 3.

24. Ibid.

9. GLOBAL AFRICA: THE LAST INVESTMENT FRONTIER?

1. See 'GEMs Equity Strategy—SSA: Improved Fundamentals Priced-In Near Term', Morgan Stanley Investment Perspectives, 8 August, 2008, p. 4.

2. Martin Meredith, *The State of Africa: A History of Fifty Years of Independence* (London: Free Press, 2005).

3. 'Africa 1.01 Unlocking Investment Potential', Renaissance Capital, July 2008.

4. British Petroleum, *Statistical Review of World Energy*, June 2008, pp. 6, 22.

5. 'What's Up in Africa', EMEA Perspectives, UBS Investment Research, 2007, p. 60.

6. Paul Stevens, *The Coming Oil Supply Crunch* (London: Royal Institute of International Affairs, 2008).

7. René Verduijn, 'The Food and Agriculture Organisation and the World Food Programme', in Adekeye Adebajo (ed.), *From Global Apartheid to Global Village: Africa and the United Nations* (Scottsville: University of Kwazulu-Natal Press, 2009), pp. 437–462.

8. 'Can Greed Save Africa?' *Newsweek*, 10 December 2007, p. 49.

9. See *The Economist*, 13 May 2000.

10. These countries are Botswana, Burkina Faso, Burundi, the Central African Republic, Chad, Ethiopia, Lesotho, Malawi, Mali, Niger, Rwanda, Swaziland, Uganda, Zambia, and Zimbabwe.

11. The National Audit Office recently concluded that the Private Finance Initiative—the main form of PPP deals in Britain—provides 'poor value for money'. The office found that £180 million of public money was being 'wasted' due to contractors charging unjustifiably high fees. National Audit Office, 'Making Changes in Operational PFI Projects', London, January 2008.

12. 'Nigeria on the BRINC?' Renaissance Capital, February 2008.

13. Energy Information Agency, 2007.

14. 'What's Up in Africa?', p. 63.

15. Yongzheng Yang and Sanjeev Gupta, *Regional Trade Arrangements in Africa: Past Performance and the Way Forward*, Working Paper no. WP/05/36 (Washington, DC: International Monetary Fund, February 2005). See also AU Commission, *Audit of the African Union 2008*, available at http://www.pambazuka.org/actionalerts/images/uploads/AUDIT_REPORT.doc.

16. Interview with author, *Sunday Telegraph*, 3 December 2006, Business Section, p. 5.

17. Robert B. Zoellick, 'A Challenge of Statecraft', speech to the Center for Global Development, Washington, DC, 2 April 2008.

18. Angus Maddison database, http://www.ggdc.net/maddison.

19. Adrian Wood, 'How Donors Should Cap Aid to Africa', *Financial Times*, 4 September 2008, p. 11.

10. AN ANATOMY OF THE ECONOMIC PARTNERSHIP AGREEMENTS

1. European Commission, 'ACP-EU Partnership Agreement Signed in Cotonou on 23 June', arts. 19–34. Supplement to *The Courier* (Brussels: European Commission), September 2000.

2. *General Agreement on Tariffs and Trade*, art. XXIV: 8(b), 5(c).

3. According to the 'Understanding on the Interpretation of Art. XXIV', 'substantially all trade' refers in the case of customs unions to the weighted average tariff rates and customs duties collected. FTAs (such as EPAs) must satisfy the provisions of WTO Article XXIV: 5.

4. Peter Mandelson, 'Comments by Peter Mandelson at the INTA Committee, European Parliament', Strasbourg, 22 October 2007, available at http://trade. ec.europa.eu/doclib/docs/2007/october/tradoc_136542.pdf.

5. *Cotonou Agreement*, art. 35.2.

6. Mareike Meyn, 'Economic Partnership Agreements: "How to Ensure Development Orientation of Trade Liberalisation and the Coherence with ACP Regional Integration Objectives"', in BMZ Discourse, *The Development Dimension of the Economic Partnership Agreements (EPAs) Between the ACP Countries and the EU* (Berlin: German Federal Ministry for Economic Cooperation and Development [BMZ], 2007). This is an overview of the factors that constrain economic integration among ACP countries, such as (a) the noncomplementary trade structure and low degree of industrialisation; (b) conflicts and political instability; (c) low macroeconomic convergence among member states; (d) supply-side constraints; (e) insufficient compensation mechanisms to limit the effects of trade diversion and revenue losses; and (f) overlapping memberships and the inconsistency of regional integration strategies.

7. East Timor, Somalia, and Cuba are classified as ACP countries but were not part of the EPA negotiations. South Africa is also part of the ACP group but has a separate trade and development regime with the EU (TDCA). The full complement of the ACP group is therefore seventy-nine.

8. The ESA was the EPA negotiation framework of sixteen Southern and Eastern African countries, including all EAC countries (which opted for an EAC negotiation framework only at the last minute). All ESA countries except Tanzania are members of COMESA.

9. See the following Overseas Development Institute (ODI) project briefings: 'The End of Current EU Preferences for Namibia: Economic and Social Impacts', May 2007, available at http://www.odi.org.uk/iedg/Publications/Namibia_Preferences_Project_Briefing.pdf; and 'The End of Botswana Beef Exports to the EU?' August 2007, available at http://www.odi.org.uk/iedg/Publications/Botswana_MMeyn_briefing.pdf.

10. 'The Costs to the ACP of Exporting to the EU Under the GSP', study commissioned by the Foreign Ministry of the Netherlands (London: ODI, March 2007), available at http://www.odi.org.uk/iedg/Research_areas/Trade_trade_policy.html.

11. 'A Development-Oriented SADC Framework Agreement', study commissioned by the Namibian Agricultural Trade Forum (ATF) (London: ODI, August 2007).

12. For each product, the schedule shows the treatment to be accorded within CARIFORUM unless a country has registered an exception. These 'exceptions' vary from about 400 tariff lines in the case of Dominica up to more than 3,600 in case of the Bahamas. Even after the end of the twenty-five-year implementation period, the CARIFORUM countries will not have a common external tariff on all of their EU-sourced imports (London: ODI, 2008).

13. How the quotas are allocated within the EPA configuration is for the countries to decide. With the exception of the Dominican Republic, no country-specific quotas were allocated.

14. This will be applied when the European Union market price of white sugar falls during two consecutive months below 80 per cent of the market price during the previous marketing year.

15. This states that both knitted and woven clothing can be produced by sourcing fabric from the most competitive supplier without losing originating status under the EPA. See Adekeye Adebajo, 'An Axis of Evil? China, the United States, and France in Africa', in Kweku Ampiah and Sanusha Naidu (eds.), *Crouching Tiger, Hidden Dragon? Africa and China* (Scottsville: University of Kwazulu-Natal Press, 2008), pp. 256–257; Anver Versi, 'At Last, a Win-Win Formula for African Business', *African Business* no. 285 (2003), pp. 12–15; and R.W. Copson, *The United States in Africa* (London: Zed), 2007, pp. 34–36.

16. South Africa has not signed an EPA but has a separate free trade agreement with the EU. Botswana, Lesotho, Namibia, and Swaziland are together in the customs union SACU, and submitted a joint EPA liberalisation offer.

17. European Commission Directorate-General for Trade, 'Six Common Misconceptions About Economic Partnership Agreements (EPAs)', (Brussels, 11 January 2008), available at http://trade.ec.europa.eu/doclib/docs/2008/january/ tradoc_137484.pdf.

18. ODI and European Centre for Development Policy Management (ECDPM), 'The New EPAs: Comparative Analysis of Their Content and the Challenges for 2008', study commissioned by the Foreign Ministry of the Netherlands, 2008, available at http://www.odi.org.uk/iedg/Projects/0708010_The_new_ EPAs.html.

19. The nineteen COMESA members are Burundi, Comoros, the Democratic Republic of the Congo, Djibouti, Egypt, Eritrea, Ethiopia, Kenya, Libya, Madagascar, Malawi, Mauritius, Rwanda, Seychelles, Sudan, Swaziland, Uganda, Zambia, and Zimbabwe.

20. South Africa, which already has a WTO-compatible trade deal with the EU, decided not to join the EPA initialled by its fellow SACU members Botswana, Lesotho, Namibia, and Swaziland.

21. Richard Gibb, 'The New Southern African Customs Union Agreements: Dependence with Democracy', *Journal of Southern African Studies* 32 (3) (September 2006), pp. 583–603.

22. This is according to 2006 data provided by South African Revenue Services.
23. Chris Stevens, 'The New Economic Partnership Agreements: Implications for SADC', paper for the Trade and Industrial Policy Strategies (TIPS), Johannesburg, South Africa, annual report 2008–2009.
24. As stated in its December 2007 Council Regulation (EC No. 1528/2007), the Council needs to act 'by qualified majority on a proposal from the Commission' in order to add or remove countries from the list of DFQF beneficiaries (chap. 1, art. 2.2).

11. AFRICA AND EUROPE: ENDING A DIALOGUE OF THE DEAF?

1. Louis Michel, 'Europe-Africa: The Indispensable Partnership', speech delivered to the European Policy Centre, Brussels, November 2007.
2. See John Akokpari, Angela Ndunga-Mavumba, and Tim Murithi (eds.), *The African Union and Its Institutions* (Johannesburg: Jacana, 2008); and *Audit of the African Union: Towards a People-Centred Political and Socio-Economic Integration and Transformation of Africa* (Addis Ababa: AU Commission, 2007).
3. For analyses of changing forms of regionalism on both continents, see Gilbert M. Khadiagala, *Europe and Africa: Fading Memories, Fraying Ties?* Occasional Paper no. 5 (Kent: Lyman L. Lemnitzer Centre for NATO and European Community Studies, 1996).
4. The members of the G8 are the United States, Russia, Japan, Germany, Britain, France, Italy, and Canada.
5. Garth le Pere, 'The New ACP-EU Cotonou Agreement: Its Main Features', *Issue* no. 9 (2001).
6. For recent analyses of EU-Africa relations, see Alex Nunn and Sophia Price, 'Managing Development: EU and African Relations Through the Lomé and Cotonou Agreements', *Historical Materialism* no. 4 (2004), pp. 203–230; Gumisai Mutume, 'Africans Fear "Ruin" in European Trade Talks', *Africa Renewal* vol. 21 no. 2, July 2007, pp. 10–13.
7. Peter Draper, 'EU-Africa Trade Relations: The Political Economy of Economic Partnership Agreements', Jan Tumlur Policy Essay no. 2 (Brussels: European Centre for International Political Economy, 2007); Richard Gibb, 'Post-Lomé: The European Union and the South', *Third World Quarterly* 21(3) (2000), pp. 457–481; Stephen Hurt, 'Cooperation and Coercion? The Cotonou Agreement Between the European Union and the ACP States and the End of the Lomé Convention', *Third World Quarterly* 24(1) (2007), pp. 161–176.
8. For a good analysis of the confusion that marked the decision on the EAC configuration, see Damas Kanyabwoya, 'Tanzania: We Are Negotiating EPA Under EAC, Says Bargainer' *The Citizen* (Dar es Salaam), 18 December 2007; Wilfred Edwin, 'EU Wants Dar to Decide Under Which Regional Bloc It Will Negotiate EPAs', *The East African* (Nairobi), 3 April 2007; and Paul Kruger, 'The Pos-

sible Withdrawal of Tanzania from the SADC EPA Configurations', *TRALAC News*, 24 April 2007.

9. Thanos Ramos, 'General Overview of the Economic Partnership Agreement Between the EC and the East African Community' (Nairobi: European Commission, 16–17 February 2009).

10. Benjamin Muindi, 'The EU Flexes Its Muscles', *The Nation*, 10 February 2010.

11. Quoted in Ben Angira, 'Threat to Reintroduce EU Import Duties', *The Nation*, 7 December 2009.

12. 'Breakthrough in EPA Talks', *The Citizen* (Dar es Salaam), 4 February 2010.

13. EU Commission Office, 'EPA Negotiations Recommence in Zanzibar', press release, Dar es Salaam, September 20, 2011.

14. European Union, 'The Interim SADC-EPA Agreement: Legal and Technical Issues and Challenges' (Tshwane, 2007).

15. African Union, 'Economic Partnership Agreements: Background—The Idea of EPA Negotiations' (Addis Ababa, 2007).

16. European Commission, 'EU-SADC Negotiations: What Has Been Achieved So Far? Future Challenges' (Tshwane, June 2010); European Union, 'The Interim SADC EPA Agreement'.

17. 'Aid for Trade and EPAs: Commissioner Ashton in Zambia', *Europa* press release, April 2009, available at http://europa.eu/rapid/pressReleasesAction.do?referen ce=IP/09/540&format=HTML&aged=0&language=EN&guiLanguage=en

18. European Commission, 'EU-ESA Negotiations' (Brussels, October 2009).

19. Suleiman Mustapha. 'ECOWAS Ministers Endorse Controversial EPA Deal', *The Statesman* (Accra), 10 October 2006; Suleiman Mustapha, 'ECOWAS Extends Deadline for EPA Negotiations', *The Statesman* (Accra), 6 December 2006; and Daniel Nonor, 'Ghana: Regional EPA Due in June', *Accra Times*, 4 March 2009.

20. ECOWAS Secretariat, 'Draft Proposals for PAPED', 23 April 2010; and 'Support to the Development Dimension in the EU-West Africa EPA', *Europa* press release, 11 May 2010.

21. In 2009, for example, there were more than ten meetings among these participants to review the negotiation processes. See ECOWAS Secretariat, 'West African Ministers Want Private Sector Involved in EPA Negotiations with the European Union', 8 May 2010; Babianae Mbaye Gahamanyi, 'West Africa in the EPA Negotiations with the European Community', *ACP-EU Civil Society Information Network*, August 2004.

22. Agritrade, 'EPA Negotiations in West Africa Continue to Face Difficulties', *Agritrade News and Analysis*, May 2010.

23. 'ECOWAS-EU EPA Negotiations Not Stalled', *Ghana News Agency*, 28 November 2011, available at http://www.ghananewsagency.org/details/Economics/ ECOWAS-EU-EPA-Negotiations-not-Stalled-ECOWAS-Official/?ci=3&ai=36 178.

24. For a summary of the negotiations, see Claude Maerten and Elisabeth Tison, 'EPA Negotiations with Central Africa', *Trade Negotiations Insight* 8(2) (March 2009); and South Centre, *EPA Negotiations in the Central Africa Region: Some Issues for Consideration* (Geneva, July 2007).

25. Agritrade, 'EPA Negotiations Between Central Africa and the EU', *Agritrade News and Analysis*, 10 March 2010.

26. Ibid.

27. Yash Tandon, 'The ESA-EU EPA Negotiations and the Role of COMESA', *Southern and Eastern African Trade, Information, and Negotiations Institute bulletin* 7(9) (4 June 2004); and African Trade Policy Centre, 'EPA Negotiations: African Countries Continental Review', review report (Addis Ababa, 19 February 2007).

28. Oxfam International, *Economic Partnership Agreements: Partnerships or Power Play?* (London, 2008).

29. Christopher Stevens, 'The EU, Africa, and Economic Partnership Agreements: Unintended Consequences of Policy Leverage', *Journal of Modern African Studies* 44(3) (2006), p. 447.

30. European Union, 'The Interim SADC EPA Agreement'.

31. Yash Tandon, 'The ESA-EU EPA Negotiations', p. 2.

32. For analyses and critiques of the CfA report, see William Brown, 'The Commission for Africa: Results and Prospects for the West's Africa Policy', *Journal of Modern African Studies* 44(3) (2006), pp. 349–374; and Cameron Duodu, 'Gleneagles: What Was All the Hype About?' *New African*, August–September 2005, pp. 34–37.

33. For analyses of Tony Blair's Africa policy during this period, see Zoe Ware, 'Reassessing Labour's Relationship with Sub-Saharan Africa', *The Round Table* 95(383) (2005), pp. 141–152; and Tom Porteous, 'British Government Policy in Sub-Saharan Africa Under New Labour', *International Affairs* 81(2) (2005), pp. 281–297.

34. Commission for Africa, *Our Common Interest: Report of the Commission for Africa* (London, 2005), available at http://www.commissionforafrica.org.

35. Todd Moss, 'Briefing: The G8's Multilateral Debt Relief Initiative and Poverty Reduction in Sub-Saharan Africa', *African Affairs* 105(419) (2006), pp. 285–293.

36. For analyses of the summit, see Penny Jackson, 'Briefing: The Commission for Africa: Gleneagles, Brussels, and Beyond', *African Affairs* 104(417) (2005), p. 658.

37. Jackson, 'Briefing', p. 658. See also a *Financial Times* (London) report on 14 July 2005 that noted: 'Some smaller European countries have voiced frustration at G8 Grandstanding. Norway, Sweden, Denmark, Luxembourg, and the Netherlands, who, collectively, are the world's most generous aid donors pointed

out that none of the G8 countries had yet reached the UN target of donating 0.7 per cent of their national income as aid'.

38. For discussion of this strategy, see Samuel S. Kingah, 'The European Union's New African Strategy: Grounds for Cautious Optimism', *European Foreign Affairs Review* 11 (2006), pp. 527–253.

39. Cited in Kingah, 'The European Union's New African Strategy'.

40. For a good analysis of EU efforts at democracy promotion, see Gordon Crawford, 'The European Union and Democracy Promotion in Africa: The Case of Ghana', *European Journal of Development Research* 17(4) (2005), pp. 571–600.

41. See Adebayo Adedeji, 'NEPAD's African Peer Review Mechanism: Progress and Prospects', pp. 241–269; Chris Landsberg, 'The Birth and Evolution of NEPAD', pp. 207–226; and Sheila Bunwaree, 'NEPAD and Its Discontents', pp. 227–240, all in Akokpari, Ndunga-Mavumba, and Murithi, *The African Union and Its Institutions*.

42. Kingah, 'The European Union's New African Strategy'. See also Charles C. Pentland, 'The European Union and Civil Conflict in Africa', *International Journal* (Autumn 2005), pp. 919–936.

43. Stephan Klingebiel, 'Regional Security in Africa and the Role of External Support', *European Journal of Development Research* 17(5) (2005), pp. 437–448.

44. Richard Youngs, 'The EU and Conflict Resolution in West Africa', *European Foreign Affairs Review* 11 (2006), pp. 333–352; UN Integrated Regional Information Networks, 'Fund to Support Peacekeepers', 16 May 2007.

45. Winrich Kühne, *How the EU Organises and Conducts Peace Operations in Africa: EUFOR/MINURCAT* Report no. 3 (Berlin: Centre for International Peace Operations, 2009).

46. Paul Redfern, 'G8 Pledges for Africa No Longer Concern the West', *The East African* (Nairobi), 11 July 2006.

47. Kate Connolly, 'Uneasy Echoes of Berlin in G8 Wall', *The Guardian* (London), 1 May 2007.

48. Government of Canada, 'Muskoka Declaration Recovery and New Beginnings' (Muskoka, 25–26 June 2010).

49. African Union and European Union, 'The Africa-EU Strategic Partnership: A Joint Africa-EU Strategy', Lisbon Declaration, Africa-EU Summit, 9 December 2007.

50. Ibid., pp. 26–27.

51. For critical analyses of the joint strategy, see Paul Engel and Marie-Laure de Bergh, 'Lisbon-EU Summit: The Day After … Prepared for a Real Change in the Relationship?' *WDEV* no. 6 (November–December 2007).

12. A CRITIQUE OF THE EU'S COMMON AGRICULTURAL POLICY

1. Déméter, *Economie et Stratégie Agricoles 2002* (Paris: Armand Colin, 2001).

2. See http://en.wikipedia.org/wiki/Common_Agricultural_Policy.

3. Peter Zander, Andrea Knierim, Jeroen J.C. Groot, and Walter A.H. Rossing, 'Multifunctionality of Agriculture: Tools and Methods for Impact Assessment and Valuation', *Agriculture, Ecosystems & Environment* 120(1) (2007), pp. 1–4.

4. See also 'EU Budget Facts and Myths' at http://europa.eu.

5. South Centre, 'A Positive Agenda for African Agriculture in EPAs', in Analytical Note SC/AN/TDP/EPA/17 (Geneva, 2008), available at http://www.southcentre.org.

6. Alan Matthews, 'Europe's Common Agricultural Policy', *Journal of European Integration* 30(3) (2008), pp. 381–399.

7. European Commission, Directorate-General for Agriculture and Rural Development, Brussels, 2009.

8. Action Aid, *Farmgate: The Developmental Impact of Agricultural Subsidies* (London, 2008).

9. Jochen Jesinghaus, 'Agricultural Sector Pressure Indicators in the European Union', in Floor Brouwer and Rob Crabtree (eds.), *Environmental Indicators and Agricultural Policy* (Wallingford: CAB International, 1999), pp. 45–55.

10. 'CAP2020', Policy Briefing no. 2 (London and Brussels: IEEP, December 2008), p. 12.

11. For example, Health 21 Hungarian Foundation, the European Network for Smoking Prevention European Cancer Leagues, the European Heart Network, and the European Respiratory Society.

12. http://www.euractiv.com/.../ngos-defy-commission-eu-2020-agenda.

13. Martin C. Whitby (ed.), *The European Environment and CAP Reform: Polices and Prospects for Conservation* (Wallingford: CAB International, 1996).

14. Andrew Moxley, Martin Whitby, and Philip Lowe, 'Research Report on Environmental Indicators for a Reformed CAP: Monitoring and Evaluating Policies in Agriculture' (Newcastle: University of Newcastle, School of Agriculture, Food, and Rural Development, 1998).

15. See Allan Buckwell, 'Economic Signals, Farmers' Response, and Environmental Change', *Journal of Rural Studies* 5(2) (1990), pp. 149–160; Whitby, *The European Environment and CAP Reform;* Michael Winter and Pete Gaskell, 'The Effects of the 1992 Reform of the CAP on the Countryside of Great Britain', report to the Countryside Commission, Countryside Council of Wales, Department of the Environment and Scottish Natural Heritage, 1997.

16. Kathy Baylis, Stephen Peplow, Gordon Rausser, and Leo Simon, 'Agri-Environmental Policies in the EU and United States: A Comparison', in *Ecological Economics* (London: Publisher, 2007).

17. Floor Brouwer and Philip Lowe (eds.), 'CAP and the Rural Environment in Transition: A Panorama of National Perspectives' (Wageningen: Wageningen Pers, 1998); Floor Brouwer, '"Agri-Environmental" Indicators in the European Union: Policy Requirements and Data Availability', in Brouwer and Crabtree, *Environmental Indicators and Agricultural Policy*, pp. 57–72.

18. Matthews, 'Europe's Common Agricultural Policy'.

19. OECD, 'Producer and Consumer Support Estimates', OECD Database 1986–2004 (Paris, 2006).

20. Slovenian Presidency of the EU, press release, 21 January 2008, available at http://www.eu2008.si/en/News_and_Documents/Press_Releases/January/0121_MKGP_AGRIFISH.html.

21. Barry K. Goodwin and Ashok K. Mishra, 'Are Decoupled Farm Payments Really Decoupled? An Empirical Evaluation', *American Journal of Agricultural Economics* 88(1) (February 2006), pp. 73–88.

22. These include Bird Life International, the European International Bureau, the European Forum on Nature Conservation and Pastoralism, the International Federation of Organic Agriculture Movements-EU Group, and the World Wildlife Fund.

23. Farming and environmental nongovernmental organisations such as Third World Network and Farm Subsidy have therefore come together with proposals to replace all current CAP subsidies with a new system. See http://www.eeb.org/EEB.

24. European Commission, *The EU Rural Development Policy: Facing the Challenges* (Brussels, 2008).

25. 'CAP 2020', p. 12.

26. See British House of Commons, EU Scrutiny Committee, *Seventh Report of Session 2007–08*, 9 January 2008, available at http://www.publications.parliament.uk/pa/cm200708/cmselect/cmeuleg/16-vii/16vii.pdf.

27. Kym Anderson (ed.), *Distortions to Agricultural Incentives: A Global Perspective* (London: Palgrave Macmillan, 2008), p. iv.

28. European Environmental Agency, *Europe's Environment: Fourth Assessment* (Copenhagen, 2007).

29. 'Opinion of the Environment, Public Health, and Food Safety Committee on Agriculture and Rural Development on the Health Check of the CAP', January 2008, available at http://www.europarl.europa.eu/sides/getDoc.do?pubRef=-//EP//NONSGML+COMPARL+PE-98.573+03+DOC+WORD+V0.//EN&language=EN.

30. Examples here include Belgium, Denmark, the Netherlands, France, and Germany.

31. Kym Anderson and Tim Josling, *The EU's CAP at Fifty: An International Perspective*, CEPR Policy Insight no. 13 (2007).

32. Panagariya Arvind, 'Alternative Perspective on "Subsidies and Trade Barriers"', in Bjorn Lømborg (ed.), *Global Crises, Global Solutions* (Cambridge: Cambridge University Press, 2004), pp. 592–604.

33. See Agricultural Policy of the United States and Food, Conservation, and Energy Act of 2008.

34. Quoted in All Party Parliamentary Group, *Why No Thought for Food? A UK Parliamentary Inquiry into Global Food Security* (London: UK Parliament Publications, January 2010).
35. Ibid.
36. Action Aid, *Farmgate*.
37. World Bank, *Development Report*, (Washington, DC, 2008).
38. OECD, *Report on the OECD Workshop on the Disaggregated Impacts of the CAP* (Paris, March 2010).
39. Matthews, 'Europe's Common Agricultural Policy'.
40. See http://www.tradingmarkets.com/.site/news/Stock%20News/1248781.
41. United Nations Development Programme (UNDP), 'Policy, Not Charity: What the Rich Countries Can Do to Help Achieve the Goals', in UNDP, *Human Development Report*, (New York, 2003).
42. European Commission, *The EU Rural Development Policy: The Common Agriculture Policy After 2013*, public debate summary report (Brussels, 2010).
43. House of Commons Hansard (pt. 0010), 3 June 2010, col. 615.
44. UNDP, 'International Cooperation at a Crossroads: Aid, Trade, and Security in an Unequal World', in UNDP, *Human Development Report*, (New York, 2005).
45. Brouwer and Crabtree, *Environmental Indicators and Agricultural Policy*.
46. See http://en.wikipedia.org/wiki/Common_Agricultural_Policy.
47. All Party Parliamentary Group, *Why No Thought for Food?*
48. Heikki Lehtonen, Jussi Lankoski, and Jyrki Niemi, *Evaluating the Impact of Alternative Policy Scenarios on Multifunctionality*, Working Paper no. 13 (CEPS and ENARPRI, 1 July 2005).
49. Arvind, 'Alternative Perspective'.

13. AU-EU SECURITY AND GOVERNANCE COOPERATION

1. Jean-François Bayart, 'Africa in the World: A History of Extroversion', *African Affairs* 99 (2000), p. 267.
2. See Adam Habib, 'Western Hegemony, Asian Ascendancy, and the New Scramble for Africa', and Adekeye Adebajo, 'An Axis of Evil? China, the United States, and France in Africa', both in Kweku Ampiah and Sanusha Naidu (eds.), *Crouching Tiger, Hidden Dragon: Africa and China* (Scottsville: University of Kwazulu-Natal Press, 2008), pp. 259–277 and pp. 227–258.
3. See, for example, Adekeye Adebajo, *The Curse of Berlin: Africa After the Cold War* (London: Hurst, 2010), pp. 175–176.
4. Mark Leonard, *Why Europe Will Run the 21st Century* (London: Fourth Estate, 2005).
5. John Ravenhill, *Collective Clientelism: The Lomé Conventions and North-South Relations* (New York: Columbia University Press, 1985), pp. 86–115.

6. See Christopher Stevens, 'Economic Partnership Agreements: What Can We Learn?' *New Political Economy* 13(2) (June 2008), pp. 211–223.

7. Harmut Mayer, 'Is It Still Called "Chinese Whispers"? The EU's Rhetoric and Action As a Responsible Global Institution', *International Affairs* 84(1) (January 2008), pp. 61–63.

8. Kofi Annan, *In Larger Freedom: Towards Security, Development, and Human Rights for All*, Report of the Secretary General of the UN for Decision by Heads of State and Government (New York, September 2005).

9. Craig Burnside and David Dollar, *Aid, the Incentive Regime, and Poverty Reduction*, Policy Research Working Paper no. 1937 (Washington, DC: World Bank, 1998), pp. 16–19.

10. Nils-Sjard Schulz, 'The G20 and the Global Governance of Development', policy brief (Madrid: FRIDE, September 2010), p. 2.

11. See Stefan Szepesi, *Coercion or Engagement? Economics and Institutions in ACP-EU Trade Negotiations*, Discussion Paper no. 56 (Maastricht: ECDPM, 2004).

12. Francis Ikome, *From the Lagos Plan of Action to the New Partnership for Africa's Development: The Political Economy of African Regional Initiatives* (Midrand: Institute for Global Dialogue, 2007), pp. 144–159. See also John Akokpari, Angela Ndinga-Muvumba, and Tim Murithi (eds.), *The African Union and Its Institutions* (Johannesburg: Jacana, 2008).

13. Alyson J.K. Bailes, 'The EU and a "Better World": What Role for the European Security and Defence Policy?' *International Affairs* 84(1) (January 2008), pp. 115–130.

14. John Kotsopoulos, 'The EU and Africa: Coming Together at Last?' policy brief (Brussels: European Policy Centre, July 2007).

15. Gordon Crawford, 'European Union Development Co-operation and the Promotion of Democracy', in Peter Burnell (ed.), *Democracy Assistance: International Cooperation for Democratization* (London: Cass, 2000), pp. 90–127.

16. Clare Short, 'Aid That Doesn't Help', *Financial Times*, 23 June 2000.

17. OECD, *Net Official Development Assistance in 2007* (Paris, 4 April 2008).

18. EU-Africa e-alert, 'EDF 10: Development Cooperation Instrument and EU Development Policy', 2008, Europafrica.org.

19. Jean-Victor Louis, *The European Union: From External Relations to Foreign Policy?* EU Diplomacy Paper no. 2 (Bruges: College of Europe, 2007), pp. 6–8.

20. Susanne Wolf and Dominik Spoden, *Allocation of EU Aid Towards ACP Countries*, Discussion Paper no. 22 (Bonn: Centre for Development Research, 2000), pp. 6–8.

21. Yvonne M. Tsikata, 'Owning Economic Reforms: A Comparative Study of Ghana and Tanzania', in Steve Kayizzi-Mugerwa (ed.), *Reforming Africa's Institutions: Ownership, Incentives, and Capabilities* (New York: United Nations University Press, 2003), pp. 37–43.

22. Louise Fawcett, 'Regional Governance Architecture and Security Policy', briefing paper (Berlin: FES, February 2006).

23. *The EU-Africa Partnership in Historical Perspective*, Issue Paper no. 1 (Maastricht: ECDPM, December 2006).

24. On the EU side, the Troika is made up of representatives of the current and incoming EU presidency, the European Commission, and the EU Council. On the African side, the Troika consists of representatives of the current and outgoing presidencies of the AU and the AU Commission.

25. 'From Cairo to Lisbon: The EU-Africa Strategic Partnership', communication from the European Commission to the European Parliament and European Council, 27 June 2007, COM (2007) 357 Final,.

26. Ibid.

27. See Akokpari, Ndinga-Muvumba, and Murithi, *The African Union and Its Institutions*.

28. See European Commission, 'Key Deliverables of the Joint Africa-EU Strategy', 1 June 2010.

29. Article 1 of the Protocol Relating to the Establishment of the Peace and Security Council of the African Union, 9 July 2002.

30. Article 6–1, Common Position 2004/85/CFSP, 26 January 2004, JO L21/25.

31. Council of the European Union, 'EU Concept for Strengthening African Capabilities for the Prevention, Management, and Resolution of Conflicts', adopted at 2760th meeting of the General Affairs Council, Brussels, 13 November 2006.

32. UN General Assembly and Security Council, *Report of the African Union/United Nations Panel on Modalities for Support to African Union Peacekeeping Operations*, December 2008, UN Doc. A/63/666-S/2008/813.

33. James Mackie et al., *Final Report of Mid-Term Evaluation of the African Peace Facility*, Maastricht, 1 December 2005, available at http://ec.europa.eu/development/Geographical/europe-cares/africa/docs/APF_Eval_final_Report-ECDPM_1DEC05.doc.

34. Ian Manners, 'The Normative Ethics of the European Union', *International Affairs* 84(1) (January 2008), p. 54.

35. 'Governance and Development Cooperation: Civil Society Perspectives on the EU Approach', briefing paper (City: Coopération Internationale pour le Développement et la Solidarité [CIDSE], August 2006).

36. CONCORD Cotonou Working Group, 'Governance', briefing paper, ACP-EU Joint Parliamentary Assembly, Ljubljana, 15–20 March 2008, available at http://www.concordeurope.org.

37. Adrian Hyde-Price, 'A "Tragic Actor"? A Realist Perspective on "Ethical Power Europe"', *International Affairs* 84(1) (January 2008), pp. 32–33.

38. Hans Morgenthau, *Politics Among Nations: The Struggle for Power and Peace* (New York: McGraw-Hill, 1993, first published in 1948), p. 6.

39. Edward Hallett Carr, *The Twenty Years' Crisis: An Introduction to the Study of International Relations* (New York: Palgrave, 2001, first published in 1939), pp. 74–75.

14. THE EU SECURITY ROLE IN THE GREAT LAKES REGION

1. Commission of the European Communities, 'EU Strategy for Africa: Towards a Euro-African Pact to Accelerate Africa's Development', October 2005, available at http://eur-lex.europa.eu/LexUriServ/LexUriServ.do?uri=COM:2005:0489:F IN:EN:PDF.

2. Bruce D. Jones, *Peacemaking in Rwanda: The Dynamics of Failure* (Boulder: Lynne Rienner, 2001); Linda Melvern, *A People Betrayed: The Role of the West in Rwanda's Genocide* (London: Zed, 2000); Roméo Dallaire, *Shake Hands with the Devil: The Failure of Humanity in Rwanda* (New York: Carroll and Graf, 2004). For analyses of the French-led Operation Turquoise in Rwanda, see Arthur Jay Klinghoffer, *The International Dimension of Genocide in Rwanda* (New York: New York University Press, 1998), pp. 82–85; and Henry Kwami Anyindodo, *Guns over Kigali: The Rwandese Civil War, 1994* (Accra: Woeli Services, 1997).

3. See René Lemarchand, *The Dynamics of Violence in Central Africa* (Philadelphia: University of Pennsylvania Press, 2009); Georges Nzongola-Ntalaja, *The Congo: From Leopold to Kabila* (London: Zed, 2002); Gérard Prunier, *From Genocide to Continental War: The 'Congolese' Conflict and the Crisis of Contemporary Africa* (London: Hurst, 2009).

4. These countries and bodies were Belgium, Britain, Denmark, the European Commission, Finland, France, Germany, Italy, Ireland, the Netherlands, and Sweden.

5. Noreen Macqueen, *United Nations Peacekeeping in Africa Since 1960* (London: Pearson, 2002); Dennis C. Jett, *Why Peacekeeping Fails* (New York: Palgrave, 2001); Cameron Hume, *Ending Mozambique's War: The Role of Mediation and Good Offices* (Washington, DC: US Institute of Peace Press, 1994); Aldo Ajello, 'Mozambique: Implementation of the 1992 Peace Agreement', in Chester Crocker et al., *Herding Cats: Multiparty Mediation in a Complex World* (Washington, DC: US Institute of Peace Press, 1999), pp. 615–642; Richard Synge, *Mozambique: UN Peacekeeping in Action, 1992–1994* (Washington, DC: US Institute of Peace Press, 1997); United Nations, *The United Nations and Mozambique, 1992–1995* (New York, 1995); Pamela L. Reed, 'The Politics of Reconciliation: The United Nations Operation in Mozambique', in William J. Durch, *The Evolution of Peacekeeping: Case Studies and Comparative Analysis* (New York: St. Martin's, 1993), pp. 275–310.

6. See Adekeye Adebajo, 'The United Nations', in Gilbert M. Khadiagala (ed.), *Security Dynamics in Africa's Great Lakes Region* (Boulder: Lynne Rienner, 2006), pp. 141–161. See also Ian Traynor and Julian Borger, 'UK Blocking Eastern Congo Force: Miliband Rejects Calls for EU Troops to Avert Humanitarian

Catastrophe', *The Guardian* (London), 12 December 2008, p. 1; Natalie Nougayrede, 'The European Union Is Balking at Sending a Peacekeeping Force to North Kivu', *Le Monde*, 21–22 December 2008, p. 11; and two seminar reports by the Centre for Conflict Resolution (CCR): 'Eurafrique? Africa and Europe in a New Century', seminar report, Cape Town, 31 October–1 November 2007, and 'From Eurafrique to Afro-Europa: Africa and Europe in a New Century', Stellenbosch, 11–13 September 2008, available at http://www.ccr.org.za.

7. The EU member states contributing to headquarters staffing needs were Austria, Hungary, Ireland, Italy, the Netherlands, Portugal, and Spain. Non-EU member states contributing to the military force included Brazil, Canada, and South Africa. Simon Duke, *Consensus Building in ESDP: Lessons of Operation Artémis*, Working Paper no. 08–7 (Dublin: UCD Dublin European Institute, July 2008), p. 15, available at http://www.ucd.ie/dei/wp/WP_08–7_Simon_Duke.pdf.

8. Bastian Giegerich and Jean-Ives Haine, 'Congo: a Cosmetic EU Operation', *International Herald Tribune*, 18 June 2006.

9. Magaret Vogt, 'The UN and Africa's Regional Organisations', in Adekeye Adebajo (ed.), *From Global Apartheid to Global Village: Africa and the United Nations* (Scottsville: University of Kwazulu-Natal Press, 2009), pp. 251–268.

15. THE EU SECURITY ROLE IN CHAD AND THE CENTRAL AFRICAN REPUBLIC

1. I thank Anja Muecke for assistance in completing this chapter.

2. UN Security Council Resolution 1778, 'The Situation in Chad, the Central African Republic, and the Subregion', 25 September 2007.

3. United Nations, *Report of the UN Secretary-General to the Security Council on Chad and the Central African Republic*, 23 February 2007, UN Doc. S/2007/97.

4. See the UNHCR website, http://www.unhcr.org/cgi-bin/texis/vtx/page?page=49e45c156.

5. See United Nations, *Report of the UN Secretary-General to the Security Council on Chad and the Central African Republic*, 23 February 2007.

6. See United Nations, *Report of the UN Secretary-General to the Security Council on Chad and the Central African Republic*, 10 August 2007, UN Doc. S/2007/488, p. 5.

7. See *Official Journal of the European Union*, 2 October 2007, L 279, p. 21.

8. There was, however, a little-known exception to these financing rules: Denmark does not participate in financing the common costs, according to the Athena mechanism. This was due to an annex that Copenhagen negotiated to the Treaty on the European Union clarifying that Denmark does not participate in the elaboration or in the implementation of joint actions. Copenhagen thus has no obligation to finance them.

9. See UN Security Council Resolution 1778, para. 12.

10. See United Nations, *Report of the UN Secretary-General to the Security Council on Chad and the Central African Republic*, 10 August 2007, para. 48.

11. See European Council, *Joint Action*, 15 October 2007, para. 1.

12. Denmark's Torben Brylle was appointed as the EU Special Envoy for Sudan from 2007 to 2010.

13. See http://www.consilium.europa.eu/uedocs/cmsUpload/080929_FACT-SHEET_EUFOR_TCHAD-RCA_version6_EN.pdf.

14. European Council, *Joint Action*, 15 October 2007, art. 9.

15. For detailed information on the political, historical, and conflict background of Chad and the CAR, see, for example, Kelly Campell, 'Central African Republic, Chad, and Sudan: Triangle of Instability?', Briefing no. 12 (Washington, DC: US Institute of Peace, 2006), available at http://www.usip.org/pubs/usipeace_briefings/2006/1222_car_chad_sudan.html; Roland Marchal, 'Chad/Darfur: How Two Crises Merge', *Review of African Political Economy* no. 109 (2006), pp. 467–482; and Paul-Simon Hardy, 'Chad: Wading Through a Domestic and Political Crisis in a Turbulent Region', situation report (Tshwane: Institute for Security Studies, 5 December 2007).

16. 'EUFOR Press Conference of General Patrick Nash', 29 January 2008, available at http://www.consilium.europa.eu/ueDocs/cms_Data/docs/pressData/en/esdp/98479.pdf.

17. See http://www.consilium.europa.eu/uedocs/cmsUpload/081210%20Force%20Strength%20by%20Nations%20inOO10122008.pdf.

18. For a more detailed description of EUFOR's logistical challenges, see Bjoern H. Seibert, 'African Adventure? Assessing the European Union's Military Intervention in Chad and the Central African Republic', working paper (Cambridge: Massachusetts Institute of Technology Security Program, November 2007).

19. Raymond Frenken, 'EU Chad/CAR Force Aims to Enhance Stability and Protection', *European Security and Defence Policy Newsletter* no. 6 (July 2008), pp. 7–14.

20. Ibid., p. 13.

21. See http://www.irinnews.org/Report.aspx?

22. See:http://www.europarl.europa.eu/sides/getDoc.do?type=MOTION&reference=B6-2008-0190&language=EN.

23. See, for example, the comment 'EUFOR in Chad and the CAR: The EU's Most Taxing Mission Yet', in International Institute for Strategic Studies, *Strategic Comments* 14(4) (May 2008), available at http://www.iiss.org.uk.

24. See http://allafrica.com/stories/printable/200806200006.html.

25. United Nations, *Report of the UN Secretary-General to the Security Council*, 12 September 2008, UN Doc. S/2008/601, para. 63 ff.

26. See United Nations, *Report of the UN Secretary-General to the Security Council*, 4 December 2008, UN Doc. S/2008/760, paras. 40, 57.

27. Ibid., paras. 47 ff., 57 ff.
28. Ibid., para. 4 ff.
29. Ibid., para. 57 ff.
30. The genesis of UNAMID in Darfur is another example of this tendency.
31. I know of no such systematic and thorough evaluation having taken place.
32. For a short appraisal of EUFOR's achievements, see also Hans-Georg Ehrhardt, 'Assessing EUFOR Chad/CAR', in International Security Information Service (ISIS) Europe, *European Security Review* no. 42 (December 2008), pp. 20–21.
33. United Nations, *Report of the UN Secretary-General to the Security Council*, 12 September 2008, para. 11 ff., and *Report of the UN Secretary-General to the Security Council*, 4 December 2008, para. 4 ff.
34. United Nations, *Report of the UN Secretary-General to the Security Council*, 12 September 2008, para. 2, and *Report of the UN Secretary-General to the Security Council*, 4 December 2008, para. 4.
35. Roland Van Hauwermeiren, 'Insecurity Reigns in Eastern Chad as the EU-UN Mission Struggles to Protect Civilians', *Oxfam International*, 10 September 2008 pp. 1–3.
36. See the MINURCAT homepage, http://minurcat.missions.org.
37. See United Nations, *Report of the UN Secretary-General to the Security Council*, 4 December 2008, UN Doc. S/2008/760, para 64 ff.
38. Surprisingly, in his report, the UN Secretary-General does not mention the plan, negotiated by the 'African Dakar Contact Group', to deploy about 2,000 Sudanese and Chadian troops to both sides of the Sudanese-Chadian border in early 2009 as a bilateral monitoring force. He clearly did not seem to consider this a reliable force. The past history of Sudanese-Chadian peace negotiations does not offer much confidence that anything reliable will result from these bilateral understandings.
39. See the MINURCAT homepage, http://minurcat.missions.org.
40. This finding confirmed a conclusion drawn by a workshop jointly organized by the Berlin Centre for International Peacekeeping Operations (ZIF) and the New York Centre on International Cooperation (CIC) titled 'Towards an Understanding of Peacekeeping Partnerships', held in Berlin in June 2008 with a number of high-level and field-experienced experts from the UN, the AU, the EU, and similar bodies. The report of the workshop concluded: 'Partnerships must be recognised for what they are: operational formulations driven primarily by political compromises, dictated by the situation at hand, both by actors in the theatre of operation and at the international headquarters level. At times, partnerships have added unnecessary levels of complexity to peace operations, negatively spread accountability across actors involved and left space for spoilers to apply 'divide and conquer' political strategies'. See http://www.zif-berlin.org/de/analyse-und-informationen/veroeffentlichungen.html.

16. FRANCE, THE EU, AND AFRICA

1. See Raymond Betts, *Assimilation and Association in French Colonial Theory, 1890–1914* (New York: Columbia University Press, 1961); Prosser Gifford, W.R. Lewis, and Timothy Weiskel (eds.), *France and Britain in Africa: Imperial Rivalry and Colonial Rule* (New Haven: Yale University Press, 1972).

2. Francis Terry McNamara, *France in Black Africa* (Washington, DC: National Defense University Press, 1989), p. 36.

3. Mort Rosenblum, *Mission to Civilize: The French Way* (New York: Harcourt, Brace, and Javonovich, 1986).

4. Jean-François Bayart, *The State in Africa: The Politics of the Belly* (London: Longman, 1993).

5. McNamara, *France in Black Africa*, p. 80.

6. Grégoire Biyogo, *Déconstruire les Accords de Coopération Franco-Africains*,vol. 1, *Par-Delà l'Unilatéralisme et l'Interventionnisme Économique, Politique et Militaire* (Paris: L'Harmattan, 2011), p. 5.

7. Ibid., p. 58.

8. For a historical background, see John Chipman, *French Power in Africa* (Oxford: Blackwell, 1989); Paul Gifford and W.R. Lewis (eds.), *The Transfer of Power in Africa: Decolonization 1940–1960* (New Haven: Yale University Press, 1982); Guy Martin, *Africa in World Politics: A Pan-African Perspective* (Asmara: Africa World, 2002); and Victor T. Le Vine, *Politics in Francophone Africa* (Boulder: Lynne Rienner, 2007).

9. Frederick Cooper, *Africa Since 1940: The Past of the Present—New Approaches to African History* (Cambridge: Cambridge University Press, 2002).

10. Agir içi-Survie, *Jacques Chirac et la Françafrique: Retour à la Case Foccart?* (Paris: L'Harmattan, 1995); François-Xavier Verschave, *La Françafrique: Le Plus Long Scandale de la République* (Paris: Stock, 1999); Samuël Foutoyet, *Nicolas Sarkozy ou la Françafrique Décomplexée?* (Bruxelles: Editions Tribord, 2009); Agir Survie, *Petit Guide de la Françafrique* (Paris, 2010).

11. Jean-Pierre Dozon, *Frères et Sujets: La France et l'Afrique en Perspective* (Paris: Flammarion, 2003).

12. Stephen Smith, *Voyage en Postcolonie: Le Nouveau Monde Franco-Africain* (Paris: Grasset, 2010), p. 26.

13. Smith, *Voyage en Postcolonie*, p. 27.

14. Antoine Glaser and Stephen Smith, *Comment la France a Perdu l'Afrique* (Paris: Calmann-Lévy, 2005).

15. Smith, *Voyage en Postcolonie*, p. 28.

16. Smith, *Voyage en Postcolonie*, p. 27.

17. Samuel Huntington, *The Third Wave: Democratization in the Late Twentieth Century* (Norman: University of Oklahoma Press, 1991).

18. Smith, *Voyage en Postcolonie*, p. 30.

19. Smith, *Voyage en Postcolonie*, p. 32.
20. Ibid.
21. Ibid.
22. Glaser and Smith, *Comment la France a Perdu l'Afrique*, p. 89.
23. Ibid.
24. 'The more things change, the more they remain the same'. An epigram coined by Jean-Baptiste Alphonse Karr in the January 1849 issue of his journal *Les Guêpes*.
25. Smith, *Voyage en Postcolonie*, p. 38.
26. Ibid.
27. Quoted in Achille Mbembe, '*Sacré Bleu!* Mbeki and Sarkozy?' *Mail and Guardian*, 24–30 August 2007, p. 24.
28. Sarkozy visited Angola in 2008 and promised President Eduardo dos Santos that no Angolan would be pursued in the trial. He reportedly pressured the magistrates to drop their charges against Pasqua's men involved in the oil-for-arms affair. In the end, however, Sarkozy was unable to protect them, and both Pierre Falcone and Charles Pasqua were convicted and sentenced for their involvement.
29. Foutoyet, *Nicolas Sarkozy ou la Françafrique Décomplexée?*
30. See Nicolas Beau, *La Maison Pasqua* (Paris: Plon, 2002). Among the powerful members of this network are Etienne Léandri, Jean-Charles Marchiani, Pierre Falcone, André Tarallo, Robert Feliciaggi, and Michel Tomi.
31. Survie, *Petit Guide de la Françafrique*, p. 39.
32. Jacques Foccart was the most important adviser on Africa in the French Fifth Republic, was named secretary-general for African affairs by Charles de Gaulle, then serving under Georges Pompidou and, later, Jacques Chirac. His *Journals de l'Élysée* were published posthumously: *Tous les Soirs avec de Gaulle, 1965–1967* (Paris: Fayard-Jeune Afrique, 1997); *Le Général en Mai, 1968–1969* (Paris: Fayard-Jeune Afrique, 1998); *Dans les Bottes du Général, 1969–1971* (Paris: Fayard-Jeune Afrique, 1999); *La France Pompidolienne, 1971–1972* (Paris: Fayard-Jeune Afrique, 2000); and *La Fin du Gaullisme, 1973–1974* (Paris: Fayard-Jeune Afrique, 2001).
33. Quoted in Survie, *Petit Guide de la Françafrique*, p. 40.
34. Quoted in ibid., p. 43.
35. Denis Muzet, 'Insécurité: Pourquoi la "Stratégie Présentielle" [*sic*] ne Fonctionne Plus—L'Absence de Résultats Disqualifie l'Occupation Intensive du Terrain', *Le Monde*, 4 September 2010, p. 17.
36. Nicolas Sarkozy, 'Discours de M. le Président de la République Devant le Parlement Sud-Africain', 28 February 2008, p. 10.
37. Ibid., p. 11.
38. Ibid.

39. Ibid.

40. Ibid., p. 7. Alain Juppé, appointed minister of defence in November 2010, claimed in a published interview that the defence accords with France's partners had already been 'updated' (*actualisé*): 'We are no longer in Africa to intervene in the internal affairs of other States'. *Le Monde*, 19 January 2011, p. 8. But the secret nature of these defence accords makes it difficult independently to verify this claim.

41. Sarkozy, 'Discours de M. le Président de la République Devant le Parlement Sud-Africain', 28 February 2008.

42. Sarkozy, 'Discours de M. le Président de la République Devant le Parlement Sud-Africain', 28 February 2008.

43. Center for Strategic and International Studies, 'Western Military Balance and Defense Efforts: A Comparative Summary of Military Expenditures: Manpower, Land, Air, Naval, and Nuclear Forces' (Washington, DC: January 2002), p. 106, available at http://csis.org/files/media/csis/pubs/westmb012302%5b1%5d.pdf.

44. European Defence Agency, *European Defense Data 2009: Facts and Figures* (Brussels, 2010), available at http://www.eda.europa.eu/defencefacts.

45. Guibert, 'Je Veux des Formes plus Modernes', p. 8.

46. Henri Burgelin, *L'Europe: Prolongement ou Alternative à une Défense Nationale?* (Paris: Publisud, 2002).

47. Ibid., p. 1.

48. 'M. Juppé: "Nous ne Sommes plus en Afrique pour Intervenir dans les Affaires Intérieures"', *Le Monde*, 19 January 2011, p. 8.

49. Martin, *Africa in World Politics*, p. 92.

50. Emmanuel Beth, 'Coopération Militaire: Facteur de Stabilité', *Revue Défense* no. 129 (Paris: IHEDN, November–December 2007).

51. Raphaël Granvaud, *Que Fait l'Armée Française en Afrique?* (Marseilles: Agone, 2009), p. 63.

52. Beth, 'Coopération Militaire'.

53. Quoted in Granvaud, *Que Fait l'Armée Française en Afrique?* p. 228.

54. Niagalé Bagayoko-Penon, 'Politique Étrangère et de Sécurité Commune (PESC) et Politique Européenne de Sécurité et de Défense (PESD) en Afrique', *CIRPES* (March 2005), p. 16 (emphasis in original).

55. Quoted in Fondation pour la Recherche Stratégique (FRS), 'Les Opérations Psychologiques au Service de la Stratégie Militaire', *Revue Défense Nationale et Sécurité Collective* no. 12 (December 2000), p. 10.

56. See, for example, Daniela Kroslak, *The Role of France in the Rwandan Genocide* (London: Hurst, 2007); and Andrew Wallis, *Silent Accomplice: The Untold Story of France's Role in Rwandan Genocide* (London: Tauris, 2006).

57. Eric Miller, *The Inability of Peacekeeping to Address the Security Dilemma: A Case Study of the Rwandan-Congolese Security Dilemma and the United Nations Mission in the Congo* (Saarbrücken: Lambert Academic, 2010), pp. 114–115.

58. European Union, 'Declaration by the Presidency on Behalf of the European Union on the Massacres in the Provinces of Ituri in the Democratic Republic of Congo', 13 October 2003, available at http://ue.eu.int/showPage.asp?id=606& lang=en1mode=g.

59. *The Economist*, 'Peacekeeping in Congo', 12 June 2003, available at http://www.economist.com.

60. Colette Braeckman, 'Les Dessous d'une "Histoire Secrète"', *Le Soir*, 27 November 2006, available at http://www.blogs.lesoir.be/colette-braeckman.

61. A. De le Grange, 'L'Europe Peine à Intervenir Autour du Darfour', *Le Figaro*, 21 September 2007.

62. Granvaud, *Que Fait l'Armée Française en Afrique?* p. 236.

63. Ibid.

64. France (1,700 troops), Ireland (450), Poland (400), Sweden (200), Austria (170), Netherlands (90), Italy (90), Spain (80), Belgium (70), Finland (60), Slovenia (15), Greece (15), Britain (4), Germany (4), Hungary (3), Bulgaria (2), Czech Republic (2), Portugal (2), Romania (2). See http://www.bruxelles2.eu/category/afrique/tchad-soudan.

65. Glaser and Smith, *Comment la France a Perdu l'Afrique*, p. 17.

66. Martin, *Africa in World Politics*, pp. 84–85.

67. Douglas Yates, *The Rentier State in Africa: Oil-Rent Dependency and Neo-Colonialism in the Republic of Gabon* (Trenton, NJ: Africa World Press, 1996).

68. AFP, 'Ouverture d'une Enquête sur des Comptes qui Appartiendraient à Edith Bongo à Monaco', 30 March 2009, available at http://www.google.com/hostednews/afp/article/ALeqM5geKpOB0CMoEoHW3rkVS6XtSMlNeQ.

69. See, for example, Kweku Ampiah and Sanusha Naidu (eds.), *Crouching Tiger, Hidden Dragon? Africa and China* (Scottsville: University of Kwazulu-Natal Press, 2008); Chris Alden, Daniel Large, and Ricardo Soares De Oliveira (eds.), *China Returns to Africa: A Rising Power and a Continent Embrace* (London: Hurst, 2008); Robert I. Rotberg (ed.), *China Into Africa: Trade, Aid, and Influence* (Washington, DC: Brookings Institution, 2008); and Ian Taylor, *China's New Role in Africa* (Boulder: Lynne Rienner, 2009).

70. George Friedman, 'The Geopolitics of France: Maintaining Its Influence in a Changing Europe', Stratfor Global Intelligence Monograph, 13 September 2010.

71. Jean-Baptiste Duroselle, *Tout Empire Périra: Théorie des Relations Internationales* (Paris: Publications de la Sorbonne, 1981).

72. Edward Gibbon, *The Decline and Fall of the Roman Empire*, edited by Hans-Friedrich Mueller (New York: Modern Library, 2003, originally published as six volumes between 1776 and 1789).

17. BRITAIN, THE EU, AND AFRICA

1. For earlier overviews, see Rita Abrahamsen and Paul Williams, 'Ethics and Foreign Policy: The Antinomies of New Labour's "Third Way" in Sub-Saharan Africa', *Political Studies* 49(2) (2001), pp. 249–264; Paul Williams, 'Britain and Africa After the Cold War: Beyond Damage Limitation?' in Ian Taylor and Paul Williams (eds.), *Africa in International Politics* (London: Routledge, 2004), pp. 41–60; Paul D. Williams, 'Britain and Africa in the Twenty-First Century', in Jack Mangala (ed.), *Africa and the New World Era* (New York: Palgrave Macmillan, 2010), pp. 37–51; and Tom Porteous, *Britain in Africa* (London: Zed, 2008). See also Kaye Whiteman and Douglas Yates, 'France, Britain, and the United States', in Adekeye Adebajo and Ismail Rashid (eds.), *West Africa's Security Challenges* (Boulder: Lynne Rienner, 2004), pp. 349–379; and Kaye Whiteman, 'The Switchback and the Fallback: Nigeria/Britain Relations', in Adekeye Adebajo and Abdul Raufu Mustapha (eds.), *Gulliver's Troubles: Nigeria's Foreign Policy After the Cold War* (Scottsville: University of Kwazulu-Natal Press, 2008), pp. 255–280.

2. David Miliband, *Hansard* (Commons), 23 January 2008, cols. 52–53WS.

3. James Mayall, 'Britain and Anglophone Africa', in Amadu Sesay (ed.), *Africa and Europe* (London: Croom Helm, 1986), pp. 52–74.

4. Christopher Clapham, *Africa and the International System* (Cambridge: Cambridge University Press, 1996), p. 88.

5. Mayall, 'Britain and Anglophone Africa', p. 54.

6. Ibid.

7. Ibid., p. 61.

8. See Linda Melvern and Paul D. Williams, 'Britannia Waived the Rules: The Major Government and the 1994 Rwandan Genocide', *African Affairs* 103(410) (2004), pp. 1–22.

9. Britain did respond to some displays of 'bad governance' by cutting its aid programmes, for example to Sudan (1991), Kenya (1991), and Malawi (1992). But this approach was not pursued consistently across Africa's authoritarian states: friendly or economically more significant regimes, in Ghana, Uganda, and Nigeria for instance, generally escaped such punishment.

10. Cited in Williams, 'Britain and Africa After the Cold War', p. 55.

11. David Styan, 'Does Britain Have an African Policy?' in *L'Afrique Politique* (Paris: Karthala, 1996), pp. 262–263, 266.

12. Cited in ibid., p. 264.

13. Ibid., p. 261.

14. For an overview, see Abrahamsen and Williams, 'Ethics and Foreign Policy'.

15. Porteous, *Britain in Africa*, pp. 54 ff.

16. From 2006 the Department for Environment, Food, and Rural Affairs (DEFRA),

not the FCO, was to play the leading role on Britain's international work on climate change.

17. Porteous, *Britain in Africa*, p. 85.

18. *Human Security Brief 2007* (Simon Fraser University, 2008), available at http://www.humansecuritybrief.info.

19. UK Home Office, Immigration Statistics, July–September 2011, vol. 1, available at http://www.homeoffice.gov.uk/publications/science-research-statistics/research-statistics/immigration-asylum-research/immigration-tabs-q3–2011/asylum1-q3–11-tabs.

20. UNDP, *Human Development Index 2007/2008*, available at http://hdr.undp.org/en/statistics. The index's total pool of 177 states did not include Somalia or Liberia, presumably owing to the difficulty of gathering data in these countries.

21. See Camilla Toulmin, *Climate Change in Africa* (London: Zed, 2009).

22. A considerable number of large companies, some of which have access to Britain's corridors of power, operate in Africa. Among the largest are British Petroleum and Shell, but others also have significant investments on the continent, including Anglo-American, BAE Systems, Barclays, British Airways, British American Tobacco, Cadbury, Crown Agents, De La Rue, Guinness, KPMG, Land Rover, Lonrho, P&O, Standard Chartered, Taylor Woodrow, Unilever, Virgin Atlantic, and Vodafone.

23. Porteous, *Britain in Africa*, p. 44.

24. *Hansard* (Commons), 23 January 2008, cols. 52–53WS.

25. Jon Lunn, Vaughne Miller, and Ben Smith, *British Foreign Policy Since 1997*, Research Paper no. 08/56 (London: House of Commons, 23 June 2008), p. 115.

26. The ten priorities are set out in 'Active Diplomacy for a Changing World', FCO white paper, March 2006, and by then—foreign secretary Margaret Beckett in *Hansard* (Commons), 8 June 2006, cols 37–38WS.

27. For an overview, see Paul D. Williams, 'Who's Making UK Foreign Policy?', *International Affairs* 80(5) (2004), pp. 911–929.

28. See Simon Bulmer and Martin Burch, 'The Europeanization of UK Government: From Quiet Revolution to Explicit Step Change?', *Public Administration* 83(4) (2005), pp. 861–890.

29. Robin Niblett, 'Choosing Between America and Europe: A New Context for British Foreign Policy', *International Affairs* 83(4) (2007), p. 639.

30. See Anand Menon, 'From Crisis to Catharsis: ESDP After Iraq', *International Affairs* 80(4) (2004), p. 644.

31. See, for example, David Keen, *Conflict and Collusion in Sierra Leone* (Oxford: Currey, 2005); and Whiteman, 'The Switchback and the Fallback'.

32. See Clara M. O'Donnell and Richard G. Whitman, 'European Policy Under Gordon Brown: Perspectives on a Future Prime Minister', *International Affairs* 83(2) (2007), pp. 255–256.

33. See Paul Williams, 'Fighting for Freetown: British Military Intervention in Sierra Leone', *Contemporary Security Policy* 22(3) (2001), pp. 140–168.
34. In 1997 there were 5,753 British personnel deployed as part of the Stabilisation Force in Bosnia. By 2004 this figure had dropped to 1,450. When British forces were withdrawn from Bosnia in early 2007, only about 600 soldiers remained. In Kosovo, London initially contributed about 9,600 personnel to the NATO mission, although this number had been reduced to about 200 by the end of Blair's term in office in 2007. Claire Taylor, Tom Waldman, and Sophie Glick, *British Defence Policy Since 1997*, Research Paper no. 08/57 (London: House of Commons, 27 June 2008), pp. 63–64.
35. UN Department of Peacekeeping Operations, http://www.un.org/Depts/dpko/dpko/contributors.
36. International Institute for Strategic Studies, *The Military Balance* (Abingdon: Routledge, annual 2001–2011). These figures do not include the invasion forces in Iraq, codenamed Operation Telic.
37. Cited in 'UK Troops "Ready to Go to Sudan"', *BBC News Online*, 25 July 2004, http://news.bbc.co.uk/2/hi/uk_news/3922109.stm.
38. David Miliband, 'Europe 2030: Model Power Not Superpower', speech to the College of Europe, Bruges, 15 November 2007, available at http://www.brugesgroup.com/MilibandBrugesSpeech.pdf.
39. The idea of EU battle groups was officially proposed at the Franco-British summit in November 2003.
40. Britain contributed about 700 of the 7,000 troops in EUFOR Althea (in Bosnia), and deployed 88 soldiers to Operation Artémis; see *Hansard* (Commons), 8 July 2003, col.698W. Although Britain did contribute to EUFOR RD (in the DRC), it contributed less than 100 soldiers. As of 10 December 2008, Britain had contributed just 4 of the 3,420 personnel deployed to the EUFOR operation in Chad and the Central African Republic.
41. Rebecca Feeley and Colin Thomas-Jensen, 'Beyond Crisis Management in Eastern Congo', strategy paper (Washington, DC: ENOUGH, December 2008), p. 6.
42. See Richard Gowan, 'From Rapid Reaction to Delayed Inaction? Congo, the UN, and the EU', *International Peacekeeping* 18(5) (2011), pp. 593–611.
43. Porteous, *Britain in Africa*, p. 106.
44. In December 2007 this was renamed the Stabilisation Unit.
45. Author's communications with British officials.
46. 'Uncertainty Awaits the UK', *Jane's Defence Weekly*, 16 May 2007.
47. See *National Security Strategy of the United Kingdom: Security in an Interdependent World* (HMSO: Cabinet Office, Cm7291, 2008), p. 40.
48. See, for example, Gareth Evans, *The Responsibility to Protect* (Washington, DC: Brookings Institution, 2008); and Adekeye Adebajo, Mark Paterson, and Jer-

emy Sarkin (eds.), *Global Responsibility to Protect*, 'Special Issue: Africa's Responsibility to Protect', 2(4) 2010.

49. For example, Brown stated that 'we now rightly recognise our responsibility to protect behind borders where there are crimes against humanity'. Gordon Brown, Lord Mayor's banquet speech, 12 November 2007, available at http://www.number10.gov.uk/output/Page13736.asp.

50. David Miliband, 'The Democratic Imperative', speech at the FCO, 12 February 2008, available at http://www.britainusa.com/sections/articles_show_nt1.asp?d=2&i=41020&L1=0&L2=0&a=47750.

51. See John Chipman, *French Power in Africa* (Oxford: Oxford University Press, 1989); and François-Xavier Verschave, *La Françafrique: Le Plus Long Scandale de la République* (Paris: Stock, 1998).

52. Africa is clearly not one of the main areas of British business concerns, with the partial exception of South Africa. In 2005, British exports to South Africa were estimated to be £3.2 billion while its investments in South Africa were £24 billion. Lagging a long way behind in second spot was Nigeria, where British exports were valued at £818 million in 2005. Porteous, *Britain in Africa*, p. 43.

53. Lunn, Miller, and Smith, *British Foreign Policy*, p. 75.

54. Porteous, *Britain in Africa*, p. 103.

55. The priority countries were the DRC, Ethiopia, Ghana, Kenya, Lesotho, Malawi, Mozambique, Nigeria, Rwanda, Sierra Leone, South Africa, Sudan, Tanzania, Uganda, Zambia, and Zimbabwe.

56. Porteous, *Britain in Africa*, p. 140.

57. DFID, *Statistics on International Development, 2002–03 to 2006–07* (London: TSO, 2007), pp. 27–29. The two sectors receiving the largest shares of this expenditure were humanitarian assistance (22 per cent) and health (21 per cent) (p. 125).

58. See Porteous, *Britain in Africa*, pp. 15 ff.

59. Ibid., p. 21.

60. Ibid., p. 24.

61. Lunn, Miller, and Smith, *British Foreign Policy*, p. 75. See http://www.gsdrc.org/go/topic-guides/drivers-of-change.

62. Lunn, Miller, and Smith, *British Foreign Policy*, p. 86. The most prominent of these have been the new embassies in Iraq and Afghanistan.

63. Tom Cargill, *More with Less: Trends in UK Diplomatic Engagement in Sub-Saharan Africa*, Africa Programme Paper no. 2011/03 (London: Chatham House, May 2011), p. 11.

64. *Hansard* (Commons), 8 January 2008, col. 138W.

65. Lunn, Miller, and Smith, *British Foreign Policy*, p. 111.

66. Porteous, *Britain in Africa*, p. 18.

67. DFID, *Statistics on International Development*, p. 124.

68. Ibid.

69. Ibid., pp. 122–123.

70. Ibid., p. 123.

71. Porteous, *Britain in Africa*, p. 60.

72. 'UK Imposes Ethiopian Aid Sanction', *BBC News Online*, 19 January 2006, http://news.bbc.co.uk/2/hi/africa/4627084.stm.

73. DFID, *Government, Development, and Democratic Politics* (London, 2007), p. 68.

74. For relevant discussions, see Paul D. Williams, 'Blair's Commission for Africa: Problems and Prospects for UK Policy', *Political Quarterly* 76(4) (2005), pp. 529–539; William Brown, 'The Commission for Africa: Results and Prospects for the West's Africa Policy', *Journal of Modern African Studies* 44(3) (2006), pp. 349–374; Stephen R. Hurt, 'Mission Impossible: A Critique of the Commission for Africa', *Journal of Contemporary African Studies* 25(3) (2007), pp. 355–368; and Porteous, *Britain in Africa*, pp. 61–80.

75. Commission for Africa (CFA), *Our Common Interest* (London: DFID, 2005), p. 61.

76. Ibid., p. 57.

77. Porteous, *Britain in Africa*, p. 139.

78. Christopher Clapham, introduction to *International Affairs* 81(2) (2005), p. 277.

79. Porteous, *Britain in Africa*, p. 71.

80. See ibid., p. 79; and Mark Bradbury, *Becoming Somaliland* (Oxford: Currey, 2008).

81. See Richard Joseph and Alexandra Gillies (eds.), *Smart Aid for African Development* (Boulder: Lynne Rienner, 2009); Ian Taylor, '"Advice Is Judged by Results, Not by Intentions": Why Gordon Brown Is Wrong About Africa', *International Affairs* 81(2) (2005), pp. 299–310.

82. Cargill, *More with Less*.

18. PORTUGAL, THE EU, AND AFRICA

1. Patrick Chabal, 'The End of Empire', in Patrick Chabal et al. (eds.), *A History of Postcolonial Lusophone Africa* (London: Hurst, 2002), p. 17.

2. Assembleia da República, 1976, p. 406.

3. António Raimundo, 'Between Europeanisation and Domestic Influences: Portugal's Post-Colonial Relations with Angola', paper presented at the fifth Pan-European Conference on EU Politics of the ECPR-SGEU, Porto, 23–26 June 2010.

4. Guinea-Bissau signed up to the first Lomé Convention in 1975; Cape Verde and São Tomé and Príncipe to Lomé II in 1979; and Angola and Mozambique to Lomé III in 1984.

5. Cavaco Silva's attachment to Africa derived from the time he served as a conscripted army officer in Mozambique in the 1970s; since then, he has remained interested in the affairs of the continent.

6. Ricardo Soares de Oliveira, 'Sobre as Relações entre Portugal e Angola ao fim do Trinta Anos: Um Ensaio Crítico', *Relações Internacionais* no. 8, 12 (December 2005).

7. M. Venâncio and C. McMillan, 'Portuguese Mediation and the Angola Conflict, 1990–1', in Stephen Chan and V. Jabri (eds.), *Mediation in Southern Africa* (London: Macmillan, 1993), pp. 100–117.

8. On RENAMO, see Alex Vines, *Renamo: From Terrorism to Democracy in Mozambique?* (London: Currey, 1996).

9. Douglas Mason, 'Contemporary Portuguese Policy in Africa', *Sub-Saharan Africa: Regional Overview* (London: Economist Intelligence Unit, December 2000), pp. 12–20.

10. From 1987, the Portuguese started investigating whether they could assist in achieving lasting peace in Mozambique. During a 1989 trip to Southern Africa, Manuel Barroso was invited by the Mozambican government to assist in searching for a peaceful formula. Contacts then developed more officially with RENAMO, and, in April 1990, the Portuguese announced publicly their desire to assist the developing peace process. See Vines, *Renamo*, pp. 143–144.

11. During the Mozambican peace process, the Portuguese tried to have the peace talks moved from Rome to Lisbon in 1991, and there was also disquiet about too much Anglophone input into the process. However, Cavaco Silva reined in Portuguese 'spoilers', mindful that Portugal had incurred a significant bill for hosting the Bicesse process on Angola, and that Portugal needed to focus on its EU presidency for the first six months of 1992. See Vines, *Renamo*, p. 144.

12. In 1992, Portuguese efforts to become involved in the Rome peace process were rebuffed by the Italian mediators and the Mozambican government in the run-up to the signing of the Rome General Peace Accords.

13. Tensions remain. For example, Angola's press centre refused to issue press accreditation for several mainstream Portuguese newspapers wanting to cover Angola's legislative elections on 5 September 2008.

14. 'Portuguese President's Visit to Mark Relations with Angola', *Angop*, 13 July 2010.

15. 'The Main Lines of Portuguese Foreign Policy', speech by António da Cruz, minister of foreign affairs and Portuguese communities abroad, Assembly of Portuguese Republic, 18 June 2002.

16. 'Africa—Foreign Policy Priority of the EU Presidency: Interview with Manuel Lobo Antunes, Portuguese Secretary of State for European Affairs', *The Courier*, September–October 2007.

17. Cravinho comes from a *retornado* family from Angola and holds a doctorate

from the University of Oxford on the agrarian strategy of the Frente de Libertação de Moçambique (FRELIMO) in Mozambique.

18. This mirrors the Institute for Strategic and International Studies' (IEEI) hosting of a network on Euro-Med—the EuroMeSco network of foreign policy
institutes (see http://www.euromesco.net) from 1995 to 2008 under a grant
from the European Commission.

19. 'Africa—Foreign Policy Priority of the EU Presidency'.

20. 'New Markets: Effort to Exploit Ties with Former Colonies Pays Dividends',
Financial Times,13 July 2010.

21. Ibid.

22. Economist Intelligence Unit, *Angola Country Report*(London, September 2010),
p. 14.

23. 'Africa's Banking Boom', *The Economist*, 18 September 2010, p. 90.

24. OECD, 'Portugal, DAC Peer Review: Main Findings and Recommendations',
(Paris: 2006).

25. Portuguese universities and research institutes have increasingly been subcontracted by the Portuguese Institute for Development Assistance (IPAD) to conduct research, analysis, and evaluation efforts.

26. Portugal also signalled that it would support other countries with which it has
historical ties—Indonesia, Morocco, Senegal, and South Africa.

27. F. Cardoso (ed.), *Diplomacia Cooperação e Negócios: O Papel dos Actores Exter-
nos em Angola e Mozambique* (Lisbon: Instituto de Estudos Estrategicoés e Internacionais, 2006), p. 40.

28. Portugal agreed a similar arrangement with São Tomé in August 2009, and the
Portuguese treasury will facilitate and underwrite the exchange-rate peg between
the dobra and the euro, which took effect in January 2010.

29. OECD, *Managing Aid: Practices of DAC Member Countries*, DAC Guidelines
and Reference Series (Paris, 2005).

30. Alex Vines, 'Rhetoric from Brussels and Reality on the Ground: The EU and
Security in Africa', *International Affairs* 86(5) (September 2010), pp. 1097–
1098.

31. Economist Intelligence Unit, *Mozambique Country Profile 2007* (London, 2007).

32. Economist Intelligence Unit, *Mozambique Country Profile 2008* (London, 2007),
pp. 26–27.

19. THE NORDICS, THE EU, AND AFRICA

1. UN Development Programme, *Human Development Report 2010: The Real Wealth
of Nations: Pathways to Human Development* (New York: Palgrave Macmillan,
2010), p. 142.

2. The Schengen Agreement was first signed in 1985, but did not take effect until
1995.

3. See, for example, Carlos Buhigas Schubert and Hans Marten, *The Nordic Model: A Recipe for European Success?* Working Paper no. 20 (Belgium: European Policy Centre, September 2005).

4. Camelia Minoiu and Sanjay Reddy, *Development Aid and Economic Growth: A Positive Long-Run Relation'*, Working Paper no. WP/09/118 (Washington, DC: International Monetary Fund Institute, May 2009), p. 11.

5. Scott Gates and Anke Hoeffler, *Global Aid Allocations: Are Nordic Donors Different?* Working Paper no. 234 (Oxford: Centre for the Study of African Economies, 2004), p. 16, available at http://www.bepress.com/cgi/viewcontent.cgi?article=1234&context=csae.

6. Jack Spence, 'South Africa's Foreign Policy: Vision and Reality', in Elizabeth Sidiropoulos (ed.), *Apartheid Past, Renaissance Future: South Africa's Foreign Policy, 1994–2004* (Johannesburg: South African Institute of International Affairs [SAIIA], 2004), p. 42.

7. Lina Soiri and Pekka Peltola, *Finland and National Liberation in Southern Africa* (Uppsala: Nordiska Afrikainstitutet, 1999); Tore Linné Eriksen, *Norway and National Liberation in Southern Africa* (Uppsala: Nordiska Afrikainstitutet, 2000); Tor Sellström, *Sweden and National Liberation in Southern Africa: Solidarity and Assistance, 1970–1994*, 2nd ed. (Uppsala: Nordiska Afrikainstitutet, 2002); Christopher Munthe Morgenstierne, *Denmark and National Liberation in Southern Africa: A Flexible Response* (Uppsala: Nordiska Afrikainstitutet, 2003). This entire series can be downloaded from http://www.liberationafrica.se/publications.

8. Norway has embassies in the following sub-Saharan countries: Angola, Côte d'Ivoire, Eritrea, Ethiopia, Kenya, Madagascar, Malawi, Mozambique, Nigeria, South Africa, Sudan, Tanzania, Uganda, Zambia, and Zimbabwe

9. There are Swedish embassies in Angola, Ethiopia, Kenya, the Democratic Republic of the Congo, Mozambique, Nigeria, Senegal, South Africa, Sudan, Tanzania, Uganda, Zambia, and Zimbabwe.

10. Denmark's embassies in sub-Saharan Africa are in Benin, Burkina Faso, Ethiopia, Ghana, Kenya, Mali, Mozambique, South Africa, Tanzania, Uganda, and Zambia.

11. Finland's sub-Saharan embassies are in Ethiopia, Kenya, Mozambique, Namibia, Nigeria, South Africa, Tanzania, and Zambia.

12. Tor Sellström, writing in Morgenstierne, *Denmark and National Liberation in Southern Africa*, p. 9.

13. Sellström, *Sweden and National Liberation in Southern Africa*, p. 34.

14. Ibid., pp. 34–38.

15. During the anti-apartheid struggle, the Swedish government distributed 1.6 billion SEK to a variety of anti-apartheid, democracy, cultural, and civil society organisations within South Africa, almost twice as much as it awarded to

the ANC. See Sellström, *Sweden and National Liberation in Southern Africa*, pp. 38–39.

16. Eriksen, *Norway and National Liberation in Southern Africa*, p. 9.

17. Ibid., p. 71.

18. Ibid., pp. 175–177.

19. Morgenstierne, *Denmark and National Liberation in Southern Africa*, p. 13.

20. Ibid.

21. See Lars-Ludvig Røed, 'Tid for tilbakebetaling' [Time to Repay], *Aftenposten*, 2 May 2009.

22. This sum does not include Swedish humanitarian or conflict, peace, and security assistance on the continent. Swedish International Development Cooperation Agency (SIDA), *Internationellt Utvecklingssamarbete: SIDAs årsredovisning 2009* (Stockholm, 2009), tab. 62, available at http://www.sida.se.

23. Government of Sweden, *Sweden and Africa: A Policy to Address Common Challenges and Opportunities*, Government Communication no. 2007/08:67 (Stockholm, 6 March 2008), p. 20.

24. Government Office of Sweden, 'A New Swedish Policy for Africa', press release (Stockholm: Ministry of Foreign Affairs, 13 March 2008).

25. Government of Sweden, *Sweden and Africa*, p. 21.

26. Ibid.

27. Ibid., p. 22.

28. Ibid., p. 21.

29. Ibid., p. 4.

30. Statistics on Norway's assistance to Africa are taken from the Norad Report Portal, http://www.norad.no/Resultater+og+kvalitetssikring/Norsk+bistand+i+tall/Statistikkportalen.

31. Norwegian Ministry of Foreign Affairs, *Klima, konflikt og kapital: Norsk utviklingspolitikk i et endret handlingsrom* [Climate, Conflict, and Capital], Stortingsmelding no. 13 (2008–2009) (Oslo: Departementenes servicesenter, 13 February 2009); and Norwegian Ministry of Foreign Affairs, *Interesser, ansvar og muligheter: Hovedlinjer i norsk utenrikspolitikk* [Interests, Responsibility, and Opportunities], Stortingsmelding no. 15 (2008–2009) (Oslo: Departementenes servicesenter, 13 March 2009).

32. Jan Speed, 'Angola: Mer enn bare business' [Angola: More Than Just Business], *Bistandsaktuelt* (Oslo), 23 December 2009, available at http://www.bistandsaktuelt.no/Nyheter+og+reportasjer/Arkiv+nyheter+og+reportasjer/Angola+%E2%80%93+mer+enn+bare+business.150632.cms. *Bistandsaktuelt* is the official news magazine of NORAD.

33. NORAD, *Norads strategi mot 2010: Utdypende analyse* (Oslo, 2006), p. 14.

34. Norwegian Ministry of Foreign Affairs, 'Satser mer på klima og fornybar energi i fattige land' [Further Emphasis on Climate and Renewable Energy in Poor Countries], press release (Oslo, 6 October 2011).

35. See, for example, Lars Inge Staveland and Siri Gedde Dahl, 'Kutter bistand til statsbusjetter' ['Cuts Budget Support'], *Aftenposten*, 5 December 2011, available at http://www.aftenposten.no/nyheter/iriks/Kutter-bistand-til-statsbudsjetter-6714290.

36. See Anne Hammerstad, 'Donors, Democracy, and Sovereignty: The Politicisation of Aid and Its Impact on African-EU Relations', in Patricia Magalhães Ferreira (ed.), *Os Desafios das Relações Europa-Africa: Uma Agenda de Prioridade* [The Challenges of Europe-Africa Relations: An Agenda of Priorities] (Lisbon: Instituto de Estudos Estratégicos Internacionais [IEEI], 2005), p. 78.

37. Danish Ministry of Foreign Affairs, *Making Progress in Africa: An Updated Analytical Overview* (Copenhagen: Africa Department, May 2007).

38. Danish Ministry of Foreign Affairs, *Afrika på Vej: Debatoplæg om regjeringens prioriteter for samarbejdet med Afrika i perioden 2007 til 2011*, background paper (Copenhagen, 2007), p. 12, available at http://www.afrika.um.dk/da/servicemenu/Debatoplaeg/RegeringensDebatoplaeg. In 2009, 60 per cent of Denmark's country-specific bilateral aid went to Africa. See Danida, *Denmark's Participation in International Development Cooperation 2009* (Copenhagen, 2010), p. 82.

39. Danida, *Denmark's Participation in International Development Cooperation 2009*, p. 82.

40. Africa Commission, *Realising the Potential of Africa's Youth: Report of the Africa Commission, May 2009* (Copenhagen: Secretariat of the Africa Commission and Danish Ministry of Foreign Affairs, June 2009), available at http://www.africacommission.um.dk.

41. Danish Ministry of Foreign Affairs, *Afrika på Vej*, p. 2.

42. Ibid., p. 3 (translated from the Danish by author).

43. Ibid., p. 12.

44. Anne Hammerstad, 'UNHCR and the Securitisation of Forced Migration', in Alexander Betts and Gil Loescher (eds.), *Refugees in International Relations* (Oxford: Oxford University Press, 2010), p. 247.

45. Danish Ministry of Foreign Affairs, *Afrika på Vej*, p. 8.

46. Danish Ministry of Foreign Affairs, *Freedom from Poverty, Freedom to Change: Strategy for Denmark's Development Cooperation* (Copenhagen, July 2010).

47. Danish Ministry of Foreign Affairs, *Priorities of the Danish Government for Danish Development Assistance: Overview of the Development Assistance Budget, 2012–2016* (Copenhagen, August 2011), p. 2.

48. For example, the Nordic Africa Institute in Uppsala, Sweden, not only played a research and policy development role for Sweden, but also brought together all the Nordic countries for common deliberations on their future Africa strategies.

49. Holger Bernt Hansen, 'Danish Experiences in Africa Relations', speech at the seminar 'Partnering with Africa', Estonian Parliament, 17 April 2008.

50. Information from interviews conducted with Norwegian Foreign Office officials in Oslo in March 2009.

51. Norway increased its aid by 55 million NKR in May 2009 and a further 42 million NKR after a meeting in Oslo between Prime Ministers Morgan Tsvangirai and Jens Stoltenberg on 16 June 2009. In total, Norway pledged 200 million NKR in aid to Zimbabwe for 2009. All the money is channelled through the UN, the World Bank, and NGOs, and will only benefit sectors, such as education, where Tsvangirai and his Movement for Democratic Change (MDC) colleagues are in control. See Norwegian Prime Minister's Office, 'Norge vil øke hjelpen til Zimbabwe' [Norway Will Increase Aid to Zimbabwe], press release, Oslo, 17 June 2009; and Norwegian Foreign Office, 'Norge øker bistanden til Zimbabwe' [Norway Increases Assistance to Zimbabwe], press release, 25 May 2009.

52. Nordic Development Fund, 'A New Focus for the Nordic Development Fund: Grant Financing for Climate Projects in the Poorest Countries', press release, Helsinki, 19 May 2009.

53. The ten countries are Benin, Botswana, Ghana, Lesotho, Mali, Mozambique, Nigeria, South Africa, Senegal, and Tanzania.

54. Jonas Gahr Støre, 'Opening Statement at 6th Informal Nordic-African Foreign Ministers Meeting', speech by the Norwegian foreign minister, Oslo, 19–20 March 2007.

55. Confidential interview.

56. Minoiu and Reddy, *Development Aid and Economic Growth*.

57. Thorvald Stoltenberg, *Nordisk Samarbeid om Utenriks: Og Sikkerhetspolitikk* [Nordic Cooperation on Foreign and Security Policy], report presented at an extraordinary Nordic Foreign Ministers Meeting in Oslo, 9 February 2009.

58. European Centre for Development Policy Management, *Towards a Joint Africa-Europe Partnership Strategy: Issue Paper II* (Maastricht, December 2006), p. 23.

20. MIGRATION AND 'FORTRESS EUROPE'

1. For a range of documents that emerged from the European Commission in the mid-2000s on the 'external' dimension of migration, see, for example, the following from the Commission of the European Communities (CEC): 'Wider Europe—Neighbourhood: A New Framework for Relations with Our Eastern and Southern Neighbours', COM (2003) 104 Final (Brussels, 2003); 'Integrating Migration Issues in the EU's Relations with Third Countries', COM (2003) 703 Final; 'Reference Document for Financial and Technical Assistance to Third Countries in the Area of Migration and Asylum, AENEAS Programme 2004–2006' (Brussels, 2003), available at http://ec.europa.eu/europeaid/projects/eidhr/pdf/themes-migration-annexe2_en.pdf; 'Intensified Co-operation on the Management of Migration Flows with Third Countries: Report by the Commission's

Services on the Implementation of the Council Conclusions on Intensified Co-operation on the Management of Migration Flows with Third Countries of 18 November 2002', SEC (2003) 815; 'European Neighbourhood Policy: Strategy Paper', COM (2004) 373 Final; and 'Migration and Development: Some Concrete Orientations', COM (2005) 390 Final.

2. Rob B.J. Walker, 'The Elusive Study of Global Change', *International Studies Review* 42(2) (1998), p. 328.

3. James Anderson, Chris Brook, and Allan Cochrane (eds.), *A Global World: Reordering Political Space* (Oxford: Oxford University Press, 1995); Jean Gottmann, *The Significance of Territory* (Charlottesville: University of Virginia Press, 1971); Bertrand Badie, *La Fin des Territoires: Essai sur le Désordre International et sur l'Utilité Social de Respect* (Paris: Fayard, 1995); Michael Bommes and Andrew Geddes, *Immigration and Welfare: Challenging the Borders of the Welfare State* (London: Routledge, 2000); Elspeth Guild, 'Moving the Borders of Europe', inaugural lecture, Catholic University of Nijmegen, May 2001; Robert Johnston, 'Out of the "Moribund Backwater": Territory and Territoriality in Political Geography', *Political Geography* 20(6) (2001), pp. 677–693; Jan Zielonka, 'How New Enlarged Borders Will Reshape the EU', *Journal of Common Market Studies* 39(3) (2001), pp. 507–536; Joan DeBardeleben (ed.), *Soft or Hard Borders? Managing the Divide in an Enlarged Europe* (Aldershot: Ashgate, 2005); Hélène Pellerin, 'Migration and Border Controls in the EU: Economic and Security Factors', in DeBardeleben, *Soft or Hard Borders?*; Andrew Geddes, 'Europe's Border Relationships and International Migration Relations', *Journal of Common Market Studies* 43(4) (2006), pp. 787–806.

4. James Rosenau, *Along the Domestic-Foreign Frontier: Exploring Governance in a Turbulent World* (Cambridge: Cambridge University Press, 1997).

5. Joseph Nevins, *Operation Gatekeeper: The Rise of the 'Illegal Alien' and the Making of the US-Mexico Boundary* (New York: Routledge, 2002).

6. Mark Purcell and Joseph Nevins, 'Pushing the Boundary: State Restructuring, State Theory, and the Case of U.S.-Mexico Border Enforcement in the 1990s', *Political Geography* 24 (2005), p. 213.

7. Barry Buzan, Ole Wæver, and Jaap de Wilde, *Security: A New Framework for Analysis* (Boulder: Lynne Rienner, 1998), pp. 106–107.

8. Neil Walker, *Europe's Area of Freedom, Security, and Justice* (Oxford: Oxford University Press, 2004).

9. Ibid., p. 11.

10. CEC, 'Policy Priorities in the Fight Against Illegal Immigration of Third-Country Nationals', SEC (2006) 1010.

11. Nazaré Albuquerque Abell, 'The Compatibility of Readmission Agreements with the 1951 Refugee Convention Relating to the Status of Refugees', *International Journal of Refugee Law* 11(1) (1999), pp. 60–83; Martin Schieffer,

'Community Readmission Agreements with Third Countries: Objectives, Substance, and Current State of Negotiations', *European Journal of Migration and Law* 3(3) (2003), pp. 343–357.

12. Council of the European Union, 'A Strategy for the External Dimension of JHA: Global Freedom, Security, and Justice', 14366/3/05 REV 3, LIMITE, JAI 417, RELEX 628 (Brussels, 2005).

13. CEC, 'Communication on Immigration and Asylum Policies', COM (1994) 23 Final.

14. Geddes, 'Europe's Border Relationships and International Migration Relations'.

15. World Bank, *Global Economic Prospects: The Economic Implications of Remittances and Migration* (Washington, DC: 2005), available at http://www.worldbank.org/prospects/gep2006; World Bank, *Close to Home: The Development Impact of Remittances in Latin America* (Washington, DC, 2007).

16. Demetrios Papademetriou and Phillip Martin (eds.), *The Unsettled Relationship* (Westport: Greenwood, 1991).

17. Ninna Nyberg Sorensen, Nicholas Van Hear, and Poul Engberg-Pedersen, *The Migration Development Nexus: Evidence and Policy Options* (Geneva: International Organisation for Migration, 2002).

18. Eight Central and Eastern European countries joined in 2004: the Czech Republic, Estonia, Hungary, Latvia, Lithuania, Poland, Slovakia, and Slovenia. Two more joined in 2007: Bulgaria and Romania.

19. Luca Einaudi, *Le Politiche dell'Immigrazione in Italia dall'Unità ad Oggi* (Rome: Laterza, 2007).

20. Federica Bicchi, *European Foreign Policy-Making Towards the Mediterranean* (New York: Palgrave, 2007).

21. See the following documents from the European Council's High-Level Working Group on Asylum and Migration: 'Résumé of the Action Plans Drawn Up by the High-Level Working Group', 11716/99, LIMITE, JAI 86, AG 37 (Brussels, 1999); 'Adoption of the Report to the European Council in Nice', 13993/00, LIMITE, JAI 152, AG 76 (Brussels, 2000); and 'Draft Action Plan for Albania and the Neighbouring Region', 7886/1/00, REV 1, LIMITE, JAI 40, AG 41 (Brussels, 2000).

22. European Council, 'Conclusions', Tampere, October 1999.

23. European Council, 'Conclusions', Seville, June 2002.

24. CEC, 'Integrating Migration Issues in the EU's Relations with Third Countries', pp. 4–5.

25. CEC, 'Reference Document for Financial and Technical Assistance to Third Countries'.

26. CEC, 'On Circular Migration and Mobility Partnerships Between the European Union and Third Countries', COM (2007) 248 Final.

27. For a comparative analysis of the implementation of EU integration measures

and laws in the domestic integration policies of member states, see http://www. integrationindex.eu.

21. THE BLACK ATLANTIC FROM OTHELLO TO OBAMA: IN SEARCH OF A POST-RACIAL SOCIETY

1. See Paul Gilroy, *The Black Atlantic: Modernity and Double Consciousness* (Cambridge: Harvard University Press, 1993).
2. See Ali A. Mazrui, *Euro-Jews and Afro-Arabs: The Great Semitic Divergence in World History*, edited by Seifudein Adem (Washington, DC: University of America Press, 2008).
3. See, for example, Frances Somers Cocks, *The Moor of St. Petersburg: In the Footsteps of a Black Russian* (London: Goldhawk., 2005).
4. See *Washington Post*, 27 May 1968. This Kennedy prophecy was also cited by the late Tim Russert in the television programme *Meet the Press* on 8 June 2008. Russert died suddenly on 13 June 2008, barely a week after the *Meet the Press* interview.
5. William Shakespeare, *Four Tragedies: Hamlet, Othello, King Lear, Macbeth* (London: Penguin, 1994, first published in 1565).
6. William Shakespeare, *The Merchant of Venice* (New York: Washington Square, 1992, first published in 1600), Act III, Scene 1.
7. There are more than 20 million asylum-seekers, refugees, and others of concern to the Office of the UN High Commissioner for Refugees (over 5 million of whom are in Africa), according to the UNHCR website. See http://www.unhcr. org/cgi-bin/texis/vtx/basics/opendoc.htm?tbl=BASICS&id=3b028097c.
8. Samuel P. Huntington, 'The Clash of Civilizations?' *Foreign Affairs* 72(3) (1993), pp. 22–49. Responses by Fouad Ajami, Kishore Mahbubani, Robert L. Bartley, Liu Binyan, and Jeanne J. Kirkpatrick, among others, were published in the next issue of *Foreign Affairs*, 72(4) (1993), pp. 2–22.
9. Samuel P. Huntington, *The Clash of Civilizations and the Remaking of World Order* (New York: Simon and Schuster, 1996).
10. See William Julius Wilson, *The Declining Significance of Race: Blacks and Changing American Institutions* (Chicago: University of Chicago Press, 1978).
11. Blacks who have served (or are serving) as senators include Hiram Revels and Blanche Bruce (both from Mississippi), Edward Brooke (Massachusetts), and Carol Moseley Braun and Barack Obama (both from Illinois).
12. Reports lamenting the end of the African 'safe haven' may be found in *New African* 367 (October 1998), pp. 16–17; and *The Economist*, 'Now for Africa', 5 July 2003, p. 9.
13. Beth Potter, 'No Vacation from Terror's Reach', *U.S. News and World Report*, 9 December 2002.

14. According to the National Urban League's *State of Black America 2007* report, black men are nearly seven times more likely to be jailed than white men. See 'State of Black America', *Washington Post*, 21 April 2007.

15. There is an epidemic of 'black-on-black violence'. A study by the Bureau of Justice Statistics found that, between 2001 and 2005, almost half the people murdered in the US annually were black; that nine of ten black murder victims were killed by other blacks; and that blacks, though composing 13 per cent of the population, were victims in 15 per cent of nonfatal violent crimes. For a report, consult Dan Eggen, 'Study: Almost Half of Murder Victims Black', *Washington Post*, 10 August 2007.

16. For example, even an insider—Lieutenant-Colonel. Stephen E. Abraham of the Army Reserve, who had been involved with the military hearings at Guantanamo Bay to determine if the detainees were 'enemy combatants'—described some of the evidence at these hearings as 'garbage' in testimony to the US Congress. See William Glaberson, 'Critic and Ex-Boss Testify on Guantanamo Hearings', *New York Times*, 27 July 2007.

17. William Blake, *Songs of Innocence and Experience* (Oxford: Oxford University Press 1970, first published in 1794).

18. George Padmore, *Pan-Africanism or Communism? The Coming Struggle for Africa* (London: Dobson, 1956).

19. Kwame Nkrumah, *Consciencism: Philosophy and Ideology for Decolonization* (London: Panaf, 1964).

20. Edward W. Blyden, *Christianity, Islam, and the Negro Race* (London: Whittingham, 1887, 3rd ed. published by Edinburgh University Press in 1967).

21. Mildred Amer, 'Membership of the 110th Congress: A Profile' (Washington, DC: Congressional Research Service, 15 December 2006).

22. Raymond Colitt, 'Brazil Aims to Show Justice Is Colour Blind', *Financial Times*, 30 May 2003, available at http://search.ft.com/search/quickSearch_Run.html.

23. See, for example, Douglas A. Yates, 'The UN Educational, Scientific, and Cultural Organisation', in Adekeye Adebajo (ed.), *From Global Apartheid to Global Village: Africa and the United Nations* (Scottsville: University of Kwazulu-Natal Press, 2009), pp. 481–498.

24. Ismael Serageldin would have stood a better chance of being elected as UNESCO's director-general had the Arab voting bloc not been split between Serageldin (an Egyptian) and a candidate put forward by Saudi Arabia. Serageldin later became the director-general of the new International Library of Alexandria, one of the most technologically advanced libraries in the world, and one with close links to UNESCO and other global cultural institutions.

22. EUROPE'S POSTCOLONIAL ROLE AND IDENTITY

1. This contribution is a new adaptation and continuation of previously published research. It is based on the following projects: Hartmut Mayer and Henri Vogt (eds.), *A Responsible Europe? Ethical Foundations of EU External Affairs* (Basingstoke: Palgrave, 2006); Hartmut Mayer, 'Is It Still Called "Chinese Whispers"? The EU's Rhetoric and Action As a Responsible Global Institution', *International Affairs* 84(1) (2008), pp. 61–79; Hartmut Mayer, 'The Long Legacy of Dorian Gray: Why the European Union Needs to Redefine Its Perspective, Responsibility, and Role in Global Affairs', *Journal of European Integration* 30(1) (2008), pp. 7–25; Hartmut Mayer, 'Declining Might in the Limelight: European Responses to New Regional Powers', *South African Journal of International Affairs* 16(2) (2009), pp. 195–214.

2. The classic 'capability-expectations gap', coined by Christopher Hill, is probably the most used concept when describing the successes and failures with regard to the EU's global role. See Christopher Hill, 'The Capability-Expectations Gap, or Conceptualizing Europe's International Role', *Journal of Common Market Studies* 31(3) (1993), pp. 305–328.

3. For comprehensive documents outlining these ambitions, see the publication of the 2010 EU-Africa summit in Tripoli, in particular the European Commission's 'Joint Africa EU Strategy: Action Plan 2011–2013' (Brussels, 2010).

4. See Mayer, 'The Long Legacy of Dorian Gray'.

5. For a more comprehensive treatment of such themes, see, for example, Damien Helly, *L'UE et L'Afrique: Les Défis de la Cohérence*, Cahiers de Chaillot (Paris: EU Institute for Security Studies, November 2010).

6. See, for example, Hanns W. Maull, 'Europe and the New Balance of Global Order', *International Affairs* 81(4) (2005), pp. 775–799.

7. See Andrew Hurrell, 'One World? Many Worlds? The Place of Regions in the Study of International Society', *International Affairs* 83(1) (2007), pp. 127–146.

8. See Hartmut Mayer, 'France, Germany, UK: Responses of Traditional to Rising Regional Powers', in Daniel Flemes (ed.), *Regional Leadership in the Global System: Ideas, Interests, and Strategies of Regional Powers* (Farnham: Ashgate, 2010), pp. 276–278.

9. Charles Krauthammer, 'The Unipolar Moment', *Foreign Affairs* 70(1) (1990), pp. 23–33.

10. See Richard N. Haass, 'The Age of Non-Polarity: What Will Follow US Dominance?', *Foreign Affairs* 83(1) (2008), pp. 44–56.

11. For example, see the European Commission's 'A Secure Europe in a Better World. European Security Strategy' (Brussels, 12 December 2003).

12. Gunnar Sjöstedt, *The External Role of the European Community* (Farnborough: Gower, 1977).

13. See, for example, Charlotte Bretherton and John Vogler, *Europe as a Global Actor* (London: Routledge, 1999).

14. François Duchêne, 'The European Community and the Uncertainties of Interdependence', in Max Kohnstamm and Wolfgang Hager (eds.), *A Nation Writ Large? Foreign-Policy Problems Before the European Community* (London: Macmillan, 1973), pp. 1–21.

15. Ian Manners, 'Normative Power Europe: A Contradiction in Terms?', *Journal of Common Market Studies* 40(2) (2002), pp. 235–258.

16. Björn Hettne and Frederik Söderbaum, 'Civilian Power or Soft Imperialism? The EU as a Global Actor and the Role of Interregionalism', *European Foreign Affairs Review* 10(4) (2005), pp. 535–552.

17. Thomas Diez and Stefan Stetter, 'The European Union and Border Conflicts: The Transformative Power of Integration', *International Organization* 60(3) (2006), pp. 563–593. See also Heather Grabbe, *The EU's Transformative Power: Europeanization Through Conditionality in Central and Eastern Europe* (Basingstoke: Palgrave, 2006).

18. Curt Gasteyger, *An Ambigious Power* (Gütersloh: Bertelsmann, 1996).

19. Sophie Meunier and Kalypso Nicolaidis, 'The European Union as a Conflicted Trade Power', *Journal of European Public Policy* 13(6) (2006), pp. 200–233.

20. Robert Falkner, 'The Political Economy of "Normative Power" Europe: EU Environmental Leadership in International Biotechnology Regulation', *Journal of European Public Policy* 14(4) (2007), pp. 507–526.

21. Parag Khanna, 'The EU—the Metrosexual Superpower', *Foreign Policy* 143 (2004), pp. 66–68.

22. This conceptual work was developed by a study group on 'Responsible Europe' assembled for Hartmut Mayer and Henri Vogt (eds.), *A Responsible Europe?* See, in particular, Andras Szigeti, 'The Problem of Institutional Responsibility and the European Union' in the Mayer and Vogt volume.

23. See Terry O'Shaughnessy, 'The European Union: A Responsible Trading Partner?' in Mayer and Vogt, *A Responsible Europe?* pp. 181–199.

24. See Mayer, 'The Long Legacy of Dorian Gray', pp. 15–16.

25. See Hartmut Mayer and Henri Vogt, 'Conclusion: The Global Responsibility of the European Union—From Principles to Policy', in Mayer and Vogt, *A Responsible Europe?* pp. 225–235.

26. Hartmut Mayer, 'The "Mutual", "Shared", and "Dual" Responsibility of the West: The EU and the US in a Sustainable Transatlantic Alliance', in Mayer and Vogt, *A Responsible Europe?* pp. 57–75.

27. See Benita Ferrero-Waldner, 'The European Neighbourhood Policy: The EU's Newest Foreign Policy Instrument', *European Foreign Affairs Review* 11(2) (2006), pp. 139–142; European Commission, 'Wider Europe—Neighbourhood: A New Framework for Relations with Our Eastern and Southern Neigh-

bours' (Brussels, 11 March 2003). See also European Commission, 'European Neighbourhood Policy Strategy Paper' (Brussels, 12 May 2004).

28. See Geoffrey Edwards, 'The Construction of Ambiguity and the Limits of Attraction: Europe and Its Neighbourhood Policy', *Journal of European Integration* 30(1) (2008), pp. 45–62.

29. See Joint United Nations Programme on HIV/AIDS (UNAIDS) and World Health Organisation (WHO), 'AIDS Epidemic Update' (Geneva, December 2004), available at http://www.unaids.org/wad2004_html_en/Epi04_05_en.htm#Top of page.

30. See Sonia Lucarelli, 'The European Union in the Eyes of Others: Towards Filling a Gap in the Literature', *European Foreign Affairs Review* 12(2) (2007), pp. 249–270.

31. See Mayer, 'Is It Still Called "Chinese Whispers"?'

32. Daniela Sicurelli, *The European Union's Africa Policies: Norms, Interests, and Impact* (Farnham: Ashgate, 2010), p. 147.

33. Ibid., pp. 148–149.

INDEX

Abéché 305
Abidjan 337
Abuja treaty 1991, *see also* EAC 92, 96, 97
Accra Agenda for Action (2008) 260
Accra AU summit and Accra Protocol (2007) 103
Accra 49, 114, 224, 261
ACHPR 60, 68, 73–4, 272
ACP countries, *see also* Cotonou Agreement; Lomé Conventions 4, 5–9, 153–4, 213–16, 227, 372, 448, 449
ADB 112
Addis Ababa 50, 61, 69, 72, 362
Adedeji, Adebayo 6, 62, chapter 4, 182
Adesina, Akin 247
AEC 46, 92, 96, 101–3, 234
AEF 87–8, 317–18
AfCHPR 60, 74–5, 272
Afghanistan 351–3
Africa Conflict Prevention Pool 355
Africa-EU Civil Society Human Rights Dialogue 273
African Americans 48, 428–39
African Charter on Democracy, Elections, and Governance (2004) 274
African Charter on Human and Peoples' Rights 75
African Court of Justice 68, 75
African Economic Research Council 108

African Standby Force 17, 53, 269, 270
AGOA 207
agriculture 84–5, 183–6, 207, 211, 212, 237–54
Ahidjo, Ahmadou 75
aid 34–7, 40, 90–91, chapter 5, 122, 124, 194, 213–14, 228–35, 249, 262–5, 273–4, 326, 328, 346–9, 357, 377–9, 388–99, 401–2, Annex A
Albania 305, 406
Algeria 78, 146, 371, 436
Allam-Mi, Ahmed 298, 309
Alliance for a Green Revolution in Africa 247
Al-Qaeda 145, 257, 369, 432, 439; Al-Qaeda of the Islamic Maghreb 330
Amin, Idi 38
AMIS 231, 262, 272
AMISOM 312
Amos, Baroness 436
Amsterdam Treaty 59, 264, 408, 413
AMU 97–8, 102, 147
ANC 389
Anglo-French 1998 St Malo meeting 39
Angola 33, 51, 209, 222, 284, 286, 290, 292, 324, 325, 348, 366, 367–72, 374–6, 380, 394
Annan, Kofi 259, 333, 435
Anyaoku, Emeka 437
AOF 87–8, 317–18
APEC 165

APF (African Peace Facility) 231, 261–2, 269–70
APRM (African Peer Review Mechanism) 113, 165, 230, 273
APSA (African Peace and Security Architecture) 269–70
'Arab Spring' 151–2
Arab states 32, 66, chapter 7
Arab-Israeli conflict 141, 150–51
Artémis, Operation 288–90, 333–4, 354
Arusha 75
ASEAN 153, 158–60, 165–6
Ashton, Catherine 60, 156, 222–3, 442
Asia-EU relations chapter 8
Asia-Europe Meetings 153, 157, 165–6
AU 8, 10, 38, 46–7, 53–4, 60–78, 96–7, 100–4, 232–5, 260–61, 268–9, 284, 292, 293, 337, 456; audit (2007) 101–4; Peace and Security Council 269–70; Special Fund 269
Australia 111
Austria 58, 111, 251, 304, 305, 312
Awolowo, Obafemi 49

Balladur, Henri 338
Ban Ki-moon 298, 302, 307–11
Banda, Hastings 49
Bandar bin Sultan 435, 436
banks 195, 376–7
Barcelona Process 144–5, 148, 411–12
Barroso, Durão 370
Barroso, José Manuel 63, 157, 369, 373
Bashir, Omar al- 9, 166, 312, 400
Belgium 38, 284, 289, 305
Bemba, Jean-Pierre 291
Ben Ali, Zine el-Abidine 152
Ben Bella, Ahmed 78
Benin 339, 400
Bentegeat, Henri 335
Berlin Conference (1884–85) 24–7, 46, 48, 91
Berlin Initiative 127
Beth, Emmanuel 331
Bicesse Accords 369

Bismarck, Otto von 25–6, 46
'Black Atlantic' and 'Black Indian Ocean' 419–20, 428, 431–3, 438–9
Blair, Tony 39–40, 228, 232, 257, 344, 347, 350, 355–6, 357–9, 362–3
Blake, William 433
Blyden, Edward W. 434
Boateng, Paul 436
Bockel, Jean-Marie 42, 326, 339
Bokassa, Jean-Bédel 38, 320
Bongo, Ali 324, 339
Bongo, Omar 326, 338–9
Bosnia 352, 354
Botswana 128, 130, 202, 208, 209, 211
Bouaké 337
Bourgi, Robert 325
Boutros-Ghali, Boutros 435
Bozizé, François 297, 339
Brazil 122, 371–2, 436
Brazzaville 87, 318
Brazzaville bloc 49–51
BRIC countries 122
Britain 5, 25–6, 28–9, 31–2, 38, 39, 57, 76, 87, 111, 123, 124, 138, 156, 187, 228–9, 240, 245–6, 251, 284, 289, 304, 333, 340, chapter 17, 372, 427, 431, 436
Brown, Gordon 40, 267, 344, 436
Bruguière, Jean-Louis 334
Bunche, Ralph 437
Burkina Faso 10–11, 339
Burnham, Forbes 35
Burundi 74, 207, 220, 293, 312
Bush, George W. 112, 145, 436

Cahora Bassa 383
Cairo Declaration and Cairo Plan of Action 230
Cameron, David 344, 363
Cameroon 74, 75, 211, 305, 339
Camões Institutes 379
Canada 111, 122, 232
Cancún 9, 41
CAP (Common Agricultural Policy) 12, 16, 56, 139, 192, chapter 12, 362

Cape Town 23, 42, 328, 390
Cape Verde 376, 380–82
Caribbean Forum 204
Casablanca bloc 49–51
Cavaco Silva, Anibal 366, 367–70
CEAO 97
CEMAC 97, 224–5
CEN-SAD 97, 302
Central African Republic 38, 224, 231,
chapter 15, 320, 331, 335, 339, 354,
371
Centre for Conflict Resolution 2, 23
Centre for Global Development 111,
115
Césaire, Aimé 48
CFA franc 97, 321
CFSP 59, 67, 125, 142, 231, 261, 270,
277, 282–4, 306, 344, 350, 454
Chad 231, chapter 15, 320, 332,
335–6, 339, 354, 371
Chalker, Lynda 346–7
Chambas, Mohamed Ibn 11
Charlemagne 54–5, 341
Cheysson, Claude 4, 5, 34, 35
China 64, 67, 122, 131, 160–66, 177,
189, 192, 258, 259, 271
Chirac, Jacques 39, 42, 326, 330,
333–4, 336–7, 339
Church of England 427
CIMAO 36
civil society 266, 273
climate change issues and talks (COP
17) 134–5, 397
Cold War 8, 35, 86, 98, 143, 257, 340,
386, 389, 390
colonialism 24–31, 34, 46–50, 85–8,
91–2, 98, 138, 324, 448–50
COMESA 97–8, 126, 129, 209, 210,
212, 220
Commission for Africa 40, 228, 356,
357, 361–2
commodity trade 90, 171–2, 180–83
Common Position on the Prevention,
Management, and Resolution of
Violent Conflicts in Africa 270

Commonwealth 28, 32, 35, 345, 357,
437
Comoros 320
CONADER (DRC) 283–4
Conference on Security and Coopera-
tion in Europe 143
conflict prevention and resolution 53,
230–32, 261, 265, 267, 269–72,
chapter 14, chapter 15, 333–8, 351–9
Congo crisis (1960s) 50
Congo Free State 26, 28
Congo, Democratic Republic of the
(DRC) 70, 74, 133, 222, 231, 278,
280–92, 320, 333–5, 339, 348, 354,
358
Congo, Republic of (Congo-Brazzaville)
205, 224–5, 290, 324, 339
Conseil de l'Entente 88
Conservative Party (UK) 344, 362–4
Cooper, Robert 350
Cooperation, ministry of (France) 321,
326, 339
Coreper (Committee of Permanent
Representatives) 69
corruption 174, 229, 284, 395, 396
Côte d'Ivoire 39, 204, 211, 223,
319–20, 322, 331, 336–8, 353
Cotonou Agreement, see also EPAs 4,
7–9, 10–12, 27–8, 33, 36–8, 90–92,
197–206, 219–25, 409
coups d'état 66
CPLP 366–7, 371–2
Croatia 305, 406
CSDP (Common Security and Defence
Policy) 261–2, 371
Cuba 51
Czech Republic 245

Dakar 42, 87, 318, 324
Darfur 8, 9, 70, 73, 163, 231, 293, 296,
297, 304, 312, 336, 353, 364
DCMD 330–1
DDR 267, 270, 281, 282–8
de Gaulle, Charles 3, 30–31, 34, 56–7,
319

de Geus, Arie 106
De Klerk, F.W. 435, 437
de Villepin, Dominique 326, 336
debt 77, 85, 174, 248, 266, 361, 370
Déby, Idriss 295, 297, 298–300,
    306–10, 336, 339
Delors, Jacques 57–8, 63, 109
democracy in Africa 173–4, 264–6,
    273, 323
Denmark 57, 58, 111, 385–90,
    395–402; Africa policy 395–8
DFID 245–6, 248, 355, 357–62
diaspora 48–9, 419–20, 435–7
Djibouti 319
Doha round, see also WTO 83–5, 161,
    192–3, 196, 229, 241, 248
dos Santos, José Eduardo 325, 368
DuBois, William E.B. 48, 49, 428–9,
    433
Dupuch, Michel 322
Durban II Racism Conference 400
duty-free quota-free imports 206–7,
    209–10, 215, 216

EAC 54, 88, 97, 207, 212, 215, 221
EAFRD 245
EAGGF 238
Eanes, António 367
East African Community/Eastern and
    Southern Africa region (ESA) 201,
    204, 209, 211, 212, 215
ECA 62, 89, 112, 129
ECCAS 91, 97–8
ECJ 57, 60, 65, 76–7
ECOWAS 6, 11, 34–5, 36, 91, 96, 98,
    100, 153, 274, 337
ECSC 55–7
EDF 6, 8, 10–11, 13, 15, 36, 38, 132,
    200, 213–14, 231, 264, 271, 273,
    292–3
EFTA 148
Egypt 50, 75, 122, 141, 145, 152, 434,
    435, 437
EIB 132
El Baradei, Mohamed 437
electricity 181, 188–9, 196

Elias, T.O. 436
energy 180–83, 188–9, 196
EPAs 7–9, 33, 35, 37, 40–41, 90–92,
    94, 101–3, 123, 127, 129–32, chap-
    ter 10, 260, 263, 456
Equatorial Guinea 224, 339, 348–9,
    372
Eritrea 348
ESDI (European Security and Defence
    Identity) 231
ESDP (European Security and Defence
    Policy) 271, 277, 344, 350, 351, 354,
    454, 456
Ethiopia 33, 35, 50, 52, 233, 312, 358,
    360–61, 422
EU enlargement 5, 59, 148, 251, 411
EU Operations Centre 271
EU Special Representative for Africa
    233, 262
EU strategic partnerships (general)
    155–7
'EU Strategy for Africa' report (2005),
    see also EU-Africa Strategy (2007)
    105, 229–31, 273, 277, 292, 455
EU-Africa Dialogue 267
EU-Africa Ministerial Conference
    (2006, Rabat) 416
EU-Africa Strategic Partnership (2005)
    268, 274
EU-Africa Strategy (2007), see also 'EU
    Strategy for Africa' report (2005) 2,
    33, 145, 232–3, 275
EU-Africa summits, Cairo, 2000 38,
    230, 268, 372; Lisbon, 2007 2, 4,
    8–9, 33, 37, 38, 40–41, 105, 107,
    155, 198, 218, 232–4, 261, 268,
    328–9, 372–3; Tripoli, 2010 2, 9, 38,
    41, 155, 218, 233, 210, 268, 328, 373
EUFOR (European Union Force) 231,
    288–92, 335–6, 354
EUMC (EU Military Command) 301
EUPOL (European Union Police Mis-
    sion) 282–3, 287–8, 290
Eurafrique idea 2–3, 11–12, 23–4,
    27–35, 40–43, 419, 457

Euratom 56, 57
euro, Eurozone 12, 59, 78, 159, 366, 381
Eurocentrism 442–3, 454–5
Euro-Mediterranean Partnership 145
Europe's position in the world (general) chapter 22
Europe-Africa Research Network 373
European Centre for Development Policy Management (EDPM) 211, 402
European Defence Agency 271
European Environmental Bureau 241
European Initiative for Democracy and Human Rights 273
European Monetary System 57
European Monetary Union 58
European Neighbourhood and Partnership Initiative 148
European Neighbourhood Policy 145, 147–9, 150, 263, 452
European Parliament 57, 58, 60, 71, 225, 246, 269
European Peace Facility 293
European Security Strategy (2003) 154, 161, 261, 350
European Union-Africa Peace Facility 231
European-African Business Forum 229
EUSEC 281–4, 287–8
'Everything but Arms' trade 37, 202, 225
External Action Service (EU) 65, 442, 454
Extractive Industry Transparency Initiative 274
Eyadéma, Gnassingbé 320

Fajemirokun, Henry 100
FDLR 287, 334
Federation of West African Chambers of Commerce 100
Finland 58, 111, 251, 305, 312, 386, 388–9
Foccart, Jacques 319, 325–6

Foley, Maurice 34
food supply and trade 85, 183–4, 207, 248, 249
Forest Law Enforcement Governance and Trade 274
Fouere, Erwan 125
Françafrique 3, 31, 33, 42, 321–4, 326, 338–9
France 2–3, 9, 17, 23–6, 29–31, 38, 39, 41–3, 51, 55, 87–9, 111, 138–41, 149–50, 156, 225, 240, 251, 284, 289, 298, 300–2, 304, chapter 16, 431
Franco-African summits 328
Francophonie 327, 339
FRELIMO 389

Gabon 42, 205, 210, 224–5, 289, 290, 319–20, 338–9
Gambia 74
Gana, Jaime 372
Ganascia, Jean-Philippe 301
Garvey, Marcus 429
GATT 7, 199, 242
Gbagbo, Laurent 336–8, 339
Gbowee, Leymah 437–8
Germany 2, 25–30, 55–6, 59, 111, 149, 151, 156, 164, 232, 240, 284, 289, 291, 304, 333, 335, 340–41, 431
Ghana 49, 75, 204, 211, 223, 265, 331, 354, 428, 436–7
Gilroy, Paul 419–20
Giscard d'Estaing, Valéry 59, 66, 338
Gleneagles summit 40, 232, 259
Global Conflict Prevention Pool 355
Global Mediterranean Policy 141–2
Gowon, Yakubu 35
Great Lakes Region, see also Congo, Democratic Republic of the (DRC); Rwanda chapter 14, 334–5, 346
Greece 58, 142, 246
Group of 20 162, 453
Group of 77 52
Group of Eight 40, 145, 228, 233, 218, 228, 232, 259, 271, 357

GSP 201–3
Guaino, Henri 3, 42, 149
Guéant, Claude 325
Guebuza, Armando 383
Guéhenno, Jean-Marie 335
Guelke, Adrian 123
Guernier, Eugène 29
Guinea 3, 30, 34, 50, 74, 332
Guinea-Bissau 372, 380, 382–3
Guyana 32

Habyarimana, Juvénal 334
Hain, Peter 356
Hallstein, Walter 55, 57
Hannibal, Abram 422
Harvard University 427, 428
Hassan II 50
High-Level Working Group on Migration and Asylum 412–20
Hitler, Adolf 30, 31, 55
HIV/AIDS 228–9
Holland, Martin 122, 123, 124–5
Holy Roman Empire 55
Hortefeux, Brice 326–7
Houphouët-Boigny, Félix 338
human rights 27, 52, 53, 74, 143–4, 264–5, 266–7, 272, 392
Hungary 240, 246
Huntington, Samuel 430–31

ICC 9, 272, 400
Iceland 148, 386
ICJ 436–7
ICRC 310,
IDA 285
IDPs 278, 296–7, 299, 300, 304, 310, 313
IGAD (Intergovernmental Authority on Development) 91, 97,
IMF 84, 107, 144, 162, 366, 453
India 122, 160–62, 177, 179, 189, 259
Indonesia 160, 177
inflation 17, 57, 85, 107, 176
Integrated Military Structure (DRC) 281, 285

Integrated Police Unit (DRC) 282
international trade, see also Cotonou Agreement; Lomé Conventions; WTO 47, 77, 84–5, 190–94, 197–216, 221, 246–50, 253–4, 449
investment 166, chapter 9, 221, 226, 336
IPAD 378
Iraq 59, 143–4, 154, 156, 351–3
Ireland 57, 59, 60, 111, 240, 304, 305, 312
Islam 147, 152, 312, 421–2, 424, 426, 431–2
Italy 29, 56, 111, 138, 140, 142, 143, 146, 251, 304
Ituri 289, 334

Jackson, General Sir Mike 353
Jakarta 160
Jammeh, Yahya 74
Japan 64, 92, 122, 232
Jews 94, 424–5
Joana, Pierre-Michel 262
Johnson-Sirleaf, Ellen 437–8
Jospin, Lionel 330
Joyandet, Alain 326
Juppé, Alain 330
Justice and Home Affairs 'pillar' 67, 142, 408–9

Kabila, Joseph 287, 333, 339
Kagame, Paul 287, 334
Kasavubu, Joseph 50
Kaunda, Kenneth 35, 74
Keita, Modibo 50
Kennedy, Robert F. 422
Kenya 74, 75, 122, 189, 208, 211, 220–21, 264, 312, 359, 426–8, 432, 434, 435
Kimberley Process 274
King, Martin Luther 437
Konaré, Alpha Oumar 61–2, 69, 77, 339
Korea, South 122
Kouchner, Bernard 298

Kufra 137
Kuwait 143

Labour Party (UK) 344, 347–51,
    355–63, 436
Lagos Plan of Action and Lagos Final
    Act 92, 96, 99–100
Lamy, Pascal 192
Latvia 251
LDCs 202, 205–8, 223, 224–5
Leopold II 25–6, 28
Lesotho 128, 130, 208, 209, 211
Liberal Democrats (UK) 356, 358
liberation struggles 78, 86, 93–4, 95,
    388, 389–91, 400
Liberia 174, 437–8
Libya 9, 38, 53–4, 134, 138–40, 146,
    151–2, 156, 320, 325, 340, 363, 364
Licorne, Operation 39, 336–8
Lisbon Treaty (EU, 2007) 4, 10, 60, 442
Lobo Antunes, Manuel 373–4
Lockerbie affair 146
Lomé Conventions 3, 4, 5–8, 27, 32–8,
    89–90, 128, 129, 139, 198, 219,
    265, 365–6
Lumumba, Patrice 50
Luthuli, Albert 437
Luxembourg 76

Maastricht Treaty (EU) 6, 58, 67, 261,
    264, 408
Maathai, Wangari 437
MacSharry reforms 242, 252–3
Madagascar 133, 207, 209, 222, 324,
    325
Madivo, Callisto 437
Maghreb 12, 15, 66, chapter 7, 230,
    452
Mahtar M'Bow, Amadou 436
Major, John 346
Malawi 74, 222
Malcorra, Susana 309
Mali 50, 53, 330, 331, 339
Malloch-Brown, Mark 357
Malvern, Lord 34

Mamba, Operation 334
Manchester, Pan-African Conference 48
Mandela, Nelson 53, 125, 426
Mandelson, Peter 41
Manley, Michael 35
Manuel, Trevor 107
Marcoussis agreement 336–7
Marshall Plan 56, 77, 95
Martin, Guy 34, 338
Mashrek 141, 145
Mauritania 70, 324, 325, 330
Mauritius 209, 222
Mayall, James 345
Mba, Léon 320
Mbeki, Thabo 9, 113, 196, 232
MEDA protocols 144, 148
media 279, 290
Mediterranean Union 42–3, 149–50
Medjauni, Mohammed 436–7
MENA, *see also* Barcelona Process
    411–12
Mengistu Haile Mariam 35
Merchant of Venice, The 423–6
Merkel, Angela 149
Mexico 122
Michel, Louis 41, 42, 93, 217–18, 332
MICOPAX 302
migration 15, 18–19, 111, 143, 145,
    230, 326–8, 348, 380, 381, 397,
    chapter 20, 431, 434–5
Miliband, David 251, 349, 354, 356,
    359
Millennium Challenge Account 112
MDG (Millennium Development
    Goals) 107, 114, 132–3, 260, 273,
    274, 347, 378
Milton, John 45–6
MINURCAT 295–300, 307–12
Mitterrand, François 338
Mobutu Sese Seko 39, 174
Moi, Daniel arap 264
Mongella, Gertrude 70
Monnet, Jean 55, 57
Monrovia bloc 50–51
Mont Valérien 300–1

MONUC 287, 288, 333, 335, 354
MONUSCO 282
Morgenthau, Hans 275
Morocco 8, 38, 50, 138–40, 144, 268, 371, 374, 377, 412–13, 416
Moussa, Idriss 70
Mozambique 33, 115, 129, 209, 211, 222, 288, 358, 368
MPLA 367–70, 389
Mubarak, Hosni 152
Mugabe, Robert 9, 38, 40, 41, 134, 164, 166, 232, 264, 267, 350, 352, 372
Multi-Donor Reintegration Programme (DRC) 288
Museveni, Yoweri 54, 83
Muskoka summit 232
Myanmar 159, 166

N'Djaména 305, 306
Namibia 128, 202, 209–10
Napoleon 55, 341
Nash, Patrick 301, 304
Nasser, Gamal Abdul 50, 138
NATO 29, 38, 56, 140, 156, 325, 329, 332, 333, 340, 368, 386, 390, 453
négritude 48
NEPAD 33, 93, 113, 165, 230, 233
Netherlands 111, 117, 138–9, 251, 284, 304, 412, 431
Neto, Agostinho 367
New Zealand 111
NGOs 73, 360, 389
NIEO 5, 32
Niger 324, 330
Nigeria 9, 34, 87, 89, 122, 177, 188, 189, 203, 205, 210, 223, 331, 437
NACCIMA (Nigerian Association of Chambers of Commerce, Industry, Mines and Agriculture) 100
Nkrumah, Kwame 4, 49–50, 88, 434
Nkunda, Laurent 287
Non-Aligned Movement 52, 140
Nordic countries 112, 358–9, chapter 19

Nordic Development Fund 399–400
North African Governance Facility 230
Norway 111, 148, 285, 385–95, 397–402, 431; Africa policy 393–95
Nyerere, Julius 35, 51–2, 75, 425

OAU 19, 33, 35, 47, 50–53, 230, 292
Obama, Barack 13, 161, 421, 425–38
Obasanjo, Olusegun 75, 113, 232
Obiakor, Chikadibia 309
ODA 346–7
ODI 202, 212
OECD 108, 113, 173, 249, 260, 279
oil and gas 32, 175–6, 180–83, 205, 258, 348, 374, 394
Okigbo, Pius 4
Olympic Games 162
Orsini di Camerota, Paolo Agostino 29
Othello 421, 423–5, 439
Ouagadougou 11
Ouattara, Alassane 337–8
Oxfam 91, 226, 250, 311

Padmore, George 49, 433–4
Paige, Rod 436
PALOP, see also Portugal 367, 378–84
Pan-African Parliament 60, 69–70, 72–3, 261, 269
Pan-Africanism 47, 48, 49, 428–9, 433
Paris Declaration on Aid Effectiveness (2005) 114–15, 260
Pasqua, Charles 325, 326
peacekeeping operations, see conflict prevention and resolution
Permanent Representatives Committee (AU) 61, 65
Ping, Jean 9, 61, 66
Pisani, Edgard 4
Poland 59, 246, 251, 304–5, 312
police 282, 299, 312, 311, 327
Polisario 320
Political and Security Committee (EU) 282, 301
Pompidou, Georges 34, 141
Port-Bouët 336
Porteous, Tom 347, 359

Portugal 26, 38, 40, 58, 59, 111, 141, 142, 232, 240, 251, chapter 18, 390
Post-Conflict Reconstruction Unit (UK) 355
Powell, Colin 436
private sector 100, 115, 187–8, 195, 226, 229, 376
PTA 97–8, 100
PTPH/DIS (Chad) 299–300, 308
public-private partnerships 187–8
Pushkin, Aleksandr 422
Qaddafi, Muammar al- 9, 47, 53–4, 66, 134, 140, 146, 152, 320, 325, 326, 340
racial issues 420–39
Ramphal, Shridath 32, 36, 437
Raphaël-Leygues, Jacques 322
readmission agreements 410
RECAMP 331
RECs 91, 95–104, 191, 234–5, 456
refugees 296–7, 299, 304, 310–11, 313, 397
regional integration, see also RECs and names of groupings chapter 4
remittances 411, 415
Renaissance Capital 188
RENAMO 368
Renovated Mediterranean Policy 142
'responsibility to protect' 356
retornados 368, 380
Rhodes, Cecil 28
Rhodesia 34, 52
Rice, Condoleezza 436
Rio de Janeiro 135
Roman Empire 341
Romania 312
Rome, Treaty of 3, 5–6, 31, 56, 89, 138–9, 217, 241, 272
Russia 177–9, 188, 232, 305, 341, 402, 422, 452
Rwanda 39, 74, 207, 220, 278, 287, 289, 290, 292, 320, 325, 330, 333, 346, 358

SACU 123, 128, 201, 207, 209, 221–2

Sadat, Anwar 435
SADC 36, 97–8, 123, 126–31, 132–3, 153, 201, 209, 220, 221–2, 284, 397, 399
Salim, Salim Ahmed 52–3
sanctions 52, 124–5, 133, 146, 159, 350, 369–70, 390
Santer, Jacques 71
Sanu, Olu 4
Sanusi Order 138
São Tomé e Principe 224, 339
Sarkozy, Nicolas 3, 42–3, 149–50, 320–21, 324–9, 336–40
Saudi Arabia 435
Savimbi, Jonas 367, 369
Schacht, Hjalmar 30
Schulz, Martin 71
Schuman Plan 55
Scotland, Baroness 436
Scramble for Africa 24–9, 34, 46
Sebha 137
Senegal 42, 75, 319,
Senghor, Léopold 31, 34, 75
September 11 attacks 145, 257, 369
Serageldin, Ismail 437
Seville European Council summit 414
Seychelles 203, 222
Shaba 38
Shakespeare, William 48, 421, 423–6
Shinkaiye, John 9–10
Short, Clare 263, 356, 357
Sicurelli, Daniela 456
Sierra Leone 39, 74, 75, 348, 350, 364
Single European Act 58
Single Market (EU) 124
Single Payment Scheme 251
Sirte Declaration 93, 96
Sisulu, Beryl Rose 390
slavery and slave trade 27, 46, 93, 420
Slovenia 244
Smith, Stephen 322–4
Soares, João 369
Soares, Mário 365
Socrates, João 370
Solana, Javier 306, 350

Somalia 112, 139, 174, 292, 297, 312, 348, 398
Somaliland 362
South Africa 12, 38, 42, 51, 52, 67, 69, 72, 78, chapter 6, 177, 179, 192, 208, 209, 228, 234, 284, 290, 347, 368, 374, 377, 383, 384, 389–90, 435, 437
South Africa-EU Trade, Development and Cooperation Agreement (TDCA) 123, 125, 127–31, 133, 155, 222
South African Development Partnership Agency 133
South Sudan 133
Soviet Union 30, 49, 142, 143, 368, 386
Soyinka, Wole 48
Spain 58, 76, 111, 138, 141, 142, 240, 246, 251, 312, 381–2
SSR 270–71, 280–88, 382–3, 396
Stabex 36, 90
Stevens, Christopher 226
Stevens, Siaka 75
stock markets 195
Stoltenberg, Thorvald 402
Strasbourg 71
structural adjustment programmes 83, 265
subsidies 84–5, 192–3, 238–54
Sudan 8, 9, 70, 163, 231, 297, 306, 312, 348, 353, 400
sugar 32, 206
SWAPO 389
Swaziland 128, 130, 133, 209, 211
Sweden 58, 111, 246, 251, 289, 304, 305, 385–93, 395–401; Africa policy 391–2
Switzerland 148
Sysmin 36, 90

Tampere EU summit 413
Taodenni 137
Tandon, Yash 227
Tanzania 35, 51–2, 75, 129, 207, 209, 220, 222, 265, 432

Telles, Francisco 370
terrorism 145, 166–7, 257, 348–9, 369, 432
Thatcher, Margaret 142
Thomann, Jean-Claude 333
Thomas, Clarence 436
Timbuktu 137
Togo 36, 332
Toubou of Tibesti 137
Touré, Sékou 3, 30, 33

transport 187
Tripolitania 137
Tsvangirai, Morgan 398–9
Tunisia 75, 138–40, 144, 151–2
Turkey 72, 141, 424
Tutu, Desmond 94, 437

UDAO 88
UEMOA 36, 97, 223
Uganda 38, 51–2, 54, 207, 220, 221, 289, 290, 312, 357
UKTI 363
UMOA 97
UNAMID 296, 303, 312
UNAMSIL 350
UNDP 273, 348, 357
Une Tempête 48–9
UNESCO 436–7
UNHCR 278, 296
UNITA 367, 368–70
United Nations 30, 39, 52, 107, 108, 132, 134, 146, 161, 163, 164, 194, 231, 259, 270, 271, 278, 280–82, 286–7, 288–93, 295–303, 307–13, 333–8, 351–3, 357–9, 363, 369–70, 387, 390, 453; Human Rights Council 272
UNMIS 312
UNOCI 336–8
US Middle East Partnership Initiative 145
US 13, 38, 48, 49, 58–9, 64, 77, 95, 111, 112, 140, 143, 145, 148, 159, 161, 192, 207, 258, 271, 284, 340, 369–70, 408, 422, 426–33, 435–9

van Rompuy, Herman 60, 156, 442
Venice 423–5
Vervaeke, Koen 233, 262
Vichy regime 2, 30, 31

Wade, Abdoulaye 9, 40, 338, 339
Washington Consensus, *see also* IMF;
    World Bank 84, 106–9, 144
Washington, Booker T. 429
Western Sahara 19, 72, 320
WFP 184
Wilson, William Julius 431
Wolfensohn, James 109
Wolfowitz, Paul 109
Wood, Adrian 194
World Bank 107–9, 144, 193, 249,
    285–8, 437, 453
World Cup 177
World War, First 27, 195, 341

World War, Second 27, 55, 95, 341
Wright, Jeremiah 430
WTO 7, 37, 64, 110, 129, 161, 192–3,
    197–204, 210, 216, 225, 229, 241,
    242, 249, 260, 453

Yaounde Conventions 3, 5, 31, 89, 139
Yugoslavia 58–9, 67, 156, 351

Zaire 38, 51, 174, 320
Zambia 35, 74, 75, 211, 222
ZANU 389
Zanzibar 221
ZAPU 389
Zenawi, Meles 361
Zimbabwe 9, 38, 40, 41, 74, 133, 134,
    164, 232, 264, 267, 348, 350, 352,
    353, 364, 372, 398–9, 437
Zoellick, Robert 193